Town and Crown

AN ILLUSTRATED HISTORY OF CANADA'S CAPITAL

INVENIRE BOOKS

INVENIRE is an Ottawa-based "idea factory" specializing in collaborative governance and stewardship. INVENIRE and its authors offer creative and practical responses to the challenges and opportunities faced by today's complex organizations.

INVENIRE welcomes a range of contributions – from conceptual and theoretical reflections, ethnographic and case studies, and proceedings of conferences and symposia, to works of a very practical nature – that deal with problems or issues on the governance and stewardship front. INVENIRE publishes works in French and English.

This is the thirtieth volume published by INVENIRE.

INVENIRE also publishes a quarterly electronic journal, found at www.optimumonline.ca.

Editorial Committee
Caroline Andrew
Robin Higham
Ruth Hubbard
Daniel Lane
Gilles Paquet (chair)

The titles published by INVENIRE are listed at the end of this book.

Town and Crown

AN ILLUSTRATED HISTORY OF CANADA'S CAPITAL

By David L.A. Gordon

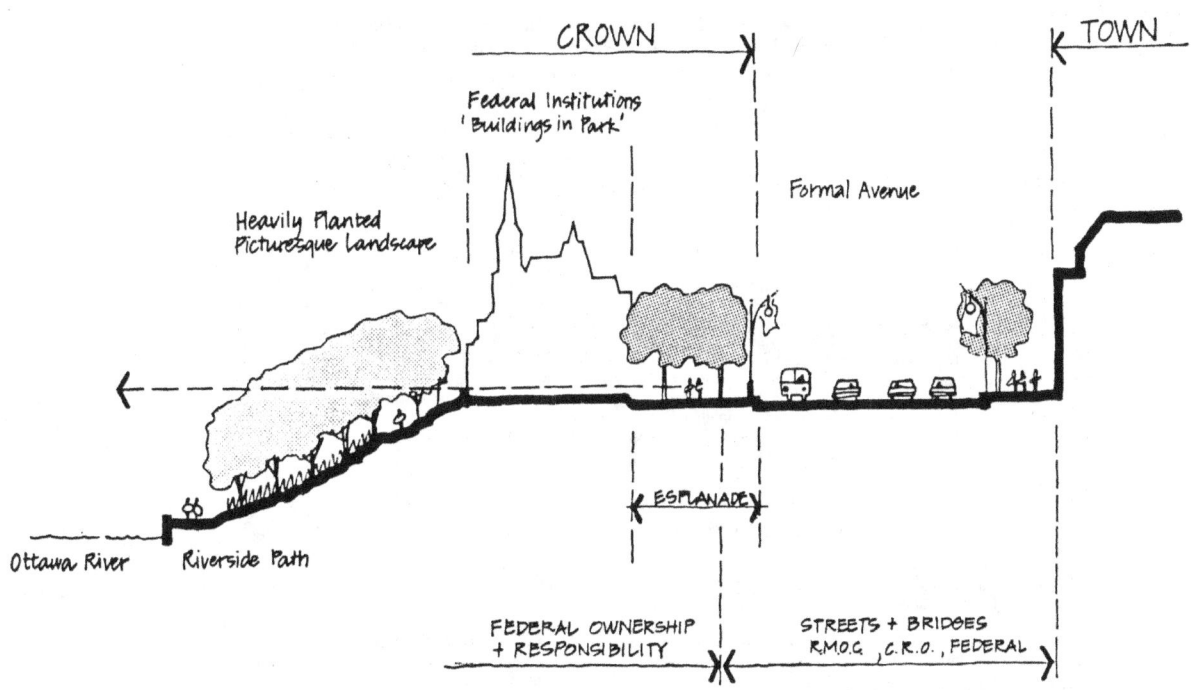

INVENIRE

Ottawa, Canada

2015

University of Ottawa **Press**
Les **Presses** de l'Université d'Ottawa

The University of Ottawa Press (UOP) is proud to be the oldest of the francophone university presses in Canada and the oldest bilingual university publisher in North America. Since 1936, UOP has been enriching intellectual and cultural discourse by producing peer-reviewed and award-winning books in the humanities and social sciences, in French and in English.

www.Press.uOttawa.ca

Library and Archives Canada Cataloguing in Publication

Title: Town and crown : an illustrated history of Canada's capital / by David L.A. Gordon.
Other titles: Illustated history of Canada's capital
Names: Gordon, David L. A., author.
Description: Reprint. Originally published: Ottawa : Invenire, 2015. | Includes bibliographical references and index.
Identifiers: Canadiana (print) 20220286655 | Canadiana (ebook) 2022028668X | ISBN 9780776638850 (softcover) | ISBN 9780776638867 (PDF) | ISBN 9780776638874 (EPUB)
Subjects: LCSH: Regional planning—National Capital Region (Ont. and Québec) | LCSH: City planning—Ontario—Ottawa—History—Pictorial works. | LCSH: City planning—Ontario—Ottawa—History. | LCSH: City planning—National Capital Region (Ont. and Québec)—History. | LCSH: Ottawa (Ont.)—History—Pictorial works. | LCSH: Ottawa (Ont.)—History. | LCSH: National Capital Region (Ont. and Québec)—History.
Classification: LCC HT169.C22 O769 2022 | DDC 307.1/2160971384—dc23

Legal Deposit: Library and Archives Canada, Third Quarter 2022
© University of Ottawa Press 2022, all rights reserved.

This book was initially published by Invenire Books in 2015. The cover design, layout and design were produced by Sandy Lynch. Cover image: Mikebrulotte (Dreamstime.com). The University of Ottawa Press reissued this book thanks to the support of Ontario Creates.

Invenire

Invenire Books, an Ottawa-based idea factory that operated from 2010 to 2019, specialized in collaborative governance and stewardship. Invenire and its authors provide creative practical and stimulating responses to the challenges and opportunities faced by today's organizations. The list is now carried by the University of Ottawa Press.

Profession: Public Servant
The Entrepreneurial Effect: Practical Ideas from Your Own Virtual Board of Advisors
La flotte blanche : histoire de la compagnie de navigation du Richelieu et d'Ontario
Tableau d'avancement II : essais exploratoires sur la gouvernance d'un certain Canada français
The Entrepreneurial Effect: Waterloo
The Unimagined Canadian Capital: Challenges for the Federal Capital Region
The State in Transition: Challenges for Canadian Federalism
Cities as Crucibles: Reflections on Canada's Urban Future
Gouvernance communautaire : innovations dans le Canada français hors Québec
Through the Detox Prism: Exploring Organizational Failures and Design Responses
Cities and Languages: Governance and Policy – An International Symposium
Villes et langues : gouvernance et politiques – symposium international
Moderato Cantabile: Toward Principled Governance for Canada's Immigration Policy
Stewardship: Collaborative Decentred Metagovernance and Inquiring Systems
Challenges in Public Health Governance: The Canadian Experience
Innovation in Canada: Why We Need More and What We Must Do to Get It
Challenges of Minority Governments in Canada
Gouvernance corporative : une entrée en matières
Tackling Wicked Policy Problems: Equality, Diversity and Sustainability
50 ans de bilinguisme officiel : défis, analyses et témoignages
Unusual Suspects: Essays on Social Learning
Probing the Bureaucratic Mind: About Canadian Federal Executives
Tableau d'avancement III : pour une diaspora canadienne-française antifragile
Autour de Chantal Mouffe : le politique en conflit
Town and Crown: An Illustrated History of Canada's Capital
The Tainted-Blood Tragedy in Canada: A Cascade of Governance Failures
Intelligent Governance: A Prototype for Social Coordination
Driving the Fake Out of Public Administration: Detoxing HR in the Canadian Federal Public Sector
Tableau d'avancement IV : un Canada français à ré-inventer
A Future for Economics: More Encompassing, More Institutional, More Practical
Pasquinade en F : essais à rebrousse-poil
Building Bridges: Case Studies in Collaborative Governance in Canada
Scheming Virtuously: The Road to Collaborative Governance
A Lantern on the Bow: A History of the Science Council of Canada and its Contributions to the Science and Innovation Policy Debate
Fifty Years of Official Bilingualism: Challenges, Analyses and Testimonies
Irregular Governance: A Plea for Bold Organizational Experimentation
Pasquinade in E: Slaughtering Some Sacred Cows

The University of Ottawa Press gratefully acknowledges the support extended to its publishing list by the Government of Canada, the Canada Council for the Arts, the Ontario Arts Council, the Social Sciences and Humanities Research Council and the Canadian Federation for the Humanities and Social Sciences through the Awards to Scholarly Publications Program, and by the University of Ottawa.

 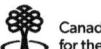

Dedicated to the memory of:

Maj. M. Laird Gordon CD
(1928-2004)

Joan W.M. (Ashton) Gordon
(1930-2013)

Both born in the Ottawa Civic Hospital and now resting in Beechwood Cemetery.
Their interest in the history of our national capital inspired this volume.

Table of Contents

List of Figures		i
Preface		v
Prologue		1
1.	A Magnificent Site (Pre-1826)	5
2.	Building Bytown (1826-1832)	35
3.	Imperial Outpost (1832-1857)	55
4.	The Queen's Choice? (1858-1867)	73
5.	Lumbertown (1868-1900)	91
6.	Crown Plans: 'Parking' the Capital (1900-1912)	119
7.	Crown Plans: City Beautiful? (1913-1920)	137
8.	Roaring Twenties (1920-1930)	161
9.	Depression and the Wartime Capital (1930-1944)	179
10.	Post-War Plans (1945-1959)	195
11.	Boom Town (1960-1969)	225
12.	Town vs. Crown (1970-1989)	255
13.	From Red Tape to Blue Chips? (1990-2011)	287
14.	Town and Crown: Lessons for the Future of Canada's Capital	319
Epilogue		333
Cast of Characters		335
Bibliographic Essay		343
Acknowledgements		351
Endnotes		353
Index		431

List of Figures

PROLOGUE
    Union Bridge over the Chaudière Falls, 1845

CHAPTER 1
1-1A Topography and River Systems of the site of Canada's Capital City
1-1B The many municipalities in the National Capital Region, circa 2000
1-1C Central Area of Hull and Ottawa, showing the Islands at the River's narrowest point
1-2   The Great Kettle and Chaudière Falls on the Ottawa River by Thomas Burrowes, 1831
1-3   Watercolour sketch of the Rideau Falls, 1826
1-4   Jean Talon's planned villages, 1667
1-5   Champlain's "Carte de la Nouvelle France" (detail), 1632
1-6   Voyageurs shooting the rapids in a birch bark canoe
1-7   British colonies: William Penn's 1682 plan for Philadelphia
1-8   Charlottetown Plan, 1791, by Thomas Wright
1-9   Lord Dorchester's Model Township Plans, 1789
1-10 Demonstration Plan for the Settlement of the Ottawa Valley, 1790
1-11 Philemon Wright (1760-1839)
1-12 Wrightstown, 1823
1-13 L'Enfant's 1791 Washington Plan
1-14 Perth Town and Park Lots, 1824
1-15 Lord Dalhousie. Dalhousie Portrait, ca. 1830
1-16 Dalhousie Purchase map, June 18, 1823 (detail)
1-17 Plan for the 'Town of Sherwood', 1822
1-18 First subdivision plan for Wright's Town, 1826

CHAPTER 2
2-1   Lt. Col. John By
2-2   1825 Elliott Map (detail)
2-3   First Camp, Bytown, September 1826
2-4   The Chaudière Falls, Ottawa River
2-5   Galt's plan for Goderich, 1829
2-6   Layout of Rideau Canal and initial Bytown townsites, 1828
2-7   Bouchette 1831 Lithograph of Bridge plan and elevation
2-8   Lady Dalhousie Crossing the Falls, 1827
2-9   Wooden Bridge across the Ottawa River at the Chaudière Falls
2-10 Bouchette's 1831 map of Bytown
2-11 Plan by Royal Engineers for a fortress protecting the north end of the Rideau Canal, 1826

CHAPTER 3
3-1   Jos. Monteferrand (1802-1864)
3-2   Union Suspension Bridge with the Chaudière Falls beyond, 1844
3-3   The ByWard Market, scene of the Stony Monday riot
3-4   Thomas McKay
3-5   New Edinburgh
3-6   1842 Plan, showing Ordnance Reserve and Canal turning basin
3-7   1848 Plan of Central Bytown (detail)
3-8   Old Christ Church on lot donated by Sparks, 1872
3-9   Old City Hall, 1857, on land donated by Sparks
3-10 Pigs on Sparks Street near Kent ca. 1857
3-11 View of Upper Town from Barrack Hill (detail), 1854.
3-12 Sarony, 1858 lithograph

CHAPTER 4
4-1   Tory mob burning the Canadian Parliament, Montréal, April 25, 1849
4-2   Canada's "perambulating" seat of government
4-3   Sir Edmund Head
4-4   Aerial view of Parliament Hill site before construction looking southeast

4-5   Aerial view of Parliament Hill with new buildings
4-6   Parliament Buildings under construction, ca. 1861
4-7   View of Parliament Buildings under construction from the Russell House Hotel, ca. 1863
4-8   Charlottetown Confederation Delegates, September 1864
4-9   Col. John H. Gray (New Brunswick)
4-10 Construction zone around Parliament Hill, ca. 1864

CHAPTER 5

5-1   Image of last raft of square timber as it approaches the Parliament Buildings, 1908
5-2   The mighty Chaudière Kettle reduced to a trickle by industrialization, ca. 1868
5-3   The Rideau Falls dammed and reduced to a thin curtain to drive McKay's mills, ca. 1870
5-4   Lumber piles and sawmills west of Parliament Hill, 1876
5-5   Piling lumber in J.R. Booth's yard, 1873
5-6   J.R. Booth and Perley's sawmills cover the Chaudiére Islands, ca. 1870
5-7   Fires in Hull and Ottawa
5-8   View from Parliament of "Bankers' Row" ca. 1889-1895
5-9   Dufferin and Sappers' bridges, looking northwest, ca. 1900
5-10 Water Delivery in Ottawa, 1870s
5-11 Ottawa Water Works, ca. 1892
5-12 Horsecar stuck in the Sparks Street mud, ca. 1880
5-13 Sparks Street, Ottawa's best retail address in 1872
5-14 Inaugural run of the electric streetcar, 1891
5-15 Chicago Waterfront from Burnham and Bennett's 1909 *Plan of Chicago*
5-16 Rideau Hall, 1868
5-17 View of the Princess' Vista cut from Rideau Hall to the Ottawa River
5-18 T.C. Keefer's Rockcliffe Park Plan, 1864
5-19 Major's Hill Park under construction; the view from Parliament Hill, ca. 1873
5-20 Lady Aberdeen was the impetus for the Ottawa Improvement Commission
5-21 Sir Wilfrid Laurier, founder of the Ottawa Improvement Commission
5-22 McMillan Commission Plan for the Ceremonial Core of Washington
5-23 Lady Aberdeen and Sir Wilfrid Laurier and their families, 1897
5-24 Ottawa Improvement Commission 1899-1902
5-25 Fleeing the 1900 fire on Queen Street
5-26 Downtown Hull after the 1900 fire
5-27 Parliament Hill as an idealized landscape for the Crown
5-28 The more prosaic of the Town: Snow on Sparks Street, 1885

CHAPTER 6

6-1   Aftermath of the Hull-Ottawa fire: April 26, 1900
6-2   The Secret of Heroism: Henry Harper's Study.
6-3   William Lyon Mackenzie King (right) with family and friend Henry Harper at Kingsmere, 1901
6-4   Unveiling of the Sir Galahad Monument in 1908
6-5   Mount Royal Park, Montréal 1877 design by Frederick Law Olmsted
6-6   Rideau Canal driveway, west of Bank Street, ca. 1912
6-7   Frederick Todd
6-8   Parks System Comparisons by Frederick Law Olmsted Jr. and Frederick Todd, 1902-1903
6-9   Parks system proposed by FG Todd, 1903
6-10 Woods in proposed Hull Park
6-11 Three 1903 Todd photos of Rockcliffe Park
6-12 Photo taken by Todd for a proposal to construct a system of parks and pathways along the Rideau River
6-13 Patterson's Creek before and after
6-14 Strathcona Park, 1912
6-15 Earl and Lady Grey
6-16 C.P. Meredith
6-17 Macdonald Gardens, 1999
6-18 Evolution of the Ottawa-Hull parks system from 1950-1990

CHAPTER 7

7-1   Subdivision sprawl in Nepean, 1915
7-2   The short term solution to the typhoid epidemic
7-3   Victoria Memorial Museum, 1908
7-4   Edward White and Aston Webb's 1912 proposal for an imperial capital

LIST OF FIGURES

7-5 Baker and Lutyens' New Delhi, 1911
7-6 The Griffin's 1913 Preliminary Plan for Canberra
7-7 Edward H. Bennett
7-8 Aerial view of Parliament Hill by Jules Guérin, 1915
7-9 Frontispiece of the 1915 Plan
7-10 Plan for the Municipal Railway Centre
7-11 Municipal plaza proposed for Ottawa
7-12 Hull Municipal Plaza, 1915
7-13 Bennett's 1915 zoning proposal for central Ottawa and Hull
7-14 Bennett's proposals for the silhouette along the Ottawa River
7-15 Centre Block of the Parliament Buildings destroyed by fire, February 1916

CHAPTER 8
8-1 Lindenlea site plan by Thomas Adams, 1919
8-2 Neighbourhood Unit, 1929
8-3 Centre Block Parliament Buildings, 1927
8-4 Comparison of Todd (1912), Bennett (1915) and Wright and Adams (1920) plans for expanding Parliament Hill
8-5 Confederation Building, 1928
8-6 City Scientific, Toronto waterfront parks plan, Olmsted Association parks design
8-7 Photo of young Noulan Cauchon
8-8 Corner rounding in the City Scientific manner, Bronson and Carling avenues, 1922
8-9 Vimy Way proposal, OTPC, 1925
8-10 War Memorial Location, 1925
8-11 Thomas Ahearn
8-12 William Lyon Mackenzie King, 1927
8-13 Cauchon's 1928 OTPC plan for Confederation Square
8-14 Ottawa Town Planning Commission's parking plan for Connaught Place

CHAPTER 9
9-1 Jacques Gréber at Kingsmere during a visit with Mackenzie King, ca. 1948
9-2 Proposal to locate the War Memorial in Major's Hill Park
9-3 Plan for Confederation Square and War Memorial
9-4 Supreme Court of Canada
9-5 King George VI, Queen Elizabeth and Mackenzie King (with umbrella) at the dedication of the National War Memorial, May 1939
9-6 Model of 1939 Plan for Downtown Ottawa by Jacques Gréber
9-7 Wartime 'temporary' office buildings, 1940
9-8 Wartime Housing Corporation Project in Ottawa Suburbs, 1945
9-9 Temporary buildings for the Dominion Bureau of Statistics in Thomas McKay's old mills on Green Island, 1940
9-10 Crowded wartime conditions in a downtown office building, 1945
9-11 Greater London Plan diagram
9-12 Urban Renewal: Toronto Regent Park Plan

CHAPTER 10
10-1 Vimy Ridge comes to the Gatineau Hills
10-2 Mackenzie King and Jacques Gréber, 1949
10-3 1950 Plan Watercolour
10-4 Proposed transportation corridors
10-5 Proposed parks system
10-6 United Nations Complex, New York 1955
10-7 Modern buildings in Beaux-Arts civic spaces
10-8 Nicholas Sparks' farmhouse, ca. 1950
10-9 1948 Population Forecast
10-10 Mayor Charlotte Whitton
10-11 Chart of Federal Expenditure
10-12 Road Cross-Sections. Gréber's designs for the main boulevards in Ottawa and Hull
10-13 Main Entrance Boulevard to the National Capital
10-14 The Queensway under construction in 1965
10-15 The Green's Creek Sewage Treatment Plant
10-16 Ottawa City Hall
10-17 Cars and Trams
10-18 National Printing Bureau, 1949
10-19 Tunney's Pasture Design Model

CHAPTER 11
11-1 Five governments signing the agreement for the Macdonald-Cartier Bridge
11-2 Approaches to the Macdonald-Cartier Bridge, 1967
11-3 Existing Conditions – LeBreton Flats, ca. 1959
11-4 Twin Aerial Photos, LeBreton Flats – Before and model
11-5 Capital Plan Brasilia – 1960
11-6 Preston Street Urban Renewal Plan

11-7   Sparks Street Mall Design
11-8   Temporary Mall, Summer, 1960
11-9   Permanent Mall, ca. late 1960s.
11-10 Proposed office towers through downtown Ottawa and Hull
11-11 (Not) Preserving the views of the Parliament Buildings
11-12 Place de Ville, 1967
11-13 The Mile of History
11-14 Confederation Square Proposal
11-15 Recommended freeway system from the 1965 Transportation Study
11-16 "It's the Downtown Distributor"
11-17 Proposal to put a King Edward Expressway in an open trench and Lowertown East urban renewal
11-18 Megastructure proposal to connect downtown Ottawa and Hull buildings
11-19 Gréber's New Town Proposals
11-20 Political Boundaries, 1974

CHAPTER 12
12-1   Megastructures: Battery Park City, New York, 1969
12-2   Place du Portage under construction in downtown Hull, 1975
12-3   Portage Bridge, ca. 1973
12-4   Douglas Fullerton, ca. 1974
12-5   Skating on the Rideau Canal in Downtown Ottawa
12-6   Rideau Mall Galleria proposal, 1975
12-7   Citizen Participation at a charette, Ottawa.
12-8   Lowertown East Urban Renewal Model, 1970
12-9   First RMOC Plan Concepts
12-10 Urban Structure Plan for Ottawa-Carleton, 1974
12-11 CRO Regional Plan, 1973-77
12-12 Tomorrow's Capital Regional Transit Structure Proposal, 1974
12-13 Urban Growth in the National Capital Region, 1890-1991
12-14 Greenbelt separation
12-15 Museum of Civilization
12-16 Confederation Boulevard Plan
12-17 Ceremonial route cross-section on Wellington Street
12-18 Parliamentary Precinct Plan, 1987
12-19 Jean Pigott

CHAPTER 13
13-1   Ottawa Region High-Tech Employment, 2004
13-2   Gatineau City Centre Plan
13-3   Bridge to Nowhere, 2001
13-4   The constant competition between RMOC and Ottawa is symbolized by their new civic buildings
13-5   Character sketch for Rideau Street, 1991
13-6   Ecological Planning and Sustainable Development: Crombie Commission Toronto Bioregion plan
13-7   700 Sussex Drive
13-8   LeBreton Flats Plan, 1990
13-9   Canadian War Museum and New Park in LeBreton Flats
13-10 Bank Street Axis Development, *Plan for Canada's Capital*, 1999
13-11 Victoria and Chaudière islands proposals
13-12 Redevelopment proposal for the north shore of the Ottawa River, 2000
13-13 Asinabka Proposal
13-14 The Metcalfe Street Widening Proposal
13-15 Ottawa 20/20 Structure
13-16 Drawing from the NCC's Core Area Plan
13-17 Parliamentary Precinct Plan, 2006
13-18 View Control Planes

CHAPTER 14
14-1   *Reconciliation*, Peace Keeping Monument, Jack Harmon, 1982
14-2   *Women are Persons*, Barbara Peterson, 2000
14-13 View of Parliament Hill from the Museum of History

Preface

This book is an illustrated history of the planning and development of Canada's capital city. It was written because, in the fall of 1994, I could not answer a question in a graduate seminar presentation on Jacques Gréber's 1950 *Plan for the National Capital*. This plan appeared to be a competent professional study, yet it was rejected by the local governments of the rural townships, where landowners intended to cover the proposed Greenbelt with suburban subdivisions lacking piped water, sewers, or even paved roads. As the research progressed, it became clear that two themes illustrated by this episode were constant throughout the history of the region: conflict between local ('Town') and national ('Crown') objectives and the need to address the effects of inappropriate development fuelled by land speculation.

The book is written mainly from the perspective of the region's 'planning history', examining the activity variously known as community planning in Canada, town planning in the UK, *urbanisme* in France or urban and regional planning in the US. It addresses the urban history of the region and some elements of its social history, although these themes are covered better by John Taylor's 1986 *Ottawa: An Illustrated History* and Chad Gaffield's 1997 *History of the Outaouais*.[1] Canada's planning history in the nineteenth and early twentieth century was heavily influenced by plans and ideas from other countries that are introduced throughout the main narrative. For example, I hope that planning historians will forgive yet another basic introduction to Ebenezer Howard's Garden City, but this background seems necessary for others to understand the origins of the Greenbelt in Canada's capital.

Since this book addressed the physical transformation of the national capital, it must be an 'illustrated' history. The story is told using a combination of images and text. Fortunately, the Ottawa Valley was extensively documented in early travellers' sketches, historic maps, archival photography and plans. The images and plans in the book are supplemented by many more resources at our companion website: www.TownAndCrown.ca.

The early 'Town-Crown' conflicts documented in this book were caused by military objectives for the Rideau Canal. In later years, much of the problem was caused by the region's status as the seat of the federal government. National governments have practical objectives for their host cities that are often similar to local governments. They need effective homes, shops, schools and transportation for the public servants. However, capital cities have additional requirements beyond the normal planning objectives for a metropolitan region. There are specialized requirements for legislatures, diplomatic districts, embassies and government offices that are relatively straightforward to provide. National governments also have cultural objectives for their capital cities that often result in museums, galleries and performance venues that can enrich both local residents and visitors. More controversially, capital city plans must often address symbolic objectives, which may affect urban design, architecture, monuments and place names. This book specifically addresses capital planning issues and short descriptions of other capital cities are provided in extended illustration captions, especially where these cities demonstrate ideas that have affected the Canadian capital.[2]

The book is the story of Canada's capital city and therefore its planning has been affected by Canada's histories and politics. It assumes minimal knowledge of even the most basic element of our heritage, both to serve the international reader, and to adapt to the sorry state of historical education of the general Canadian audience. Short biographies of familiar historical figures are included in the "Cast of Characters" in the appendix to avoid breaking the flow of the main argument, and I hope that professional historians will forgive me for re-ploughing ground on the selection of Canada's capital and the country's Confederation that has been much better tilled by others.[3]

The spatial perspective of the book includes both sides of the Ottawa River, to cover the entire National Capital Region. With rare exceptions,[4] most academic and professional publications about the region are limited by local, provincial and linguistic boundaries. Even the plans of 'regional' governments in the Ottawa Valley routinely have blank spaces on the other side of the river. The research for this project aggressively sought archival and current sources of both the Outaouais and Ottawa areas, and the research team always had staff fluent in both official languages.

Temporally, the book is arranged in chronological order, covering the period from 1800-2011, with small extensions outside this period to reinforce the main narrative. The research for the period before 1975 required about fifteen years of archival work, while the last two chapters relied on documentary evidence, newspapers and over 30 key-informant interviews. The primary research is strongest on the planning and development issues. In these areas we tried to leave no stone unturned and no file un-opened.

I am not a professional historian, so when the story strays outside the areas where we conducted primary research, I consulted expects in these fields to guide my interpretation of the enormous secondary literature. As an additional check, parts of the research were tested by previous publication as articles in peer-reviewed historical journals and chapters in books that are listed in the notes. The project also benefited from insightful reviews of the entire manuscript by four anonymous referees, who provided detailed comments that have materially improved the organization of the book and the incisiveness of the contents.

The research that is the foundation of the book is documented in end notes and supported by a bibliographic essay to guide future scholars. The complete bibliography, which is over 100 pages, is available at the book's website, TownAndCrown.ca, in a form that is electronically searchable.

Finally, the growth of the metropolitan population and the expansion of planning activity meant that the last chapters cover more material, but with less focus on individual actors. Community planning has become a much more collaborative and inclusive activity in recent years and the era of "great men making great plans" is in the past. This monograph stops just short of current events and avoids judging current actors. However, the book concludes with some judgments about past projects and ideas that might inform the future of Canada's capital city.

Prologue

Blow breezes blow, the stream runs fast, the rapids are near and the daylight's past.
Canadian Boat Song, traditional arrangement, 19th c.

The delegates of the Confederation conferences barely saw the outline of their new capital city when they arrived on All Hallow's Eve in 1864. They had spent the fourth day of their triumphant tour of the united provinces of Canada steaming leisurely from Montréal up the trade route of the Algonquin and Outaouais peoples. They drank in the autumn colours of the Ottawa Valley and sang the *Canadian Boat Song*. It was getting dark when they docked at the foot of John By's canal, and Ottawa's citizens conveyed them to the Russell House Hotel in a torchlight parade.[5] It was just as well that the delegates arrived in the dusk, since Ottawa was a crude place in 1864. The torchlight procession was necessary, since the city lacked the most basic urban amenities, such as gaslights, paved streets, piped water and sewers. The Toronto *Globe*'s correspondent cattily noted that:

a hard frost during the night had abolished the mud, and in a few hours done more good than all City Council could have accomplished in twelve months. ...[6]

The next day broke sunny and clear, and the civic officials ensured that the delegates from the united Canadas and four Atlantic colonies got the best possible introduction to the site of the proposed capital city. They all boarded the steamer *England* for a river tour. Even the Torontonians were impressed. "The sun shone out gloriously, gilding land and water and rendering the scenery as beautiful as it can be."[7] Prince Edward Island's Edward Whelan noted that:

the buildings to be dedicated to the use of the Parliament and the Government Offices, now nearly completed and ready for use, could be seen to much greater advantage on the river than in the city.[8]

At first, the *Globe*'s correspondent thought that the falls of the Rideau River might be the great attraction, while the Ottawa men proudly pointed out Thomas McKay's sawmills and factories perched on that precipice.

But the best was yet to come. The boat turned around and steamed up river:

to the foot of the Chaudière Falls, as near as the current would permit. Our Guests gazed their fill on the seething, boiling devil's cauldron, and pronounced it the most beautiful scenery witnessed by them since Montmorenci Falls.

After landing at the Wright family's village in Canada East, "a pleasant drive for a mile or so through the bush" took them back to Thomas Keefer's elegant suspension bridge over the steaming Chaudière and on to the new Parliament Buildings.

The *Globe*'s correspondent opined:
the morning's proceedings afforded a good opportunity of judging Ottawa. The delegates, upon the whole, I think, were agreeably

Union Bridge over the Chaudière Falls, 1845
(Source: LAC C-005250 Watercolour by: Godfrey N. Frankenstein)

surprised and pleased by the substantial appearance of the city …[9]

They were surprised, perhaps, because the recently re-branded "City of Ottawa" had only just began to shed Bytown's reputation as a rough, boozy, lawless frontier settlement.

The guides saved the most impressive sights for last, since the new Parliament Buildings were splendid, even in their incomplete state. The Fathers of Confederation were treated to a scrumptious luncheon in the Picture Gallery of Stent and Laver's gothic masterpiece. As the sunlight streamed in through the glass ceilings, the delegates proposed enthusiastic toasts to their new country. Canada West's John A. Macdonald was somewhat the worse for wear after the previous night's festivities (not for the last time …), so it fell to Alexander Galt to formally announce the news that all Ottawa awaited:

… that Ottawa has been selected by the conference as the seat of government for the Confederation. (Loud cheers). That selection has not been made without some reference to the future … capital of British North America (Loud cheers).[10]

The delegates were in an expansive mood, clearly enjoying the opportunity to engage in nation-building, rather than the partisan inter-provincial bickering of the past decade. Colonel John Gray of PEI summed up the opinion of the delegates:

They had been much delighted today with what they had seen. Nature and art had combined to render this fair city peculiar attractive; and as regarded this superb structure in which they were now assembled, and which not only rivaled the Tuileries of Paris, but in his opinion, even the Houses of Parliament on the Thames … (cheers), they all agreed that it was but a fit and proper building for the purpose to which it was to be devoted, one in which should site the representatives of a free people, who soon would have their territory washed by the Atlantic at Halifax and the Pacific at Vancouver island. (Cheers.) It needed no prophet to foretell that the day was coming when they would take their place among the first nations of the world.[11]

The Confederation delegates' fervent optimism about Canada's future is clear and they must have been pleased to watch their dreams unfold across the continent in the decades ahead.

Unfortunately, the opportunity to build a proud capital city for the new nation slipped away, despite the remarkable natural beauty of the site and the handsome Parliament Buildings. Almost everything that the delegates admired on that glorious autumn day in 1864 was maimed or destroyed in the years ahead, through greed, indifference, incompetence or simple lack of planning. The forests were clear-cut; the Chaudière islands covered with factories, their boiling falls dammed up; the air filled with sulphurous fumes; the mighty river's water rendered poisonous by human and industrial waste; the elegant bridge rotted; and many of the young city's buildings burned, including the magnificent Gothic pile they lunched within.

Canada's capital city was an embarrassment to its leaders and people at the end of World War II. It took a determined effort over the next half century to begin to put it right, a task that was made more difficult by more than a century of struggle between the interests of the Town and Crown.

CHAPTER 1
A Magnificent Site (Pre-1826)

Start from the north pole; strike a bead for Lake Ontario; and the first spot where the glacier ceases and vegetation begins – that's Ottawa –
American directions on where to find Canada's capital, 1857.[12]

The site of Canada's capital city is a great river valley that was covered by the Laurentide glacier 20,000 years ago. The 2,000 metre thick glacier ground the last remains of the ancient mountains into gently rolling hills. The great weight of the ice depressed the land, so that when the glacier melted during a global warming 12,000 years ago, an arm of the Atlantic Ocean which geologists named the Champlain Sea quickly inundated the area. The land slowly rebounded after the glaciers melted away, and the sea retreated, leaving deposits of clay, alluvium and sand beaches miles away from the river that now drained the valley.[13]

The hills to the north of the valley were left with thousands of lakes, inter-connected by fast-flowing streams, while the water in the flatter lands to the south created many bogs and wetlands. Vast quantities of water drained through the young

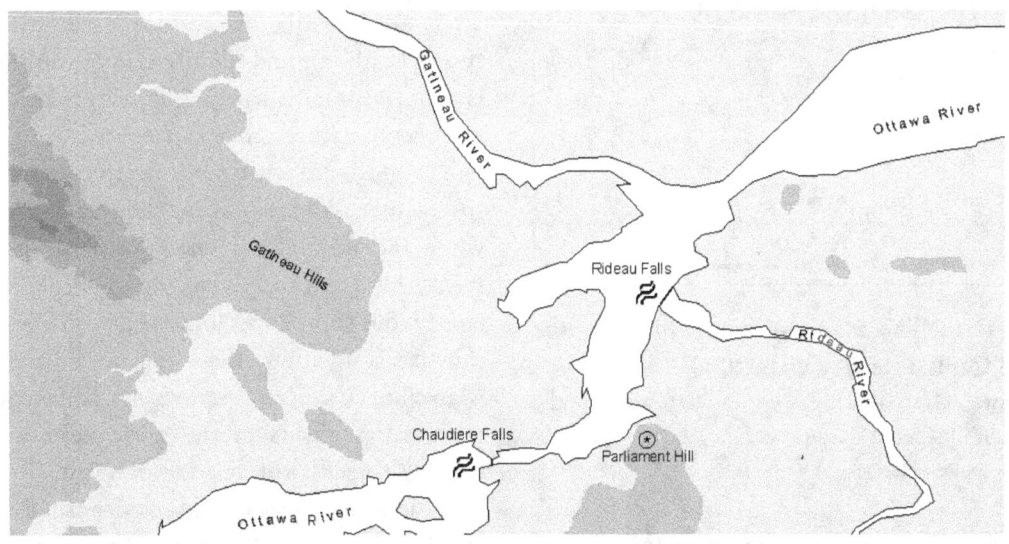

FIGURE 1-1A: **Topography and River Systems of the site of Canada's Capital City**
The hills north of the river and the cliffs on the south shore are the dominant topographic features of the region.
(Drawing by Michelle Nicholson)

river system, where the streams had not yet worn comfortable channels through the valley. Today, the rivers still leap over falls, run down boiling rapids and make sharp turns through breaks in the rock formations.

Canada's capital was established at the place where three young rivers meet (Figure 1-1A). The great east-west river (now known as the Outaouais or Ottawa), narrows from over two kilometres in width to barely 400 metres. It slips through a gap between the Gatineau hills on the north side of the valley and three cliffs to the south. The river roars through the gap with considerable force, cutting channels that created several islands. The force of the water carved out a great hollow in the rocky ledges, where the water once boiled and spray rose in a plume that was visible from several kilometres upstream (Figure 1-2).

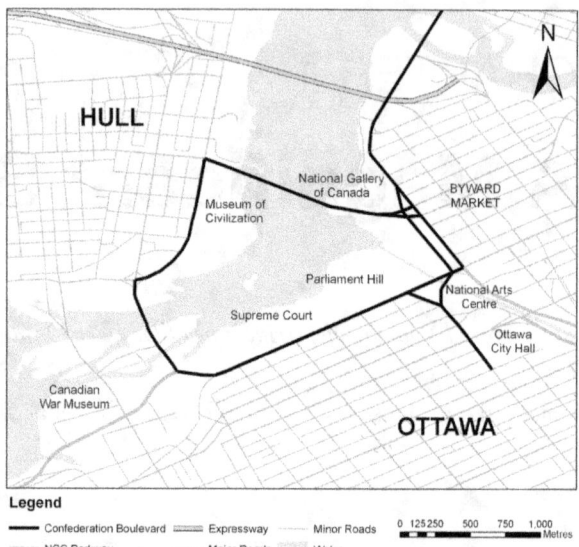

FIGURE 1-1C: **Central Area of Hull and Ottawa, showing the Islands at the River's narrowest point**
(Drawing by Andrew Morton)

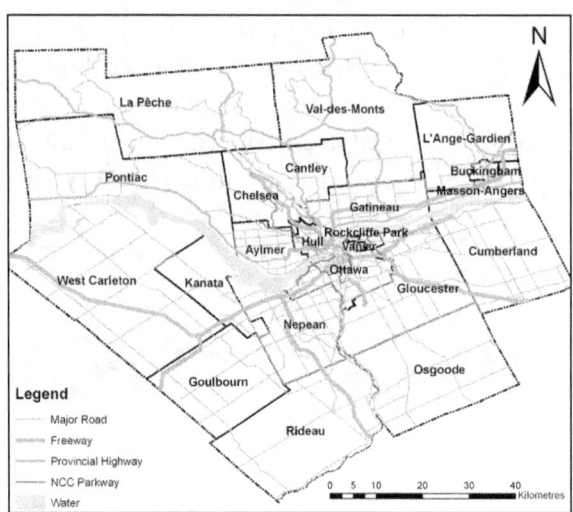

FIGURE 1-1B: **The many municipalities in the National Capital Region, circa 2000**
The Ottawa River, flowing west to east, divides the provinces of Québec and Ontario.
(Drawing by Andrew Morton)

The river flowing from the south (now called the Rideau) ran quietly through the forests before falling over the cliffs in a waterfall so perfect that it looked like two white curtains (*rideau*) divided by a central island (Figure 1-3). The river from the north (the Gatineau) roared down a steep valley studded with rapids and falls, only to flatten out at its mouth, making a smooth entrance to the great river.

The region's climate has fluctuated over the past 10,000 years. In the past two centuries, the area has experienced a temperate, continental climate. There are four distinct seasons – a relatively brief spring with annual floods and a summer that is (for visitors) surprisingly warm and humid, with temperatures that can exceed 30ºC (86ºF). Fall is glorious, with moderate temperatures and spectacular landscapes in the maple-clad hills, while the winter is a serious affair, with frozen rivers, temperatures averaging -11ºC (12ºF), and continuous snow cover for four months.[14] Although the site is at about the same latitude (45ºN) as Marseilles or Milan,[15] it does not benefit from the moderating effects of the great freshwater lakes located just 200 km. to the southwest.

The post-glacial inland sea deposited alluvium and clay soils in the great river valley and the lands to the south. These soils were suitable for agriculture, but the clay layers were susceptible to major landslides. The rocky hills to the north of the valley were scraped bare and hold shallow

FIGURE 1-2: The Great Kettle and Chaudière Falls on the Ottawa River by Thomas Burrowes, 1831
Surveyors and engineers from this era were trained to produce accurate perspective sketches to record local conditions. Their watercolour drawings are the closest thing we have to colour photographs of these sites.
(Source: Thomas Burrowes, Archives of Ontario I0002124)

FIGURE 1-3: Watercolour sketch of the Rideau Falls, 1826
Samuel de Champlain must have seen almost exactly this view, two centuries before.
(Source: Thomas Burrowes, Archives of Ontario I0002118)

brown soils deposited by the forests over the past centuries. Spruce and fir trees similar to those in northern Canada dominated the first forests. After the climate and soils improved, the forests slowly changed to support many stands of magnificent white and red pine. The valleys and moderate slopes were cloaked with maple forests, with the silver and sugar maple predominating.[16]

The many streams and wetlands were ideal habitat to an industrious aquatic rodent, the beaver (*castor canadienesis*), which built thousands of dams and ponds throughout the region. The forests could support a wide variety of mammals including abundant white-tailed deer and moose.[17] This rich wildlife habitat could also support small quantities of people.

The First Nations

The great river valley was unfit for human habitation prior to 11,000 years ago, due to the effects of the ice and inland sea. The archaeological evidence indicates that aboriginal peoples have inhabited the valley for about 6,000 years.[18] The woodland peoples such as the Algonquin and Nipissing occupied the great river valley in two manners. It appears that most families lived a semi-nomadic existence in one of the watersheds north or south of the great river valley, hunting and gathering wild food on a regular cycle, and establishing summer and winter camps as required. These groups survived by sophisticated hunting techniques, harvesting deer and using relatively simple spears and bows for weapons.[19]

Another group of aboriginal peoples supplemented their hunting and gathering by trading for useful objects from other bands. There is clear archaeological evidence that the nations in the Ottawa River valley were trading with other groups from north of Lake Superior and northern New York State. The great river was the main east-west route for this trade, and the aboriginal peoples that engaged in this trade developed skills in building and operating the birch bark canoe, a lightweight watercraft that was ideal for long voyages on these broken rivers. At impassable rapids or waterfalls, the canoes would be removed from the river and carried (portaged) around the obstacles. The portages were quite dangerous ambush sites during periods of conflict between nations. The best natural fortress along the river – a cliff-edged island surrounded by rapids (Morrison Island, near today's Pembroke) has been occupied for almost 6,000 years, and is perhaps the only permanent aboriginal settlement in the valley.[20]

First European Contact

French explorer Jacques Cartier reached the St. Lawrence River in 1534-1535, visiting villages founded by the Iroquois people south of Stadacona (Ville de Québec). Cartier's westward progress towards (he hoped) China was stopped by impassable rapids on the St. Lawrence, now named the Lachine Rapids. He visited the Iroquois' stockaded village at Hochelaga, built on a large island beside the rapids. After climbing the extinct volcano behind the village, which he named Mount Royal (Mont Réal), Cartier could see the mouth of another great river flowing to the west, but that was as close as he got to the Ottawa River.[21]

The next European explorer was Samuel de Champlain, who arrived at Stadacona in 1603, to find a victory celebration underway. The Algonquin-speaking bands of the Ottawa and St. Lawrence valleys had driven the Iroquois back into the lands to the south.[22] When Champlain arrived at the Lachine Rapids in July 1603, there was no sign of the Iroquois village of Hochelaga.[23]

It appears that the Iroquois settlements along the St. Lawrence River had been wiped out in one of the periodic wars that were a feature of the aboriginal peoples' struggle to control territory. Champlain made an alliance against the Iroquois with the Algonquin-speaking bands because he needed their assistance in exploring the interior of the continent and in establishing the colony of New France along the St. Lawrence River. Under Champlain's leadership, the French established settlements at Québec (1608), Trois Rivières (1634) and Montréal (1642) where the townsite eventually adopted Jacques Cartier's name for the mountain.[24]

Champlain had several town planning precedents available when he established settlements in New France. French kings had implanted well-planned fortified towns (*bastides*) to control their southern provinces in the fifteenth century.[26] Champlain had also visited many Spanish colonial towns while commanding a Spanish ship from 1599 to 1601. These towns were laid out according to the Spanish planning regulations known as the Laws of the Indies, which provided specifications for site selection, fortification, plazas, principal streets and the size of lots.[27]

Champlain's earliest settlements, Sainte Croix, NB (1604) and Port Royal, NS (1605) were simple fortified villages.[28] These first two settlements were abandoned, but Québec (1608) grew organically from an irregular street plot in Lower Town to include a citadel on the cliffs above.[29] The plan for Louisbourg (1720), on Cape Breton Island, provides a good example of French colonial fortress town planning. The massive fortifications were designed using the techniques of Sebastian Vauban, while the small town within the walls is laid out with Renaissance street patterns and public squares. Montréal's early fortified-grid plan (1642-1720), faces the St. Lawrence River, following the *bastide* model.[30] The French built similar planned towns in the Mississippi valley in St. Louis, Mobile, and New Orleans. The French Quarter in New Orleans is perhaps the best remaining example of French colonial town planning. Bienville and Pauger's 1822 plan for New Orleans has an attractive central plaza (now Jackson Square) and adjacent gridded neighbourhoods that have retained their charm as the French Quarter.[31]

Champlain built trust among his aboriginal allies by assisting them in their military expeditions against the Iroquois, where the French muskets proved to be terrifyingly effective weapons. He also built a network of guides and interpreters by sending young Frenchmen to live with individual bands in the interior. Two of these guides, Étienne Brûlé and Nicolas de Vignau, were probably the first Europeans to visit the site of Canada's future capital city. Brûlé[32] had been placed with the Huron nation in 1610. He traveled to their lands via the Grand River of the Algonquins,[33] Lake Nipissing and Georgian Bay. After Brûlé reported to Champlain in 1611, Vignau[34] was embedded with the Algonquin's Kichesipirini band, which used their fortress at Morrison Island to control trade along the Grand River. Vignau returned to Paris in 1612 claiming to have reached a northern sea (Hudson's Bay) where he found the wreck of an English ship. His report caused a small sensation and the King dispatched Champlain to explore the route.[35]

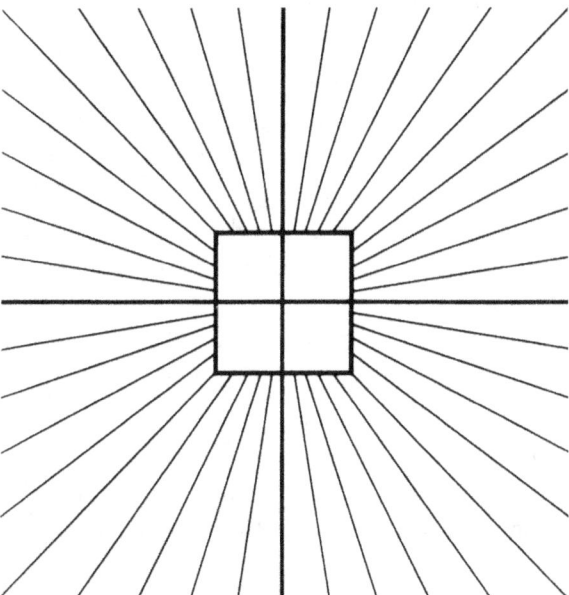

FIGURE 1-4: Jean Talon's planned villages, 1667
French colonial authorities made some innovative settlements plans. Most settlers in New France lived on long, narrow farm lots along the St. Lawrence River. To encourage the population to live in inland communities, Jean Talon developed three villages 10 km. northwest of Ville de Québec. The village designs for Charlesbourg, Bourg Royal, and L'Auvergne (1667) are based on farm lots radiating out from a central square.[25]
(Source: Hodge and Gordon, 2014, Figure 3.4)

Champlain and Vignau set out from Montréal in late May 1613 to explore the 'Grand River of the Algonquins' and search for the northern sea. They reached the site where the three rivers met on June 4, and Champlain was charmed by the place (Figure 1-2):

> ... at its mouth there is a wonderful waterfall; for, from a height of twenty or twenty-five fathoms, it falls with such impetuosity that it forms an archway nearly four hundred yards in width. The Indians, for the fun of it, pass underneath this without getting wet, except for the spray made by the falling water. There is an island in the middle of this river, which like all the land round about is covered with pines and white cedars. When the Indians wish to enter this river, they go up the mountain, bearing their canoes, and carry half a league.[36]

The French described the falls (Figure 1-3) as a curtain (*rideau*) and this name was also attached to the river. They named the next falls the "Chaudière," following the Algonkian name '*asticou*' for a kettle pot:

> A league thence we passed a rapid which is half a league wide and has a descent of six or seven fathoms. Here are many small islands which are nothing more than rough, steep rocks, covered with poor, scrubby wood. At one place the water falls with such force upon a rock that with the lapse of time it has hollowed out a wide, deep basin. Herein the water whirls around to such an extent, and in the middle sends up such big swirls, that the Indians call it **Asticou**, which means 'boiler.' This waterfall makes such a noise in this basin that it can be heard from more than two leagues away.[37]

When the explorers reached the Kichesipirini fortress, the Algonquins refused to convey Champlain to Hudson's Bay and de Vignau recanted his claim to have reached it the year before.[38] Bitterly disappointed, Champlain returned downriver, stopping again at the Asticou:

> *Continuing our journey, we arrived at the Chaudière falls, where the natives celebrated their usual ceremony, which is as follows. Having carried their canoes to the foot of the fall, they assemble in one place, where one of them takes up a collection with a wooden plate into which each puts a piece of tobacco. After the collection, the plate is set down in the middle of the group and all dance about it, singing after their fashion. Then one of the chiefs makes a speech, point out that for years they have been accustomed to make such an offering, and that thereby they receive protection from their enemies; ...When he has finished, the orator takes the plate and throws the tobacco into the middle of the boiling water, and all together utter a loud whoop... they would not think they could have a safe journey, unless they had performed this ceremony here, more particularly since their enemies, not daring to go farther on account of the bad trails, waited for them at this spot and surprised them...*[39]

Champlain made another voyage up the Grand River in 1615-16, following Brûlé's route to the Hurons and reaching Georgian Bay and Lake Ontario. After this great voyage, he remained in Québec, strengthening the French colony along the St. Lawrence until his death in 1634. His last map (1632) skilfully incorporated his own observations and those of his associates, sharing a detailed knowledge of the Grand River of the Algonquins (Figure 1-5).

The early agricultural settlements in New France grew slowly, and were concentrated in the St. Lawrence valley. Large land grants were made to absentee *seigneurs* in France, who were supposed to improve the land, but often made little progress. The colony survived mainly on the fur trade, and the River of the Algonquins was the most important route for the aboriginal allies of the French to bring beaver pelts to Montréal.[40] However, the trade in the valley suffered disastrous setbacks in the 1640s. Contagious diseases such

FIGURE 1-5: Champlain's "Carte de la Nouvelle France" (detail), 1632
Sault 77 is the Chaudière, while 91 is the Rideau River. The river flowing to the north is the Gatineau.
(Source: Library and Archives Canada, National Map Collection NMC 51970)

as smallpox and tuberculosis were carried into the native population by explorers and missionaries, with devastating effects. The weakened Algonquins were attacked everywhere along the river by their Iroquois enemies, who had been provided with firearms by the Dutch traders from Fort Orange (Albany). Mohawk war parties set ambushes at both portages at the Chaudière in 1642, and by 1647 they had conquered the Kichesipirini fortress at Morrison Island. The Iroquois drove the handful of remaining Algonquins into refuge at Montréal and Trois Rivières.[41]

The Iroquois drove the Huron bands away from the south shore of Georgian Bay in 1649, and the Outaouais (Ottawa) people retreated from the bay's north shore to the Straits of Makinac, near the entrance to Lake Michigan. The French fur trade completely dried up, placing the colony in severe financial distress. Luckily for New France, the Outaouais stepped into the breach to organize the trade to the northwest. The Outaouais[42] were a trading nation and expert at long canoe voyages. In 1654, a flotilla of perhaps 120 natives traveled from Lake Michigan, down the Grand River to Montréal, bearing furs to trade for European goods. The Outaouais returned in greater numbers each year, and the French established a fortified trading post at Lake Temiskaming to protect the Grand River route. As the fur trade flourished again, the French began to refer to the route as the "Rivière des Outaouais." Ironically, the Grand River of the Algonquins became known as the Ottawa River, named after a people that had never inhabited its valley.[43]

Nobody consulted the remaining Algonquins about the name change, of course. The European colonizers of the 17th century habitually attached their own names to everything they 'discovered,' even if the rivers and lakes had other names from the aboriginal peoples who had traveled them for centuries. The few shattered remains of the Algonquin peoples initially clung to their French havens along the St. Lawrence, where they were further decimated by disease and alcohol. No records exist about the complete extinction of the bands that lived along the Madawaska, Gatineau and Rideau rivers, although some Algonquins appear to have fled far to the north, to intermingle with the Cree. The French kept the trading route open along the Ottawa River, and a few Algonquins began to return to their ancestral lands on annual hunting expeditions from the St. Lawrence.[44]

The Ottawa Valley in the 18th Century

The colony of New France struggled for survival throughout the 17th and 18th centuries. Although French explorers ranged throughout North America, settlement was still concentrated in the St. Lawrence valley in the 1600s. The large semi-feudal estates granted to French settlers (*seigneuries*) developed slowly due to limited immigration from France. Although a Petit Nation *seigneury* had been granted in 1674 in the Ottawa valley close to Montréal, the lands were not settled until 1801.[45]

The French established more advanced settlements to control the fur trade on the Great Lakes and Ottawa River, including Fort Frontenac (1673) at the outlet of Lake Ontario,[46] Fort Michimilakinac (1681) at lakes Huron and Michigan and Fort Niagara (1725). White settlement was generally prohibited in the Ottawa valley, but the portages at the Chaudière saw plenty of traffic as the huge voyageur canoes headed up and down the river (Figure 1-6). While the Ottawa Valley lay dormant, additional French colonies were established in Acadia (New Brunswick and Nova Scotia), Isle St. Jean (Prince Edward Island) and Louisiana.

Although the French and British colonies were at war almost continuously from 1754 to 1783, the Ottawa valley was never touched by the conflicts. Battles raged up and down the Lake Champlain

FIGURE 1-6: Voyageurs shooting the rapids in a birch bark canoe
Frances Anne Hopkins made this painting following her own 19th century wilderness travels up the Ottawa River, with her husband, who was a Hudson Bay Company manager.[47]
(Source: Oil painting by Frances A. Hopkins (1838-1919), Library and Archives Canada C-002774)

and St. Lawrence River corridors, first between the French and the British in the Seven Year's War from 1754-1763. The tiny French population of 80,000 (Canadien and Acadian) had little chance against the 1,500,000 in the British colonies to the south, and New France fell into British hands after the defeat of the garrisons of Québec (1759) and Montréal (1760).

The British were interested in promoting settlement outside the St. Lawrence Valley, but wished to protect the fur trade and their relations with their aboriginal allies. The Royal Proclamation of October 1763 set out a new imperial policy for development. While the *seigniorial* system was left intact, only the British Crown (imperial government) could purchase land from the aboriginal nations, and all new settlement was required to be on these Crown Lands. The proclamation established procedures for Crown purchases from the First Nations, prohibited unauthorized white settlement in 'Indian Territory' and attempted to prevent the purchase of poorly-defined parcels by encouraging cadastral surveys at the township level before settlement.[48]

The British authorities had several examples of good town planning to draw upon from their settlement of North American colonies. Renaissance planning ideas influenced English settlement in North America in the new towns established from New York to Georgia. These towns usually employed a modified grid layout of streets combined with public squares. They followed the pattern set by the fashionable residential districts of English cities in the mid-17th century, especially Georgian London. Philadelphia, Pennsylvania (Figure 1-7) and Savannah, Georgia are particularly good examples.

Philadelphia 1682 plan (Figure 1-7) includes a central square and four neighbourhood squares set in a street grid. This structure was later recommended in Québec's 1789 town planning regulations.[49]

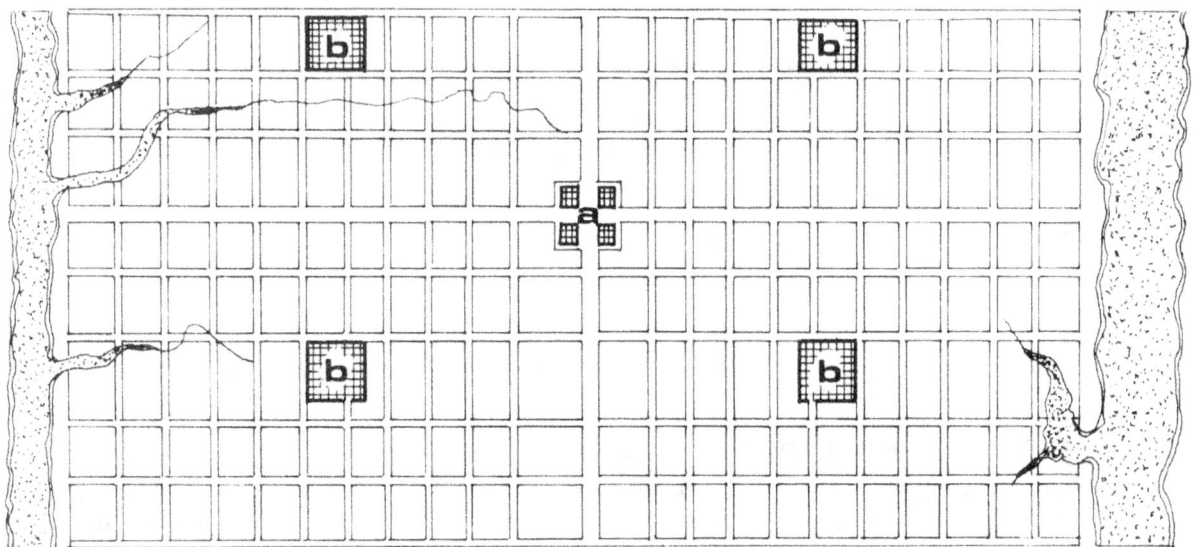

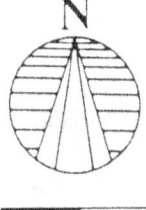

FIGURE 1-7: British colonies: William Penn's 1682 plan for Philadelphia
Note the central square (a) and the four neighbourhood squares (b).
(Source: Hodge & Gordon, 2014, Figure 2.13)

Philadelphia's central north-south and east-west streets reflect the *cardo* and *decamanus* from classic Roman town planning principles.[50] Each of these streets was 30m (100 feet) wide, and the main east-west road (now Market Street) stretched about 3 km (2 miles) between the Delaware and Schuylkill rivers. Penn's plan provided enough expansion area for the city to expand for almost 200 years.[51] The combination of wide major streets and neighbourhood squares was used elsewhere in the British colonies, including Charlottetown, PEI (Figure 1-8).

The British did not have a chance to put their new policies into action before the American Revolutionary War put the frontier in flames again. An American army marched north along the Lake Champlain corridor in 1775 and captured Montréal. However, few *Canadiens* supported the invasion and General Richard Montgomery was defeated and killed at Québec on December 31, 1775. Québec

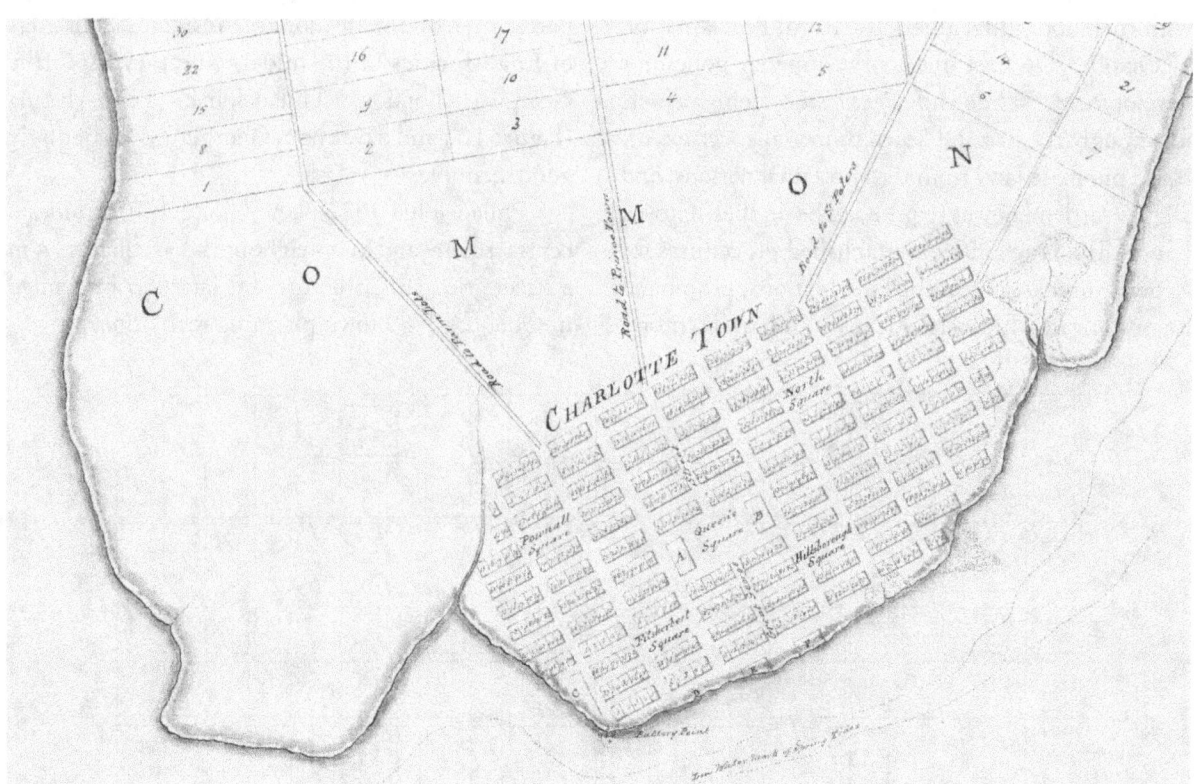

FIGURE 1-8: Charlottetown Plan, 1791, by Thomas Wright (detail)
When the British began to establish permanent settlements in other parts of North America in the mid-18th century, the new communities were developed according to plans prepared by surveyors and military engineers. These were usually based upon a rectangular grid of streets and carefully surveyed. This was the method for the original town sites for Charlottetown (1768), Saint John (1783), and even on the steep hillsides of Halifax (1749)[52]. These plans typically allowed space for a church, a governor's residence, barracks and parade grounds, a cemetery, and warehouses, and were sometimes surrounded by a palisade.
Captain Charles Morris prepared the 1768 plan for Charlottetown, revised in 1791 by surveyor Thomas Wright.[53] Note that central square, commons, four neighbourhood squares, and suburban 'park' lots.
The garrison commons neighbourhood and larger suburban lots were common features of Québec's 1789 town planning regulations, and later settlements in Upper Canada, but not Ottawa.[54]
(Source: Library and Archives Canada NMC 34291)

Governor Guy Carleton drove the Americans out of the province the following spring, but the British lost the war in the southern campaigns.

Governor Carleton faced a different invasion at the end of the war, as British regiments, their Iroquois allies and Loyalist residents from upper New York State poured across the new border as refugees in 1783. The retired troops were settled as a buffer along the United States border, in new townships hastily surveyed along the north shore of the St. Lawrence River and eastern Lake Ontario.[55] The new farm lots and townsites like Kingston were surveyed quickly and simply to put land grants in the hands of the Loyalists at the lowest possible expense to the Crown.[56] The results were uninspired rectangular grids of 200-acre farm lots, unrolled across the forests.[57]

By 1789, the entire St. Lawrence Valley was surveyed into townships between Montréal and Kingston. Governor Carleton (now Lord Dorchester) wished to improve the quality of community planning prior to the settlement of the Ottawa valley, and issued new regulations that called for the layout of towns in each township.[58] There were to be two basic models – the ideal inland township should be ten miles square, and have a one square mile town at its centre, while the standard waterfront township should be nine miles by twelve, and have its town centred on the river (Figure 1-9). The town planning regulations were quite detailed, requiring a central four-acre square and four other squares at the centre of each quadrant of the town. Minimum lot sizes were specified (one acre for town lots, and 24 acres for suburban park lots) and road

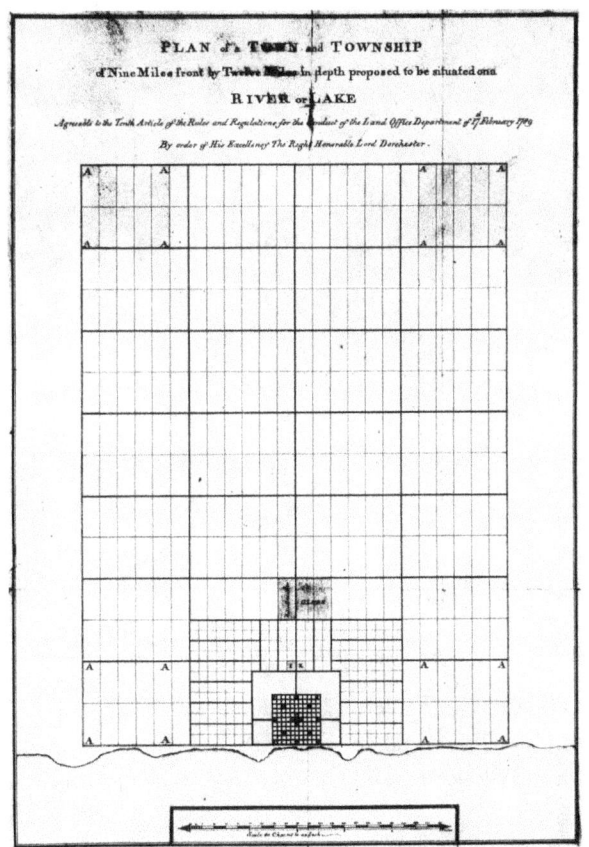
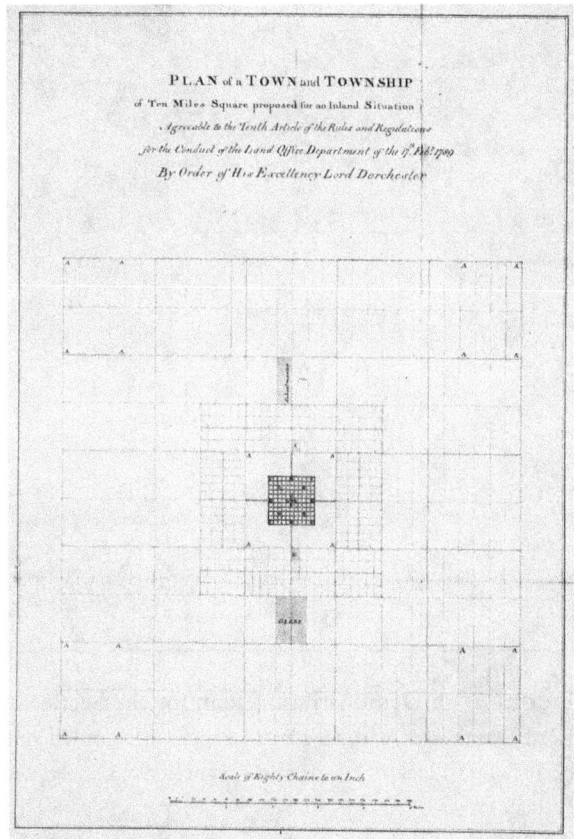

FIGURE 1-9: Lord Dorchester's Model Township Plans, 1789
Plan for a town situated on a river or lake (left); ideal design for an inland township (right).
(NMC 7427/28/29/30)

widths established (96 feet for principal streets and 60 for minor roads). Social planning considerations were addressed by creating lots for "places of Divine worship," a school, court-house, farmers' market, prison, poor-house, hospital, and common burying ground. Finally, each town was to be surrounded by a reserve belt, one-half mile wide, for "works of defence if necessary or such other disposition as shall be thought proper in a future period."[59]

The Surveyor-General's office supplied an illustrative scheme showing how these model townships might be deployed for the settlement of both sides of the Ottawa Valley. New townships were designated (but not surveyed) every nine miles along the riverfront, named after British dukes (e.g., Buckingham, Cumberland, Gloucester) or English towns (Hull, Hawkesbury, Eardley) (Figure 1-10). Not for the first time, budget considerations outweighed community planning ideals, and the townships were surveyed in much simpler format, if they were surveyed at all. The problem was that the cash-strapped provincial government was

FIGURE 1-10: **Demonstration Plan for the Settlement of the Ottawa Valley, 1790 (detail)**
Lord Dorchester's model plans were simply copied onto this plan. The actual surveys of the area were not much better due to lack of funds and inexperienced surveyors. Note the Gloucester and Cumberland townships near the Rideau River.
(Source: Province of Québec, Surveyor-General's office, February 22, 1790, Archives of Ontario)

giving away all the land for free, so the surveying costs were a dead loss to the Crown treasury. All the standard 200-acre farm lots could be laid out in a 100 square mile township by cutting perhaps twelve straight lines through the bush, and hammering in wooden pegs at intervals of ten surveyor's chains (660 feet). But laying out a town required careful work to find the right location, and then marking scores of lines and hundreds of small lots with considerably more accuracy. The extra surveying substantially increased costs to the Crown since it received no revenue for this work and the town sites were rarely laid out. For example, there were only three planned towns (Brockville, Johnstown and Cornwall) for the nine Loyalist townships along the St. Lawrence River.

To increase settlement and decrease its costs, the cash-strapped provincial government tried to pass the costs of the surveying along to the settlers, by establishing a "leader and associates" system. A leader who promised to survey and settle on area according to the new regulations could apply to a provincial Land Board for huge grants of land.[60] Proposals to settle entire townships (64,000 acres) were not unusual, and if the Loyalists were involved, the government might assist with some of the basic surveying costs. More controversially, the province began to accept proposals from Americans to settle the inland townships, far from the border, despite concerns about where the new settlers' loyalties might lie in the event of another war.

The new province of Upper Canada (Ontario) was mostly inhabited by aboriginal bands and Loyalists settlers when it was established in 1791. The new government quickly accepted an application for a township by George Hamilton, a Loyalist veteran who claimed to represent 143 prospective settlers from the St. Lawrence Valley.[61] The provincial government dispatched John Stegmann to survey Nepean, Gloucester and North Gower townships along the Rideau River. Hamilton and his associates were granted Nepean Township, south of the Ottawa River and west of the Rideau. Stegmann completed his survey in 1794, but Hamilton's settlers took one look at the lands and decided to stay on the St. Lawrence.[62]

Unfortunately, Nepean was Stegmann's first large-scale surveying assignment and his plans were rather irregular. One set of lots was oriented towards the Rideau River and another range were oriented to the Ottawa. The roads didn't meet up and lot boundaries were muddled.[63] His survey of Gloucester Township, across the Rideau from Nepean, was even more awkward. It had one set of lots fronting the Ottawa, another fronting the Rideau (not aligned with Nepean) and a third set at an acute angle, where the two rivers met.[64] The irregular road patterns established by these surveys were not a major difficulty in isolated rural areas, but created problems as these two townships grew into a major city.

The Upper Canada government tried to settle the Rideau River townships after Hamilton's land grant had been revoked for lack of action. Many Loyalists along the St. Lawrence had not yet received their full grants, and their children had also been promised land when they came of age. The Fraser family used their extra Loyalist grants to control many of the best lots along the Rideau in Nepean Township, including all the lands at the mouth of the river, where Canada's Parliament Buildings stand today. The families were holding the land for speculative gain, and a small market emerged in Loyalist land grants, with property trading for between 10 shillings and £1 per acre. Other prominent speculators in Nepean were John Crysler, a farmer from the Morrisburg area who bought 1,800 acres, and the American industrialist Robert Randall, who bought potential mill sites. None of this speculative activity led to even one homestead. Nepean's first European settler took up residence over seventeen years after Stegmann's survey.[65]

First European Settlement in the Outaouais Valley

The aboriginal family pulling their little bark sleigh down the ice-covered Ottawa River was surprised to meet Philemon Wright's settlement party in March 1800. Although Wright's four families had made good time after leaving Massachusetts in February, the boiling open water of the Long Sault rapids had delayed them. Their axe-men cut a 10 km. road through the woods north of the rapids, so the oxen could drag the heavily-laden sleighs ahead in the deep snow. Wright's settlement party had lost several valuable days, and when the caravan re-assembled on the river, the spring ice was dangerous. As Wright recounted, the aboriginal family:

> *... looked at us in astonishment, as seeing our habit, manner and custom, and more especially at our cattle, – they viewed us as if we had come from some distant part, or from the clouds, – they were so astonished walking round our teams, as we were then halted, and trying to make discourse with us concerning the ice, but not a word could we understand ... he immediately went to the head of our company without the promise of fee or reward, with his small axe, trying the ice at every step he went, as if he had been the proper guide or owner of the property.*[66]

Of course, it is not surprising that the aboriginal peoples felt that the great river was their property, since it had served as their main travel route for centuries. With the aid of their new guide, Wright's party arrived safely at the Gatineau River on March 7, covering the last 100 km. in six

Figure 1-11: Philemon Wright (1760-1839)
Wright would have been considered a good candidate to receive land grants compared to other speculators, because he was an experienced farmer, had some capital and a strong desire to build a community. He was a popular leader with a vision of an agricultural utopia for his settlers, but somewhat inept as an entrepreneur. His company, Philemon Wright and Sons, tried to control all commerce near the Chaudière, but flirted with bankruptcy several times. The family's extensive land holdings and restrictive policies showed in the development of the lands on the north shore of the river. See the Cast of Characters for more information.
(Source: Portrait by John James, Library and Archives Canada, C-011056)

days. These sixty people were the first European settlers of Hull Township, on the north shore of the Ottawa River.

The Lower Canada government had granted Wright ownership of thousands of acres in the township under the "leader and associates" settlement system. The new British government wished to promote European settlement of the interior of the Ottawa Valley, but avoid any cash costs. So the settlement 'leaders' were given vast areas in exchange for surveying the lands, laying out towns, building roads and establishing social infrastructure such as schools and churches. Philemon Wright's associates were the families of three of his relatives, one other unrelated family and ten hired men. They received smaller land grants of about 1200 acres, most of which they transferred back to Wright in exchange for his expenses in setting up the settlement.[67]

The Founding of Wrightstown

Wright's objective was to establish a model agricultural community that could benefit his extended family for generations to come. Although Hull Township was to be populated by 'independent farmers' like the four original families, Wright intended to establish all the businesses and services that would meet their needs. He organized the settlement carefully, purchasing some land in 1796 and touring Lower Canada in 1797. Wright brought potential associates with him for a detailed assessment of the agricultural capability of the proposed Hull township in 1798 and 1799, accidentally encountering the forest resources that would save their settlement in the future:

> ... we climbed to the top of one hundred or more trees to view the situation of the country, which we accomplished in the following manner, we cut smaller trees in such a manner as to fall slanting, and to lodge in the branches of those large ones, which we ascended, until we arrived at the top. By this means we were enabled to view the country, and also the timber, and by the timber we were enabled to judge of the nature of the soil, which we found to answer our expectations.[68]

The site Wright selected for the original village was level and well-drained land on the north shore of the river at the foot of the Chaudière Falls. That first year was spent developing good relations with the aboriginal peoples, clearing and planting land, building houses and surveying the township into farm lots. In 1802, Wright built grist and sawmills using the Chaudière waterpower and by 1804, his village boasted a blacksmith's shop, a shoemaker's shop, tailor shop and bake houses.[69] The buildings were laid out on either side of a village green in the manner of Wright's native New England.[70] Wright did not lay out streets and lots in the village he named Columbia Falls, because it was a company town. Wright owned the entire site between the Gatineau River and the Chaudière Falls. He intended to keep it for his family, leasing some buildings to the merchants and residents. Not surprisingly, the settlement soon became known as "Wright's Village" or "Wrightstown" (Figure 1-12).

The associates cleared land and started farms north of the village, but progress towards self-sufficiency was slow. In 1806, the settlers owned 1921 acres in Hull Township and the Wrights owned 12,190.[71] By this time, Philemon had spent his entire $20,000 capital surveying the lands, building the roads and village, and purchasing the food and supplies needed by the settlement in its early years. Wright's expenses remained greater than his agricultural revenues in 1806 and he was growing desperate:

> As I had now been six years in the township of Hull, and expended my capital, it was time for me to look out for an export market to cover my imports; no export market had been found as not a stick of timber had been sent from that place down these dangerous Rapids.[72]

Wright's men cut down some of the best oak and pine trees, and then trimmed and squared the logs on the ground with their axes. The square timber was dragged out of the bush by oxen, and assembled into rafts on the Ottawa River. In the summer of 1806, Philemon and his sons navigated the rafts down the river, though the treacherous Long Sault and past other rapids in the channel north of the island of Montréal. A month later, they floated into Québec City, but it took until November to sell their timber rafts to ship captains returning to Britain. The timber market was uncertain, but the trade brought in some cash that Wright could use to pay off his debts to the Montréal suppliers.

Wright's settlement began to prosper, with the labourers and farmers spending the winter in the bush cutting timber and the summer tending to agriculture. The land under cultivation grew slowly, new farmers were attracted to the Township, and Wright could pay his labourers year-round. He added a school, church and the Columbia Hotel to the village, which served tourists inspecting what was considered a model agricultural settlement by the 1820s.[73]

The 1823 drawing by Captain DuVernet (Figure 1-12) shows the mill and tavern at Wrightstown in

Figure 1-12: Wrightstown, 1823
This beautiful (and accurate) watercolour of Philemon Wright's village was painted by Capt. Henry DuVernet, an engineer with the Royal Staff Corps, who was constructing canals further down the Ottawa River.
(Source: Library and Archives Canada C-000608)

the foreground with the Columbia Hotel and village green beyond. Philemon Wright or his company owned everything visible in the image. The settlement never expanded beyond this scattering of buildings, since Wright intended it to remain a model agricultural village. The records don't show much opposition to this paternalism in the early years, since the other settlers were busy with their farms and Wrightstown met their immediate needs. If the Ottawa Valley had evolved into the agricultural utopia that its founder had intended, then Wrightstown might have evolved into a form of the genteel New England village that Philemon remembered from his youth. Unfortunately for Wright's dreams, the development of the Valley took another direction and a different type of settlement was needed.

The Square Timber Trade

Wright was lucky. His desperate 1806 raft trip coincided with Napoleon's continental blockade, which cut off most of Britain's traditional timber supply areas in the Baltic. Prices soared, and the British government moved quickly to establish an additional supplier, placing duties upon foreign square timber that encouraged the trade in the North American colonies. New suppliers emerged in New Brunswick and along the St. Lawrence and Ottawa rivers. They floated the square timber down to ports at the river mouths, where they attempted to sell their rafts to British timber merchants. Prices fluctuated dramatically, and if too many rafts arrived, some timber might go unsold.[74]

Philemon Wright hated the risky square timber business, but it saved his settlement. On May 8, 1808, a fire destroyed all his mills, grain and the winter's production of sawn lumber. All that was left was seven bushels of flour and the timbers afloat in the river. Wright immediately took the timber rafts to Québec, using the proceeds to build a new sawmill and buy supplies to get his settlement through the winter. Over the next three years, he sent his men into the untouched woods on the south banks of the Ottawa River to cut out the finest pine and oak timbers, replenishing his capital to rebuild the agricultural village.[75]

Other landowners along the Ottawa noticed Wright's activity and quickly began to copy it.[76] There were few barriers to entry to the timber trade, as most farmers could unhitch their oxen from the plough to pull timber out of the forest during the winter. There were no prohibitions on cutting timber on Crown lands in the early days, so the best trees were stripped from publicly-owned lands.

The largest landowners, like the Wright and Papineau families, hired workers to cut their timber during the winter. The earliest lumberjacks were often young men from French Canadian farms. After the timber near the settled areas were cut, the men spent the winters living in shanties built deep in the woods and floated the timbers out on the spring runoff. A certain lawlessness prevailed on the edge of the frontier and the lumberjacks routinely cut trees from the vast Crown Lands and unoccupied properties of absentee owners. The work was difficult and dangerous, and a 'cult of masculinity' developed among the shantymen, rafters and lumberjacks. Disputes were settled with fists, far from the eyes of the law.[77]

The square timber industry was dangerous for the landowners too. The British government stimulated colonial production by sharply increasing duties on foreign square timber in 1812 and 1814, but booms and busts in the supply caused prices to be unstable, and Philemon Wright nearly went bankrupt on a couple of occasions. In addition, the 'Big Kettle' at the Chaudière was a major obstacle to the timber trade in the Upper Ottawa Valley. The rafts were destroyed going over the falls, and the timber had to be gathered up and re-assembled on the river below. Ruggles Wright solved the problem in 1829, building a timber slide in the channel beside their lands at the Chaudière. This proved to be a profitable enterprise until the provincial government built another slide on the south side of the river in an early example of competition between local and national interests.[78]

Few settlers in the Ottawa Valley grew rich on the timber trade, because the greatest profits went to the British merchants at the ports. The trade contributed little to the development of the region, other than stabilizing the farm economy by providing some winter employment and cash income. The square timber trade was quite wasteful, with perhaps one third of the tree's useable wood left to rot on the ground, and nobody thought of re-planting the forest. In the early 19th century, trees were the enemies of settlers, to be cut down or burned to clear the lands, with the stumps rotting in the fields for a decade before they could be pulled out. Obtaining a little cash for some of the best timber was an unexpected bonus.

The early Ottawa Valley sawmills were tiny and mainly served local needs, so most of the wood was exported in the form of large timbers or huge planks known as 'deals.' The export trade grew slowly, collapsed after the end of the war in 1815, and grew again until 1825, when it accounted for over half of the value of all exports from the Canadas. However, the big expansion of the industry would not occur until the late 1820s, when river improvements and access to Crown lands made the business more lucrative, and competition for resources and labour much more intense.[79]

The War of 1812

The War of 1812 did not touch the Ottawa valley, but it affected its planning and development for the next half century. It also affected every decision about the future location of Canada's capital city. The US entered the war at the height of Napoleon's power in Europe, when the Canadas were defended by only six battalions of British troops, some Canadian militia and their aboriginal allies. The Royal Navy maintained a base in Halifax, but Montréal and Upper Canada were beyond its protection.[80,81] Britain could not send any troops from Europe, and most of the border areas were inhabited by French Canadians or recent American settlers.

The United States expected an easy victory, a "mere matter of marching" according to Thomas Jefferson.[82] However, the American military leadership was weak, and some of the state militias were reluctant to fight on foreign soil. Major-General Isaac Brock, the Governor of Upper Canada defeated one American army at Detroit and engaged another at Queenstown on the Niagara frontier. But Brock was killed leading the charge up Queenstown Heights, and the Americans very nearly conquered Canada the next year.

With most of the British troops engaged on the Niagara frontier, another American army sailed across Lake Ontario on April 27, 1813 and captured York (Toronto), the capital of Upper Canada. After the retreating troops blew up Fort York, the Americans burned the Upper Canada legislature and sacked the town.[83] To rub salt into the wounds, the Americans sailed across Lake Ontario, and captured Upper Canada's capital again in August, but there were no government buildings left to burn.[84] The difficulties of defending York from an American naval attack would reduce its chances at becoming the Canadian capital in the future.

While the British were withdrawing from western Ontario, the Americans launched a two-pronged attack to seize Montréal during the fall of 1813. One army marched up the Châteauguay River into Lower Canada, and another sailed down the St. Lawrence River. The first army was defeated by a small force of Canadian militia led by Lt. Col. Charles de Salaberry at the Battle of Châteauguay, only 200 km. south of Montréal.[85]

Meanwhile, the British forces stationed in Kingston chased the 7,300 troops in the other American army down the St. Lawrence, to prevent the invaders from capturing Montréal. The small force of 900 British regulars, 300 Canadian militia and 30 Mohawk warriors caught up to the Americans at John Crysler's farm, just below Morrisburg, on November 11, 1813. The three US brigades turned to crush their pursuers, but discovered that they were no match for the disciplined British regular troops on the open fields of Crysler's farm. The Americans suffered heavy casualties and were driven across the St. Lawrence River to starve over a harsh winter.[86]

The British and Canadians also suffered significant losses, but they saved Montréal because the American army was only a two-day march along an undefended road to the city when it was caught and defeated. Although the Crysler's Farm battlefield is a mere 45 miles south of Philemon Wright's village, the swath of wilderness between the St. Lawrence and Ottawa rivers shielded the northern valley from attack.[87]

The war dragged on for another year with a nasty stalemate continuing on the Niagara frontier, while British forces from Halifax captured most of Maine. Upper Canada was avenged when the Royal Navy sailed up Chesapeake Bay with a force of marines and regular troops from Halifax for a surprise attack in August 1814. They captured Washington, burned the Capitol, White House, and other government buildings in retaliation for the sack of Niagara frontier settlements and York, the capital of Upper Canada.[88]

When the British captured Washington in 1814, the city was barely 20 years old (Figure 1-13). The 1790 selection of a site on the Potomac River for the federal capital of the United States was a compromise. The new country's seat of government had temporarily been located in Philadelphia and New York and these rival cities both staked their claim. However, the Potomac had the virtue of being the dividing line between the rural southern states and the more urban north.[89]

With the Napoleonic War drawing to a close in 1815, the British were able to turn their full attention across the Atlantic. Since all possibility of an easy conquest of Canada had evaporated and the Napoleonic blockade had been lifted, the American appetite for the war waned. In the Treaty of Ghent, both parties agreed simply to return to the original borders.[93, 94] However, the celebrated "undefended border" between Canada and the United States did not emerge until the late 19th century. In fact, both sides prepared for another war in the decades following 1815, and Britain invested huge sums of money defending the frontier of its North American colonies from another American invasion.[95] Military strategy affected settlement policy, infrastructure design and the location of the seat of government for decades to follow.

The War of 1812 was a minor sideshow in the British imperial sphere, but it was a near disaster for the Canadas. A few months after the peace, Sir James Yeo, the British naval commander on the Great Lakes, considered, in private correspondence, how the British survived the war owing to "… the perverse stupidity of the Enemy, the Impolicy of their plans; the disunion of their Commanders and lastly, between them and their Minister of War."[96]

Yeo considered that the Americans' main 'Impolicy' had been their failure to cut off the British supply line along the St. Lawrence River from Montréal to Kingston. It was clear that James Monroe, the new American Minister of War, fully understood Upper Canada's strategic weakness. Monroe and his new generals prepared a new plan to exploit the river for the 1815 campaign, which was cancelled due to the Treaty of Ghent. After Monroe became president in 1817, new military roads were quickly completed along the American banks of the St. Lawrence and new canals reached lakes Champlain, Ontario and Erie. These were ominous signs that the Americans were preparing for the next war.[97] The British planned ahead, too.

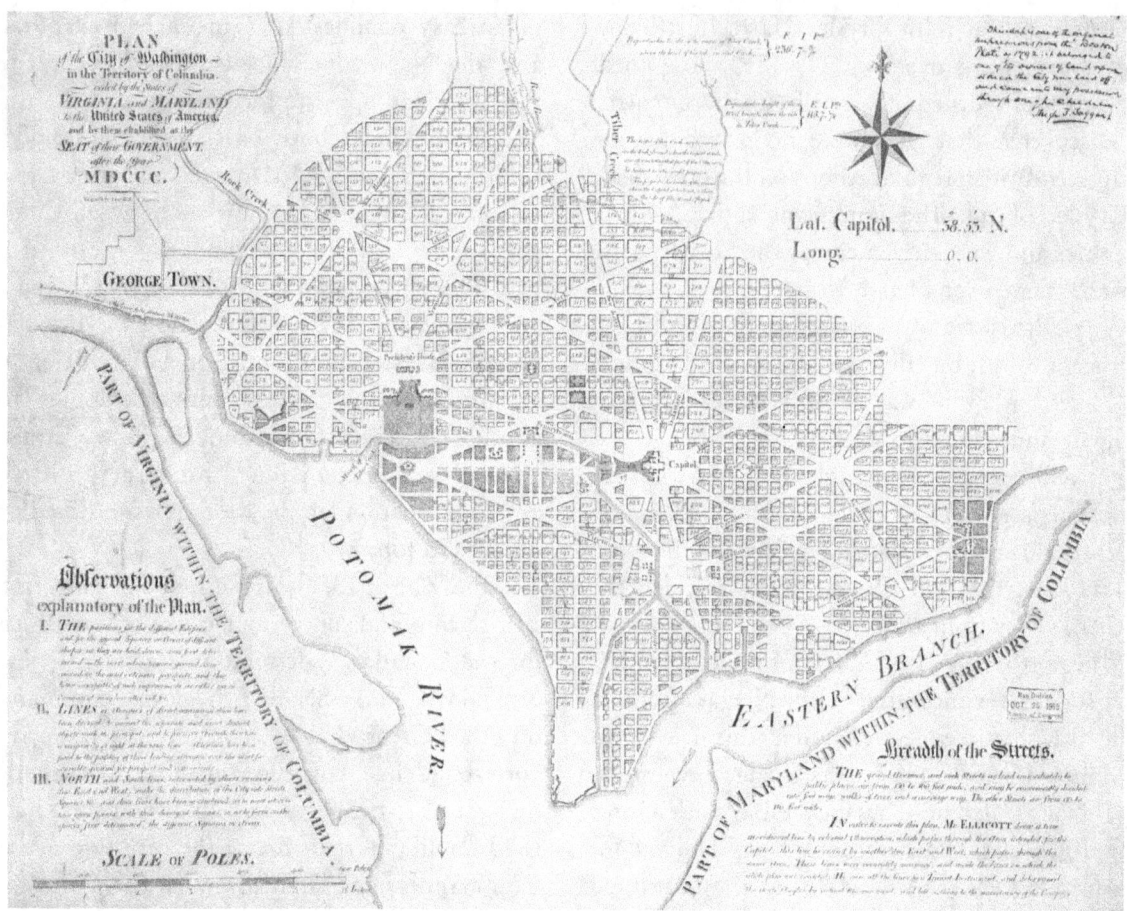

FIGURE 1-13: L'Enfant's 1791 Washington Plan
L'Enfant's Washington plan, as revised by Andrew Ellicott in 1792 Washington.

Congress had the power to designate a ten-mile square as a federal district, under its direct control, but it needed a survey to establish its limits, acquire land and sell lots. President Washington requested the assistance of Major Pierre Charles L'Enfant (1754-1825), a French military engineer then practicing architecture in New York.[90] L'Enfant surveyed the site and produced a preliminary plan during a six-month period in 1791. His plan combined wide axial boulevards with a tight grid of blocks. L'Enfant was quite familiar with radial boulevards, since he had grown up near Versailles. He designed the new roads to connect up high points in the land north of the Potomac. The intersections of the boulevards were reserved for major institutions, with the highest hill reserved for the Capitol building and another nearby knoll for the president's house. A broad mall would connect the Capitol to the river, with a monument to George Washington at its centre.[91]

The government hoped to finance the construction of the capital city by the sale of lots, but had little initial success. Neither the Capitol nor the White House was complete when the government relocated from Philadelphia in 1800. Broad avenues were cut through the forest, with a few buildings scattered along their length. Visitors ridiculed the city for the next 50 years, and it was not until the US Civil War that it began to feel like a real city.[92] Although Washington's implementation was painfully slow, its planning and governance ideas were influential in the years ahead. After the break-up of the European empires, many new nation-states and provinces considered building their own capital cities, sometimes on green-field sites like Washington. Other countries, including Canada, considered the idea of a federal district to govern their capital cities.

(Source: Library of Congress, Prints and Photographs, LC-USZ62-120270)

The Duke of Wellington's Plans and the Smyth Report

The Duke of Wellington was a British national hero after the armies under his command defeated Napoleon at Waterloo in June 1815. After the war ended, Wellington was placed in charge of imperial defence policy as Master-General of His Majesty's Ordnance (1819-27) and commander of the Army (1827-28). The British Ordnance was a powerful, semi-independent authority that manufactured weapons and built fortifications throughout the British Empire.[98] Although Wellington never set foot in North America, he listened to the advice of trusted subordinates. One of his friends, the Duke of Richmond, was appointed Governor General of Canada in 1818. Like every other British officer who examined the defence of the Canadas, he recommended that the St. Lawrence supply route be replaced by the Ottawa River and a canal to Lake Ontario.[99] By 1819, the Duke of Wellington had turned his attention to Canadian defence and, following Richmond's reports, recommended a start on the Ottawa River canals by troops of the Royal Staff Corps.[100]

George Ramsay, Lord Dalhousie, became Governor General in 1820. He was an experienced officer, like most of his predecessors, and also toured the Canadas to inspect their fortifications. However, the most influential defence plan was prepared by Major General Sir James Carmichael Smyth, a military engineer who had served on Wellington's staff in Spain and at Waterloo. Smyth's committee toured all of British North America, but they were particularly concerned about protecting Upper Canada and Montréal, which were the only colonies beyond the reach of the Royal Navy. The Smyth Committee condemned the selection of York (Toronto) as the seat of government of Upper Canada, since the war experience demonstrated that it could not be defended:

> ... *We cannot avoid expressing upon the subject of York our regret that it should ever have been selected for the capital of Upper Canada. It offers no advantages that we are aware of, either of a civil, military or commercial nature ... Kingston appears to us to be the natural capital, in a military point of new, and being the point whereas the most important of the proposed canals will meet, its commercial importance must proportionally increase. If Kingston could be made the Seat of Government, the Civil Military and Naval authorities would be more collected, and it appears to us, with the happiest effects to His Majesty's Service.*[101]

The Smyth Commission concluded that Kingston's defences were adequate, but recommended that the wooden fort on Point Henry and its supporting towers be replaced by stone structures. They also recommended additional towers to protect the entrance of the proposed canal from Kingston to the Rideau River.[102] Smyth's Commission confirmed the decision to start on the Ottawa River canals and recommended the Rideau and Cataraqui rivers as the route for the second canal, citing a ludicrously low estimate of £145,000 helpfully provided by the provincial government.[103] After consulting with the provincial officials, Smyth reported:

> *We regret, however, to say that there does not appear to be the slightest chance of any pecuniary aid from the Province. The settlers are very poor and the Province of Upper Canada is yet in its infancy.*[104]

The government of Upper Canada may have been in its infancy, but they were clever enough to maneuver the British Ordnance into committing to paying the entire cost of the Rideau Canal using a 'low-ball' estimate prepared by a provincial surveyor. The proposed canal had obvious civilian uses and a similar venture for the Lachine Canal outside Montréal was entirely funded by the provincial government of Lower Canada.[105] However, by the time the Ordnance had its own engineer on site for a detailed review, the Rideau Canal had been approved by the Westminster Parliament and firmly lodged in British military strategy.

Wellington's staff looked about for a military engineer with experience in canal building and the Canadas. They found Lieutenant-Colonel John By, retired on half-pay, and brought him back into active service in March 1826 to build the Rideau Canal. Although Parliament baulked at the total of £1.14 million estimate for defence works for all of Upper Canada, it did approve £5,000 for preliminary planning for the Rideau Canal. By was ordered to proceed to Canada immediately, prepare more detailed estimates, and to retain civilian contractors to build the canal with dispatch. Since his orders came from the Duke of Wellington, who was commander of the Army, Master of the Ordnance and had a seat in Cabinet, By had no reason to doubt their authority. He arrived in Montréal in June 1826 to begin planning, and agreed to meet Governor General Lord Dalhousie at the mouth of the Rideau River in September to examine the Ottawa River terminus of the canal.[106]

The Richmond Settlement

Military settlement of the lands between Kingston and the Ottawa River was the second element of the plans for the defence of Upper Canada. This followed the tradition established after the American Revolutionary War, when retired troops and Loyalist refugees were settled along the St. Lawrence River, Lower Canada's Eastern Townships, New Brunswick's St. John River valley and several Nova Scotia counties.

When the War of 1812 ended, several British regiments were nearing the end of their overseas service. Since post-war economic prospects in England looked dim, many officers and men accepted offers of generous grants of land in Upper Canada and assistance in their settlement. The 99th and 100th Regiments were settled in new townships stretching north of Kingston to the Ottawa River. Many regimental officers retired at half-pay pensions, providing leadership and an immediate social hierarchy for the new settlements.[107]

The military settlers were provided with supplies and benefited from some advance planning. Most settlers were granted both a town lot and farm lots that varied in size according to rank. The surveyors laid out town sites in Perth (1816), Richmond (1818) and Lanark (1820). The townsite plans were variations on a simple square grid (Figure 1-14), which largely ignored local terrain and streams. In Perth, sites were reserved for a courthouse, a public school, several churches, and a public burial ground. Town lots were 1-2 acres, and ten-acre 'park' lots were provided for grander country villas for the officers and other gentry.[108]

Perth was settled by cutting a road north from Brockville's townships, but Richmond was to be settled by a road cut west from the Ottawa River. The 99th Regiment arrived at the Chaudière Falls in early August 1818, and pitched tents on the 'flats' beside the portage on the south side of the river. They renamed the portage site 'Richmond Landing' after their patron, the recently appointed Governor General of the Canadas.

The site where the 99th Regiment landed in 1818 was previously known as Bellow's Landing, after the proprietor of a nearby tavern. It was a key location, since it was the head of navigation for the Ottawa River. Even the most nimble canoes needed to be portaged around the boiling Chaudière Falls. A small locked storehouse was located near the portage, so that goods shipped from Montréal could be left for settlers in the inland district.

The flats and adjacent lots were owned by Robert Randall, an American industrialist and land speculator who had been released from debtor's prison in Montréal before the settlers arrived. Randall had settled in the Niagara region in 1798, where he established a forge and purchased a mill. He traveled widely throughout Upper Canada and the Ottawa Valley seeking additional lands. In the early 1800s, established entrepreneurs could obtain large land grants at no cost, merely by applying to the provincial government and expressing some interest in developing them.

A MAGNIFICENT SITE (PRE-1826) 27

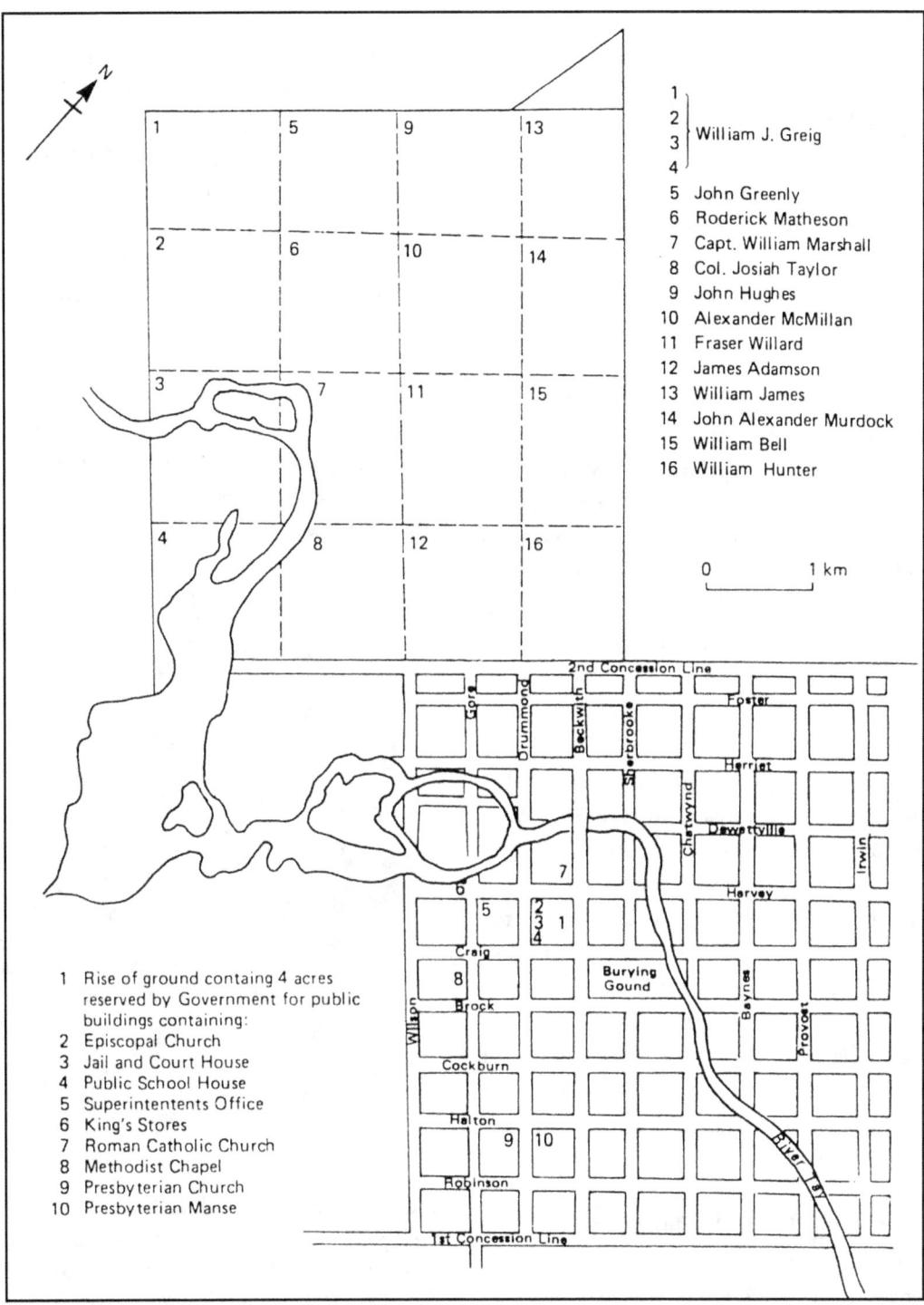

FIGURE 1-14: Perth Town and Park Lots, 1824
The military settlement in the Upper Ottawa Valley included three planned towns. Perth was located on an attractive site on the Tay River. By 1880, the large suburban 'park' lots granted to its 'gentry' were being subdivided to accommodate the town's growth.
(Source: Reid, R., 1990, Map 1)

In 1807, Randall traveled by canoe from Kingston to the Ottawa River to explore the surveyed townships. He discovered iron ore in Hull Township and discussed opening another foundry and mill at the Chaudière. Randall petitioned for hundreds of acres of land in Nepean Township, Hull Township and the islands and broken-front lots at the Chaudière. Randall received title to the lands in 1809, but never visited them. Later in 1809, one of his creditors had him thrown in debtor's prison in Montréal, where he remained for seven years.[109]

It is likely that nobody in the area knew, or cared, about the identity of the owner of the flat lands south of Chaudière portage in 1818. Almost the entire Nepean Township was in the hands of absentee owners in that era and there was no local record of land titles.[110] Settlers simply camped where they could, and cut timber and roads where needed. Richmond was expected to become the major entrepôt of the Rideau River and its plan had 120 large park lots; Perth had 16 park lots and there was no settlement planned for "Richmond Landing."

While women and children camped on the flats, men cut a rough road through the forest some 30 km to the Richmond townsite at the confluence of the Rideau and Jock rivers.[111] The settlers followed down the road a few weeks later, building storehouses, simple cabins and an inn before the winter set in. They also cut an extension of the Richmond Road a further 47 km. to Perth, which was declared the capital of the new Bathurst District in 1822. Perth became the administrative centre for the Upper Canada townships as far west as the Rideau River.

Richmond and Dalhousie

The Duke of Richmond only just reached the settlement named in his honour during his 1819 tour of the new defence works in Upper and Lower Canada. A rabid fox bit him while inspecting the new forts south of Montréal, but hydrophobia symptoms did not emerge until a week later, as he approached the small village named after him. The Duke's condition deteriorated overnight and he died outside Richmond village on August 28, 1819.[112]

Lord Dalhousie (Figure 1-15) was just completing his appointment as Governor General of Nova Scotia when news of Richmond's tragic death arrived. He was posted to Québec as the new Governor General and Commander-in-Chief for the Canadas. Dalhousie continued the inspection of Canadian defences the next summer, reaching Wrightstown on August 19, where Philemon Wright charmed him. While examining Richmond Landing, he noticed the high bluff of land to the east, and predicted that it would one day house the seat of government.[113] The cliff-top site admired by the Governor General is now known as Parliament Hill.

FIGURE 1-15: Lord Dalhousie, ca. 1830
George Ramsey, 9th Earl of Dalhousie (1770-1838) was a British General who served with the Duke of Wellington in Spain. He began a career as a colonial administrator with appointments as Lieutenant-Governor of Nova Scotia (1816-1820), governor of British North America (1820-1828) and military commander of India. See the Cast of Characters for more details.
(Source: Library and Archives Canada C-005958, Portrait by Sir John Watson-Gordon)

Dalhousie hated the Richmond Road and regarded most of Nepean Township as a "useless waste" because it was all the property of absentees, which the Crown could not recall or force into settlement.[114] However, the leadership of the half-pay officers in the military settlements impressed the new Governor General. He dined with them at both Richmond and Perth, openly discussing his plans for developing the Valley. One of the officers he dined with was Captain John LeBreton of the Royal Newfoundland Regiment, who had served with some distinction in the War of 1812. LeBreton had received grants in Nepean and March Townships in 1819, calling his homestead "Britannia" in deliberate contrast to "Columbia Falls" established downriver by the Yankee, Philemon Wright. LeBreton constantly attempted to expand his holdings and had assembled over 9,000 acres by 1822, although he had only cleared about 20 on the western edge of Nepean Township.[115]

Unfortunately for LeBreton, his acquisition of Richmond Landing proved to be a serious blow to his reputation. A few months after Dalhousie's 1820 visit to the Richmond settlement, Robert Randall's lands at the Chaudière were put up for sheriff's auction for non-payment of debts to his solicitors.[116] LeBreton traveled by canoe and horseback from the Ottawa River to Brockville to attend the auction and purchased the lots for £499 on December 10, 1820.[117] The following spring, LeBreton visited Québec and attempted to sell half the lands to Dalhousie for £3,000, which was an enormous sum in those days.

The Governor General was outraged that a half-pay officer like LeBreton would attempt to gain a large speculative profit from the Crown by taking advantage of the discussions at his Richmond dinner the year before. He accused LeBreton of breach of confidence, threw him out and supported legal expenses of the family that operated the tavern at Richmond Landing from his own pocket.[118]

LeBreton's brazen speculation angered Dalhousie, but his title to the lands near Richmond Landing held up in the courts, despite repeated legal attacks by both Randall and the Crown. The Governor General ensured the Crown's control of the adjacent Ottawa riverfront in 1823 when he purchased the adjacent waterfront lots to the east for £750 from Hugh Fraser, the son of the original Loyalist grantee. This act of foresight placed the lands north of today's Wellington and Rideau streets in public ownership, including the great riverside bluff that is now Parliament Hill (Figure 1-16).[119]

LeBreton's attempt to flip his lot at Richmond Landing for an enormous profit made Dalhousie an implacable enemy, which was a serious problem in the early nineteenth century. The Governor General blackened LeBreton's reputation and supported the tavern keepers occupying his lands.[120] LeBreton plowed ahead anyway, and subdivided his lands into the "Town of Sherwood" in 1822 (Figure 1-17). However, Dalhousie publicly disputed his title to the property and LeBreton had no takers for his lots. The Governor General also organized a timber slide on the south side of the Ottawa River that made development of mills on LeBreton's shore more difficult.[121]

Dalhousie's purchase of the remainder of the riverfront allowed the engineers to consider other options for the terminus of the Rideau Canal that did not involve paying LeBreton's price. Although Richmond Landing (the future LeBreton Flats) was an obvious location for a village to support the canal works, the land would lie fallow for over a quarter-century while LeBreton proved his title in the courts and waited for development of the town to head in his direction.[122]

Lord Dalhousie's hostile attitude towards land speculators was another serious outcome of this relatively minor dispute with LeBreton. The Governor General's later policies would sometimes be more concerned with preventing profiteering than with promoting sound development.

One other land parcel was cleared on the south side of the Ottawa River in the early 1820s.

John Burrows Honey had acquired the 200-acre farm lot south of the Fraser's river frontage in 1817. Unlike the absentee landowners in the area, Honey cleared a portion of his lands, built a small house and attempted to farm the property (see Lot "C" on Figure 1-16). In 1821, Honey sold the lot for £95 to Nicholas Sparks, a labourer working for Philemon Wright. It was later reported that he bought the lot sight unseen, and wept when he saw the poor condition of the land.[123] Much of the area, which is now Ottawa's downtown core, was a combination of a mixed forest of hemlock and beech with cedar swamp and 'beaver meadow' in low-lying areas.[124]

On the north side of the Ottawa River, the first townsite plan for 'Wrightstown' was an 1826 survey prepared for the Wrights' holdings on the island created by Brewery Creek and the Gatineau River (Figure 1-18). The plan may have been prepared to meet Lower Canada's requirement for a town plan as part of the "leader and associates" scheme for settlement. The plan had small square blocks, similar to the 1816 plan for Perth (Figure 1-14), and a couple of narrow streets were laid out that survive to this day.[125] This plan may have been used by Philemon Wright to lease land, since he preferred not to sell lots in the townsite. Ruggles Wright replaced it with a more practical plan in 1840.[126]

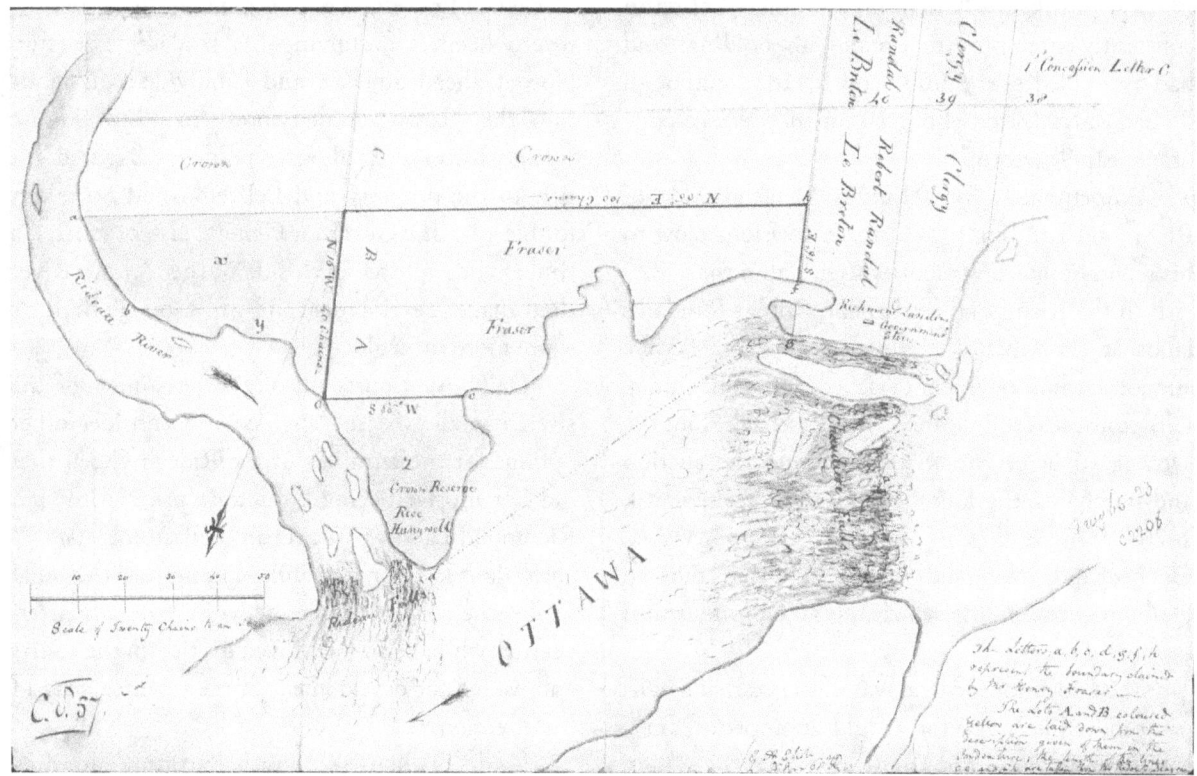

FIGURE 1-16: Dalhousie Purchase map, June 18, 1823 (detail)
Lord Dalhousie purchased two undeveloped lots, A and B, from the Fraser family to control the rest of the Ottawa riverfront after Capt. John LeBreton had bought the key Richmond Landing site. The adjacent Lot C was later purchased by J.B. Honey and sold to Nicholas Sparks (North is at the bottom of this plan).
(Source: Library and Archives Canada NMC 79949, drawn by G.A. Eliot)

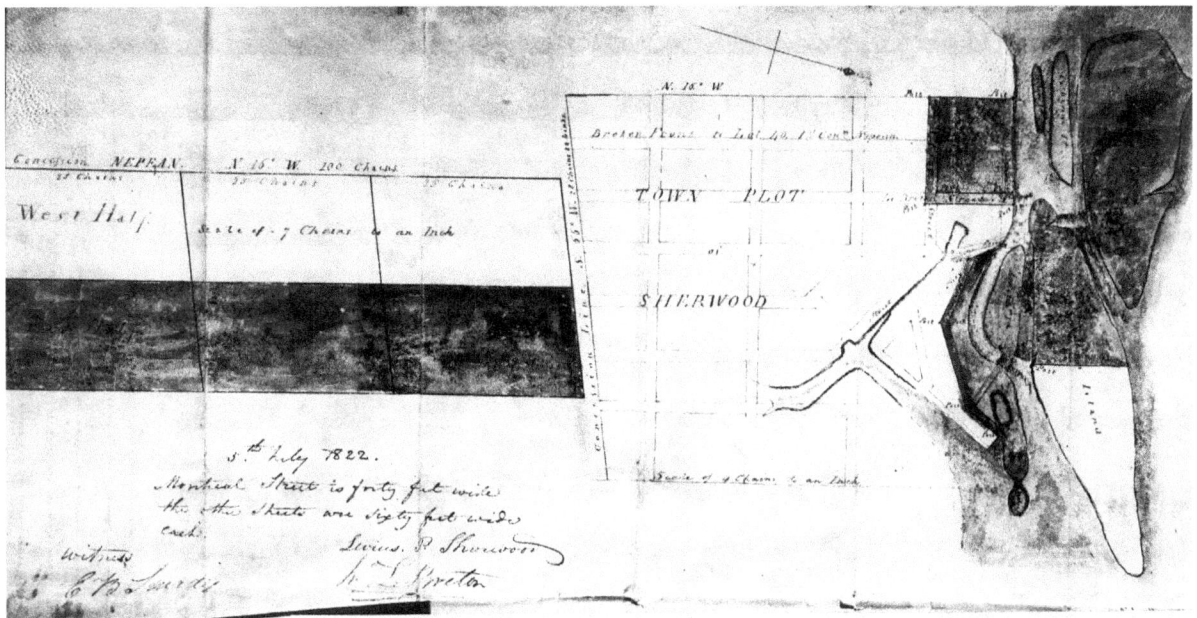

FIGURE 1-17: **Plan for the 'Town of Sherwood,' 1822**
Captain John LeBreton proposed subdividing his lands near the Chaudière Islands (right) but had no takers due to a dispute with Governor General Dalhousie.
(Source: Library and Archives Canada NMC 3974)

Reflections

Canada's capital has a magnificent natural setting that reflected the frontier energy of the new country. Although the aboriginal inhabitants of the Ottawa valley left few permanent settlements, their attachment to the river and stewardship of their lands might have set a good example for the woods-based industries in future generations.

Although the Ottawa valley was near the French settlements along the St. Lawrence, it was closed to European settlement for over 200 years. When the British opened the valley to settlement in the 19th century, the lands were in the same natural state that they had been during the time of the first European contacts with the aboriginal peoples described by Champlain in 1613. So the British colonial authorities had the opportunity to learn from over two centuries of settlement in North America. Their 1789 land planning regulations appear to have absorbed many good ideas for the design of towns and townships.

However, while good physical planning is an important component for long-term success in new community development, it is only one part of the solution. Short-term financial and political difficulties can be major obstacles for effective implementation of town planning principles. Raw land in the Ottawa Valley had nearly no monetary value in 1800, since the government was giving away huge quantities of it for free. Under these conditions, it should have been possible to set aside the lands needed for public spaces, roads, and community facilities. Yet the desperate financial position of the colonies meant that they could not afford miniscule cash costs to survey the property and protect the lands needed for public facilities in towns.

Before we condemn the early administrators, it should be remembered that Upper and Lower

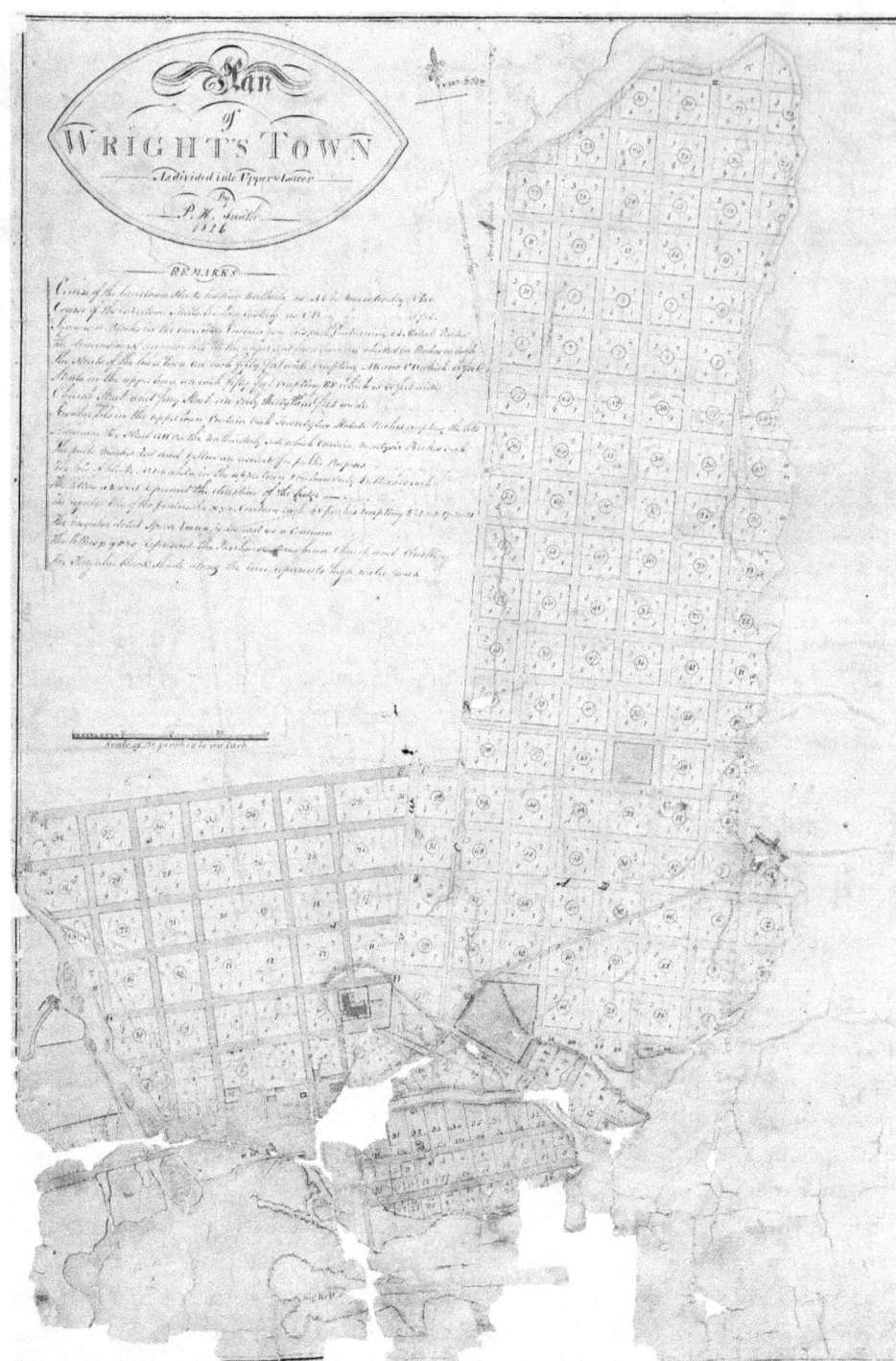

FIGURE 1-18: **First subdivision plan for Wright's Town, 1826**
There was little development of this early plan for the Hull area because the Wright family preferred to lease property, rather than sell.
(Source: Library and Archives Canada NMC 1443, drawn by P.H. Smith)

Canada were essentially rural settlements until the 20th century. The important work was to get the farm lots laid out and the settlers to work clearing the land, so the colony could feed itself. The rural township surveys accomplished that objective tolerably well. In comparison, planning and surveying towns was expensive and could wait; so it often did. The problems arose when the necessary planning was not done in advance of townsite development.

A second important difference from Canada's 21st century experience was the importance of military issues. For both aboriginal peoples and European settlers, almost every generation had a war. The consequences of losing were severe – forced migration, destruction of property, violent death or near extinction. Military considerations were therefore primary inputs into decisions about overall settlement patterns, communication routes, the location of towns, and the detailed design and fortification of urban areas. The military establishment often had the best access to capital and professional expertise, so civilian development made use of their planning and infrastructure during peacetime.

One important similarity with current ideals is the interest in property ownership. Land ownership meant wealth and power in eighteenth century Europe, and it was confined to privileged nobility. British North American settlements used land ownership as an incentive for rural settlement. Owning property and a home were powerful motivations for the citizens of the new country. Farmers and ordinary townspeople worked hard to clear their lots and build their own houses. For middle-class people like retired army officers, it was possible to obtain ownership of vast areas (5,000 acres was not uncommon) that would be equivalent in size to the estates of the most powerful noble families in Europe.

It took a few decades for the aspiring gentry to realize that mere ownership of uncleared land was not the equivalent of wealth. The more astute speculators understood that a single mill might produce more cash than hundreds of acres of wilderness. But there were few outlets for investment capital in the new colonies, so land ownership and speculation became considered as both a right and widespread occupation of all classes and professions. When land speculation became too widespread, it sometimes delayed development in key locations, or scattered it across the landscape in a 'leapfrog' manner that was inefficient for infrastructure and defence. The distribution of raw land and promotion of its settlement was a principal task of 19th century governments in Upper and Lower Canada.

When the development of the Ottawa valley finally got underway in the early 19th century, these influences – the primacy of rural development, military considerations, and land speculation – would shape some of the first settlements.

The early European settlement history of the Ottawa Valley is a study in contrasts. Along Lower Canada's north shore, there was slow but steady progress towards a model agricultural community under the paternalistic leadership of the Wright family. The provincial government got the type of settlement it wanted, without investing a penny since the "leader and associates" undertook all the expenses of development in exchange for enormous land grants. However, the Wrights were focused upon agricultural pursuits, with little interest in developing more than a market village.

The early settlement of Nepean and Gloucester townships on the south side of the Ottawa River was much slower and haphazard, even though the lands were surveyed six years before the Wrights arrived. Upper Canada paid for the surveys, but its development policies were less effective, since the large land grants to Loyalists who had already settled along the St. Lawrence River led to chronic problems with absentee landowners who held the lands for speculative profit.

The second development phase of the Upper Canada townships was dominated by military concerns, following the near-disaster in the War of 1812. The Perth and Richmond settlements had the advantage of some advance planning, modest military supplies and financial support. While Perth developed into a charming county town, Richmond's intended role as the centre of the Rideau River settlement was usurped by later development at Ottawa.

Lord Dalhousie's hostile attitude towards land speculation along the Rideau and Ottawa rivers was a serious outcome of his minor dispute with Captain John LeBreton. Since Upper Canada was barely five years removed from the end of the war, the Governor General likely viewed these matters through the lens of his role as Commander-in-Chief for the British forces in the Canadas, rather than as the head of a civil government promoting settlement. LeBreton's attempt to make a 1,200 percent speculative profit, while perhaps no worse than the conduct of any other landowners of the era, seemed unbecoming to a half-pay army officer in a society preparing for another war. The dispute might have blown over with little effect, except that Dalhousie's later policies would sometimes be more concerned with preventing land speculation than with promoting proper urban development in a region that would soon experience rapid growth due to construction of military infrastructure.

These policies could be an early example of friction between the local residents, or 'Town,' and the imperial government representing the 'Crown.' Conflicts between 'Town' and 'Crown' would be a constant issue in the Ottawa Valley for the next two centuries.

CHAPTER 2

Building Bytown (1826-1832)

... a valuable locality for a considerable village or a town ...
– Governor General Lord Dalhousie's instructions to Lt. Col. John By, 1826[127]

When Lt. Col. John By (Figure 2-1) reached "Wright's Town"[128] on September 21, 1826, he found a small frontier community of perhaps 1,000 people, struggling to become an agricultural service centre and the forwarding post for the precarious Ottawa Valley timber trade. The lands on the Lower Canada side of the Chaudière were almost entirely owned by Philemon Wright's family. The Upper Canada side of the Ottawa River was mainly untouched wilderness in the hands of absentee landlords, chief among them the Crown's riverfront property purchased by Dalhousie in 1823. A tavern and storehouse were located at Richmond Landing,[129] and Nicholas Sparks had cleared one-third of his 200 acres[130] (Figure 2-2). There were perhaps two other square timber houses and a few log cabins in the entire Nepean Township, and fewer across the Rideau River in Gloucester Township.[131]

FIGURE 2-1: Lt. Col. John By
Lieutenant-Colonel John By (1783[132]-1836) was a career army officer and military engineer. He was the principal designer of the Rideau Canal (now a UNESCO World Heritage site) and founder of the settlement that became Bytown, and later, Ottawa. For further details, see the Cast of Characters.
(Source: Library and Archives Canada C-028531)

FIGURE 2-2: 1825 Elliott Map (detail)
Detail from a preliminary survey for the northern terminus of the Rideau Canal by the Royal Engineers. 'Wright's Town' is to the upper centre; Nicholas Sparks' farmstead is in the lower centre. The north boundary of Sparks' land is Wellington Street today; the Canal entrance was eventually built at 'Sleigh Bay' at the lower right, rather than Richmond Landing at the centre.
(Source: Library and Archives Canada NMC 3163, sketch by G.A. Elliot)

By and his small engineering team[133] established a base camp at Sleigh Bay on the Upper Canada side of the river, opposite Wright's settlement (Figure 2-3). The campsite's location was not an accident, since an earlier reconnaissance by the engineers (Figure 2-2) had indicated that this bay might be considered a suitable entrance for the canal.

Lord Dalhousie joined By's team on September 25, during a tour of Canadian military defence works and canals.[134] The Governor General landed at Wright's Town where "my old friend Philemon had his house all ready for us."[135] Dalhousie was engaged in debilitating political conflict with the Lower Canada legislature for the previous four years, so he seemed to relish returning to his roots as a military commander planning the defence of Upper Canada.[136] He took a detailed technical interest in the canal design and spent September 25 hiking through the woods with the engineers to examine the proposed route for the canal entrance from the Ottawa River. Although it must have pleased Dalhousie that the entrance would be located on lands he purchased in 1823, Col. By was not patronizing his governor with the proposed

FIGURE 2-3: First Camp, Bytown, September 1826
This sketch, attributed to Lt. Col. By, shows the Royal Engineers headquarters for construction of the Rideau Canal, on its first day.
(Source: McCord Museum, M386)

location. Sleigh Bay was the foot of a small ravine that cut through the cliff to a beaver meadow eighty feet above the river. A flight of locks could be built there more economically than at any other spot except for LeBreton's property at Richmond Landing. Dalhousie's dispute with LeBreton made it unlikely that the Governor would pay his £3000 asking price, even if those lands did offer the opportunity for a second flight of locks to bypass the Chaudière for commercial traffic to the upper Ottawa River.[137]

Dalhousie and By could not resist Sleigh Bay on that fall morning in 1826, because they were army officers siting a military canal, and the western edge of the ravine was formed by a rocky bluff with a sheer cliff falling 180 feet to the Ottawa River. It was the dominant landscape feature of the area, and a natural fortress similar to Cape Diamond at Québec City. If the Rideau Canal entered the Ottawa River at Sleigh Bay, it could be guarded by a citadel that would be far stronger (and much less expensive) than the forts planned for the Kingston end of the canal.[138] Any competent military officer would attempt to seize and control such a spectacular site for a fortress, as Dalhousie had done in 1823. The Royal Engineers and the Board of Ordnance would continue to hold the lands into the 1850s, when Barrack Hill became Parliament Hill.[139]

The next day, Dalhousie and By examined Richmond Landing and the Chaudière, where the Governor General approved By's proposal for a timber chute similar to the one constructed by Ruggles Wright on the opposite bank. By also argued that a bridge across the river would be needed to connect the canal head to Wright's mills and workshops and the raw materials on the north side. At this time, no major river had been bridged in British North America. By had studied the site carefully, preparing a sketch (Figure 2-4), and proposed a chain of seven bridges hopping across the islands.

Dalhousie approved the daring bridge scheme, reasoning that it would reduce the cost of canal labour and materials and could become a toll connection between the two provinces.[140] That evening, Dalhousie extended his thoughts about the civilian use of the canal zone in a letter to By that contained detailed instructions to lay out a town site adjacent to the canal works. Since this letter is essentially the charter for the original plan of our nation's capital, it is worth examining in its entirety:

Falls of the Chaudière on Ottawa
26 Sept 1826

My dear Sir:
I cannot but approve in the strongest terms of the suggestion you propose for a bridge acrofs [sic] at the broken rocks and islands here. The advantages are obvious and the expense a trifle, as preparatory [sic] to the great works you are appointed to superintend. If any sanction is necessary, I give it in the fullest manner.

I take the opportunity of meeting you here to place in your hands a sketch plan of several lots of land which I thought it advantageous to purchase for the use of Government, where this Canal is likely to be carried into effect. These not only contain the site for the head lock but they offer a valuable locality for a considerable village or town for the lodging of artificers and other necessary assistants in so great a work.

I propose that these should be clearly surveyed and laid out in lots of two to four acres, to be granted according to the means of settlers and to pay a ground rent of 2/6d per annum to the Crown annually. The location to contain the positive condition of building a house within twelve months from the date of the ticket and to place the house on the line of streets according to plan to be made of it. Allow me to caution you against the immediate rush of applicants for these lots that will be made. Make particular inquiries as to individuals and others before you consent to their petitions. It will be highly desirable to encourage half pay officers and respectable people should they offer to build on these lots.

As the purchase was made by me for the public services and has already been approved, I place the whole in your hands for the purpose I have now explained.

I have the honour to be, my dear Sir Your's faithfully Dalhousie [141]

Although these lands were located in Upper Canada, under the civil control of Lt. Governor Sir Peregrine Maitland, Dalhousie probably felt justified in issuing these instructions because he had personally purchased the property, the deeds were registered in his name, and the construction of military works was under his control as the commander-in-chief for British North America. His concern about preventing speculation was understandable, given his experience with LeBreton, but also because absentee owners holding land for speculative purposes had hindered development throughout Upper Canada including Nepean and Gloucester townships. Leasing lands at nominal rates was appropriate for a construction camp, especially when huge capital expenditures are about to be made by the government that will make the surrounding area vastly more valuable. The proposed annual rent of 2s/6d for a two-acre lot was trivial and appears to be well below market value, since Nicholas Sparks sold adjacent land for £200/acre in December 1826.[142]

None of the four major towns that were first developed in Upper Canada (Kingston, Toronto,

FIGURE 2-4: The Chaudière Falls, Ottawa River
This picturesque view, attributed to Lt. Col. John By, is also an engineering study for the location of the Chaudière bridges.
(Source: Library and Archives Canada C-000614; Toronto Public Library; JRR 1405)

London, and Hamilton) followed Lord Dorchester's model design and it is unclear if Dalhousie knew of the planning regulations. These early Ontario gridiron town plans had no aesthetic pretensions. Their aims were primarily functional: to provide for fast, orderly development, the equitable distribution of land, and basic public land needs at the lowest possible cost of surveying the lots. Since most of the lots were to be given away, there was no revenue to offset the costs of more complex plans that might provide public amenities.

Two early community plans broke this parsimonious tradition: Guelph in 1827 and Goderich in 1829. These two towns were to anchor the development of 400,000 ha of land, the Huron Tract, in western Ontario. The private developer of these towns, the Canada Company, had an incentive to create attractive plans, since they wished to sell town lots. Plans for both of these places, usually credited to John Galt, adopted the idea of a radial pattern of streets converging on a town market (Figure 2-5).

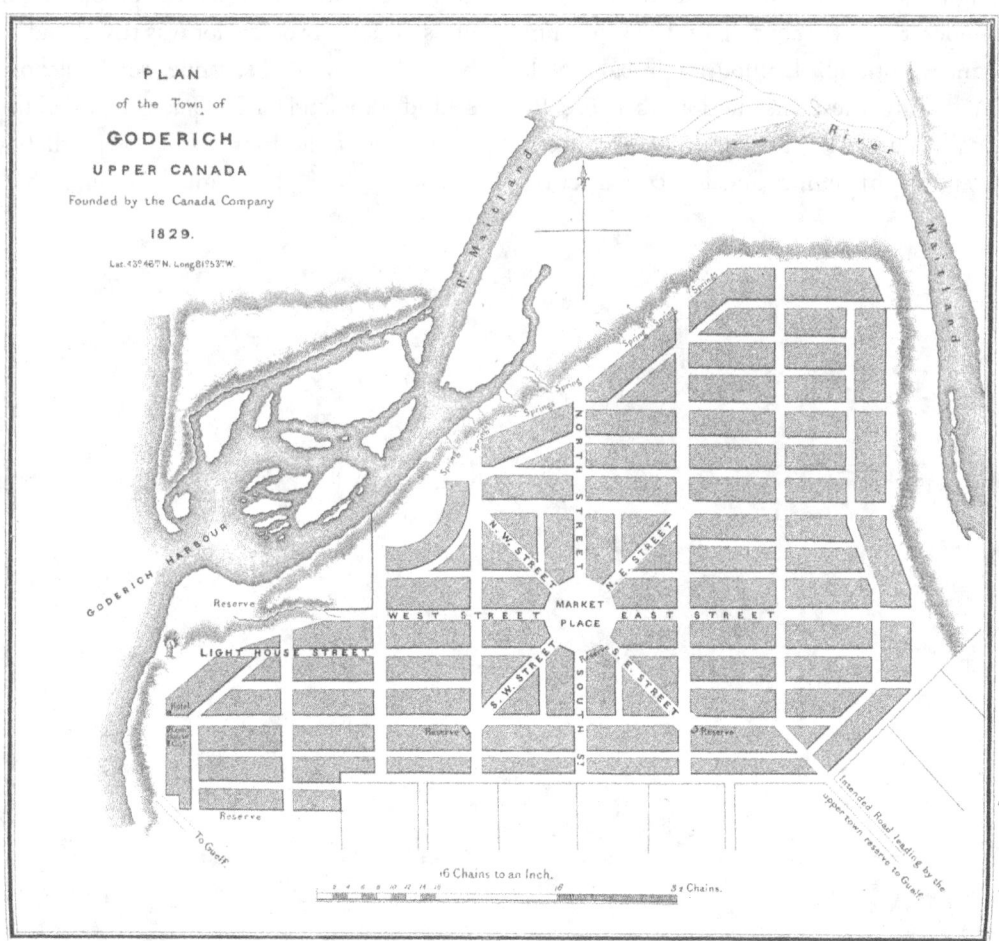

Figure 2-5: Galt's plan for Goderich, 1829
Goderich was arranged around an octagonal central market square. As in Renaissance designs, a grid pattern was used for local streets.[143] John Galt is known to have been influenced by the town-planning approaches used by the Holland Company, which acquired rights to develop upper New York State. The latter development was supervised by Joseph Ellicott, whose brother had succeeded L'Enfant as the planner for Washington. Thus, the plans for Guelph and Goderich are descended more from L'Enfant's plans than from Georgian England.[144]
(Source: Joseph Bouchette, *The British Dominions in North America* (London: Longmans, 1831))

On September 27, 1826, Dalhousie presided at a small opening ceremony for the project. Thomas McKay, the head mason for the Lachine Canal, had accompanied By to Wright's Town to identify sites to quarry stone for the Rideau works. McKay prepared a great block of stone for the first arch of the Chaudière bridges, which Dalhousie tapped into place, confiding to his diary:

A Royal salute from two field six pounders added grandly to the scene at that wild & romantic spot. I took my departure at that moment, having made a commencement of three great works. They will prove to immense importance in that young country, become the means of establishing markets for produce, create a circulation of money in coin, and lead to an assemblage of labourers who will most assuredly settle in that part, now a tract of forest & waste lands.[145]

Col. By invited the Governor General to return in a year to walk across the bridges, which was a bold suggestion given the uncertain design and scale of the crossing.[146] Work on the first spans of the bridge commenced immediately, with Thomas McKay as the contractor.

The Early Townsite

Although Kingston was the largest town in Upper Canada and the site of a major military garrison, Colonel By decided to establish his headquarters at the Ottawa River end of the Rideau Canal, because that terminus was closer to Montréal. In the autumn of 1826, the woods on either side of the entrance valley at Sleigh Bay were cleared, and a construction camp was started to accommodate the hundreds of labourers who flooded into the area in search of wages. The townsite was laid out in a few weeks in October 1826, starting with a street along the south side of Dalhousie's lot. West of the canal, the new street was named in honour of the Duke of Wellington, Dalhousie's former commander and By's current Master of Ordinance. East of the entrance valley, the base line was called Rideau Street. Wellington Street would connect the entrance locks to the Chaudière Bridge and Richmond Landing, while Rideau Street connected the canal to the Rideau River (Figure 2-6).

Since the large bluff beside the Entrance Valley was reserved for future barracks and military use, only a smaller promontory was available for immediate settlement in the lands west of the canal. The area was known as Upper Town, and By leased these sites to the "respectable people," following Dalhousie's instructions.[147] The bluffs immediately east of the Entrance Valley were also reserved for military purposes. The commander's house was built there at By's expense, so the site became known as Colonel's Hill.[148]

The lands north of Rideau Street were named Lower Town and divided into lots by John McTaggart, a surveyor on By's staff. Most lots were not inhabitable because they were in the remains of a cedar swamp.[149] But with hundreds of labourers flooding in, By had the Lower Town swamp drained in the spring of 1827, and these lots were quickly taken up.

The surveyor's chain (66 feet or 20 m.) was the basic unit of measurement for rapid layout of the town-sites on Dalhousie's lands. Wellington and Rideau streets were established as 1.5 chains wide (99 feet) and other street rights of way were one chain. In Lower Town, George, York and King Edward streets were laid out with 1.5 chain widths to accommodate a canal drainage ditch (the ByWash), a farmer's market (ByWard Market) and a grand avenue respectively. Given the intense demand for lots, By decided to make them smaller than the 2-4 acres suggested by Dalhousie. Most early blocks were laid out in lots one chain wide (66 ft.) and 2-3 chains deep (132-196 ft.). Later lots were only 1.5 chains deep (99 ft.), the typical size for an urban parcel.

The large initial lots were mainly leased to the canal staff and contractors like McKay at the lowest rate. The merchants who leased the smaller lots at £4 to £6 per annum bitterly resented the difference and launched petitions and lawsuits to allow them to purchase their lots.[150]

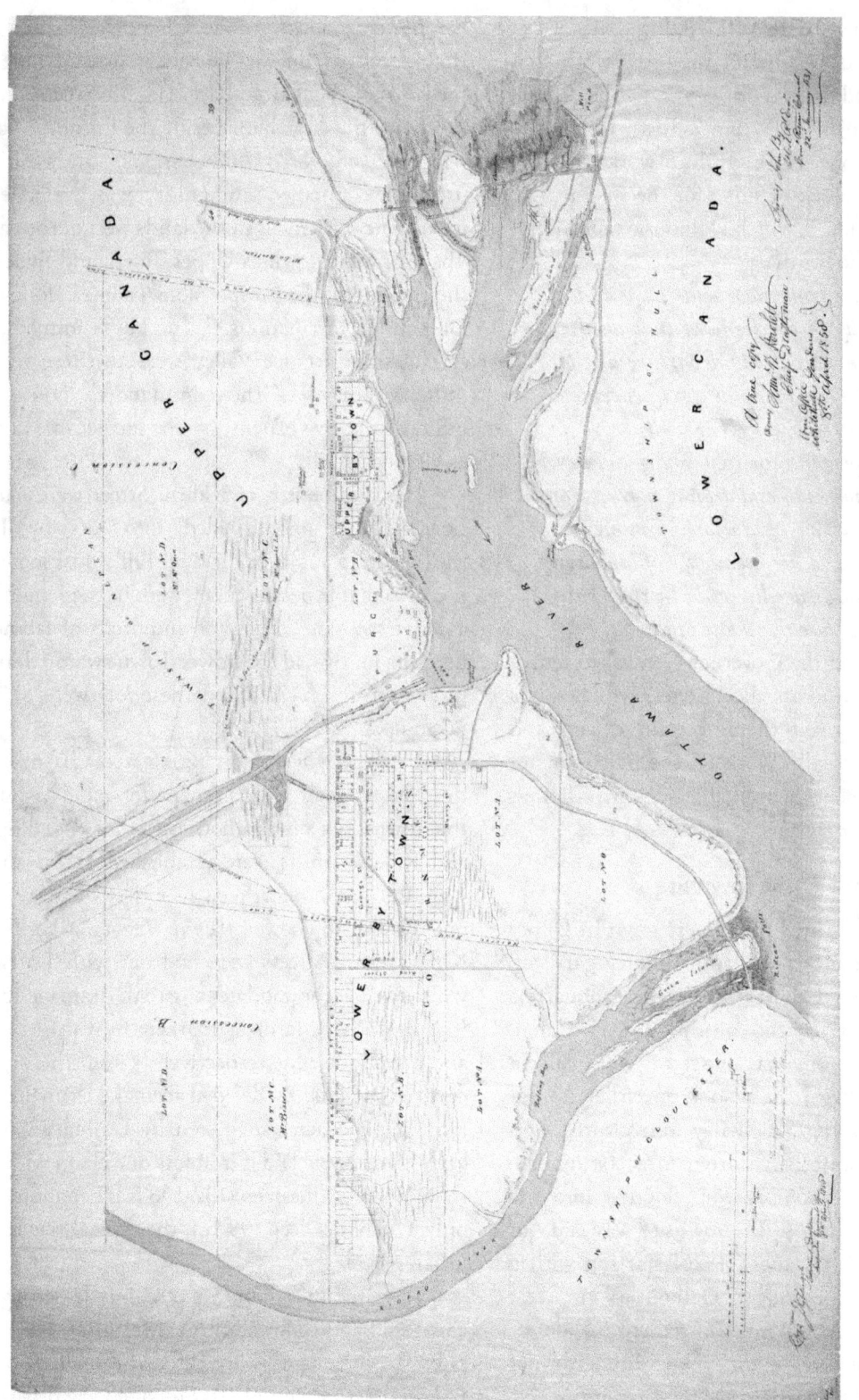

Figure 2-6: Layout of Rideau Canal and initial Bytown townsites, 1828
The essential structure of the frontier settlement is already in place, only two years after the start of construction. Working class 'Lower By Town' is east (left) of the Canal; the military barracks are on the hill in the middle and the middle class district is to the west (right).

(Source: John By, Lt. Colonel Royl. Engrs. Com'g. Rideau Canal, June 26, 1828. Library and Archives Canada, NMC 130131)

In November 1826, several of the private land owners in the township came forward to offer lands for construction of the canal, expecting that the works would make their remaining land much more valuable. Nicholas Sparks agreed to donate 200 feet on either side of the canal and moved the concession street on the south side of his lot to the north side. Sparks thereby gave up sixty-six feet on the north side of his farm lot, but his land would face Wellington and Rideau streets, which would be improved at government expense.[151]

Since the canal works would be entirely located in Upper Canada, the local enabling legislation had to come from its Legislative Assembly. The statute passed by the legislature introduced the purpose of the project as: "for the Transport of Naval and Military Stores. ... Will tend most essentially to the security of this Province by facilitating measures for its defence."[152] The act granted broad powers to the officer charged with construction of the canal, permitting him to survey and build dams, tunnels, bridges and roads, and to seize land for the "intended Canal, Locks, Towing Paths, Rail-ways and other Constructions and Erections."[153]

Curiously, the statute did not specifically mention land for fortifications, even though security and defence were the main objects of the legislation. Within months, this omission was to cause problems, since Dalhousie's purchase was not large enough to accommodate a proper 19th century fortress. In addition to walls, ditches and earthworks, a fort from that era needed a glacis, or cleared area, for the guns to do their deadly work. The Royal Engineers requested another eighty-four acres west of the canal from Nicholas Sparks, but they could not agree upon a price with the owner. While some of this land was required for a boat turning basin at the head of the locks, the remainder was clearly for military use as a southerly extension of the Barrack Hill fortification site.[154] Col. By expropriated the extra land from Sparks, and the resulting lawsuits lasted over twenty years.[155]

Early Bridge and Canal Construction

Thomas McKay continued to work on the first span of the Chaudière bridges over the winter of 1826-27, and also erected a handsome stone Commissariat building for the Royal Engineers in the Entrance Valley.[156] The pace of construction picked up in the spring and summer of 1827, after contractors began work on excavation for the canal and construction of the entrance locks. The new construction camp appears to have acquired a name that spring, when it was first reported as Bytown following a banquet in Kingston.[157] Town-site improvements accelerated after the arrival of two companies of the Royal Sappers and Miners from England. The Sappers built themselves stone barracks and store buildings on the hill, and a modest stone house for Colonel By and his family on the opposite side of the valley. A wooden civilian barracks was built at the corner of Rideau and Sussex streets.

A bridge across the canal excavation was another obvious need, and the soldiers quickly erected a stone arch bridge at Rideau Street, just past the head lock. The Sappers' Bridge was solidly constructed, with a 19 foot (5.8 m) roadway and masonry parapets.[158] A two-foot plank sidewalk was suspended over the north side to provide a safer pedestrian way across the narrow bridge, which become quite busy after more buildings were erected in Upper Town and the Chaudière bridges were completed.

The Chaudière bridges were the first to join Upper and Lower Canada and an extraordinary feat of early 19th century civil engineering. The Union Bridge was actually a set of seven spans crossing the channels and islands at the Chaudière Falls (Figure 2-7). Lord Dalhousie described the spans in his diary as:

... It commences from the North side, near to Philemon Wright's mills ...

No. 1 and 2 Bridges are stone arches, dry built but coped with lime & large stones on edge; each arch is 57 feet.

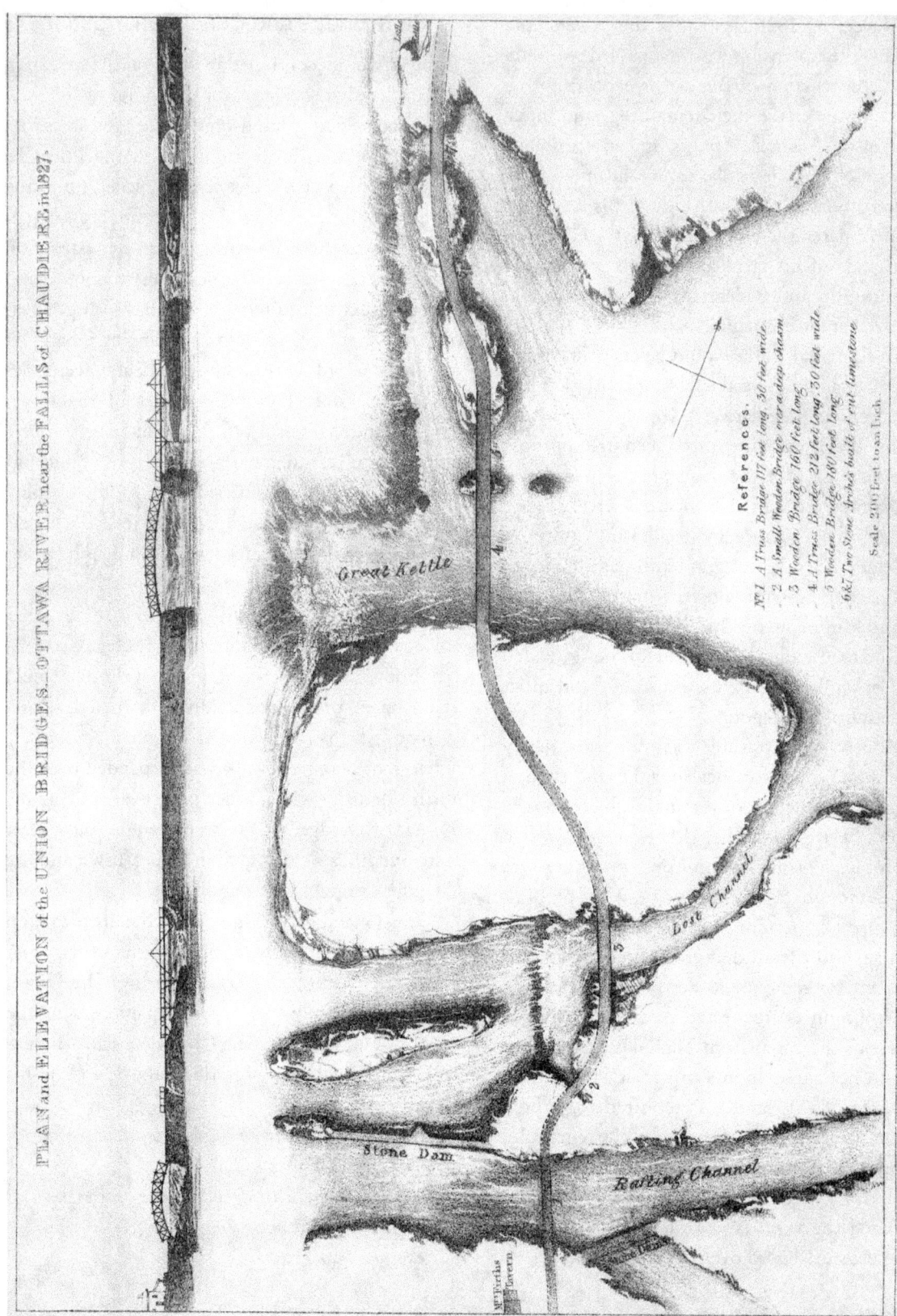

FIGURE 2-7: Bouchette 1831 lithograph of Bridge plan and elevation
(Source: Library and Archives Canada C-036203)

No. 3, a long straight Bridge of wood, rough beams, two supports fixed on the flat rocky bed, 186 feet.

No. 4 is to be a wooden Bridge 212 feet span with an easy spring of arch 20 feet; there is however now only a temporary suspension bridge to facilitate the preparations & give a walking passage to people employed. Of this I must refer to the drawing, only saying that it is a support on 3 cables, with planks on pathway and a hand rope to hold by. I have ordered a model of this which I intend to send to Dalhousie Castle.

No. 5 is a straight bridge 164 feet in length, with three supports.

No. 6 a wooden arch 117 feet long, spring 9 feet. This and No. 4 are done on a mechanical principle common in America. The uprights tie together, in triangular divisions, and give great strength to the beam or arch on which the path rests. It is not pleasing to the eyes, but that will not be considered if it answers in more material points.[159]

As Colonel By had promised, Lord Dalhousie could walk across the river when he returned to lay the foundation stone for the canal in September 1827. However, the crossing was more perilous then either man expected. The 212-foot span across the face of the falls proved quite difficult to bridge. Support piers were out of the question, since the current was swift and a 300-foot sounding line did not touch bottom in the 'kettle.' The engineers shot a thin rope across the chasm with a small brass cannon, pulled thicker ropes across, and threaded wood planks to make a rather unstable suspension bridge for construction purposes. Lord Dalhousie wobbled across this rope bridge on September 26, 1827. He and Colonel By were called back to accompany the plucky Lady Dalhousie, who became the first woman to cross the bridge (Figure 2-8), to

FIGURE 2-8: Lady Dalhousie Crossing the Falls, 1827
Col. By and the Governor General assist her across the precarious bridge over the roaring Chaudière.
(Source: Library and Archives Canada C-002173; sketch by Robert Bouchette)

her husband's surprise and delight: "I admit it was a bold thing for a Lady, but I was satisfied before of the safety of it."[160]

The Governor General was perhaps a bit too confident in his engineers' infallibility. Nineteenth century engineering was more craft than science, with much trial and many errors. By had designed an innovative wooden truss bridge to spring across the gap (Figure 2-9). Chains were drawn across the gap to assemble the truss, but two snapped in April 1828, throwing the workmen into the river, where at least one was drowned. The builders then tried eight-inch ropes suspended over trestles supported by a scow anchored in the channel. A strong summer gale sent the scow downstream, destroying the bridge again. The engineers didn't give up; they ordered enormous iron chains with ten-inch links from the naval stores in Kingston. These held up long enough to assemble the truss bridge, which opened in October 1828.[161]

FIGURE 2-9: Wooden Bridge across the Ottawa River at the Chaudière Falls
Two previous bridges fell during construction. This one, although "not pleasing to the eyes," lasted until it collapsed in 1836 due to lack of maintenance.
(Source: Library and Archives Canada C-016331, sketch by John Burrows)

The Chaudière bridges should have made Captain John LeBreton's property at Richmond Lands much more valuable, but Lord Dalhousie and Colonel By continued to dispute his title and cut him out of development. The approach to the bridge was secured by the purchase of a small lot from the adjacent landowner, Sherwood, and the tavern and storehouse on LeBreton's lands were relocated there at government expense. Although LeBreton had prepared a subdivision plan for his "Town of Sherwood" in 1822, he did not have clear title to the land until a court decision handed down in August 1828, a few days before Dalhousie retired from Canada. LeBreton jubilantly placed this advertisement in the Perth newspaper:

Town of Sherwood
In consequence of the decision of the Court of Kings Bench held at Perth on the 20th instant, providing the subscriber's indisputable title to that valuable tract of land in the township of Nepean, formerly known by the name of Richmond Landing (at present the Town of Sherwood) and adjoining to By Town, reports prejudicial to the title of the said land having been maliciously circulated by a personage of high rank and responsibility, have heretofore prevented the subscriber from disposing of said land. The situation is most beautiful and salubrious, being on the south side of the Chaudière Falls, with the Grand Union Bridge abutting on the centre of the front and leading through the main street. It is replete with mill sites, and for commerce no situation on the River Ottawa can equal it. The subscriber is determined as much as possible to confine his sales to persons of respectability.
Britannia, Ottawa River.
26th August 1828.[162]

Alas, no 'persons of respectability' came forward to purchase, since Upper Town and Sparks' property were more attractive. Colonel By continued to cut LeBreton out, refusing to pay for the road right-of-way across his property to the bridge. The 1836 collapse of the main bridge span meant that LeBreton's land was once again a backwater, and he had to wait for the 1844 opening of the new Union Bridge to market his lots. The first buildings in "LeBreton Flats" were mainly middle class homes that were an extension of the Upper Town community.[163]

As construction expanded, the Ordnance allowed the poorest Irish labourers to build a second construction camp south of Lower Town, along the northeast edge of the canal excavation. This temporary camp was called Corktown, after the Irish home county of many emigrants. They built sod huts and earth burrows in their native tradition.[164] The workers had dangerous jobs, getting crushed in excavation, blown up by explosions, and dying of malaria by the hundreds while pushing the canal through the fetid swamp known as the Cranberry Marsh. John MacTaggart estimated that one in ten Corktown residents died in the first two years of the job.[165]

The Rideau Canal's political support in Britain seemed solid, because the chief promoter of the plans to fortify the Canadas, the Duke of Wellington, had been British prime minister since January 1826. Work paused in the winter of 1827-28 to allow the Ordnance Department to review Colonel By's much higher estimates for the completion of the canal to a standard that fit the new steamboats that were plying the St. Lawrence and Ottawa rivers.[166] An Ordnance committee approved By's mandate and a local commission led by Nova Scotia Lieutenant-Governor Sir James Kempt approved the steamboat plan in June 1828. The work raced forward again with construction along the entire route.[167]

When Lower Canada Surveyor-General Joseph Bouchette visited the Ottawa Valley in 1828, Bytown had probably surpassed Wrightstown in size, with perhaps 940 people living in Upper and Lower towns. Bouchette's map (Figure 2-10) and description of the site flattered the young settlement:

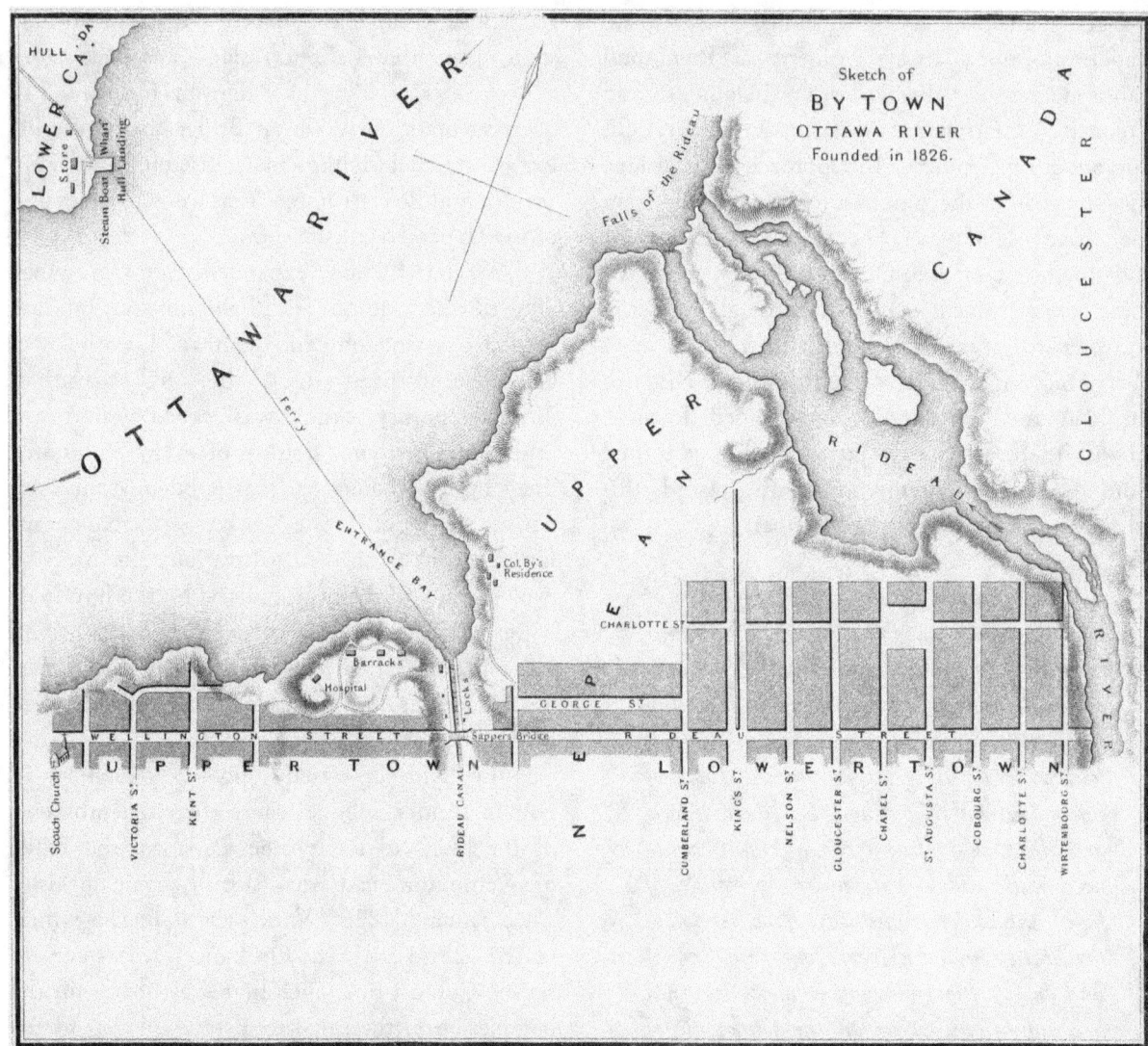

Figure 2-10: Bouchette's 1831 map of Bytown
This map made the town-site look more orderly than it probably was at the time. Compare the minimal nature of Bytown's non-plan to 1829 Goderich from the same publication (Figure 2-5). Bytown had a larger population at the time, and much less thought in its planning.
(Source: Library and Archives Canada NMC 15506)

> ... The streets are laid out with much regularity, and of a liberal width, that will hereafter contribute to the convenience, salubrity, and elegance of the place. The number of houses now built is not far short of one hundred and fifty, most of which are constructed of wood, frequently in a style of neatness and taste that reflects great credit upon the inhabitants. On the elevated banks of the bay, the hospital, an extensive stone building, and three stone barracks, stand conspicuous; and nearly on a level with them, and on the eastern side of the bay, is delightfully situated the residence of Colonel By, the commanding royal engineer on that station. From his veranda the most splendid view is beheld that the magnificent scenery of the Canadas affords.[168]

Although Bouchette could be impressed by the rapid progress of construction, Bytown's town-site plan was a terrible mess. The farm lots from the 1794 survey collided at odd angles – some were laid out at right angles to the Ottawa River, and some orthogonal to the Rideau River, with many irregular lots along their shores. The Ordnance lands were subdivided with streets and blocks based upon the 66-foot chain, while the private lands of Sparks and Louis Besserer had 60 foot streets and narrow lots. So the surveyed blocks met at awkward angles and none of the major streets lined up.

The Rideau Canal works made things worse, since they cut through the survey grids at an angle. The lands reserved for the canal and fortress left a broad, empty swath disconnecting the two town-sites. The Sappers Bridge was sensibly built at a right angle to the canal, but it therefore could not connect Rideau to Wellington Street, and the Barrack Hill reserve deflected the road from the bridge far south of Wellington, creating the Barrack Hill Bulge.

The town-site layout made social tensions worse in the town. The rigid spatial segregation and stark contrast between the Protestant, Anglo-Scots elite on the high ground in Upper Town and the Catholic French/Irish labourers in Lower Town swamps caused constant jealousy, friction and political strife in the decades ahead. The canal and a large swath of Crown land separating the two communities made it too easy for the gentility to ignore severe problems in Lower Town and Corktown.

The financial arrangements for early Bytown may have been appropriate for a construction camp, but they did not work for a growing settlement. Short-term leases did not encourage tenants to build permanent homes or maintain their property in either Wright's Town or Bytown. And the token rents in Bytown did not produce enough income to fund proper town infrastructure.[169] The Ordnance managed to build a well and market shed in both Upper and Lower Town, but that was about the limit of the initial town-site improvements. The private builders could make few public improvements because their contracts were closely specified for the Canal Works. So the Royal Engineers and Sappers and Miners mostly built the meagre town-site improvements during the limited time that was not devoted to the canal. On the Lower Canada side, the Wright family completed some village improvements, when not tending to their farms and timber businesses.

The institutional frameworks for the frontier towns were also hobbled by their location and the Ordnance requirements. Both Wright's Town and Bytown were border towns, far from their provincial capitals, and were given little financial or institutional support. Upper and Lower Canada did not know how to co-operate for bridges, river improvements, municipal governments or law enforcement. Lower Canada assumed that Philemon Wright would take care of disputes.[170] The Upper Canada government assumed that the British Ordnance would be handling problems in their camp, but the nearest courts and jails were in Perth, almost 80 km. away by a poor bush road.

British authorities could produce a good colonial town plan if they put their mind to it in advance, as we saw in Philadelphia and Charlottetown. Perth and Richmond look like a model of foresight and good town planning, when compared to Bytown.[171] But the growing settlement at the head of the Rideau Canal suffered from the worst aspects of both construction camp impermanence and military site control. The combination was dysfunctional for a frontier town, and completely inappropriate for planning a capital city.

Of course, Colonel By never thought that he was building a capital city, or even a frontier town. He was focussed on the extraordinary engineering challenges of building the Rideau Canal through the wilderness. Dalhousie's September 1826 town-site instructions were incomplete, conflicting, and arrived at the last minute. The Governor General did not do the necessary work with the Upper Canada government to establish a town at the end of the Rideau Canal, despite his earlier insight that his land purchase might someday hold the seat of government. The oversight was perhaps minor at the time, but it caused problems in the decades ahead.

Construction of the Rideau Canal was an extraordinarily difficult task, requiring engineering innovations that are now recognized as part of a UNESCO World Heritage site.[172] After Colonel By's redesign of the canal to accommodate the new steamboat technology was approved in 1827, construction re-started along the entire route. Each section was given to a different private contractor so the entire waterway would be available for military use as quickly as possible.[173] The Royal Engineers travelled up and down the route from their Bytown headquarters to monitor the work and solve problems.

Thomas McKay, the builder for the initial flight of locks to Ottawa, discovered a quarry site in the Entrance Valley, which sped up construction and increased his profit on the contract. He would re-invest his earnings in purchasing the land east of the Rideau Falls and his masons would build many other stone structures in the area. Other contractors were not so skilled or so lucky. The New York contractor who submitted the lowest bid for the dam at the Hog's Back Rapids had never worked with masonry before and he abandoned the project after his first effort washed away in 1828. It was rebuilt under the direct supervision of Colonel By, with the assistance of Philemon Wright's woodsmen.[174]

Inexperienced contractors initially won the excavation projects. They hired the unskilled labourers who flocked to Bytown, mainly recent Irish immigrants. The contractor digging the cut for the canal above the entrance locks had to be replaced when he could not complete the work, and Philemon Wright replaced another contractor who could not build an embankment along the swampy ground on the edge of Dow's Lake.[175]

Even worse problems emerged on the contracts further upstream from Bytown. "Swamp fever," now recognized as malaria, broke out along the entire canal project in 1828. Scores of labourers died of the disease and construction was halted on some segments of the canal that summer because there were no men fit to work. The hospital on Barrack Hill was full and the two doctors on the project were overwhelmed. Col. By and his chief clerk, John McTaggart, were both sick for months.[176]

While the engineers were busy with the frantic activity up and down the canal route, the construction camp at their headquarters was growing into a frontier town at a fast rate. Lower Town attracted the French Canadian lumbermen as well as the mainly Irish canal labourers. Shops and taverns to serve these communities and the canal and timber contractors were established along Rideau, Sussex and George streets, on land leased from the military. But although the Ordnance was the landlord, Bytown lacked a civil authority to administer the community and keep the peace.

As early as May 1827, the Governor was petitioned to appoint magistrates to administer the new town because the peace was "most dreadfully disturbed and lives and property being in danger day and night by drunken and riotous persons employed on the canal."[177] A public meeting was held in March 1828 to appoint 'public officers' to administer the town, but it was all unofficial, since the Bytown settlement was administered from Perth as an unincorporated part of Nepean Township, in the Bathurst District. The new magistrates and the 'council' were mostly from Protestant Upper Town, because it was bad for business if the Lower Town shopkeepers arrested their own customers. Bytown had no courthouse or jail, and few people would volunteer to be constables, since friends of the arrested men sometimes assaulted the constables in revenge. Transporting prisoners 80 km. through the woods to jail in Perth was a dangerous job. If the accused could escape across the river to Lower Canada, neither the magistrates nor the constables had the jurisdiction to retrieve them. As a result, Bytown developed a culture of lax support for the rule of law for the next decade.[178]

Like most frontier settlements of the era, Bytown had dirt streets, and residents dug latrines in the rear of their lots. Refuse was fed to pigs, or dumped in the streets, and water was brought up by barrel from the rivers below the town-site. Others preferred to draw from Lower Town's By Wash, which was a dangerous source, since it was also used for canal, storm and sanitary drainage.

Since the settlement was not incorporated and most land was leased, there was no municipal body to make other improvements. Colonel By had provided the most basic infrastructure, clearing some roads, building wells and erecting two market sheds. The engineers could fund improvements that were related to the canal, like Sapper's Bridge, but other town-site improvements were funded by the rents paid for lots on Ordnance land. They had been set at low rates to encourage development, so there was little cash for infrastructure. In 1830-31, these funds were used to make street drains, construct a public wharf and build a bridge over the Rideau River connecting Sussex Street to the new sawmills on Green Island.[179]

The canal made rapid progress after 1828. The flight of eight locks in the Entrance Valley and the Hog's Back Dam were both completed in 1831. The Royal Engineers also prepared separate plans for the fortification of the Rideau Canal during this period. Colonel By built defensible blockhouses at most of the lock stations as part of the canal contracts, but other military works needed separate funding from the British Treasury. The Royal Engineers prepared plans for fortresses at both ends of the canal in 1828-30. In October 1830, Colonel By was ordered to prepare plans for a permanent fortress on Barrack Hill (Figure 2-11), capable of resisting a sustained siege, similar to Halifax, Québec and Kingston. By's plan had extensive ramparts and required most of Sparks' land.[180] Construction of the great stone redoubt at Kingston's Fort Henry began in 1832, but the Bytown citadel was not funded at the same time. However, the Ordnance officers clung to the site tenaciously over the next two decades in expectation that it would be funded in the future.[181]

The last element of the Rideau waterway to be finished was the great stone arch dam at Jones Falls in the wilderness north of Kingston. When it was completed in late 1831, it was the highest dam in North America.[182] The canals and lakes behind the dam were navigable by the next spring. Colonel By took his family and fellow engineers on the inaugural voyage from Kingston, arriving at Ottawa in the steamboat *Pumper* on May 29, 1832.[183] Colonel By handed over the completed canal to the British Ordnance Department and prepared to return to England.

The British Treasury had spent almost £800,000 in Eastern Ontario over a six-year period.[184] Hundreds of men were employed in construction, and contractors like Thomas McKay and Philemon Wright made small fortunes that they reinvested in the region. Colonel By followed their lead, purchasing nearly 800 acres of the vacant lands south of Nicholas Sparks' farm lot for £1200 shortly before he left.[185] Since he invested his salary in the property after completion of the canal, no hint of personal impropriety can be raised, but it seems clear that even By wished to profit from the increase in land values as the new town developed.

When Colonel By departed for England in October 1832, he expected to be hailed for completing construction of a complicated military canal through difficult wilderness conditions. However, the Duke of Wellington had been defeated as British Prime Minister in November 1830 and the new Reform government had little interest in colonial defence. John By returned home to discover that a Parliamentary committee had censured him in his absence for exceeding his grant by £22,000 in 1831. With his political and military sponsors out of office, he was unable to clear his name.[186] He retired to his English home in a fruitless attempt to recover his health, which had been damaged by malaria. John By never returned to his Canadian estate, passing away in 1836 at age 52.[187]

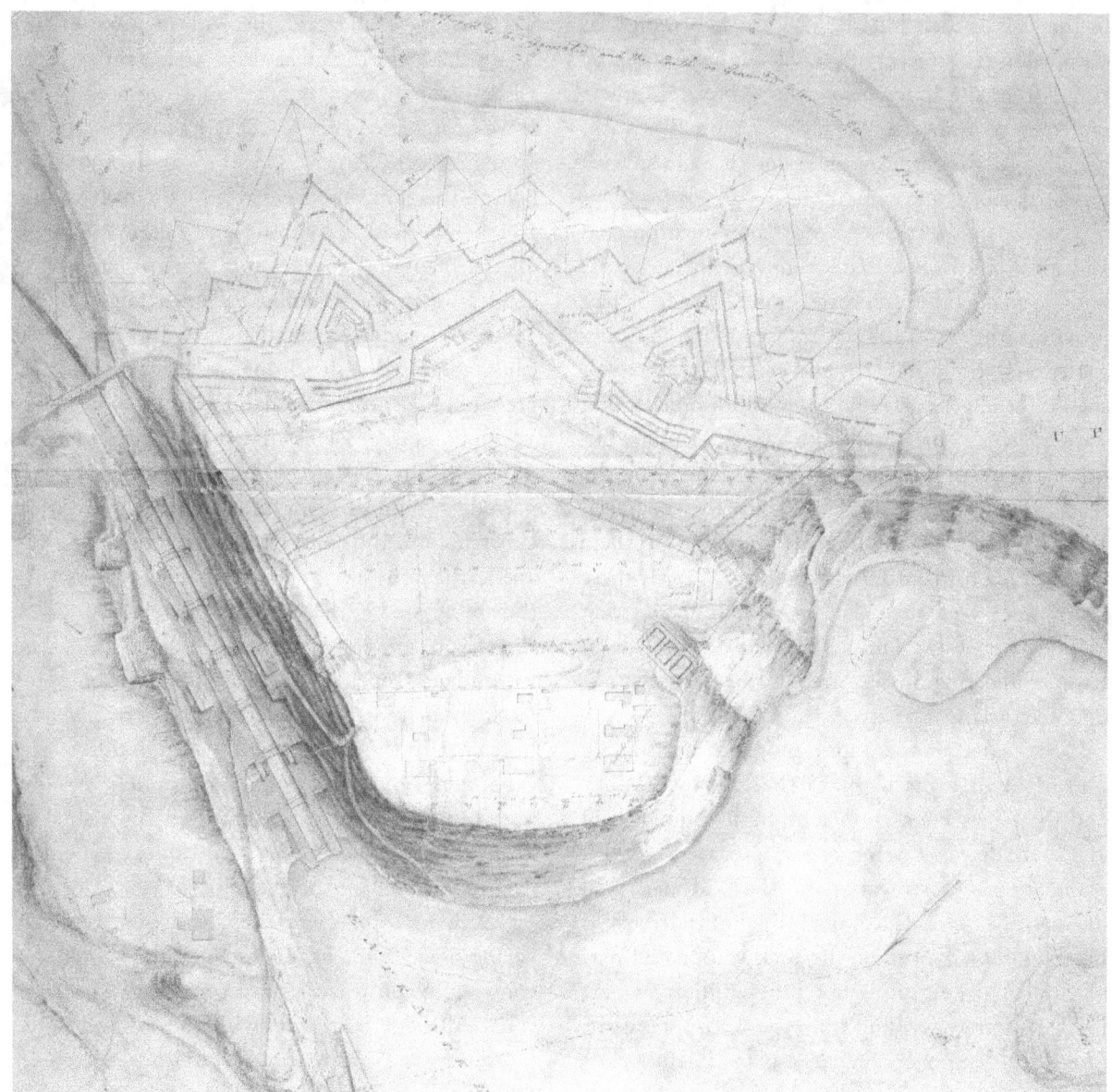

Figure 2-11: Plan by Royal Engineers for a fortress protecting the north end of the Rideau Canal, 1826
The high ground in the centre of the image was Barrack Hill, later Parliament Hill.

The Ordnance needed to keep this plan secret because the *Rideau Canal Act* did not permit acquisition of lands for military purposes. Nicholas Sparks' lands (top half of the map) were seized to allow room for construction of the outworks and glacis for this citadel. The courts returned the lands to Sparks in 1847.
(Source: Library and Archives Canada, NMC 17423)

Reflections

The British officers pursued their military engineering objectives in Upper Canada with tenacity and admirable technical skill. Colonel By was a fine engineer, and completing the Rideau Canal was an extraordinary achievement. Unfortunately, the Ordnance's record in town planning was much weaker. Some of the blame for the failures in this area must reside with Lord Dalhousie. Although he showed considerable foresight in purchasing Fraser's lot in 1823, the Governor General did not provide his engineers with the provincial legislation needed to meet the military engineering objectives.[188] Secondly, although Dalhousie recognized that the canal would require a town-site, he failed to provide the necessary financial arrangements or legislation to support the development and operation of a town. Perhaps because of his experience with LeBreton, the Governor General was too focused on preventing speculative gain, and the short-term, nominal leases he advocated caused continual trouble for By and the Ordnance. While it was good public policy to retrieve the property from speculators who did not pay rent or build upon their lots, Lower Town residents who did build were deprived of economic security and a vote in elections by the short-term leases. They responded with political lobbying, numerous lawsuits, and civil disobedience that absorbed too much administrative time and effort. Worse, most leaseholders built for the short-term, with inexpensive wooden structures that did not last.

The physical planning for Bytown also caused numerous problems. The location of the main town-site in a swamp containing the canal drainage ditch was a serious mistake. Although the Lower Town land was eventually drained, building lots were not available at a crucial time, the streets were a quagmire for decades, and the By Wash was an obstacle and health hazard.

What could the British have done better at Bytown? The imperial authorities were perfectly capable of planning a community in coordination with a military objective, such as a fortified harbour at Halifax or a soldiers' settlement at Perth. The key was a small amount of foresight – 'planning' – before construction. The first step was to recognize that a town-site was needed – an insight that Colonel By appears to have missed, and Lord Dalhousie came to rather belatedly. The second step would be to get the cooperation of the civil authorities in establishing a town. This was Dalhousie's responsibility and he missed the best chance. Since the Upper Canadian legislature desired the commercial benefits of the Rideau Canal but obstinately refused to pay even a penny towards its construction, Dalhousie could have negotiated for their assistance in establishing a town that would ensure the development of the Upper Canadian side of the Ottawa River. He needed legislation to acquire land for civil and military purposes, to govern a town-site during construction of the canal and turn it over to a proper local government after the works were complete.

The third step would be to estimate the likely population of the settlement and the land area required for its initial establishment and expansion. By should have been able to estimate the construction force he needed, and there would be ready precedents for the necessary size of a frontier town-site from Perth or Kingston.[189] The next step would be to examine the ground looking for land suitable for town-site development, which could have been done at the same time as preliminary surveys for the entrance works of the canal.

The obvious site for the town was the land between the Entrance Valley and Richmond Landing, which would have placed the civilian settlement between the Canal and the bridge to Wrightstown. The land for the fortress might have been reserved, and a single town-site constructed on the good land in Upper Town from Wellington Street southwards. Nicholas Sparks' land should have been expropriated, or in the absence of appropriate legislation, purchased in advance of the announcement of where the entrance would be.[190]

In a similar case, George Washington spent several weeks arranging for the purchase of land in the Georgetown area prior to L'Enfant's first survey for the American federal capital. This allowed the American government to purchase the necessary land for low prices and arrange for land exchanges for half the plotted lots. Washington's prestige and the uncertainty over the exact location of the capital allowed him to stare down most of the speculators and embarrass them into supporting a project that was in the national interest.[191] Dalhousie might have followed a similar strategy to assemble the Ottawa town-site. The Crown might also curb speculation in town lots by a repurchase requirement if building did not commence, or by having long-term leases at market value that converted to freehold tenure some period after construction of a building. Financial arrangements of this type would reward entrepreneurs who made long-term investments in the town with stable land titles and the voting franchise.

Next, the engineers needed to prepare a site plan for the town-site, laying out streets and blocks, and setting aside lots for key public functions like markets, court houses, schools, parks and places of worship. The list of facilities from the 1789 provincial land planning requirements[192] would have been a good start. Setting aside lots for public purposes when land was essentially free would have saved the future town years of sectarian squabbling over land purchases. Drawing a town plan would only require a few days' work by a surveyor, and if By's engineering staff did not have much experience in this field, they might have requested assistance from the provincial Inspector General, or simply adapted one of the standard provincial plans (Figure 1-9) to the topography.

Finally Colonel By and Lord Dalhousie needed to plan for the physical and political transition from a construction camp to a town. The Ordnance may have needed authority over the townsite during the construction period, but if so, it needed to accept more responsibility for the policing, health, planning and infrastructure of the settlement. While the military did build a jail and hospital for their own purposes on Barrack Hill, these might have been located so they could be transferred or shared with the civilian authorities upon completion of the work.[193] The lack of attention to the transition from a military camp to a civilian settlement continued almost two centuries of conflict between 'Crown' and 'Town' in the Ottawa Valley.

CHAPTER 3
Imperial Outpost (1832-1857)

The main objection to Ottawa is its wild position, and relative inferiority to the other cities named. But this wild position is a fault which every day continues to diminish. The present population may be called 8,000 or 10,000, not of the best description.
– Governor-General Sir Edmund Head explaining why Ottawa might not be suitable as a national capital, 1857[194]

Bytown after Colonel By (1832-1857)

The construction camp at the head of the Rideau Canal had grown rapidly from 1826, and numbered perhaps 1,000 residents in 1832.[195] The canal was only part of the reason for the boom, since the square timber trade in the Ottawa Valley was also showing remarkable growth at the time. Although Philemon Wright's family pioneered this business, many other landowners followed their lead, farming in the summer and cutting timber in the winter. Other small operators entered the trade, hiring French Canadian lumberjacks to cut the trees and float the timber down river. It was still common practice to cut trees on Crown lands and unoccupied private property, and certain lawlessness prevailed in the woods. After 1826, Upper and Lower Canada allowed cutting trees on unsurveyed Crown lands in the Ottawa Valley, provided that duties were paid, and the government began to auction off limited areas for timber cutting.[196] Bytown quickly passed Wright's Town as the centre for supplying the timber trade after many independent merchants broke the Wright family monopoly. The Lower Town contractors were already supplying the Rideau Canal contractors, and they extended their services to the timber camps. The many taverns, restaurants, and bawdy houses that served the canal labourers also proved to be quite attractive to the lumberjacks and rafters, so Lower Bytown housed a mixed population of Irish and French Canadian labourers in the early 1830s.[197]

Bytown's status as a settlement continued to be uncertain in 1832. After the Royal Engineers departed, the British Ordnance department operated the canal and managed its lands with a much reduced military staff. The 'Corktown' construction camp along the bank of the canal was cleared, and some of the residents, mainly Irish, moved into Lower Town, looking for homes and work. The Ordnance department continued to administer most of the leased land in Lower Town, but the leaseholders agitated for the right to buy their properties.

The Ottawa Valley received a second shock in the summer of 1832, as cholera arrived with the immigrants travelling upon the new canal. The epidemic quickly spread to Lower Town and the barracks, so a Board of Health was established in response to the crisis. A cholera hospital was built at the foot of the locks, but it was little more than a windowless shed to quarantine the dying victims from the rest of the population. All the local victims were from Lower Town and many were the poorest Irish. The fever struck again in

1834 and since many of the immigrants were also Irish, local prejudices were further inflamed, with similar results.[198]

The Shiner's War[199]

The poor Irish immigrants in Bytown were getting desperate in the mid-1830s.[200] The canal jobs had disappeared, they were crowded into Lower Town tenements, and were beset by disease. The best remaining jobs were in the timber trade, where French Canadians had held almost all the jobs in the woods and on the water for decades. Some of the more aggressive Irish immigrants, known as Shiners[201] set about to take these jobs by brute force. They were aided by unscrupulous timber merchants, such as Peter Aylen and Walter Beckwith, who wanted to expand their operations using violent intimidation. This was possible because the Ottawa Valley was on the frontier of Canadian settlement in 1834. There were no police; only a handful of part-time magistrates and some volunteer constables, and the nearest courts were in Montréal and Perth.

Beckwith employed about forty Shiners, who engaged in terror tactics in the woods near Pembroke and increasingly against the homes of the French Canadian workers in Lower Town.[202] Peter Aylen assumed leadership of the Shiners in 1835 by the savagery of his tactics and the impertinence of his affronts to the Anglo-Scots elites in Upper Town.[203] The Shiners began to attack and demolish the rafts manned by French Canadians on the rivers. Although some French Canadian crews began to resist, most notably those led by Joseph Monteferrand (Figure 3-1), the Shiners had control of much of the Ottawa River by the summer of 1835. When the rafters returned to Bytown after the spring drive, public authority collapsed almost completely. Those who opposed the Shiners were assaulted, or had their houses and businesses burnt. A constable who attempted to arrest a Shiner wanted for rape was beaten senseless in the street, surrounded by citizens afraid to intervene. The remaining magistrates were powerless to make arrests or convey prisoners to Perth for trial.[204]

Figure 3-1: Jos. Montferrand (1802-1864)
A legendary lumberjack and Canadian hero, who as a foreman for an Outaouais timber contractor, often led the resistance to the Shiner assaults.[205] Canada Post issued this stamp in 1992 to commemorate "Big Joe Mufferaw's" exploits.
(Source: Library and Archives Canada, Postal 1365; Copyright: Canada Post Corporation)

The Upper Town residents watched, appalled, as Bytown slid towards anarchy. The settlement had always been rowdy and drunken fights in Lower Town were not unusual. But by midsummer the Shiners had taken over the Union Bridge, threatening travelers and demanding payment. By October, the gentry had seen enough and organized a vigilante group, the Bytown Association for the Preservation of the Peace. Nightly patrols by armed citizens were established, and money was raised for constables' fees and other expenses to prosecute felons. Appeals to the provincial government in Toronto for assistance failed, but the magistrates were able to regain a semblance of control on the streets.[206]

Aylen's most ambitious political move was an attempt to seize control of the local government. On January 2, 1837, he led a gang of Shiners into the annual meeting for Nepean Township, got himself elected to council, and demanded that the other positions go to people he approved. When the constables intervened, the Shiners rioted, severely beating a merchant and also James Johnston, the proprietor of Bytown's first newspaper.[207] The *Bytown Independent* further angered the Shiners, who shot up Johnston's house and ambushed him on Sappers' Bridge. Johnson escaped with minor wounds and his assailants were arrested, but Aylen publicly boasted they would soon be freed. At last, the military intervened, lending 30 soldiers to escort the prisoners to Perth. The Shiners regrouped and attacked the Perth jail a few weeks later, freeing the three accused men. This flagrant affront to the powers in the district capital finally energized the civil authorities. The escapees were re-captured a few days later and were imprisoned for attempted murder.[208]

Following the rebellions in York and Lower Canada in 1837-38 the military garrisons were more willing to go to the aid of the civil authorities. Armed civilian special constables patrolled the streets in Bytown during the rebellions and the Shiners' violence gradually tapered out. By 1840, Peter Aylen understood the constraints from the new regime and sold his property in Bytown. He moved to Aylmer in Lower Canada, where he became a respectable businessman.[209]

The Shiners' War damaged Bytown's already sketchy reputation at a critical time. In the aftermath of the rebellions, Upper and Lower Canada were to be joined together in 1840. It was rumoured the new Governor General, Lord Sydenham, would locate the capital city of the new union in a central place, perhaps in Upper Canada. The new *Bytown Gazette* and its owner-editor, Dr. A.J. Christie, pushed this idea hard, publishing over 25 articles promoting Bytown as the ideal site for the seat of government between 1836 and 1842.[210]

Christie was also the Conservative candidate for Bytown's seat in the new union's legislature, until Lord Sydenham made his first visit to Bytown on September 23, 1840. The Governor General requested that the local candidates withdraw in favour of his favourite, William Derbishire from Québec.[211] Christie promptly withdrew and nominated Derbishire for the Conservatives. Sydenham's candidate for Hull and Aylmer was Charles Dewey Day, lawyer to Philemon and Ruggles Wright, and a vigorous enemy of the Shiners.[212] Although the Valley's few electors sent both Derbishire and Day to the Legislature,[213] Sydenham awarded the seat of government to Kingston, privately dismissing Bytown as:

> *Altho' presenting considerable advantages from its position away from the Frontier, or at the mouth of the Rideau, it is so very small a place, would require such vast increase of Buildings & is altogether so remote from thickly settled Districts that I cannot consider it fit for the purpose at the moment.*[214]

The Town of Bytown

Having lost the seat of government, the Bytown leaders set themselves a more attainable objective – getting out from under the yoke of the British Ordnance and becoming an independent municipality that was dominant in the Ottawa Valley. The union of the Canadas and the Wrights' stranglehold on the Township of Hull assisted these objectives. The Wrights' ownership of virtually all the land on the north side of the Union Bridge retarded the development of Hull, since the family had neither the resources nor the inclination to make municipal improvements. Although the Wrights were still powerful timber merchants, they were now merely one family among many involved in the trade, and were soon surpassed by some of the more aggressive firms. The new communities of Aylmer and Buckingham, just outside the Wright's lands, welcomed these new entrepreneurs. Although Aylmer briefly threatened Wright's Town as the *entrepôt* of the Outaouais, Bytown quickly surpassed them both.[215] However, the Wrights' large landholdings ensured that the Township of Hull would continue as the local government on the north side of the river.

The Shiners' War caused the Bytown residents to lobby harder for their own municipal government and courts, rather than continuing to be governed from Perth as part of Bathurst District. The first step was the creation of the new Dalhousie District, established by an act passed on March 6, 1838.[216] The act would take effect when a new jail and courthouse were built, but the Bytown residents disputed the location of a courthouse for over a year, until Nicholas Sparks donated a plot east of the canal in Lower Town. Then arranging an architect and contract took another year, with the Tory *Bytown Gazette* declaring scandals every step of the way.[217] Further construction delays bumped the declaration of the proposed Dalhousie District past the last sitting of the Upper Canada legislature. Luckily for Bytown, the United Canada's Baldwin-Lafontaine ministry supported new local governments across the two former provinces.

Dalhousie District was finally inaugurated in Lower Town's new courthouse on August 9, 1842. The new District Council acted as a local government for Bytown and the surrounding townships on the south side of the Ottawa River.[218] The Upper Town elites maintained control of the new government with the aid of the Tory farmers, while most Lower Town residents could not vote since they leased their lands from the Ordnance. Thomas McKay was elected reeve, and Upper Town's George Baker represented Nepean Township.[219] The magistrates gave up their municipal powers but continued as justices of the peace, who could try minor cases in their own courthouse.

The new government of the United Canadas, with its capital in Kingston, was more attentive to the needs of the Ottawa Valley than the previous regimes in York and Ville de Québec. The Outaouais received a circuit court, which sat in Aylmer, so cases no longer needed to be heard in Montréal.[220] And the Union government built a magnificent suspension bridge across the Chaudière Falls (Figure 3-2) to replace the wooden truss that had collapsed in 1836, due to a lack of proper maintenance after the Royal Engineers departed.[221]

The Roman Catholic Church noted the growth in the Ottawa Valley and the removal of the border between the provinces of Upper and Lower Canada. It created a new Diocese of Bytown in 1847, combining parishes on both sides of the Ottawa River that were previously administered from Québec and Kingston. Notre Dame Basilica on Sussex Street became the dominant architectural feature on the Lower Town landscape. The church also established the General Hospital (1846) and the College of Bytown (1848), both located in Lower Town. The Catholic Church set an example for the rest of the region, making an early commitment to bilingualism to meet the needs of its mixed French Canadian and Irish congregations.[222]

The next step for full control of Bytown's affairs by its residents would be the incorporation of the town as a municipality. As Bytown's population approached 5,000 in the 1840s, its status as an unincorporated village within the rural Dalhousie District chafed, since York and Kingston were already incorporated as cities. An incorporated town would have an elected council and mayor that could levy taxes, improve streets, and organize police, fire protection and public health measures.

FIGURE 3-2: Union Suspension Bridge with the Chaudière Falls beyond, 1844
This is the remarkable vista that greeted the Fathers of Confederation in 1864. The treed islands, waterfalls and elegant bridge were all destroyed within decades to foster industrial development of the area.
(Source: Library and Archives Canada C-005040, watercolour by Frederick Preston Rubridge)

There was a strong sectarian angle to the incorporation debate. The Protestant Anglo-Scottish elite in Upper Town controlled Dalhousie District with the aid of the Tory farmers from the townships. They wanted to control the new town council too, even though they were greatly outnumbered by the Catholics, Irish and French Canadian residents of Lower Town. The Upper Town Tories used their power in the provincial legislature to fix the property requirements for standing for office and voting at a high rate and to gerrymander the ward boundaries of the proposed new town in their favour.[223]

The Tory scheme almost worked. The Legislature passed the bill to incorporate the Town of Bytown on July 28, 1847, and four Lower Town Reformers and three Upper Town Tories were elected. The councillors elected John Scott as the first mayor, voting on straight sectarian lines.[224] The new council passed bylaws to establish constables, regulate nuisances and begin repairs on the Lower Town market.[225]

But the sectarian interests that bedevilled Bytown quickly went back into play. The Tories regained control of the town council after 1848 by exploiting French-Irish differences in Lower Town, electing John Bower Lewis and Robert Hervey as mayors in 1848 and 1849. Although Council had initially met in the Court House in Lower Town, in August 1849, the Tory councillor Nicholas Sparks[226] moved that the Upper Town market be converted into a City Hall. The wooden Upper Town market on Elgin Street erected in 1848 sat empty, unable to compete with the ByWard Market in Lower Town. The Lower Town representatives were outraged by the proposed move and forced the next meeting to be held at the ByWard Market. The Tories had a majority at the next meeting and forced relocation of the city government back to the abandoned Upper Town market shed, where it remained until the building was replaced by a proper City Hall on the Elgin Street site in 1877.[227]

Although Bytown now had a Mayor and a Town Council, the new local government could not overcome the sectarian divisions between Tory and Reform, and Anglo-Scots, French-Canadian and Irish. To make matters worse, the Orange Order was stirring up religious hatred with an anti-Catholic campaign.[228] Although the General Hospital's nuns had acted heroically in the 1847 typhus epidemic, tending to hundreds of infected Irish immigrants, William Pitman Lett, editor of the *Orange Lily and Protestant Vindicator*, attacked the nuns and the hospital in August 1849 for attempting to indoctrinate the sick.[229]

Bytown was a municipal powder keg in September 1849. Even the simplest civic functions – building a courthouse, city hall or hospital, or tending to the dying victims of an epidemic – were rife with sectarian disputes.

The Stony Monday Riots, 1849 [230]

Social and economic pressures were increased by a downturn in the timber trade and a general recession in 1849. So when it appeared that the seat of government of the United Canadas might relocate from Montréal following the Tory riots over the *Rebellion Losses Bill*, there was considerable interest in attracting the government jobs to Bytown. The Governor General was touring Upper Canada considering new sites for the capital. A bipartisan committee chaired by Bytown's Member of the Legislative Assembly (and former mayor) John Scott was established to prepare an address to Lord Elgin on the town's advantages for the seat of government. However, the Bytown Conservative Party stood with their Montréal colleagues in opposition to the Governor. After the Tory mayor Robert Hervey refused to order a town meeting to discuss the address, the Reform council members called a public meeting for Monday, September 17 in the ByWard Market in Lower Town. The Mayor countered by setting a rival meeting for that Wednesday to be held in Upper Town, and the Tories announced that they would make their views known in any forum.

When the Monday meeting began at the ByWard Market (Figure 3-3), both sides were armed with stones and guns, and reinforced by men from outside the town. The proposed address on Bytown's advantages as the seat of government was read, but a fight broke out that quickly escalated into a shower of stones, and then gunfire. The Reformers were driven from the market square, with one man killed and thirty wounded by the fusillade. Mayor Hervey called out the troops from Barrack Hill, and directed the arrests of a score of Reformers, including his predecessor as mayor, MLA John Scott. The victorious Tories then seized control of the public meeting and adopted an address condemning the Governor General's actions in Montréal.[231]

Both sides spent the next day re-arming and gathering recruits. By Wednesday, the entire Ottawa Valley seemed to be mustering for battle. Reformers from the Gatineau Valley brought muskets, pistols and three small cannon from Philemon Wright's armoury in Hull to the Lower Town market.[232] Tory farmers from the southern townships converged on Upper Town, bringing their own muskets and cannon. Almost 2,000 armed men faced each other across the Rideau Canal, but Bytown's divided town site kept the two groups apart. Between them, on Sappers' Bridge, stood fifty soldiers of the Royal Canadian Rifles with fixed bayonets and a pair of cannon. The soldiers were supported by additional guns on Barrack Hill, trained on both sides of the canal. Both parties looked into the cannon's mouth and paused, narrowly averting a bloodbath. Eventually both sides dispersed, firing their weapons into the air.[233] Not surprisingly, Lord Elgin decided to visit other towns, and the seat of government soon relocated to Toronto.

FIGURE 3-3: The ByWard Market, scene of the Stony Monday riot
A meeting to advocate Bytown as the seat of government for the United Canadas dissolved into a pitched battle leaving one dead and thirty wounded on this site on September 17, 1849.
(Source: Library and Archives Canada C-010533; painting by Franklin Brownell)

The debate over Bytown's suitability for the capital of Canada was only coincidentally responsible for the Stony Monday riot. Almost anything might have sparked a social explosion in Bytown in 1849.²³⁴ However, the riot demonstrated that Bytown was not cohesive enough to seriously pursue the seat of government in 1849, and it further blackened the town's reputation for violence and lawlessness.²³⁵

Bytown in the 1850s

The Canadian economy recovered in 1850-51 and by 1852 timber production in the Ottawa Valley had almost returned to the previous peak levels of 1845-46.²³⁶ But most of the urban population growth took place in Bytown during the 1840s and 1850s, since the new District of Hull stagnated under the Wright's ownership.²³⁷ The new Bytown Town Council focused on public infrastructure to catch up with the population growth, during the 1850s. The Council built wood plank sidewalks, graded some streets and built 'drains' (covered ditches that acted as crude storm sewers) through about half of Lower Town. They also experimented with a few gas lamps on Sussex and Rideau streets, which were emerging as the main business areas.²³⁸ The Council also considered, but did not adopt, a fire-protection bylaw, which was not wise public policy in a town built almost entirely out of wood.²³⁹

All of this activity was initially directed by a Town Council that was disabled by its disputes with the British Ordnance Department. The Ordnance wanted its lands to be tax-exempt and to keep control over Sappers' Bridge and the streets on Ordnance land – about half the town. When the provincial incorporation bill did not meet their requirements, the Ordnance used its imperial powers to have the bill struck down by the Queen in late 1849. Bytown had to start again with a new municipal act from the provincial legislature.[240]

The town also took an active role in attempting to diversify the local economy beyond the difficult and cyclical square timber trade, which supported few full-time jobs. One proposal was to pursue export markets for sawn lumber. Several of the early settlers had built small sawmills to serve the local market, including Philemon Wright at Wright's Town and Jean St. Louis on Green Island at the Rideau Falls. Thomas McKay (Figure 3-4) bought the Green Island sites in the 1830s and established a flourmill and a cloth factory. He also developed the Village of Edinburgh (Figure 3-5) on adjacent land to provide a community for his managers and workers. He built a larger sawmill there in 1847, hoping to serve the American market.[241] Although McKay had established a successful export business by 1849, no other local entrepreneurs followed his lead, since most of the families had their limited capital tied up in the square timber trade.[242]

While no local businessmen would invest in the Ottawa Valley lumber export trade, a couple of American entrepreneurs built sawmills on the edge of the Ottawa River at the Chaudière. However, the rushing waters beside the islands and in the great falls themselves had not yet been touched. Most of the sites with the best potential for waterpower were Crown 'hydraulic lots' in the river, located within the boundaries of the new Town of Bytown. In 1852, Richard W. Scott, an enterprising Reform mayor, began to market the water lots to visiting American industrialists. The mayor arranged that two syndicates would have no local competition in a public auction of the most valuable 'hydraulic lots' at Victoria and Amelia islands. So Harris, Bronson & Co. and

Figure 3-4: Thomas McKay
Thomas McKay (1792-1855) began his career in Ottawa as a master mason and contractor as the Rideau Canal, but soon became an industrialist and land developer for the lands north of the mouth of the Rideau River. He designed and built Rideau Hall in 1838 as his personal estate. After his death, his home was purchased by the governor-general; the residence and the remainder of his estate was developed as Rockcliffe Park by his son-in-law, Thomas Keefer (see Cast of Characters).
(Source: Library and Archives Canada PA-125208)

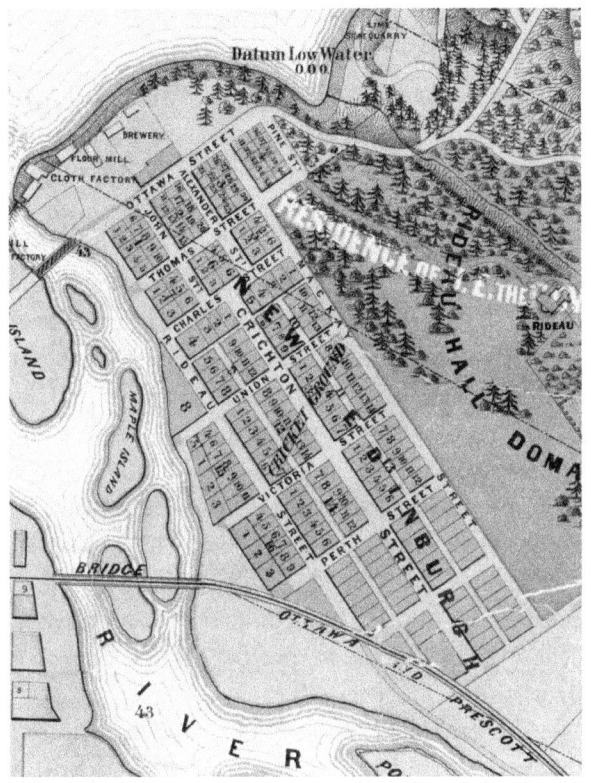

FIGURE 3-5: New Edinburgh
Thomas McKay laid out the main streets in New Edinburgh as a simple grid, parallel to the north bank of the Rideau River. Although his industrial complex expanded quickly during this period, the village grew slowly, with just 144 people in the 1851 census. Following McKay's death in 1855, his son-in-law, T.C. Keefer pushed development forward. He hired local engineer Robert Surtees to subdivide the land between McKay Street and the river into smaller lots served by rear lanes.[243]

New Edinburgh's narrow streets, rear lanes and 19th century homes create attractive streetscapes, and the neighbourhood was declared a Heritage Conservation District in 2001.[244] Thomas McKay's industrial village has become a desirable inner city neighbourhood.
(Source: T.C. Keefer's Rockcliffe Park Plan, 1864 (detail); Library and Archives Canada NMC 17613)

Perley & Pattee both were able to buy the water lots for one shilling over the £50 upset price on September 1, 1852, provided that they agreed to build sawmills.[245]

Rigging the auction of a public resource would probably land a mayor in jail today, but in the mid-19th century, this practice was merely good economic development by a town that was desperate to find employment for its restless and growing population. Mayor Scott's law practice soon began to represent the new lumber barons, and his memoirs fondly recall his role in fixing the auction that led to their fortunes.[246] By 1857, the transformation of the Chaudière Falls from natural wonder to industrial power supply was underway. In that same year, Richard Scott was elected to the Canadian provincial legislature, where he would play the key local role in the further diversification of the economy of the Ottawa Valley, by attracting the seat of government for Canada.

The Bytown & Prescott Railway Fiasco

Most civic infrastructure work trickled to a halt in the mid-1850s because of disastrous municipal investments in the Bytown and Prescott (B&P) Railway. The cream of the Bytown merchant class incorporated the B&P with Thomas McKay's son-in-law John MacKinnon as president. The corporate secretary was Robert Bell, owner of the *Bytown Packet*. Council promptly invested £15,000 ($75,000) in the line on October 1850.[247]

The B&P was a fiasco from the start: undercapitalized, badly planned, poorly designed and shabbily constructed. The line was routed so that it could enter Bytown though McKay's New Edinburgh village and new sawmill at the Rideau Falls. The passenger station was inconveniently located at the north end of Lower Town, and freight could not connect to the new sawmill sites on the Chaudière Islands.[248] A second municipal loan of $200,000 was required in 1853 to build the Lower Town terminus. These loans absorbed the young town's borrowing power in the late 1850s and early 1860s and other municipal infrastructure lagged.

The first Bytown and Prescott train arrived on December 25, 1854, but the station did not open until 1855. The line went into receivership in 1861, and the municipality lost every penny of its investment, crippling the local government's spending power for several years.[249]

The Town of By becomes the City of Ottawa

Although the municipality of Bytown was in dire financial straits in 1855, the settlement continued to grow, and had probably passed 10,000 people by this time,[250] most of them concentrated in Lower Town. The municipality petitioned the provincial government for the town to become a city, so that it might enjoy the additional powers under the *Municipal Corporations Act*.[251] The Reform mayors who requested the change in status might soon have regretted it, since the Tory members in the legislature rigged the ward boundaries again to give an advantage to the less populous Upper Town. This set of ward boundaries lasted over a century, helping continue the social conflicts well into the 20th century.[252]

The new municipality was given a new name – The City of Ottawa – upon its January 1, 1855 incorporation. There was little local affection for the old name, because of lingering memories of disputes with Colonel By and the Ordnance over land leases.[253] The second reason for the name change was that "Bytown" had become somewhat synonymous with lawless behaviour from its construction camp origins. The municipal council hoped for a more dignified image in 1854, more appropriate for a city that aspired to be the capital of a nation that was expanding to the west. So the Council commemorated the 200th anniversary of the descent of the Ottawa First Nation down the river in the city's new name.[254]

Town vs. Crown: The Ordnance Question

While sectarian tensions mounted in Bytown in the 1830s and 1840s, there was one issue that could unite the local factions: a common dislike for the Board of Ordnance, which still owned much of the land in the centre of the city. The Ordnance control of the land leases in Bytown and the differential rents that favoured the original lessees from By's staff and contractors were a constant source of jealousy, friction and legal action. The tenants began a rent strike in 1835, and many other lessees in the Lower Town did not improve their properties. After the Ordnance refused to grant By the land on which he had built his house on Colonel's Hill in 1835 and further refused to compensate him for its £700 cost of construction, other lessees concluded that they would never get ownership of their buildings.[255]

The canal had brought jobs, fat contracts and much infrastructure, all paid for by the British Treasury. But once the canal was complete, the local citizens saw no further benefits from the Crown presence in the area, and wanted ownership of their leased lots and control of their town. The political control and land issues were intertwined because only property owners could vote.

The Ordnance saw it differently, of course. They regarded the Rideau Canal as a partially completed military defence scheme, still in need of fortification against a powerful enemy that had nearly succeeded in conquering the colony less than twenty years earlier.[256] Construction of the canal itself was merely the first phase of a strategic plan personally devised by an imperial hero – the Duke of Wellington, who had defeated Napoleon, became Master of the Ordnance and then Prime Minister. The fortification at the south end of the canal in Kingston was under construction at considerable expense during the 1830s and 1840s, while the Ordnance Land debates raged in Bytown. Land was reserved for the defence of the north end of the canal, fortification plans had been prepared, and a budget established for the works.

All that remained was for funding to be approved by the British Treasury. Any competent military authority would resist giving up land near Barrack Hill for what they regarded as private speculative gain by the local population that they were trying to protect.

However, if the Ordnance wanted control over the lands near their proposed fortress, they should have realized that power usually has responsibility attached to it. While the Royal Engineers had done a barely adequate job of construction camp development and a poor job of town-site planning in the canal phase, the Ordnance managed the transition from a construction camp to a municipality in an abominable manner. They were always behind on the necessary enabling legislation, town-site planning, and basic infrastructure, and in managing relations with the residents. For example, the By Wash canal drainage ditch was a constant nuisance in the Lower Town and eventually become a hazard to public health. It was entirely located on Ordnance Lands, yet it was crudely inserted into the town-site plan and never properly enclosed as a storm sewer.[257]

The Ordnance officers may also have enjoyed the degree of control they could exercise over the town as landlord. They likely regarded leasing land as a normal state of affairs in urban areas, since even London aristocrats leased land from the Duke of Westminster.

However, the culture in Upper Canada was quite different from London. Widespread land ownership was the norm and residents were used to receiving Crown land for free or a nominal sum. Land speculation was a national pastime and major source of wealth – people wanted to repeat the success of Nicholas Sparks and Louis Besserer, who were already selling small house lots for over double the price they paid for their entire farms. The Lower Town residents also saw the lease system as a means of reducing their political influence, because some Upper Town residents got their lands in fee simple or as perpetual leases and could therefore vote in elections. Even the Tory editor A.J. Christie was passionately opposed to the lease system on ideological and practical grounds, organizing a petition to the new Union government to allow the lessees to buy their lots.[258]

The petition and advocacy by the Tories[259] made the Ordnance nervous, so they approached the new Canadian administration for a bill that would formally 'vest' the Crown lands purchased by Lord Dalhousie into the control of the Ordnance rather than the new province. The local landowners had friends in the legislature, so the vesting act also required the Ordnance to dispose of all lands not required for canal purposes at terms extremely favourable to local residents.[260]

The Ordnance commissioned a new survey by Donald Kennedy to lay out the rest of the town site (Figure 3-6) and commenced selling the occupied lots to the existing tenants and disposing of vacant lots by public tender.[261] But the Ordnance refused to return Sparks' land south of Wellington Street, so he put his claim into the hands of the Shiners in the days just before the new Dalhousie District courts were opened. On March 23, 1844, Sparks recruited some raftsmen, supplied them with brandy and seized a vacant house built by the Ordnance on the west side of the Canal. The canal staff were beaten when they tried to repossess the property and a party of soldiers in transit to Montréal were pressed into service to prevent a riot and retrieve the property.

When brute force didn't work, Sparks simply prepared a subdivision plan for the rest of his property in Ordnance hands and sold lots, encouraging the purchasers to occupy the sites south of Barrack Hill. The Ordnance responded with lawsuits, and Sparks' friends in the Legislature forced a special enquiry on the issue.[262] The Ordnance were now trapped by the wording of the 1827 *Rideau Canal Act*, and had to prove that they needed Sparks' land for canal purposes. They presented a fanciful plan that required all 88 acres as a turning basin for great rafts of lumber. The legislative committee was not fooled and ruled in favour of Sparks, recommending arbitration for a

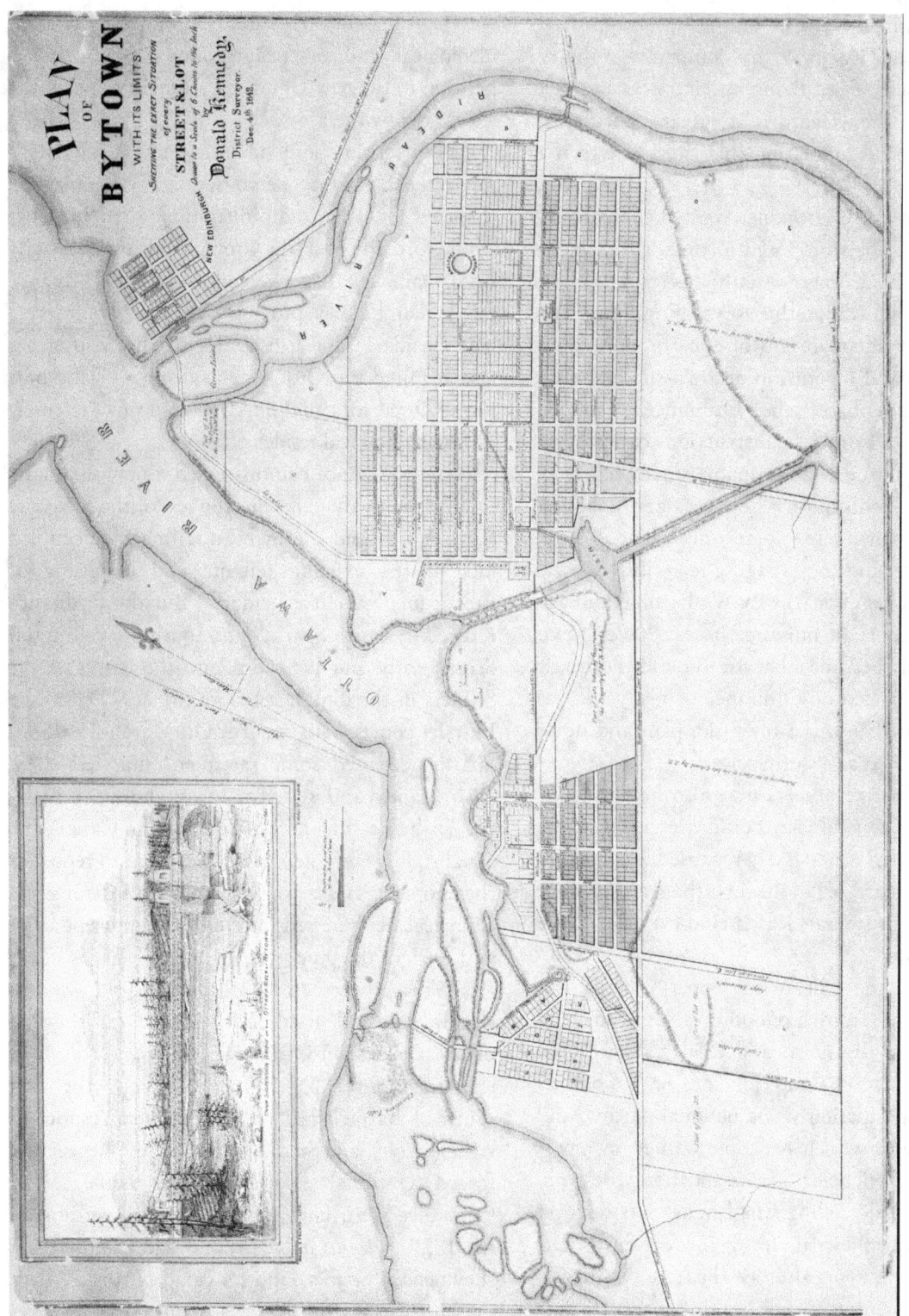

FIGURE 3-6: 1842 Plan, showing Ordnance Reserve and Canal turning basin

This plan was prepared to facilitate the sale of Ordnance land not required for canal or military purposes. Note the deflection of Wellington Street below Barrack Hill and the reserve of Nicholas Sparks' land.

(Source: Library and Archives Canada, NMC 22556/57; drawn by D.A. Kennedy)

price, which was set at £25,000 in March 1847.²⁶³ The settlement was too rich for the peacetime Ordnance, and Sparks reclaimed his land.²⁶⁴

The return of Nicholas Sparks' lands destroyed the British Ordnance's hopes to fortify Barracks Hill, but improved the town-site plan for Bytown. The great swath of vacant space between Upper Town and Lower Town (Figure 3-6) would gradually be eliminated, leading to a more continuous urban fabric divided only by the Rideau Canal.

The canal itself was the final chapter in the Ordnance's unhappy relationship with Bytown. The waterway was rarely used to move troops, but did have a brief period of commercial success before the advent of the railroads in the 1850s. The Ordnance began to lose money on its operation²⁶⁵ and turned it over to the Board of Works of Upper and Lower Canada in the spring of 1857, leaving town just before the new City of Ottawa became capital of the United Canadas.²⁶⁶

Nicholas Sparks, Land Developer

Sparks recognized the potential value of his remaining lands and commenced the subdivision of the rest of his property, laying out 25-foot wide lots fronting onto streets that were only 60 feet wide²⁶⁷ (Figure 3-7). Sparks was an astute entrepreneur: these narrow dimensions increased his lot yield and initial profit, but they caused many subsequent problems for the municipal government. Unfortunately, Louis Besserer, who owned the lot east of Sparks', also followed his narrow survey dimensions.

Sparks also promoted institutions, functions and amenities that enhanced the marketability of his properties and increased the value of his assets.²⁶⁸ In 1828, he donated a lot for the St. Andrews Presbyterian Church on Wellington Street, opposite Upper Town. He also donated a valuable lot on the edge of the escarpment for the Anglican Christ Church (Figure 3-8) and when fundraising for the building stalled, he matched

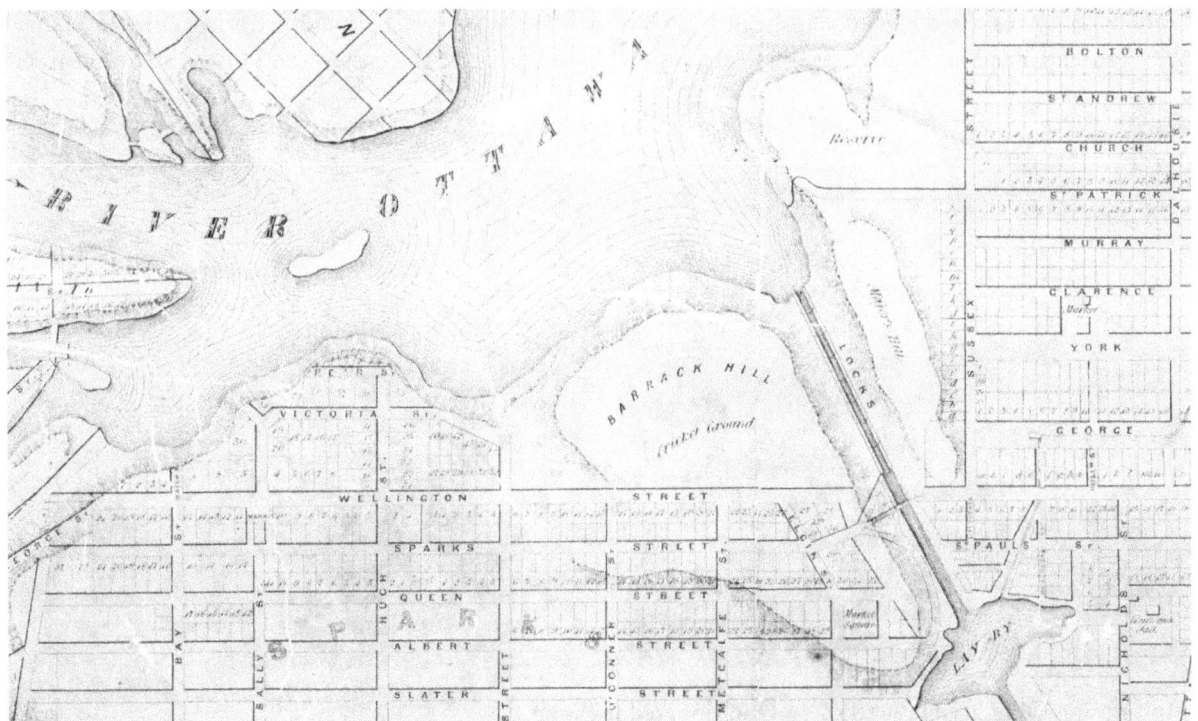

FIGURE 3-7: 1848 Plan of Central Bytown (detail)
All of Sparks' land is subdivided with narrow streets and small lots.
(Source: Library and Archives Canada NMC 22567; drawn by W.A. Austin)

FIGURE 3-8: Old Christ Church on lot donated by Sparks, 1872
The Anglican Church Cathedral was later erected on this lot, solidifying the hold of Upper Town on the Anglo elite.
(Source: Library and Archives Canada C-03317)

the donations from the parishioners.[269] These early moves reinforced Upper Town's status as the home of Bytown's Anglo-Scottish elite, and led to the high-end neighbourhood's gradual expansion southward onto Sparks' land. After the Ordnance lots on the bluff overlooking the river were leased, elite settlement expanded into Sparks' land to the south along the cliff overlooking Le Breton flats.[270]

Banks and hotels followed in the decades ahead, although Lower Town's Sussex and Rideau streets were the initial commercial hub of the settlement (Figure 3-9).

Sparks had prepared subdivision plans for his remaining lands even before they were returned to him in May 1847.[271] However, lot sales were slow along his new Sparks Street, and most of the land south of Barrack Hill still remained vacant countryside. It could even boast pigs rummaging along the western end of its muddy track as late as 1857 (Figure 3-10). Sparks had sold a cluster of lots that were developed for small commercial buildings at the eastern end of the street, near the

FIGURE 3-9: Old City Hall, 1857, on land donated by Sparks
This building failed as a market, but the Bytown Council designated it as City Hall, with Sparks casting the deciding vote as an alderman.
(Source: Library and Archives Canada, C.B. Powell fonds, C-002185)

canal. Several structures had been built in Upper Town, but the area was still essentially a small residential subdivision (Figure 3-11).

When Nicholas Sparks died in 1862, he had not quite succeeded in developing his property into a family fortune. In the long term, the Ordnance expropriation of Sparks' lands might have indirectly benefited the family, although they certainly did not see it that way at the time. Since Sparks did not regain control of the central property until 1848, he had been prevented from selling lots for the low-intensity purposes which had characterized his previous activities. His family was to amass a considerable fortune selling the remaining lots later in the century.[272] What prompted this change in fortune was the 1858 announcement that Ottawa was to be the seat of government of the United Province of Canada. At a stroke of the Queen's pen, Sparks' lands moved from the periphery of a lumber town to being at the centre of a capital city.

FIGURE 3-10: **Pigs on Sparks Street near Kent ca. 1857**
This image is perhaps the earliest known photograph of the Ottawa area; pigs were common on the city streets, since there was no municipal trash removal. Note the simple wooden buildings, dirt streets and open space at the time Ottawa was selected as capital; rearranging the street system was possible at this moment.
(Source: Harry Walker, Library and Archives Canada, C-011384)

FIGURE 3-11: View of Upper Town from Barrack Hill (detail), 1854
The buildings in the centre are along Wellington Street.
(Source: Library and Archives Canada C-000601, Lithograph by E. Whitefield)

The End of the Imperial Era

The development of Wright's Town (Hull) and Bytown (Ottawa) were both impeded by the stubborn actions of monopolistic landowners during the period 1826-1857. The Wright family's focus on maintaining an agricultural seigneury with a side business in timber, and their refusal to sell land on the island of Hull, meant that Bytown quickly surpassed their settlement as the service centre for the canal. This decline in status occurred even though the British government built a bridge across the river to Wright's village. As a result, the adjacent village of Aylmer began to compete for municipal institutions and development on the north side of the river.

The withdrawal of the British Ordnance department and Bytown's incorporation as the City of Ottawa mark the end of a quarter-century when imperial interests dominated the development of the south side of the river. By the mid-1850s, the Canadas were forty years removed from the last war, and the threat of American invasions appeared to have receded, although it would re-open after the American Civil War only a decade later. The Rideau Canal was the most expensive project undertaken by the Ordnance, but interest in colonial defence had waned in Britain, and the Ordnance Department itself was wound up in 1855.[273]

Reflections

The engineers and Ordnance should have planned for the transfer of the town site to civil authority in an orderly manner. Colonel By was in a minor conflict of interest as the magistrate of the town, but the military should not have withdrawn from responsibility for maintaining the peace until proper civilian institutions were in place in the town – a separate judicial district, gaol, magistrates and constables. Similarly, the Ordnance should have supported the establishment of a local government prior to the end of construction, rather than impeding it. Once again, poor physical planning impeded proper social planning – if the initial town site had been developed in Upper Town, it would have been much easier for the Ordnance to retain control of its canal and fortress sites while ceding authority to a local government on the lands between Barrack Hill and the Chaudière bridges.

The separation of Upper and Lower Town exacerbated class, religious, and ethnic divisions, increasing social tensions in an already unstable situation. It also created needless competition between the two town sites about which should contain civic facilities such as the market, town hall, post office or courthouse. New public facilities are usually a focus of civic pride and development, but in Bytown each decision was delayed and riven with sectarian conflict.

Despite these problems and lost opportunities, the proposed new capital still enjoyed an extraordinary site, on a great river at the edge of the wilderness, as we can see from the remarkable 1858 Sarony lithograph (Figure 3-12). Hull was a small industrial village, and to the south, Sparks Street was flanked by a few farm fields and lands recently cut-over for timber. To the north and west were the new lumber mills; and beyond, the great expanse of an, as-yet, undeveloped Canada. Hull and Ottawa were still lumber towns in the bush, with aspirations for the future. All was to change when, by royal declaration, the perambulating capital of Canada finally "found refuge in a certain modest village-town, perched meekly on high bluffs and intervening valleys, between the spray and roar of two headlong river-falls. The town of By became the city of Ottawa..."[274] Although the 'Town-Crown' conflict over the Ordnance's military objectives subsided in the late 1840s, a new requirement for a capital city soon created new friction in the relationship.

FIGURE 3-12: Sarony, 1858 lithograph
Although published in 1858, the fieldwork for this lithograph was likely conducted the previous fall, so this view shows us the settlement almost exactly at the time of its choice as the capital of the Canadas.
(Source: Library and Archives Canada C-002813)

CHAPTER 4

The Queen's Choice? (1858-1867)

... a subarctic lumber village transformed by royal mandate into a political cockpit ...
– Goldwin Smith[275]

Even Bytown's most ardent boosters in 1841 would never have imagined that only three decades later, it would be the capital city of a country that stretched from the Atlantic to the Pacific and Arctic oceans. But the political context for Wright's Town and Bytown was changing quickly as the two settlements grew in the 1840s. The British government had decided to combine the two colonies of Upper Canada (Ontario) and Lower Canada (Québec). The 1840 *Act of Union* set off a bitter, 27-year battle among six cities to become the seat of government of the United Canadas. The new City of Ottawa was an unlikely winner of this capital city contest in 1857. It also received a surprising bonus after Confederation in 1867, when Ottawa was designated as the seat of government of the new Dominion of Canada.

Seat of Government Debates

There was little experience anywhere with the process of selecting a capital city in the early 19th century. Most lands were part of an empire, and the seat of government was where the throne of the monarch was located. New colonies or provinces might have a governor, with an administrative seat usually located on the coastline to allow easy communication with the imperial capital, like Halifax, Boston, Helsinki or Rio.[276]

The United States signalled that selecting a capital for a federation could be a difficult task in a democracy and might create a surprising result. Boston, New York and Philadelphia were the largest cities and main contenders for the American capital; nobody would have guessed tiny Georgetown, MD as the site. But the 13 founding states had to choose the location of their seat of government, and Boston was at the extreme north of the new country, too far from the southern states. New York was the largest city, and designated by the Congress as the temporary seat of the new federal government in 1788. But many Americans were suspicious of New York's Tory past or jealous of its mercantile class. The compromise was to be a site somewhere along the Potomac River, which divided the northern and southern states, with Philadelphia as the interim seat of government until the new capital was ready. New Yorkers watched glumly as the federal government left for Pennsylvania in 1790, their regret assuaged by massive profits in the assumption of public debt held by their financiers.[277]

George Washington had selected the site for the District of Columbia and Pierre L'Enfant prepared a preliminary plan by 1791, but it took years to get the basic infrastructure of a capital city ready. Philadelphia hung onto the federal government for as long as it could, but the legislation establishing the federal district had cleverly put a firm 10-year limit for the interim capital[278] and the federal officials struggled to get a basic capitol building and president's residence ready by 1800. Washington, DC took more than a century to grow into L'Enfant's grand plan. It was initially ridiculed for its wide avenues and vast distances between public buildings.[279] But the 17 years between the end of the American Revolutionary War and moving into a permanent federal capital began to look like quick work, compared to the experience of other nations in the 19th and 20th centuries, including Canada.[280]

Kingston and Montréal

Bytown was not seriously considered for the seat of government when the colonies of Upper and Lower Canada were united in 1841. Governor General Lord Sydenham personally selected Kingston as the first capital of the United Canadas, rejecting the competing claims of Ville de Québec, Montréal and Toronto. Bytown's reputation as a remote and somewhat lawless frontier town hurt its chances.

The legislators never accepted the Governor's choice, complaining constantly about the poor accommodations and rent gouging. The young Charles Dickens judged Kingston:

> ... *a very poor town, rendered still poorer in the appearance of its market-place by the ravages of a recent fire. Indeed, it may be said of Kingston, that one half of it appears to be burnt down, and the other half not to be built up. The Government House is neither elegant nor commodious* ...[281]

No efforts were made to plan or improve Kingston as the seat of government and the city lost its political champion due to the poor condition of the capital's streets. Lord Sydenham's horse stumbled and fell on him in September 1841 and the Governor General died within a few weeks. His successor, Sir Charles Bagot, disliked Kingston from the start and his health declined precipitously after arrival. He was dead of heart disease within a year. Sir Charles Metcalfe fared little better, wasting away from cancer after his arrival in 1843.

Although Kingston seemed hazardous to vice-regal health, it was not the Governor General, but the legislature, directed by the historic coalition of Robert Baldwin and Louis-Hippolyte Fontaine that took the initiative to transfer the capital to Montréal in 1844.[282] Although Kingston had a central location within the united province, it was too small, too Protestant and not a comfortable place for the francophone delegates of Lower Canada. The transfer of the government ruined the municipality, which had borrowed heavily to build a city hall worthy of its status as a capital city.[283]

Montréal seemed like a good political compromise at first, since it was the largest city in British North America and almost as central as Kingston. The city was bilingual, bicultural and had never been the capital of either province. But in 1849 some segments of Montréal's Anglo commercial elite, angry about the financial burden of the *Rebellion Losses* bill during an economic recession, openly called for Canada to be annexed by the United States. A Tory mob burned the legislature building and pelted Governor General Lord Elgin with stones and rotten eggs as he made his escape[284] (Figure 4-1). Only the ceremonial mace and the portrait of Queen Victoria survived the blaze. The mace was wrested from a leader of the rioters by two citizens and returned to the Speaker, while a clerk who rushed into the flaming legislative chamber saved the painting.[285] The parliamentary library and legislative papers were destroyed, crippling the Canadian administration.

Montréal's reputation as a host for the seat of government was ruined and Parliament fled the city, never to return.

FIGURE 4-1: **Tory mob burning the Canadian Parliament, Montréal, April 25, 1849**
(Source: Library and Archives Canada C-073717, detail from drawing by C.W. Jeffreys)

The Perambulating Capital

Lord Elgin left Montréal and travelled through Upper Canada to test the idea of moving the seat of government. Bytown ruined its chances at the prize on September 15, 1849 when a public meeting called to invite the Governor General degenerated into the Stony Monday riot. Not surprisingly, Lord Elgin declined to visit Bytown.[286] The Canadian Parliament was removed to Toronto on a temporary basis.

The legislature then entered a perambulating stage, alternating between Toronto and Québec every four years (Figure 4-2). The disadvantages of this arrangement were soon recognized, but the politicians were simply unable to agree upon a city to host the seat of government.[287] The issue consumed vast amounts of the legislature's time and energy, pitting every community against its rivals, and threatening the delicate new coalition led by John A. Macdonald and Georges-Étienne Cartier.

Macdonald's Gamble

In April 1856, the Department of Public Works reported that suitable parliament building sites were available in Toronto, Kingston, Ottawa and Québec, and that the new facilities should cost approximately £300,000, excluding the cost of grounds.[288] But despite debating the issue of the better part of a month, the legislature could not select a capital city. The closest they came to a decision was when the Legislative Assembly narrowly voted for a permanent seat of government in Québec, but the Legislative Council (upper house) refused to approve the annual budget until the £50,000 appropriated for new buildings was deleted.

After the legislators were exhausted, the government proposed an unusual method to resolve the issue. Rather than push Kingston, his own hometown, Macdonald suggested binding arbitration by the Crown. Any city could put forward a proposal to become the capital, and the Legislative Council would refer the choice to the Queen for a decision. Macdonald cunningly added a motion "providing a sum of money (not to exceed £225,000) for the erection of the necessary buildings."[289] Macdonald and Cartier were able to get their shaky coalition to vote on the funds for the buildings in advance, even though their alliance would disintegrate on every vote for a city, due to local partisanship.

The arbitration proposal diverted all the partisan energy into preparing 'memorials' to the Queen outlining the advantages of their community as the seat of government. Hamilton, Toronto,

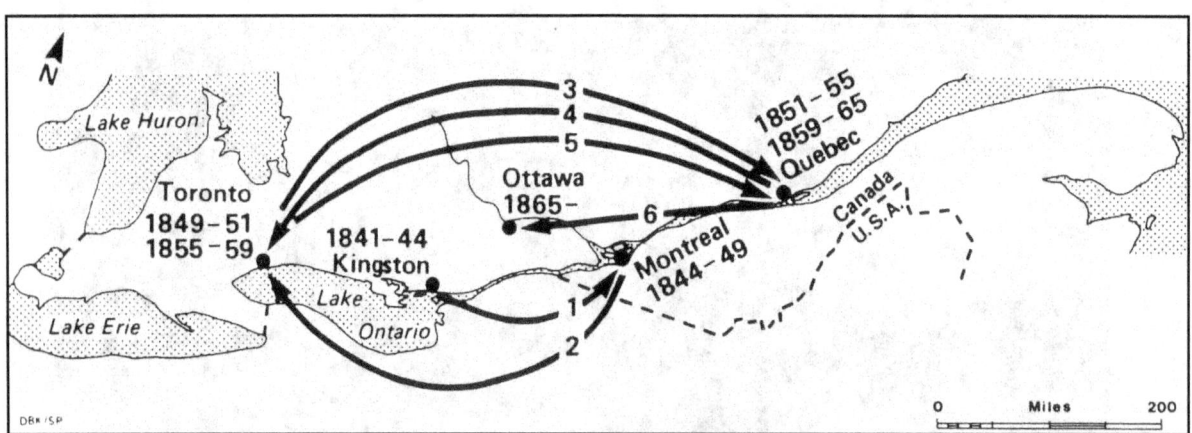

FIGURE 4-2: Canada's "perambulating" seat of government
(Source: Knight, 1991 Figure 1)

Kingston, Ottawa, Montréal and Québec all prepared documents presenting the case for their city. Ottawa's memorial was drafted by Richard W. Scott, a former mayor and the city's current member of the Legislative Council.[290] Its introduction caught the bitter flavour of the seat of government debate:

> ... *Since the union of Upper and Lower Canada, in the year 1840, the subject of the adoption of a permanent site for the seat of Government has continuously agitated the public mind, and has annually give[n] rise to excited and protracted debates in the Legislature of the country, gradually developing bitter feelings of jealousy in the two sections of the province, and at times, almost threatening a dissolution of the union ...*[291]

Ottawa argued that it was centrally located, could easily be defended, had a good site for the Parliament Buildings and that the city would welcome the seat of government. However, all of the other cities made the same claims in their memorials.[292] But Ottawa's conclusion concisely argued the political advantages of choosing their new city:

> ... *situated as Ottawa is, within the territory of Upper Canada, but connected with the lower province by the "Union" suspension bridge, with a population of French and British origin equally balanced, the political and social effect of its selection would be to forever set at rest any feelings of jealousy on the part of either section, and would tend more firmly to cement a union which has already been productive of the happiest results; a conclusion your memorialists are warranted in asserting from the frequently expressed opinions of the Lower Canadians that, next to the place they felt immediately interested in, they preferred Ottawa, and to which, moreover, they have never urged an objection in Parliament; and Upper Canada would have no cause of complaint, since the pledge that the seat of Government should be permanently placed within the territory of Upper Canada, said to have been tacitly given by the late Lord Sydenham when carrying out the union, would be fulfilled ...*[293]

The memorials of the six cities were shipped off to London in mid-1857. With a general election expected in the fall, Macdonald wrote privately to London, suggesting that the Queen not give her decision for eight to ten months.[294] With the seat of government issue cleverly deferred, Macdonald and Cartier won a narrow election victory in late 1857, with a majority of the seats in Canada East (Québec), but only a minority in Canada West (Ontario), the stronghold of George Brown's Reform party.

Head's Secret Advice: 'the least objectionable place'

Although the choice of a seat of government was officially referred to Queen Victoria for a decision, the surviving documents indicate that her Governor General, Sir Edmund Head (Figure 4-3) made the crucial recommendations. His 1857 memorandum on the issue appears to be the decisive document, stating:

> *Ottawa is the only place which will be accepted by the majority of Upper and Lower Canada as a fair compromise. With the exception of Ottawa, every one of the cities proposed is an object of jealousy to each of the others. Ottawa is, in fact, neither in Upper nor Lower Canada. Literally it is in the former; but a bridge alone divides it from the latter. Consequently its selection would fulfil the letter of any pledge given or supposed to be given, to Upper Canada at the time of the Union. The population at present is partly French, and partly English and Irish. The settlement of the valley of the Ottawa is rapidly increasing, and will be at once stimulated by making it the capital ...*

> ... *The **main objection to Ottawa is its wild position, and relative inferiority to the other cities named**. But this wild position is a fault which every day continues to diminish. The present population may be called 8,000 or 10,000, **not of the best description**. It will be six years before the Government can be actually transferred thither, and the settlement of the fertile country on the Ottawa would be accelerated by the very fact of the certainty of such transfer, even before it took place ...* [emphasis added]

Head summarized several memoranda on the defence of the capital, which was still an important issue, with the Oregon boundary dispute only a few years past:

> ... *In a military point of view (I speak of course with submission to higher authorities), Ottawa is advantageously situated. Its distance from the frontier is such as to protect it from any marauding party, or even from a regular attack, unless Montréal and Kingston, which flank the approach to it, were previously occupied by the enemy. Stores and troops could be sent to Ottawa either from Québec or Kingston, without exposure on the St. Lawrence to the American frontier ...*

> ... *A secondary consideration, but one of some importance as affecting the popularity of the choice, is the fact that the Rideau Canal, now handed over to the Provincial Government, would probably increase its traffic, and become more productive by the transfer of the seat-of-government to Ottawa. At present this great work is a dead loss so far as money is concerned ...*

> ... *It may be added, that as Kingston stands at the outlet of the canal on Lake Ontario, the probable increase of traffic by this route would in some degree compensate Kingston for the preference of a rival city ...*

Head concludes his brief with the local political arguments, which were the strongest concern, given the deadlock of the past fifteen years. It is hardly a ringing endorsement:

FIGURE 4-3: Sir Edmund Head
Sir Edmund Walker Head (1805-1868) was one of the most successful colonial administrators to serve in the British North America. He was Lieutenant Governor of New Brunswick from 1854 to 1861. The seat-of-government issue was a major political problem during his early regime and Head's confidential advice on this topic was perhaps the most influential support for the surprising selection of Ottawa as the capital city of the Canadas (see Cast of Characters for more information).
(Source: Library and Archives Canada C-119677; painting by Theophile Hamel)

... On the whole, therefore, I believe that **the least objectionable place is the city of Ottawa**. *Every city is jealous of every other city except Ottawa. The second vote of every place (save, perhaps, Toronto) would be given to Ottawa. The question, it must be remembered, is essentially one of compromise. Unless some insuperable bar exist to its selection, it is expedient to take that place which would be most readily acquiesced in by the majority ...*

... If Québec were taken, all Upper Canada would be angry at the choice. If any place in Upper Canada (with the exception of Ottawa) were taken, all Lower Canada would raise an outcry ...

... If Ottawa is chosen, Montréal will acquiesce in the choice, and the majority of Upper Canada will not in any way resist, for to them it is a partial triumph. The whole matter is a choice of evils, and the least evil will, I think, be found in placing the seat-of-government at Ottawa. Whichever section predominates, and however far westward the commerce of Canada may extend, Ottawa will be a convenient position ...[295] [emphasis added]

Head crossed the Atlantic to advise Whitehall on the issue, and kept mum upon his return in November 1857. The Colonial Office's recommendation for Ottawa was in the Queen's hands in early December, and on December 31, 1857, the Colonial Secretary wrote to Head that:

I am commanded by the Queen to inform you that in, the judgement of Her Majesty, the City of Ottawa combines greater advantages than any other place in Canada for the permanent Seat of the future Government of the Province, and is selected by Her Majesty accordingly.[296]

Ottawa was called "The Queen's Choice,"[297] but a century of research has revealed a more complex situation with the key advice given confidentially by the Governor General and potential strategy from the elected local leaders.

Ignoring the Queen's Choice

Macdonald managed to keep the seat of government decision secret until mid-January, 1858, and then leaked it to the *Toronto Colonist* before George Brown's *Globe* could comment. Ottawa reacted with jubilation and City Council quickly offered free offices to accommodate the Legislature and civil service until the new buildings would be constructed.[298] But the other cities were surprised by the "Queen's Choice" and the overall reaction was far from favourable.[299]

George Brown realized that he could use the Ottawa decision issue to destroy Cartier's Québec base and bring down the government. When the legislature finally met, the politicians could not agree on where the capital should be, but on July 28, 1858 a 60-54 majority agreed "that in the opinion of this House, the City of Ottawa ought *not* to be the permanent seat of government of this province."[300] This motion was interpreted by many observers as an insult to the Queen, who had been asked to make the choice. It was certainly embarrassing to the Legislature that had made the request.

The Macdonald-Cartier government resigned and Governor General Head invited George Brown to form a new administration, which was defeated in the House two days later. Brown expected an election, but Macdonald then performed his most infamous political manoeuvre, the "double shuffle," re-arranging all his ministers and requesting that Head call on the "Cartier-Macdonald" administration to form a government. Brown was outraged, and the Reformers redoubled their opposition to the current state of the Union. But Macdonald concluded that the seat-of-government issue was pure political poison and he wasn't going to drink it again. He told Richard Scott, Ottawa's champion, that the city would have to find its own support, and that its prize was slipping away. While Scott lobbied the other members, Macdonald prevented the seat-of-government issue from re-appearing throughout 1858.

When the 1859 session began in Toronto, Ottawa's chances seemed to be fading. There was talk of a wider Confederation in the air, and the location of the capital might be re-opened again. In a desperate attempt to hold the Canada East votes, it was proposed that the seat of government should be moved to Ville de Québec until "the necessary arrangements shall have been completed" in Ottawa.[301] After a furious lobby, Richard Scott also persuaded a handful of Eastern Ontario and Montréal Reformers to change their votes and save Ottawa's designation as the seat of government in a crucial vote early on February 11, 1859. After dragging in every absent and sick member at 1 a.m., the Ottawa partisans prevailed with a majority of only five votes.[302]

Other Reformers then attempted to stop the project by refusing to vote the funds for the buildings, only to find that Macdonald had out-foxed them three years earlier, with the almost-forgotten approval for £225,000. With the Ottawa location precariously fixed, the government moved rapidly, issuing a notice of a design competition for the Parliament Buildings on May 7, 1859.[303] Architects were only given until August 1, 1859 to submit drawings, since the government wanted to get a shovel in the ground before the legislature could change its mind yet again.

Parliament Buildings

The site chosen for the legislature was obvious: Barrack Hill was the most prominent land in the city and Lord Dalhousie was reported to have mentioned it as a future site of the seat of government as early as the 1820s.[304] Thanks to Dalhousie's purchase, the hill was entirely in Crown ownership and appeared to be large enough to accommodate the needs of the government of the United Canadas for some time. The 1858 instructions for the Parliament Buildings architectural competition did not envision any alternative sites.[305]

Most of the plans submitted for the competition did not even acknowledge Nicholas Sparks' 10-year old subdivision of the lands south of Wellington Street and the few buildings erected in the vacant land (Figure 4-4). The winning designs for the

Figure 4-4: Aerial view of Parliament Hill site before construction looking southeast
There was little development opposite Parliament Hill and Metcalfe Street was undeveloped.
(Source: Sarony lithograph 1858, Library and Archives Canada C-002813)

Centre Block and Library (Fuller and Jones) and flanking departmental blocks (Stent and Laver) placed the buildings on the cliff edge of Barrack Hill to take advantage of the site's visual prominence and the vista from the Ottawa River (Figure 4-5). The original Centre Block and its campanile, the Victoria Tower, were fitted to the bluff, rather than sited to terminate a north-south axis extending from one of the narrow dirt streets of Sparks' 1848 subdivision. Fuller and Jones rejected such Beaux Arts design concepts, reasoning that Gothic architecture was particularly important for the Barrack Hill site, which drops as a craggy precipice into the river to the north.[306] Carolyn Young concludes that,

The Barrack Hill plateau became a giant pedestal for buildings which, like High Renaissance sculptures, were meant to be seen in the round. The architects fully exploited the principle of the Picturesque in the flamboyant, almost free-standing, polygonal library above the cliff. Their approach reflected a long-standing and constantly evolving aesthetic tradition of interrelationship between architecture and landscape.[307]

The Parliament Buildings were such a leap beyond the small-town architecture on the adjacent Sparks subdivision that nobody suggested that the two plans be integrated. With hindsight, if connections between town and Parliament Hill were needed, this was the time to secure them, since the local government and adjacent landowners were co-operative and expropriation costs would have been minimal. Close scrutiny of the 1858 Sarony lithograph (Figure 4-4) reveals a Metcalfe

FIGURE 4-5: Aerial view of Parliament Hill with new buildings
Stent and Laver put a flap over Sarony's 1858 lithograph to illustrate their competition entry, which placed first for the Departmental Buildings. In 1862, they revised the lithograph to incorporate this view of Fuller and Jones' winning entry for the Centre Block.
(Source: Library and Archives Canada C-002812)

Street that was merely a narrow dirt track lined by perhaps a half-dozen small buildings. But the 1859 architects were merely designing a legislative and administrative complex for a small colony, rather than creating a plan for the capital city of a large nation-state. Wellington Street served as a boundary between Crown and Town, demarcated by a substantial stone wall built on the south side of Parliament Hill.[308]

Construction on Barracks Hill commenced in late 1859. The 1,600 construction workers were a boost to Ottawa's economy but it was quickly evident that Macdonald's 1857 appropriation would not be enough to finish the project. The original 1856 Department of Public Works rough estimate was £300,000 (about $1.5 million in 1858 dollars)[309] for the buildings alone, but the legislature had only approved £225,000 ($1.1 million) for the entire project. The competition brief called for building cost targets of:

The Parliament Building	$300,000
Two Departmental Buildings	$249,000
Governor General's Residence	$100,000
Building total	$640,000 [310]

This $640,000 excluded foundations, heating systems, furniture and landscaping. The government had started the competition before proper soil surveys were carried out, and conditions were far worse than expected – with much excavation in solid rock. By the time the Prince of Wales arrived to lay the cornerstone of the Parliament Buildings in September 1860, the project was in serious financial trouble, since most of the building budget had been spent on foundations.[311] The Governor General's residence was dropped and the contractors built the walls of the first floor of the main building to show some progress in 1861. The Department of Public Works employed the new technology of photography to prove to the politicians in Québec that some construction was under way.[312] Samuel McLaughlin was retained to document progress, creating beautiful, large-scale images that were displayed in Québec (Figure 4-6).

But the cash ran out in September 1861 and the work was stopped, severely damaging Ottawa's economy. The walls and tower of the Parliament Building were capped and 1,300 workers were laid off. Commissioner of Public Works Joseph Cauchon

FIGURE 4-6: Parliament Buildings under construction, ca. 1861
(Source: Library and Archives Canada C-003040; Samuel McLaughlin photograph)

estimated that $1,424,882 had been spent or owed, so the project was already almost one-third over budget.[313] While a Royal Commission was investigating the scandal, the opposition pounced in the Legislature in Québec, suggesting that the project be abandoned.[314] The commission reported that there had been irregularities in the contracts, and criticized deputy commissioner of Public Works, Samuel Keefer, for starting construction when he was aware that "the style of the buildings was too expensive for the funds set aside."[315] Keefer and three of the architects were dismissed.

If the buildings had been delayed even another six months, they might still be a half completed ruin on Barrack Hill, and Ville de Québec might be the capital of Canada. But the Legislature voted another $300,000 for construction in the 1863 budget, provided that proper contracts were put in place. Construction re-started in April 1863, and progressed rapidly that year (Figure 4-7), while the American Civil War raged and Macdonald, Cartier and Brown dreamed of a larger confederation.

FIGURE 4-7: View of Parliament Buildings under construction from the Russell House Hotel, ca. 1863
Note the vacant lots on Wellington Street. The Fathers of Confederation saw a half-completed complex during their November 1864 visit described in the Prologue.
(Source: Library and Archives Canada PA-181436)

Confederation and the Capital

Although the Cartier-Macdonald administration managed to resume construction on the Parliament Buildings in 1863, the bitter sectional rivalries most evident in the seat of government debates continued to paralyze the legislature. Reformers from Canada West (Ontario) wanted out of the 1841 Union, to obtain representation by population and control of local affairs. In 1864, George Brown chaired an all-party parliamentary committee to investigate constitutional reform, recommending the "federal principle" to overcome sectional rivalries. Ontario and Québec might be separated again, but confederated with other British North American colonies.

Of course, confederation was not a new idea, with an 1826 proposal by Nova Scotia Attorney General Uniake and Lord Durham's 1839 report still within memory. Uniake proposed a federation of Nova Scotia, New Brunswick, PEI, Lower Canada and Upper Canada, with Ville de Québec as the seat of government. Québec was viewed as a central location in the proposed nation, easily accessible by water from all colonies.[316] Although Uniake's confederation proposal did not find support, his observation that Québec was a central location for a capital was still common in 1864, with the Grand Trunk Railway connecting Toronto and Québec, and the Intercolonial Railway proposed to link Halifax to Québec.[317]

George Brown's Reform Party had pursued a federal union since 1859, and the time finally seemed right in 1864, as four successive ministries failed in the Canadian legislature. In 1864, he offered to join his bitter rivals Macdonald and Cartier in a coalition government to seek a federal union of all the British North American provinces.[318] Brown also had a change of heart on Ottawa as the seat of government. Although he had previously been a virulent critic of the site and every penny spent on the Parliament Buildings, Brown expressed a completely different view to Macdonald after a visit in August 1864:

*The buildings are magnificent; the style, the extent, the site, the workmanship, are all surpassingly fine. But they are just **five hundred years in advance of the time**. It will cost half the revenue of the province to light them, to heat them, and to keep them clean. Such monstrous folly was never perpetrated in this world before. But as we are in for it I do think the idea of stopping short of completion is out of the question. I go in for tower, rotunda, fountains and every conceivable embellishment. If we are to be laughed at for our folly at least let us not be ridiculed for a half-finished pile.*[319]

As it happened, the Maritime provinces were willing to discuss the confederation proposal in 1864, since they were mired in their own seat-of-government controversy. New Brunswick and PEI had once been part of a larger Nova Scotia, before they were separated in 1769 and 1784, respectively. Arthur H. Gordon, Lieutenant Governor of New Brunswick, was pursuing a new Maritime Union in 1863-4, with the support of the Colonial Office. But, as in the United Canadas, some early discussions foundered on the location of the seat of government. New Brunswick and PEI were jealous of Halifax, and would not consider it as the seat of government, while PEI insisted that Charlottetown must be the capital city, even though it was not accessible in the winter months. But Gordon was persistent and managed to get the three legislatures to agree to hold a conference to discuss Maritime Union in the summer of 1864. To their surprise, the legislators of the United Canadas asked if they might join the discussions.

A conference was hastily arranged for September 1864 at Charlottetown, the only place the PEI delegation would meet (Figure 4-8). The seat-of-government issue is surprisingly absent from the 1864 Confederation debates. The various records of the Charlottetown conference debates contain no mention of where the capital of the new confederation might be located.[320] This is

FIGURE 4-8: Charlottetown Confederation Delegates, September 1864
(Source: Library and Archives Canada C-000733, detail from G.P. Roberts photograph)

remarkable, since the issue had recently hamstrung Maritime Union discussions and paralyzed the legislature of the United Canadas for over a decade. We can only speculate that the delegates assumed that the seat of government would be located somewhere in the United Canadas, which brought three million people to the Confederation, versus the 650,000 in the Maritime provinces.

The delegates reconvened in Ville de Québec in October 1864, to continue the discussions. Québec was the seat of government of the United Canadas at the time, and the delegates met in a dowdy reading room in the temporary Legislative Assembly building.[321] Once again, the provincial delegations negotiated *in-camera*, and without extensive official minutes or records of the debates. But we have some notes by the executive secretary and some of the delegates.[322] Macdonald and Cartier carefully controlled the agenda for the conference, meeting each night to prepare motions for debate the next day. Most of the debate swirled around the composition and powers of Parliament and the financial arrangements for Confederation. On October 26, 1864 (the second last day of the conference), Macdonald introduced a motion:

> 52. *The Seat of Government of the Federated Provinces shall be Ottawa, subject to the Royal Prerogative.*[323]

The motion was adopted unanimously, and there is no official record of any debate on the issue.[324]

Given the controversy over the seat-of-government issue for the United Canadas and the proposed Maritime Union, the lack of debate on resolution 52 at the 1864 Québec conference seems a mystery at first glance. But Macdonald left us a clue, with his next motion, also adopted unanimously:

> *53. Subject to any future action of the respective Local Governments, the Seat of the Local Government in Upper Canada shall be Toronto; of Lower Canada, Québec; and the Seats of the Local Governments in the other Provinces shall be as at present.*

It was a clever compromise of municipal interests. Toronto, Québec, Fredericton, Charlottetown and Halifax all received provincial legislatures, and Québec, the potential federal capital, continued to receive the short-term advantage of the government of the United Canadas until Ottawa was ready. Kingston was by then a bit player, and its most prominent politician, Macdonald, supported Ottawa. Finally, Montréal was still tarred by the disgraceful 1849 riots, and its principal politician, Cartier, also supported Ottawa.

For the Maritime cities, Ottawa was not a commercial rival in any way, unlike Québec or Montréal. The Maritime provinces all got to keep their capitals and given the balance of geography and population (650,000 vs. 3,000,000 for Canada), there never was any realistic choice of a Maritime federal capital. Finally, the choice of Ottawa came with a brand new set of Parliament Buildings, paid for at vast expense by the taxpayers of the United Canadas.[325] So it appears that the Maritime delegates simply acquiesced to Ottawa, and bargained hard for other benefits like reduced public debt, an early start on the Intercolonial Railway and increased representation in the Commons and Senate.

The demeanour and tone of debate was another startling difference in comparing Confederation speeches to the earlier seat-of-government debates. The seat-of-government issue seemed to bring out the worst in mid-19th century politicians and their newspapers, with outright boosterism for their home towns combined with vicious criticism of competing cities and their inhabitants. In contrast, the Confederation debates seemed to elevate those same politicians into a more statesmanlike demeanour. While the "Fathers of Confederation" may have bargained hard behind the closed doors in Charlottetown and Québec, their public speeches at the many evening banquets and balls were suffused with goodwill and a spirit of nation-building. The staggering quantity of champagne supplied by the Canadian delegation probably helped build the camaraderie, but there was also much talk of extending the new nation from sea to sea by acquiring the Hudson's Bay Company lands and incorporating British Columbia into the federation.[326]

The concept of a broader confederation probably improved Ottawa's position as a capital city. Rather than being considered as a frontier town at the western edge of the confederated provinces, Ottawa could now be viewed as the gateway to the new territories to the northwest, and a more central position in a nation that was destined to extend from "ocean to ocean."[327] But Montréal could make similar arguments, so it appears that the new Parliament Buildings were an important advantage for Ottawa.

The confederation advocates travelled to Halifax, Saint John and Fredericton after the Charlottetown conference and to Montréal, Toronto and Ottawa after the Québec meeting. These trips were the first time many of the delegates had visited the other provinces, and helped build goodwill towards Confederation, which would come under severe attack in the Maritime provinces. But the glorious October 31, 1864 visit must have clinched Ottawa's position as the capital of a new country in the hearts of many delegates. They steamed up the river from Montréal, enjoying the fall colours in the Ottawa valley. The delegates were met by a huge torchlight parade to escort them to the Russell House hotel, where "it seemed as if the whole population of Ottawa had turned out on the occasion, sending out rapturous cheers after cheer as welcome notes to their guests…"[328]

Although the "Fathers of Confederation" agreed to Ottawa as the capital of Canada, the seat-of-government issue would not die during the ratification debates in the Maritimes. New Brunswick's John H. Grey (Figure 4-9) recommended a federal district for Ottawa, following the Washington model.[329]

More seriously, Ville de Québec was still favoured by several newspapers, and Joseph Howe, the leader of the anti-confederation forces in Nova Scotia, pressed for Halifax as the capital.[330] While the confederation resolutions were in London for imperial approval, the *New York Times* stirred up controversy by reviving rumours that the seat of government would be relocated to either Québec or Montréal.[331] These reports were groundless, since the Colonial Office fully supported Ottawa and there was no record of debate of the issue in the 1866-67 London conference. However, the Québec conference resolution was subtly adjusted in the drafting of the 1867 *British North America Act* to read:

16. Until the Queen otherwise directs, the Seat of Government of Canada shall be Ottawa.[332]

Therefore, the "Queen's Choice" was enthroned in Canada's constitutional legislation, ensuring that any future seat of government debates would need approval at the highest level.

Ottawa Becomes a Capital City

Many workers were again laid off following the completion of the first stage of the construction of the Parliament Buildings in 1866. Their loss to the local economy was offset somewhat by the 300-400 "permanent" civil servants of the United Canadas who began to arrive in late 1865. As *Picturesque Canada* put it, "the peripatetic carpet-bag existence of government officials ceased, and the nomad tribes of the various departments settled down permanently under their own vine and fig-tree."[333] Although this may be hard to believe today, the East and West Blocks of the Parliament Buildings included the offices of the entire Canadian civil service. They were nearly completed in the fall of 1865, although the area around Parliament Hill looked like a construction zone for years (Figure 4-10). These new offices were a significant improvement on the scattered, rented buildings in Québec.[334] Since Ottawa lacked most municipal services, the government provided its own for the

FIGURE 4-9: Col. John H. Gray (New Brunswick)
New Brunswick's John Hamilton Gray (1814-1889) appears to have been the only Father of Confederation to have raised the issue of governance of the new federal capital. He reviewed the America legislation and recommended a federal district similar to Washington, to ensure that the new federal government would have a say in the local administration of the capital city. It appears that nobody listened at the time, but poor relations between 'Crown' and 'Town' caused problems for the new capital city for the next century.
(Source: Library and Archives Canada C-018884)

FIGURE 4-10: Construction zone around Parliament Hill, ca. 1864
The Parliament Buildings were splendid, but the surrounding town was not inspiring.
(Source: Library and Archives Canada, C-000610, detail from Samuel McLaughlin photograph)

buildings, with a water pump-house on the river, sanitary sewers and flush toilets. Gaslights and the telegraph were installed by 1866, when the local services were improved.[335] Initially, however, the new capital could not provide middle-class housing to accommodate the civil servants. Many joined the politicians who gathered in the city for the first session of Parliament in 1866 in hotels and rooming-houses.

Construction of the Centre Block was far from complete when the politicians from the United Canadas met in their new Parliament House for their only Ottawa session in June 1866. The central tower was not finished, and the gorgeous (and fireproof) parliamentary library would not be completed until 1877. But the politicians pronounced themselves well pleased with the new parliamentary chambers, which were a vast improvement over their temporary quarters in Kingston, Toronto or Québec.[336] Luckily, the chambers had been designed with room to expand, so they would be able to accommodate the House of Commons and Senate of the new dominion in 1867.

There were no public celebrations for the opening of the new buildings in June 1866 because Ottawa was an armed camp during the parliamentary session. Soldiers were stationed everywhere throughout downtown and Parliament Hill because of invasion threats from the Fenian Society. Thousands of Irish nationalists had been recruited from the Union Army at the end of the American Civil War. They attacked New Brunswick in April 1866, but were driven off, although the raid helped rally support for Confederation in the Maritimes.[337] But the

Canadian government was caught unprepared when another Fenian brigade invaded the Niagara peninsula on May 31, 1866, capturing Fort Erie and defeating the local militia twice before they were forced to withdraw to Buffalo in June. A third brigade of 1,600 Fenian troops invaded Canada from Vermont, just as the legislature convened for the first time in Ottawa. The entire militia from Montréal, Eastern Ontario and the Eastern Townships were called out to protect the frontier. News that the Québec militia had driven these raiders back across the border on June 7, 1866 was greeted with public acclaim in the new capital.[338]

Although a Fenian plot to blow up the Parliament Buildings was intercepted in late 1866,[339] the threat of invasion had lessened by mid-1867, and municipal governments across the new country planned public celebrations for the first "Dominion Day." Ottawa City Council declared July 1, 1867 a public holiday but, in a portent of future problems, initially declined to fund any festivities.[340] Less than a decade earlier, the Ottawa Council had offered large sums to provide buildings to attract the seat of government to Ottawa, but now that the prize was secure, many councillors did not want to spend even $500 to celebrate the birth of the new nation, suggesting that the federal government cover the cost.

Reflections

Two hundred years after Washington DC, we can see that controversy, conflict and compromise are common elements in selecting a capital city for a federal nation. Canberra was a compromise between Sydney and Melbourne; New Delhi between Kolkatta and Mumbai; Brasilia between Rio and Sao Paulo.[341] Canada's seat-of-government conflict must have appeared unusual in 1860, but Montréal, Toronto and Québec played roles similar to New York, Boston and Philadelphia in the debate over the location of the American capital city. The Canadian seat of government could easily have gone to Montréal, if its Tories had not rioted, or Québec, if construction of the Parliament Buildings had been delayed until 1864.

It is now clear that both Sir Edmund Head and Sir John A. Macdonald favoured Ottawa, but it is hard to disentangle their roles in developing the strategy for selecting the seat of government, since we have no record of their private conversations. The clever domestic political manoeuvring and confederation consensus-building have Macdonald's imprint, but the idea for binding arbitration by the Crown may have come from the more cerebral Head. The Governor General certainly took a significant constitutional risk in supporting Macdonald and Cartier after the infamous "double shuffle" and handled the Colonial Office with authority and skill on the seat-of-government issue.

In retrospect, appropriating the £225,000 for the buildings at the same time as making the referral to Queen Victoria was a crucial decision. It was a typical example of a low estimate to get a 'shovel in the ground'; and it worked as a tactic, but only just. The walls of the Centre Block were built up just high enough that when the money ran out in 1861, McLaughlin's photographs could hint at the gothic grandeur of the Parliament Buildings. Because the political support needed to build a capital city can be consumed in selecting a site, an independent means to get construction started on infrastructure and public buildings is an important implementation tool.[342]

The politicians and civil servants sitting in the relative urban comfort of a 'temporary' capital like Melbourne, Philadelphia, or Québec rarely want to move to a smaller, boring and incomplete community in a remote location. Sometimes the relocation can be delayed for decades, like the 1960 move from Rio to the inland capital of Brasilia, which was a feature of Brazil's constitution since 1891.[343] An incomplete move, such as Tanzania's proposed switch from Dar es Salaam to Dodoma, can be even worse, because politicians, civil servants and diplomats must maintain a presence in both cities.

It also helps if the new capital is grazed by beautiful buildings that inspire pride in the new nation. We owe Keefer, Fuller, Jones, Stent and Laver a debt of gratitude for sticking to their designs to construct the Parliament Buildings, even at the cost of their jobs. The buildings were the main feature inspiring patriotism in Canada's capital for decades, starting their good work with the Confederation delegates' visit in 1864. It can be hard to get national support to finish a capital city when the buildings look cheap and temporary, as the United States found out in the 19th century, and Australia in the 20th century. Their temporary legislature buildings did not help their cause.

Although the Canadian Parliament Buildings were beautiful, the opportunity to plan a more attractive capital city was missed in 1859. Ottawa had much vacant land near Parliament Hill and the local government and landowners were at their most receptive in the late 1850s due to the competitive nature of the selection process. Wider streets, public open spaces and important vistas could only have been reserved at minimal cost at that time. The 1859 design competition produced beautiful buildings, but lacked a larger vision, perhaps because Ottawa became a national capital in two separate but close steps. The architects were only asked to design buildings for a province of 3.5 million people and Barrack Hill looked big enough to accommodate the provincial government of the day, with room for a bit of expansion. The winning designs concentrated development on the Hill and separated the 'Crown' from its 'Town' with an elegant fence. A broader vision might have emerged from a similar competition only five years later, when Ottawa was designated as the capital of a much more ambitious confederation. Washington DC's plan seemed impossibly grand and incomplete in 1860, but it turned out to be less difficult to fill in a half-completed grand plan than to retrofit the industrial towns that grew up in Ottawa and Hull.

During the 1850s, there was not much hint of the tensions between Town and Crown that develop in most capital cities. The competition between cities caused by the arbitration process encouraged the municipalities to unite locally in pursuit of the prize. The Ottawa citizens and local government focused on the prestige and economic benefits that the seat of government would bring to their young city, even offering financial incentives for the legislation to relocate. After the capital had been secured, the valuable construction completed and the jobs permanently relocated to Ottawa, the familiar pattern of Town-Crown conflicts began again.

The events of 1857 and the establishment of the Dominion of Canada had a profound impact on the character of Ottawa and, to a lesser extent, Hull. The seat of government of the United Province of Canada was a boost to the small settlements on the banks of the Ottawa River. But little of this potential was apparent in Ottawa or Hull in 1867. In fact, for the remainder the 19th century, most of the region's economic rationale and vitality was generated by enterprises involved in the woods industry. This new lumber 'Town' turned its back (both literally and symbolically) upon the 'Crown's' lonely presence on Parliament Hill.

CHAPTER 5
Lumbertown (1868-1900)

... it looks as if it were at 't' other end of nowhere
– Frances Monck, 1864 [344]

For much of the 19th century, the Ottawa Valley's economic base and vitality were generated by enterprises involved in the forest industries. The square timber trade pioneered by the Wright family peaked in 1863 as the last great stands of the prized old-growth white pine were cut down in the upper Ottawa Valley. The export trade had shrunk by half within a decade, and many firms went out of business in the 1880s. The last 'crib' went down the Ottawa timber slides in 1908 [345] (Figure 5-1).

The region's industrial base was saved by switching products from square timber to sawn

FIGURE 5-1: **Image of last raft of square timber as it approaches the Parliament Buildings, 1908**
Note the lumber piled along the river's edge. The Upper Town houses at the top of the cliff were acquired in 1912 to provide sites for expansion of federal offices, the Supreme Court and the National Library.
(Source: Library and Archives Canada, C-005068, Pittaway & Jarvis Photograph)

lumber, switching markets from Britain to the US and exploiting the waterpower of the Chaudière Falls (Figure 5-2). Ottawa Mayor Richard Scott enticed a group of American investors to purchase the hydraulic lots on the Ottawa River for bargain prices in 1852.[346] The waterfalls and boiling rapids were soon diverted into the mills and the adjacent islands were covered with industrial buildings[347] (Figure 5-2 and 5-3).

FIGURE 5-2: The mighty Chaudière Kettle reduced to a trickle by industrialization, ca. 1868
Dams diverted all the water to mills and timber slides. Note the height of the lost falls compared to the three-storey buildings on their edge and the destruction of the remarkable view that captivated the Fathers of Confederation only four years earlier (Prologue).
(Source: Library and Archives Canada, PA-012556; Detail of image from the W.J. Topley Collection)

FIGURE 5-3: The Rideau Falls dammed and reduced to a thin curtain to drive McKay's mills, ca. 1870
Note the comparison to the powerful falls seen by Champlain and the Fathers of Confederation (Figure 1-3).
(Source: Library and Archives Canada, PA-008346; detail of image from the W.J. Topley Collection)

These were boom years for the new cities. Between 1851 and 1871, Ottawa's industrial employment rose from 747 to 2,744 while the population tripled from 7,760 to 21,545.[348] In comparison, the federal civil service did not exceed 1,000 until after 1900.[349] The output of saw mills doubled in the early 1860s and doubled again by 1871 (Figure 5-4 and 5-5).

The square timber trade had made little impact upon the urban landscape in Hull and Ottawa, with the exception of the timber slides. In comparison, the lumber trade transformed the waterfront on either side of the Ottawa River. The boiling kettle at the Chaudière Falls was lined with mill buildings (Figure 5-6). Sawdust and waste from the mills were either burnt or dumped in the Ottawa River. The screaming noise from the thousands of saws could be heard throughout the downtown and on Parliament Hill. But the most visible changes were the enormous piles of lumber, stacked to dry on the islands, both banks of the river and across LeBreton Flats. The piles were

FIGURE 5-5: **Piling lumber in J.R. Booth's yard, 1873**
The piles are almost 20 m. high, taller than every private building in Ottawa. Despite the risk of fire, there were no municipal regulations on how close lumber could be piled, since the Hull and Ottawa councils were both controlled by lumber interests.
(Source: Booth Family Collection, Library and Archives Canada, PA-012494)

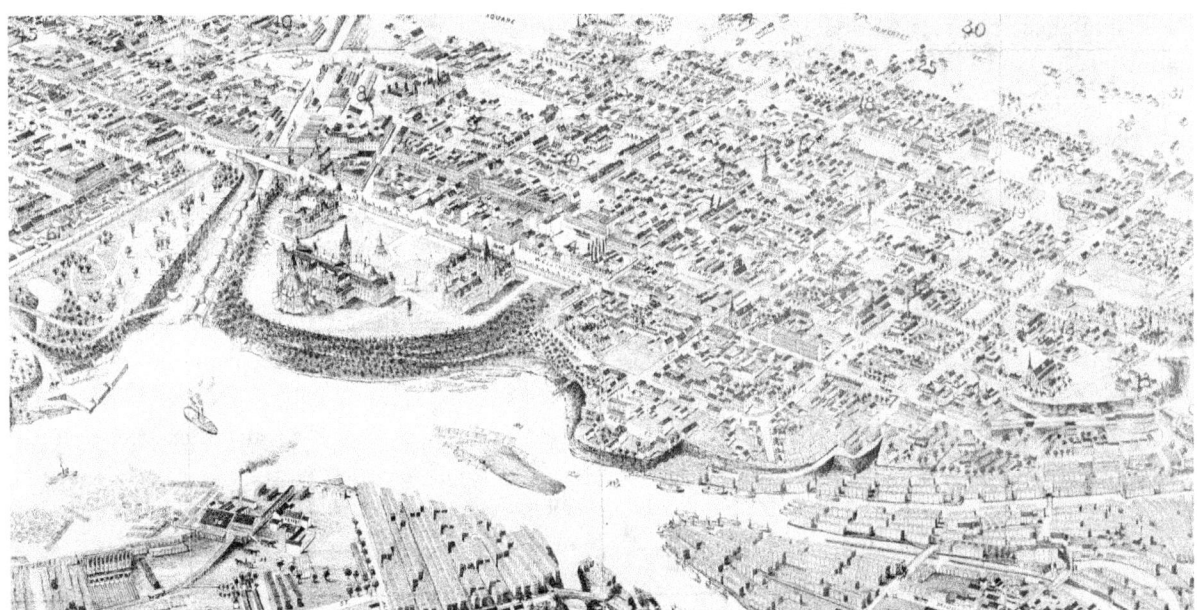

FIGURE 5-4: **Lumber piles and sawmills west of Parliament Hill, 1876**
The riverfront and Chaudière Islands are completely covered by enormous piles of lumber. E.B. Eddy's sulphite pulp mill is located directly across the Ottawa River from the Parliament Buildings.
(Source: Detail from lithograph by Brosius, 1876, Library and Archives Canada, C-015971)

FIGURE 5-6: J.R. Booth and Perley's sawmills cover the Chaudière Islands, ca. 1870
(Source: Library and Archives Canada, PA-012497, detail of image from the W.J. Topley Collection)

often as tall as a six-storey building (Figure 5-5). At first glance, the vast lumber yards look like European streets in the birds'-eye views of the era (Figure 5-4).

The Ottawa River mills were North America's largest lumber suppliers in the late 19th century, reaching their markets first by canal barge, and then by railway. J.R. Booth was one of the few Canadian entrepreneurs to enter the Ottawa lumber trade. He rented a mill from the Wright family in 1857 and got his first big break the next year when he won the contract to supply all the timber for the Parliament Buildings.[350] Booth's sawmill was the world's largest when it burned in 1893. He rebuilt a larger mill only to see it burn again in 1900 and in 1903.[351]

The mill owners made considerable fortunes for their New England investors and some of the money remained in the region, as the Bronson, Perley, Eddy, Maclaren, and Booth families eventually put down local roots.[352] These 'lumber barons' became the new local elite, following the example of Thomas McKay, who had served in the provincial assembly from 1834 until his death. Alonzo Wright served in the Canadian Parliament from 1863-1891, G.H. Perley represented Ottawa in the Ontario legislature, and E.B. Eddy was elected to the Québec Assembly from 1871-1875. Eddy then served on Hull's municipal council from 1875-1891, including several terms as mayor. The Maclaren family were similarly prominent on the Buckingham municipal council from 1865-1906.[353]

The lumber barons had more local influence in the Ottawa area than the Canadian government by virtue of their personal fortunes, property tax payments, large local employment and connections to the municipal governments. Under their influence, Ottawa and Hull remained industrial centres with a hint of the frontier.

The lumber industry also posed a considerable danger to their host communities. The City of Hull had eight major fires between 1880 and 1933 (Figure 5-7), while Ottawa had big fires in 1874, 1900 and 1903. While fire was a common hazard in 19th century cities, the region's lumber industry made the risks higher and fires more intense.[354] The mill owners sometimes provided free green lumber for their employees to rebuild their homes, but the result of the frequent fires was that the 19th century built heritage in Hull and the LeBreton Flats was minimal, and working class neighbourhoods were dominated by inexpensive, quickly-built wooden houses with shingle roofs.

Alas, the boom was not sustainable, because the lumber barons did not replant the trees.[355] The forests of the Ottawa Valley produced their largest yield of white pine in 1881 and thereafter declined in the face of relentless clear-cutting.[356] In reaction, J.R. Booth's Canada Atlantic Railway was extended to new timber resources in distant parts of Eastern Ontario and deposited logs at his Le Breton Flats rail terminus. For a while, this strategy supported the continued growth of the region's industrial sector but, by the late 1890s, the sawn lumber business was in decline.[357]

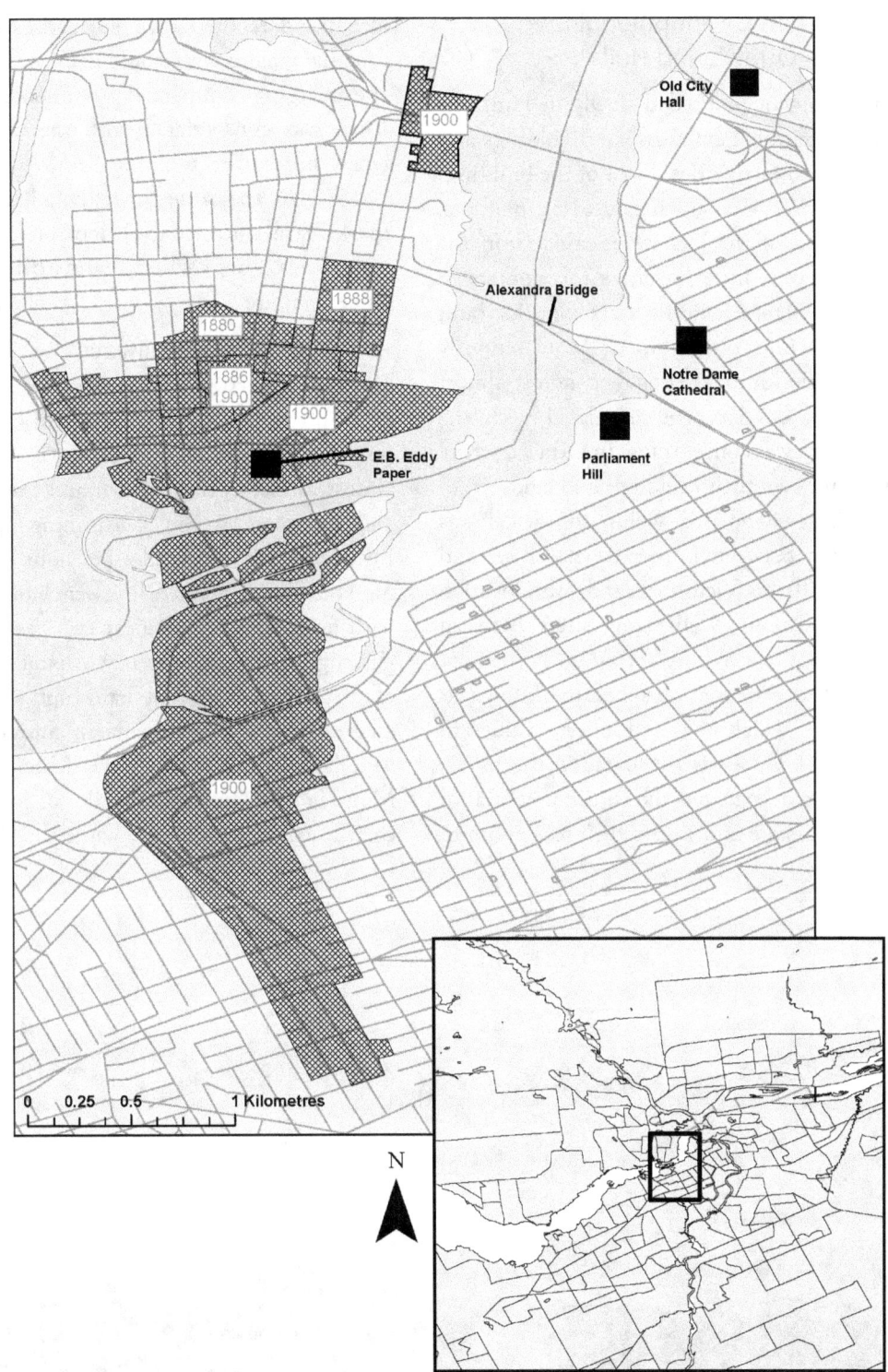

FIGURE 5-7: **Fires in Hull and Ottawa**
Large sections of Hull had previously burned in 1875, 1880, 1886 and 1888. A pressurized municipal water supply for fire fighting was finally installed after the 1900 disaster.
(Source: Drawing by Anthony Hommik, based on Ouimet 1996, Taylor 1979)

Urban Development in Ottawa and Hull

Urban development proceeded slowly in Hull due to the Wright family's extensive land holdings and disinterest in real estate sales. Most of the buildings in Hull were narrow wooden houses on half-lots. Since almost all of the lots were leased from the Wrights, there was little incentive for workers to improve their homes. Middle class families built elsewhere in Aylmer or Ottawa.[358] More seriously for Hull's position in the regional economy, almost all commercial development associated with the lumber industry was concentrated in Ottawa, where investors could own their buildings and land.[359]

Ottawa's newly-opened Wellington Street was the connection between Lower Town's shops and the lumber mills on Victoria Island. The location of eight banks along Wellington Street between Bank and Metcalfe streets, fronting on Parliament Hill, established a district that became known as "Bankers' Row" (Figure 5-8). Property values in Nicholas Sparks' Upper Town soared in the 1870s, as entrepreneurs recognized the future potential of the new nation-state and invested in real estate to accommodate their own enterprises and those of potential tenants who would flock to the new capital. The emerging commercial prominence of the Upper Town was consolidated with the construction of a new post office building in 1875, and city hall in 1877. At the same time, the adjacent blocks of Sparks Street attracted lumber brokers, insurance companies, booksellers, and other corporate offices (Figure 5-9).

Railways

The railway system in the Ottawa Valley was in crisis in the 1860s. The "Fathers of Confederation" travelled to Ottawa by steamboat because it was almost as fast as the Bytown and Prescott Railway and far more scenic.[360] Running speed on the B&P was only nine miles per hour due to lack of maintenance. The entire line went bankrupt in 1865, with no freight for the next two years and limited passenger service to the new capital city. The City of Ottawa almost went bankrupt with the B&P, and its capital investments in municipal services were hobbled for years by the debt.[361] Toronto and Montréal had over 2,000 miles of rail service into their hinterlands in 1860, while the Ottawa Valley

FIGURE 5-8: View from Parliament of "Bankers' Row," ca. 1889-1895
(Source: Library and Archives Canada, PA-008490; W. J. Topley photograph)

FIGURE 5-9: Dufferin and Sappers' bridges, looking northwest, ca. 1898
Note the many streetcars and horse-drawn cabs.
(Source: Library and Archives Canada, C-003778)

was stuck with only its narrow-gauge track to Prescott until the forerunners of the CPR reached Hull in 1877 and Ottawa in 1880.[362]

The Ottawa Valley rail system expanded chaotically in the 1880s and 1890s when lumber baron J.R. Booth built his own railway system to connect to his American timber markets. The Canada Atlantic Railway (1882) built stations beside the Rideau Canal, first at Elgin Street, then at Rideau. Booth's Ottawa, Arnprior and Parry Sound Railway (1896) built a terminus at his mill site in LeBreton Flats. Outaouais industrial interests built the Pontiac and Pacific (1886) and the Ottawa and Gatineau Valley (1892) railways and the CPR finally added a 'high speed' connection from Ottawa to Montréal in 1898.

There was no planning and no coordination of this expansion, the railroad system in Ottawa and Hull was a mess by the end of the 19th century. Freight yards were scattered across the region; the main east-west lines ran at-grade along Catherine Street; there was only one connection across the Ottawa River and passenger service arrived at five different terminals, making transfers between lines difficult.

The railway system may have worked for its industrial promoters, but it was unpleasant for the many small residential neighbourhoods trapped next to the tracks and yards, and awkward for passengers. The system did not serve Ottawa's function as a seat of government well, depositing visitors some distance from Parliament Hill, with their first impressions of Canada's capital city dominated by declining industrial areas and freight yards. The 1909 Union Station, built beside the Rideau Canal at Rideau Street, reduced the passenger connection problem (CP remained in LeBreton Flats and Hull), but the shabby arrival sequence continued into the 20th century.

Municipal Services

The urban infrastructure in Hull and Ottawa was significantly behind that of other central Canadian cities when the seat of government was relocated to the region. The contrast with the previous capital cities of the United Canadas – Québec, Toronto, Montréal or even Kingston – was not favourable (Table 5-1).[363] All these cities had piped water since the early 1850s but homes and businesses in the new capital had to rely on water delivered in barrels by horse cart (Figure 5-10). Piped water arrived in Ottawa in 1874 and in Hull in 1886.

Residents and visitors also had to endure the consequences of the absence of a municipal sewage system. The advent of summer often brought a problem that was to plague the city for several months: disease caused by "disgraceful sanitary arrangements."[364] The causes were evident to all: polluted water in the cellars; earth-closets that needed to be cleaned; smelly backyards behind buildings.[365] Human waste was removed by horse cart, if it wasn't just thrown into the streets, since Ottawa's primitive sewer system did not receive its first trunk lines until 1872. Hull would wait for sewers until 1880, almost three decades after Québec.

To make matters worse, the sewage was discharged untreated into the Ottawa River not far from the water intakes, so a supply of *safe*

TABLE 5-1: **Municipal Infrastructure Comparison**

	Ottawa[366]	**Toronto**[367]	**Kingston**[368]	**Montréal**[369]
Incorporated	1847 (Town) 1855 (City)	1834 (City)	1838 (Town) 1846 (City)	1831 (City)
Piped Water	1872	1841	1847	1801
Water Treatment	1932	1912		1918
Sewers	1857	1840		1840
Sewage Treatment	1961	1911	1957	
Paved Streets	1895	1861		
Sidewalks	1845		1830s	
Gas Lights	1854	1844		1830
Electric Lights	1885	1882		1886
Omnibus		1849		1861
Horse Cars	1866	1861	1877	1861
Electric Streetcars	1891	1894	1893	1892
Police	1866	1834 (Town)	1841	1818
Jail	1842	1800	1844	

FIGURE 5-10: Water Delivery in Ottawa, 1870s
Horse-drawn barrels were barely adequate for hauling drinking water, and almost useless for firefighting.
(Source: Library and Archives Canada, C-013323; watercolour by J. H. de Rinzy)

drinking water had to wait for decades.[370] Public health problems, including fatal typhoid epidemics, continued well into the 20th century. Ottawa's water filtration plant opened in 1932, a quarter century after Toronto's.[371] Ottawa's infant death rate was double that of other large cities in Ontario in 1900, partly due to problems with the water supply, almost four decades after Toronto received pure water (Figure 5-11).[372]

The streets were also a shameful comparison with those of other cities. Toronto may have been known as "Muddy York" early in the century, but Ontario's capital had gas streetlights widely installed in 1841 and Jarvis Street was first paved in 1848. Ottawa had a few gas lamps on Sussex and Rideau streets after 1854, but to conserve funds, Council only lit them during the dark phases of the moon. By 1871, the gas lamps were lit nightly, and the weak whale-oil lamps on other downtown streets were phased out two years later.[373] Before Hull got downtown gaslight in 1878, the streets were lit only by the glow from adjacent windows.[374]

Lowertown Ottawa had been a swamp until the 1830s, and its streets still had serious drainage problems decades later. They were essentially impassable in the spring because of the deep mud and accumulated human waste of the winter. The city government made slow progress draining these streets, and had technical troubles with early road surfacing (Figure 5-12). The first proper asphalt pavement was laid on Sparks Street in 1895 (Figure 5-13).[375]

FIGURE 5-11: Ottawa Water Works, ca. 1892
This system provided pumped water for fire fighters, but its intake was from Nepean Bay, adjacent to sanitary sewer outlets. City Council ignored engineering reports recommending a pure water supply from the Gatineau Hills.
(Source: Library and Archives Canada, C-006278, C.B Powell fonds)

FIGURE 5-12: Horsecar stuck in the Sparks Street mud, ca. 1880
The mud was too thick for the street railway to operate, so cart-wheels were attached to the cars every spring.
(Source: Library and Archives Canada, detail from image C-017827)

FIGURE 5-13: Sparks Street, Ottawa's best retail address in 1872
The view outside Bate & Co., the capital's leading grocery store; Sparks Street had surpassed Sussex as the prime shopping street, but note the dirt roadbed, wooden plank sidewalk and lack of street lights.
(Source: Library and Archives Canada, C-006987, C.B Powell fonds)

Ottawa and Hull's public infrastructure developed slower than that of other Canadian cities because their local governments started later and were dominated by industrial concerns. Ottawa was financially crippled by its disastrous investment in the B&P railway, and the lumber barons who controlled the two cities simply were not interested in creating the urban amenities demanded by the commercial and financial elites in Toronto and Montréal, let alone in capital cities in other countries.

The two cities began to catch up to their provincial rivals in the late 1880s, when the hydro-electric power available from the Chaudière became a regional advantage. Local entrepreneurs Thomas Ahern and Warren Soper experimented with electrical engineering. They provided Ottawa with electric street lights in 1885, only a year after Toronto.[376]

Although Montréal and Toronto's horse drawn trams began in 1861, five years ahead of Ottawa, Ahern and Soper opened an electric streetcar route in 1891, a year ahead of the other cities[377] (Figure 5-14). They took over the entire Ottawa tramway system and electrified it in 1894, building their own streetcars in local factories. The Ottawa Electric Railway (OER) was an immediate success, quickly expanding from Rockcliffe Park to Britannia.[378] Hull never had horsecars, but it quickly adopted the new technology, chartering the Hull Electric Railway (HER) in 1895. Unfortunately, the two companies were intense competitors and the two streetcar systems were never connected, providing an early example of the interjurisdictional conflict that plagued the region in the 20th century. The OER built a bridge across the Chaudière in 1896, but would not allow the HER to use it. In response, the Hull council would not allow the OER even to build a turn-around loop in Hull. The HER extended two lines across the new Alexandra Bridge in 1901, with a connection to Ottawa's Union Station, but the Ottawa council would not permit the Hull cars to run on Ottawa's streets. Passengers were left to transfer as best they could and this disconnect would last for over a century.[379]

The horsecar, electric streetcar, electric light and private gas distribution systems demonstrate that Ottawa Valley entrepreneurs could provide infrastructure quickly and efficiently, although the provincial border was a barrier to true regional networks. In contrast, 19th century utilities provided by the local governments arrived late, were under-capitalized, poorly engineered and badly managed. Much of the blame for these problems must rest with the precarious financial situation of the municipal governments and the narrow self-interest of the industrial elites that controlled them. This situation would change later in the 20th century, but the track record of the municipal governments did not inspire the confidence of the national government early in the new century.

FIGURE 5-14: Inaugural run of the electric streetcar, 1891
The privately-owned Ottawa Electric Railway was a leader in this new technology.
(Source: City of Ottawa Archives, detail from image CA-1510)

Rebellion of the Aristocrats (1868-1900)

Governor General the Viscount Monck hated Ottawa from the start:

> It seems like an act of insanity to have fixed the capital of this great country away from the civilization, intelligence and commercial enterprise of this Province, in a place that can never be a place of importance and where the political section of the community will live in a position of isolation and removed from the action of any public opinion. My confident belief is that Ottawa will not be the capital four years hence.[380]

Monck refused to travel by the rutted dirt track leading from the Governor General's residence at Rideau Hall to Parliament. He kept a small boat to travel on the Ottawa River instead. Monck joked with Fanny Meredith, wife of one of the first deputy ministers, about joining him in a plot to blow up the new Parliament Buildings so they could be rid of the place.[381] Lord Dufferin, who followed Monck as Governor General, also preferred Québec, and spent as much time there as possible.[382]

The opinion and presence of the Governors General still mattered in the mid-19th century. After Confederation in 1867, they were empowered to only govern according to the wishes of the elected Prime Minister on domestic issues. But the Governor General remained the chief representative of Canada on international and imperial issues. Foreign affairs were handled from London, so Ottawa had no embassies until the 20th century.

The Queen's representative during the latter half of the 19th century was typically a British nobleman with an interest in promoting ties to the Crown and Empire. Several Governors General also vigorously promoted Canadian unity and identity, touring the young country and encouraging cultural and sporting activity with their patronage. These interests sometimes resulted in vice-regal initiatives in the planning of Canada's capital.

The civil service was also unhappy about relocating from Québec, but they had no choice. Although moving from city to city every four years to follow the "perambulating capital" was inconvenient, at least Montréal, Toronto and Québec had a stock of decent middle-class houses and some basic municipal services such as piped water, sewers, and paved streets. It was a struggle to set up a household in Ottawa, which had been a frontier town only 30 years earlier and whose municipal services had yet to catch up to the older, larger cities.[383] The comparison to sophisticated world capitals such as London and Paris was dreadful.

Paris was generally regarded as the world's most beautiful capital city and the model of urban sophistication in the late 19th century. In comparison Washington was incomplete and London grew "more by fortune than design."[384] The parks, boulevards and urban services built in the French capital were the most extensive in Europe.[385] In 1853, Emperor Napoleon III made Baron Georges-Eugène Haussmann *Prèfet de la Seine*, responsible for transforming Paris from a medieval labyrinth into a healthy, functional and grand imperial capital. In less than 20 years, Paris gained 110 km. of new boulevards, 640 km. of paved streets, 50,000 street trees, 14 new or reconstructed bridges and numerous new markets, town halls, churches and theatres.

While Haussmann is chiefly remembered for his beautiful boulevards, he also tripled Paris' water supply from pure sources, built 400 km. of sewers and expanded the city's parks from a mere 19 ha. to over 1,800 ha. It was an astonishing program of public works, implemented with innovative financing schemes and enormous loans, which eventually caused Haussmann's removal.[386] Paris was also the centre of excellence in architecture. The École de Beaux-Arts became the world's leading design school, with students flocking to its ateliers to learn architecture and large-scale urban design.[387] As a result of its leadership in infrastructure, architecture and urban design, Paris became the dominant model for the new South American capital cities, a strong precedent for the reconstruction of Washington and an inspiration for the North American City Beautiful movement.[388]

City Beautiful Movement

The first plans to improve Canada's capital were affected by a movement to make North American cities more beautiful at the end of the 19th century. Ottawa and Hull were not the only industrial cities whose appearance disappointed their elite citizens. 'Civic Improvement' societies found a model in Chicago's 1983 World's Columbian Exposition. The design team for this world's fair, led by Daniel Burnham, produced a plan that drew on classical European architecture and urban design traditions from Paris and Rome. Their "White City" left many visitors awestruck in comparison to their hometowns, and inspired new civic centers and boulevards across the continent. The key players from the Columbian Exposition team were re-assembled for the 1903 McMillan commission plan for Washington, and City Beautiful plans were also prepared for commercial cities like Cleveland (1903), San Francisco (1904) and Chicago (1908).[389]

Other designers prepared City Beautiful plans for Maisonneuve (1905), Toronto (1906), Kitchener (1914), Calgary (1914), Regina (1914) and Edmonton (1915). Despite Chicago's success, the aesthetic objectives of most City Beautiful plans were rarely implemented in Canadian commercial cities,[392] where later activists pushed for affordable housing and infrastructure reforms.[393]

However, some City Beautiful techniques were appropriate for improving capital cities, like Regina's Wascana Centre, where parks and urban design improvements helped create a dignified and attractive setting for the provincial government.[394]

FIGURE 5-15: Chicago Waterfront from Burnham and Bennett's 1909 *Plan of Chicago*
The Chicago plan, prepared by Daniel Burnham and Edward Bennett,[390] was the most comprehensive and influential of the City Beautiful plans, addressing infrastructure, parks and urban design issues at both regional and local scales. Bennett was later invited to prepare a plan for Canada's capital. This plan of the central area shows parks, waterfront improvement and a railway relocation that were implemented, but the grand civic centre was not.[391]
(Source: Burnham and Bennett, 1909, plate CX)

Rideau Hall

Although living in Ottawa may have been disagreeable for most of the civil service, it was considered a hardship post by the vice-regal couples of the day. Lady Monck had been warned to "keep out of it [Ottawa] as long as you can…" She only stayed for one night during her husband's first residence in the new capital.[395] Lady Dufferin described Ottawa as:

> … *a small town, with incongruously beautiful buildings crowning its insignificance. A very bad road leads to Rideau, which is a long, two-storied villa, with a small garden on one side of it and a hedge which bounds our property on the other.*[396]

The vice-regal residence, Rideau Hall, was a small country villa leased from the estate of Thomas McKay in 1864. It had few improvements at first, other than the long, two-storey wing added in 1865 (Figure 5-16). The Canadian government finally bought the house in 1868, and many additions were made over the next decades, without improving the coherence of the floor plan.[397] The eighty acre (35 ha.) estate surrounding Rideau Hall was in poor shape, having been let go in the decade following McKay's death. The house originally had a spectacular site overlooking the Ottawa River and Bytown but adjacent trees grew up and closed the views. Each of the succeeding vice-regal couples made additions to the gardens, most working in the picturesque English landscape style.[398]

FIGURE 5-16: Rideau Hall, 1868
The Monck family is seated in the new garden. Thomas McKay's original 1838 bow-fronted villa is at the left side of the image. The new wing of rough Gloucester stone made no effort to match McKay's fine masonry. Any British nobleman's country house would be far grander.
(Source: Library and Archives Canada, C-005966, detail from photo by Samuel McLaughlin)

The Marquis of Lorne and Princess Louise attempted to raise the cultural tone in the frontier capital. The Governor-General promoted Canadian arts and science, founding a Canadian Academy for the Arts (1880) and the Royal Society of Canada (1882). Lorne pushed hard for a National Gallery and the Academy moved out of its temporary quarters in an Ottawa hotel into the old Supreme Court building in 1882.[399] Princess Louise, an accomplished amateur artist, created watercolours of scenes in the capital and her travels across the country.[400] She also opened a view from Rideau Hall to the Ottawa River that became known as the "Princess' Vista" (Figure 5-17). But Queen Victoria's daughter returned to Britain in 1880 after she was severely injured when their sleigh overturned on a rutted road outside the gates.[401]

Perhaps it is not surprising that the politicians and Governors General paid so little attention to the capital during its first years, since they fled as soon as parliamentary sessions ended. Even the Prime Minister left, since there was no official residence until almost a century after Ottawa was selected as the capital. Canada's first Prime Minister, Sir John A. Macdonald, owned a variety of houses in his native Kingston,[402] but he purchased his first Ottawa residence in 1883, a quarter-century after his government announced the capital. Earnscliffe was perched on a bluff overlooking the Ottawa River, not far from Rideau Hall. By coincidence, the Prime Minister's house had also been designed and built by Thomas McKay.[403]

The truth is that Ottawa was a one-industry town in the mid-19th century, and that industry was lumber, not government. The politicians and 350 civil servants occupied only the picturesque triptych of gothic buildings on Parliament Hill. The legislators typically spent only a third of the year in Ottawa. They boarded in hotels like the Russell House, and fled the day that the House of Commons rose.[404] So the politicians and civil servants barely made a dent in the society of "one of the roughest, booziest, least law-abiding towns in North America."[405]

Figure 5-17: View of the Princess' Vista cut from Rideau Hall to the Ottawa River
(Source: *Picturesque Canada*, by George M. Grant, Library and Archives Canada, detail from image C-082887)

The Governors General and their wives toured the country constantly, filling their diaries with accounts of Canada's natural wonders, and spending as much time as possible in the more civilized confines of Montréal and Québec. When they were trapped in Ottawa, they promoted Canadian sports, so Rideau Hall acquired a skating rink, toboggan run and a curling rink for entertaining guests during the long winters. Skating parties were important social occasions in the late 19th century.[406]

Meanwhile, back in downtown Ottawa, the growth of both the nation and the scope of federal government caused continual increases in the civil service, which soon leapt over the wall on Parliament Hill in search of rented premises on the upper floors of Wellington and Sparks streets. In 1883-86 the federal Department of Public Works erected a new building at Wellington and Elgin streets to accommodate the overflow.[407] Construction of the new office building was surrounded by scandals similar to the Parliament Buildings. It exceeded its budget by almost 100 percent, was completed three years late and a Conservative MP, Thomas McGreevy, was found to be a silent partner of the contractor. McGreevy was previously accused of corrupt dealings as the contractor for the Parliament Buildings[408] and was related by marriage to Public Works minister Hector Langevin. News of kickbacks to the contractor and 'gifts' to DPW officials were too much for the public to bear, even in the patronage-riddled Macdonald administration, so the minister and chief engineer were forced to resign.[409] Ironically, the building was later named after the disgraced minister, but the scandal forced reforms of the public service to reduce corruption in building projects. However, the Langevin Building was the last federal office building erected in the 19th century. All further civil service growth had to be accommodated in rental premises elsewhere in the city.

Of course, the new buildings were only the most visible impact of the seat of government upon Ottawa. The social structure of the city changed more radically than the townscape. The civil service added perhaps three hundred well-paid, well-educated families to the city's middle and upper-middle classes.[410] The presence of Governors General drawn from the British nobility eventually grafted an entirely new social strata to the lumber town. When in residence at Rideau Hall, the Governor General and his retinue were the centre of the new Ottawa social world in the late 19th century, brilliantly described by Sandra Gwyn in her book, *The Private Capital*, drawn from diaries from the era.[411] Upper Town lost some of its status as an elite residential area when both the Governor General and the Prime Minister chose residences near Rockcliffe.

Rockcliffe Park

It took a long time for Rockcliffe Park to become Ottawa's most fashionable suburb. Thomas McKay had purchased the farm lots in the 1830s and developed New Edinburgh, but his families' homes were the only houses on the rest of the property when he died in 1855. McKay's son-in-law, Thomas Coltrin Keefer, managed the estate and supervized its planning and development.[412] By 1864, he had prepared a promotional brochure and a plan for the subdivision of the estate into park, villa and estate lots, in the English picturesque tradition, with McKay Lake preserved as a decorative element[413] (Figure 5-18).

However, Rockcliffe Park grew quite slowly in the 19th century, despite the prestige of the Governor General's new residence. Upper Town and Sandy Hill were more conveniently located to downtown and Parliament Hill. The key improvement was the 1893 extension of the electric streetcar to the area, providing a fast and comfortable connection to the city. The service had to be good, because Ottawa Electric Railway owners, Thomas Ahern and Warren Soper, built large homes in Rockcliffe. Other industrial families followed them after the 1900 fire and federal expropriation of Upper Town for the expansion of the parliamentary precinct.

Rockcliffe Park was incorporated as a separate village in 1908, and established policies encouraging single family homes set on large lots in a lush landscape and prohibiting commercial development. The village became popular for senior civil servants in the inter-war years, and the large houses built by the industrialists were converted into ambassadorial residences after World War II.[414]

Washington of the North?

The first embellishments to the new capital beyond Parliament Hill were an initiative of the newspapers and city government. The Major's Hill, east of the Rideau Canal, had been reserved by the Crown for Ordnance purposes and then for the Governor General's 'palace.' After Rideau Hall became the

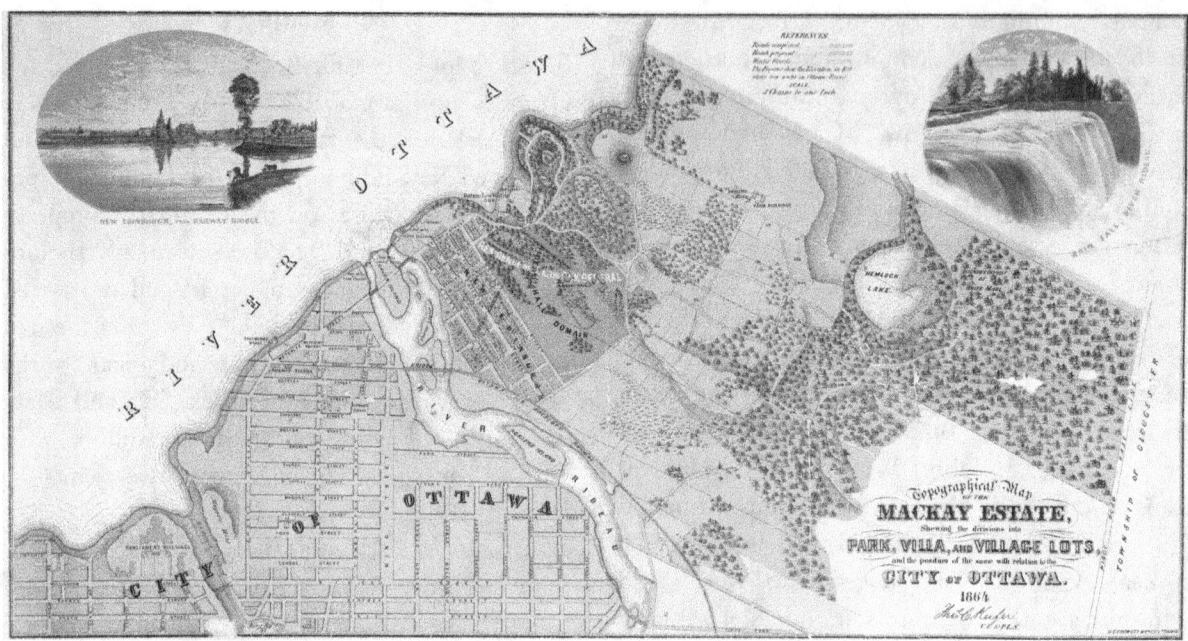

Figure 5-18: T.C. Keefer's Rockcliffe Park Plan, 1864
(Source: Library and Archives Canada, NMC 17613)

permanent vice-regal residence, City Council lobbied to be granted the land as a site for a new city hall, without success.[415] However, a proposal for a public park on the Major's Hill received federal support and the Department of Public Works leased the land to the city in 1874[416] (Figure 5-19). City Engineer Robert Surtees designed the original park, which was completed in 1876 at a cost of $10,000. Unfortunately, some of Surtees' rustic cedar embellishments began to decay within six years. City Council had little interest in funding the operations or maintenance of public parks, and returned Major's Hill to the Department of Public Works in 1885, a mere nine years after it opened.[417]

The official neglect of Canada's capital began to change in the spring of 1893, with the arrival of a new Governor General, Lord Aberdeen. Perhaps more importantly, his energetic wife, Ishbel Gordon (Figure 5-20), accompanied him to Canada (see Cast of Characters). The Aberdeens, like those before them, were disappointed by Ottawa. In January 1895, she noted "We are very sorry to leave Montréal. Ottawa means exile emphasized, accompanied by a feeling of hopelessness. Happily Ottawa does not mean Canada, nor does it represent Canada."[418] However, rather than staying away from the city as much as possible, Lady Aberdeen decided to make the best of an Imperial bad lot: "As Montréal is now hopelessly lost as a capital, everything possible should be done to push Ottawa."[419]

Lady Aberdeen found an ally in her quest to improve the capital in Wilfrid Laurier (Figure 5-21), the new Leader of the Opposition (see Cast of Characters). He did not have a good early impression of the capital, writing to his confidante, "Here I am chained to this detested place for many weeks to come …"[420] When Laurier arrived in Ottawa for the national convention of the Liberal Party on June 19, 1893, he was met by a crowd of supporters at the station. Speaking from the back of his Pullman car, he addressed the assembly, ending with:

I consequently keep a green spot in my heart for the city of Ottawa, and when the day comes, as it will come by and by, it shall be my pleasure and that of my colleagues I am

FIGURE 5-19: **Major's Hill Park under construction; the view from Parliament Hill, ca. 1873**
(Source: Library and Archives Canada, C-002261; detail from the W.J. Topley photograph)

FIGURE 5-20: **Lady Aberdeen was the impetus for the Ottawa Improvement Commission**
Making Canada's capital more beautiful was just one of the many projects for this ambitious social reformer, who started the Victorian Order of Nurses and championed the National Council of Women.
(Source: Library and Archives Canada,: PA-028880; S. J. Thompson photograph)

sure to make the city of Ottawa as attractive as possibly could be; to make it the centre of the intellectual development of this country and above all the **Washington of the north** [emphasis added].[421]

The speech made headlines in the newspapers and left an indelible impression on many of those who heard it.[422] Laurier repeated his promise when he arrived in Ottawa in August 1896, as newly-elected Prime Minister. "Washington of the North" became the slogan for Ottawa's improvement as a national capital. It held some promise, since the American city was finally emerging as a proper capital after a century of ridicule and slow development.[423]

FIGURE 5-21: Sir Wilfrid Laurier, founder of the Ottawa Improvement Commission

For Laurier, a capital city that inspired pride among Canadians was simply a policy that helped promote national unity.

(Source: Library and Archives Canada, William Lyon Mackenzie King fonds, C-005599)

Washington's McMillan Commission Plan

A Canadian prime minister would not use the American capital city as a good example for most of the century. Pierre L'Enfant's 1792 Washington plan had almost been abandoned in the late 19th century. A railway station had been built on the Mall, in front of the Capitol, government buildings were popping up everywhere, the Washington monument was sited off the axis of the Mall to reduce foundation costs and the proposed parks were not built.[424] In the absence of a municipal government, the American Association of Architects, the local Board of Trade and parks advocates lobbied for a new plan for Washington during the 1890s. In response, Senator James McMillan, chair of the Senate Committee for the District of Columbia, established an expert commission including architects Daniel Burnham and Charles McKim (of Chicago World's Fair fame), sculptor Augustus Saint Gaudens and landscape architect Frederick Law Olmsted Jr.. After their appointment to the Senate Park Commission, Burnham led them on a whirlwind tour of Paris and Rome. Many photographs of European precedents illustrated their 1902 report and Olmsted prepared drawings comparing the parks systems of London, Paris, Boston and Washington.[425]

The design team rescued L'Enfant's plan and updated it slightly for the 20th century. Burnham convinced the president of the B&O Railroad to move its terminal off the Mall and designed a magnificent new station just northwest of the Capitol building. McKim cleverly re-aligned the Mall to make it look like the Washington Monument had been built where L'Enfant proposed it. He also provided sites for the future Lincoln and Jefferson memorials and the Federal Triangle. Olmsted designed a regional parks system that included waterfronts, the Rock Creek Valley and the ceremonial core of the Mall. Parkways connected the open spaces, similar to his firm's Emerald Necklace in Boston.

The Senate Parks Commission had no legislative authority to implement their plan, so they embarked on a major campaign to influence the President, Congress and the public. The best commercial illustrators were retained to create colour paintings of the plans and huge 'before-and-after' scale models of the Mall. President Teddy Roosevelt opened the exhibition of paintings and models at the Corcoran Museum of Art, creating a big splash in the newspapers. The Commission followed up with lavish articles in mass circulation magazines, including dramatic colour lithographs in *National Geographic*.

The 1902 McMillan commission report combined elements of the City Beautiful (Figure 5-22) and the Parks movements, and its comprehensive approach and wide dissemination affected planning across North America.[426] Although the formal axes of the Mall are the most famous elements of the plan, Olmsted's regional parks system proposals had the most immediate effect on Canada's capital, since one of his former apprentices, Frederick Todd, was retained to assist the Ottawa Improvement Commission in 1903.

The Ottawa Improvement Commission

Although City Council had abandoned Major's Hill Park, two patriotic aldermen, Fred Cook and Robert Stewart, established a civic committee to study the plans to embellish other capitals in the British Empire and their financial arrangements.[427] By October 1897, City Council prepared a petition to the federal government suggesting that it had inadequate funds to meet the needs of a seat of government because the Crown property within the city was exempt from local property taxes. Citing the example of London, where the UK government paid municipal taxes on its properties, the Ottawa Council suggested that the federal government pay it an annual grant, and the city would then provide an adequate water supply, fire protection and parks.[428] Ottawa's proposal arrived at the same time that the new prime minister was considering Lady Aberdeen's proposal to improve the capital.

Laurier became friends with the Aberdeens, and they collaborated on a strategy for Ottawa's

FIGURE 5-22: McMillan Commission Plan for the Ceremonial Core of Washington
This plan recovered the ceremonial core of L'Enfant's 1792 design in the City Beautiful style.
(Source: Report of the U.S. Senate Park Commission, 1902; Plate VII; watercolor by Francis L.V. Hoppin)

improvement (Figure 5-23). The Countess invited the Lauriers for a picnic on Nepean Point in the fall of 1898, during the last days of her Canadian appointment. They dreamed of making Ottawa a better capital, as noted in one of the last entries in Lady Aberdeen's' diary:

> *I must own to beginning to feel quite a sneaking fondness for the place itself, in spite of its shabby old Government House put away amongst its clump of bushes & in spite of dirty old tumble down Sussex Street, to drive over which always needed an effort, although it was an effort almost daily repeated.*
>
> *Perhaps this fondness is not altogether unconnected with a scheme for a grand improvement of Ottawa which lies very near our hearts & which if carried out would make her one day a very queen of capitals. The idea is to get a [town] plan made & adopted...*
>
> *Sir Wilfrid is quite taken with the idea & came over the place with me to inspect it one day ... he was not only enthusiastic about it but seemed to think it possible to undertake at a much earlier date than we had ventured to hint at. We only said "Look fifty years ahead" get a plan made whereby such a scheme may ultimately be developed & which will prevent eyesores of buildings being put up meanwhile & thus preventing it.*
>
> *Mr. Fielding [the Finance Minister] says "Get Ottawa put under a Commission like Washington & I am with you". Probably he is right for the Ottawa civic authorities have not been very wonderful up to now ...*[429]

It took less than a year for Laurier and Finance Minister W.S. Fielding to respond to the proposals from Ottawa and Lady Aberdeen. On August 11, 1899, the Ottawa Improvement Commission [OIC] was formed, with Fielding introducing the bill to Parliament[430] (Figure 5-24).

The *Act Respecting the City of Ottawa* addressed both Lady Aberdeen's initiative and the local

FIGURE 5-23: **Lady Aberdeen and Sir Wilfrid Laurier and their families, 1897**
(Source: Library and Archives Canada, C-003775)

government's complaints. The new OIC could cooperate with the City of Ottawa for:

> ... *the improvement and beautifying of the said city, or the vicinity thereof, by the acquisition, maintenance and improvement of public parks, squares, streets, avenues, drives or thoroughfares, and the erection of public buildings in the said city or in the vicinity thereof.*[431]

The Commission was granted $60,000 per year for at least 10 years to accomplish these objectives, and given the power to acquire or expropriate any property required for their purposes.[432]

The federal government did not agree to the City of Ottawa's demand that it pay property taxes on its growing portfolio of land, or to provide the city with a cash grant to make improvements. Instead, it appointed the Mayor of Ottawa as one of the four OIC commissioners. The national government also agreed to maintain the Union Bridge, three bridges across the Rideau Canal and sidewalks in front of federal buildings. It also agreed to pay for its share of improving Wellington Street, should the city decide to pave it. However, the federal government also withdrew the small annual payments to the city for water supply to federal buildings.[433]

Figure 5-24: Ottawa Improvement Commission 1899-1902
Chairman Henry Bate is top row centre and engineer Robert Surtees, who designed the OIC's original parks is bottom row, second from the left.
(Source: A. Gard, *The Hub and the Spokes*, 1904, p. 50)

The OIC's first chairman was Sir Henry Bate, the local grocer who had welcomed Laurier to Ottawa on the day he made his "Washington of the North" promise.[434] The other commissioners were local businessmen C.R. Cunningham, Joseph Riopelle and Mayor Thomas Payment (Figure 5-24) The OIC was expanded to six commissioners in 1902, with the appointment of Senators Louis-Joseph Forget, Francis T. Frost, and William Hingston. It appears that most of the appointed commissioners were prominent Liberals, with the exception of Sir William Hingston, who was a Conservative and former mayor of Montréal.[435] The commissioners served without payment and "at the pleasure" of the Cabinet, which meant that there was no policy for regularly changing the membership of the OIC, except for the mayor. The commissioners were supported by administrative staff from the civil service, and retained the consulting advice of the Dominion botanist, Dr. William Saunders, and Robert Surtees, the former City Engineer and designer of Major's Hill Park.[436] The OIC's work had just begun when the region suffered its greatest disaster.

The 1900 Hull/Ottawa fire

An overheated chimney in north Hull caught fire on a breezy morning in April 1900. As the winds picked up during the morning, the fire quickly went out of control, blowing southwards towards the Chaudière. The Hull firefighters were overwhelmed, desperate calls were sent out for assistance to Ottawa and Montréal, but by lunchtime, over half the city had been destroyed.[437] The lumber piles in the Chaudière then created one of the largest urban fires in Canadian history (Figure 5-25). The blaze

FIGURE 5-25: Fleeing the 1900 fire on Queen Street
Residents saved what they could throw on wagons as the flames roar behind them.
(Source: Booth Family Collection, Library and Archives Canada, PA-120334)

leapt the Ottawa River, destroying everything on the Chaudière Islands except J.R. Booth's main sawmill, which was saved by his company firefighters and a new sprinkler system. The fire then tore into western Ottawa and, devoured everything on LeBreton Flats. Luckily, the wind was blowing towards the southwest and the fire could not climb the cliff to Sparks Street or Parliament Hill. But the blaze destroyed the western neighbourhoods before running out of fuel near Dow's Lake and the Dominion Experimental Farm.[438]

The fire killed seven people, left 15,000 people homeless, and destroyed an area about five kilometres long and one kilometre wide, including all of downtown Hull (Figure 5-26). It was also a turning point for the local forest products industry. Most of the small lumber firms that were burnt out left the business, and only Booth and Eddy rebuilt their sawmills. It was obvious that the lumber piles were a major cause of the disaster, and Parliament considered attaching conditions to its $410,000 relief grant to require municipal legislation prohibiting the piles.[439] But Hull and Ottawa city councils were poorly funded and dominated by the forest industries, which were their largest employers and biggest source of property tax revenues. Many aldermen represented business interests and, while they might issue large municipal loans and grants to railways that would benefit the corporations, they usually would not approve commercial property

FIGURE 5-26: Downtown Hull after the 1900 fire
(Source: Library and Archives Canada, PA-023233)

tax increases, capital expenditures or restrictions on business activity. So the only restriction upon the lumber piles was a 60-foot set back from other property, but since the streets were 60 feet wide in the area, the bylaw had no practical effect. The council declined to place any regulations for fireproof housing construction in the areas near the mills, and would not even replace the city's steam fire engine that was destroyed in the blaze.[440]

E.B. Eddy had already begun diversification into the pulp and paper businesses in 1886, converting the Chaudière waterpower from sawmills to mechanically grind logs into wood pulp. He built a sulphite mill for chemical production of pulp and started paper production opposite Parliament Hill in 1890. J.R. Booth converted some of his sawmills to pulp and paper production after the 1900 fire.[441] Unfortunately, both these plants were west of the downtowns and Parliament Hill, so the prevailing winds often blew the smoke and sulphur fumes into the centre of Ottawa and Hull.

Reflections

The juxtapositions of the lumber town and national capital were evident throughout the area around Parliament Hill and appear in photographs and plans of the early years of the period (Figure 5-27). These images clearly illustrate the conflict between the commercial ambition of the 'Town' and the national objectives of the 'Crown'. Contemporary accounts describe Parliament Hill and the downtown main streets with a background of constant noise and acrid smoke from the nearby sawmills and pulp factories. The streets were mired in mud in spring, choked by dust in the summer, and shoulder-high snow banks in winter (Figure 5-28), but the adjacent shop windows were heaped with fine consumer goods.[442] These were perhaps common sights in many Canadian cities of the era, but the degree of contrast between raw public realm and refined private or government premises seemed unusually strong in Ottawa and Hull. The contrast

FIGURE 5-27: Parliament Hill as an idealized landscape for the Crown
(Source: *Picturesque Canada*, 1882, p. 163; Library and Archives Canada, C-011259)

FIGURE 5-28: The more prosaic reality of the Town: Snow on Sparks Street, 1885
(Source: Library and Archives Canada, C-002186; Samuel Jarvis photograph)

eventually inspired efforts to improve the function and appearance of the capital city.

The motives for the involvement of the imperial aristocrats in planning Canada's capital changed over time. Some governors general appeared to be influenced by a desire for simple comforts in a cold, muddy and somewhat backward lumber town. Suggestions of driveways from the vice-regal residence to Parliament Hill, and picturesque vistas and attractive grounds in Rockcliffe Park seem motivated by these rather selfish concerns.

A second motivation may have been representation of imperial power. Lord Dalhousie's purchase of the future Parliament Hill and Sir Edmund Head's promotion of the site for the Parliament Buildings seems to be based in that tradition. Later proposals by Lady Aberdeen seem rooted in a desire that Ottawa become a worthy capital of a dominion of the British Empire. When the British Empire was at its zenith, in the 1890s and early 1900s, it did not seem unusual for some aristocrats to simultaneously promote imperialism, local culture, town planning and social reform in Canada. Lady Aberdeen and the Marquess of Lorne appeared to operate in this tradition of *noblesse oblige*, which we shall see again with Earl Grey in the early 20th century.

The initiative in planning Canada's capital began to switch to its prime ministers at the turn of the century, beginning with Sir Wilfrid Laurier's Ottawa Improvement Commission. Laurier's main motivation was to create an attractive capital city to promote Canadian unity, an objective also pursued in the early 20th century by Prime Minister Sir Robert Borden. The evidence from their speeches and papers indicate that both these politicians combined a mild form of Canadian nationalism with respect for the British Empire. This combination, not unusual in the Edwardian era, allowed for co-operation with the vice-regal initiatives for planning the capital city.

At the local government level, the new City of Hull was almost completely focused on its industries and providing basic urban services for its citizens. Although the City of Ottawa had fought vigorously for the *benefits* of the seat of government designation in the 1850's, it was mainly concerned with the *costs* of the capital by the end of the 19th century. The city's tax revenue concerns, unwillingness to invest in embellishment and poor infrastructure became constant sources of friction in Town-Crown relations in the 20th century.

Clearly, the contrast between the imagined form of a national capital and the reality of Ottawa prompted much negative and disappointed commentary. Canada is dotted with raw towns that grew overnight, but few were faced with such tremendous expectations. Eventually, the contrast between the picturesque architecture on Parliament Hill (Figure 4-10) and the rough condition of the rest of the lumber towns became so great that the federal government began to invest its own cash in embellishing the public spaces of the capital city. The Ottawa Improvement Commission was the first step in the direction of the federal government taking the lead in the planning and development of the National Capital Region, a trend that would peak in the middle of the next century.

CHAPTER 6

Crown Plans: 'Parking' the Capital (1900-1912)

Ottawa is not a pretty place, save about the parliament buildings.
–William Lyon Mackenzie King, 1900

Town and Crown tensions were reduced a bit after the federal government began to invest its own funds in planning and improving Canada's capital city. The City of Ottawa's mayor was made a commissioner of the new OIC, which included 'Town' input into 'Crown' planning in a refreshing change from previous decades. And the federal agreement to expend its own cash on civic improvements soothed local concerns, so the Crown became the prime actor over the first two decades of the 20th century.

Starting in 1900, the OIC made the capital more beautiful by building new public spaces, guided by the ideals of the 'Parks Movement' described below. But the first year of the new century also saw the arrival of William Lyon Mackenzie King, who was destined to become Canada's longest-serving prime minister and the most important champion for improving the national capital.

Ottawa dismayed King when he arrived in May 1900 as a young civil servant in the Department of Labour.

> ... *the first glimpse of the city was from the lately fire swept district and it was gloomy enough. The business part of the town is small and like that of a provincial town, not interesting, but tiresome ... Ottawa is not a pretty place, save about the prlmt. bldgs. [Parliament Buildings] and has all the non-attractions of a small town.*[443]

Only weeks before, King had been enjoying the splendours of summer in Paris and Rome, so Canada's capital must have been a rude comparison (Figure 6-1).

But the future prime minister soon found solace in the beautiful landscapes of his new home – cycling in the Gatineau hills in the fall and skating on the Ottawa River during the long winters. King joined the Canadian civil service in 1900 and advanced to the rank of Deputy Minister at the astonishingly young age of 26. He hired his University of Toronto classmate Henry Harper as his secretary and they shared rooms near Parliament Hill (Figure 6-2).

During his first Thanksgiving in the capital, King and Harper cycled to Kingsmere Lake, set in a small bowl of low hills. He was enchanted by the wilderness setting so close to the city: "It is very lovely here and being again with the trees, the stars, the birds, the breezes and the skies makes one's heart rejoice"[444] (Figure 6-3).

King returned every year of his life. He built a simple cottage in 1903, and bought additional

FIGURE 6-1: Aftermath of the Hull-Ottawa fire, April 26, 1900
A startling scene welcomed the future Prime Minister William Lyon McKenzie King upon his arrival in Ottawa.
(Source: Booth Family Collection, Library and Archives Canada, PA-121793)

FIGURE 6-2: The Secret of Heroism: Henry Harper's Study
Henry Harper's study in the apartment he shared with W.L. Mackenzie King. Note the print of "Sir Galahad" by Sir George Frederick Watts on the wall above his desk, which inspired his memorial (Figure 6-4).
(Source: Library and Archives Canada, PA-126945)

land over the next half century to ensure that its privacy would be preserved. Landscaping his Kingsmere estate became the future prime minister's favourite hobby. He spent weeks every year directing the layout of the gardens and other landscape projects. Mackenzie King also took a keen interest in improving the landscape of Canada's capital city throughout his career (see Cast of Characters).

King also developed a strong interest in the statues and monuments in the capital, starting with a tragedy that affected him deeply. During a 1903 skating party, Bert Harper died in a valiant, but futile attempt to save Bessie Blair, a young woman who had fallen through weak ice into the Ottawa River. Despite warnings from bystanders, he jumped into the swiftly-flowing water and was swept under the ice with Bessie. His last words were, "What else can I do?"

King was devastated by his personal loss, inspired by his friend's heroic death, and determined to ensure his sacrifice would not be forgotten. Accordingly, he led the campaign for a monument to Harper's heroic death. The statue, "Sir Galahad," was erected just outside the gates to Parliament Hill.[445] King wrote a small book, *The Secret of Heroism*, to celebrate Harper's romantic chivalry.[446] These actions provide us with insights into King's intellectual and emotional make-up, and also provided him with experience in establishing memorials. The book and statue were to resonate throughout his interventions in planning a capital worthy of Canada and national war memorials worthy of her military heroes of the two World Wars.

FIGURE 6-3: William Lyon Mackenzie King (right) with family and friend Henry Harper at Kingsmere, 1901
(Source: Library and Archives Canada, PA-124433)

FIGURE 6-4: Unveiling of the Sir Galahad Monument in 1908
King is second from the left. Most visitors to Canada's capital walk briskly by the small statue of Sir Galahad on the Wellington Street sidewalk, just outside the central gates to Parliament Hill. Few are aware of its connection to William Lyon Mackenzie King, Canada's longest serving prime minister (Figure 6-2).
(Source: Library and Archives Canada, C-003184)

The Parks Movement

Mackenzie King's embrace of landscapes and outdoor recreation was not unusual in the late Victorian age. These values were core elements of an early planning tradition, the Parks Movement.

Most Canadian parks were not part of the initial planning of their communities. The first plans for towns in eastern Canada provided for market squares, church yards, and military parade squares, but not public recreation areas. Plans for communities in Western Canada usually provided for neither squares nor parks. In many North American cities, some of the earliest landscaped open spaces emerged from rural cemetery precedents built outside cities such as Boston (Mt. Auburn, 1831), Montréal (Mount Royal, 1852), Ottawa (Beechwood, 1873) and Toronto (Mt. Pleasant, 1876). The grounds of the cemeteries were beautifully landscaped, according to plans designed by gardeners or civil engineers – because the landscape architecture profession had not yet emerged. Regular visits to the graves of family became a social activity rather like a picnic. The next step was to provide a public park for similar recreation, without the trip to the rural cemetery.

Indeed, the idea of space being set aside for public recreation only began to take hold in Britain in the 1840s and during the 1860s in the United States. Canada's first public parks to be supported by municipal funding were established less than a decade after those in Britain and around the same time as those in US cities. A major stimulus was the transfer of military reserves held by the British colonial government to the local government. Toronto's Exhibition Park started this way in 1848, as did Kingston's City Park (1852), Hamilton's Gore Park (1852), Halifax's Point Pleasant Park (1866) and Ottawa's Major's Hill Park (1873). Other Crown transfers created the Toronto Islands (1867), London's Victoria Park (1869), Montréal's Isle Ste. Hélène (the site of Expo 67) in 1874, and Vancouver's Stanley Park (1886). All of these park areas were on the periphery of their respective communities at the time.

As Toronto's parks chairman said in 1859, public parks offered "breathing spaces where citizens might stroll, drive, or sit to enjoy the open air."[447] The outlook reflected a desire to create a natural setting, often along with an appreciation of horticulture. The Public Garden in Halifax is an example of the latter; Mount Royal Park in Montréal an example of the former (Figure 6-5).

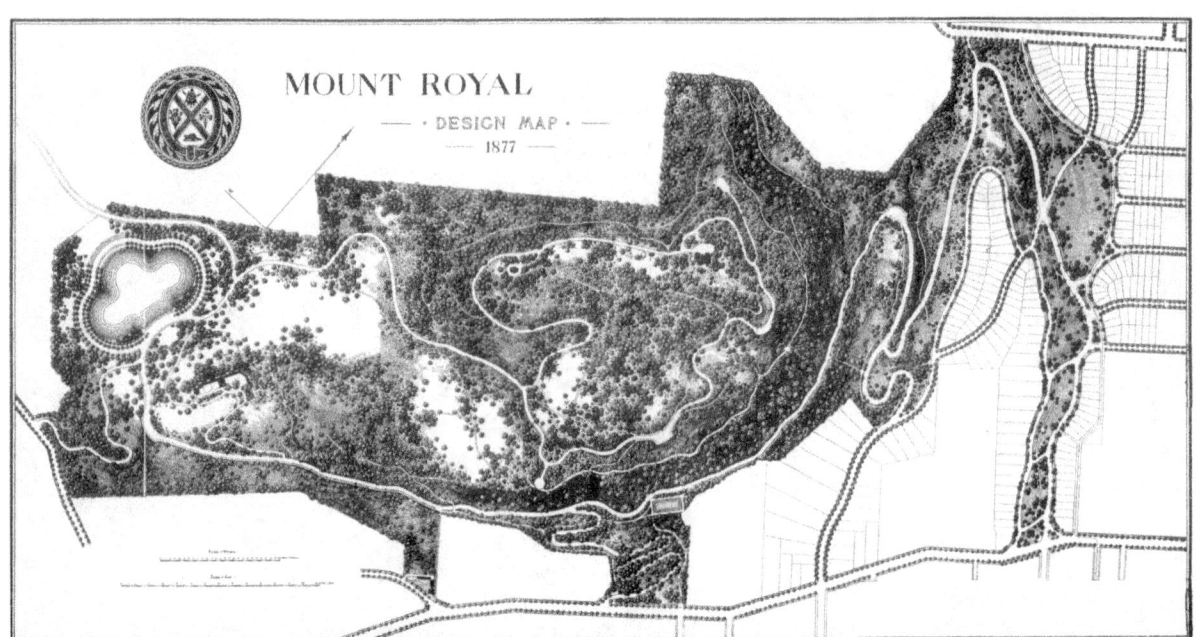

FIGURE 6-5: **Mount Royal Park, Montréal 1877 design by Frederick Law Olmsted**
Mount Royal Park, purchased by the city in 1872, is significant among Canadian urban parks because its original design was by Frederick Law Olmsted, who had designed Manhattan's Central Park. He urged Montréal to "bring out the latent loveliness of [the] mountain beauty and retain the wilderness and sense of seclusion."[448] Olmsted's firm went on to prepare plans for parks at Niagara Falls, for Stanley Park in Vancouver, and for Rockwood Park in Saint John.[449]
(Source: Frederick Law Olmsted, *Mount Royal,* Montréal, 1881)

The Ottawa Improvement Commission

The new Ottawa Improvement Commission (OIC) was strongly influenced by Parks Movement ideals and creating new open spaces in the capital was their main area of activity in their first years.

At first, there was general acclaim for the OIC's work. The commission cleared away the underused industrial buildings on the west bank of the Rideau Canal, and built a parkway that was not only popular but also improved the view from the train when entering the capital (Figure 6-6). The OIC undertook these improvements without professional design assistance, relying on its superintendent, former Ottawa City Engineer Robert Surtees, and construction foreman Alex Stuart.

The OIC's ambitions exceeded its $60,000 annual budget.[450] In early 1903, the commission had committed an additional $15,000 to projects under construction, and had short-term plans to invest $271,500 more. The commissioners decided to prepare a general plan and detailed cost estimate for all the improvements it intended to undertake. Most importantly, they decided that the OIC would seek permission to borrow money to carry out this extensive plan.[451] Chairman Bate and Senator Frost approached the Minister of Finance with the proposal. By June 1903, they could report success – the Minister was supportive. The OIC requested permission to issue bonds to the extent of $250,000 and to secure the services "of a first

FIGURE 6-6: Rideau Canal driveway, west of Bank Street, ca. 1912
New parks along the Rideau Canal by the Ottawa Improvement Commission.
(Source: Library and Archives Canada, detail from image PA-010848)

class landscape architect." Within two weeks, the commission's superintendent approached Montréal consultant Frederick Todd (Figure 6-7) for assistance.[452]

FIGURE 6-7: Frederick Todd
Fredrick Todd apprenticed in the famous landscape architecture firm founded by Frederick Law Olmsted, and opened his own office in Montréal in 1900. He designed many of the best Canadian parks in the early 20th century (see Cast of Characters). We can only wonder how much better the OIC's parks system might have been had Todd been their consulting landscape architect and planner from 1903 until its successor, the Federal District Commission, hired its first designer in the mid-1930s.[453]
(Source: McCord Museum, Wm. Notman & Son photo II-175018)

Todd's 1903 Preliminary Report

In retaining Todd, the OIC procured the services of a sole practitioner with excellent training but little experience in the turbulent politics of capital city planning. Todd's report was a preliminary plan for a regional parks system encompassing a 300 sq. km. area on both sides of the Ottawa River.[454] His introduction contains some of the most compelling justifications for planning written in the era:

You may ask, is it reasonable to look so far ahead as one hundred years or more, and to make plans for generations in the distant future? We have only to study the history of older cities, and note at what enormous cost they have overcome the lack of provision for their growth, to realize that the future prosperity and beauty of the city depends in a great measure upon the ability to look ahead, and the power to grasp the needs and requirements of the great population it is destined to have.[455]

Todd's report was based upon two principles that ran against the OIC's self-perceived agenda: one, the plan was not just restricted to Ottawa, and second, the Canadian capital should **not** emulate Washington. His vision was grander, not limited "… to the purely arbitrary boundaries of City, Town or Province, but have been guided alone by what would seem to be a wise provision for future parks and boulevards, commensurate with the importance of the Capital City of the Dominion."[456]

His regional view incorporated not only both sides of the Ottawa River, but included lands that were outside the boundaries of the City of Ottawa and the province of Ontario.

Secondly, Todd debunked the notion that the planning of Ottawa should make it the "Washington of the North." His reasoning explains the considerable differences in the sites of the two cities, but also reflects his naturalistic design style:

Many of the beauties of Washington are certainly well worthy of imitation, but it would be a mistake to copy too closely, even if it were possible, the plans which have proved so successful there, for the location of the two cities is so absolutely different, that what has made the beauty of one, might mar the beauty of the other. Washington stretches over a gently undulating country, Ottawa is broken by steep terraces and picturesque cliffs. The Potomac winds its way quietly through the city of Washington, while the Ottawa and Rideau Rivers rush through Ottawa by leaps and bounds. The Government buildings of Washington are of the Colonial type of architecture, as best suited to long stretches of comparatively level ground. Your Government buildings are pure Gothic, the style which is perhaps better suited than any other to a picturesque site. Thus it is absolutely impossible to treat these two cities in the same manner.[457]

Todd writes approvingly of L'Enfant's 1791 plan and the recommendations of the 1902 McMillan Commission plan, released only a few months before Todd received his commission.[458] It is not surprising that Todd was familiar with the McMillan Commission plan, considering it was widely publicized and his colleague F.L. Olmsted Jr. (1870-1957) was the principal consultant for its open space system (Figure 6-8).

The remainder of Todd's introduction contains much unsupported optimism regarding Ottawa's future growth and prospects, a characteristic typical of City Beautiful planning and in tune with his clients' interests.[459] He correctly noted that creating a plan for Ottawa as the capital would differ from planning a purely commercial city. On one major assumption however, Todd would be proven wrong –Ottawa was not destined to become a great manufacturing city as a result of its "immense water power." It may not have been apparent that the lumber industry was already in decline in 1903.

The remainder of Todd's *Preliminary Report* presents a general scheme for a regional parks system, containing elements ranging from large-scale to small-scale improvements (Figure 6-9):
- large natural parks or reserves,
- suburban parks,
- boulevards and parkways,
- waterway parks-bathing, and
- city parks and squares and playgrounds.[460]

The OIC was probably not expecting a recommendation that they should acquire thousands of acres of woods, but Todd incorporated original forests to "provide a place where nature may still be enjoyed, unmarred by contact with humanity." He recommended acquiring lands with "picturesque and diversified scenery," including 2,000 acres in the Gatineau Valley and the lands surrounding Meech Lake (Figure 6-10).[461]

Perhaps sensing that the OIC would be hostile to the wilderness parks proposal, Todd stressed the low maintenance required for such reserves. Citing London's Epping Forest to prove his point, he exhorted the Commission to provide the large future population of Ottawa with:

… large areas of untamed forest which can be set aside forever for the enjoyment of people who wish to get away for a day from the crowded city, who wish to wander in the woods where the wildest birds are at home, and where nature's mossy carpet is still luxuriant and unworn? Would these future generations, could they be consulted, object to bearing, if need be, the whole expense of making such reserves?[462]

Todd cited the "mental, physical and moral" benefits of access to these reserves as a change from the "exacting cares of business and the impure air of crowded streets" using the rationale frequently employed by proponents of the Parks Movement, with its roots in Olmstedian planning.[463]

Todd supported the OIC's proposal to extend Rockcliffe Park as its first suburban park project. He recommended that the commission purchase adjacent land and undertake minimal improvements to its natural condition, illustrating his suggestions

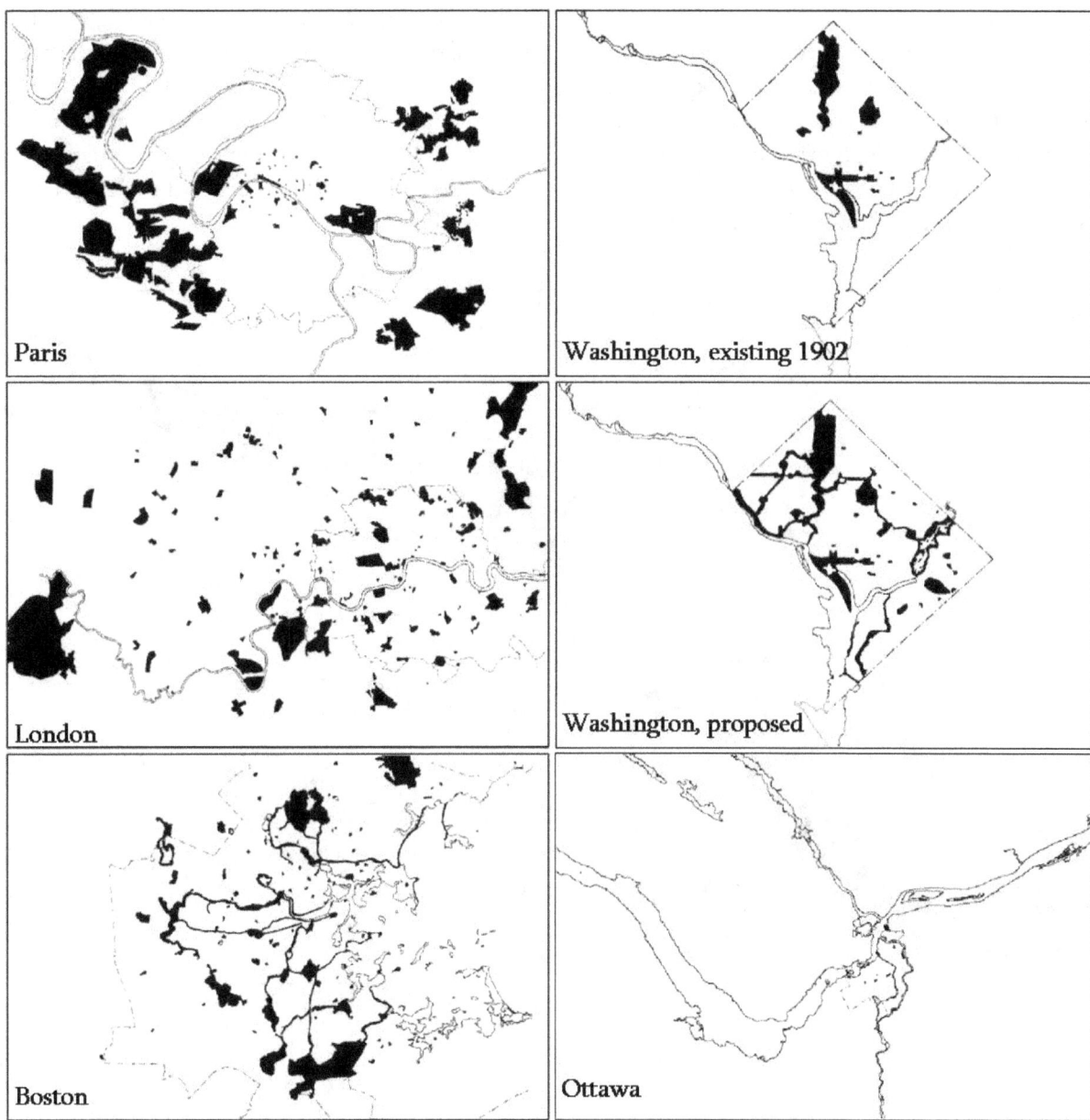

FIGURE 6-8: Parks System Comparisons by Frederick Law Olmsted Jr. and Frederick Todd, 1902-1903
Note the tiny amount of park space in Canada's capital in comparison to the other cities, despite its location next to much undeveloped land. The drawings show the parks systems of major cities at the same scale. The Paris, London, Boston and Washington drawings were prepared by Frederick Law Olmsted Jr. as part of the 1902 McMillan Commission plan. The Ottawa plan was reconstructed to recreate Todd's 1903 drawing at the same scale.
(Source: McMillan Commission report, 1902; image rendered by Jeffery O'Neill)

with several photographs (Figure 6-11). He also recommended that a second suburban park, approximately 100-200 acres in size, be established west of the built-up area of Ottawa, and the Experimental Farm south of the city be maintained as public open space. The southern area would also be complemented by 40-70 acres of woods on either side of the Rideau River. In keeping with the regional scope of his report, Todd also recommended a park adjacent to neighbouring Hull, outside the jurisdiction of the OIC. Establishing these parks would create a balanced ring of intermediate-sized suburban parks on all four edges of the 1903 built-up area (Figure 6-9).

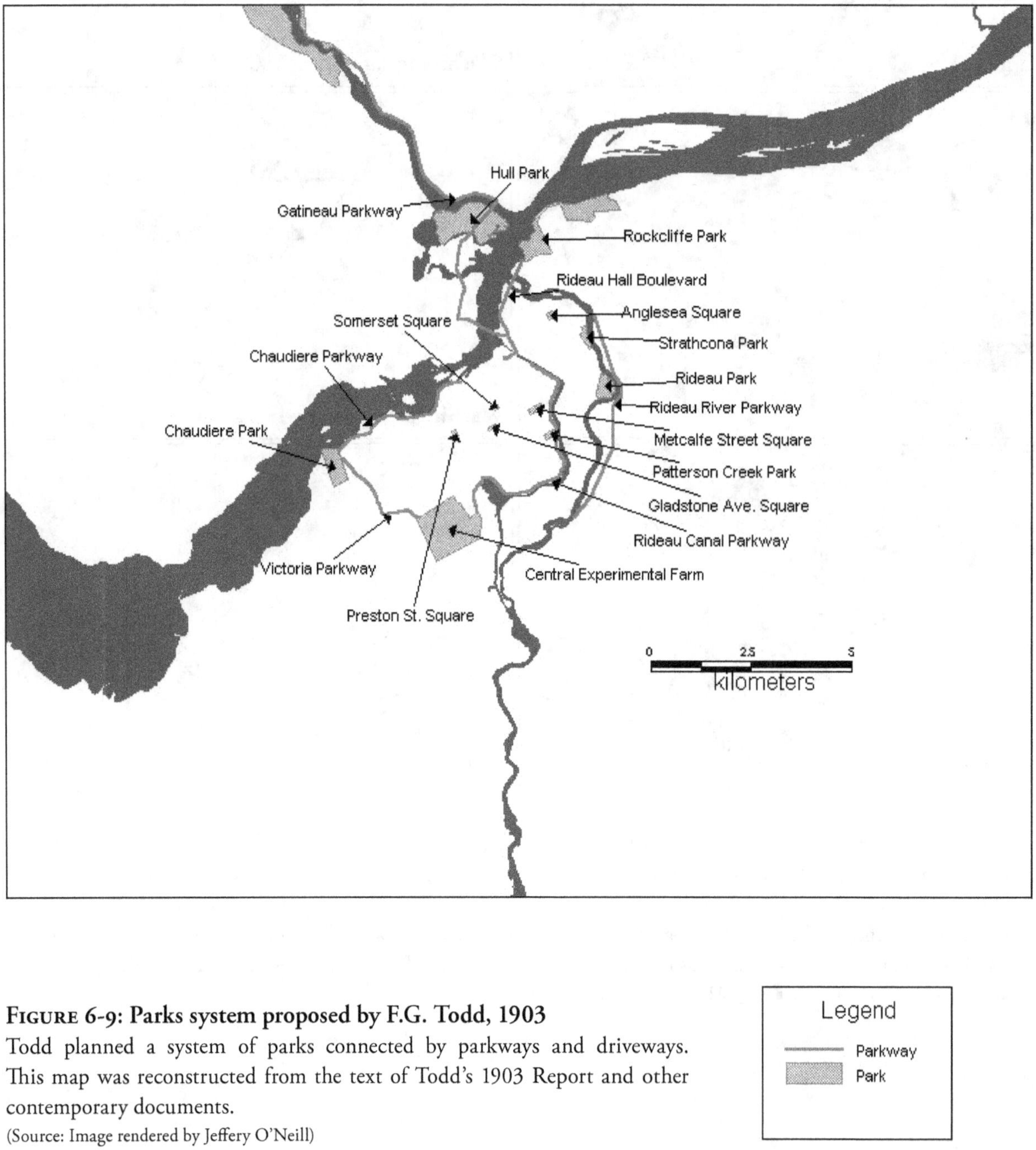

FIGURE 6-9: Parks system proposed by F.G. Todd, 1903
Todd planned a system of parks connected by parkways and driveways. This map was reconstructed from the text of Todd's 1903 Report and other contemporary documents.
(Source: Image rendered by Jeffery O'Neill)

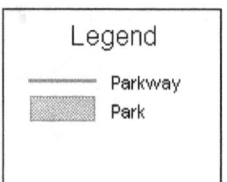

FIGURE 6-10: Woods in proposed Hull Park
Frederick Todd's original photograph of the woods in proposed Hull Park; located at the junction of the Ottawa and Gatineau rivers. The image gives important clues about Todd's design intentions for the park system to be a place of natural beauty, rest and recreation for residents in the best tradition of the Olmsted firm. Other cities would spend decades and enormous funds to create landscapes like this – all that Canada's capital had to do was stop cutting them down for firewood.
(Source: F.G. Todd, 1903 collection of the NCC)

FIGURE 6-11: Three 1903 Todd photos of Rockcliffe Park
Left: Rockcliffe Park, path through the woods
Top right: Rockcliffe Park driveway circle
Bottom right: View of the Ottawa River from Rockcliffe Park Drive
(Source: F.G. Todd, 1903, p. 27-30)

Todd recommended inter-connecting these parks and forest reserves with a system of parkways and boulevards. The OIC had already begun street improvements along the west bank of the Rideau Canal, and had built King Edward Avenue to connect Parliament to the Governor General's residence in Rideau Hall, adjacent to Rockcliffe Park. Although this new boulevard provided the safe passage to Parliament desired by the governors general, it ignored the scenic possibilities of a route along the cliffs on the edge of the Ottawa River. Todd provided a preliminary description and photographs for the river route. He also recommended parkways along the Ottawa and Rideau rivers to connect other elements of the preferred parks system (Figure 6-12).

Within the city, Todd called for landscaping a number of small parks and squares, intending these for rest and relaxation. He warned against attempts to display the gardener's "ability to design curious and fantastically shaped flower beds, which unfortunately, cannot always be classed as artistic."[464] Instead, he recommended small playgrounds and the natural treatment of open spaces. While the city already owned several un-landscaped parcels for these purposes, Todd recommended immediate purchase of the Patterson's Creek lands adjacent to the Rideau Canal (Figure 6-13). He concluded with general advice and suggestions that addressed the future design for parks, boulevards and driveways, praising the beautiful natural shores and fine woods adjacent to the centre of the city.

Todd was gently critical of the OIC's initial work to date, stating that:

Real landscape art is nothing if it is not conservative of natural beauty, and does not consist alone in building rustic bridges, or in arranging plants or trees, but is rather the fitting of landscape for human use and enjoyment in such a manner as will be most appropriate and beautiful.[465]

To guide the development of parkways, Todd suggested that: "if the road seems to wiggle on ahead without apparent reason, like a gigantic serpent, the curves will appear unnatural, meaningless and annoying."[466] He concluded with a plea for such park improvements to be carried out on a systematic basis "in strict accordance to a pre-arranged plan."[467]

Unfortunately, the OIC was simply not prepared to pay for landscape architectural services when some design and construction supervision was available within its own staff. Planning and aesthetic arguments in favour of professional design assistance only appeared to hold sway with the commissioners when they needed financial or political approvals.[468]

FIGURE 6-12: Photo taken by Todd for a proposal to construct a system of parks and pathways along the Rideau River
In one of the great lost opportunities of the national capital, the OIC could not obtain the small capital grant needed to acquire these lands at the same time they bought the Ottawa River frontage.
(Source: F.G. Todd, 1903, *Report to the Ottawa Improvement Commission*, p. 22)

FIGURE 6-13: Patterson's Creek before and after
Left: Frederick Todd's photo of Patterson's Creek in 1903, used as a storage basin for lumber flowing down the Rideau system
Right: Patterson's Creek a decade later, following landscaping by the Ottawa Improvement Commission
(Source: Left: F.G. Todd, 1903. Right: *Special Report of the Ottawa Improvement Commission*, 1913, p. 18)

In practice, the OIC did its own design work, extending the Rideau Canal Driveway, completing Strathcona Park along the Rideau River (Figure 6-14) and Somerset Square downtown. It carried out over $1.2 million in capital improvements between 1900 and 1912, with the projects designed and supervised by engineer Surtees or construction superintendent Stuart.[469]

Although Todd was not involved in any of these initiatives, the new greenery sprouting throughout the city delighted its citizens and the Laurier government. The OIC also improved a downtown avenue and built two bridges across the Rideau River to provide a circuitous route connecting the Governor General's residence to Parliament Hill.[470] The commission's budget was increased to $100,000 per year in 1910, and the prime minister continued to aid it by personally lobbying the Canadian Pacific Railway to donate land for a park.[471] Although Laurier was satisfied with the work of the OIC, criticism of Ottawa planning gradually grew in the first decade of the century. Surprisingly, much of this criticism was sponsored by a new Governor General, Earl Grey, and by a Laurier appointee to the OIC, C.P. Meredith.

Earl Grey (Figure 6-15) was dismayed by the absence of a comprehensive plan for the improvements to the national capital. He built support for better planning by inviting British town planning advocates such as Raymond Unwin to speak in Ottawa. The Governor General personally sponsored a cross-country speaking tour by landscape architect Thomas Mawson, and Henry Vivian, MP, an advocate of social reform and garden cities.

Raymond Unwin, co-designer of the Letchworth and Hampstead Garden Suburb, visited Ottawa in 1910. In his public address, he made several tactful suggestions as to how the national capital might be improved by better planning and design.[474] English landscape architect Thomas Mawson was less discreet during his visits. He was complimentary about Ottawa's splendid natural setting, but publicly criticized the OIC's work as:

> ... rustic work, ... curly walks, sprawling patterns or specimen trees and shrubs. Now, really, why do you do this sort of thing? How can you admire it?[475]

Mawson vigorously pursued a commission to plan Canada's capital, returning to the city on several occasions to give public lectures.[476]

Figure 6-14: Strathcona Park, 1912
The wiggly walkways in the OIC's Strathcona Park along the Rideau River were much criticized by visiting designers.
(Source: Library and Archives Canada, PA-009927; W.J. Topley photograph)

Figure 6-15: Earl and Lady Grey
Both Governor General and Lady Grey closely followed Ottawa planning issues and personally designed some of the vistas in Rockcliffe Park.[472] The Greys succeeded in pushing the OIC to build an improved parkway connecting to the vice regal residence along the crest of the embankment on the Ottawa River. The new road was named Lady Grey Drive when it opened in 1914.[473]
(Source: Library and Archives Canada, C-030723; Galbraith Photo Co.)

Colborne Meredith (Figure 6-16) coached Mawson's criticism of the OIC's work.⁴⁷⁷ By 1910, the Commission had become a bit stodgy, and there was a whiff of scandal concerning their operations.⁴⁷⁸ If Prime Minister Laurier wanted the young Meredith to stir things up, he got more than he bargained for. After the Ottawa Improvement Commissioners ignored his suggestions that they hire design consultants,⁴⁷⁹ Meredith started a well-coordinated lobby to destroy their reputations and take control of a new plan for the nation's capital.⁴⁸⁰ Following the 1911 victory of Robert Borden's Conservative Party in the federal elections, he formed a loose affiliation with Mawson and Ottawa engineer Noulan Cauchon to pursue the consulting contract for the new plan.

Meredith's objective was to establish an elite commission of technical experts to supervise the preparation of a comprehensive plan. His model was based upon Washington's successful experience with the 1902 Senate Parks Commission (McMillan Commission).⁴⁸¹ Newly elected Prime Minister Borden turned Meredith's lobbying to his political advantage. After Mawson's criticism, Sir Wilfrid Laurier defended the OIC from the opposition benches in Parliament, claiming that Todd's long-forgotten 1903 *Preliminary Report* had guided the Commission.⁴⁸² Meredith responded by sending Borden a detailed and confidential memo that not only critiqued the Todd report section by section, but also attacked the OIC in the severest terms:

> ... the Commission has, from the first, carried on its work in a most un-businesslike way, and persists to continue doing so notwithstanding all the criticisms that have been made, and are content to have the general park scheme, the engineering work and the designing of structures requiring artistic training done by a so-called superintendent, who is nothing more than a bricklayer.⁴⁸³

Borden asked for permission to include Meredith's analysis of the 1903 *Report* in a government policy paper on Ottawa planning. Meredith agreed, either not understanding the furor his remarks would cause, or perhaps relishing it. The policy paper included a Royal Architectural Institute of Canada memoranda, the criticism of Unwin and Mawson, the entire text of the Todd report, and Meredith's critique.⁴⁸⁴ With headlines proclaiming *"Merciless Analysis of Commission's Work,"*⁴⁸⁵ it was front-page news in the Ottawa newspapers.

FIGURE 6-16: C.P. Meredith
Colborne Powell Meredith (see Cast of Characters) was an Ottawa architect appointed by Sir Wilfrid Laurier to the OIC in 1910. He quickly became a prominent critic of the OIC.
(Source: *Who's Who and Why*, 1914)

The OIC responded by mounting a public relations campaign and co-opting Frederick Todd. The Commission issued a beautifully printed report, lavishly illustrated with pictures of its new parks and driveways.[486] Todd was offered the design and supervision of park improvements for a seven-acre site on abandoned cemeteries in downtown Ottawa. Not coincidentally, the lands lay directly across the street from Prime Minister Borden's new house. Todd designed a charming urban park, with a shelter on the highest point and a view to Parliament Hill (Figure 6-17). Without blushing, Laurier's Liberal OIC appointees named it Macdonald Gardens, after the famous leader of the Conservative party and Canada's first prime minister. The Commission also sent its workmen to improve the grounds of Borden's home. The political gestures and low-level bribery did not work. The new prime minister may have been flattered, but he continued to cut the OIC out of future planning initiatives.[487]

Reflections

It is tempting to over-estimate the importance of Todd's 1903 *Preliminary Report*, given its stirring prose. And the OIC's refusal to implement it, which was so thoroughly documented by Meredith, gives it somewhat tragic status. Later observers treat Todd's role in the planning of the capital quite sympathetically, although they perhaps exaggerate his contribution somewhat.[488] Meredith was right: Todd's 1903 report was not a comprehensive plan. It was a preliminary study, based upon several weeks of fieldwork.

Yet the $489 the OIC spent on Todd's advice certainly gave both 'Crown' and 'Town' value for their money. An impartial overview from a skilled designer can sometimes help local residents see their home more clearly or a national government to see their place in the world. Todd's 1903 *Preliminary Report* was influential because he captured the *genius loci* of Ottawa. His suggestions to respect the

FIGURE 6-17: Macdonald Gardens, 1999
Todd's only built legacy in Ottawa, Macdonald Gardens, is neglected and almost unknown today. Fortunately, Todd's landscape and belvedere have survived and the hospital buildings that bordered the park have been renovated into apartments and townhouses.
(Source: David Gordon, 1999)

unique natural setting of the city and its Gothic-revival Parliament Buildings, and his advice to avoid any literal planning of a "Washington of the North," still resonate today. Todd's regional approach and admiration for natural systems reflect modern ecological planning principles. His plan for an inter-connected parks system reflects the best of the Olmsted tradition and was adopted in every subsequent plan. Following the 1903 report, this parks system was thoroughly implemented over a seven-decade period (Figure 6-18). Finally, Todd's advocacy of long-term planning for the welfare of future generations inspired future generations of Ottawa planners.

A final evaluation of Todd's participation in the planning of Canada's capital must be tinged with regret over a lost opportunity. The naïve young consultant evolved into a prominent landscape architect and town planner. One can only wonder how much better the parks system in Canada's capital might have been, had Todd been the OIC's consulting landscape architect and planner from 1903 until its successor agency hired its first professional designer in the mid 1930s.[489]

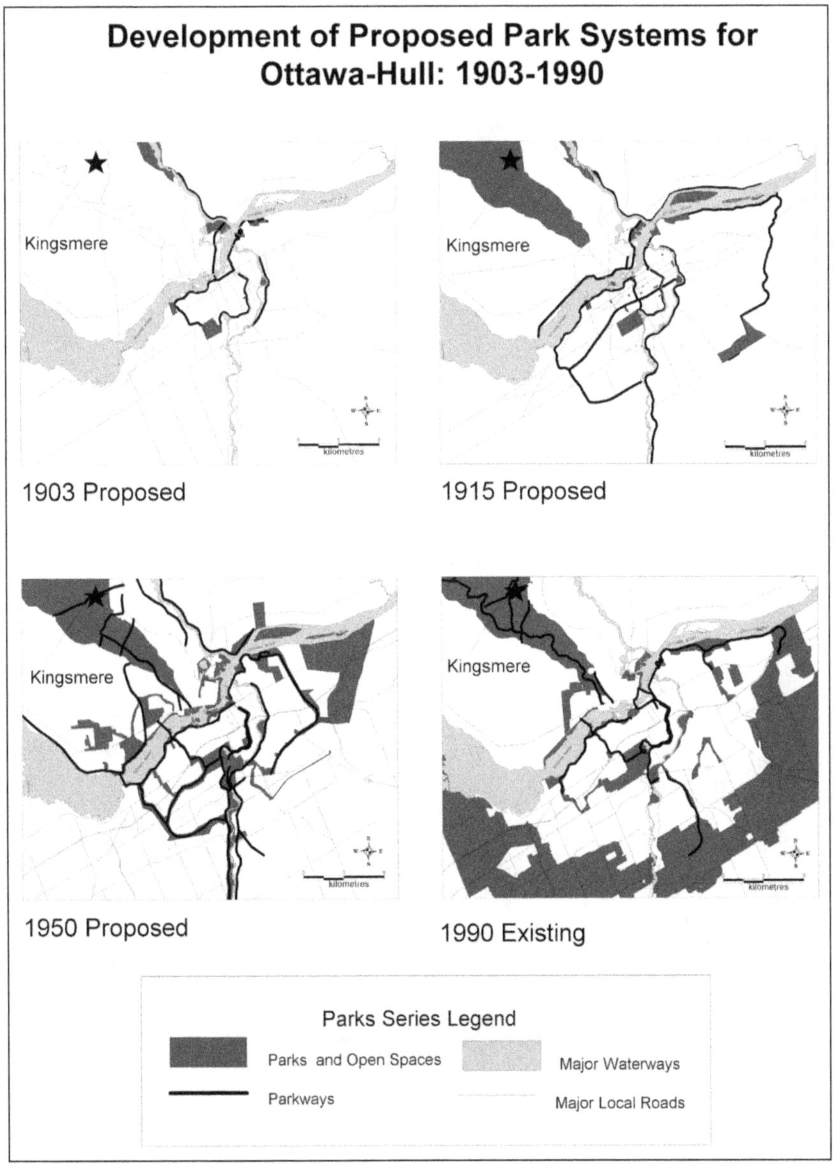
Development of Proposed Park Systems for Ottawa-Hull: 1903-1990
Kingsmere
1903 Proposed
Kingsmere
1915 Proposed
Kingsmere
1950 Proposed
Kingsmere
1990 Existing
Parks Series Legend
Parks and Open Spaces
Major Waterways
Parkways
Major Local Roads

FIGURE 6-18: Evolution of the Ottawa-Hull parks system from 1950-1990

(Source: Gréber 1950, NCC 1992 base map; drawn by J. O'Neill)

CHAPTER 7

Crown Plans: City Beautiful? (1913-1920)

But what Ottawa leaves in the mind is a certain graciousness – dim, for it expresses a barely materialised national spirit – and the sight of kindly English-looking faces, and the rather lovely sounds of the soft Canadian accent, in the street.
– Rupert Brooke, 1913[490]

The Crown's first efforts at improving the capital resulted in many new public parks and Todd's innovative plan that extended planning across the Ottawa River into Hull. The second decade of Crown planning continued this inclusionary trend, with the mayor of the City of Hull joining the Ottawa mayor as 'Town' representatives in federal planning for the national capital. However, the federal government remained the major proponent of planning for the region, and its proposals for a federal district eventually met implacable opposition from local and provincial interests in Hull and the Outaouais region.

Hull and Ottawa both grew rapidly after the 1900 fire, but the two cities followed different paths, with Hull becoming more specialized as a working-class industrial town, and the increasing importance of the federal government in Ottawa. Hull almost doubled in population, from 14,000 in 1901 to 24,000 in 1921,[491] and fewer people worked in the sawmills. The J.R. Booth and E.B. Eddy pulp and paper plants were joined by the Woods textiles factory, a cement plant, a small iron and steel foundry and a meat packing plant. The new industries helped diversify the Outaouais economy, and Hull became the fourth largest city in Québec.[492] Hull remained a city of small, wooden houses on narrow lots in working-class neighbourhoods. Its local government was dominated by the tasks of massive reconstruction after the great fire and accommodating rapid growth, but the city was still small enough that its lack of infrastructure did not present insuperable problems.[493]

Rapid growth and poor infrastructure led to a public health disaster on the Ontario side of the river. The urban population in Ottawa and its adjacent townships more than doubled from 1901 to 1910, passing 100,000 people. The new electric streetcars intensified commercial development along Sparks, Rideau and Bank streets. However, the streetcar's greatest impact was to encourage extensive suburban development outside the built-up area. Rockcliffe Park and Eastview (now Vanier) emerged at the ends of two lines into Gloucester Township, but the 1900 Britannia streetcar into Nepean Township had the greatest effect. The Ottawa Electric Railway established a popular amusement park on Britannia Bay, some 11 km. from downtown.[494] Farm lots were divided up into subdivisions all along this route, with many 25 x 100 foot cottage lots on dirt roads.

Much of the best farm land in Nepean was lost to these speculative ventures, scattering subdivisions across the northern half of the township[495] (Figure 7-1). Anybody could subdivide their land and sell lots, with no government approval needed. The speculative frenzy peaked in the years prior to World War I, with enough land subdivided in the Ottawa area to serve a population of 1,600,000 at the densities of the existing built-up area. Most subdivisions had only a light sprinkling of houses for years.[496]

Subdivision mania also struck Western Canadian cities, and Vancouver and Calgary almost went bankrupt by servicing tens of thousands of vacant lots.[497] Nepean had a cheaper solution to the problem – it simply would not build piped water and sewer services, leaving the residents to cope with wells and privies. The rural township councils were happy that the farmers were able to sell their land at a profit and placed few obstacles in the way of subdividers. But they were also unwilling to incur debt or raise taxes to service land. If the subdivisions got too crowded and their wells were polluted, then they had to be annexed by the adjacent city.

Ottawa annexed three Nepean subdivisions (Bayswater, Hintonburg and Mechanicsville) from 1907-1911, even though the city was stretching its finances to service the remaining vacant lands within its boundaries.[498] The city pumped its water, untreated, from the centre of the Ottawa River, opposite Hintonburg. In 1910, New York civil engineer Allan Hazen recommended that the city chlorinate the water immediately to protect public health, and then either develop an alternate supply from the Gatineau lakes or filter the river water. Unfortunately, the city council was more concerned about costs and the effects of chlorination upon the taste of the water, and declined to act.[499]

The first typhoid epidemic struck in January 1911, with 983 cases reported and 83 deaths. Provincial and federal investigators both laid the blame upon the city's waterworks. Raw sewage from privies in Hintonburg ran down a small creek into Nepean Bay (Figure 7-2). Contaminated water was distributed through the city's water system because an emergency valve was left open in the main intake in Nepean Bay to maintain fire pressure.[500] The city engineer insisted that a new intake pipe would solve the problem, and the local medical health officer blamed the victims, noting that most of the deaths occurred in the poorest districts, "which were the most unsanitary localities."[501]

City council still refused to chlorinate the water, but it did order regular tests of the water supply. Unfortunately, civic officials ignored the repeated reports that the water was contaminated in the summer of 1912, replacing the technician responsible for the testing. The second outbreak struck at the peak of the tourist season, with complaints from local businessmen about the effects of the bad news on visits to Ottawa. Astonishingly, the city's medical officer of health issued a bulletin declaring the epidemic to be over, when the tests showed the opposite. New deaths continued into the fall, because both the old and new intake pipes leaked, allowing more raw sewage from Nepean Bay into the water system. Another 1,378 people contracted typhoid and 91 more people died.[502]

Blaming the victims wouldn't work this second time around. The medical officer of health and the city engineer were fired, and from the evidence in the judicial enquiry, they were lucky not to face criminal charges.[503] Mayor Hopewell also fired City Solicitor Taylor McVeity when he started asking too many questions about the city engineer's cash contributions to the mayor's election campaign. Hopewell eventually resigned and McVeity was elected mayor in 1914.[504]

Public confidence in the capacity of the municipal government reached a new low after the typhoid epidemics. Ottawa electors voted 7,335 to 2,942 in favour of the city becoming a federal

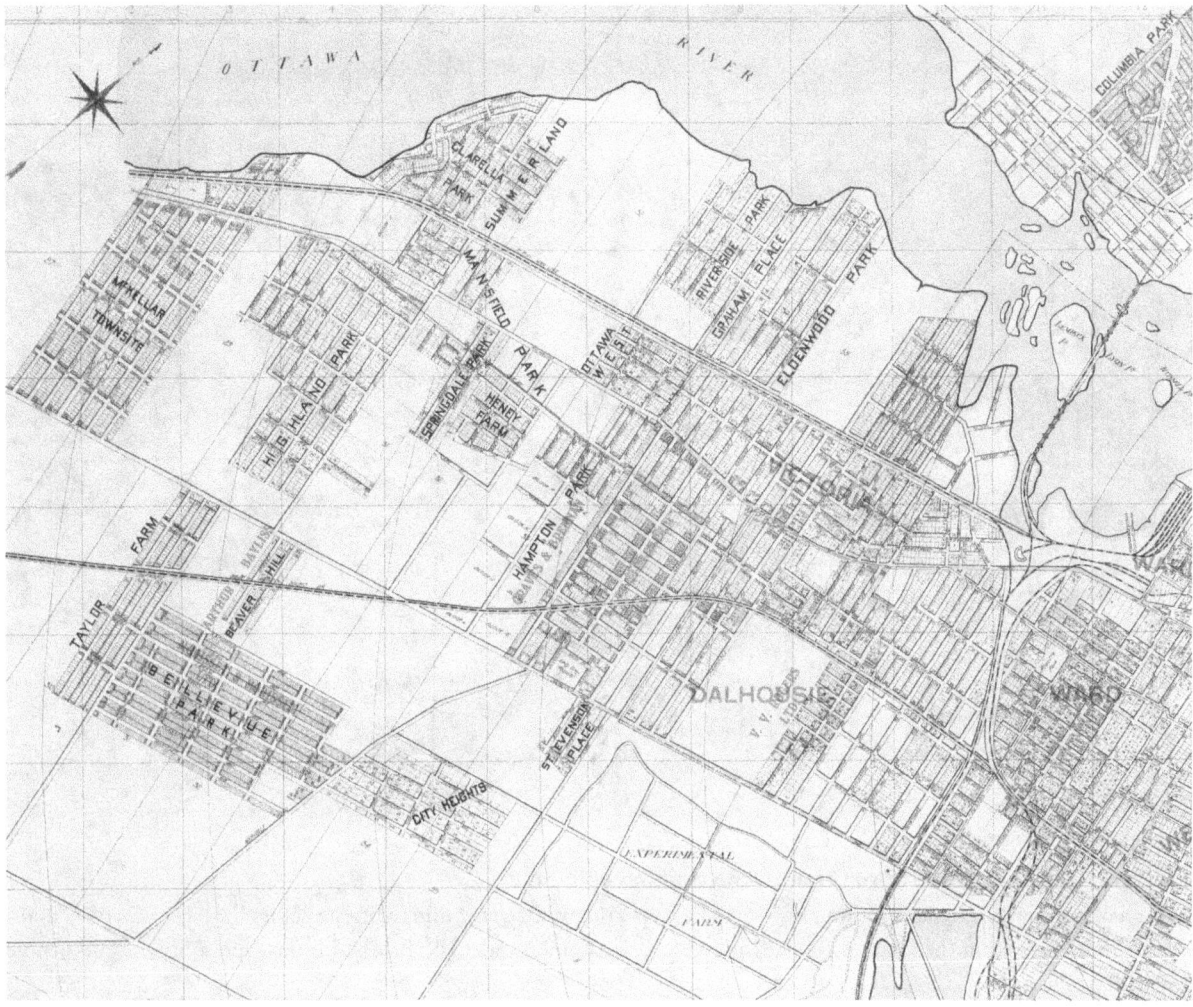

FIGURE 7-1: **Subdivision sprawl in Nepean, 1915**
Un-serviced, uncoordinated subdivisions leap-frogging across the landscape. The Britannia streetcar line runs along Richmond Road, about one-third from the top of the map. Hintonburg and Nepean Bay are in the top right corner, along with Lemieux Island, site of the city's ill-fated water supply.
(Source: LAC NMC 16998)

district in a non-binding 1912 referendum.[505] A true federal district was unlikely at that time since the francophone Outaouais was enraged by Ontario's attack on French language schools, so Hull would not consider abandoning Québec's protection of its culture.[506] However, the epidemics sparked a renewed interest in municipal reform, where technical commissions and boards of control would check the power of city council. None of this speeded up Ottawa's procurement of a pure water supply. Arguments at city council between proponents of filtering the river water versus an aqueduct from the Gatineau lakes swirled for a decade. The cheaper river filtration option eventually won, and the City of Ottawa opened the Lemieux Island filtration plan in 1932.[507]

FIGURE 7-2: The short term solution to the typhoid epidemic
Instead of preventing raw sewage from flowing into Nepean Bay, Ottawa builds a bridge across the bay to carry its main water intake pipe from the Ottawa River. The two previous pipes under the Bay had leaked, poisoning 2,500 people and killing 174.
(Source: City of Ottawa Archives; image CA 006062)

New Federal Buildings but No Federal Planning

While the Ottawa Improvement Commission (OIC) was busy building parks across the capital, another federal agency began to change the face of Ottawa. The Department of Public Works (DPW) had recovered from the Langevin Building scandals and had been constructing attractive new federal buildings across the country.[508] Ottawa was long overdue for new government accommodation, since only one building had been added since the construction of the Parliament Buildings in 1866. The national population had increased from 3.7 to 7.2 million from 1871 to 1911 and the number of civil servants in Ottawa had more than doubled from 1901 to 1911 alone.[509]

The first step in the expansion of the federal presence was to spin out public institutions into their own buildings including the Public Archives (1905-07), the Royal Mint (1906-08) and the Victoria Memorial Museum (1905-08). These buildings were designed by the Department of Public Works in a "Tudor Gothic" style that harmonized reasonably well with the Parliament Buildings[510] (Figure 7-3). The Mint and Archives were sited on Sussex Street, and the larger museum was built about 1.5 km south of Parliament Hill. Although Frederick Todd had suggested Sussex Street as a good location for government buildings, neither the OIC nor the DPW made any attempt to plan the location of the new institutions in a coordinated manner.[511]

The expansion of the civil service and the judiciary in the new century had created urgent requirements for more office buildings and a new home for the Supreme Court. The Department of Public Works decided to group these new structures on a long, narrow site on Sussex Street, across from Major's Hill Park. Given the prominence of the site and the program, the DPW decided to hold an architectural competition, the first in the half-century since the Parliament Buildings. The competition was open to Canadian architects, and the rules suggested "some phase of Gothic would better harmonize with existing structures."[512] The Montréal firm of Edward & W.S. Maxwell were announced as winners of the competition in September 1907, but the DPW did not proceed with the design, to the consternation of the architectural profession. The Supreme Court was dropped from the program, and the DPW designed the Connaught Building (1913-16) in its own Tudor Gothic style.[513]

FIGURE 7-3: Victoria Memorial Museum, 1908
This museum was designed for the federal governments' geology and natural history collections, but the fine art gallery was also squeezed in for a half century. The museum was built on poor soil and the stone tower at left began to lean away and was removed in 1916. It was replaced by a lightweight glass tower in 2011.
(Source: LAC C-009273)

The DPW realized that the small remaining site on Sussex Street did not hold the space required for the expansion of the federal buildings and turned its gaze towards the Upper Town lands on the cliffs north of Wellington Street. These lands had more dramatic possibilities for an extension of the parliamentary precinct to the west, but the property needed to be re-assembled by the Crown, since it had been leased or sold by Colonel By in the 1820s. The federal government expropriated the original Upper Town properties in 1912.[514]

The DPW sought preliminary urban design advice on the layout of the buildings from Frederick Todd of Montréal and Edward White of London, England. Todd produced a simple site plan with general advice to match the building style and materials to the Parliament Buildings.[515] White almost stole the commission by allying with the noted English architect Aston Webb, who had redesigned the Buckingham Palace façade, Pall Mall and the Admiralty Arch in London. Webb was a master of the English 'Grand Manner' and produced a design that would bring imperial Whitehall to Ottawa, with domes, colonnades and arches in the best classical style[516] (Figure 7-4).

The 1912 White-Webb design must have been tempting to the friends of the British Empire in Sir Robert Borden's Cabinet. Its classical architecture and planning had become an international symbol of sophisticated urban design for national capitals, pioneered in Paris, but also adapted in Edwardian London and Washington's 1902 McMillan Plan[517] (Figure 5-22). This classical design vocabulary was dominant in plans for other capitals in the British Empire, including Herbert Baker's 1911 designs for Pretoria, Lutyens and Baker's 1911 plans for New Delhi and the Griffins' 1912 plan for Canberra.[518]

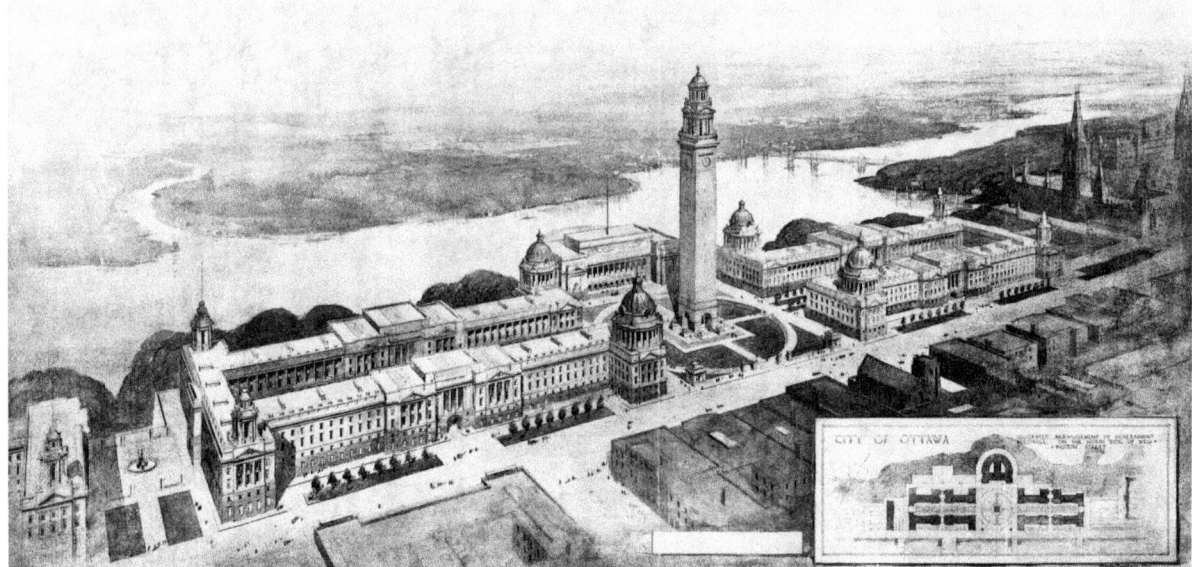

FIGURE 7-4: Edward White and Aston Webb's 1912 proposal for an imperial capital
Edward White and Aston Webb's 1912 proposal for an imperial capital north of Wellington Street in London's Georgian style. The existing West Block is just visible on the left of the rendering, and is ignored in the site plan.
(Source: LAC NMC 5451)

The City Beautiful in New Delhi, 1911

The site for the new capital of India was proclaimed by King George V at the Delhi Durbar in 1911. It was a controversial move, because Kolkata (Calcutta) had been the seat of the imperial government. Delhi was centrally located and had been an ancient capital of the Pathan and Mughal empires, but it had less commercial power than Kolkata or Mumbai. The colonial government was able to impose this plan as a result of its strong power over local and national development.

The original New Delhi Plan (Figure 7.5) was prepared by a small Town Planning Committee (1912-1913), with expert British consultants. English architect Sir Edwin Lutyens led the design team and designed the most prominent building, the Viceroy's Palace. He had a distinguished career as a designer of English country homes, and had designed the centrepiece of London's Hampstead Garden Suburb.[519] He was assisted by Herbert Baker, who had executed many important commissions in South Africa, including the Union Buildings.[520] Baker was given the commission for the Secretariat Buildings, which house civil service offices.

Lutyens brought plans of Paris and Washington to Delhi to assist in the 1913 designs of the imperial capital.[521] The Delhi plan incorporated a classical central axis, the Rajpath, and hexagonal geometry, part of an unusual early 20th century urban design

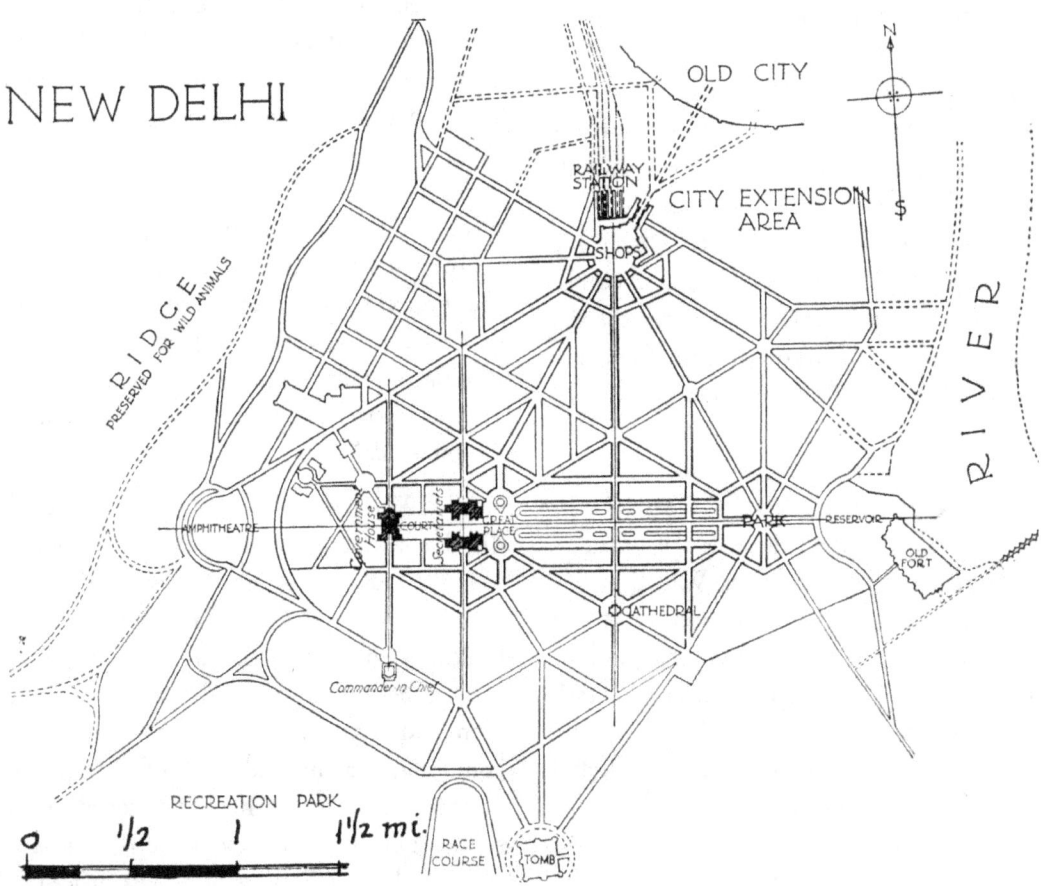

FIGURE 7-5: Baker and Lutyens' New Delhi, 1911
This image was in the drawing collection of Canada's National Capital Planning Service from the post-war period.
(Source: NCC Box 4666, Historic Plans and Photos file, Image 4666-23-5)

motif.[522] Baker designed the massive Secretariat Buildings as a pair that frame the approach to the Viceroy's Palace. In a famous urban design dispute, Baker constructed the slope of the Rajpath as a ramp that provided convenient access to his buildings. The slope of the ramp had the unfortunate effect of cutting off the view of Lutyen's palace as a visitor approached it along the central axis.[523]

The new capital was not inaugurated until 1931, over a decade late.[524] New Delhi functioned as an imperial capital for less than two decades. Following the declaration of the Republic of India in 1948, the buildings became the capitol complex of the new federation.[525]

Canberra, 1912:
The City Beautiful in Australia

Australia was created as a federal state in 1901, without a designated seat of government – neither Melbourne nor Sydney was acceptable to its counterpart. After a thorough survey for a suitable site, the new federal government chose some sheep farms in the Canberra area in 1908.[526] The Australian Capital Territory (ACT) was carved out of the state of New South Wales as a separate district responsible to the national government, following the example of the District of Columbia in the United States.

In 1912, Australia commissioned an international design competition for a plan for its capital.[527] It was lucky to get three designs as good as those submitted by the finalists, Walter Burley Griffin (US), Eliel Saarinen (Finland) and Alf Agache (France). Walter Burley Griffin's design for Canberra (Figure 7-6) is now recognized as a classic, but it emerged from a controversial competition process that was boycotted by Commonwealth and Australian architects.[528] Griffin (1876-1937) was a landscape architect from Chicago and had practised in Frank Lloyd Wright's office. He emigrated to Australia with his wife, the architect Marion Mahoney Griffin, who had collaborated on the winning design.[529]

Unfortunately, the Griffins had little success implementing their plan. World War I put most of the work on hold, and although Griffin was a talented designer, he had little background or enthusiasm for the political and financial battles required to build the city. Griffin only managed to revise his plan and stake it out on the site. His contract was not renewed in 1920, and he left Canberra disillusioned and dispirited by the lack of progress.[530] It took a sustained effort after the Second World War to develop the capital city. Griffin's original plan, superbly fitted into a bowl of hills, was largely built out in the 1960s. The new Parliament House opened in 1988.

The best aspect of Canberra is its adaptation to the landscape. On paper, Griffin's plan appears like a relic of the "City Beautiful" era with grand boulevards and civic centres, but the experience on the ground is quite impressive. The central land axis and the radiating avenues focus attention on the Parliament House, while the lake and hills create a unique landscape with a powerful sense of place. Canberra's development is a landmark in 20th century Australian urban planning.[531] However, the project's early years were a classic example of a "good plan/poor implementation" scenario, lacking the political support, financial strategy and administrative expertise needed for development of a capital city.[532]

The 1913 Ottawa Competition

The Department of Public Works included Webb-White's proposal in an international competition for the Supreme Court and new departmental buildings that was announced in 1913. However, the competition assessors disliked the White-Webb plan and inserted a clause into the competition conditions leaving the style of the buildings up to the architects.[533] The DPW received sixty-one submissions with a wide variety of architectural styles and site planning proposals. The jury short-listed six firms (none of them particularly famous) before the competition was placed on hold, never to re-open.[534]

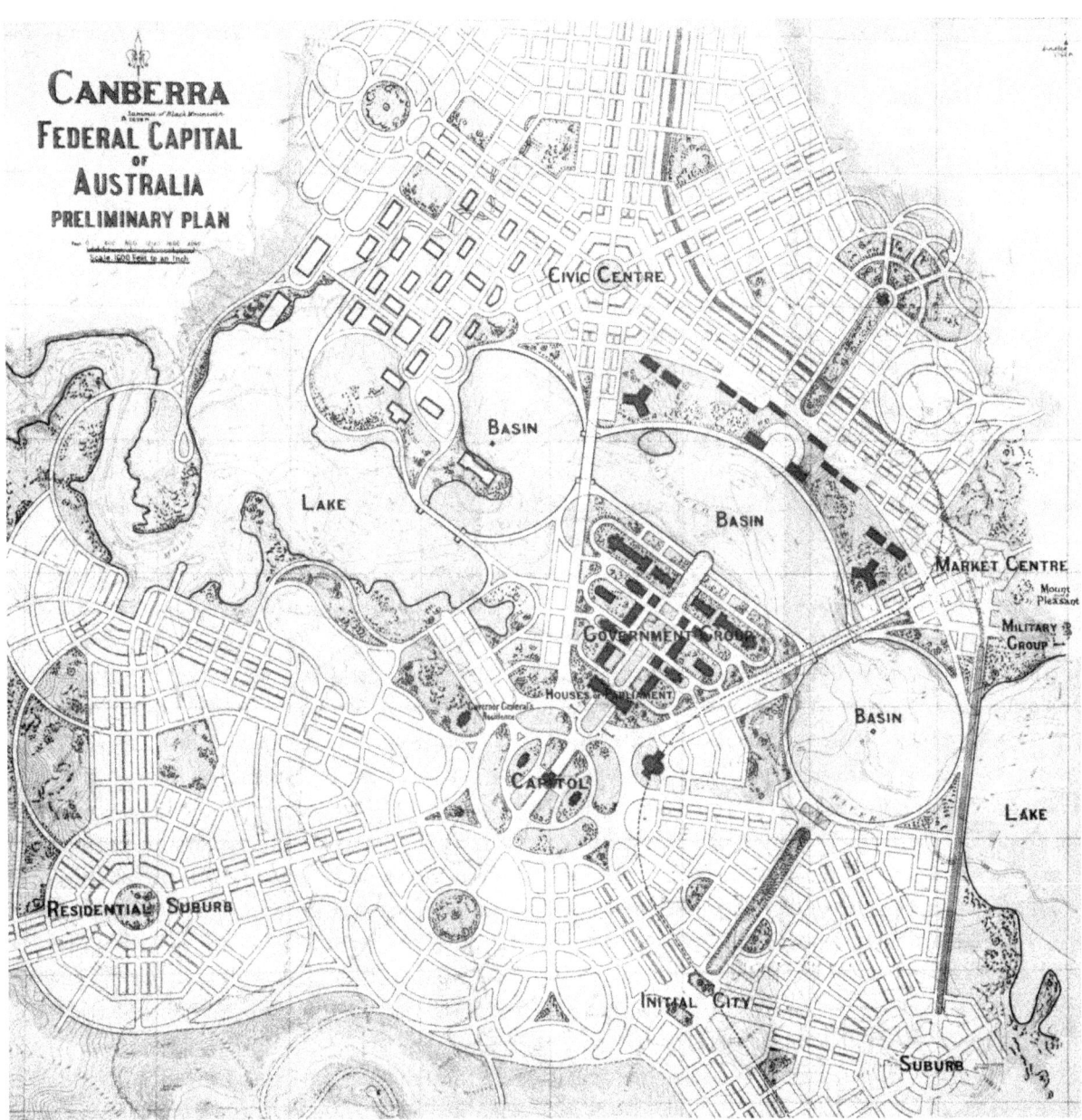

FIGURE 7-6: The Griffin's 1913 Preliminary Plan for Canberra
(Source: Australia, 1913)

The 1913 competition was unsatisfactory for two reasons: the proposed classical style and its limited scope in urban design. It is not clear whether White or Webb had ever visited Ottawa, but their proposal repeated the mistakes of 1859, being completely disconnected from the rest of the city. It also seemed to misinterpret the spirit of the place that had been noted by Todd. The grand classical ensemble proposed did not seem connected to any notions of a Canadian identity, and clearly was unsympathetic to the existing Parliament Buildings. Even Thomas Mawson, the English landscape architect closely associated with classical urban design, felt that the White-Webb scheme was inappropriate for Ottawa, and for Canada, recommending "the picturesque quality that the present parliament buildings undoubtedly possess ..."[535]

Secondly, the DPW's building-centred approach did not address the fundamental problems of the Canadian capital city. Well-designed public buildings are a necessary component of a capital, and can even be a major source of national identity and pride, as we saw with the new Parliament Buildings. However, Ottawa was an unsatisfactory capital city because of the conditions beyond Parliament Hill. These problems could be best addressed by a new technique – a comprehensive plan for the capital city as suggested by Lady Aberdeen in 1898. Although no Canadian city had yet prepared a comprehensive plan in 1914, there were recent capital city precedents from Washington (1902), New Delhi (1911) and Canberra (1912). The comprehensive plans for San Francisco (1904) and Chicago (1909) were also widely distributed in monograph formats.[536]

While the DPW competition was underway, the new Conservative government had also been considering a wider plan. The national and city governments retained Noulan Cauchon to prepare the preliminary surveys and topographic maps needed to shape a comprehensive plan for Ottawa. Meredith, Mawson and Cauchon intensified their lobbying for an expert commission to prepare the new Ottawa plan, on the 1902 Washington model.

Meanwhile, Prime Minister Borden and his advisors had other ideas.

The Federal Plan Commission

Borden was uncomfortable with the idea of a commission of architects over whom he would have no political control. He also wanted a plan that covered both Ottawa and Hull. So the government appointed a Federal Plan Commission (FPC), in September 1913, to:

> ... draw up and perfect a comprehensive scheme or plan looking to the future growth and development of the City of Ottawa and the City of Hull, and their environs, and particularly providing for the location, laying out and beautification of parks and connecting boulevards, the location and architectural character of public buildings and adequate and convenient arrangements for traffic and transportation within the area in question.[537]

The government's first choice to chair the commission was Sir William van Horne, a famous president of the Canadian Pacific Railway who was also active in promoting town planning in Montréal. But van Horne declined, so the government turned to Herbert Holt, another prominent Montréal railway executive, banker and Conservative Party activist.[538] The mayors of Ottawa and Hull were ex-officio members. Montréal lawyer Sir Alexander Lacoste, Toronto real estate developer Robert Home-Smith and Toronto architect Frank Darling were the other commissioners. All three were strong Conservative Party supporters.[539] The federal government agreed to pay half the costs of the Commission, while Ottawa and Hull were to split the remainder, based upon the relative proportions of their populations.[540]

The Commission's first activity was the selection of consultants. Darling and Home-Smith were the only members of the group with direct experience in town planning and they likely had considerable influence in the selection process. At the turn of the century, Frank Darling was one of Canada's most respected architects. He was a director of the Toronto Civic Guild of Art, which sponsored two plans for that city in the City Beautiful style. Home-Smith developed large portions of the western edge of Toronto. He also served on the Civic Guild and was a Toronto Harbour Commissioner. The Harbour Commission had recently prepared a comprehensive plan for the Toronto waterfront with Frederick Law Olmsted Jr. as a consultant. The plans were vigorously implemented under the direction of its chief engineer, E.L. Cousins.[541] Home-Smith approached Olmsted for advice regarding the new Federal Plan Commission and Holt interviewed him in Montréal in November 1913.[542] Prime Minister Borden had personally interviewed Thomas Mawson in December 1912, but his senior staff had doubts about Mawson's suitability for the job. Although Mawson was involved in seven planning projects in Canada during 1912, he preferred to work from his English studio with local associates, making occasional visits to clients during his trans-Atlantic speaking tours.[543]

The Federal Plan Commission's first appointment was its consulting engineer. Although Noulan Cauchon had just completed the preliminary surveys for the Ottawa plan, he was not chosen for the job. He was likely regarded as a bit of an eccentric. His frequent articles in the *Ottawa Citizen* newspaper criticized the OIC and advocated all kinds of city planning schemes. Instead of Cauchon, the Commission appointed E.L. Cousins, chief engineer with the Toronto Harbour Commission,

FIGURE 7-7: **Edward H. Bennett**
Edward H. Bennett (1874-1954) was America's leading City Beautiful planner when he was retained by the Federal Plan Commission in 1913. Daniel Burnham recruited him after his graduation from Paris' École des Beaux Arts and they were co-authors of the San Francisco (1905) and Chicago (1909) plans (see the Cast of Characters for his biography).
(Source: Underwood & Underwood photograph, courtesy of the Art Institute of Chicago)

whose work was well known to the Toronto-based members of the FPC. The Commission then chose Chicago architect Edward Bennett as its chief planning consultant. In December 1913, Darling and Home-Smith would likely have been familiar with Bennett's work from their Civic Guild plans. Bennett visited Darling and Cousins in Toronto before his interview, and traveled with them to meet Holt and the other members of the Commission in Ottawa. When word of the appointment leaked out, Meredith resigned from the OIC in protest, sending a strongly worded letter to Prime Minister Borden and an angry letter to his mentor Frank Darling.[544]

Prompted by Cauchon, the *Ottawa Citizen* ran a story complaining that Canadian and British town planners were excluded in favour of an American. Holt defended the Commission's choice in a letter to the Cabinet, later partially released to the newspapers:

> ... I am sure that you will appreciate that the work of City Planning involves broad generalising study in economics and design, which requires the services of an expert who has made a special study of this work and has extensive previous knowledge. The Commissioners, after an exhaustive investigation, arrived at the conclusion that Mr. Bennett was the best man for the position, having had the knowledge and experience necessary to make studies and plans of such important work as contemplated for the Federal Capital. The Commissioners also considered that it is most important to have as their expert a man who has a thorough architectural training and who specialized in City Planning, and came therefore to the conclusion that Mr. Bennett's experience and the knowledge which he has gained at the Beaux Arts, which is acknowledged to be one of the greatest Architectural Colleges in the world, eminently fits him for the position.
>
> The Commissioners would have preferred appointing a Canadian for this position if they could have found a man considered *competent and with sufficient practical experience to work out a plan which would be of credit not only to Ottawa but to the whole Dominion of Canada.*[545]

Despite the outcry from disappointed local competitors, the Federal Plan Commission probably made the right choice in 1913. In hindsight, the protests against Bennett's Ottawa appointment by Mawson and the disappointed local contenders appear somewhat ironic. Rather than choosing a leading British practitioner supported by the local elite, the Federal Plan Commission appointed a polite, self-effacing man who was born in England, educated in France, and thoroughly familiar with the latest American techniques.

What could be more Canadian?

Bennett's Approach to the Ottawa-Hull Plan

Bennett never hid his City Beautiful influences, despite the criticism the movement endured post 1910. We have a clear record of his approach to the Ottawa-Hull plan in a speech he gave to the elite Canadian Club in April, 1914. In an hour and a half lecture illustrated by 95 lantern slides, he clearly set forth his philosophy of city planning:

> ... to create conditions of life such that the maximum of health, happiness and efficiency of the citizens may be obtained; to create and foster in the minds of all citizens the sense of entity of the city and the interdependent relationship of the various elements of the city, and thereby to promote a spirit of co-operation.
>
> A city may be said to be a setting for the lives of its inhabitants, and this setting may be one in which the influences are deleterious or, on the contrary, one in which the stimulus is given on every hand to a beautiful expression of life; I use the term 'beautiful' in its broadest sense. Whether this be during the working hours or those of play, the influence of harmonious and orderly surroundings is constantly active and it is fair to say that the

production of orderly and harmonious or, in other words, beautiful surroundings is one great aim of the City Plan ...[546]

Bennett was un-apologetic about his approach, perhaps because he believed that it was rooted in the best traditions of city design and that it incorporated modern technical advances in planning. One quarter of his lecture was devoted to a history of city planning, drawing on the experiences of European capitals such as London, Vienna, Rome, Berlin and, especially, Paris. The next section of the speech covered recent American experiences illustrated by Burnham's work in the 1893 Chicago World's Fair and Cleveland, and Bennett's plans for San Francisco, Chicago, Portland, Minneapolis and Brooklyn. While Bennett showed a few slides of his plans' trademark watercolour renderings, most of the discussion focused upon the technical aspects of planning: railway relocation, street design, regional park systems, traffic congestion and zoning. He described how each of these elements was being implemented in selected cities. Finally, Bennett expounded upon the design of capital cities, with particular reference to the 1902 McMillan Commission for Washington.[547]

Bennett concluded with a review of the site of the Canadian capital, comparing it to the river edges in London, Paris, Berlin and Budapest. His final slides compared the Gothic splendour of the Parliament Buildings on the bluff over the Ottawa River to the best elements of Princes' Street in Edinburgh. This comparison was a particularly adept political touch, given the Scottish background of many members of the Canadian elite. Overall, the slide show was a strong performance, driving home Bennett's wide-ranging familiarity with appropriate urban design precedents, combining these with mastery in technical planning and implementation. However, the *Ottawa Citizen's* report of the speech portended future problems. Noulan Cauchon's story attacked Bennett for his architectural approach to planning and lack of attention to housing for the poor.[548]

How the 1915 Plan was Prepared

A foreign consultant preparing a master plan can expect political and technical problems without an adequate local presence, as Thomas Mawson discovered in Calgary.[549] So the Federal Plan Commission appointed Canadian engineer A.E.K. Bunnell to manage its Ottawa office in December 1913. He reported directly to Bennett and Cousins, and supervised a team of engineering assistants and draftsmen who prepared the surveys and detailed technical analyses of the site. Bennett and Cousins made several trips to Ottawa for meetings with the Commission and staff during 1914. They maintained daily contact by letter, telegram, overnight courier and the occasional use of that relatively 'new' business communications device, the long-distance telephone.[550]

E.L. Cousins prepared the railway, utility and waterway sections of the plan from his Toronto office, where Darling, Home-Smith and Bennett visited him. Cousins and Bennett collaborated on the road plans. All the urban design, zoning, parks and government building analyses were completed in Bennett's office in Chicago. Frank Darling made two trips to Chicago to review these plans. Bennett retained Jules Guérin for watercolour renderings of the capital in the luminous style that Guérin had used in the Chicago plan. In the best tradition of the École des Beaux Arts, Bennett and his staff did a *charrette* (an intense period of design or planning activities) over the 1914 Christmas holidays to complete the drawings before the year-end deadline.[551]

The initial output was a group of 27 drawings that hung in an exhibition at a downtown Ottawa office building in January 1915. The plans included technical analyses of land uses, population densities and growth, and railway and streetcar traffic, but Jules Guérin's renderings probably stole the show.[552] His watercolour aerial perspectives, some as large as six feet by three feet, presented bird's-eye views of the regional park system and the future central areas of Ottawa and Hull (Figures 7-8 to 7-11).

After feedback from the Commission and senior federal and municipal officials, the technical drawings were modified and the text of the final report was prepared. Bennett wrote a first draft in early 1915, incorporating sections by Cousins on the engineering issues. A comparison of the draft manuscript to the final report suggests that the Commissioners ordered a complete re-working of the introductory portion of the plan to incorporate their political concerns.[553]

Components of the Plan for Ottawa-Hull

The thorough technical analysis underlying the plan stood the test of time for the most part. Bunnell prepared population projections indicating that the Ottawa-Hull regions would grow from 125,000 to 250,000 by 1950. These were almost exactly correct, despite the upheavals in the intervening years.[554] Bennett's staff and Cousins prepared forecasts of streetcar and railway traffic based upon comparisons with other North American cities. Bennett personally carried out research on the growth and space required for government offices based on proportional comparison to Washington. The one forecast where the planners were radically wrong concerned the future role of the automobile. While Bennett believed that the horse was on its way out, in 1914 the automobile was still an expensive luxury. The capital's plans for automobile roads focused on inter-regional highways and daily commuting was to be accommodated by an expansion of the streetcar network.

The 1915 FPC report contained most of the components that the leading authorities of the time, Thomas Adams and Frederick Law Olmsted, Jr., suggested should comprise a comprehensive plan.[555] It included:
- a regional parks and forest reserves system,
- a parkway and playground plan,
- street layouts for future suburban expansion,
- regional passenger and freight railway plans,
- regional highway plans,
- new plans for street railway lines,
- utility analysis,
- waterway and flood analysis,
- plans for federal and municipal government buildings,
- a central business district plan, and
- a preliminary zoning scheme.

The parks provisions included many of the suggestions in Todd's 1903 report, but Bennett also recommended the acquisition of the Gatineau hills north of Hull. Guérin's rendering of this wedge of hills almost reaching the river formed the frontispiece for the plan (Figure 7-9). The railway plans recommended removal of the east-west freight line through the centre of the city, and its replacement by a limited access highway. Passenger service was to be consolidated in a union station opposite the Château Laurier hotel.

The planning team forecast the future streetcar congestion downtown, and recommended a streetcar subway under Wellington Street to relieve the pressure. Bennett devoted considerable effort to untangling the knot of streetcars, trains and vehicular traffic near the downtown bridges over the Rideau Canal. His solution involved the widening of Elgin Street, clearing the west bank of the Rideau Canal to create a new plaza, and the cutting of a new diagonal road and bridge from Laurier Avenue (Figures 7-10 and 7-11). This was the only new road proposed to be cut through the built-up area.

Bennett's analysis of the government centre was based upon its historical and natural context. Despite his Beaux Arts training, he did not insist upon an axial approach to Parliament Hill in the manner of the proposed civic-centre of his 1909 Plan of Chicago or the 1902 Senate Parks Commission report for Washington. In fact, Bennett avoided the temptation to adopt a formal approach to Parliament Hill from the south and specifically rejected Washington as an urban design precedent. He suggested that while a perpendicular axial vista was

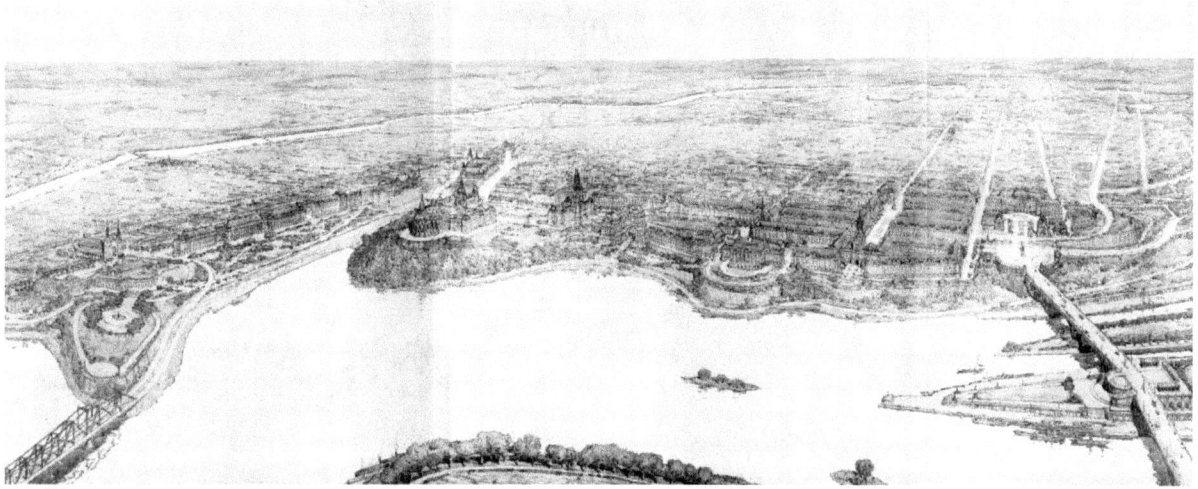

FIGURE 7-8: Aerial view of Parliament Hill by Jules Guérin, 1915
The Parliamentary Precinct and Wellington Street are rendered in the Château style. This image may have influenced Mackenzie King, who later became a strong advocate of this style for Ottawa. The bridge at right is similar to the Portage Bridge built sixty years later.
(Source: Bennett, 1915; Drawing 15)

FIGURE 7-9: Frontispiece of the 1915 Plan
Frontispiece of the 1915 Plan shows a bird's-eye view of the future capital city, looking north. Note the Gatineau Hills extending almost to the river.
(Source: Bennett, 1915; Drawing 1, by Jules Guérin)

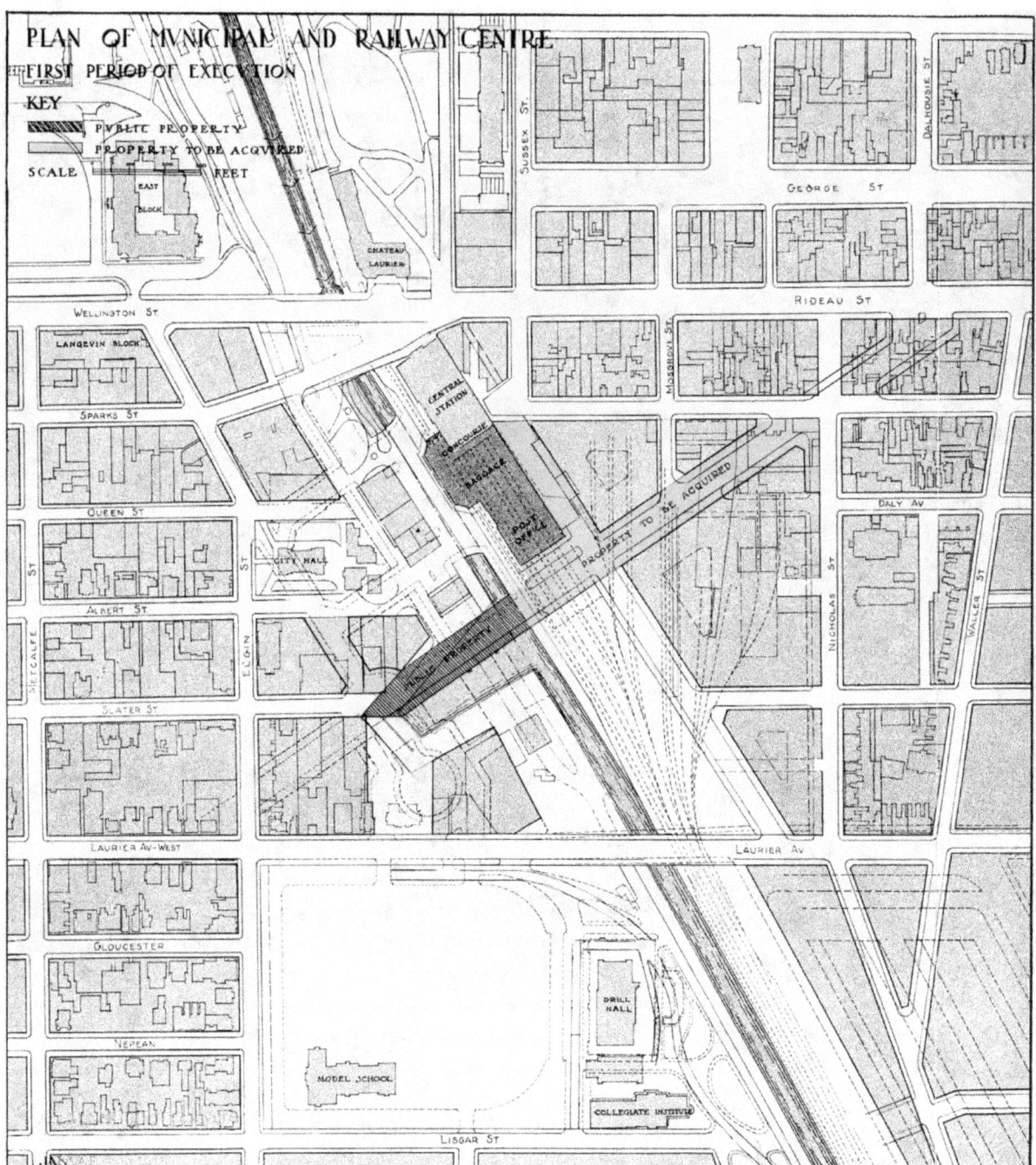

FIGURE 7-10: **Plan for the Municipal Railway Centre**
Plan for the Municipal Railway Centre, involving the widening of Elgin Street and the cutting of a new diagonal road from Laurier Avenue.
(Source: Bennett, 1915; Drawing 6A)

appropriate for classical architecture, for optimum effect, Ottawa's Gothic Revival buildings should be viewed on a diagonal axis. Bennett recommended a widened Elgin Street and proposed a plaza along the canal as appropriate ceremonial approaches for this purpose (Figure 7-11).

Although he did not include it in his plans, Bennett suggested that the approach to Parliament Hill from the south might also be improved:

Unfortunately, the relation that ought to exist between the Government buildings and the street system of the city was not recognized at the time the Parliament Buildings were erected. The lack of a main axial approach, such as would result if Metcalfe Street was a wide avenue on a line with the axis of the Victoria Tower, is much to be regretted.[556]

That final sentence, which was almost an afterthought in the 1915 plan, was later to cause some difficulty in planning Ottawa's downtown, as future prime ministers pursued City Beautiful visions.

Plans for both the downtown and the suburbs included both Hull and Ottawa. Hull was to have its own civic centre and new bridges across the Ottawa River (Figure 7-12). In downtown Ottawa, the federal government buildings were planned to extend along Wellington Street to the west

FIGURE 7-11: **Municipal plaza proposed for Ottawa**
The Château Laurier hotel (1907, upper right) was a model for the architectural style of other important buildings, such as the proposed city hall (middle left).
(Source: Bennett, 1915; Drawing 5)

(Figure 7-8), with municipal buildings down Elgin Street to the south-east (Figure 7-11). Guérin's renderings illustrate some neo-classical buildings associated with the City Beautiful style, combined with others drawn in the manner of the new Château Laurier (Ottawa) and Château Frontenac (Québec) hotels. The railway hotels created something of a Canadian national style in the first half of the century (Figure 7-11). The Château style was vigorously promoted by the Canadian railways for its hotels across the country, so Holt may also have had some influence in the iconography.[557]

The zoning provisions of the plan (Bennett called them district control) reviewed current practice in both Europe and America. Bennett recommended separating the city into six districts:
a. industrial areas,
b. general railway and transport areas,
c. a central business district to include retail, wholesale and light industry,
d. a central residential district,
e. an outer or general residential district, and
f. a suburban residential district at present unplatted [*unsubdivided*].[558]

FIGURE 7-12: **Hull Municipal Plaza, 1915**
Hull gets a civic centre in the City Beautiful mode, but with buildings rendered in the Château style. Note the Alexandra Bridge replaced by a more elegant suspension bridge, and another new bridge in the foreground, approximately in the location of the 1973 Portage Bridge.
(Source: Bennett, 1915; Drawing 7)

The inner circle in the zoning plan (Figure 7-13) was a central business district, with the next ring demarcated for central residential development. Three heavy industrial districts were proposed for locations marked 'a' and 'b' on Figure 7-13, their siting intended to reduce the amount of discomfort from smoke and odours, and provide good access to the relocated freight railway yards and highways.[559]

Finally, Bennett personally prepared studies of the silhouette of the capital's skyline from six locations (Figure 7-14). To protect the prominence of the Parliament Buildings in the skyline, he included height limits for each section of the downtown in the zoning plan.

What the 1915 Report did *not* include were any plans for housing, particularly housing for the poor. Bennett was certainly aware of the

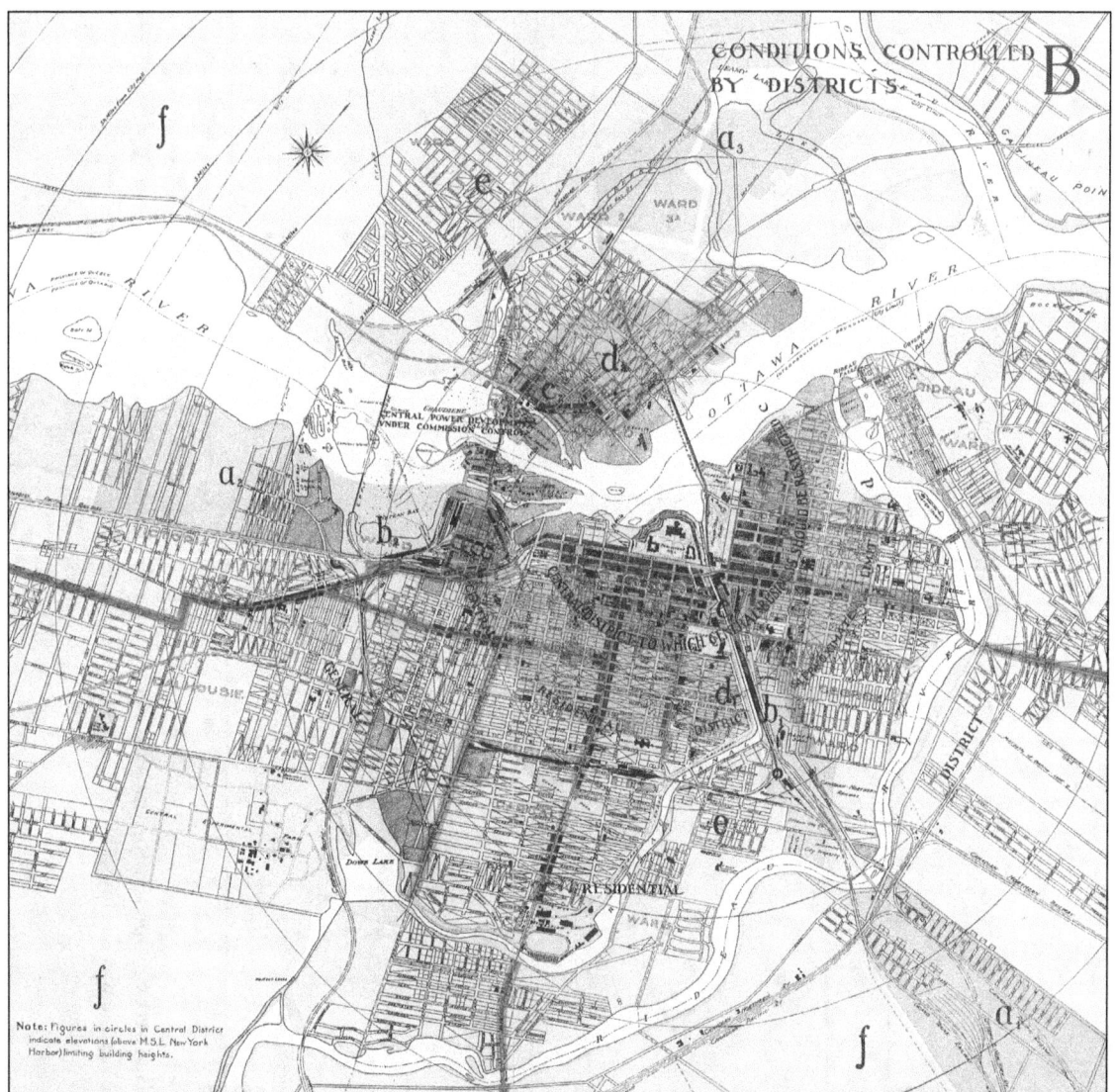

FIGURE 7-13: Bennett's 1915 zoning proposal for central Ottawa and Hull
Bennett's 1915 zoning proposal for central Ottawa and Hull was one of the first Canadian zoning proposals.
(Source: Bennett, 1915; Drawing 19B)

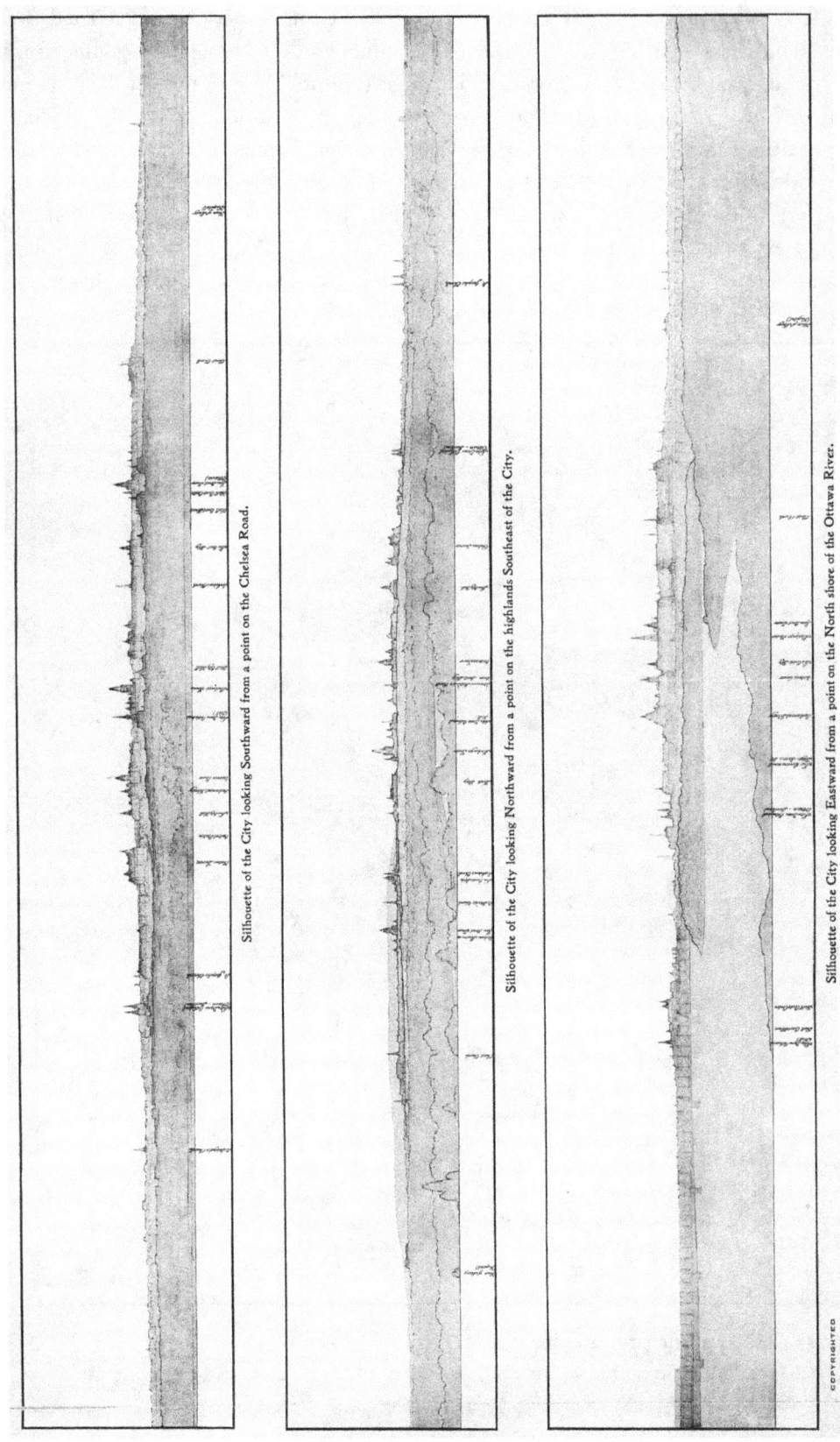

FIGURE 7-14: Bennett's proposals for the silhouette along the Ottawa River
This picturesque skyline was destroyed by private developers in the 1960s.
(Source: Bennett, 1915; Drawing 17)

unsuitable residential conditions some parts of the region offered, and the planning team's population density analyses hint at the problems. However, the order in council establishing the Federal Plan Commission did not encompass housing issues, and it is doubtful that the commissioners were inclined to address them.[560] City Beautiful plans rarely gave more than token consideration to housing, since housing reform was seen as a separate movement at the time.[561] The discussions of suburban housing and street standards included in Bennett's original draft were edited out of the FPC's final report, just as Burnham's text on housing was removed from their *Plan of Chicago*.[562]

Implementation Provisions

The Commissioners themselves, with assistance from their advisors in the civil service, appear to have prepared the implementation provisions of the 1915 plan. The first and foremost recommendation of the Commission was:

> *We are of the firm opinion that the future improvements in the area about the Capital of Ottawa and Hull should not be attempted without first establishing a Federal district and securing for the Federal authority some control of local government.*[563]

This recommendation is coupled with a description of the operation of the District of Columbia but lacks any discussion concerning the future relationship of the cities of Ottawa and Hull, or the provinces of Ontario or Québec.[564] The federal district proposal was a hot political issue in the region for a decade, and Ottawa citizens had voted in favour of the idea in a 1912 referendum.[565]

The commissioners also recommended the reorganization of the railway network, a comprehensive plan for the government buildings, and zoning, as proposed by Bennett and Cousins. The FPC regarded the railways as the most important technical problem in the plan, and they were probably correct. Traffic in Ottawa was choked by over 100 level crossings in the downtown area. Multiple passenger stations and freight yards scattered throughout the city decreased the efficiency of the railway network. The plan recommended that the new Federal District Commission "be placed in complete control of the railway situation within the limits of the district," and the acquisition and control of all existing tracks and terminals.[566] Given that Herbert Holt was the president of a prominent railway company, this recommendation was both radical, and an indication of serious coordination problems between the railways.[567]

The Federal Plan Commission Report

The final report of the Federal Plan Commission consisted of 158 pages and 24 fold-out drawings. Unfortunately, FPC staff made three mistakes during the printing of the report. The crest gilt-stamped into the cover contained an error in the arms of one of the new provinces, leading to more complaints about absentee American consultants. More seriously, the French translation of the report and a proposed 'popular' version were not immediately printed, although funds were already budgeted for their production. As a result, the Federal Plan Commission report was neither widely distributed, nor available on time in both the dominant languages used in Canada.

The report was printed by the end of 1915, but it was not tabled in Parliament until March 10, 1916. It was not an auspicious time. The war in Europe was going badly and the Centre Block of the Parliament Buildings had burned in a spectacular fire the preceding month (Figure 7-15). The report received a few brief reviews in the press. Having completed its limited mandate,[568] the Federal Plan Commission disbanded.

In a capital transfixed by war, the plan quickly sank from sight. The only reminders of its existence were Guérin's watercolour paintings which hung in Ottawa City Hall for several years. Eventually, they were removed, for fear of damage during the hurly-burly of the municipal nomination meetings of the day. The drawings were shipped to the office of the Commission of Conservation in the federal government, where they were eventually misplaced.[569]

FIGURE 7-15: Centre Block of the Parliament Buildings destroyed by fire, February 1916
Although some of the damaged walls were still standing the next morning, they had to be demolished in the weeks that followed.
(Source: LAC PA-173113)

Planning the City of Ottawa

The City of Ottawa's planning initiatives were modest during the early 20th century. The 1910 building code allowed construction of buildings up to ten floors. In 1914, city council passed a bylaw that limited buildings height to 110 feet above grade, implementing one of the FPC proposals before the report was released.[570] The height limit copied the US federal government's regulations to control the height of buildings in Washington. In turn, the American regulations were based upon Parisian building codes that limited the height of many buildings to the width of the adjacent street. Many of the avenues in L'Enfant's 1793 plan for Washington are 110 feet wide, generating a similar height limit.[571]

The direct transfer of the Washington regulation to Ottawa was particularly unfortunate for Sparks Street, with its 60-foot wide right-of-way. Fortunately, the orientation of the Upper Town street grid some 32 degrees off north ensured that "east-west" roads like Sparks Street received some afternoon sun. The City of Ottawa's construction code and height limit combined to set the scale of buildings in Upper Town for over a half century and to protect long-range views of the central tower of the Parliament Buildings.

Reflections

The conventional explanations of why the 1915 plan was 'put on the shelf' include: the nation was focused on the war,[572] any expenditure in Ottawa was diverted to rebuilding the Centre Block,[573] and a City Beautiful plan was inappropriate for Ottawa.[574]

The first two points were valid excuses for inactivity in the short term. However, the war ended in three years, and many plans were made for improving the country upon the return of its veterans.[575] Why not a suitable national capital for a 'nation forged in fire'?

Secondly, the Centre Block, including the new Peace Tower, was rebuilt by 1925. The country was still in an expansionary mood in the mid-1920s. Why did the federal government not proceed with the rest of the plan for Ottawa?

A partial answer might be that the political aspects of the Commission's work were naïve, and not conducive to effective implementation in an environment of increasing 'Town-Crown' tension. The FPC conducted its meetings in English, without an interpreter, even though the mayor of Hull spoke only French.[576] The Commission was comprised entirely of prominent Conservatives, and the plan was commonly referred to as the 'Holt Commission report'. When the Tory government fell in 1920, the Commission had been dissolved for five years. There was nobody left to advocate the plan to the new Liberal administration.[577]

Third, the Federal District proposal ran into implacable local opposition in Québec. It was a complete non-starter in the City of Hull and the Province of Québec. Both city and province were fiercely opposed to any potential loss of territory or sovereignty. The Hull City Council was so incensed by the proposal delivered in the English version of the report that it refused its contractual obligation to pay for a share of the report. The federal government sued for the money in the Exchequer Court and won. Hull appealed to the Supreme Court of Canada, which upheld the appeal on a technicality. The federal government launched an appeal to the Judicial Committee of the Imperial Privy Council before eventually dropping the case.[578] This extended dispute over a small sum was hardly the foundation for a new era of co-operation between 'Crown' and 'Town'.

Opposition to City Beautiful planning may have more explanatory power in the long-term disappearance of Bennett's plan. Although Meredith and Cauchon made the usual complaints about the City Beautiful approach after Bennett was selected, their criticism has the taint of sour grapes. Their champion, Thomas Mawson, was equally identified with the City Beautiful style, but without the detailed technical competence and interest in zoning shown by Bennett in all his plans since Chicago. Also, Cauchon had suggested diagonal boulevards and a civic centre in his earliest Ottawa sketches, and his plans for Hamilton were replete with City Beautiful touches.[579]

Thomas Adams' opposition was a more serious obstacle to the 1915 Plan. He was appointed the Town Planning Advisor to the federal government's Commission of Conservation (see Cast of Characters). Within the emerging North American planning community in 1914, Adams was perhaps equal in eminence to Bennett, but opposite in approach. If Bennett could be considered the leading City Beautiful planner of the day, Adams was equally prominent as a proponent of the 'City Scientific.' Adams revealed his position immediately after the Holt Commission report was tabled in 1916. The next issue of the Commission of Conservation journal contained his article stating:

> Had the **British** method of preparing a town planning scheme been adopted the plan and scheme to give it effect would have been prepared simultaneously, but the Federal Commission adopted the simpler **American**

method of preparing a plan and making a general report, leaving the detailed scheme and the financial considerations for subsequent consideration. The work still to be done in this direction is as important and as large in extent as that which the Commission has accomplished, and the value obtained from the plan and report would be commensurate with the activity shown in proceeding with the second stage and preparing an actual town planning scheme. But even the Federal Plan cannot be properly carried out without a provincial town planning Act, so that in Ottawa, as elsewhere, the greatest urgency is in getting legislation [author's emphasis].[580]

We might take Adams' comments about 'the British method' with some caution. Patrick Abercrombie, editor of the leading British journal *Town Planning Review*, described the FPC report as: "one of the most elaborate and full City Planning reports which has appeared for a town in the British Empire."[581] There was also praise from France: Jacques Gréber featured the plan in his influential book, *L'Architecture aux États Unis*.[582] These observers found the City Beautiful urban design approach to be appropriate for a national capital plan.

Adams implemented his own projects in Ottawa, and they reflected his different priorities for community planning across Canada. He founded local branches of the Civic Improvement League and the Town Planning Institute and promoted affordable housing and control of suburban subdivisions.[583] Adams designed the 1919 plan for Lindenlea, an Ottawa garden suburb that served as a demonstration project for the first federal affordable housing program.[584] By 1920, Adams had regrets that the 1915 FPC plan had been shelved, but still insisted that its methods were inappropriate:

With proper building regulations capital will be less timid and will be attracted to the city. The prevailing assumption that town planning is merely an aesthetic fad is shown by these statements to be entirely wrong. It is on economic grounds that we need town planning and proper zoning. Orderly development and health will produce beauty without seeking beauty as an end in itself.[585]

These words, written by the federal government's chief town planning advisor, must surely have been the end of the Holt Commission's plan.

CHAPTER 8
Roaring Twenties (1920-1930)

... We may not come to have the largest, the wealthiest or the most cosmopolitan Capital in the world, but I believe that with Ottawa's natural and picturesque setting, given stately proportions, and a little careful planning, we can have the most beautiful Capital in the world.[586]
– Prime Minister W.L. Mackenzie King, 1928

The 1900-14 building boom did not resume immediately after World War I. A deadly worldwide influenza epidemic sapped the nation's strength, and the Canadian economy and housing market had a hard time re-integrating the returning veterans. The federal government started an affordable housing program with Thomas Adams planning Ottawa's Lindenlea neighbourhood as a demonstration project (Figure 8-1). Hull and Nepean Township saw expansion of inexpensive subdivisions, with minimal services and little thought to their design, despite the widely promoted ideas for garden suburbs and the neighbourhood unit (Figure 8-2) that were emerging in Britain and the US.[587] Thomas Adams' 1929 Regional Plan for New York and environs promoted the neighbourhood unit concept, and its first prominent application was Radburn, NJ, a garden suburb designed by Henry Wright and Clarence Stein.[588] Radburn made extensive use of culs-de-sac based on London's Letchworth and Hampstead Garden Suburb.

The industrial restructuring of the Outaouais continued, with the final collapse of the lumber industry, decline in pulp production and expansion of paper making. Canadian International Paper entered the Outaouais in 1925, building a huge paper plant in Gatineau, 10 km. east of Hull.[589] This was the first plant to be properly sited, downwind of the urban area, and its large labour force pulled unserviced suburban development east of Hull into the rural areas of Point Gatineau and Gatineau.

Expanding Parliament Hill

Within Ottawa, the federal government was initially focused upon rebuilding and expanding Parliament Hill rather than improving the capital city. Reconstruction of the Centre Block had started immediately after the 1916 fire under the direction of architects John Pearson and Omer Marchand. They expanded the space within the building almost 50 percent by adding another storey and extending the floor plan at the rear of the building. Pearson kept the basic elements of main facade, but reduced the extent and exuberance of Fuller's Gothic detailing. The biggest change was the new Peace Tower, which soared to almost 100 m. (296 ft.) above grade, almost twice the height of Fuller's more ornate Victoria Tower that was destroyed in the fire. The taller tower was a good change, since the Mackenzie Tower added to the West Block

FIGURE 8-1: Lindenlea site plan by Thomas Adams, 1919

Thomas Adams' 1919 design for Lindenlea is a fine example of a garden suburb, incorporating some of the best site planning ideas of the British Garden City movement. The nine hectare (22 acre) site was a demonstration project for the federal government's first affordable housing program. Adams re-planned the area, replacing the grid proposed by the Ottawa Housing Corporation for the steep and rocky site between Beechwood Avenue and Rockcliffe Park. His plan provided modest homes in an attractive setting, with a community hall, small parks system, a wading pool, tennis court and playground. The ample open space system took up 12 percent of the site.[590] The plan provided for a streetcar line, which was extended in 1921.[591]

Adams' plan provided 168 lots, which were sold for $340 to $595. Unfortunately, the overall effect was initially marred by the Ottawa Housing Corporation's construction of identical houses on almost every lot,[592] but these have been expanded and much-modified by the owners over the years. Lindenlea is today a pleasant and green inner-city neighbourhood, and nobody would guess that it was Canada's first federal low-cost housing project.[593]

(Source: *Journal of Town Planning Institute of Canada* (JTPIC), Volume 1(3), April, 1921); reproduced with permission with permission of the Canadian Institute of Planners)

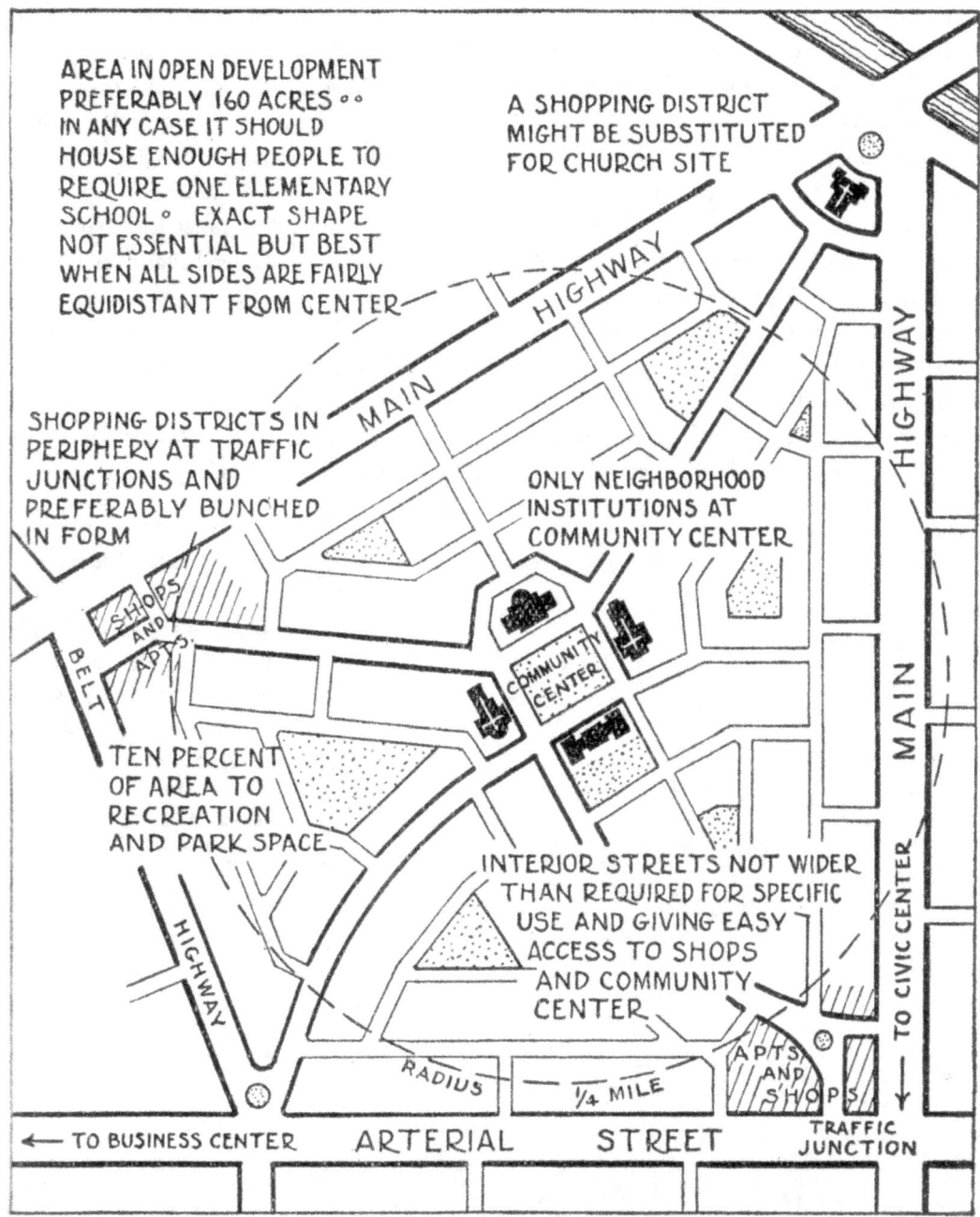

FIGURE 8-2: Neighbourhood Unit, 1929
Clarence Perry's 1929 proposals, showing the central school and park, with sites for two places of worship. Shops and apartments are at the corners, and everything is within a radius of a 10-minute walk.

The neighbourhood unit concept emerged in the 1920s, led by sociologist Clarence Perry.[594] His concept was for residential areas to be organized in units with enough people to require one elementary school, or about 64 ha. A typical neighbourhood unit might have a radius of about 400 m or a five-minute walk to its centre. Major traffic streets bound the area, not pass through it, providing safer conditions for the children using the school and playground at the centre.

(Source: Clarence Perry, "The Neighbourhood Unit," in *Regional Survey of New York and Its Environs*, (New York, 1929), vol. 7)

in 1878 had been slightly taller than the original Victoria Tower, leading to some confusion about the focus of the Parliament Hill group. The taller Peace Tower signalled that the building where Parliament sat was the symbolic centre of the capital (Figure 8-3). Although Parliament returned to the new Centre Block in 1920, construction of the Peace Tower was not completed until the Diamond Jubilee of Confederation in 1927 (Figure 8-12).[595]

The new floor space in the Centre Block was not enough to meet the post-war needs of the federal government, and the Department of Public Works once again cast its gaze upon the lands west of Parliament Hill, which had been expropriated in 1912. The 1913 international design competition had been abandoned, and DPW chief architect Richard Wright and Thomas Adams prepared a new site plan. Adams was an outspoken critic of City Beautiful urban design principles, so it was perhaps surprising that his 1920 plan incorporated some of the formal and symmetrical plans prepared in Edward Bennett's Federal Plan Commission report to accommodate two office buildings that were designed by the DPW staff (Figure 8-4). The new Confederation Building made one other concession to the Federal Plan Commission report: its roof was designed in the Château style that was recommended by Bennett (Figure 8-5).[596]

FIGURE 8-3: Centre Block, Parliament Buildings, 1927

Centre Block, Parliament Buildings was designed by John Pearson and J. Omer Marchand. The Peace Tower was the dominant element on the Ottawa skyline until the mid-1960s.

(Source: Canada. Dept. of Interior, Library and Archives Canada, PA-034205)

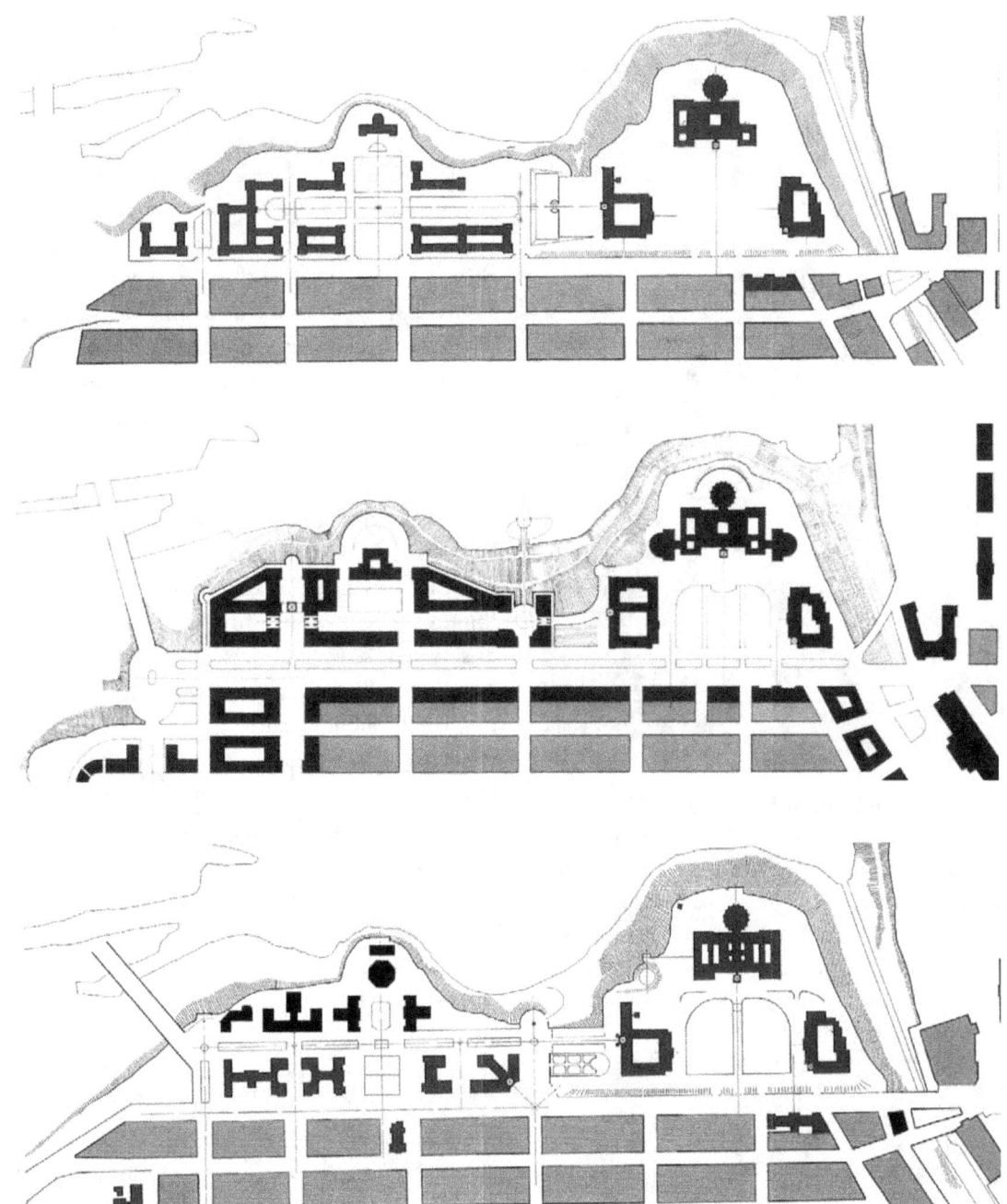

FIGURE 8-4: **Comparison of Todd (1912), Bennett (1915) and Wright and Adams (1920) plans for expanding Parliament Hill**
All three plans extend the axis of Bank Street (middle of site) to the river. Adams (1920, bottom of drawing) incorporates Bennett's proposals for an east-west axis formed upon the Mackenzie Tower of the West Block, and a north-south axis from the Supreme Court site to Wellington Street. Adams' drawing was used to site the Confederation (1928) and Justice (1934) buildings on Wellington Street.
(Source: du Toit Allsopp Hillier, *Parliamentary and Judicial Precincts Area: Site Capacity and Long-Term Development Plan*, (Ottawa, ON: DPW, 2006), p. 114-5)

FIGURE 8-5: Confederation Building, 1928
Confederation Building, Ottawa was designed by the DPW with a roof in the Château style as recommended by Edward Bennett. The building base incorporated some Tudor Gothic details similar to DPW's pre-WWI Sussex Street buildings, but somehow it seems to work, creating a building that is compatible with the adjacent Parliament Buildings.

(Source: Canada. Dept. of Interior, Library and Archives Canada, PA-049843)

Adams, Cauchon and the City Scientific

In the early 20th century, public concerns about the efficient operation of cities were addressed by engineer-planners like Harland Bartholomew and Noulan Cauchon as part of the City Scientific movement.[597] George B. Ford first coined the term at a 1913 conference:

> ... except on the aesthetic side, city planning is rapidly becoming as definite a science as pure engineering ... it is becoming more and more obvious that the best way to secure a city plan which will be lastingly satisfactory from all points of view and really comprehensive is to put the work in charge of several experts – one an engineer, one an architect, and one, perhaps, a social expert.[598]

City Scientific planners and engineers built impressive city-wide infrastructure systems for fresh water, sewerage, electricity, gas, paved streets, railways and electric streetcars. These initiatives improved public health and the quality of life for most urban citizens, giving credibility to the multi-disciplinary teams of planners involved. But their real breakthrough was in devising plans to accommodate the rapid increase in private automobiles in North American cities after the Great War. The newly developed discipline of traffic engineering and the City Scientific movement reshaped North American cities to work with the automobile after 1920.[599]

City Scientific public works projects of the early 20th century might address a variety of objectives simultaneously. For example, the 1912 waterfront plan (Figure 8-6) of the Toronto Harbour Commissioners (THC) not only built a new port, but also installed major sewers, built popular public parks along the western and eastern beaches, and a landscaped boulevard along the entire waterfront.[600]

Cauchon became Thomas Adams' ally in a decade-long effort to establish planning across Canada using methods from the City Scientific, rather than the City Beautiful. Adams was the founding national president of the TPIC in 1919,

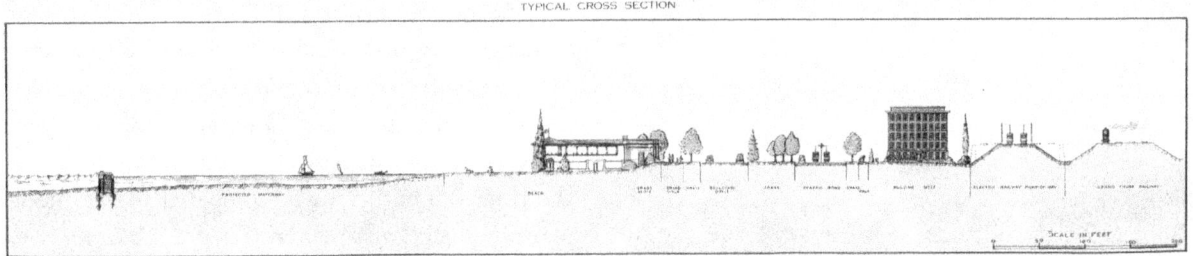

FIGURE 8-6: City Scientific, Toronto waterfront parks plan, Olmsted Associates parks design
(Source: *Journal of the Town Planning Institute of Canada* (JTPIC) Volume 2, November 1922; reproduced with permission. of the Canadian Institute of Planners)

with Cauchon as a national vice president. Their TPIC constitution defined town planning as: "the *scientific* and orderly disposition of land and buildings in use and development with a view to obviating congestion and securing economic and social efficiency, health and well-being in urban and rural communities."

Adams' typical emphasis on "social efficiency, health and well-being" is matched by Cauchon's City Scientific influences in "obviating congestion" and the "scientific and orderly disposition of lands." This definition was placed on the masthead of the *Journal of the TPIC* and guided Canadian planners for much of the first half of the century.[601]

By 1920, increased automobile traffic made a congested mess of the area outside Parliament Hill, making the area a candidate for City Scientific planning. Traffic was always snarled at Connaught Place, the deck between the two bridges connecting Rideau with Wellington and Sparks Street. The addition of the new Union Station and Château Laurier hotel to the existing post office, Russell House Hotel, and City Hall made the congestion worse. Edward Bennett's innovative plan for a central municipal plaza on Elgin Street (Figure 7-10) sat on the shelf with the rest of the FPC report. Ironically, while interfering with the implementation of Bennett's plan, the Great War – together with William Lyon Mackenzie King's imagination – was to be the catalyst for implementing change. King returned to Ottawa as the new leader of the Liberal party in 1919, and became prime minister after the 1921 election.

Meanwhile, Noulan Cauchon had lost any opportunity for consulting contracts with the national government with his intemperate public remarks, so he repositioned himself as an expert on local infrastructure problems, such as Connaught Place, and as a critical commentator on federal planning issues. He promoted his views using access to newspapers and to the *Journal of the Town Planning Institute of Canada*, and his positions as the Chairman of the Ottawa Town Planning Commission (OTPC) and TPIC President.

The Ottawa Town Planning Commission

When the OTPC was established by city council in April 1921, Noulan Cauchon (Figure 8-7) was selected as its founding chairman.[602] During the early 20th century civic reform era, commissions were often established to provide expert advice on important issues, at arm's length from part-time elected city councils. The capital's elites sometimes took a dim view of the business practices of their elected council, an opinion reinforced by the 1913 typhoid epidemic caused by the city's botched implementation of its water supply system.[603] Establishing a planning commission was one method to insulate planning decisions from the rough and tumble world of ward politics. It was also a way to obtain long-term leadership not typically available in municipal government – Ottawa had 19 different mayors from 1900-1935.[604] In contrast, Cauchon served continuously as OTPC chairman for 14 years from its inception.

Unfortunately, the Ontario legislation that empowered municipal planning commissions at the time was rather weak compared to the model planning acts of the day.[605] The *Planning and Development Act, 1917*[606] **permitted** municipalities to establish planning commissions and to adopt general plans and land subdivision controls, but it did not **require** them to do so, or to entrust the council's approval authority to a commission.[607] From the beginning, Cauchon realized that the role of the OTPC would be:

> *a persuasive one – we have to persuade the city council to act upon our recommendations – that these are in the public interest ... I do not feel that one has any moral right to impose even 'improvements' upon the people who pay for them against their will. Safety lies in convincing them.*[608]

In a good start, Ottawa City Council granted the OTPC a modest annual budget of $10,000,[609] which allowed the commission to engage architect John Kitchen and a draftsman to support its activities.

The six original members of the Ottawa Town Planning Commission were clearly drawn from the city's elite. They included Cauchon, W.M. Southam

Figure 8-7: Photo of young Noulan Cauchon
(Source: Library and Archives Canada, PA-177046)

(owner of the *Ottawa Citizen*), H.E. Lemieux (*Le Droit*), Alderman E.D. Lowe, Alderman L.P. Whyte and Charles Hopewell, the former mayor for Ottawa from 1909-1912.[610] Southam's paper published many of Cauchon's planning articles, while Lemieux's paper was the principal French-language daily; Hopewell was also an original member of the Civic Improvement League.

From 1921-34, the OTPC met monthly, producing many planning reports that advocated ideas to improve Ottawa.[611] The commission reported to the city's Board of Control, a group of councillors that was elected city-wide and had primary oversight of the municipality's finances. The requirement for the board's approval often restricted the OTPC to smaller-scale, practical improvements, as opposed to the grand visions that Cauchon advocated as president of the TPIC.[612] The OTPC focused its actions entirely upon City Scientific concerns regarding automobile traffic, parking, infrastructure and zoning.[613] Cauchon began with smaller-scale improvements but soon brought forth a broad range of infrastructure issues for consideration during the OTPC's second year. Early projects focused on making the city's traffic flow function more efficiently, rounding corners to eliminate hazardous intersections resulting from the collisions of the grids of many unplanned subdivisions (Figure 8-8).

At first, the OTPC received favourable reviews. In 1922, Mayor Plant stated:

Cauchon had already done more for Ottawa than most people realized and he had done what money could not buy. He had drawn up plans which would not cost much money to execute and would ... make the Capital city a better place in which to live.[614]

The Mayor's speech also acknowledged that council had made planning mistakes in the past, but the current situation of having the OTPC as an advisor made council "entirely sympathetic with the work of town planning."[615] Cauchon would receive a lot of sympathy for the OTPC, but not much else.

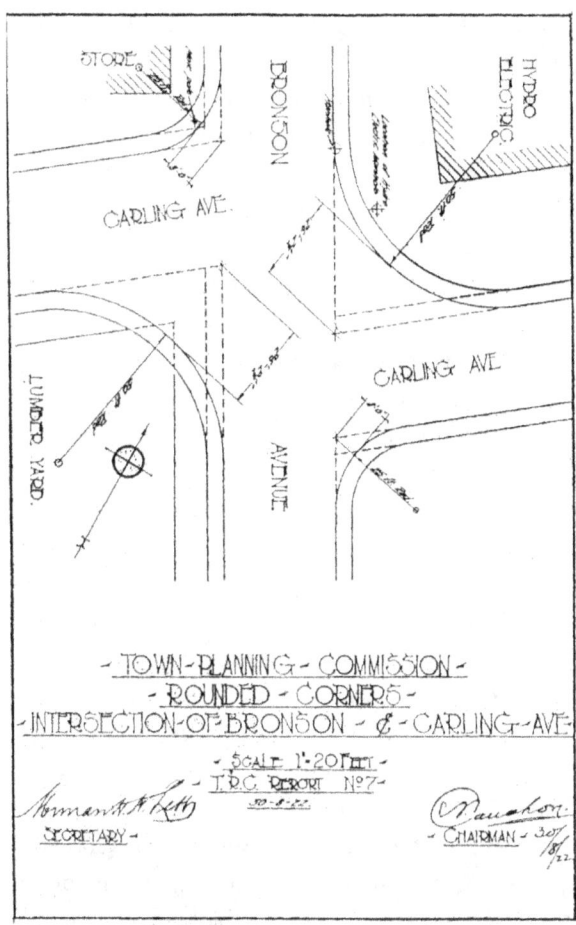

FIGURE 8-8: Corner rounding in the City Scientific manner, Bronson and Carling avenues, 1922

(Source: OTPC Report No. 7, August 30, 1922, Library and Archives Canada, MG30 C-105, Vol. 4)

Preparation of a general plan was conspicuously absent from the OTPC's list of activities. The Federal Plan Commission had recently prepared a comprehensive plan at considerable expense and the document still sat on the shelf. Bennett's plan was largely ignored by the OTPC and the federal government also paid it little attention until the Confederation Square project began in the late 1920s. Although another comprehensive plan was probably premature, the OTPC did consider comprehensive zoning as a technique to deal with Ottawa's haphazard mix of residential areas with stores, factories and garages. By 1922, the OTPC reported that:

> ... *zoning powers should be more explicit and positive, not negative as at present, and the provisions governing them should be coordinated to facilitate application and advantage being taken of same. The zoning powers should be such that a Plan Commission could determine what and where structures and activities be allowed and placed.*[616]

City council adopted the OTPC's initial recommendations and agreed to retain Cauchon as a consultant who would direct the preparation of a comprehensive zoning plan.[617] Cauchon toured the city, speaking frequently on the health, financial and economic benefits of zoning.[618] OTPC staff prepared 59 area zoning plans which covered most of the city, using a symbolic code that Cauchon promoted as a standard for the country.[619]

In February 1926, after three years of preparation and substantial local press coverage,[620] the commission submitted a comprehensive zoning bylaw for the City of Ottawa for Council's approval. Cauchon's introduction stated that zoning is primarily based upon the biological demands for an environment that will maintain health and efficiency.[621] Council seemed favourable at first,[622] but its public meetings attracted fierce opposition from private property owners.

The principal attack came from real estate developers, sales agents and some homeowners, represented by the Ottawa Property Holders Association. Landowners were opposed to most limitations that might affect the development of their property and publicized that the bylaw created over 90 new offences that could be punished by fines or prison.[623] As the rhetoric heated up, the forceful Cauchon adopted a lower profile in the public debate; his assistant, John Kitchen, negotiated with the OPHA and Ottawa Real Estate Board.[624] Kitchen made some progress with the Real Estate Board, negotiating agreement on light and air provisions,[625] but the property industry remained divided and city council stalled.

Ontario's weak planning legislation did not help the matter, since the 1917 act did not enable zoning bylaws. The City of Kitchener had received special provincial legislation to adopt a zoning bylaw prepared by Thomas Adams' assistant, Horace Seymour.[626] But Kitchener's experience was not easy and the adjacent City of Waterloo also had a difficult time with zoning.[627] Faced with political opposition and uncertain implementation, Ottawa City Council left its draft zoning bylaw to sit on the shelf.[628] Cauchon was bitterly disappointed, attacking his opponents during his retiring speech as TPIC President in 1926:

> ... *while it may involve in some cases a little sacrifice of anti-social liberty, it protects the most anti-social libertarian from the depredations of his neighbors. We cannot go on forever destroying life and building values because of a few thoughtless or predatory individuals wish to do as they like with the face of the earth for their own profit and without regard to the welfare and convenience of their neighbours.*[629]

Cauchon might have felt even worse if he had known that Ottawa's comprehensive zoning bylaw would not be finally approved until 1965, almost three decades later.

The failure to implement the zoning bylaw was disappointing, but Cauchon should have been on stronger technical ground with railway relocation schemes. There was no doubt that Ottawa's badly sited cross-town railway tracks were a major problem, as identified in Edward Bennett's plan.[630] Following a suggestion first made by Cauchon in 1912,[631] the OTPC recommended that the cross-town tracks be relocated south of the built-up area, and the resulting corridor used for a through traffic road. Despite the Commission's detailed reports indicating the financial benefits of the removal scheme,[632] council took no action on the proposals. A 1924 scheme to connect the city's two railway stations with a tunnel under Wellington Street also stalled.[633] These last plans required the co-operation of two competing railways and the local government. All three actors involved looked to the federal government for a substantial investment to solve the problem, but the national government's priorities were elsewhere.

Designing the Town-Crown Edge

Cauchon prepared three schemes for new public spaces near Parliament while he was chairman of the OTPC. The first and most ambitious was Vimy Way, named after the famous victory of the Canadian Corps in the Great War (Figure 8-9). The plan featured a riverside parkway cut into the cliff behind Parliament Hill, and a second bridge across the Rideau Canal to connect a street to the front of the Parliament Buildings. The eastern terminus of the parkway was a proposed traffic circle named Courcelette Place, after another World War I battle.[634] In the adjacent park, Cauchon proposed to erect statues to Lt. Col. John By and the Governor General Lord Byng, former commander of the Canadian Corps.[635]

Despite its patriotic wrapping as a war memorial and a hint of City Beautiful place-making, the Vimy Way plan was essentially a local traffic distribution scheme designed to unclog automobile congestion in the Ottawa downtown. The federal government declined to support the project, voicing strong concerns about local traffic running so close to both sides of the Parliament Buildings.[636] The Vimy Way proposal was never implemented,[637] but Cauchon's proposal to enlarge Connaught Place by demolishing the three small blocks east of Elgin Street was the beginning of Confederation Square.

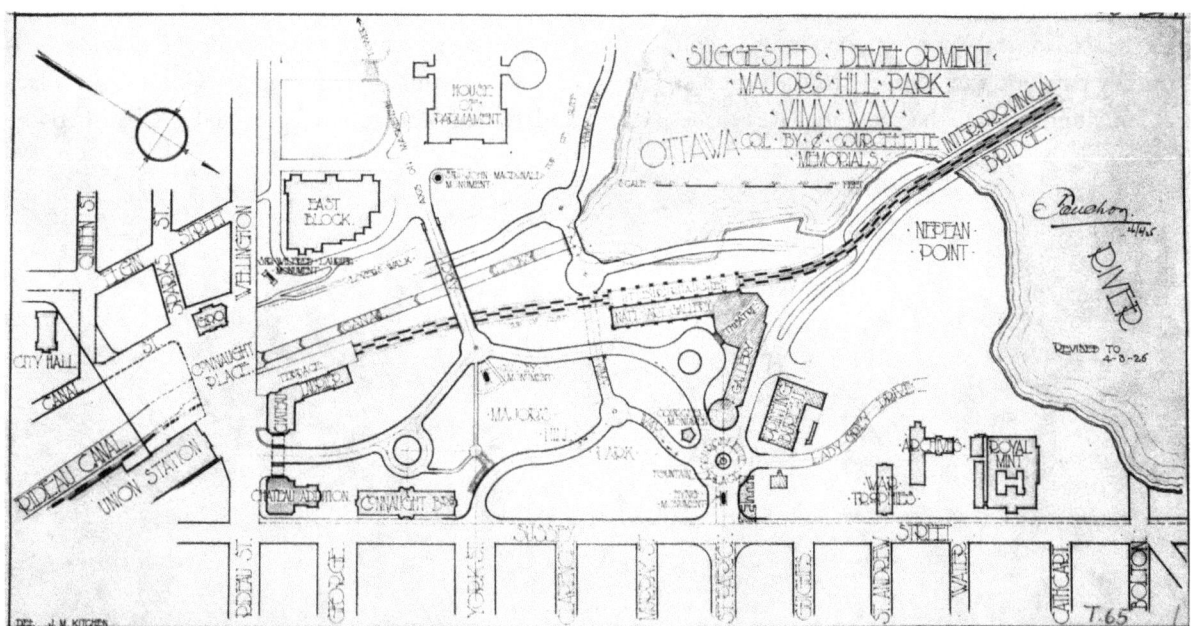

FIGURE 8-9: Vimy Way proposal, OTPC, 1925
Vimy Way was to be a riverside parkway cut into the cliff behind the Parliament Buildings (top of drawing). Note the proposal for a bridge across the canal locks to create a new road between the East and Centre Blocks of Parliament.
(Source: Library and Archives Canada, detail from image NMC 15774; drawing by J.M. Kitchen)

National War Memorial

Prime Minister Mackenzie King had his own plans for a national war memorial in Ottawa. But first, there was the need to decide on the appropriate means of commemorating Canada's wartime role in the nation's capital. Some local citizens preferred the utilitarian to the symbolic and favoured buildings like community centres. Thus, an initial plan in 1919 called for the construction in Ottawa of a Memorial Hall intended to hold some 2,000-4,000 persons. A select committee that included Thomas Adams and Noulan Cauchon recommended the FPC plan be ignored, and the auditorium be built on Elgin Street beside City Hall.[638] At the national level, the focus was on memorials whose size and allegorical form communicated the power and sense of the common purpose of a united Canadian people. Indeed, there were two such structures: one at Vimy Ridge in France and the proposed National War Memorial in Ottawa. For Vimy, a patriotic gaze that looked back to France and the site and events of that nation-forming battle dictated the location.[639] For the National War Memorial in the capital, a similarly patriotic view influenced the proposed site at Connaught Place. The memorial was to be part of a concerted effort to enhance Ottawa's image as a truly national capitol complex.

This was quite evident in the terms of reference for the "National Commemorative War Monument" released by the Minister of Public Works in February 1925.[640] The design competition was open to architects, artists, and sculptors who were British subjects or citizens of her Allies during the Great War. The government provided a budget of $100,000 as well as explicit directions on the spirit and purpose of this important project. The memorial was to be "expressive of the feelings of the Canadian people as a whole, to the memory of those who participated in the Great War and lost their lives in the service of humanity." There was no question about "the most appropriate centre in the Capital" for the monument:

> *The location on Connaught Place, between the Château Laurier, Post Office and Central Station would seem to be the most suitable, and the monument could take the form of a column or other design which might be considered most appropriate for this location.*

An accompanying map of Connaught Place and five photographs (Figure 8-10) identified the

FIGURE 8-10: War Memorial Location, 1925
This photograph was included in the instructions for the international design competition for Canada's war memorial. The site on Connaught Place was personally selected by Prime Minister Mackenzie King.
(Source: Department of Public Works, 1925, Figure 2)

favoured site on the widened bridge-deck, just above the edge of the Rideau Canal. This was the site that Prime Minister Mackenzie King had insisted on a month before the announcement of the terms of reference.[641]

A Federal District Commission if necessary, (but not necessarily a Federal District ...)

The proposals to create a federal district in the Ottawa area, similar to Washington, also caught Cauchon's attention at an early stage.[642] The idea gained credibility after a successful 1912 referendum in Ottawa and becoming the lead recommendation in the 1916 *Federal Plan Commission Report*.[643] Cauchon championed a federal district for Ottawa and Hull for over a decade, featuring it in a 1919 speech to the American City Planning Institute and articles in the *Journal of the Town Planning Institute of Canada*.[644] His most visionary federal district scheme was to relocate the seat of government to the Gatineau Hills, to create, Canberra-like:

> ... a city of 'straight streets, with avenues of trees already grown and boulevards already sodded.' There would be no Bank streets and Sparks streets up there, only magnificent buildings, trod by happy children and noble men and women, 'planned by government town planners,' who would put all their genius into 'making the new city the most beautiful city in the world.'[645]

But despite Cauchon's ethnic background, he seemed blind to the serious concerns of French-speaking Canadians in the region. Québec politicians were not willing to forsake the protection that the culture and language afforded by their local and provincial government. Mackenzie King, ever the policy wonk, also liked the federal district idea, but his political antennae were more finely-tuned to the objections, so he moved cautiously. In 1927, Mackenzie King renamed Laurier's Ottawa Improvement Commission as the Federal District Commission (FDC), expanded its budget and mandate, and installed the dynamic Ottawa businessman Thomas Ahern (Figure 8-11) as its chairman. But he did not create a new political entity similar to the District of Columbia or the Australian Capital Territory.

Although Ahern was 72 at the time of his appointment, the new FDC chairman increased the pace of improvements to Ottawa.[646] The electric utilities tycoon immediately started pushing for a new parkway through Ottawa and Nepean's western suburbs and the completion of the Champlain Bridge to Aylmer. When the project stalled because of property acquisition problems, Ahern bought the necessary lands for the bridge approaches

FIGURE 8-11: Thomas Ahearn

Thomas Ahearn was the local electrical entrepreneur who Mackenzie King appointed to lead the new Federal District Commission (see Cast of Characters).

(Source: W. J. Topley photograph detail, 1903; Library and Archives Canada PA-012222)

himself. Island Park Drive and the Champlain Bridge opened in late 1928. Not surprisingly, they were attractively decorated with the latest electric lights.[647]

The mood in Parliament was expansive in the late 1920s, since the economy was in good shape and federal expenditures on reconstruction of the Parliament Buildings ended with the completion of the Peace Tower. The federal government could finally consider other plans to improve the capital – and even the Leader of the Opposition suggested that the FDC's funding was perhaps too little![648] Perhaps 1927 was a particularly good year for advancing plans to enhance the nation's capital, since the country was also in a patriotic mood as a result of the Diamond Jubilee celebration of Confederation. The festivities on July 1, 1927 (Figure 8-12) were impressive and inclusive: laying of a corner-stone of the new Confederation Block on Parliament Hill; dedication of the Peace Tower carillon; planting of a maple tree by the wife of the Governor General, Viscountess Willingdon; a live nation-wide radio broadcast of a speech prepared by King George V and delivered by the Governor General; and commemoration of former Prime Minister Sir Wilfrid Laurier in a ceremony at his

FIGURE 8-12: William Lyon Mackenzie King, 1927
Prime Minister Mackenzie King presides over the celebration of the Diamond Jubilee of Confederation in 1927 from the re-built Parliament Buildings. Ottawa electrical engineer and FDC Chairman Thomas Ahearn built a cross-Canada radio network to transmit King's speech.
(Source: Library and Archives Canada, PA-027622)

tomb in the Notre Dame cemetery.[649] In August, the Prince of Wales unveiled a statue honouring Laurier, Mackenzie King's mentor, at the southeast corner of the Hill that overlooked Connaught Place, King's imagined focal-point of the emerging nation-state.[650] These 1927 events did much to reinforce the commemorative and performance functions of Parliament Hill and, to a degree, they also reinforced Mackenzie King's other initiatives in downtown Ottawa.

The new Peace Tower was even more prominent on Parliament Hill than the Victoria Tower that it had replaced (Figure 8-3). In the 1915 Federal Plan Commission report, Edward Bennett regretted that the older tower was not on axis with Metcalfe Street. Prime Minister King was thoroughly familiar with Bennett's ideas,[651] and began to consider concepts that would improve the view of the new tower from downtown. King had his staff investigate the cost and feasibility of widening Metcalfe Street. The US consulate was also interested in the proposal, which might have increased the prominence of its new embassy building on Wellington Street near Metcalfe. Members of King's staff were quite negative on the idea, citing the cost of acquiring the properties and the historic buildings involved.[652] The Metcalfe Street widening was quietly dropped, although it would emerge again in the future.

Meanwhile, King maintained the momentum to create a grand plaza at Connaught Place. When the abandoned Russell House Hotel burned down in a suspicious fire late in 1927, the prime minister blocked the owner's proposal to rebuild and expropriated the entire block. Holding aloft Bennett's 1915 plan in the House of Commons as he introduced the legislation, he proposed a $3 million fund to transform Connaught Place into a grand "Confederation Square."[653] Although the opposition parties now protested such a large expenditure on dreary Ottawa, King drove the bill through, delivering what he regarded as one of his finest speeches to the Commons:

... We may not come to have the largest, the wealthiest or the most cosmopolitan Capital in the world, but I believe that with Ottawa's natural and picturesque setting, given stately proportions, and a little careful planning, we can have the most beautiful Capital in the world. So I would ask my fellow members of this House of Commons to view not only with sympathy but with enthusiasm a project which everyone will recognize as beyond the consideration of party, that has for its object solely and wholly the development and beautification of Ottawa as the Capital of this great Dominion, something that will give some expression of all that is highest in the idealism of the nation and something which those from beyond our gates and those who may follow in future years will come to recognize as an expression in some degree of the soul of Canada today.[654]

Mackenzie King knew that he had made an impression. His diary for that day recorded his assessment of his rhetorical powers, political astuteness, and vision:

Spoke for an hour in all, and with little effort and I believe on the whole to good effect ... I did not meet with an interruption and held the attention of the House fairly well ... There is now 3 millions, a large sum, which should mean real and vast improvements within the next two years – a quite different Ottawa in the heart of the city. It is really a great achievement, and future generations will thank me for it.[655]

With Parliament on side, King's next steps were to acquire land from the local government and commission an appropriate design for the new square.

Town Lands for Crown Designs

The prime minister pressured the Ottawa City Council to expand the proposed Confederation Square site by demolishing its existing City Hall and police station, and expropriating buildings on the east side of Elgin Street to create a wide boulevard to the south.[656] The mayor and council reluctantly agreed to relocate City Hall in the future, perhaps lured by Edward Bennett's 1915 image of a magnificent new City Hall dominating the new plaza (Figure 7-11).[657] Whatever the reasons, city council's agreement marked the beginning of 20 years of high-handed treatment of the local government by a federal government determined to remake the historic core of the city in its own image.[658]

Even with money and backing in hand, Mackenzie King was unable to find a design that was both functional and monumental enough for his taste. The FDC had few professional staff and limited consulting planners or landscape architects on call. The architects and engineers in Public Works had constructed many handsome federal buildings, but had little experience with large-scale urban design and reconstruction of the type seen in some American and European cities.[659] Toronto architect Henry Sproatt, a member of the War Memorial jury, advised King that Cauchon's OTPC plan for the Confederation Square seemed to be the best of a bad lot (Figure 8-13).[660]

However, Cauchon's constant criticism of the FDC as chairman of the City of Ottawa's Town

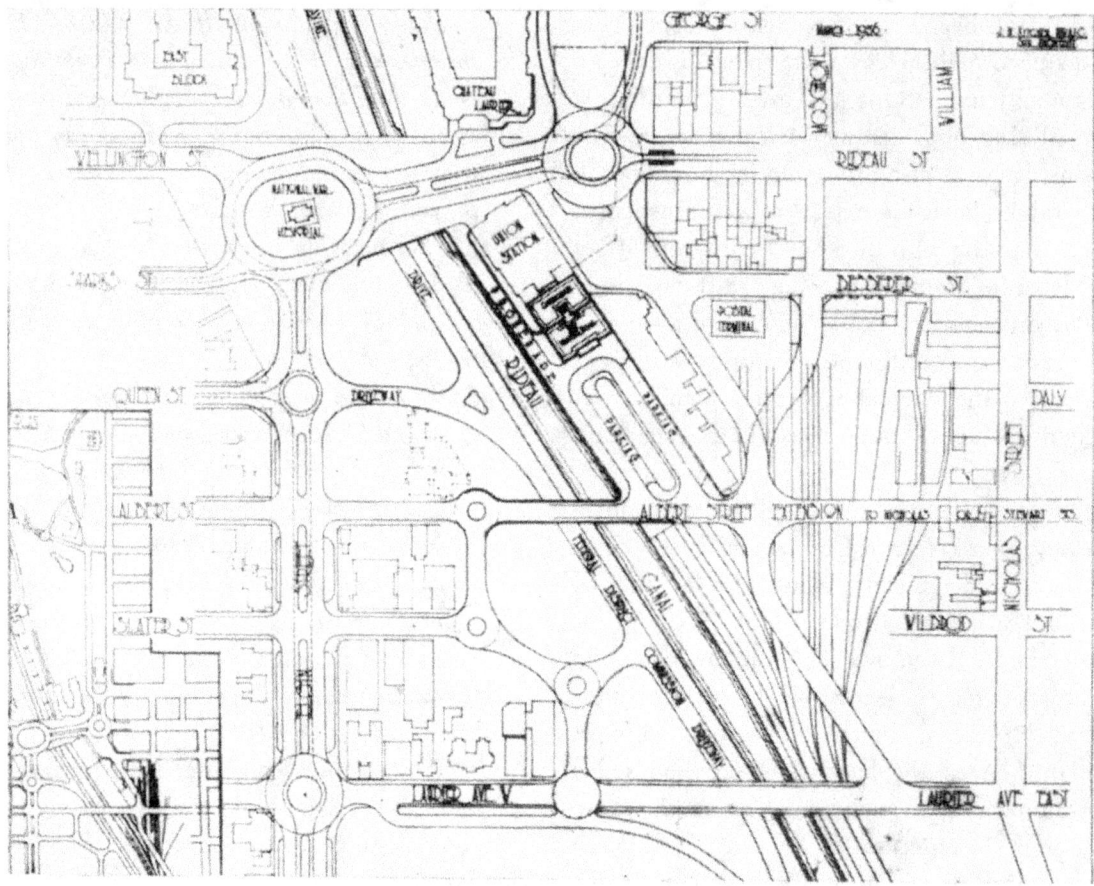

Figure 8-13: Cauchon's 1928 OTPC plan for Confederation Square
The plan was filled with City Scientific ideas such as placing the war memorial in the centre of a traffic roundabout.
(Source: Gréber 1950, p. 185)

Planning Commission annoyed King. Then Cauchon prepared a plan to create a parking lot at Connaught Place, on the very site that the Prime Minister had designated for the War Memorial (Figure 8-14). The OTPC built the scheme, garnering compliments from local newspapers about how it improved traffic flow and parking in the area.[661] This conflict was the sort of dispute that led Mackenzie King to refer to Cauchon as "too local in his outlook, had not the vision for the large expanse."[662]

During the first half of the 20th century, Canada probably lacked urban designers with high-level professional skills to unravel the complicated knot of infrastructure at Confederation Square. The decision to connect Sparks and Rideau streets by Sappers' Bridge still haunted the city a century later. Six streetcar lines, two bridges, several streets, a railway and a canal all collide within the space of two blocks. Mackenzie King's requirement that the National War Memorial be dropped into the node defeated the local designers. The architects could not make the infrastructure work and the engineers could not produce a dignified space for the memorial.

With design issues at an impasse, the *real politik* of electoral politics intervened to put the project on hold: Mackenzie King lost the national election of 1930 as the Great Depression gripped the country. In a series of wrong-headed decisions, new Conservative Prime Minister R.B. Bennett slashed the FDC's infrastructure budget, reduced its payroll and replaced Ahearn as chairman. The Federal District Commission did not recover until after World War II.[663] The capital building would have to wait.

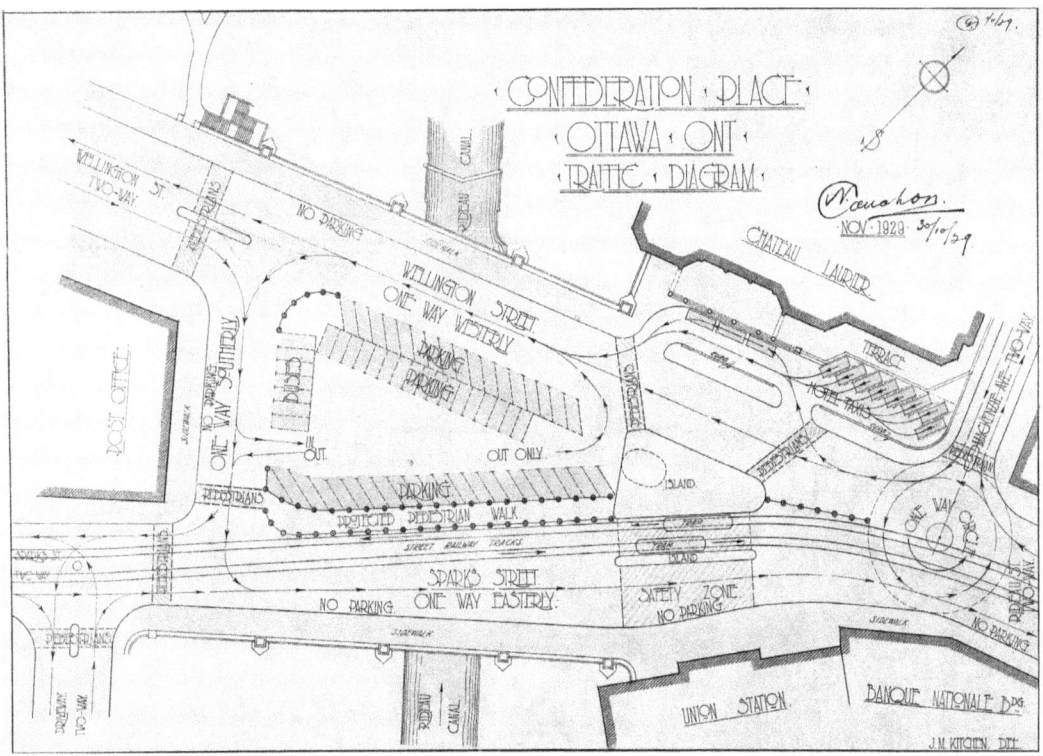

Figure 8-14: Ottawa Town Planning Commission's parking plan for Connaught Place
This was the proposed location of the National War Memorial commissioned by the federal government in an international design competition.
(Source: Library and Archives Canada, NMC 22631; drawing by J.M. Kitchen)

Reflections

'Town-Crown' conflicts became more intense in the 1920s as the City of Ottawa acquired its own voice in planning issues through the OTPC. Cauchon's commission focused on local issues with a practical approach derived from his engineering background and City Scientific sensibility. In contrast, the federal government focused on national objectives and symbolic content, informed by a City Beautiful approach. The dispute over the design of Connaught Place/Confederation Square was a classic 'Town-Crown' conflict, with the municipal government advocating a parking lot that would provide immediate relief for a small local problem while the federal government had symbolic objectives for a large national issue – commemorating the sacrifices of thousands of Canadian citizens in a world war. Planning and development had become so complicated in Ottawa that the Crown would no longer simply impose its will on an issue of national importance, even with ample funding and the direct personal leadership of the prime minister. It would take another decade before the federal government would complete its plans for a National War Memorial.

CHAPTER 9

Depression and the Wartime Capital (1930-1944)

... No form of a memorial could be more worthy of the service and sacrifice given in the war than to give the Capital of our country as worthy a place amongst the national capitals of the world as Canada occupies amongst the nations as a nation.[664]
– Prime Minister W.L. Mackenzie King

The worldwide depression hit the local governments particularly hard, since they relied so extensively on property taxes. In 1929, Nepean Township had finally started construction on the water and sewer line for the Westboro area, which had been desperately needed for over a decade. The Depression collapsed the township's revenues as people defaulted on their taxes, and the township could not sell its infrastructure bonds. Nepean acquired many vacant lots among the sparsely populated subdivisions from the pre-1914 real estate speculations, but the abandoned lots could not be sold at any price. The township government teetered on the brink of bankruptcy in 1936[665] and the experience so traumatized the rural councillors that they refused to consider debt financing for infrastructure in the decades that followed.

Poverty and hard times were so severe in the Outaouais that landowners and other citizens began to cut the trees on the hills beyond Hull for firewood. Mackenzie King, now in Opposition, helped establish a lobby group, the Federal Woodlands Preservation League, to oppose the destruction of the forests.[666] He used his political position to push the issue in the House of Commons and obtain national publicity on the issue:

I think hon. Members would be horrified if they could see what has happened within the last two years within a radius of ten or fifteen miles of the city of Ottawa. Whole hillsides which face the approaches to Ottawa from other parts of the country have been completely denuded of their trees. There have been left devastated areas which are nothing else but barren rocks and eroded soil. In some cases cut slash has been left on the roadside to the extent that it presents a serious fire hazard. Streams and springs are drying up, and the wild life of woods and waters disappearing... Anyone who takes a trip up the Gatineau will be horrified at the extent of the destruction which has occurred. A very fine scenic route from Montréal via Mont Laurier to Ottawa has in its near approaches to the capital been absolutely destroyed.[667]

The League was rewarded with positive publicity and a federal government report which recommended the purchase of 2,000 acres immediately.[668] King was prime minister again by the time the report was published, with a reforestation plank in his election platform.⁶⁶⁹ The prime minister smoothed the way for the Federal District Commission (FDC) to take action in Québec, and Parliament authorized construction of a national parkway in the Gatineau. The FDC purchased over 6,500 hectares (16,000 acres) by 1939.⁶⁷⁰ The Federal District Commission also acquired land to expand Jacques Cartier Park along the Ottawa River, but there were no grand federal public works projects in Hull. The up-river logging camps closed and the mills cut back their hours.⁶⁷¹

The FDC's efforts in the Gatineau Hills during the 1930s were a good start, but Todd's idea of a wilderness park was expanded even further in the 1950 plan for the capital.⁶⁷² King often invited Gréber to stay in Gatineau Park at Kingsmere, his private retreat. The park became a great green wedge of over 35,000 hectares, bringing the wilderness to within a couple of kilometres of Parliament.

In Ottawa, all non-federal building construction collapsed.⁶⁷³ City council was not interested in urban planning if no urban development was occurring, and cut the budget of the Ottawa Town Planning Commission in 1932.

Noulan Cauchon and his committee soldiered on, meeting irregularly on a voluntary basis, but council was not listening. To make matters worse, all of the OTPC's drawings and files were destroyed in a fire at Ottawa City Hall.⁶⁷⁴ When Cauchon died in October 1935, the Canadian planning movement was in dire straits, due to the impact of the economic depression. The Town Planning Institute of Canada (TPIC) had flourished in the 1920s, even after it lost financial support and Adams' leadership on the closure of the Commission on Conservation in 1923. Unfortunately, the Depression destroyed the Institute's membership revenue; national conferences ended in 1930; the Institute's journal ceased publication in 1931, and the organization folded in 1932.⁶⁷⁵ Local interest in urban planning collapsed without the leadership of Thomas Adams, Cauchon and the TPIC office. It would not revive until the 1950s.

Connaught Place becomes Confederation Square

Although Mackenzie King lost the 1930 election, he urged his successor, Prime Minister R.B. Bennett, to prevent the City of Ottawa from wriggling out of its agreement on Confederation Square.⁶⁷⁶ Once again, fire came to Mackenzie King's aid. In March 1931, the Ottawa City Hall burned and the cash-strapped municipality negotiated with the federal government to obtain accommodation.⁶⁷⁷ The city was offered 'temporary quarters' in a nearby federal building and was housed there for the next 20 years, while debate raged within council about the site of the new city hall. The site for Confederation Square was not clear, but all progress in developing the grandiose project ground to a halt in the face of the grim economic realities of the Depression years, which generated vacant lots rather than grand architectural or monumental designs.

The federal Department of Public Works continued to build in Ottawa, even as the rest of the country slipped into depression. The momentum of the late 1920s federal building boom carried several projects through into the early 1930s, including the completion of the Confederation Building (1928-31) on Parliament Hill and the classically designed National Research Council building overlooking the Ottawa River on Sussex Drive. But most projects were cancelled in 1932, as R.B. Bennett's Conservative government slashed government capital expenditures, reduced relief programs, and raised taxes in a misguided attempt to balance the budget as the economy declined. These disastrous policies made Canadian conditions worse, but fortunately Franklin D. Roosevelt's economic recovery program using public works was clear by 1933. Canada's 1934 *Public Works Construction Act* launched the construction of new federal buildings across the country.⁶⁷⁸ In Ottawa, the DPW designed and built the Justice Building (1934-37) in the Château style similar to its neighbour on Wellington Street. Although the style of the Confederation Building had been greeted with howls of criticism in the late 1920s from the architectural community (which supported a modern classicism),[679] the Justice Building appears to have been erected without controversy. Any work was welcome in 1935.

With Mackenzie King's return to power in 1935 and the faint promise of a more prosperous economy, he dusted off his plans for Confederation Square. But before this, he had to face the embarrassment of delays in the erection of the National War Memorial on what was formerly Connaught Place.[680] An English sculptor, Vernon March, had won the design competition in 1926, but died in 1930. His six brothers and a sister completed the memorial in 1932. Their task finished, they were disappointed to find that Canada and Ottawa were not ready for the memorial. It was put on temporary display in London's Hyde Park, where it was met with general public acclaim.[681] The planning disaster continued when it was found that the deck of Connaught Place was not strong enough to hold the memorial. The sculpture was placed into storage in England, pending resolution of the Confederation Square design.

While the appreciation of Londoners might have been satisfying, Canadians and Ottawans must have questioned when their memorial would be brought to Canada. The problem was that the prime minister was still determined that it ought to be the centrepiece for the proposed Confederation Square, citing as precedents the Nelson monument in London's Trafalgar Square and the Arc de Triomphe in Paris.[682] His war memorial was ready; all that was missing was an appropriate urban design.

Mackenzie King found the designer he needed while he was on a 1936 tour of the Paris World's Fair site. Mackenzie King requested a tour of the site for the Canadian Pavilion. The director was not available on short notice, so the chief architect, Jacques Gréber (Figure 9-1), escorted the Prime Minister. The two

FIGURE 9-1: Jacques Gréber at Kingsmere during a visit with Mackenzie King, ca. 1948
Jacques Gréber was one of France's leading urbanists, completing important commissions in architecture, urban design, landscape architecture and urban planning. After graduation from the École des Beaux Arts, he worked in Philadelphia, beginning a lifetime of trans-Atlantic projects that included plans for Montréal and Québec as well as many projects in Canada's capital (see his biography in Cast of Characters).

King often invited Gréber to stay at Kingsmere. Gréber was a talented landscape designer in the classical style, and advised King in the layout of the more formal parts of the grounds of his cottage estate, including the design of the balustrade upon which he rests in this image.
(Source: Canada. National Capital Commission; Library and Archives Canada, PA-203045. © National Capital Commission; Reproduced with the permission of the National Capital Commission)

men connected on a personal level immediately. King re-arranged his schedule to interview Gréber the next day and invited him to come to Canada to prepare plans for Ottawa's core.[683]

During his 1937 Ottawa visit, Gréber quickly produced a series of designs for Ottawa's core that resolved many issues. He combined Bennett's formal building compositions with the basic elements of Cauchon's circulation plan.[684] Despite this propitious start, Gréber ran afoul of Mackenzie King when he suggested that the traffic congestion in the square was so severe that the adjacent Major's Hill Park on Nepean Point would be a better location for the war memorial (Figure 9-2). King forcefully over-ruled the architect, a somewhat predictable outcome given his last decade of planning. A chastened Gréber returned to his hotel room to try another design:

I was almost fired. The monument should not be in the centre of turmoil; it should be in a quiet, calm and restful place. Nepean Point would have been much better, you see. So I made a sketch and showed it to Mr. King. He said that it is beautiful, but it is too late. The government and parliament have decided that the monument will be there, so it will be there. I didn't want to be fired, you know, so I obeyed.[685]

All was forgiven when King saw the next sketch, which set the memorial at the centre of the square (Figure 9-3). The prime minister gushed:

The moment I saw the Monument at the head of Elgin St. – on an elevation, which could be seen from the new Knox Church, and facing down the grand avenue, I at

FIGURE 9-2: Proposal to locate the War Memorial in Major's Hill Park
Gréber suggested a peaceful site in Major's Hill Park, but the prime minister wanted a highly visible monument in Confederation Square.
(Source: 1950 Gréber Plan, plate 115)

once saw that I had my Champs Élysées, Arc de Triomphe and Place de la Concorde all at a single stroke. As I pointed out to Gréber it made a magnificent approach to the parliament buildings, if regiments were parading from Cartier Sq. they wd. be thrilled beyond measure, marching towards the face of the Monument & past it on one side to the Prlt. Bldgs. or on the other to the City in an opposite direction.[686]

This time there was no hesitation. Gréber's revised design for Confederation Square was quickly built, in readiness for the approaching Royal visit of 1939. In a matter of months, the central post office was demolished, and then rebuilt to face the new square. The city widened Elgin Street into a grand boulevard and removed its streetcars, replacing them with buses at federal expense. Finally, the War Memorial was safely installed on solid ground in the centre of Gréber's triangular plaza.

The prime minister also micro-managed the other federal building projects in the late 1930s. King personally intervened on Ernest Cormier's

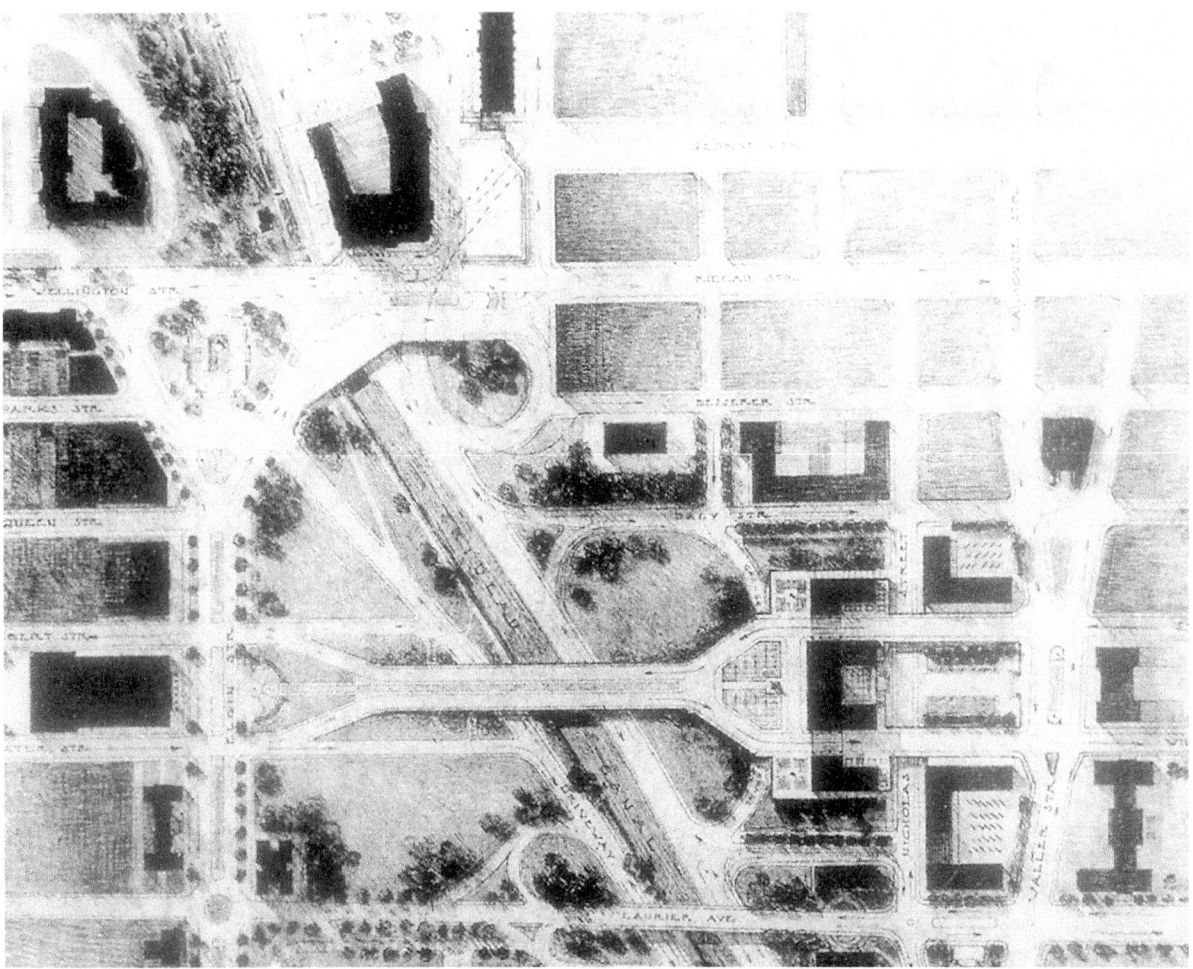

FIGURE 9-3: Plan for Confederation Square and War Memorial
This 1949 sketch shows Confederation Square, the War Memorial, and Elgin Street as built. The Mackenzie King Bridge (centre) was built in the 1950s.
(Source: 1950 Gréber Plan, plate 156)

design for the Canadian Supreme Court, insisting that its flat roof be replaced by one done in the Château style recommended by Bennett (Figure 7-11):

> *After the opening proceedings, spent three-quarters of an hour with Mr. Cormier, the Architect of the new Supreme Court building, and Mr. Cardin. I was distinctly disappointed with the plan of the building. Far too much of the modern note about it. I told the architect plainly that parts of the exterior looked more like a factory than a Court, and that the interior stair-case looked like so many boxes piled up instead of an ornamental and dignified entrance to the Court Chambers. The whole modern trend is copied from Moscow, and is an endeavour to regiment buildings as people are regimented. There is a monotonous uniformity of style about them all. I said a Supreme Court building should stand for dignity, strength, fine proportions and be classical of the best period.*[687]

The new Supreme Court and Post Office show Gréber's moderating influence on King's conservative architectural tastes. Both buildings were originally designed in the modern classical style, with flat roofs. Although King got his steeply pitched copper roofs, the architects were able to preserve most of their modern, stripped classical detailing below, which reflected Gréber's direction. Cormier, a skilled designer, was able to make the roof appear to be clearly separate from his more Modern composition (Figure 9-4).

Figure 9-4: Supreme Court of Canada
Clever detailing by architect Ernest Cormier made Mackenzie King's steeply pitched copper roof float above the masonry.
(Source: Library and Archives Canada, PA-134972)

A Royal Opening for King's Square

On May 21, 1939, over 100,000 people packed Confederation Square for the dedication of the National War Memorial by King George VI and Queen Elizabeth[688] (Figure 9-5). Mackenzie King wrote the King's speech. Once again, his diary affords remarkable insights into his personal views about what he clearly considered to be 'his' monument.[689] Moreover, he referred time and again to the "Sir Galahad" monument erected in 1905 to commemorate the heroic death of his friend, Henry Harper (Figure 6-4). He compared "this War Memorial which is the largest monument in the Capital, the most significant in Canada," to that of Galahad, "the first in the way of an idealist monument to find its place in the Capital." He also turned to the book he had written on the occasion of Harper's death – *The Secret of Heroism* – concluding that the similarity between the national wartime sacrifice and that of Harper's heroic deed was such that the National War Memorial might well be entitled, "The Secret of National Heroism."[690] And given these personal associations, it is not surprising that he was convinced of the correctness of his past decisions:

> What is particularly interesting is that I had to do, at the outset, with the character of the Memorial, its location, the competition by which the choice was made, with increase in its size, and have had everything to do of late with determining its approaches, surroundings, etc. I had thought, at one time, that I might have occasion to prepare a speech to deliver myself, if when the time of the unveiling came, I should then be in office. Little did I dream that the speech which I would write would be one for the King himself to deliver. That, too, came as it were a part of a plan …

Predictably, the speech that the prime minister drafted for King George VI at the unveiling echoed many of the Mackenzie King's private thoughts, addressing the symbolism of the monument for the nation.[691] The monarch's speech touched on all of prime minister's ideological and emotional prompts. He referred to "this beautiful Capital" and "the noble Memorial to Canada's spirit and sacrifice in the Great War"; he acknowledged the "symbolism" evoked by "The Response" of "zeal … chivalry … the voice of the nation's conscience … the very soul of the nation." But as Mackenzie King had suggested, King George alluded to the monument's educational role for the nation:

> … This Memorial, however, does more than commemorate a great event in the past. It has a message for all generations and for all countries – the message which called forth Canada's response. Not by chance do the figures of Peace and Freedom, which crown its summit, stand inseparable. Peace and Freedom cannot long be separated. It is well that we have, in one of the Capitals of the world, a visible reminder of so great a truth.

The timing couldn't have been better. A mere three months later, Canada entered the Second World War, the patriotic fervour of the Royal Visit having helped swell the volunteer ranks of the Canadian armed forces.

The 1939 Gréber Downtown Plan

Mackenzie King encouraged Gréber to expand his studies to include most of downtown Ottawa.[692] Gréber extended the Confederation Square designs to include a new city hall and complex multi-modal transportation terminal, adding automobile circulation to Bennett's 1915 scheme. Gréber's model shows the railway passenger station retained but the freight yards adjacent to the canal removed (Figure 9-6). This design was perhaps the best proposal to rebuild the Ottawa downtown, while keeping the railway passenger station as close to Parliament Hill as possible.

The 1939 plan also provided a new site for Ottawa City Hall, in a public square at Wellington and Lyon Streets, opposite the new Supreme Court. This was the original Upper Town market location provided by Nicholas Sparks and Colonel By, but

FIGURE 9-5: King George VI, Queen Elizabeth and Mackenzie King (with umbrella) at the dedication of the National War Memorial, May 1939

(Source: National Film Board of Canada. Photothèque, Library and Archives Canada, C-002179)

its clear association with Upper Town re-immersed the proposed location in Ottawa's local politics. The city hall proposal for Wellington and Lyon Street was rejected by a majority of the Ottawa ratepayers in 1939. City council then attempted to buy the Normal School (teacher's college) from the provincial government, without success.[693]

The outbreak of war put all the downtown plans on hold, but the prime minister held onto his dream of a better national capital.

Wartime Capital

World War II quickly increased activity in downtown Ottawa. The number of civil servants almost doubled from 1939 to 1941, absorbing all the private offices.[694] Two large groups of wooden 'temporary' offices were quickly built at Cartier Square and on the Upper Town lands adjacent to the Supreme Court (Figure 9-7).[695] Gasoline rationing and the rapid increase in employees caused transit ridership to reach record levels,

FIGURE 9-6: Model of 1939 Plan for Downtown Ottawa by Jacques Gréber
This model shows the broad, diagonal view of Parliament Hill along Elgin Street. The train station would be expanded and relocated to a platform above the tracks.
(Source: 1950 Gréber Plan)

with the result that Ottawa's aging streetcars were packed.

Hull's population grew 12 percent from 29,000 to 33,000 from 1931-41, while Ottawa grew 22 percent from 127,000 to 155,000 in the same period.[696] There was little additional residential space built in the Depression, so cities just became more crowded. The Wartime Housing Corporation built a few new homes on the immediate edges of Ottawa's built up area (Figure 9-8), but most of the population growth was accommodated by doubling and tripling up households in existing housing units.

Office space became a desperate need as the military and civil service population expanded. More wooden 'temporary' buildings were erected on every piece of parkland and vacant space in the downtown (Figure 9-7). Only Parliament Hill and Nepean Point were spared. Mill buildings abandoned by the lumber and textile industries were hastily converted into office space (Figure 9-9), and more staff were jammed into poorly lit,

FIGURE 9-7: Wartime 'temporary' office buildings, 1940
The wartime 'temporary' office buildings under construction in downtown Ottawa, many of which were still in use in the 1970s.
(Source: Library and Archives Canada, C-068666)

Figure 9-8: Wartime Housing Corporation Project in Ottawa Suburbs, 1945
Too little, too late – these small homes were some of the first built since the Depression.
(Source: Library and Archives Canada, C-079396)

Figure 9-9: 'Temporary' buildings for the Dominion Bureau of Statistics in Thomas McKay's old mills on Green Island, 1940
(Source: Library and Archives Canada, PA-151669)

crowded spaces (Figure 9-10). Some of the industrial buildings proved useful for government laboratories and studios for the National Film Board (NFB), but the National Research Council had expanded far beyond the capacity of its classically designed headquarters on Sussex Drive. Rather than jamming temporary buildings onto the site, the NRC took an innovative approach to expansion. It bought a farm on the eastern edge of the city and built a low-density campus of inexpensive laboratory buildings serviced by buses and automobiles. The buildings were designed in a stripped down version of the International Style and were the first Modern architecture in the national capital.[697]

Of course, few people complained about the conditions in the capital city because there was a war going on, and life was undoubtedly better in Ottawa than in the battlefields of Italy or Normandy. The NFB produced a short film that stressed how everyone in the national capital was pulling together for the war effort, in a city that had transformed itself into the "nerve-centre of Canada."[698] The capital's crowded conditions did not abate after peace was declared, since there was much work for the national government in demobilization, veteran's affairs and reconstruction.

Reconstruction Plans for 'Town and Crown'

The Canadian government released plans for post-war reconstruction of the nation in 1944, including a significant role for community planning. France and Britain were then planning the reconstruction of their shattered cities during the same period. Jacques Gréber was supervising the re-planning of Le Havre and Nord-Normandie,[699] but the most ambitious efforts were Patrick Abercrombie's 1943 *County of London Plan* for its urban area and the 1944 *Greater London Plan* for the region.[700]

The *Greater London Plan* (Figure 9-11) quickly emerged as another influential model plan for capital cities in the post-war period. It was a full realisation of Ebenezer Howard's "Social Cities" regional scheme with a greenbelt and satellite new towns.[701] This type of plan had been tried in Moscow in the 1930s, and the English government had taken the first steps to assemble the London Greenbelt

FIGURE 9-10: Crowded wartime conditions in a downtown office building, 1945
(Source: Library and Archives Canada, PA-144878; Chris Lund photograph)

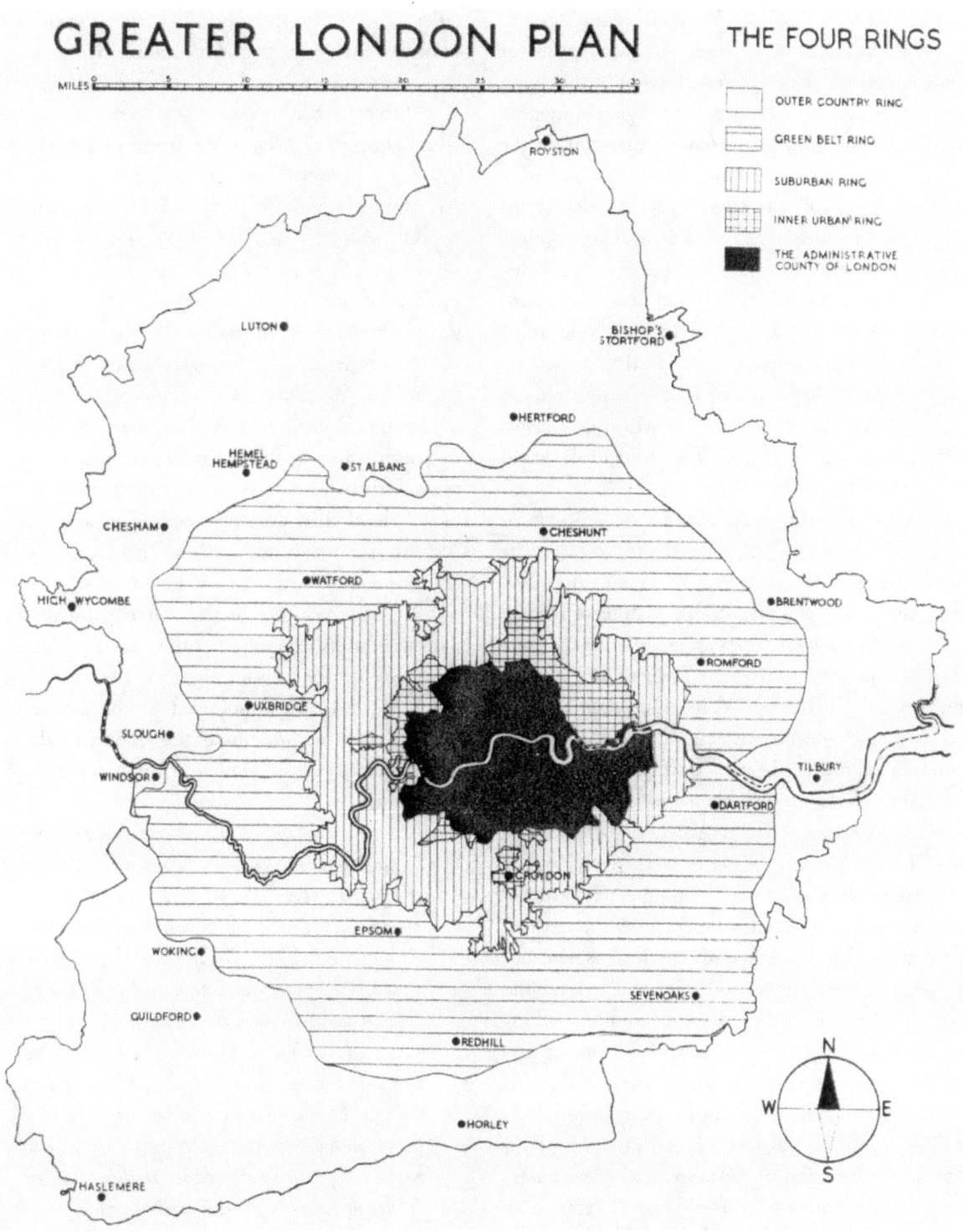

FIGURE 9-11: Greater London Plan diagram
The 1944 Greater London Plan's greenbelt and new towns became a powerful model for post-war reconstruction of other capital cities, including Ottawa.
(Source: Abercrombie, 1945)

in the 1930s, using development regulations.[702] Abercrombie's plan was poised for rapid post-war implementation. The first new town built following the *Greater London Plan* was Stevenage, planned by Gordon Stephenson, Abercrombie's assistant on the 1946 *County of London Plan*. Clarence Stein took the neighbourhood unit from Radburn back across the Atlantic to Stevenage[703] and a powerful regional planning paradigm was complete: greenbelts, radial transportation corridors and new towns with residential areas developed in neighbourhood units. Important metropolitan-scale planning variations on garden city/new town themes appeared in capital cities such as Helsinki (1946), Ottawa (1950), Stockholm (1952) Washington (1961), Seoul (1964) and Paris (1965).[704]

Urban renewal was the other important planning concept that affected post-war reconstruction. It emerged in the mid-1920s, when the *avant-garde* European architects formed the CIAM (*Congrès Internationaux d'Architecture Moderne*), to develop the new theories for building and planning.[705] The CIAM regarded the historical city as inefficient and obsolete. They continued to refine its planning theories during the economic depression of the 1930s, when little building took place in Europe or North America. After World War II, the Modern planners were ready with a well-elaborated theory for planning a new kind of city, codified in a manifesto known as the "Athens Charter."[706] Their message about the obsolescence of historic city centres and the need to rebuild using Modern planning principles found a willing audience in the reconstruction of European and Japanese cities destroyed by war (Figure 9-12).

Canada's cities did not suffer from war damage, but the Advisory Committee on Post-War Reconstruction noted extensive "congestion, deterioration, misuse and blight" in Canadian communities.[707] It recommended broad-scale housing programs to accommodate the backlog of housing demands caused by the Depression and the war, new housing to meet projected population growth, and the reconstruction of housing in the older parts of cities. The committee also advocated the need for comprehensive community planning to direct this reconstruction and new urban development.

'Town-Crown' disputes over local development issues continued, even in the midst of a world war. The federal government recognized the tremendous strain the war effort placed on the national capital and a parliamentary joint committee recommended action to reduce the fiscal burden of tax-exempt property on the municipal governments in the region.[708] King supported the grants in lieu of property taxes and special status for Ottawa even though other members in Cabinet felt that other Canadian cities would be jealous and demand similar treatment.[709] The prime minister was still attracted to the idea of a federal district, suggesting it in a speech in the House of Commons, but the loud negative reaction from Hull kept the idea in abeyance.[710]

As Canada's role in the war expanded, more nations established embassies in Ottawa, reinforcing King's desire for a more dignified capital city. On April 21, 1944 he announced to the House that Canada's commemoration of the Second World War would be the redevelopment of the national capital as a whole:

... as a memorial to the service and sacrifice of men and women who have participated in the present war, a capital city which would be a model to other cities and other countries. As now we had the War Memorial symbolical of the last war, as the memorial of this war, the National Capital in the form of a greater Ottawa, with the Ottawa River running through the heart of the Capital instead of being a boundary on one side. It would be a great symbol of the elements that have gone to make the present Canada what it is, and the future of Canada what it will become ...[713]

Once again, the prime minister was attempting to mobilize the Canadian patriotic spirit and desire to commemorate the wartime sacrifice, to pursue his objective of developing an attractive national capital city. King wasted little time in launching the project. Only days after Japan's surrender Jacques Gréber was recalled from France to develop a new plan.⁷¹⁴ King himself announced that:

> ... *the government has decided that no form of a memorial could be more worthy of the service and sacrifice given in the war than to give the Capital of our country as worthy a place amongst the national capitals of the world as Canada occupies amongst the nations as a nation.*⁷¹⁵

Reflections

Although Mackenzie King was yet again turning to wartime sacrifice and patriotic spirit to further his Crown plans for improving the national capital, this time the scale had expanded. No mere incremental addition of a plaza around a monument; the memorial was to be the 'Town' itself. At last, Ottawa was to be transformed into a capital that expressed "the soul of Canada today."⁷¹⁶

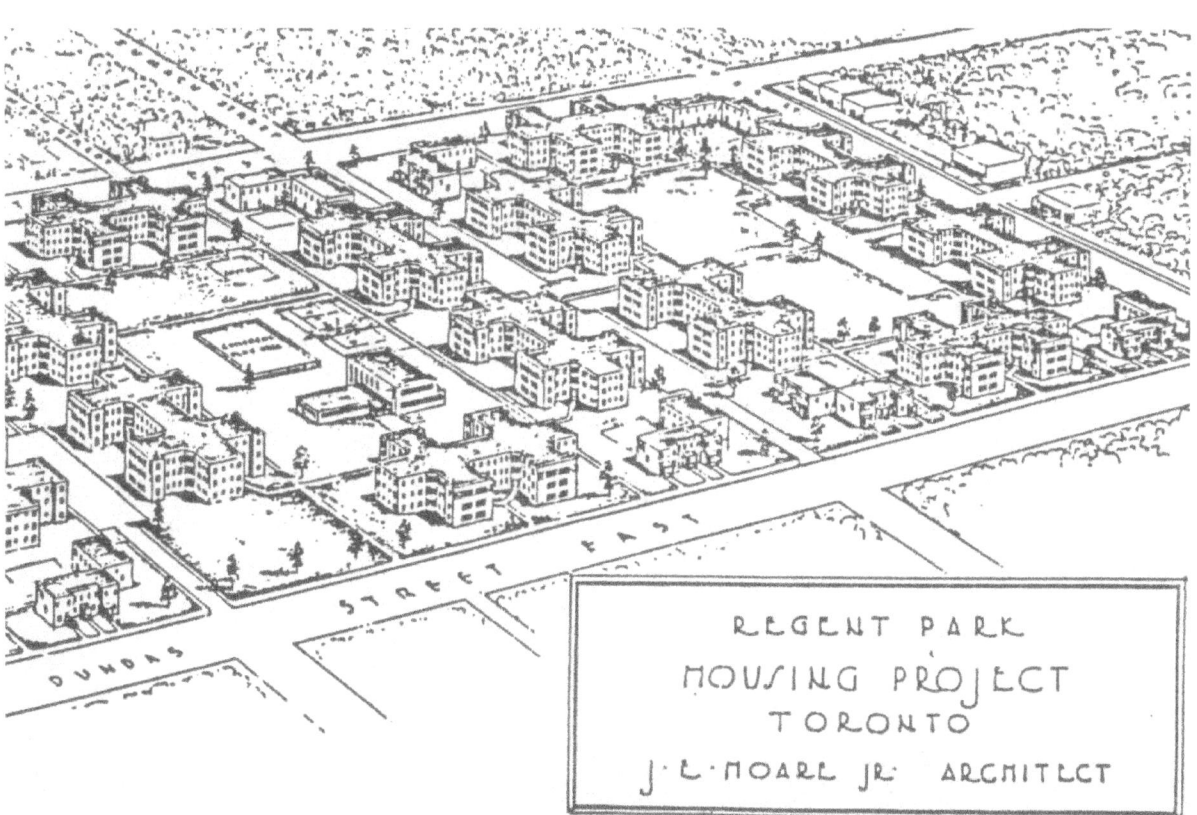

FIGURE 9-12: Urban Renewal: Toronto Regent Park Plan
Urban renewal emerged in Canada after recognition that many of the buildings in the central areas of larger cities were over fifty years old and needed major repairs.⁷¹¹ "Blighted" conditions could also be found among older industrial buildings, many of which were being abandoned for suburban business parks. The federal government established a program for financing 'slum clearance' projects, in an attempt to replace the worst of the substandard buildings with new public housing. The leaders of social reform, such as Catherine Bauer and Humphrey Carver, initially supported urban renewal.

Planning for the first Canadian project, Toronto's Regent Park, started in the 1930s and had solid public support when construction started in 1948.⁷¹² Many blocks of 19th century housing in poor condition were demolished to create a master-planned project with 2,100 public housing units. Similar projects were begun in most North American cities.
(Source: Albert Rose, *Regent Park: A Study in Slum Clearance,* (Toronto, ON: University of Toronto Press, 1958))

CHAPTER 10
Post-War Plans (1945-1959)

... I was in a state of disbelief when I saw our national capital. The town looked like an unkempt, decaying village. Hideous telegraph poles leaning over the main street. A dismal place; to call it provincial would have been a compliment.[717]
– Alan Gotlieb, 1957

Ottawa and Hull were a national embarrassment at the end of the Second World War, and the capital was a poor reflection of a country that emerged from the global conflict as a middle power. Although only a handful of nations maintained embassies in Canada prior to 1939, many more wished to have a diplomatic presence in Ottawa after the war. They found a capital city that did not represent the character of its host country, or the ambitions of its leaders. Canada's civil service was crammed into industrial buildings abandoned due to the Depression and the collapse of the lumber industry. 'Temporary' wooden office buildings crowded most downtown parks and the lawn of the Supreme Court. The pre-1914 streetcars were worn out, their tracks were in terrible shape and the road system was a jumble, cut up by numerous railway tracks. Housing was overcrowded, with deteriorated wooden structures in Hull, LeBreton Flats and Lowertown remaining from cheap reconstruction after the late 19th century fires. The newest homes were scarcely better, with un-serviced, incomplete subdivisions scattered across Nepean and Gloucester townships without a single paved road in the suburban area. As a final indignity, the entire region used the Ottawa River as an open sewer for household and industrial waste.

Prime Minister Mackenzie King's proposal to transform this urban muddle into a capital worthy of Canada was an extraordinarily ambitious war memorial, especially given the many previous failures in planning the region.

Mackenzie King's legacy

Mackenzie King was determined that the new plan for the capital should make the breakthrough that had eluded his predecessors for the previous half century. He established a National Capital Planning Committee (NCPC), independent of the FDC, with representatives appointed from across Canada and also from the architectural and engineering professions.[718] The prime minister chaired some early meetings of the committee, and frequent references in his personal diary show that he followed its every move. Despite King's heavy workload with post-war reconstruction, Gréber recalled that the prime minister often took extensive time off his schedule when his planner visited from France:

King was so interested in the work that he almost forgot the daily routine of his work to talk with me about things. He wanted to know what kind of man I was – to check my intentions. He understood that I had a clear program. I don't know that I had any other client that helped me so well. He took me several times to his place in the mountains, with his dog. ... He asked questions that were really touching. The kind of questions that a father would ask his son ...[719]

Gréber was installed as consultant to the National Capital Planning Service (NCPS), with an ample budget, numerous staff and a wide mandate. For associates, he recruited John Kitchen, Noulan Cauchon's aide from the Ottawa Town Planning Commission, and Édouard Fiset, a Québec architect and his former student from Paris' *Institut d'urbanisme*. Landscape architects, engineers, technicians and an information officer rounded out the NCPS staff, which was perhaps the only full-time professional planning organization in Canada in 1945.[720] In conjunction with the newly-formed Community Planning Association of Canada, the NCPS embarked on a public-relations program to promote both the idea of urban planning and the plan for the national capital.[721]

Gréber's scope of work was widened from the 1937-39 downtown design to encompass an expanded National Capital Region of over 900 square miles.[722] In effect, the NCPC's task was to simultaneously prepare a regional land use plan for both Ottawa and Québec sides of the river, a regional infrastructure plan for Ottawa and Hull and an urban design for the downtown area. Gréber's first important act was to brief the Senate and the House of Commons on the scope of work and precedents from other major plans. He asked the parliamentarians to set their sights high, and warned them that it would take several years to produce a comprehensive plan.[723]

The NCPS staff spent two years preparing background studies for the region, assisted by senior officials from federal departments. This task was a civic survey of the kind advocated by Patrick Geddes,[724] examining natural systems, history, demography, land use, housing conditions, infrastructure, and open space. The railway system was strangling the capital, with over 250 level crossings and blocked streets in the built-up area,[725] so the NCPC retained a leading railway consultant for assistance.[726] Similarly, the NCPC shared the cost of a civil engineering study with the City of Ottawa, because the entire region emptied raw sewage into the Ottawa River.

The NCPS staff frequently consulted with Ottawa and Hull municipal officials, and provided planning advice to some of the adjacent municipalities, who had no professional staff. A 300-page draft report was completed in 1948 and circulated to numerous agencies for comment.[727]

Gréber gave speeches to service clubs, professional organizations and municipal councils and gave numerous press conferences and radio interviews in both English and French. The NCPS information service also prepared press kits, brochures, and a summary report in both official languages that resulted in scores of newspaper articles across Canada. The National Film Board produced three newsreels and a large-scale model that went on tours across the country (Figure 9-6).[728] The public relations campaign and the project's status as a war memorial helped the country view the national capital plan in a positive light at a time when other cities were also starved for investment. Even the *Calgary Herald* supported Ottawa's improvement.[729]

Gréber devised a remarkable scheme to cut a memorial terrace on a rocky bluff at the south end of the Gatineau Hills. A great granite tower recalling France's Vimy Ridge monument would be visible from Parliament Hill, only three miles away (Figure 10-1). Visitors to the monument itself would have a fine view of the national capital from the terrace, which Gréber compared to the vista from the Piazzale Michael Angelo near Florence.[730] Gréber's associate, Montréal architect Éduoard Fiset explained the details of the design with some exuberance. Speaking of visitors as "pilgrims," Fiset referred to the essential elements of the grandiose projects: a large "light-flooded" terrace carved out of the side of the mountain; a wall inscribed with the names of "our heroic soldiers" and their military engagements; a central tower facing the city and bearing the arms of Canada and of the nine provinces; a bronze-doored chapel containing a large black marble slab gold-inlaid with the plan of the future Capital; a vista of the Ottawa River, the cities of Ottawa and Hull, and "the picturesque or proud stateliness of the steeples and towers." From this perspective, the "pilgrim" will have revealed the grand purpose of the project:

> *He will realise that the whole life and collective efforts, henceforth planned and harmonized, are a tribute to a sacred memory. He will understand that the slow re-organization, the painstaking upheaval, which some day will ensure a setting worthier of the statue of Capital City of a large country, will have been undertaken in commemoration of the men whose supreme sacrifice will have given Canada a new and powerful impulse toward the attainment to the status of a great nation.*[731]

In the short term, however, Gréber and others simply recommended that "1939-45" be inscribed into the existing war memorial as a temporary measure. The World War II veterans were opposed, wanting a separate memorial to commemorate their service, but Mackenzie King championed Gréber's Gatineau memorial terrace until the end of his prime-ministerial career.[732]

Mackenzie King's health was failing in 1948, but he remained prime minister until the draft plan was released. His last act in Cabinet was to stack an expanded FDC with supporters of the plan and push an appropriation of $25 million into the government's financial plans.[733] King retired in 1948, but continued to sit in the House of Commons where he promoted the draft plan. On the eve of his last day in Parliament in April 1949, King gave interviews about the plan to the

FIGURE 10-1: **Vimy Ridge comes to the Gatineau Hills**
Sketch by Jacques Gréber showing the proposed Second World War memorial located in Gatineau Park.
(Source: Gréber 1950, Fig. 197)

Ottawa and Montréal press. The city models and plan display were placed in the main corridor of the Centre Block, so the MPs and press could not miss them after the House was adjourned for the federal election. King staged his last parliamentary photo-op touring the models with Gréber (Figure 10-2).[734]

Alas, Mackenzie King did not live to see the final version of his plan tabled in the House of Commons. He died in 1950, just before the national capital plan was released. There was no doubt that the 1950 *Plan for the National Capital* was his personal legacy. He contributed its foreword just before his death:

To be worthy of Canada's greatness, its Capital must be planned with far-reaching foresight ... It answers the urgent needs for wise community planning and efficient traffic and transportation facilities; it corrects deficiencies resulting from unplanned undertakings in the past; it enhances the possibilities of that which is, as yet, unspoiled ... The plan cannot fail, given due appreciation and support, to result in the attainment of a Capital City of which Canadians of our own and future generations will be increasingly proud.[735]

FIGURE 10-2: Mackenzie King and Jacques Gréber, 1949
King and Gréber tour the models of the draft *National Capital Plan*, on the former prime minister's last day as a parliamentarian, April 29, 1949. The display was set up just outside the House of Commons to catch the MPs on their way home for the federal election.
(Source: Library and Archives Canada/Duncan Cameron fonds/PA-201981 © Library and Archives Canada. Reproduced with the permission of Library and Archives Canada)

Components of the 1950 Plan

The *Plan for the National Capital* was published in 1950 in two volumes: the extensively illustrated 300 page *General Report,* and an *Atlas* of 20 colour plates in large format. Both volumes contained watercolour renderings and charcoal sketches prepared by Gréber and Fiset in the best Beaux Arts manner (Figure 10-3).[736]

The first half of the *Report* contained the background studies that surveyed the region. The proposals that followed built upon previous plans by Todd, Bennett, Cousins, Cauchon and upon Gréber's 1938 scheme. They included the following elements:

- relocation of the railway system and industries from the inner city to the suburbs,

FIGURE 10-3: 1950 Plan Watercolour
This beautiful watercolour drawing of the 1950 master plan was included as a 55cm x 44cm colour plate in the oversized Atlas that accompanied the *Plan for the National Capital* report. Jacques Gréber also prepared a larger colour rendering of the region. The French government commissioned an Aubusson tapestry of the regional plan as a gift to Canada in thanks for its support during the war.[737]
(Source: Gréber Atlas 1950, Plate 9)

- consolidation of five railway stations to union stations in Ottawa and Hull,
- construction of new cross-town boulevards and bridges,
- decentralization of government back offices and laboratories to the suburbs,
- slum clearance urban renewal of the LeBreton Flats district,
- expansion of the urban area from 250,000 to 500,000 in neighbourhood units,
- surrounding of the future built-up area with a greenbelt, and
- a wilderness park in the Gatineau hills and a parks system along the canal and rivers.

The railway relocation was the key element that unlocked the rest of the plan. Removing the east-west Canadian National line and its adjacent industry in the centre of Ottawa re-connected the road grid, separated noxious industries from residential areas and provided rights of way for cross-town boulevards. Relocating the two railway stations to the suburbs permitted construction of a true union station with good road access and freed up 22 acres of yards in the heart of Ottawa for a convention centre, shopping and a hotel. The tracks leading to the station were replaced by a parkway along the east bank of the Rideau Canal. These proposals were an elaboration of the previous plans by Cauchon and Cousins, except for the station relocation, which was not contemplated as late as the 1939 Gréber downtown plan. The CNR right-of-way was proposed as the main east-west boulevard. The north-south Canadian Pacific Line was proposed as a new truck bypass of the downtown. These two radial routes were to be complemented by a ring road just inside a proposed greenbelt with two new bridges across the Ottawa River (Figure 10-4).

Government departments and national institutions that were essential for diplomatic or parliamentary purposes were to be located in high-quality masonry buildings close to Parliament Hill. Research laboratories, back office functions and administrative departments were to be decentralized to four suburban office parks in Ottawa, and the King's Printer was to move to Hull. This decentralization would allow the many "temporary" war-time buildings to be removed from the central city and free up sites for national institutions such as a library, theatre and art gallery. It would also allow many civil servants to purchase inexpensive suburban houses with a short drive to work.[738]

The planning staff were concerned about overcrowding throughout the city and poor housing conditions in the LeBreton Flats district of Ottawa. Many families were doubled up in houses after the war and the planners proposed to take advantage of the federal government's new housing program to facilitate suburban houses on long-term mortgages. The new residential population of the capital was to be accommodated in suburban neighbourhood units (see chapter 8), using the model proposed by Clarence Perry and implemented in Radburn, New Jersey before the war.[739] Gréber's team did not design these residential areas. Instead, they employed land use planning to estimate locations for approximately 50 neighbourhood units of 5,000-7,000 people.[740] It was intended that the local governments prepare their own secondary plans for these neighbourhoods.[741] Urban renewal and slum clearance were proposed for LeBreton Flats, although this was not a priority of the plan.[742]

A greenbelt approximately four km. wide was planned to surround the suburban areas to control the outer limits of urbanization. Growth beyond the 500,000 to 600,000 people anticipated within this greenbelt was to take place in satellite towns in the rural area, although the locations of these towns were not designated in 1950. This proposal was clearly based upon Ebenezer Howard's 1898 Garden Cities scheme.[743] It also drew upon Patrick Abercrombie's *Greater London Plan*, especially in the proposals for the greenbelt to be implemented by development regulations.[744]

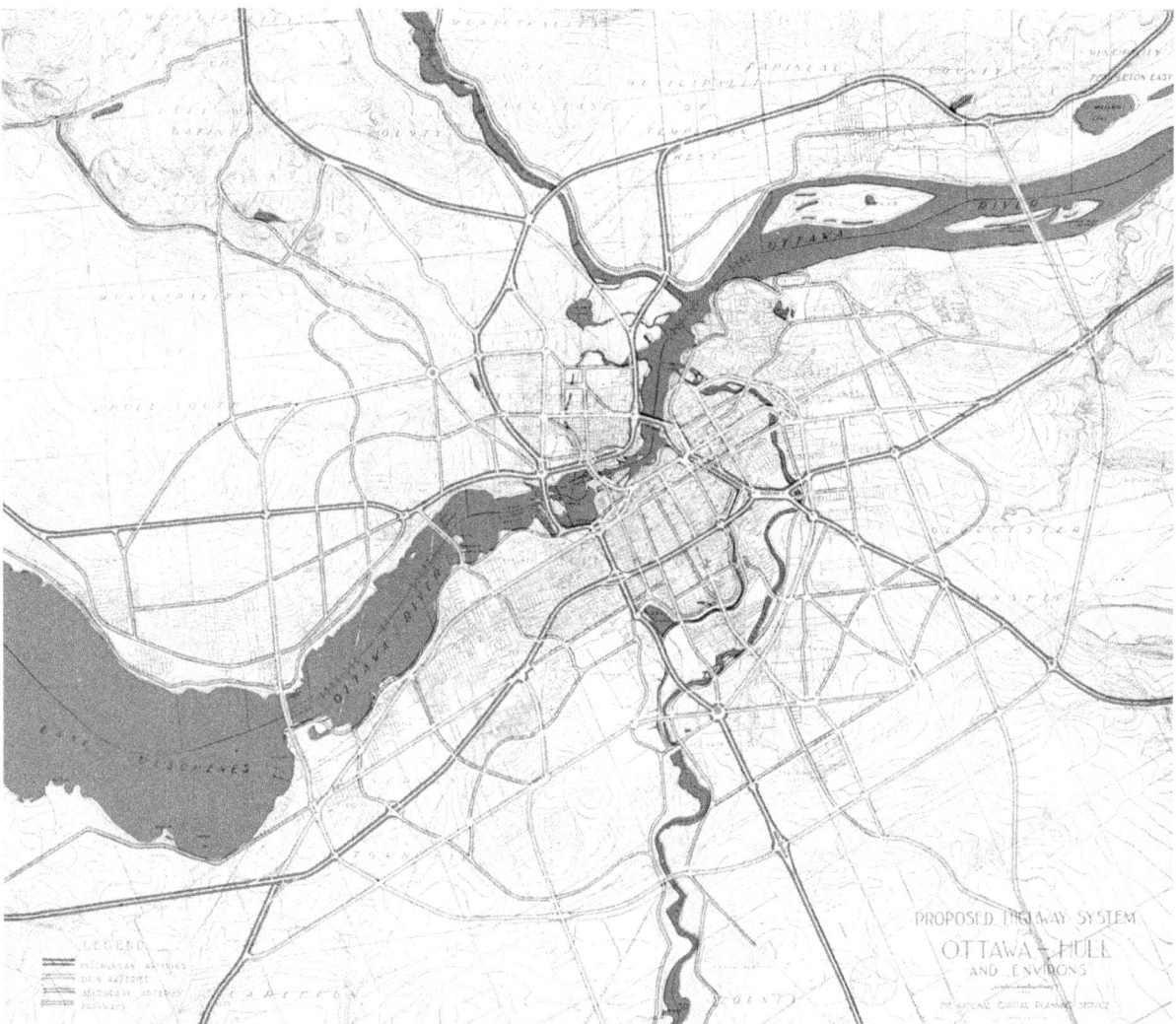

FIGURE 10-4: **Proposed transportation corridors**
Note the ring road to act as a traffic bypass, and the additional bridges proposed at the inner edge of the Greenbelt. The NCC acquired the right of way for many of these corridors in the 1950s, which helped transit planning decades later.
(Source: Gréber Atlas 1950, Plate 26)

Many of the open space proposals of the 1950 plan were first put forward by Frederick Todd in 1903.[745] Gréber recommended that the parkway system be expanded to the limits of the greenbelt and that Gatineau Park be extended as a green wedge almost to the downtown core (Figure 10-5). The riverside open spaces and parkways in Hull would require clearance of that city's rapidly-declining primary industries, including sawmills, a match factory and paper mill. These industries had long been targeted for removal by federal parliamentarians, not only because of the undignified backdrop they provided to Parliament Hill, but also because they polluted the river and air, and were a great fire hazard. To underscore the continuing danger, the logs piled on the river's north shore went up in flames in 1946, during preparation of the plan, severely damaging the main bridge to Ottawa.[746]

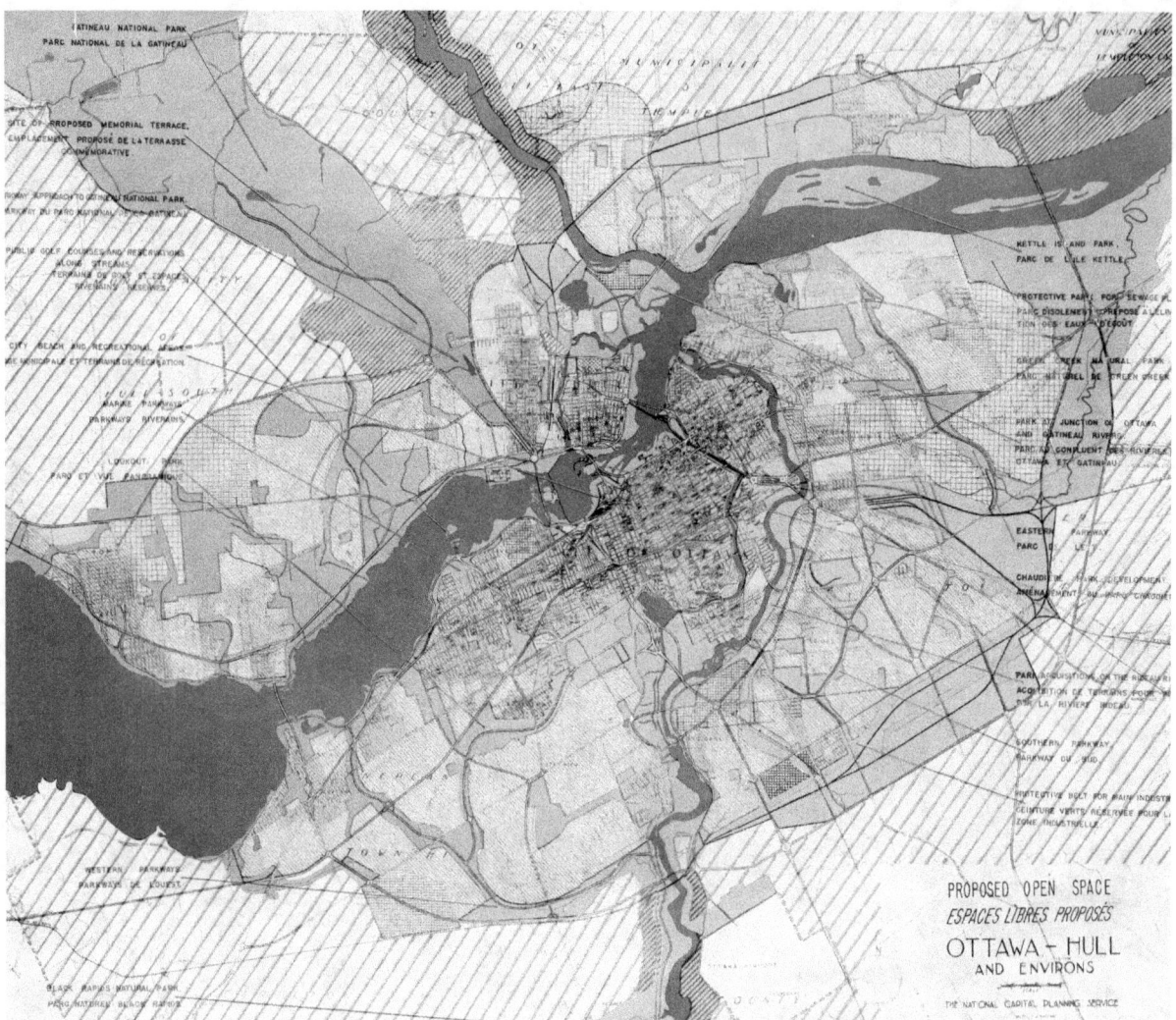

FIGURE 10-5: **Proposed parks system**
The proposed open space system included the green wedge of Gatineau Park, a green belt on both sides of the river, and parkways along the rivers and canals.
(Source: Gréber Atlas 1950, Plate 17)

Despite the Beaux Arts renderings, the proposals of the Plan for the National Capital largely conformed to the "Athens Charter" of the 1933 *Congrès Internationaux d'Architecture Moderne* (CIAM).[747] In mid-20th century, the ideas of the CIAM appeared to be fresh and democratic, especially when compared to the excesses of the City Beautiful and Beaux Arts traditions.[748] Although he was not a Modernist designer, Gréber incorporated many Modern planning elements: land use segregation, parkways, decentralization, reduced densities, urban renewal, open space and the neighbourhood unit. The CIAM Charter was a rather general list of the best techniques from the 1930s, but it is still surprising how closely Gréber's planning methods fit those recommended by the Modern movement, given that he is principally regarded as a Beaux-Arts *urbaniste* and rival of Le Corbusier.[749]

Gréber's planning embraced the CIAM without adopting their urban design manifesto. Gréber's urban public spaces typically avoided the huge super-blocks and free plans of Modern projects like Brasilia or New York's new United Nations headquarters (Figure 10-6). He preferred formal streets, blocks and public plazas, in the Parisian tradition. The 1950 models show Modern buildings in Beaux-Arts civic spaces (Figure 10-7). Gréber cloaked his modernity in Beaux Arts representations. The models, watercolours, sketches and tapestry were beautiful objects, which, for politicians like Mackenzie King with conservative aesthetic tastes, perhaps made the plan easier to accept.[750]

FIGURE 10-6: United Nations Complex, New York, 1955
The CIAM's leader, Le Corbusier got his big break in capital-city planning in 1947 when he was appointed to the Board of Design for New York's United Nations Headquarters, chaired by Wallace Harrison.[751] The Rockefeller family purchased the small site on the East River to provide a Manhattan address that was attractive to the UN. Le Corbusier influenced the design process and developed a plan following Modern principles with Brazil's Oscar Niemeyer and Canada's Ernest Cormier. Five streets were closed and the buildings razed to create a super-block, and much of the land was left as open space. The UN offices were housed in the Secretariat Building, a 39-storey rectangular slab-block with glass curtain walls. [752]

Construction of the high-profile UN project was complete by 1951, by which time Le Corbusier had already been appointed to revise the design for a new Indian provincial capital at Chandigarh while Niemeyer became the principal architect of Brasilia in 1956.[753]

Le Corbusier never designed a Canadian building, but the federal government's architecture made the transition to this Modern style in the post-war era with the National Printing Bureau (1949, Figure 10-17), the National Library (1955) and the Sir Charles Tupper building in Confederation Heights (1957).[754]
(Source: United Nations Photo/ES; Photo # 399515)

FIGURE 10-7: **Modern buildings in Beaux-Arts civic spaces**
Modern classical architecture in a framework of pre-modern public spaces: the 1950 model shows a City Hall (centre) and Art Gallery (top) at either end of the Mackenzie King Bridge. Only the bridge was built. The regional government centre, adjacent to the Laurier Bridge (centre left) became the new City Hall in 2001.
(Source: Gréber 1950, 218)

Ignoring Built Heritage

The federal planning legacy in the Modern era had a profound effect on downtown Ottawa and Hull. One aspect was a bias against older, existing buildings. Gréber had complained about some of the functional problems of the existing setting: in particular, the lack of parking and the generally inferior quality of the architecture. These comments were coupled with a post-war surplus of office space. Demobilization of the wartime civil service had left some older buildings empty in the downtown core. The 'temporary' office buildings that the government had constructed to meet wartime needs were now available for federal use: some survived in use for another thirty years! The result was the abandonment and demolition of many older, privately-owned buildings in the core and their replacement by parking lots or structures in downtown Ottawa and Hull. [755]

The bias against older buildings of no particular architectural merit was most evident in the demolition of the Nicholas Sparks farmhouse

(Figure 10-8). The house had survived since the earliest phase of settlement on Sparks Street, albeit much extended and altered for commercial use. Today, it would have been considered of exceptional heritage value because of its age, architectural integrity, and historical associations. But, in the late 1940s, it was seen as a rundown property standing in the way of the West Memorial Building, the new home of the Department of Veterans' Affairs and one of the key buildings directly resulting from the Gréber plan. It was a victim of a common mid-20th century blind spot: the failure to recognize the importance of remnants of the former built form.[756] The inherent bias towards demolition and redevelopment also prevailed in private sector responses to new development opportunities.

FIGURE 10-8: Nicholas Sparks' farmhouse, ca. 1950
The home of the land developer who owned most of downtown Ottawa was demolished in the early 1950s, during an era when built heritage was rarely protected.
(Source: Library and Archives Canada/ PA-057395)

Connecting Downtown to Parliament Hill

Gréber's 1950 plan continued to stress the diagonal views of Parliament Hill suggested by Todd and Bennett as appropriate for the Gothic Revival buildings on a picturesque cliff-top site. He developed a second, long-range diagonal view of Parliament Hill from Nicholas Street as the principal entrance to downtown from the southeast, a prospect enjoyed to this day by drivers exiting from the Queensway or skaters on the Rideau Canal.[757] However, the idea of a Metcalfe Street widening "was repeatedly brought to our attention," so Gréber discussed its disadvantages at some length. The 1950 plan contains over a page of text that summarizes the idea's deficiencies:

- The broken vertical profile of Metcalfe Street precluded a satisfactory view of the Peace Tower.
- Metcalfe Street would need widening at the intersection with Wellington Street.
- Expropriation of costly and historic buildings would be required.
- Elgin Street was better for traffic circulation than Metcalfe because of its connections at its extremities.
- The widening of Elgin Street and Confederation Square had already been started.
- The diagonal view from Elgin Street was preferred for aesthetic reasons.[758]

Gréber placed great emphasis on the last point, and his credibility on this issue would be strong, as a Beaux-Arts graduate and professor. He insisted that the classic axial approach along Metcalfe Street was not appropriate for Ottawa on aesthetic and symbolic grounds. However, more pragmatic factors were equally damning: Metcalfe Street's uphill approach and uneven grade prevented a clear sight-line of the entire Peace Tower from the street. Unless Metcalfe and cross-streets such as Sparks Street were re-graded and many historic buildings removed, the result would be a truncated perspective of the Peace Tower and Parliament Buildings, similar to Lutyens' disappointment with the Rajpath in New Delhi.[759] Gréber's arguments prevailed in 1950, but the Metcalfe Street axis would emerge again a half century later.

Early Implementation of the 1950 Plan

During the period 1945-48, Prime Minister Mackenzie King took several important steps to ensure that the new plan would be implemented. The fate of the 1915 plan prepared by Edward Bennett's team had demonstrated that talented designers and a comprehensive plan were necessary, but not sufficient, for success. Rapid implementation of a plan required that an agency do a good job of managing politics, finance and planning simultaneously. Gréber's team needed their political champion to establish political and financial strategies for long-term implementation. Mackenzie King was infamous for micro-managing the details of previous plans, but he was 72 years old in 1946 and the end of his political career was clearly in sight. Other methods would be needed to ensure the completion of his legacy for the national capital.[760]

Making the national capital itself the country's World War II memorial was a powerful first step to acquire public support. Mackenzie King ensured direct political support from across the nation with his final action as prime minister, signing an Order-in-Council that appointed his handpicked supporters to an enlarged Federal District Commission. Prominent citizens from each province were appointed to the FDC, which was chaired by Frederic Bronson, a leading Ottawa businessman. The National Capital Planning Committee (NCPC) and its staff were transferred to the FDC in 1946.[761] The FDC maintained its federal political support with regional appointments and constant public relations. Newsreels about the national capital plan played in cinemas across Canada; Gréber and Fiset made programs for CBC Radio, and a model of the national capital plan toured the country with a display. School children from across Canada were encouraged to submit essays about their vision of a national capital and the winning students were brought to Parliament Hill.[762] The press coverage from across Canada was largely favourable, and political support for the plan continued even after Mackenzie King retired in 1948 and the Liberal party was defeated in 1957.[763]

For financial stability, Mackenzie King ensured an early start on the plan's implementation by establishing a $25 million National Capital Fund via a Cabinet decision. It was agreed that $2.5 million would be put in the estimates for 1948 and annually thereafter, using executive powers to avoid a potentially divisive debate similar to the 1928 disputes over Confederation Square.[764] The 1950 plan did not have a financial analysis of its proposals. Instead, the FDC submitted annual financial reports and estimates of future capital spending to the Treasury Board. The FDC and NCC hired expert landscape architects, planners, engineers and project managers, eventually developing a reputation for good fiscal management. As their organizational competence increased from the 1930s through the 1950s, they were given responsibility for maintaining the grounds of all federal buildings in the National Capital Region, project management of infrastructure and land use planning approval for federal properties.[765]

The FDC's good managerial reputation allowed it the room to move quickly to implement elements of the Gréber plan. The FDC began the railway relocation and a bridge across the Rideau Canal even before the plan was released in 1950. The railways were not expropriated. Instead, the FDC built new and better lines and yards in the suburbs, and exchanged them for their downtown rights of way. Land was acquired at rural prices for the yards, industrial parks and road rights of way needed to complete the infrastructure. The FDC then entered into a cost-sharing agreement with the Ontario government and the City of Ottawa for the construction of the cross-town boulevard planned for the former CNR right of way, which was named the Queensway.[766]

Political relations at the local level were not always so smooth. Ottawa and Hull were given strong links to the plan by appointing both their mayors to the FDC and councillors and senior staff to the NCPC. Ottawa's major complaint, the fiscal impact of tax-exempt federal property, was addressed (if not satisfied) by adjustments to the grants-in-lieu formula in 1944 and 1950.[767] The major political issue on the Québec side was the continuing spectre of a federal district similar to Washington or Canberra, which remained completely unacceptable to Québec politicians at all levels. But Mackenzie King, ever the policy wonk, continued to favour the federal district idea, perhaps because of his academic training and reform background. After a 1946 front-page editorial challenge by a Hull newspaper, the prime minister finally reversed his position and opposed a federal district.[768] Gréber and the NCPC staff constantly stated that a federal district was not needed, citing Paris, London, New York and Philadelphia's regional plans, but the issue continued to cloud politics in Québec.[769]

In contrast, the City of Ottawa supported the FDC by establishing the Ottawa Area Planning Board (OAPB) in 1947 to control unregulated suburban expansion. However, the suburban townships continued to approve low-density subdivisions without municipal services. The city reacted in 1948 by attempting to annex all the land to the proposed inside boundary of the Greenbelt.[770]

Rural Resistance

Gloucester and Nepean townships were outraged at the City of Ottawa's attempted seizure of their most valuable lands by annexation of all lands within the proposed Greenbelt. The areas proposed for annexation contained most of their urban population, commercial assessment and many of the institutions of the semi-rural townships, including Nepean's historic township hall. The townships fought the annexations in the local and provincial arenas and at the Ontario Municipal Board (OMB). The problem was that the rural township councils wanted to hang onto the commercial assessment and residential subdivisions on the edge of the urban area, but they did not want to go into debt to pay for the necessary urban piped services and paved roads. The Ontario Municipal Board ruled in favour of the annexation in January 1949, but Nepean Council filed an appeal.[771]

With the OMB ruling in its pocket, the City of Ottawa finally sat down to negotiate with the angry townships. The city agreed to back off from the approved annexation boundaries and to absorb only the areas in Nepean that were urbanized and in need of piped services. In Gloucester, they also annexed the areas where the FDC was building the new rail yards and industrial parks. The townships agreed to zone the remaining land inside the Greenbelt as 'rural.' Unfortunately, the agreement did not solve any of the urban planning and servicing issues, which promptly re-appeared in the 1950s and 1960s in even more difficult form. The ill will created by the unilateral actions by Ottawa (and their implicit support of the federal government) would last for decades. The municipal politicians and staff argued constantly in 1950, and the Nepean Clerk had the locks changed on the township hall to deny Ottawa employees access to the expropriated offices.[772] Nepean's official history concluded:

> In future years, the 1950 annexation would be seen in the township as a rape. Some other means of achieving unified planning control would have to be found ...[773]

Although the townships had agreed in 1950 to zone their lands rural, there was nothing to prevent them from re-zoning to urban uses and approving subdivisions in the future. The rural township councils were openly sympathetic to the plight of the farmers whose land had been designated for the Greenbelt. While the proposed Greenbelt would allow them to continue their farm operations indefinitely, many farmers wanted the opportunity to profit by selling their land to speculators or dividing it themselves into suburban house lots.

Gloucester and Nepean councils refused to incorporate the Greenbelt into their zoning bylaws and began permitting un-serviced subdivisions in its proposed location.[774] The Ottawa Planning Area Board found that it was powerless to prevent these rural subdivisions if they were supported by the local governments. The Nepean Township reeve defiantly referred to the Greenbelt as the "weed belt" and suggested that it be covered with half-acre lots using wells and septic tanks for servicing.[775] The Greenbelt was not popular with the Québec provincial government, either. It was quietly dropped on the north side of the river.[776]

After six years of conflict, it became clear that the Ontario and Québec planning legislation was not strong enough to establish a greenbelt by regulation, as in the London model.[777] The federal government could not force the recalcitrant rural townships to adopt its plan, since it did not have the constitutional jurisdiction to act on planning and development matters. The provincial governments did have the jurisdiction, but were not interested in investing any political or financial support to assist the federal government's pet project of an upgraded national capital.

The FDC was making good progress on the infrastructure projects, because the City of Ottawa was eager to accept the millions of federal dollars to assist their rebuilding program. And the new federal payments in lieu of property taxes removed the city's major complaint from the previous decade, although there will always be suggestions that the formula should be improved.[778] However, the implementation of the 1950 plan as a regional plan was clearly in jeopardy by 1955, due to the opposition of local governments.

A Surprising Post-war Boom

By 1955, it slowly became clear that the demographic and economic growth forecasts that were the foundations for post-war planning were too modest. If we stand in the place of the 1948 planners, it is hard to fault them for their caution. The demographers saw that the population of the capital region had doubled from 125,000 to 250,000 between 1915 and 1946. As a result, they extended the line on the graph to forecast a regional population of 500,000 sometime between 1995 and 2020[779] (Figure 10-9). The war-time expansion of civil servants must have looked like an aberration compared to the Depression years before.

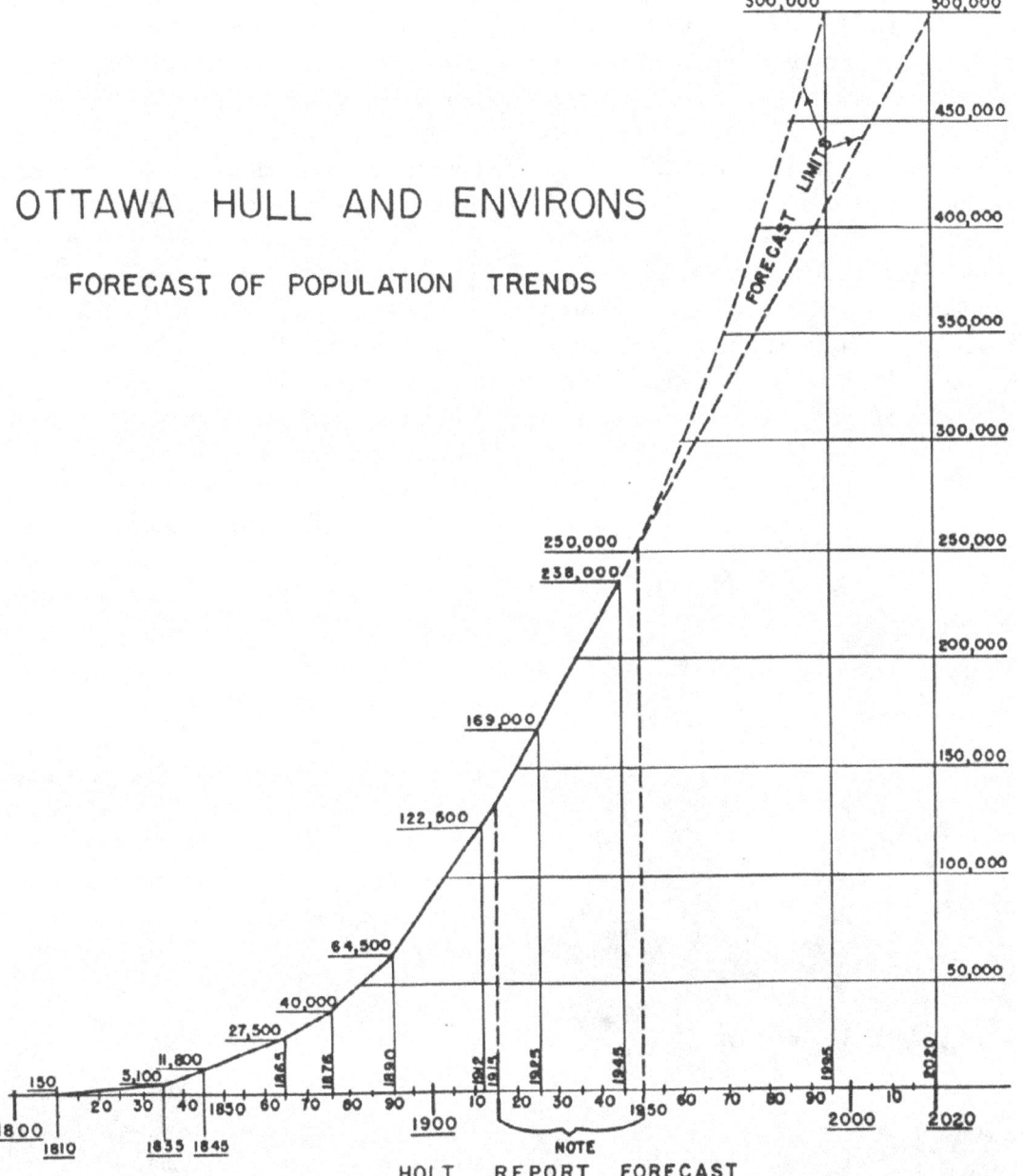

FIGURE 10-9: 1948 Population Forecast
This graph demonstrates one of the most influential errors of the Gréber plan. The demographers noted the remarkable accuracy of the 1915 'Holt Report' forecast, and simply extended this trend line into the future. The unprecedented Baby Boom and post war economic expansion pushed the regional population past the 500,000 level shortly after 1961, rather than the 1995-2020 in the forecast.
(Source: Gréber, 1950, Figure 19, p. 51)

Unfortunately, the past turned out to be an unreliable guide to the future in this case. The 1950s economic boom was completely different from the epidemic and recession that followed the First World War. The post-war reconstruction policies developed in 1944 led to a sustained economic expansion that provided jobs for the returning veterans and an influx of European immigrants. Louis St. Laurent's government helped fuel the boom with national infrastructure projects like the Trans-Canada Highway, the St. Lawrence Seaway, and the northern Distant Early Warning radar line. A strong, confident nation also reinforced social infrastructure, supporting Medicare, provincial equalization and cultural institutions such as the CBC, Canada Council and the National Film Board.[780] Transforming Canada's capital city was one part of the nation-building projects of the era.

In Ottawa itself, the number of civil servants dipped only slightly in the immediate post war years, then quickly climbed as the federal government expanded its services to Canadians.[781] The post-war households began to produce children in record numbers, creating the Baby Boom.

Although the 1955 demographers did not have the census results to prove it,[782] the physical evidence of the boom was all too evident as houses mushroomed in the un-serviced plots in Nepean Township and in Ottawa's new subdivisions such as Alta Vista. Property owners in Gloucester and Nepean could still chop up farm fields into house lots and dirt streets using the ancient 'metes and bounds' system because the rural township councils refused to adopt even the most basic subdivision controls.[783]

The City of Ottawa re-established its planning capacity in the mid-1950s, adding professional staff to the Works Department to manage the development of its suburban lands.[784] Ottawa Mayor Charlotte Whitton (Figure 10-10) forged an uneasy alliance with the Federal District Commission (FDC) to build desperately needed new roads, bridges and sewers and to relocate the railroads. The colourful mayor was once overhead loudly declaring that "Ottawa's largest problem was SEWERS" during a royal visit to the National Gallery, much to the embarrassment of the vice-regal staff.[785]

FIGURE 10-10: Mayor Charlotte Whitton
Charlotte Whitton became the first female mayor of a major Canadian city in 1957 and was a central figure in Ottawa's post-war urban expansion; see Cast of Characters for a biography.
(Source: Library and Archives Canada/ Capital Press/Charlotte Elizabeth Whitton fonds/PA-121981 © Library and Archives Canada. Reproduced with the permission of Library and Archives Canada)

The City of Ottawa believed that land proposed for suburban development should be annexed to the city and serviced with roads and utilities. The city and the FDC attempted to control rural subdivision through the Ottawa Area Planning Board, but ultimately failed when faced by the determined opposition of Nepean and Gloucester township councils. After the unserviced development began to sprawl across the lands proposed for the Greenbelt, the federal government finally realized that it did not have the jurisdiction or powers needed to build the capital city it desired.

Renewing the Federal Commitment to a National Capital

The FDC still reported directly to the prime minister in 1956 and Louis St. Laurent responded to the local government issues the same way that Mackenzie King had in 1944. He appointed an all-party committee of the Commons and Senate to investigate and make recommendations on the situation.[786] The record of the committee's public hearings is a clear demonstration of the political and economic difficulties in implementing a plan for development of a capital city. Every local government and scores of stakeholders presented briefs[787] to the committee that outlined their many frustrations in managing the growth of the metropolitan area and the frictions between the 'Town and Crown' actors involved in the process.

The key presentations were those of the Federal District Commission, the City of Hull and the City of Ottawa. The FDC brief was essentially a detailed progress report on the implementation of the 1950 plan, with a request for more resources to carry on. Hull wanted more federal investment on the north shore of the river – more jobs, not just parks. The City of Ottawa's brief was written and delivered by Charlotte Whitton herself. She outlined the many problems caused by the rapid development of the federal capital and the strains in the city's finances as it struggled to accommodate growth and provide basic services. She was a harsh critic of the federal government's lack of respect for local rights. But the mayor also stressed the city's cooperation with the FDC in building a better capital city for Canada. Ottawa wanted a lot more money and more local say in the planning process.

The joint parliamentary committee was a successful exercise in building consensus for action at the federal level. The bipartisan committee strongly supported the FDC's work and the implementation of the 1950 plan. By 1956 it was clear that the $25 million National Capital Fund would not be large enough; inflation, expropriation of the Greenbelt, and more accurate cost estimates of required infrastructure substantially enlarged the cost of the plan. Almost $20 million had been spent by 1957, and a further $70 million was estimated for the next decade. The joint Senate-Commons committee recommended that the FDC's annual capital grant be at least doubled.[788]

The committee recognized that there was a serious jurisdictional issue at stake since municipal affairs were clearly a responsibility of the provincial governments under the 1867 *British North America Act* which served as Canada's constitution. The federal government had no jurisdiction over local governments on municipal development issues, leading to the problems predicted at the Confederation conference 90 years earlier by New Brunswick's J.H. Gray.[789] The joint committee recommended that the federal government co-operate with the provincial departments and expected them to persuade the local governments. But their proposed new legislation died on the order paper as Parliament was dissolved.[790]

At this point, a seismic shock to Canadian federal electoral politics interrupted consideration of the joint committee's report. Prairie populist John Diefenbaker won a minority government in 1957, ending a period where the Liberal Party held power for 22 straight years, and 46 out of the previous

61 years. In 1958, Diefenbaker's Progressive Conservatives won the largest parliamentary majority in Canadian federal history, building upon his vision for northern development and stressing his belief in "unhyphenated Canadianism."

A regime change of this magnitude could well have been the end of Laurier and Mackenzie King's dream of a more dignified capital city. Faced with the opposition or lukewarm support of an Ontario premier, Ottawa mayor and rural township reeves from the Conservative Party and a Union Nationale Québec premier, Diefenbaker might have wound up the FDC if the national capital had been regarded as a Liberal Party project. But Mackenzie King had done a good job positioning the capital city as a war memorial with national priority and the FDC's national outreach about the 1950 plan kept the issue before the country in a positive light. Similarly, if the FDC had been corrupt, ineffective or a Liberal patronage agency, it might have been disbanded or ignored, as Laurier's OIC was bypassed by Robert Borden's new Tory administration in 1911. However, the FDC and its planners had a reputation for sound financial management and for technical excellence in planning and engineering. The agency did not have many dramatic completed projects to show in 1957, but they were well underway on a wide range of infrastructure proposed by a widely-admired plan, with good project management.

Building a national capital that would inspire pride among all Canadians appealed to Diefenbaker's patriotism, and his majority government responded with surprisingly strong support. The 1958 Throne Speech marked a new beginning for the capital. Diefenbaker's government made a new *National Capital Act* a priority for his administration and the new legislation went further than the recommendations of the Joint Committee. The Federal District Commission was to be replaced by a National Capital Commission (NCC), with stronger powers, a larger budget and larger area of jurisdiction in the two provinces.[791]

Eliminating "federal district" from the name of the agency finally addressed Québec's fear of annexation of the Outaouais. The NCC's Board included distinguished Canadians appointed from every province and representatives from Ottawa and Hull. FDC chairman Lt. Gen. Howard Kennedy continued as Chair of the NCC, but Diefenbaker put his stamp on the organization by appointing several Conservatives to the new board. Diefenbaker also used a prime ministerial warrant to appoint the distinguished urban planner (and Saskatchewan native), Eric Thrift, as the new general manager of the agency.[792]

On June 18, 1958 Diefenbaker made a startling announcement in Parliament. Rather than depend upon the goodwill of the provinces, local government and land owners to establish the Greenbelt, the new NCC would be granted the power to borrow funds to purchase the land, and if needed, to expropriate them.[793] The NCC's negotiating position in purchase transactions was enhanced by its new powers to expropriate land. Over 14,000 ha. of land were acquired through negotiation or expropriation, and 2,500 ha. were controlled by federal agencies. In total, about 93 percent of the land was purchased.[794] The farmers and speculators who held the land received agricultural values for their property, without the profits they anticipated from future suburban subdivisions. Although most farmers were given the right to continue their operations indefinitely for nominal rent, some were angry to lose title to their lands which had been owned by several families for generations.

When Harold Munro's land in Gloucester Township was expropriated in 1959, he challenged the action in court, claiming that the expropriation was beyond the jurisdiction of the Parliament of Canada. The legal decisions that followed were eventually appealed all the way to the Supreme Court of Canada. In 1966, the Supreme Court made a strong ruling in favour of the Crown, with the judge stating that:

I find it difficult to suggest matter of legislation which more clearly goes beyond local or provincial interests and is the concern of Canada as a whole than the development, conservation and improvement of the National Capital Region in accordance with a coherent plan in order that the nature and character of the seat of the Government of Canada may be in accordance with its national significance.[795]

The highest court in the land had ruled that the construction of a national capital was a proper activity for the federal government, and that it could use its spending and expropriation powers to support the objective. Diefenbaker's initiative was an expensive and inelegant solution to the jurisdictional problems of planning the Canadian capital, and the heavy hand of expropriation would continue to cause outrage in the years ahead. But given the weakness of the federal constitutional position for municipal planning and Québec's opposition to a federal district, it was perhaps the only solution that gave the national government some control over its destiny in its own capital city. Canada would become the largest landowner in the new National Capital Region, and the Crown would exercise its rights to plan for the orderly development of its property. The NCC used its land ownership, expropriation power and infrastructure budget to shape urban form according to its plan.

The Greenbelt on the Ontario side of the Ottawa River was acquired or expropriated rapidly at the end of the 1950s, just ahead of the developers. It was intended to provide visual relief and some recreational amenities to suburban residents, but the Greenbelt also was intended as a site for the airport and federal research facilities that required large tracts of land and would benefit from a non-urban location.[796] The Greenbelt became home to the Defence Research Board, the Communications Research Centre, the Agricultural Research Centre, the Defence Providing Grounds and other federal facilities. More importantly, the Northern Electric Company (later named Bell Northern Research, Northern Telecom and Nortel Networks) was sold a 28-hectare site in the western Greenbelt to develop its research laboratories.[797]

The Federal Boom

With new powers and an expanded budget, the NCC moved rapidly to implement the Gréber plan in the late 1950s and early 1960s. The agency worked closely with Ottawa and Hull, which were often pleased by the deluge of federal dollars to improve their infrastructure and parks. The 1950 *Plan for the National Capital* was probably the most thoroughly implemented Canadian plan of the 20th century. By 1970, when most of the plan had been completed, the NCC had spent $244 million or ($1.9 billion in 2014) from 1947-1970 to acquire land and build parks, roads, utilities and other infrastructure (Figure 10-11).[798]

Freight railways and their associated industries were relocated to suburban sites by the late 1950s. The "Main Eastern Entrance Boulevard" was to replace the railway along the Rideau Canal (Figure 10-12). This was to be a classic eight-lane European multi-way boulevard, similar to those which grace Paris and Barcelona. Gréber had also planned a broad parkway for the former CN Rail right of way (Figure 10-13). The "Cross-Town Parkway" was designed as a hybrid of a European boulevard and North American parkway. It was intended to act as the capital's main east-west traffic artery. While these boulevards are now regarded as an elegant and efficient method of accommodating large volumes of traffic with a positive impact on adjacent lands,[799] they seemed a bit old-fashioned in the 1950s. When the Ontario Department of Highways agreed to fund part of the construction of the route in 1957, they insisted that the new provincial expressway standards be applied to the roads. Gréber was now 75, and his annual planning consultation in Ottawa had less impact.[800] The provincial, city[801] and NCC

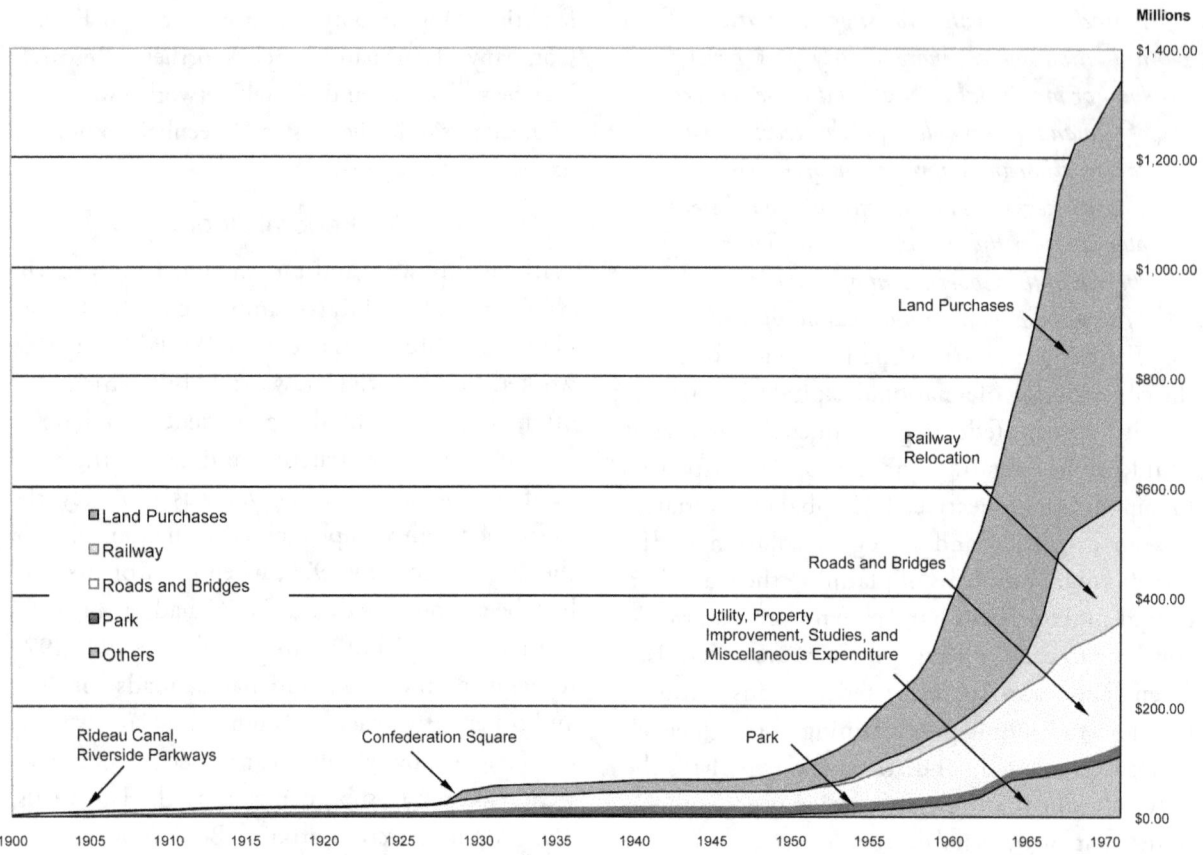

FIGURE 10-11: **Chart of Federal Expenditure**
NCC Cumulative Capital Expenditure by Project Type
(Source: FDC/NCC Annual Reports (1952-71), adjusted for inflation)

highway engineers enthusiastically embraced the freeway design proposed by leading American traffic engineering consultants DeLeuw Cather and Company.[802] Gréber's Cross-Town Parkway was re-named the Queensway in honour of Queen Elizabeth II, who dedicated the $35 million project in October 1957.[803] The NCC provided the land and planted the lush landscaping, most of which was destroyed in subsequent widenings of the expressway (Figure 10-14).

The NCC had more control over the design of its own parkway network, which was substantially upgraded and expanded in the 1950s and 1960s. The original OIC "scenic driveways," designed for horse and carriage traffic, were upgraded for low-speed automobile use. New parkways were built along the Ottawa River and Rideau Canal, with gentle curves, generous landscaping and careful attention to scenic views of the rivers, Gatineau Hills and Parliament Hill. The parkway corridors accommodated later additions of walkways and bikeways, creating the country's largest network of cycle routes.

FIGURE 10-12 **Main Entrance Boulevard to the National Capital**
This is Gréber's plan for the Main Entrance Boulevard to the National Capital. The photograph on the left shows the railway right-of-way selected by the NCC planners as the main route for the boulevard. The model to the left shows the main road from Montréal and the new rail station boulevard meeting at a grand boulevard lined with apartments and national offices; the boulevard follows the canal past a national stadium and an expanded Université d'Ottawa, creating a diagonal view of the Gothic buildings on Parliament Hill, perfectly framed in the Picturesque style. The view is partly visible today from the Rideau Canal and Nicholas Street, which functions as a long expressway ramp from the Queensway to Laurier Avenue.
(Source: Gréber, 1950, Figures 132 and 133, pp. 174-5)

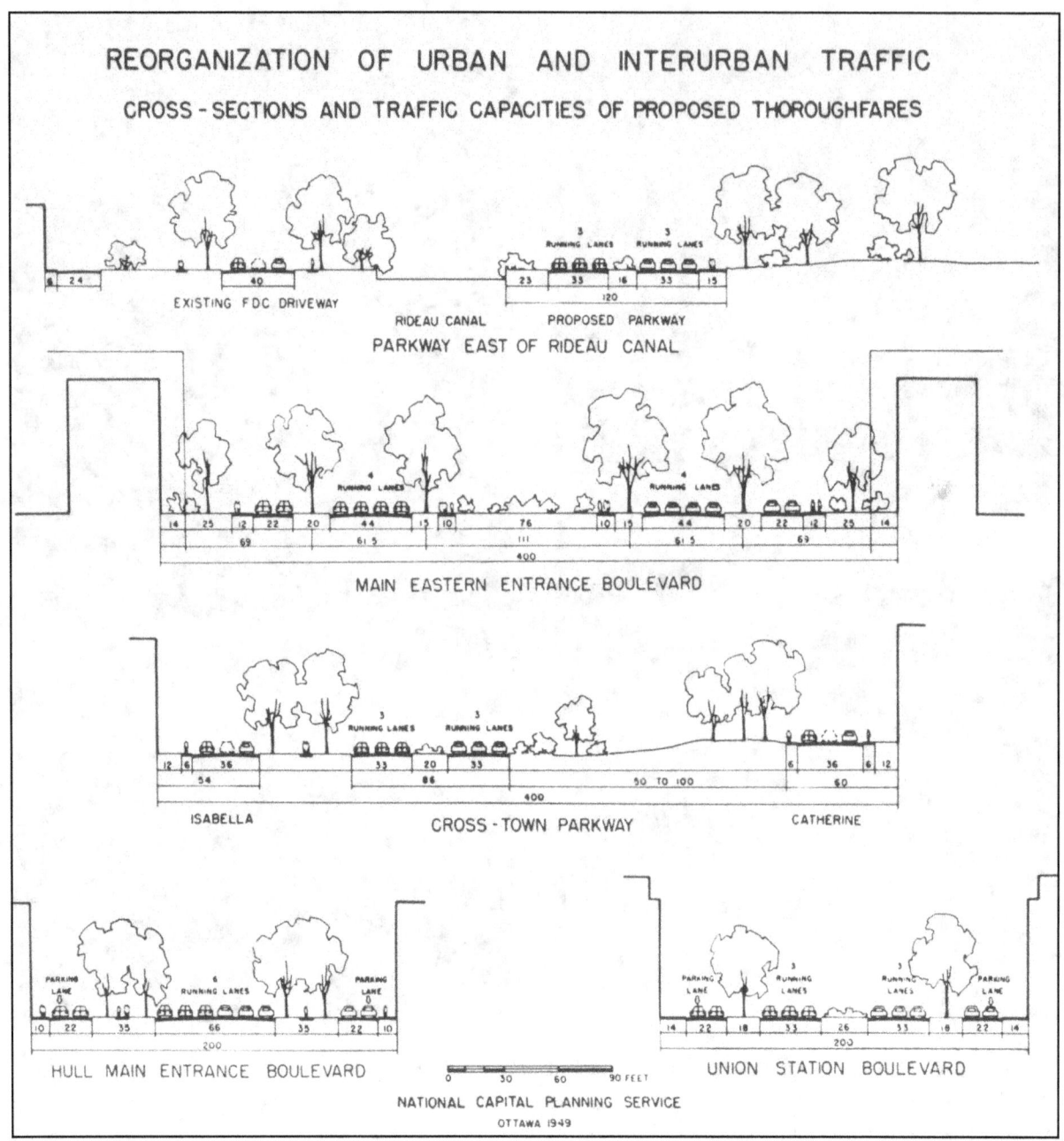

FIGURE 10-13 Road Cross-Sections. Gréber's designs for the main boulevards in Ottawa and Hull
The "Main Eastern Entrance Boulevard" above to replace the railway tracks and freight yards beside the Rideau Canal. The "Cross-Town Parkway" was to replace the east-west CN tracks, along the route now followed by the Queensway. Note the generous formal tree planting in the landscaped medians, the 6-8 lanes of through traffic and the local traffic lanes adjacent to the buildings which line the boulevards. These follow the best European traditions from Paris and Barcelona.
(Source: Gréber, 1950, Figure 145, p. 187)

FIGURE 10-14: The Queensway under construction, 1965
The cross-town CN railway tracks relocated by the NCC were replaced by this provincially funded expressway, rather than the parkway and boulevards recommended in Gréber's 1950 plan. Originally designed as a four lane expressway, it was later widened to six lanes by removing the parkway landscaping.
(Source: Canada. Dept. of Public Works; Library and Archives Canada/ PA-135171); © Library and Archives Canada. Reproduced with the permission of Library and Archives Canada)

The Golden Era of Federal-Local Co-operation in Ottawa

Charlotte Whitton pushed the policy of federal contributions to local public works to new heights in the 1950s and early 1960s (Figure 11-1). The OIC and FDC had always been leaders in beautifying the capital through open space, and most parks in Ottawa and Hull were acquired or landscaped with federal funds. Whitton's administration co-operated closely with the FDC and NCC on planning issues, and the City of Ottawa's first Official Plan, adopted in 1951, was simply the roads diagram from Gréber's 1950 report.[804] The mayor's price for this co-operation was massive federal funding for infrastructure. The City of Ottawa did not contribute a penny to the parkways and only minimally to the Queensway. Almost all bridges were federally funded on the grounds that they were inter-provincial or crossed the federally-owned Rideau Canal, or railways that had been relocated by the FDC.[805] Similarly, city arterials such as Carling Avenue, Smyth and Heron roads typically received 50 percent FDC/NCC funds if they partially served federal lands or buildings.

The FDC and NCC also cooperated with the city to develop new industrial parks. The federal government paid most of the costs for the industrial areas relocated near the railways, and co-operated with the municipal government for the city's industrial park near Russell Road.[806] Most surprisingly, the FDC shared the cost of planning the long-overdue trunk sewer system. The federal government made substantial contributions to the construction of the big pipes and the Green's Creek sewage treatment plant, which opened in 1963[807] (Figure 10-15).

FIGURE 10-15: The Green's Creek Sewage Treatment Plant
The City of Ottawa finally stopped pouring raw sewage into its namesake river in 1963, following the opening of this treatment plant built with federal cash and land subsides just inside the eastern boundary of the Greenbelt. Gatineau was even slower, starting sewage treatment in 1982.
(Source: Library and Archives Canada/, CMHC Collection, Detail from image negative no. 13255 – 2 and 3)

Ottawa City Hall

The City Hall that had been planned for Confederation Square never arrived because Ottawa City Council simply could not agree on a site. The federal government offered free land and construction assistance but the old political divisions between Upper Town and Lower Town tore the council apart on the issue. Gréber prepared plans for city hall at two prominent sites at either end of the Mackenzie King Bridge, or at Cartier Square, or on Lyon Street, but none could acquire majority support on Council.[808]

By 1955, the only place the council could agree upon was the old city hall site that had been pledged to the federal government after the 1931 fire, although the FDC had already landscaped the property as a park. Ottawa launched a national design competition for a new city hall on the old site, much to the annoyance of the FDC. In November 1955, the FDC chairman offered Mayor Charlotte Whitton her favourite federal site, Green Island at the mouth of the Rideau River, in exchange for clear title to the old city hall site. The new site was part of Thomas McKay's original sawmill complex, overlooking Rideau Falls.[809] McKay's industrial buildings declined in the early 20th century and the federal government used several abandoned factories as departmental offices during World War II. The National Capital Commission removed most of the remaining industrial buildings and created several attractive riverfront parks in the 1950s and 1960s.

In January 1956, Rother Bland Trudeau of Montréal won the design competition and a contract for the city hall on the Confederation Square site, but Whitton drove a deal through council to move the building site to Green Island. The architects were ordered to modify the design of their building to suit the new site.[810] John Bland and Charles Trudeau (brother of the future prime minister) designed a sleek building that was raised above the island on columns, in the best Modern style (Figure 10-16), a strong contrast to the Gothic or Château style of most federal buildings at that time.

The new city hall and parks helped raise the status of Thomas McKay's former industrial village in New Edinburgh. The neighbourhood was further improved when the NCC closed the original O&P railway line in 1965, in preparation for a road connection to Hull. Middle income families began to purchase and renovate the village's older houses and later defeated the NCC's plan to connect the Vanier Parkway to the new Macdonald-Cartier Bridge via the former railway right of way.

Figure 10-16: Ottawa City Hall
A modern slab floating above the *tabula rasa* – Le Corbusier might have approved. The box sticking out the front held the Council Chambers, later named Whitton Hall. The Rideau Falls are in the foreground; also note the ramps from the Macdonald-Cartier Bridge in the upper right, ready to connect to the Vanier Parkway, via a bridge that was to be built on the alignment at the decommissioned O&P Railway.
(Source: City of Ottawa Archives, CA- 8638)

Post-war Transit Planning

Unfortunately, plans for local roads, transit and land use were not well coordinated in the post-war period. Roads were maintained and occasionally planned by the engineers in local works departments. Transit was provided by separate private franchises in Hull and Ottawa, and the systems barely interconnected. When the Hull streetcar franchise ended in 1945, Hull residents voted in a referendum to replace it with a bus service.[811] The Ottawa Electric Railway's (OER) transit system had been overtaxed during the Second World War, and a few used 1911-era Toronto streetcars were the only additions to its fleet during this period. All new routes since 1921 had been served by buses. In 1948, with the end of its franchise in sight and no prospects for renewal, the OER's private owners dropped their plans for capital investment in the tram system. After Ottawa ratepayers voted to buy the transit system for $6 million, they received some relatively new buses and a streetcar system that was almost worn out.[812] The city established the Ottawa Transportation Commission (OTC) to manage the system and sought advice on its future.

In 1948, the OTC's engineering consultant recommended against new streetcar lines, cut unprofitable streetcar routes and recommended buses for new suburban routes. The commission promptly acquired the bus lines from Nepean, Eastview and Gloucester to give itself a transit monopoly. In the downtown area, the OTC began to experiment with trolley buses, which cost one-third the price of new streetcars and did not require tracks. The FDC reluctantly agreed to new overhead wires on Wellington Street, to reduce the pressure on Sparks and Queen, where a double-parked vehicle or a breakdown by one of the ancient streetcars would bring transit to a standstill[813] (Figure 10-17).

FIGURE 10-17: Cars and Trams
Parked cars and streetcars jam Sparks Street, ca. 1950. The narrow streets from Nicholas Sparks' subdivision were not wide enough for two-way traffic and streetcars.
(Source: Library and Archives Canada/ PA-165231)

Ottawa transit ridership plummeted by 23 percent between 1946 and 1953, despite the addition of the new bus routes, while automobile ownership more than doubled over the same period.[814] Rapid suburban development and the end of wartime restrictions on gasoline and automobile purchases led to similar declines and the death of streetcars systems in almost every North American city.[815] It appeared that the OTC would soon be in a crisis that required both a major capital contribution and an annual operating subsidy from the city. The municipal government began to intervene in the OTC's operations, with Mayor Whitton cutting the salaries of commission members and opposing further expenditures on new trolley bus lines.[816] As ridership and revenue continued to free-fall in 1957, the OTC proposed that the system be converted entirely to buses to reduce the operating deficit. A major consulting report commissioned by the city confirmed that buses were even cheaper than trolley coaches and did not require tracks, overhead wires or electric power distribution.[817] Faced with million dollar annual deficits, city council pulled the plug on the remaining trolley system in August 1958 and the last streetcars held a parade on Sparks Street on May 2, 1959.[818]

Suburban expansion

The NCC and Department of Public Works also made rapid progress on the decentralization of federal buildings to the suburbs during the 1950s and early 1960s. The relocation program had several objectives:

- to move federal functions that did not require access to Parliament (laboratories, printing, research units, tax returns) away from the expensive land in the congested core,
- to replace temporary war-time offices with inexpensive new buildings,
- to allow civil servants a short commute by automobile from the new suburbs, and
- to reduce the capital's exposure to an attack with nuclear bombs, which was a significant civil defense concern in the 1950s.[819]

Hull was the first area to benefit from the decentralization, when Ernest Cormier's design for the National Printing Bureau began construction in 1949, after a half-century of lobbying for a larger federal employment presence. Cormier's building signalled the change in the architectural style of Federal buildings. The offices in the front of the building were designed in the stripped classical style that Cormier employed for his original Supreme Court building proposal, but the printing plant at the rear of the building was a Bauhaus – inspired wall of glass and steel[820] (Figure 10-18).

The Modern style was a good fit with the decentralization program. Freed at last from Mackenzie King's conservative taste, federal architects could dispense with copper roofs and masonry construction in favour of lighter, less-expensive steel, glass and brick buildings. The suburban office nodes at Tunney's Pasture, Confederation Heights and Montréal Road had much in common with 1950s university campus design: low-rise Modern buildings were set in lots of green space, with plenty of free parking.[821] These suburban office campuses became the home of line agencies and research organizations such as Public Works, Health, Statistics Canada, CMHC, Revenue and the Post Office, while national cultural facilities and "command-and-control" functions such as Finance, Treasury Board, the Privy Council, Defence and the Bank of Canada remained near Parliament Hill (Figure 10-18).

Adjacent lands were designated for private development of new neighbourhoods where the new federally-insured, long-term mortgages ensured that veterans and middle class families could purchase a new house in a green suburb located only a few minutes' drive from work.[822]

FIGURE 10-18: National Printing Bureau, 1949
Hull's first federal building shows the transition in architectural style from stripped classical offices (left) to the Modern industrial building (right). Architect Ernest Cormier was working with Le Corbusier on the Modern design of the UN Headquarters (Figure 10-6) while the Printing Bureau was developed.
(Source: Library and Archives Canada/ PA-146193, G. Lunney photograph)

Unfortunately, the original rural township surveys in Nepean and Gloucester had irregular geometries and no interconnection across the Rideau River or across the Ottawa River with Québec. As a result, the suburban arterial road network is fragmented. These suburban residential areas were designed on the neighbourhood unit principle, where each area had its own elementary school, park and local shopping centre. Often, a collection of these neighbourhoods supported a high school and larger community shopping centre. Westgate, Ottawa's first suburban shopping centre, opened in 1954.[823]

This decentralization of jobs, housing, and shopping was further accelerated by rapid construction of new suburban roads for automobile travel. The suburban neighbourhoods largely were built in the locations suggested in the 1950 plan, but the local governments did not build the radial street patterns suggested by Gréber (Figure 10-4), preferring to extend the original rural grid, using conventional North American traffic engineering practices.

The 1950 plan enthusiastically pushed universal auto mobility and bus transit as a transportation strategy, rather than the urban streetcar network proposed by Bennett and Cousins in 1915.

The rural townships had their hands full managing the transition from farms to modern suburbs and could provide little support for roads or utilities. Most local governments were scrambling to accommodate rapid growth caused by the post-war boom. Municipal planning was minimal and most eastern Ontario townships did not adopt official plans until the late 1960s.[824] The local governments in the Québec portion of the region adopted their first plans in the 1970s.[825]

FIGURE 10-19: Tunney's Pasture Design Model
This field was near the western edge of the capital in 1949. It was planned as a suburban campus for new buildings for the Department of Health and the Dominion Bureau of Statistics, whose laboratories and offices did not need to be adjacent to Parliament.
(Source: Library and Archives Canada/NCP 1202 Container 2000783685; reprinted with permission)

Reflections

The early professional reviews of the 1950 plan were mixed. Many Canadian architects and landscape architects wanted the plum commission and resented Gréber as foreign consultant.[826] Once the project was underway, it was highly visible and often regarded as the most important Canadian plan in progress.[827] Advocates of Modern architecture attacked the plan and the early building designs vigorously, perhaps incited by the plan's Beaux-Arts presentation.[828]

An early critique came from Harold Spence-Sales, director of McGill University's urban planning program, and Canada's only professor of planning in 1949. He believed that "our National Capital is a small city that can only support a limited amount of grandeur, or become a hollow spectre."[829] Spence-Sales recommended even more decentralisation then Gréber:

Only when the population of the capital grows far beyond 500,000 – and the spacious urban area and its surrounding Greenbelt are no longer able to contain such an increase – do the proposals admit that satellite development may be necessary. An eventuality unforeseeable for generations![830]

Spence-Sales opposed the scale and grand urban design elements of the plan, invoking the criticisms usually deployed against City Beautiful projects:

> *In essence the plan derives its heroic qualities from forces at play to create a capital city after a bygone European concept. That stateliness transplanted to other climes may produce a mirage of magnificence, neither achieving the essential qualities of its origins, nor reflecting the cultural complexities of the countries to which it is applied ... The pursuit of the ideal of visual beauty may have obscured the significance of the structure of Canadian cities.*[831]

The Achilles heel of the Gréber plan was its population projection. The post-war Baby Boom and rapid government expansion were unforeseen by the planners, the national demographer who prepared the forecast, and also by critics such as Spence-Sales.[832] The land use planning was correct – the 1950 plan did accommodate the proposed 500,000 people within the Greenbelt, but the population grew so fast that that the opportunity to absorb suburban growth with stand-alone new towns in the London manner was lost.

Perhaps the most perceptive contemporary critique came from the prominent Modernist Toronto planner Hans Blumenfeld. He identified the low population projections, praised the freight railway relocations and parks system, and criticized the closing of the downtown rail station. He believed that Gréber had gone too far in pushing the private automobile, and predicted that Ottawa might become as automobile dependent as Los Angeles.[833] Although closely identified with Modern architecture and planning, Blumenfeld was surprisingly sympathetic to the urban design objectives of the 1950 plan.[834] His conclusion was a rebuke to the critics of the City Beautiful:

> *Gréber rightly emphasized that the desire for beauty is not the preserve of upper-class snobs, but a basic and universal human need. As influence and leisure time increase, the value of the esthetic qualities of the National Capital Region created by the Master Plan will rise from year to year.*[835]

Today, it is tempting to dismiss the 1950 plan, and Jacques Gréber, as relics of the past. Any plan rendered in watercolour paintings, charcoal sketches and a tapestry invites classification as part of the abandoned City Beautiful movement, and Gréber's Beaux Arts background only reinforces this first suspicion. A closer reading of the plan reveals a remarkable montage of themes:

- a civic survey of Geddesian thoroughness;
- a parks system inspired by Olmsted and Todd;
- grand downtown boulevards and plazas that echo the City Beautiful's Burnham and Bennett;
- a Greenbelt and satellite towns in the Garden City tradition of Howard and Abercrombie;
- City Efficient railroad, expressway, utility and zoning proposals from Cauchon and Cousins;
- CIAM land use planning and urban renewal proposals, and
- suburban planning using Perry's neighbourhood unit.

Many of the ideas were adapted from previous plans (generously acknowledged) and few of the theoretical approaches are original. Gréber's accomplishment was to weave a plan using the best threads of the many planning movements from the first half of the century, avoid the worst excesses (except for LeBreton Flats) and package the proposals in a manner that facilitated implementation. A rich and determined client, served by a powerful and skilled development agency, ensured that the Crown's plea would be thoroughly implemented, despite the rigorous opposition of the rural townships.

Conflict with the City of Ottawa and the City of Hull in the immediate post-war era was muted by the great flood of federal cash invested in desperately-needed infrastructure projects. The Crown also had an overwhelming advantage in technical capacity during the 1950s, which was an era when professional expertise was highly valued. Their advantages would begin to diminish in the decades ahead as the Crown's largesse receded and the Towns developed their own professional and political voices.

CHAPTER 11

Boom Town (1960-69)

The political context for building Canada's capital city changed during the 1960s. As a young federal civil servant in the 1950s, Pierre Elliott Trudeau referred to Ottawa as "an English capital" because of its culture and working language. Ottawa offered little to interest a brilliant, bilingual Québec native in this era, and Trudeau quickly returned to Montréal.[836]

Ottawa's reputation as an English capital city became increasingly inappropriate during the rise of Québec nationalism in the "Quiet Revolution" of the 1960s.[837] One of the first visible changes was the flag that flew throughout the capital city. The British Union Flag had flown from Parliament Hill from 1867 until 1945. It was replaced by the Red Ensign, the flag that Canadian troops fought under during World War II. However, the Ensign combined the British Union Flag with Canada's coat of arms, and was not popular in Québec. Prime Minister Lester Pearson promoted a new flag that was a uniquely Canadian symbol and, after much controversy, the red and white maple leaf flag was raised over the Peace Tower on Parliament Hill on February 15, 1965.[838]

The change in flags was just the first symbol of the changes in the country's governance arrangements in the decades ahead. Canada's constitutional odyssey grappled with increasing Québec nationalism, even as the nation swelled with pride over the 1967 centennial of Confederation, commissioning monuments and memorials across the country.[839] Although many elements of Canadian governance were in flux during the 1960s, provincial governments remained fully in control over municipal development and planning during a period of rapid urban growth. The federal government's influence over the capital city would depend upon its land ownership, funding power and the creativity of its plans and programs.

Local Governance and Planning in the Capital Region

Although Toronto and Winnipeg had shown leadership in creating new structures for metropolitan governance, the National Capital Commission (NCC) remained the only regional planning agency operating in the Ottawa-Hull area during the boom years leading to 1969. Most local governments in the Ottawa Valley had minimal roles in planning the redevelopment and urban expansion of the region during that era because they often lacked political will and staff resources to act. The federal government had established the Community Planning Association of Canada (CPAC) as an advocacy organization to encourage municipal planning, and a National Capital Region Branch was formed in 1955. The CPAC brought together planning enthusiasts from across the region, along with representatives from realtors, industrialists, architects, historic preservation and social service advocates. It was open to a wider variety of interests than the Professional Town Planning Institute of Canada, and often included a few women.[840]

Progress in establishing local planning capacity was painfully slow outside Ottawa. The Federal District Commission (FDC) and NCC planners assisted Hull throughout the 1950s, and Nepean retained a consultant to produce a zoning bylaw in 1959.[841] But Nepean's rural council was engaged in "growth without planning," and almost its entire area inside the Greenbelt was haphazardly subdivided before the township adopted a municipal plan in 1970.[842] Gloucester Township fared slightly better, getting neighbourhood plans prepared by NCC staff and consultants approved just before their lands inside the Greenbelt were subdivided in the mid-1960s.[843]

The City of Ottawa was the only local government with in-house planning capacity in the early 1960s. The Planning Branch expanded from a one-person operation in 1957, extending its activity beyond subdivision co-ordination and roads. Since the city's lands were almost entirely built out by this time, the staff did not prepare a comprehensive plan for the entire municipality.[844] Instead, they prepared plans for urban elements that needed shaping during the redevelopment process such as roads (1953), parks (1959) and housing/urban renewal (1958-60). City council finally adopted a city-wide, comprehensive zoning bylaw in 1962,[845] almost 40 years after Noulan Cauchon's draft had been set aside. Local land owners now understood the value of some restrictions on building height and land use in adjacent properties, and council wanted control over redevelopment. Since the zoning bylaw essentially protected existing uses, virtually all redevelopment after 1962 would have to come before council for a re-zoning approval.

The new zoning bylaw made a significant change to the permitted building heights downtown, increasing them to 150 feet (46 m.) above grade, from the 110 feet (34 m.) enacted by the city in 1914 during the work of the Federal Plan Commission. The city retained the consulting advice of Britain's Sir Robert Matthew and Philadelphia's Edmund Bacon, who both argued that the new height limit was appropriate.[846] The 1927 Peace Tower was in fact higher than the 1866 Victoria Tower that Edward Bennett planned for (347 ft. or 106 m. above grade). The Peace Tower would remain the dominant feature in the Ottawa landscape, because Parliament Hill was the highest point of land in the downtown, so the NCC did not object to Ottawa's new policy.

New Federal Investment for Hull

In the federal subsidy game, Hull started later and slower than Ottawa, but would play as well as its southern neighbours during in the 1960s and 1970s. The National Capital Planning Service acted as Hull's planning agency for much of the 1950s, assisting the municipality with staff and funding for site plans, urban renewal studies and the draft of its first municipal plan. The FDC acquired or landscaped several Hull parks and areas along Brewery Creek and the Ottawa River in the 1960s.[847] The city also requested federal assistance for new roads and bridges.

Hull took the lead in the greatest (and last) example of intergovernmental co-operation in the region, the Macdonald-Cartier Bridge. The 1950 plan had called for replacement of the Alexandra and Lemieux Island railway trusses with modern road bridges. By 1958, Gréber was publicly advocating replacing the Alexandra Bridge, which was hopelessly congested after being jury-rigged to take a single lane of traffic in each direction following the removal of Hull's streetcar tracks. A brief endorsed by Ottawa, Eastview, Hull and 27 other Québec municipalities petitioned Prime Minister Diefenbaker for a new bridge to replace the 1901 structure, which had been damaged in the 1948 fire at the Eddy plant. The brief stressed the complete unsuitability of the bridge and its Ottawa approaches for truck traffic.[848] The City of Ottawa and FDC both had traffic engineering studies in hand that emphatically recommended a new bridge before 1965.[849] Since roads and bridges were actually a provincial responsibility, the federal government asked that Ontario and Québec be involved. It took over a year for the five parties to complete a cost-sharing agreement (Figure 11-1), which seems lightning-fast today.

The project consultants made an innovative recommendation. Rather than replace the Alexandra Bridge, a completely new span was proposed just east of the Rideau Falls and Brewery Creek, thus avoiding the tortuous approaches to the existing bridge along the Nepean Point cliffs. Instead, the new bridge could be connected to the abandoned right of way of Thomas McKay's Ottawa and Prescott railway, making a direct connection to the Queensway at the new Ottawa rail station. This elegant proposal solved three problems at once: truck traffic would be routed down an existing rail corridor, Hull residents would have convenient road access to the new rail station, and the Alexandra Bridge could remain open for light traffic. As a bonus, the new bridge

FIGURE 11-1: **Five governments signing the agreement for the Macdonald-Cartier Bridge**
The high-water point of intergovernmental co-operation in the development of the region was reached on February 27, 1961, when (left to right) representatives of the Ottawa, Ontario, federal, Québec and Hull governments signed the cost-sharing agreement for a new bridge across the Ottawa River. Charlotte Whitton signs for Ottawa, while René Lésvesque, Minister of Public Works signs for Québec! Hull Mayor Armand Turpin (extreme right), Hull MP Oswald Parent (third from left) and NCC General Manager Eric Thrift (above, extreme left) look on.
(Source: Bibliothèque et Archives nationales du Québec- Gatineau; Oswald Parent collection P. 58-150)

would also connect to King Edward Boulevard and Lower Town.

The two provincial governments started work on the bridge, while the NCC began to build the four-lane road (now the Vanier Parkway) along the former railway line from the Queensway to Sussex Drive (Figure 11-2). But the parkway connection was missing when the new bridge opened on October 15, 1965. Thomas McKay's former industrial village, New Edinburgh, had gentrified, and the residents liked the new access to the Rideau River created when the tracks were removed behind two blocks on Stanley and Crichton streets. They lobbied the City of Ottawa and their MP to have this key riverside parcel remain as a park, and succeeded, stopping the Vanier Parkway at Beechwood Avenue. Although this result was delightful for that small corner of New Edinburgh, it was a disaster for Lower Town, Rideau Street and Sandy Hill, as the huge modern transport trucks rumble down 19th century streets that are completely unsuitable for this use. Twenty blocks were blighted in these neighbourhoods to improve the prospects of two blocks of another area, with no solution in sight 40 years later. This was the beginning of a period of neighbourhood resistance to transportation projects that continues to this day.

FIGURE 11-2: **Approaches to the Macdonald-Cartier Bridge, 1967**
This model shows planned approaches to the Macdonald-Cartier Bridge from the Hull side. Note at the top left a proposed bridge across the Rideau River to connect to the Vanier Parkway, following an abandoned railway line. This connection was dropped at the last minute leaving large trucks to trundle through 20 blocks of downtown neighbourhoods.
(Source: Canada. Commission de la Capitale nationale. Services d'information;[850] Library and Archives Canada Mikan no. 4198933; ©Library and Archives Canada)

A New Railway Station

Although removal of the mid-town rail yards to Walkley Road was an obvious improvement, removal of the downtown freight yards on Rideau Street would have to wait until the location of a combined passenger station was agreed to in the 1960s. Gréber had prepared detailed plans for a downtown multi-modal passenger terminal at the Rideau Street site as early as 1939.[851] The motivation for the relocation of the passenger station was complicated by the Canadian Pacific Railway's discomfort in working from a "Union Station" owned and operated by its fierce rival, Canadian National.[852] The relocation was also a part of a general interest in removing all the railway tracks from downtown Ottawa and Hull, since their hundreds of level crossings interfered with traffic movement and steam engines belched soot over the adjacent buildings.[853] The final argument was the need for better automobile access to the station. The 1909 Union Station had excellent streetcar access and was within walking distance of Parliament Hill, but by 1960, many rail passengers arrived by car or taxi, and Union Station was the point of maximum traffic congestion in the region.

After several false starts, the station was built at the Riverside Drive/Vanier Parkway/Queensway interchange, nearly 3 km. south of the 1909 building. John Parkin's new station was a dramatic contrast to the Beaux Arts terminal on Rideau Street. The Massey Medal-winning design is an icon of Canadian Modern architecture, incorporating a huge steel truss to cover the entrance way and station.[854] The new station had excellent automobile access for Ottawa from the day it opened, but passengers could no longer walk to downtown destinations and the rapid transit connection waited until the 1990s. Since the railways had previously announced the end of separate passenger services to Hull, the new station would also serve the Outaouais. It was proposed to be connected by the Vanier Parkway and a connection to the Macdonald-Cartier Bridge, which was never completed.

Although the new station is only 3 km. from its former downtown site, over time, the relocation of the passenger terminal emerged as a planning error. While functionally connected to the downtown (taxi and express bus connections take less than 10 minutes), moving the train station to the inner suburbs seems symbolically wrong today. In retrospect, Gréber's 1939 plan seems much better, removing the freight yards, covering the train sheds and connecting the station to Hull and Ottawa streetcars.[855]

Bad Ideas from the 1960s I: Urban Renewal

Urban renewal was a common local planning activity across Canada in the 1950s and 1960s because generous funding was available from the federal Central Mortgage and Housing Corporation to remove housing that was in poor condition and to rebuild deteriorated neighbourhoods. The inner cities in National Capital Region had many deteriorated houses because many inexpensive wooden buildings from the turn of the century were reaching the end of their useful lives. Hull, Ottawa and Eastview all launched urban renewal studies that involved extensive building condition inventories and social surveys. Ottawa's urban renewal surveys were by far the most extensive. In 1958-59 the city staff examined 13 areas, including 168 blocks and over 6,000 dwelling units.[856] The surveys were overseen by an expert consulting panel chaired by Gordon Stephenson (University of Toronto), with John Bland (McGill) and Jean Issalys (Hull).[857]

The city's 1959 survey analyzed the 13 study areas and ranked LeBreton Flats as the neighbourhood most in need of urban renewal (Figure 11-3). The municipal reports cited the large proportion of run-down and severely deteriorated housing units and the indiscriminate mix of industrial, residential and commercial uses left over from the area's rapid re-building after the 1900 fire[858] (Figure 11-3).

Figure 11-3: Existing Conditions – LeBreton Flats, ca. 1959
Left – Mixed industrial/residential buildings, from Urban Renewal Survey
Right – Wooden house at 619 Booth Street
(Source: Left – City of Ottawa, *Urban Renewal*, Figure 132; Right – DPW Collection,[859] Library and Archives Canada, Mikan no. 3932663)

The city staff dropped LeBreton Flats from their municipal urban renewal program because on April 18, 1962, the NCC expropriated the lands "as a site for government buildings and further development of the Ottawa River shoreline." Most of the expropriated lands were railway yards, streets and industrial buildings (Figure 11-4) but the site also included homes for approximately 225 families. The tight-knit, working-class community was devastated and the residents were scattered across the city when the buildings were demolished in 1965.[860] The NCC retained Walter Gropius' firm, The Architects' Collaborative, to prepare a preliminary plan in 1963, and Cabinet approved the relocation of the Department of National Defence (DND) from their "temporary buildings" on Cartier Square in 1964. The initial plans called for the country's largest office complex but, after consultation with city officials, a revised plan by an Ottawa firm (Figure 11-4) was unveiled in April 1967 containing high-rise residential buildings and the DND headquarters.[861]

The LeBreton Flats proposal was capital city planning in the Modern style, somewhat reminiscent of Brasilia.[863] The Modernist approach exemplified by Brasilia was the dominant design model for the monumental core of capital cities after the 1950s[864] (Figure 11-5). In LeBreton Flats, the railway yards were relocated, parks were built along the river and the parkway was connected to Wellington Street during the 1960s. But the rest of the project stalled in 1969 when the federal government announced that the DND would move into a new building beside the Rideau Canal downtown.[865] The Flats sat empty while the federal government looked at new office locations in Hull.[866]

The City of Ottawa continued with its own urban renewal program, focusing upon the next areas on its list of sites that needed substantial interventions – Preston Street and Mechanicsville. Council declared Preston Street an urban renewal area in 1963, and expropriated 15 acres to create a site for a high school and public housing[870] (Figure 11-6). Ottawa continued with several urban renewal projects in the central area throughout the 1960s, while Hull completed its urban renewal study in 1964 and began expropriating housing near rue Sacré Coeur.[871]

FIGURE 11-4: **Twin Aerial Photos, LeBreton Flats – before and model**
Top: Air photo of LeBreton Flats before expropriation viewed from high over downtown, looking west, from the City of Ottawa's urban renewal study. Note the rail yards and declining industry surrounding the site and cutting it off from the river.
Bottom: Model of 1967 Modernist plan by Balharrie-Helmer-Strutt. The riverfront parks and parkway were built but development of the remainder of the site stalled when the Defence headquarters stayed downtown.
(Source: Top – City of Ottawa Archives. CA 008544; Bottom – NCP collection,[862] Library and Archives Canada, Detail from image Mikan no. 3932658, reprinted with permission)

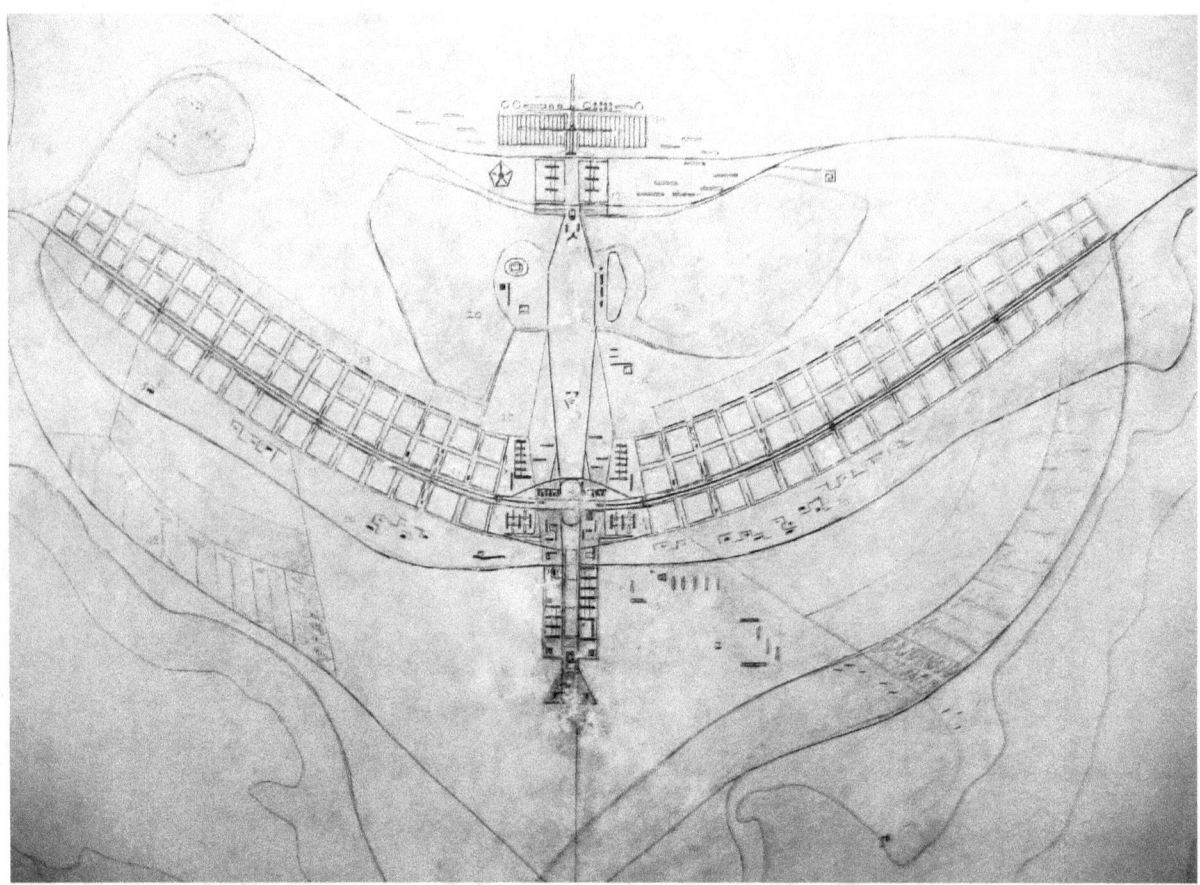

FIGURE 11-5: A Modern Capital Plan – Brasilia 1960
Brazil's 1891 Constitution called for a capital city to be established in the central plains of the vast country, but the seat of government stubbornly remained in Rio de Janeiro until a 1956 presidential election campaign by Juscelino Kubitschek.[867]

Brasilia's chief architect was Oscar Niemeyer, who had collaborated with Le Corbusier on the design of Rio's 1936 Ministry of Education building and the 1950 UN Headquarters.[868] Just ten days after the implementation agency was formed, Niemeyer started a national design competition to create the Brasilia plan. Lucio Costa's winning Plano Piloto (pilot plan) looked like a huge airplane, with the government buildings arranged along a monumental north-south axis and residential super-blocks deployed along a curving east-west expressway.

Brasilia had a schedule and a plan, but no budget. Implementation was driven by the absolute requirement for the 1960 opening ceremony at the end of President Kubitschek's term. Since this was only three years past the selection of Costa's plan, construction proceeded at a breakneck pace, with most of the costs picked up by the national government. Brasilia's Modernist plan was influential in the 1960s and was designated as a UNESCO World Heritage Site in 1987.[869]

(Source: Brazil, Governo do Districto Federal / SEDUH)

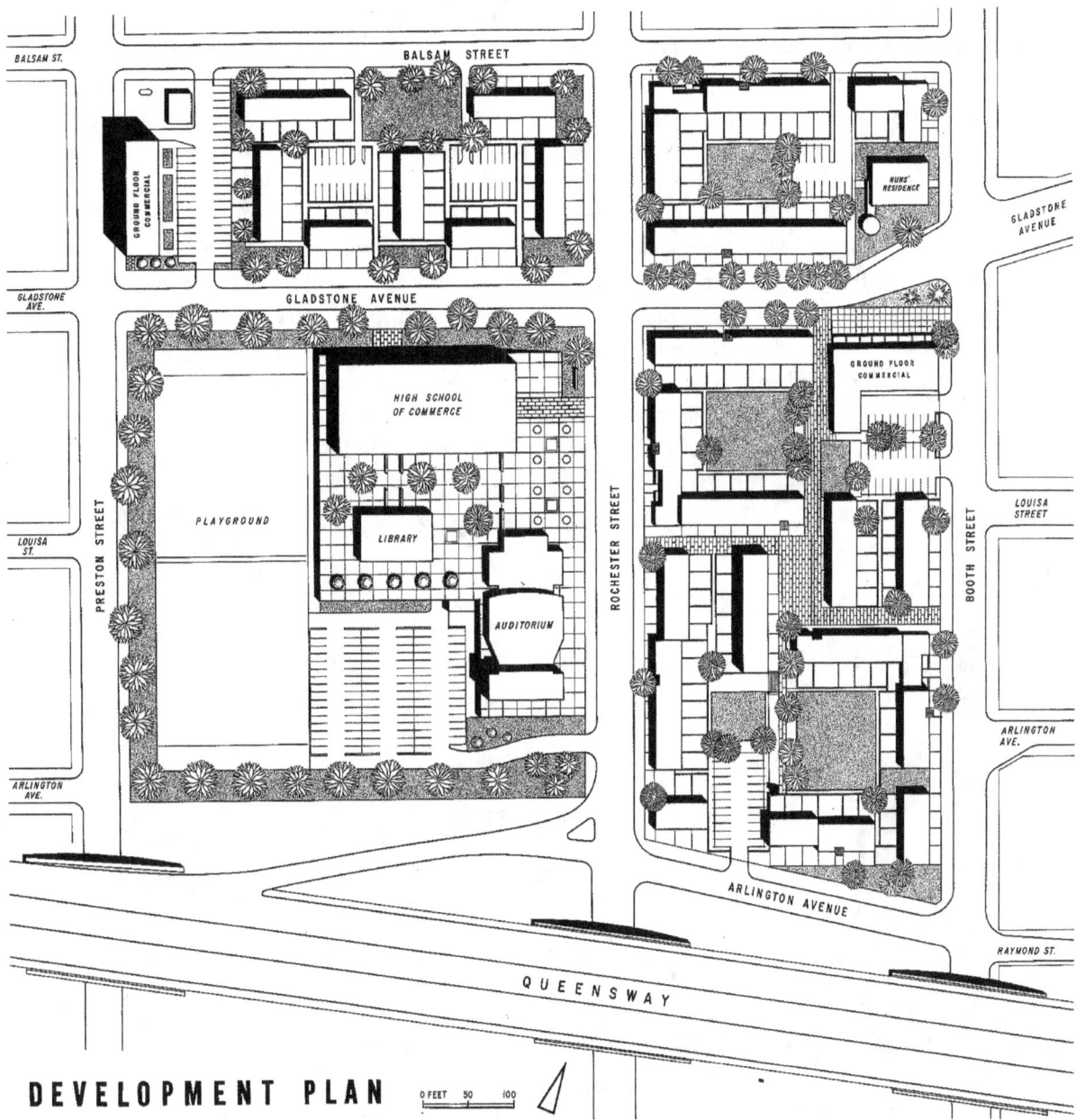

FIGURE 11-6: Preston Street Urban Renewal Plan
This was the first of several urban renewal plans by the City of Ottawa, where buildings in poor condition were expropriated to be replaced by public housing, institutions and commercial uses.
(Source: *Ottawa Urban Renewal*, Figure 29, p. 80)

Sparks Street Mall

The Sparks Street merchants and landowners reacted quickly to the May 1959 removal of the streetcars and the shift to shopping centres with an innovative proposal to counter the appeal of the new suburban malls. During the fall of 1959, the Ottawa Board of Trade organized a trip to Toledo for businessmen and public officials to see "what many had never seen before, a pedestrian precinct in the heart of downtown."[872] On their return, some of the Ottawa merchants were enthusiastic about the concept and formed a Sparks Street Development Association to improve the area. A local architect, Watson Balharrie, published a sketch of how Sparks Street might look, if developed as a pedestrian mall[873] (Figure 11-7). Moving quickly, the Development Association raised $15,000 from their members based upon a proportional scale related to the assessed value of their property. They lobbied Ottawa City Council, which matched their grant, and passed the bylaw to close the street from June until September.[874]

A downtown pedestrian mall was a radical planning idea in 1959. Of course, there were numerous historic precedents for pedestrian areas from the pre-automobile era and these plans were well known among urban designers in the late 1950s.[875] But as the prevailing planning methods from the Modern movement stressed rapid

FIGURE 11-7: Sparks Street Mall Design
Original Balharrie sketch of temporary mall, 1959.
(Source: Sparks Street Research Committee, p. 3)

automobile movement via expressways, the modern street was considered to be essentially medieval in its function and form and, thus, obsolete. Henceforth, pedestrians were to be separated from vehicular traffic and accommodated in "streets in the air," underground concourses or footpaths in parks.

Europe provided several precedents for pedestrian streets. The British New Towns of Stevenage and Harlow had central shopping areas with pedestrian malls, adapting an American suburban type of retail space to new English downtowns.[876] In 1958, Kalamazoo, Michigan created North America's first pedestrian street, designed by Victor Gruen, quickly followed by the Toledo mall that the Ottawa merchants visited.[877]

From the outset, the Sparks Street Mall was an initiative of the local merchants and the city government. The NCC donated some design services to prepare an initial plan for the mall, and its Director of Planning sat on its design committee. But the program and design were locally-driven, with Balharrie donating his time to prepare a design.[878] The architect and the design committee worked quickly to prepare plans for a temporary pedestrian mall: the asphalt was painted in bold stripes to imitate the paving in European squares; benches were brought in; the NCC loaned some trees from its nursery, which were placed in concrete planters. Five restaurants opened sidewalk cafes, the Ottawa Tourist Office built a small information kiosk and the NCC put its model of downtown Ottawa on display under an awning by Confederation Square. The temporary mall was a model of Modern design on a shoestring budget (Figure 11-8).

Although many were sceptical during the planning, the Sparks Street Mall quickly filled with pedestrians and was an obvious success from the day it opened.[879] The merchants quickly lobbied for repeat performances in the following years and a 1963 Citizen's Committee recommended that a permanent mall be built. The City of Ottawa paid half the cost and established a Mall Authority in 1965. The four-block permanent mall, designed by Balharrie, opened in June 1967, just in time for the tourist invasion celebrating the centennial of Canada's confederation. The Sparks Street Mall continued to be a success into the early 1970s, and the concept was extended west of Bank Street when the adjacent blocks were redeveloped for federal offices. It also helped popularize pedestrian malls for other Canadian cities.

In Canada, Ottawa's Sparks Street led the way in popularizing pedestrian malls. Calgary opened the Eighth Avenue mall in 1969, and Vancouver pedestrianized Robson Street. Soon after, Windsor, Sherbrooke, Montréal, Kingston, Edmonton, St. John's, Regina, and Toronto tried temporary summer malls on their main streets. Many of the schemes were an initial success, but most did not become permanent.[880] Instead, Montréal and Toronto developed extensive underground passageways interconnecting their subway stops, and Calgary built a network of second-storey pedestrian bridges.

A small federal cultural precinct emerged at the east end of the mall, at Confederation Square. After the failure of a 1952 architectural competition for a new building on Cartier Square, the National Gallery was relocated in 1960 to an interim office building on Elgin Street, just south of Sparks.[881] The federal government's Centennial project, the National Arts Centre, opened on the opposite site of the Square in 1969. These important institutions added to the cultural life in Ottawa, but they hardly contributed to the street life in Confederation Square. The National Gallery was housed on the upper floors of the office building and the National Arts Centre turned its back on the Square, with its main entrance fronting on the Rideau Canal.

FIGURE 11-8: Temporary Mall, Summer, 1960
The asphalt on Sparks Street was painted to resemble European paving and street furniture was trucked in to make a surprisingly successful public place. Today, we would call this technique "tactical urbanism."
(Source: NCC 1968, p. 11)

FIGURE 11-9: Permanent Mall, ca. late 1960s
The traditional main street attempts to compete with the new suburban shopping malls. Attractive 1960s street furniture, but heritage buildings re-clad in Modern materials by private owners.
(Source: NCC)

Bad Ideas from the 1960s II: Downtown Towers

The new downtown office blocks were rarely the elegant departmental buildings suggested in Gréber's plan because the NCC lost control of federal building initiatives in the mid-1960s. Although all federally-constructed buildings were subject to design review by the NCC, the Department of Public Works (DPW) began to lease space from private developers to accommodate the rapid growth of the civil service at a lower cost.[882] The private developers erected quite ordinary commercial buildings to meet the demand.

In the mid-1960s, Robert Campeau, a politically-connected suburban developer, destroyed the new downtown plans of both the City of Ottawa and the NCC. Campeau was a prominent federal Liberal with close ties to Public Works Minister George McIlraith,[883] and he was also involved in an on-going feud with Conservative Mayor Charlotte Whitton.[884] He briefly considered running against Whitton, and then publicly supported the campaign of controller Don Reid in hopes that "this dictatorship will cease."[885] Reid ousted the combative Whitton in a divisive campaign.[886]

The new mayor took office in January 1965, and within weeks, Campeau made an unsolicited offer to buy the city-owned parking lots on the site of the former Ottawa Transit Commission (OTC) garage at Lyon and Albert streets. He offered $851,000 for the entire block, located in the former warehouse district, several blocks west of the downtown boundary in the city's new zoning bylaw. Despite opposition from downtown merchants, a negative vote by city council and two subsequent higher bids, the Board of Control, led by Mayor Reid, pushed the sale to Campeau through.[887]

Within weeks, the Opposition was asking questions in Parliament about whether Campeau had a deal with the federal government for office space. Campeau was soon back with a proposal to build a hotel and office tower on the site. He announced: "We have planned the towers to meet the present height limits, but we hope to build them higher."[888] He returned in two months with towers 225 feet high, a 50 percent increase over the height limit. City council approved these plans, despite the vigorous opposition of its own planning staff and of the NCC.[889] The NCC, supported by the city's planners, appealed the zoning amendment to the Ontario Municipal Board (OMB), which was once again unsympathetic to arguments about the need for a graceful national capital, ruling in favour of the municipal council.[890] Ironically, the NCC's case had been undermined when federal Public Works Minister McIlraith announced that there should be new emphasis on building space for government offices in downtown buildings.[891]

The City of Ottawa planners were appalled as their downtown plans were wrecked only a year after they had been approved. It was now understood that the new city council would approve almost any request to exceed the 150 foot height limit in the downtown, and the federal Department of Public Works was openly working at cross-purposes with the NCC. City council was thrilled at the prospect of property and business taxes from the proposed private towers, rather than tax-exempt government buildings. Public Works could lease cheap office space fast, since only federally-owned buildings needed to go through the NCC's design review approval process.[892]

Within days of city council's approval of the new towers, Robert Campeau revealed that he had bought the adjacent block. Emboldened by his success at the OMB, Campeau proposed a re-zoning for office towers that would be 450 feet (137 m.), triple the height limit, and over 100 feet (30 m.) higher than the Peace Tower.[893] City council approved this rezoning too, despite the objections of its own Planning Board, and the NCC once again appealed the decision to the OMB. With their downtown building height policy in tatters, the city's planning staff and the NCC asked the OMB to delay, while it completed a new downtown plan.[894]

The 1969 *Ottawa Central Area Study* prepared by the Washington firm Hammer Green Siler proposed office towers throughout the Ottawa downtown, and also in downtown Hull[895] (Figure 11-10). The consultants' study contained some pious language and a sketch (Figure 11-11) about the importance of preserving views of the Parliament Buildings. They proposed a complicated height limit that was shaped like a bowl, centred on Parliament Hill, with taller buildings permitted at some distance from the Hill. The consultant's maps indicated that a 300 foot (91 m.) building should be permitted on Campeau's new site. But when the 'bowl' was translated into a bylaw for approval by city council, some ambiguous wording allowed Campeau to propose a 375 ft. (114 m.) tower. The NCC appealed council's actions to the OMB and lost again.[896] By now, it was public knowledge that the federal government would be the tenant of the Place de Ville, and Campeau was persuaded

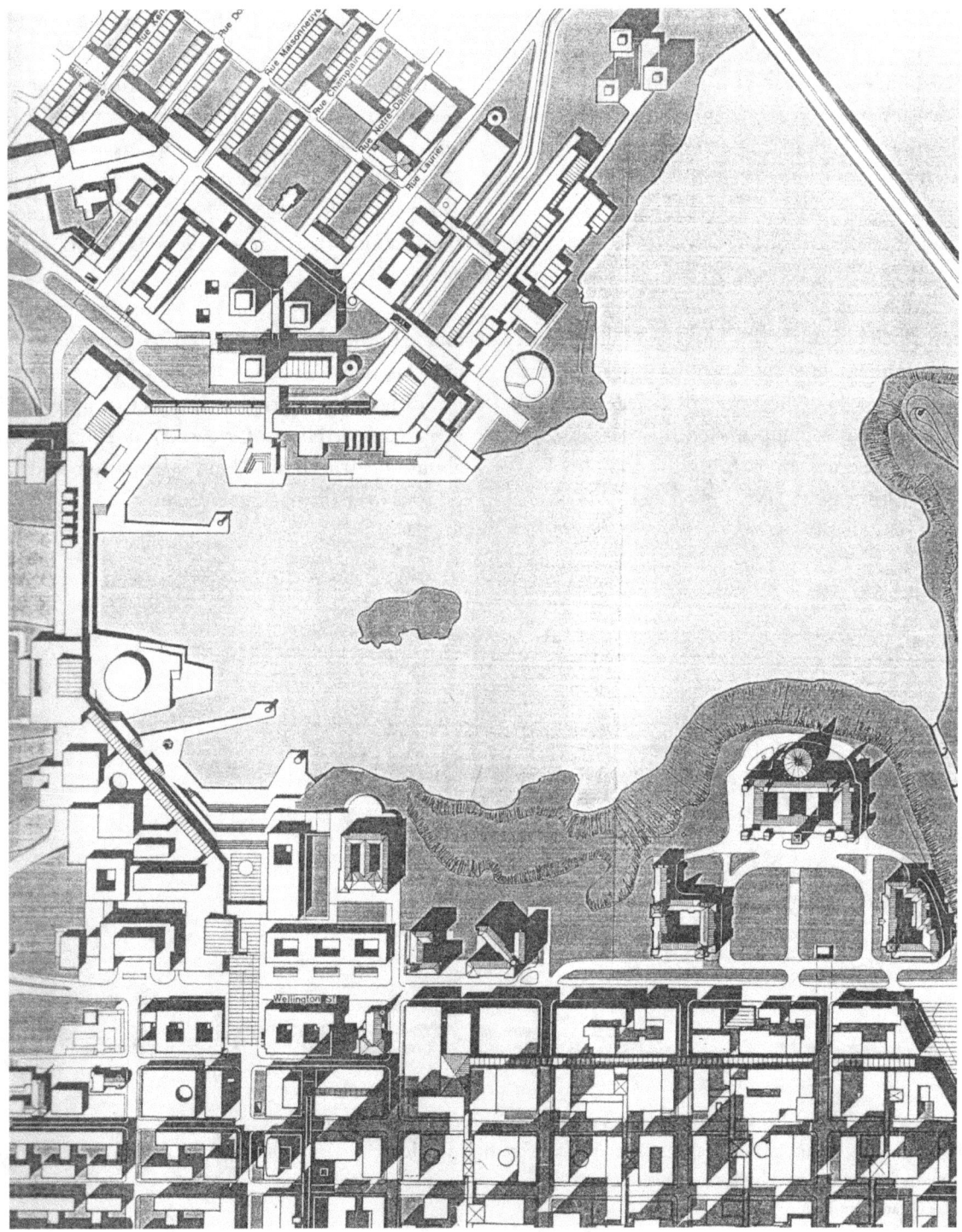

FIGURE 11-10: **Proposed office towers through downtown Ottawa and Hull**
(Source: Ottawa Central Area Study, 1969)

to reduce its height to 342 feet (104 m.), exactly the height of the Peace Tower. Although this concession would cost him ten floors of offices, the developer would soon get his reward, in major buildings on the north side of the river.

City council was delighted that the new office towers sprouted throughout the downtown in response to its new zoning bylaw and the demand from the federal government and trade associations for new space. Although two fifteen-storey office buildings produce the same property tax revenue as one thirty-storey tower, Ottawa was proud to join the ranks of cities with high-rise buildings.[897] Campeau fed this desire to join the 'major leagues' by naming his complex Place de Ville, hinting at I.M. Pei's Place Ville Marie in Montréal, and sheathing his towers in black glass, like Mies van de Rohe's iconic Seagram Building in New York and the Toronto Dominion Centre in Toronto. But the design of the Ottawa buildings were disappointments, as were most of the cheaply-built private towers that followed. The net result, a decade later, is almost precisely the skyline that the 1969 consultants warned against (Figure 11-12).

The tall towers on the skyline of New York and Toronto project a credible image of their cities as their countries' financial centres. The tall buildings that destroyed the picturesque skyline of Parliament Hill in Ottawa speak equally plainly about the triumph of land speculation and local politics over the national interest.

FIGURE 11-11: (Not) Preserving the views of the Parliament Buildings
This sketch was meant to illustrate the worst-case scenario of potential harm that might be caused to the capital's skyline by indiscriminate high-rise development. It proved to be painfully accurate.
(Source: Ottawa Central Area Study, 1969)

FIGURE 11-12: Place de Ville, 1967
The first phase of the project that breached the downtown height limits. The second phase is under construction to the right of the black glass towers. Note the wartime "temporary" buildings on the mid-right and the new riverside parkway skirting the empty LeBreton Flats.
(Source: LAC; Credit: Hans-Ludwig Blohm / Hans-Ludwig Blohm fonds; PA-145782; © Library and Archives Canada. Reproduced with the permission of Library and Archives Canada)

Restoring the Historic Downtown

The urban renewal ethic embedded in Modern planning of the post-war period was quite unsympathetic to the built heritage of the previous century. Le Corbusier's infamous Plan Voisin called for the demolition of central Paris, and the planning charter of the influential (CIAM) recommended against any attempts to conserve older districts.[898] Urban renewal programs were the instruments used to remove "obsolete" districts, and they often took a *tabula rasa* approach, typically demolishing all the buildings in an area to create a clean site for radically different new development designed in the Modern style. The urban renewal programs of Hull, the City of Ottawa and the NCC were no different from any other North American municipality in these respects. The few heritage advocates were regarded as quaint enthusiasts, and had to struggle to preserve individual structures. For example, the Ottawa Historical Society spent years advocating the preservation of Ottawa's oldest building, Thomas McKay's 1827 Commissariat Building, beside the Rideau Canal entrance locks.[899]

Given the anti-historical tone of the early 1960s, the NCC's "Mile of History" project was an extraordinary and innovative project. The commission established a Historical Advisory Committee in 1960, and began the first wide-scale inventories of heritage buildings in the region.[900] The Sussex Street buildings were a prominent site on the ceremonial route travelled by the governors general from Rideau Hall to Parliament Hill, and both Lady Aberdeen and Lady Grey had advocated that Sussex Drive be improved. By 1960, the roadbed was finally smooth, but the adjacent buildings were decaying. Rather than tearing them down to create sites for new Modern buildings, the NCC acquired the properties and restored them, creating shops and professional offices along a widened sidewalk and tree-lined street. The architects also created a charming set of urban courtyards in the service areas behind the buildings[901] (Figure 11-13).

Figure 11-13: The Mile of History
Courtyards in the service areas behind the Sussex St. buildings, linking to the ByWard Market.
(Source: NCC)

When the planners looked behind the Sussex Drive courtyards, they rediscovered the ByWard Market, which was struggling as a wholesale food district and occasional farmers' market. The widespread distribution of supermarkets, shopping centres and suburban warehouses had made the ByWard Market obsolete, and similar districts were often bulldozed in the 1960s. But the planners thought that the scale and activity of the market were charming, and made a crucial decision: they simply left the area alone to evolve in its own way. While most of downtown Ottawa and Hull were scheduled for cataclysmic transformations in the 1960s, the 1969 downtown study recommended against urban renewal in the ByWard Market. It suggested that any new buildings respect its historic scale and street orientation and that the area be considered for heritage preservation in the future.[902] This was heroic restraint in the era of Modern megastructures, and paid off handsomely in the future.

The "Mile of History" had an impact far beyond its seven blocks along Sussex Street. It set a precedent that was followed across Canada for restoring a historic district, rather than individual buildings. The plan focussed upon improving streets and blocks, and drew attention to the ceremonial route that was to become important in future planning policy. Finally, the project protected the ByWard Market, allowing it to evolve organically into one of those lucky circumstances where doing nothing is the best policy.

Bad Ideas from the 1960s III: Downtown Expressways and Urban Renewal

Unfortunately, the successful outcomes of the original Sparks Street Mall and the Mile of History were the exceptions to most downtown planning ideas from the 1960s. Looking back, we can be thankful that most of the proposals from this era remained on paper. The prevailing Modern planning concepts called for rigorous separation of land uses and traffic types, so that each could be developed to maximum efficiency and speed of movement. This usually meant that the street level was reserved for unobstructed vehicular movement, and pedestrians were relegated into underground passageways or above-ground walkways. For example, noting the success of the Sparks Street Mall, one design team proposed that it continue underground, beneath Confederation Square, and then across the canal and over Sussex Street by bridges[903] (Figure 11-14).

On a larger scale, the City of Ottawa was delighted by the Queensway, and led the Ottawa-Hull Transportation Study, which called for a network of freeways throughout the region (Figure 11-15). This plan proposed a north-south King Edward expressway and an east-west "Downtown Distributor" that would require expropriation and demolition of around 20 blocks[904] (Figure 11-16). This was the ultimate plan for a new "Autowa," with unlimited high-speed vehicular travel throughout the region. The "Downtown Distributor" (Figure 11-16) was the worst variety of 1960s megastructure, requiring complete demolition of a row of nine blocks south of Laurier Avenue, to be replaced by an underground expressway, with a bus transitway, parking decks and new office buildings above. The newspapers were excited, and Ottawa City Council began to expropriate and demolish the route westward from Elgin Street.[905]

This was the era of big urban renewal plans, and most North American cities have similar examples of freeway and downtown plans.[906] Calgary and Minneapolis both carried out programs to separate pedestrian movement in pedestrian malls, second-floor walkways and enclosed bridges, which were popular in their chilly winters. But few plans were as audacious as the 1969 *Ottawa Central Area Study*.[907] The new height limits in this study were one of the most conservative elements, compared to its detailed proposals to build an expressway in an open trench parallel to King Edward Avenue and demolish the adjacent blocks (Figure 11-17). More audacious proposals would connect most of downtown Ottawa buildings with a pedestrian skyway system, and carry the mega-structure across the Chaudière Islands to a complex in downtown Hull (Figure 11-18). This was 1960s mega-structure planning on a grand scale. Although the drawings look somewhat frightening today, the massive redevelopment plans for both downtowns also signalled a new era of thinking about the national capital; the role of Hull and the other Québec municipalities was changing. After decades of demands, the Outaouais would receive a major component of federal investment and jobs.

FIGURE 11-14: **Confederation Square Proposal**
Pedestrians from the Spark's Street Mall were to be directed under Confederation Square. The National War Memorial would be a small island in the traffic interchange above.
(Source: Parkin and Associates, 1962)

FIGURE 11-15: **Recommended freeway system from the 1965 Transportation Study**
This proposal would have destroyed large portions of downtown Ottawa. The radial expressways at the bottom left and right were deflected into the Greenbelt.
(Source: Ottawa-Hull Transportation Study, 1965)

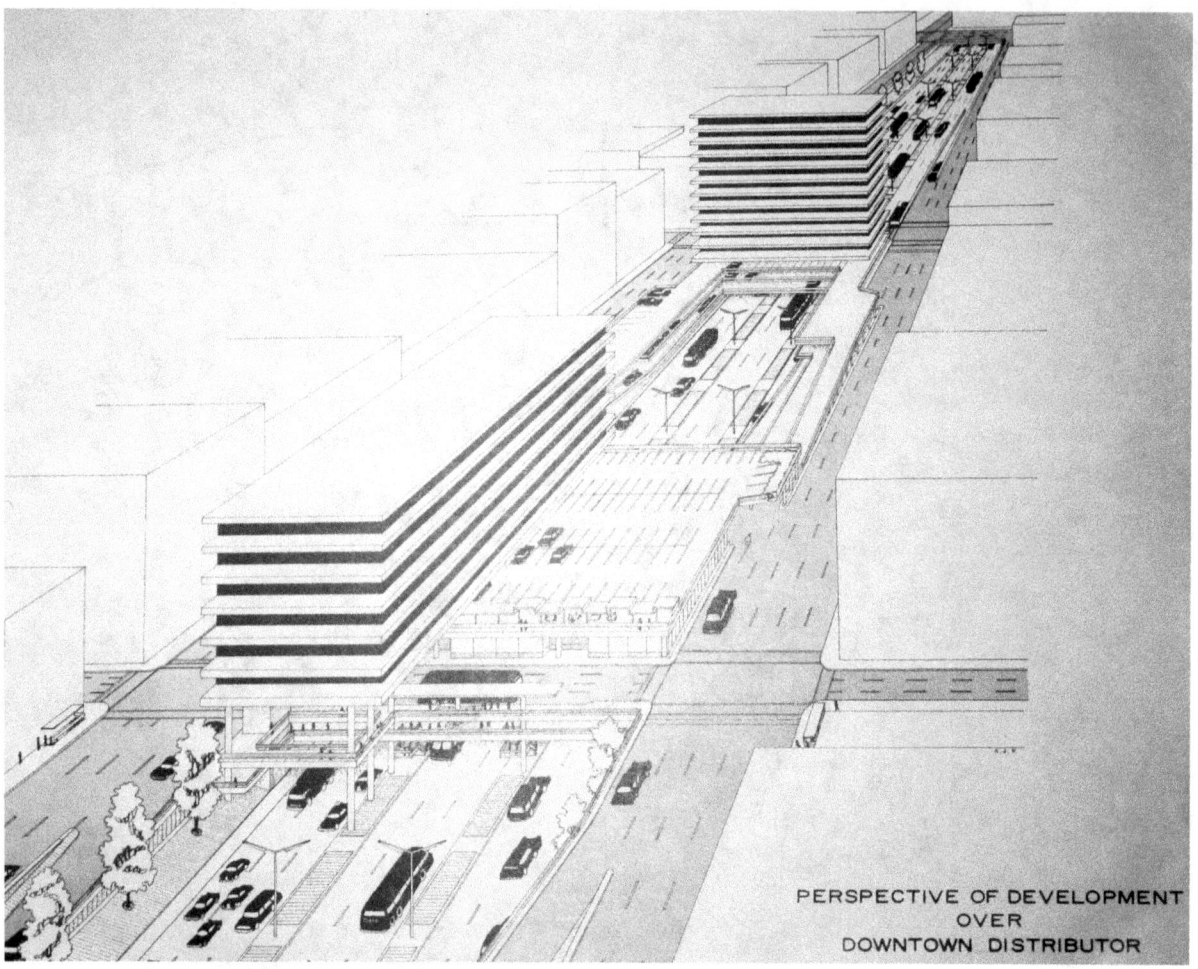

FIGURE 11-16: "It's the Downtown Distributor"
Nine blocks between Laurier and Gloucester would be destroyed to create this underground expressway with above grade garages.
(Source: Ottawa-Hull Transportation Study, 1965)

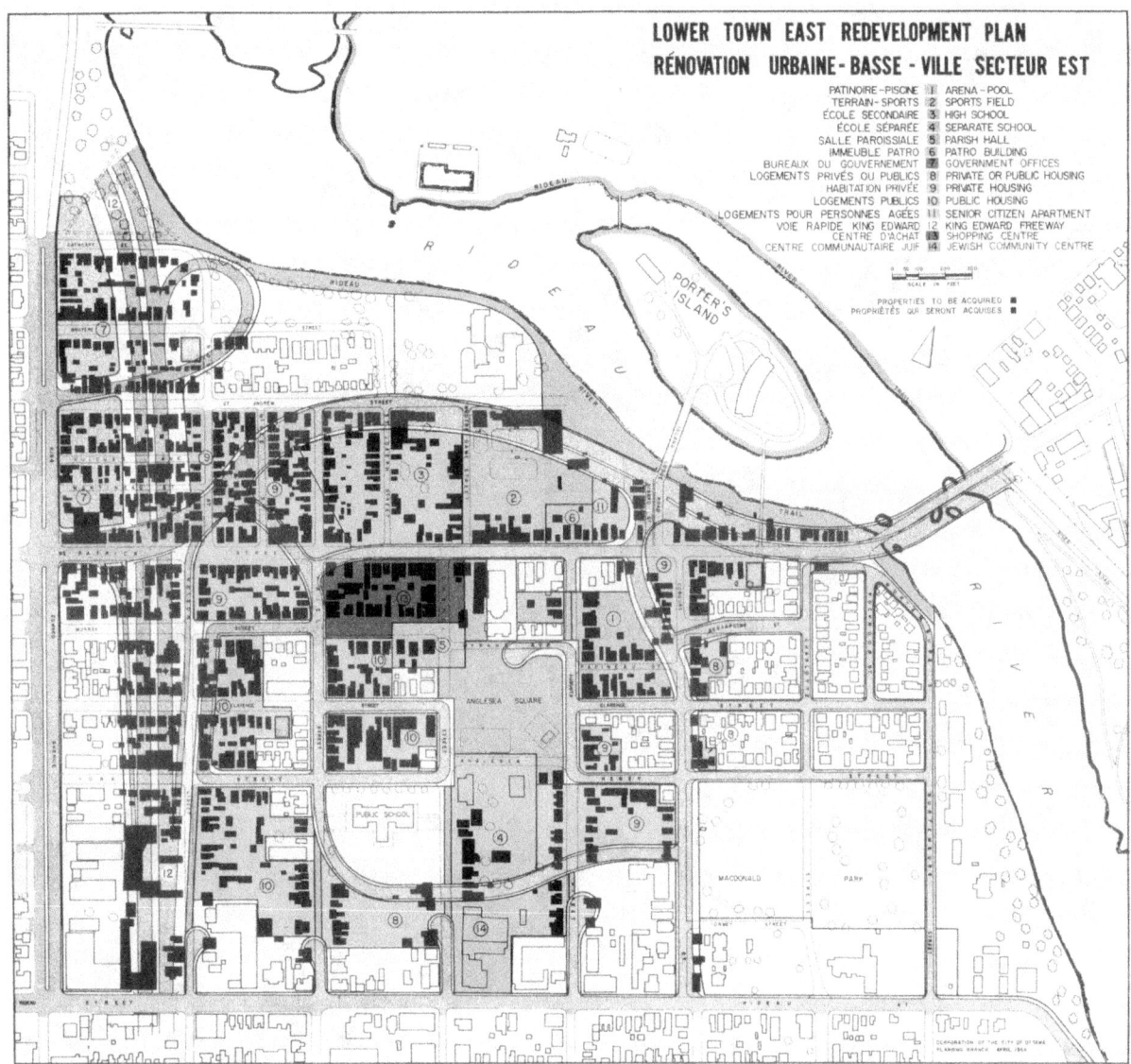

FIGURE 11-17: **Proposal to put a King Edward Expressway in an open trench and Lowertown East urban renewal**
Scores of homes in Lowertown (areas marked in grey) were expropriated and demolished by the City of Ottawa to clear the route for this expressway (above). The initial proposals were to replace the older row houses with public housing. The project was cancelled after election of neighbourhood-based councillors in 1968 and 1970, but the area took over a decade to re-build.
(Source: City of Ottawa, *Lowertown East Urban Renewal* Project, 1970)

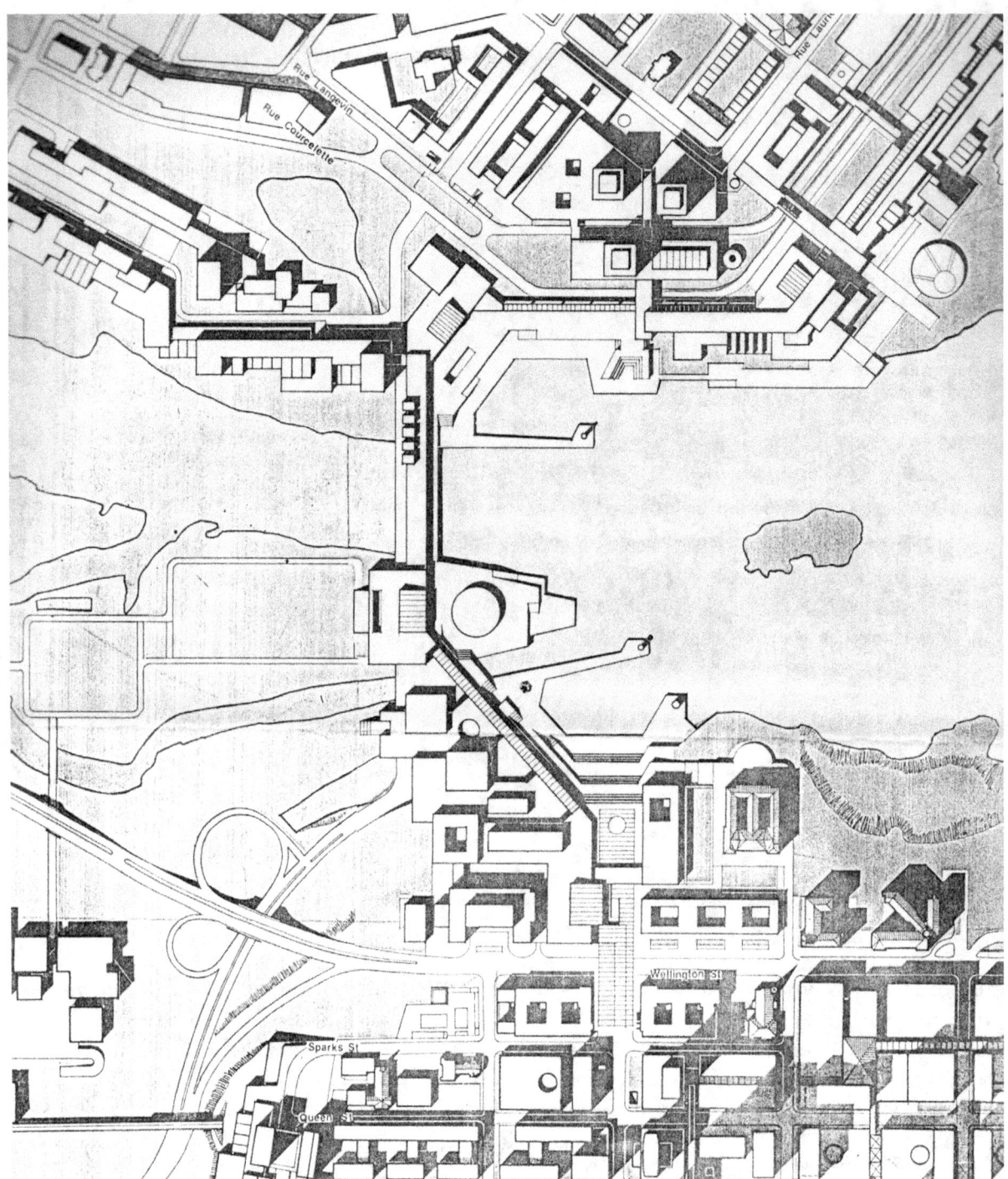

FIGURE 11-18: Megastructure proposal to connect downtown Ottawa and Hull buildings
Office buildings in downtown Ottawa and Hull were to be connected by upper level pedestrian bridges. Much of downtown Hull was demolished and rebuilt in this manner in the early 1970s.
(Source: Ottawa Central Area Study, 1969)

Jumping the Greenbelt

After the 1961 census was released, the NCC knew that the population forecasts of the 1950 Gréber Plan had been overtaken by the Baby Boom. They commissioned new demographic forecasts and land use projections as a better foundation for the many downtown and transportation studies underway.[908] With the area within the Greenbelt essentially full by 1963, and the Blackburn and Bell's Corners "hamlets" within the Greenbelt underway, the NCC planners prepared a quick estimate of where future population growth might occur in the following decades.[909] The report's sketch maps for potential growth outside the Greenbelt served as guides to savvy land speculators, who bought or optioned the farms adjacent to the Greenbelt. A group of doctors optioned the lands west of the Greenbelt and house builder William Teron was able to buy them out in 1955 for a small sum to create the original Kanata land assembly. The farms to the south were snapped up by a consortium including Nepean Reeve Aubrey Moodie, while the Greenberg family's Minto firm bought large properties to the east, in Orleans.[910]

Kanata was the first satellite community established outside of the Greenbelt. In 1959, Teron purchased 1,295 hectares of land just west of the Greenbelt to build a 'new town.'[911] Teron planned Kanata at a low density, with high quality design values.[912] The first neighbourhood, named Beaverbrook, proved popular with employees of Bell Northern Research (BNR), the Communications Research Centre (CRC) and Microsystems International, whose labs were on the edge of the Greenbelt in adjacent Nepean.

William Teron and the March Township Council targeted Kanata as a high-tech community from the beginning. Teron named his first industrial subdivision 'Technology Park' and aggressively pursued Atomic Energy of Canada Limited (AECL) as the lead tenant, with the direct assistance of March Township.[913] The local government was soon targeting other technology industries for its own industrial parks, attracting Mitel and Digital Equipment Canada among many others.[914]

Kanata initially appealed to high technology employees because of its proximity to BNR and CRC, high neighbourhood design standards and excellent recreational opportunities at the doorstep. But Teron was undercapitalized and could not afford the infrastructure investments needed for the Greenbelt new town. Ottawa developer Robert Campeau took over the project in 1970, but the residents and council pushed him to keep the high community planning and development standards.[915]

The rural municipalities did not have an adequate property tax base to support the infrastructure costs of rapid suburban residential development. Industrial development helped reduce the fiscal impacts of growth, so most local governments planned for large industrial parks.[916] But only March Township and Teron targeted the emerging technology industries. The rest of the local governments were focused upon traditional commercial and manufacturing tenants; as noted by Nepean's chief planner: "No one knew we would be the high-tech capital, we were just trying to obtain the same types of regular industry as everyone else …"[917] The NCC and local government planners were so busy accommodating the expansion of federal employment that few people noticed the steady suburban growth of the high technology industries during the 1960s and 1970s.[918]

New Federal Plans for the Suburbs

The Crown's 1950 plan anticipated that growth outside the Greenbelt would be accommodated in satellite towns, following the London, Paris and Stockholm models. But Gréber's team did not specify the location of the future towns in the 1950s because it was expected that they would not be needed until after 1995. Gréber did some quick sketches of possible new locations in 1959[919] (Figure 10-19). In the early 1960s, the NCC realized that they would need a regional planning strategy for the area outside the Greenbelt since land developers were already building new subdivisions.

Following the European new towns model, the NCC expected to develop these satellite communities in conjunction with the Central Mortgage and Housing Corporation (CMHC), the federal government's housing agency. CMHC was undertaking large scale land assemblies and developing suburban projects across Canada during this period, often in collaboration with the local governments.[920] The two agencies selected Macklin Hancock's firm, Project Planning Associates (PPA), to lead the research for the new satellite townsites. Hancock was ideally suited for the job, as he had planned Toronto's Don Mills – then regarded as Canada's model suburban community.[921] Hancock was a landscape architect/planner, and his team brought a sophisticated approach to examining the rural landscape outside the Greenbelt. They used the ecological analysis pioneered by Ian McHarg to evaluate the suitability of the rural lands for urban development. Their report recommended sites for five new satellite communities in Ontario, to complement the two Québec communities that were not yet full.[922]

PPA's plan was over-run by events, since by the time it was completed in 1967, the land for the first stage satellite towns had been gobbled up by

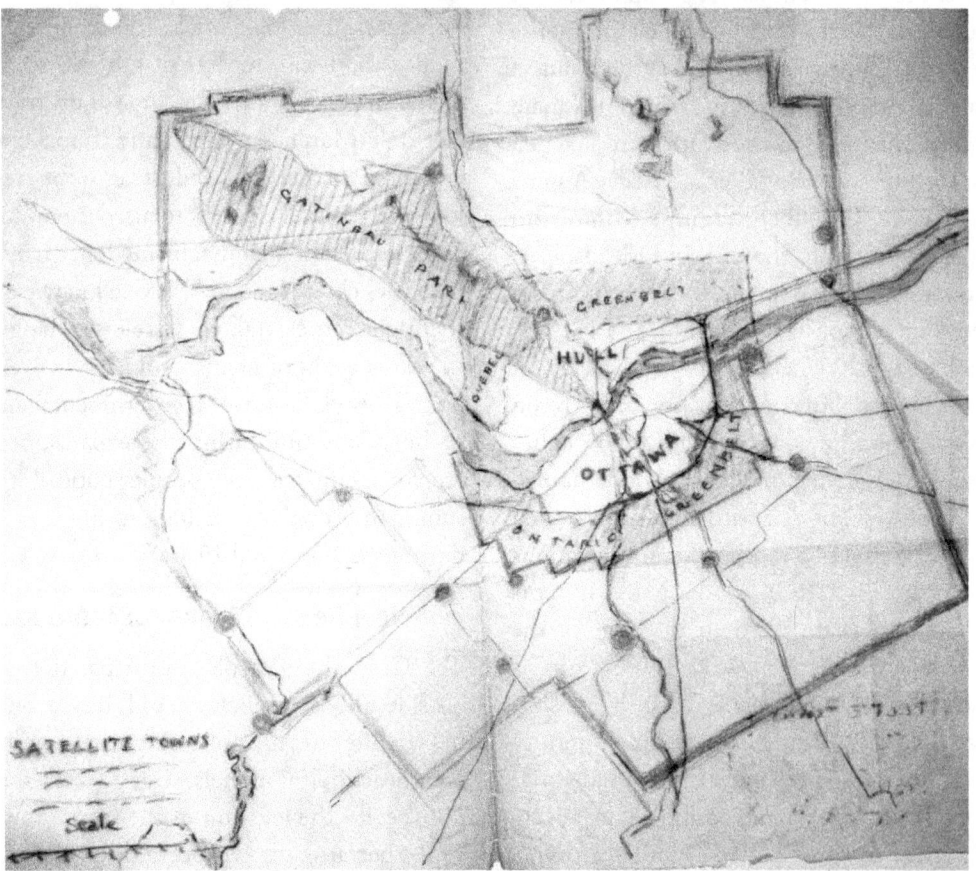

FIGURE 11-19: Gréber's New Town Proposals
This sketch plan, circa 1959, illustrates Jacques Gréber's first draft of a plan to expand the urban area past the Greenbelt, using satellite New Towns (red dots) in the manner of Abercrombie's 1944 Greater London Plan.
(Source: NCC corporate files)

speculators. And the political circumstances had changed by the late 1960s: any plan that showed most of the regional growth occurring in Ontario ran against federal political objectives to promote the development of the Outaouais in the National Capital Region. The landscape analysis of the 1967 plan continued to inform environmental planning for the region, but the development plan was never adopted.

The New Role of the Outaouais

Hull politicians and business organizations had been clamouring for a larger share of federal investment and employment for decades, since they recognized that the lumber and pulp industries that were the foundation of the local economy were in decline.[923] However, changes in the national political landscape were instrumental in achieving these long-term economic objectives. Pierre Trudeau, the new leader of the Liberal Party, won a huge majority government in the 1968 federal election, with the threat of separation in Québec a major campaign issue.[924] The Crown's attitude towards the Outaouais changed almost overnight.

Trudeau made his close ally, Jean Marchand, the Minister of Regional Economic Expansion. The NCC reported directly to Marchand, rather than the prime minister. Trudeau and Marchand introduced a broader role for the Outaouais at the February 1969 federal-provincial conference, changing the definition of the Canadian capital from Ottawa to a "National Capital Region" covering both sides of the region. They also stressed that the new region should be fully bilingual so that all Canadians "may have a feeling of pride and participation in, and attachment to their Capital."[925]

Many actions followed rapidly to start the new Outaouais initiative. The LeBreton Flats project was put on hold, and Marchand announced that the federal government was acquiring 2.4 hectares (6 acres) in downtown Hull in May 1969.[926] The Ottawa *Central Area Study*[927] showed a connection across the Chaudière Islands to a massive redevelopment of downtown Hull. Finally, the NCC prepared a report outlining the objectives for a 15-year plan to redevelop Hull.[928]

The burst of physical planning activity was matched by major policy initiatives. The Royal Commission on Bilingualism and Biculturalism released its final report in 1969, and an entire volume of its recommendations addressed the role of the national capital. The National Capital Commission was to become the federal agency responsible for ensuring that the new National Capital Region presented a thoroughly bilingual face to the nation.[929]

Local Government Reform

All this federal activity provoked the Ontario and Québec governments to complete local government restructuring that had long been under consideration on both sides of the Ottawa River. The City of Ottawa constantly complained about the infrastructure and service problems caused by the failure of the 1950 annexation to give it control over all the lands within the Greenbelt. The Ottawa Planning Area Board had proven completely inadequate for regional planning, and metropolitan Toronto provided an example of a federation of local governments that was considered quite effective in managing regional infrastructure and planning issues. The need for some form of coordination became more obvious as urban development spread outward from Ottawa to include parts of many other municipalities – Eastview (later Cité Vanier), Rockcliffe Park, Nepean, Gloucester and March townships.[930]

Rather than order more annexation, the Ontario government established a regional federation, the Regional Municipality of Ottawa-Carleton (RMOC) in January 1969 (Figure 11-20). Dennis Coolican, former reeve of Rockcliffe Park, was appointed its first chairman, but the Ottawa delegation would have voting control over the regional council. The RMOC would be

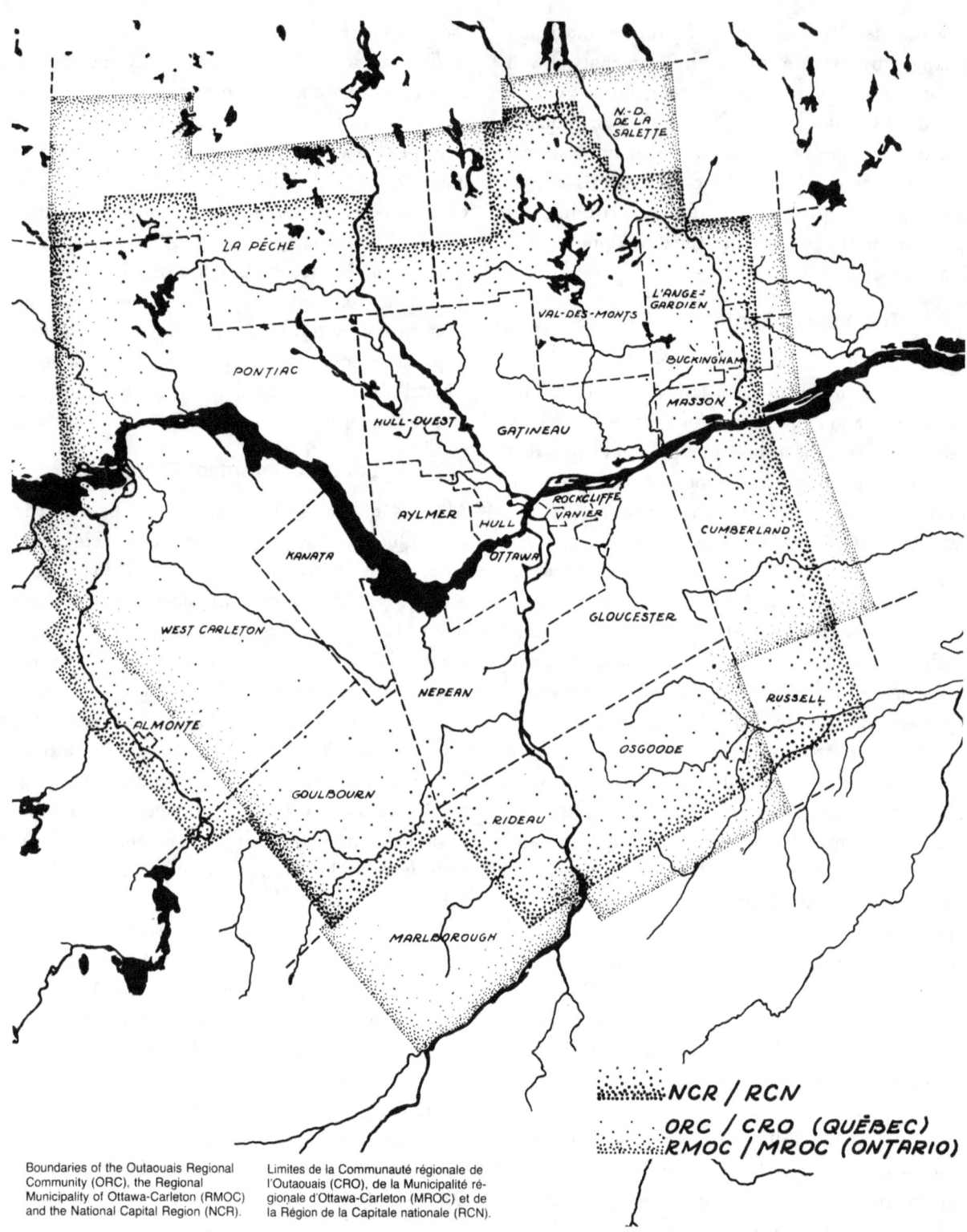

Boundaries of the Outaouais Regional Community (ORC), the Regional Municipality of Ottawa-Carleton (RMOC) and the National Capital Region (NCR).

Limites de la Communauté régionale de l'Outaouais (CRO), de la Municipalité régionale d'Ottawa-Carleton (MROC) et de la Région de la Capitale nationale (RCN).

FIGURE 11-20: Political Boundaries, 1974
Jurisdictional overlap at its maximum complexity in 1974.
(Source: Fullerton, *Capital of Canada*, 1974, vol. 1)

responsible for regional infrastructure, police, regional planning and public transit.

The situation in the Outaouais was somewhat similar, with additional concerns about the cultural and territorial integrity of the region, due to the aggressive action of the federal government. The province's Dorion Commission examining the Québec-Labrador boundary added the question of the Canadian National Capital Region to its mandate in May 1967. After hearing from many local stakeholders, the commission's 1968 report criticized the Québec government for keeping such a low profile in the Outaouais.[931] It suggested a stronger provincial presence to counteract the influence of the federal government. Long-time provincial MNA Oswald Parent pushed the Québec government to centralize its regional offices in downtown Hull, and the provincial government announced a large new office building and courthouse in October 1968. The project was expanded further after the federal government announced its plans in May 1969.[932]

Urban development in the Outaouais had spilled outside Hull into large sections of Aylmer and Gatineau Township by the late 1960s. The Outaouais region had inter-municipal coordination problems similar to the Ottawa-Carleton area, but with an additional layer of concern about the need for economic development, following the decline of its traditional industrial base. By 1969, the provincial government was preparing plans for regional governments for Montréal, Ville de Québec and the Outaouais. All three new regions were federations, providing a new layer of government to coordinate the actions of the local municipalities. The *Communauté régionale de l'Outaouais* (CRO) would include ten urban and rural municipalities covering an area of 2,410 square km., roughly covering the National Capital Region within Québec (Figure 11-20). The CRO was established on January 1, 1970, with responsibility for regional infrastructure, transit, regional planning and economic development.

The political difficulties in developing Canada's national capital area had become immensely more difficult by the end of the 1960s. The era of simple project coordination between Ottawa, Hull and the NCC was at an end, as the urban development spilled outside the areas anticipated by Gréber's 1950 plan. Building this new regional metropolis now included participation of two provincial governments, two regional governments and scores of local municipalities. The potential for 'Town-Crown' conflicts was greatly increased by this complex political environment. As these new local and regional governments developed their own urban and regional planning capabilities, the National Capital Commission would inevitably lose influence in shaping the development of the Canadian capital.

Reflections

Most elements of Gréber's *Plan for the National Capital* were implemented by the end of the 1960s. Several of the strengths of the 1950 plan are hard to discern today, and can only be appreciated by comparison to the immediate post-war conditions. The relocation of the freight railways and their associated yards and industrial development has been an unqualified success. The railways, the local road network, industries and adjacent neighbourhoods all are better after the move. It is hard to imagine how Ottawa would function without the Queensway, which is the spine of the expressway and express bus network. Similarly, the Ottawa River is much less polluted following the NCC and local governments' investment in sewage treatment and clearance of some of the abandoned riverfront industrial sites.

In the downtown area, the LeBreton Flats urban renewal proposal in the 1950 plan followed the worst traditions of this genre, with even more destructive schemes to follow from the local governments. Similarly, relocation of the railway passenger station from downtown Ottawa seemed like a good idea in 1948, but the new station location left rail travel at a comparative disadvantage.

The 1950 plan also accelerated the transformation of the National Capital Region from a compact, transit-dependent metropolis to a more decentralized, car-oriented metropolitan area. This was thought to be an advantage at the time, and the new suburban neighbourhoods, office parks, expressways and parkways were appreciated by the Baby Boom families – a new detached house seemed better than a crowded apartment, and the convenience and flexibility of a car was appreciated in comparison to the old streetcars.[933] There was little criticism of these trends in the 1960s[934] and most plans by the local governments pushed automobility even further. The assumptions about car dependence would not be seriously questioned for another 30 years, as the era of cheap gas, affordable homes, large families and easy driving on the Queensway continued into the 1980s.[935]

Finally, it is hard to miss the 1950 plan's open space network. The parkways are magnificent, with wonderful views along the Ottawa River and Rideau Canal. The Greenbelt and the many parks built by the NCC and its predecessors contribute to an attractive capital for visitors and a high quality of life for its residents. Gatineau Park is an extraordinary natural resource reaching almost to the core of the urban area. The Greenbelt creates a strong edge to the inner urban area and a gracious entrance to the capital by road and air. The pleasant environment and quality of life fostered by these improvements are essential conditions for attracting high technology workers and tourism, the two industries the new regional governments pursued to expand their economic base beyond federal employment in the ensuing decades. However, the multiple jurisdictional overlaps created by the new regional federations would intensify 'Town-Crown' conflicts in the years ahead.

CHAPTER 12
Town vs. Crown (1970-1989)

The 1960s ended with increasing evidence of Québec's dissatisfaction of its status with the Canadian federation. The sovereigntist *Parti Québécois* was founded in 1968; labour unrest increased and, shockingly, political violence broke out in Montréal, including the 1969 bombing of the Stock Exchange injuring 27 people.[936] The bombings continued until 1970, culminating in the *Front de Libération du Québec*'s (FLQ) October kidnapping of a British diplomat and killing a Québec Cabinet minister. Ottawa and Montréal became armed camps and the federal government called out the armed forces to maintain order during the October Crisis. Although political violence ended, the federal government under Pierre Trudeau remained focused upon changing the governance arrangements in the decades ahead.[937]

The 1970s and 1980s were a period of constant and bitter conflict between national objectives and local priorities for the development of the metropolis in the Ottawa Valley. 'Town-Crown' disagreements during the 1950s and 1960s had been ameliorated by a great river of federal funds to implement the Gréber plan. The Crown largesse did not stop as abruptly at the completion of the Rideau Canal in the 1830s, but after the 1950 plan reached its completion, the leadership of federal planners was increasingly questioned. The local governments gradually developed their own expertise and began to respond to municipal priorities. The addition of regional governments and regional planning agencies on both sides of the river in the 1990s further reduced the justification for the national government to lead the planning for the entire area. However, the NCC was proud of its expertise and leadership role, and plunged ahead with its grand plans.

The Transformation of Downtown Hull

After decades of demanding federal and provincial investment, the City of Hull saw its wish come true in the 1970s with astonishing speed, but at an overpowering scale. The federal and provincial governments competed to erect massive office buildings in Hull's downtown to advertise their presence in a region that had been previously ignored. After Hull's City Hall burned in 1970, the local government joined the large-scale redevelopment efforts by expanding its urban renewal plans to build a large new municipal building on adjacent lands donated by the NCC.[938]

The lands proposed for redevelopment included the south side of Rue Principale and the neighbourhood squeezed between the downtown and the riverfront industries. Most of the area consisted of two-storey wooden houses built after the 1900 fire and rented by working-class families. The general area had been proposed for redevelopment in the 1964 *Hull Master Plan*, but the municipality had started its urban renewal program on a smaller scale in the residential areas to the north. The federal and provincial governments stepped in to expropriate 7.5 hectares (18.6 acres) in downtown Hull, displacing 3,400 people living in 924 houses.[939]

The many poor families displaced from the area were offered only small relocation allowances, since their landlords received the property expropriation grants. These relocation allowances were nowhere near enough to buy a new home in Hull or even secure adequate replacement rental housing, and the supply of new public housing was inadequate.[940] In March 1969, over 300 citizens marched on city hall to demand assistance for residents forced to relocate. The Catholic Bishop of Hull had formed the *Assemblée générale de l'île de Hull* (AGIH) for social organizing in downtown Hull, and the organization took up the residents' cause. However, faced with the clear determination of the region's commercial elite and the federal, provincial and local governments to proceed with the destruction of the neighbourhood, all the AGIH could do was negotiate better terms for the relocation of renters and compensation of homeowners.[941,942]

The federal government moved quickly, with the Department of Public Works starting construction of Phase I of Place du Portage in 1970, and subsequent phases in 1972 and 1973. These projects were enormous interconnected concrete office buildings, designed as mega-structures by Montréal firms that had been involved in projects like Place Bonaventure.

Megastructures are a type of urban design that focuses on flows of people and vehicles and linkages between buildings.[943] Prominent examples were Le Corbusier's 1933 plan for Algiers, the 1960s plans for downtown Philadelphia,[944] the "Plus 15" walkway systems in Minneapolis, Calgary and Winnipeg, and the vast network of underground shopping concourses that link downtown office buildings and subway stations in Tokyo, Toronto and Montréal. Perhaps the most spectacular megastructure ever attempted was incorporated in the 1969 Master Development Plan for Battery Park City at the southern tip of Manhattan (Figure 12-1).

A building megastructure is an inflexible, all-or-nothing concept that requires large up-front public investments. Few building megastructures of the type envisioned in 1969 for Ottawa-Hull were ever built, even on a small scale, except as hospitals or research institutions. Although the "Plus 15" sky walks and underground passageway systems may offer comfortable walking conditions for office workers in poor weather, megastructures have been criticized for abandoning the grade level to vehicles and moving the public life of the street into privately controlled shopping concourses.[946]

Hull's Portage buildings had very large floor plates, but were relatively modest in height, stepping up to 18 floors (Figure 12-2), in conformity with limits proposed in the 1969 Hammer Green Siler study. The first phase of Place du Portage opened in 1973, and by 1975, the ubiquitous Robert Campeau had started construction of an even larger complex, Terrasses de la Chaudière, four blocks to the west. Campeau's project included a hotel, shops and two federal office towers rising to 28 floors.[947]

Québec and Hull were concerned that their projects were behind schedule and the federal government was becoming an overwhelming presence in the Outaouais. Liberal Cabinet minister Oswald Parent (MNA for Hull from 1956-1976) pushed his provincial government to move faster,[948] and Québec eventually contracted with the private

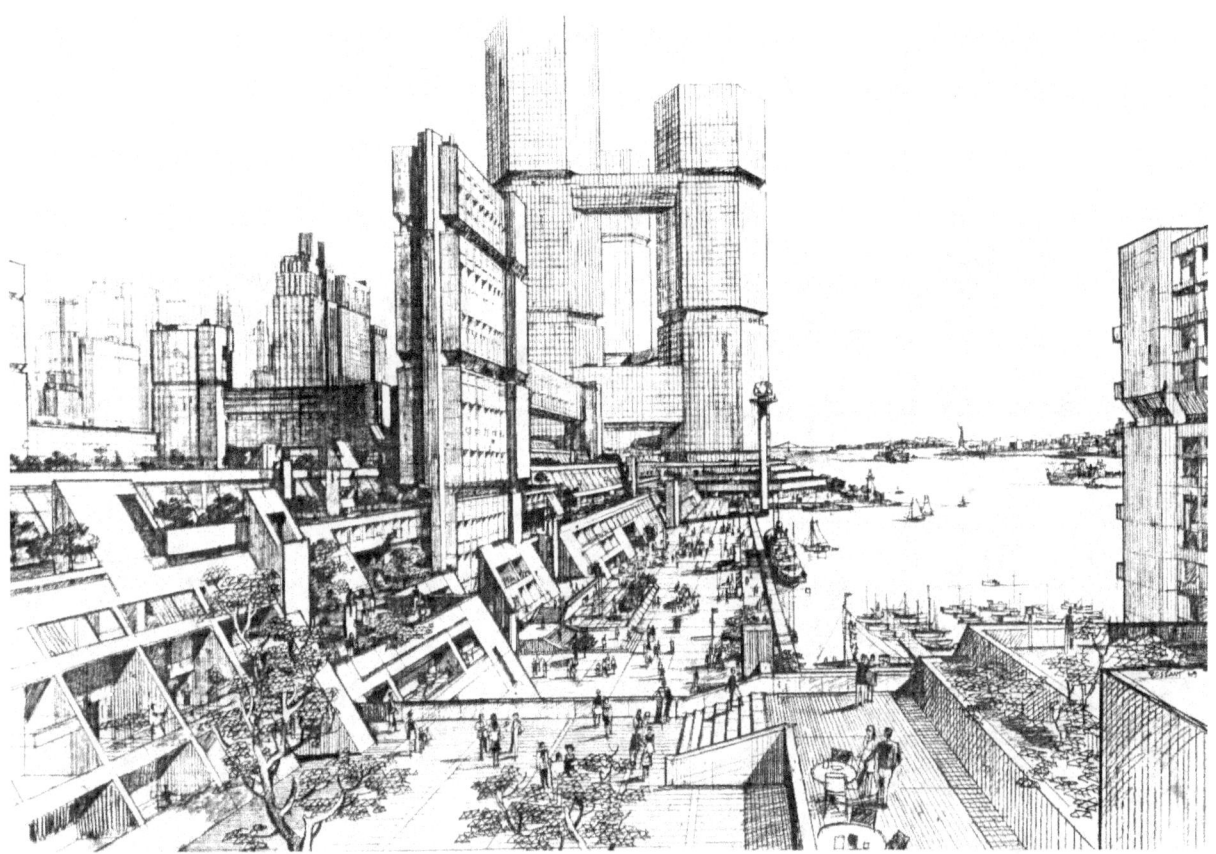

FIGURE 12-1: **Megastructures: Battery Park City, New York, 1969**
This 1969 megastructure proposal looks a bit like a space station moored to the south end of Manhattan. The plan envisioned a single building complex that was wildly different from the remainder of the Manhattan building fabric. The megastructure was to be tied together by a central pedestrian spine, an enclosed seven-story structure that would run for approximately 1.5 km along the entire length of the project. Although the expensive and complex spine was never started and only part of one housing pod was built, the concept influenced the 1969 Ottawa Central Area Study (Figures 11-10 and 11-18) and Place du Portage (Figure 12-2). Battery Park City's megastructure plan was dropped in 1979, in favour of a traditional streets and blocks concept that became a model for urban design in the 1980s and 1990s.[945]
(Source: Conklin & Rossant, Phillip Johnson and Wallace McHarg Roberts, *Battery Park City 1969 Master Development Plan*. Rendering by J. Rossant)

developer Cadillac-Fairview to build its courthouse, offices and shops in 1975. The private contract probably saved the provincial building, since the *Parti Québécois* (PQ) defeated the Liberals in the 1976 Québec elections and the new sovereigntist provincial government was not interested in building better connections to the federal capital. The sole PQ MNA elected in the Outaouais was Jocelyne Ouellette in Hull, who was appointed Minister of Public Works and made responsible for the project. Cadillac-Fairview had the building under construction with a binding contract and the project could not be cancelled without enormous losses. So the provincial government simply completed the

FIGURE 12-2: Place du Portage under construction in downtown Hull, 1975
The boom of pulp logs in the foreground is a reminder of Hull's previous economy. The closure of the antiquated E.B. Eddy sulphite pulp plant in Hull removed the source of the capital's worst air pollution, and also eliminated the need for the picturesque log drives on the Ottawa River.
(Source: Canada. Dept. of Public Works; Library and Archives Canada, PA-145782; © Library and Archives Canada)

building. In a deft political touch, it was named in honour of Joseph Montferrand, the legendary lumberjack (Figure 3-1), famous for thrashing his Anglo opponents in the 1830s Shiner Wars.[949]

Hull's *Maison du Citoyen* is perhaps the most attractive building complex of the area, with a public library at street level, a pleasant atrium and an outdoor courtyard.[950] Hull connected its civic building to a hotel and conference centre that incorporates an adjacent heritage building. However, the overall impact of all the projects has been to drain the life off the streets of downtown Hull,[951] which are now largely reserved for vehicular traffic and service vehicles. The federal, provincial and municipal buildings were all interconnected by second-level pedestrian passageways, parking garages and large internal shopping centres, with little access to the streets. Internal circulation is comfortable in all weather and the malls and food courts bustle with activity during weekday lunch hours. However, Hull's downtown is strangely deserted on evenings and weekends, in marked contrast to the roaring social activity of the 1950s and 1960s, when it attracted hordes of Ontario residents to its bars and nightclubs.[952]

The NCC did its best to stitch the various parts back together with investments in public spaces and bridges. The most important step was purchasing 18 hectares (44.5 acres) of surplus riverfront properties from E.B. Eddy Co., which was reducing the scale of its industrial operations. These became Laurier and Taché-Montcalm parks, almost doubling Hull's riverfront public access. The NCC also developed and landscaped the *Théâtre de l'Île*, perhaps the most charming small open space in Hull.[953] More surprisingly, the NCC contributed almost $220 million for new municipal infrastructure, including the entire cost of the new Portage Bridge[954] (Figure 12-3) and substantial portions of new roads, transit facilities, water filtration plants, trunk sewers and a sewage treatment plant. As a result, the Outaouais region finally stopped pouring raw sewage into its namesake river in 1983.[955]

The frenetic redevelopment of downtown Hull added almost 20,000 new public-sector jobs in the 1970s, accelerating that city's transition from a manufacturing to a service economy.[956] The proportion of federal employment on the Québec side of the region went from 3 percent in 1968 to 20 percent in 1986.[957] This was not quite the 25 percent promised to match the Outaouais' share of the metropolitan population, but it was certainly a major statement by the federal government. The Portage and Terrasses towers on the north shore were unmistakeable evidence of a strong federal presence in the Outaouais.[958]

FIGURE 12-3: Portage Bridge, ca. 1975
The new bridge provided a direct link between Wellington Street and the federal offices under construction in Hull.
(Source: City of Ottawa Archives, CA 10693)

Federal Initiatives in Downtown Ottawa

The commitment to grow federal employment in the Outaouais put an end to building large federal office buildings in downtown Ottawa. The last federally-developed project was the much-delayed Department of National Defence headquarters (1969-74), which survived an attempt by Robert Campeau to replace the proposed design with a single, cheaper black glass tower.[959] Although federal employment in Ottawa actually declined slightly from 1971 to 1976, fears of empty private office buildings were not realized because the massive LeBreton Flats complex was put on hold, and the 'temporary' wooden office buildings were demolished, some thirty years after the war ended. The Supreme Court and Cartier Square finally got their lawns back.

While the NCC's attention was mainly directed to Hull in the early 1970s,[960] the agency pursued small-scale projects in downtown Ottawa, led by a new Chairman and General Manager, Douglas Fullerton (Figure 12-4). Fullerton, a Glebe resident, built good relations with some downtown neighbourhoods with early experiments in traffic calming, constructing recreation paths and the Rideau Canal skating rink. The traffic calming was an historic accident, since the OIC had landscaped Clemow and Monkland avenues in the Glebe neighbourhood in the early 20th century as part of an uncompleted parkway network. The City of Ottawa proposed that the six-lane Carling Avenue be extended through the neighbourhood to bring traffic into the downtown. The Glebe residents, including former mayor Charlotte Whitton, opposed the project, and Fullerton declined to hand over the NCC streets. Instead, he retained local architect John Leaning to prepare one of Canada's first traffic calming plans.[961]

Recreational pathways were another innovative NCC initiative that improved the local quality of life. The agency built a 50 km. network of riverside paths in the early 1970s and expanded the network continuously in the following decades.[962] The paths were popular for walking, jogging and recreational cycling during the weekends, but to the surprise of traffic engineers, they also developed into weekday bicycle commuting routes, accommodating a hardy group that cycle through most of Ottawa's cold winters.[963]

Transforming the Rideau Canal into the world's longest skating rink[964] was an inspired idea, apparently coming directly from Fullerton (Figure 12-4). The city government had previously experimented in a few locations but the NCC made the first attempt to freeze and clear the entire downtown canal in 1971. It was an immediate hit with downtown residents and employees, and the 'rink' was quickly extended to Dow's Lake. In subsequent years, civil servants began to skate to work, and the frozen canal became a signature visitor attraction, celebrating Canada's winter heritage[965] (Figure 12-5).

Figure 12-4: Douglas Fullerton, ca. 1974
The NCC Chairman (1969-73) skating on the Rideau Canal.
(Source: NCC)

FIGURE 12-5: **Skating on the Rideau Canal in Downtown Ottawa**
The immensely popular skating venue has an inspiring diagonal view of Parliament Hill on its last stretch, perfectly framing the Gothic buildings on the bluff. The canal later became a centrepiece of the Winterlude Festival.
(Source: NCC)

The Rideau Area Project

The traffic calming, bikeways and canal skating were charming, but downtown Ottawa had a much larger problem: its shopping district was declining. The initial success of the Sparks Street Mall masked the collapse of the downtown's formerly dominant position in the region's retail market. Ottawa, like most North American cities, had unwittingly weakened its downtown by allowing development of many suburban shopping centres in the previous two decades. The Central Business District's (CBD) share of primary retail expenditure dropped from 71 percent in 1950 to 28 percent in 1970, with a further decline expected as Nepean's massive Bayshore Centre opened in 1973.[966] Although the Sparks Street Mall seemed to be holding its own in 1970 by switching its market to downtown employees and visitors, the Rideau Street department store strip was showing signs of distress.

The 1969 *Ottawa Central Area Study*, commissioned by the city and NCC[967] proposed that the land freed up by relocation of the railway freight yards be used to rejuvenate the downtown. The 3.6 ha. (8.8 ac.) site was in a prime location in the core, extending to within one block of Rideau Street. In October 1972, local MP and Liberal Finance Minister John Turner announced that the federal lands would be used to revitalize the downtown. Although Ottawa Mayor Pierre Benoit was a Progressive Conservative, he continued the tradition of a grateful city accepting federal largesse, stating:

> *My most sincere best wishes for the success of this undertaking. I hope this exercise will serve as a model for the cooperation that can and should be undertaken between the federal and municipal levels of government.*[968]

Benoit was content to let the federal government lead the project, and also be responsible for the entire cost. The project process would eventually be a model, but not in the manner Benoit might have imagined.

Mayor Benoit's quiet strategy looked wise in the short term, since the project cost quickly escalated. A group of private developers, including the leading department store, T. Eaton Company, assembled a large block in Centretown, which they proposed to demolish in order to build a downtown shopping centre. The federal government realized that this project would cause the collapse of the Rideau Street project, and bought out the developer's site in 1973 for $22 million, inviting them to relocate to the Rideau Area.[969]

With the site, developer and anchor tenant now in hand, the NCC proceeded to lead the planning in the same manner that federal government had used in the previous decades. They placed a highly qualified professional architect-planner in charge of the project and retained the best Canadian design talent to produce a bold vision. Although the Rideau Area project team was ostensibly co-chaired by the NCC's Deputy General Manager and the city's Commissioner of Community Development, it appears that the NCC's Roderick Clack assumed control of the project from the start. He drove the development forward aggressively in the style of the NCC planners of the 1960s.[970]

Although Clack was an accomplished urban designer in his own right,[971] he commissioned Diamond and Myers, one of North America's most innovative architectural firms, to prepare a concept plan for the Rideau Area. The firm was closely connected with the urban reform movement in Toronto[972] and responsible for Edmonton's HUB building, a 300 m.-long galleria that transformed a nondescript street into the lively core of the University of Alberta campus. Diamond and Myers proposed that Rideau Street's historic buildings be enclosed in a large downtown arcade in the style of the celebrated galleria in Milan or Naples. The arcade would connect the Ogilvy, Caplan and Bay department stores with the new Eaton's store[973] (Figure 12-6). Traffic would be deflected to a new street to the south, and a north-south galleria

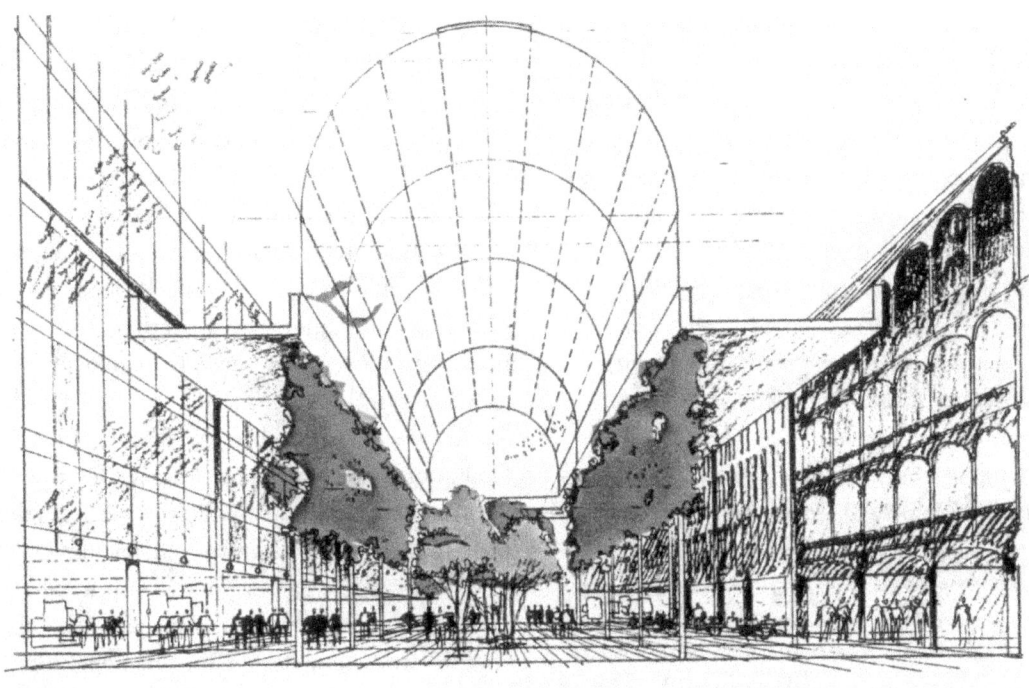

Figure 12-6: Rideau Mall Galleria proposal, 1975
Diamond and Myers' proposal to connect the department stores on Rideau Street with a pedestrian galleria similar to Toronto's Eaton Centre.
(Source: NCC)

would connect the new shopping complex to the edge of the ByWard Market.

The existing merchants and new developer strongly supported the galleria plan, sensing the commercial possibilities.[974] However, the new mayor, Lorry Greenberg, hated the way the NCC controlled the project in September 1975:

It was fascinating to watch Greenberg hitting out in every direction, searching out things he was certain were going on he felt the city had a right to know about. It was even more fascinating to watch Rod Clack break down under the pressure. Finally, he lost his cool, totally, and left the meeting. Yet Greenberg kept us all there for hours going over the project. Belligerent as hell, and every bit as arrogant as Clack, he was still a breath of fresh air.[975]

Greenberg had worked for his family's Minto development firm before he became a community activist, and promptly seized control of the city's team, firing the commissioner, re-assigning staff and demanding new plans. When the NCC planners continued to favour the galleria plan, the mayor went over their heads, demanding that they be fired too.

If Fullerton had still been at the helm of the NCC, his deft touch with the Ottawa local government might have calmed the waters. He had been replaced by two short-term appointments from the senior levels of the civil service, Edgar Gallant and Pierre Juneau, who had little rapport with the strong-willed mayor. Greenberg demanded that the NCC hand over control of the project and its multi-million-dollar budget to the city, and attempted to cap the city's financial contribution at $800,000. Not surprisingly, first Gallant and then Juneau refused.

The personal, professional and political animosity between Ottawa and the NCC became so great that the Rideau Area project effectively collapsed in early 1977. Pierre Juneau rescued the project by inviting a gifted Vancouver mediator, Harry Lash, to review the situation, and design a new organizational structure and planning process. Lash played shuttle diplomat between the obdurate parties and broke the deadlock in six months. He brought the RMOC (which owned Rideau Street), into the management of the project, and drew in the developer, Viking-Rideau, which had previously only interacted with the NCC. The most important move was to have the three governments jointly retain Lloyd Sankey as project coordinator. Sankey was an architect, but he acted as a facilitator, not as supreme designer for the project. The project office consulted scores of stakeholders, held dozens of committee meetings and four open houses to gather public input and review alternative designers for the project. The objective was to produce a design for the rehabilitation of Rideau Street that the three levels of government could agree to. Greenberg tried to wiggle out of cost-sharing, without success. The principle was established that if the local government wanted a share of control, then it should share the costs. Sankey's skilful facilitation led to a tripartite agreement in May 1979, which was perhaps the first example of the City of Ottawa, RMOC and NCC working together for a common goal.[976]

The compromise design for Rideau Street had a transit-mall to suit RMOC and semi-enclosed sidewalk canopies to provide some shelter for shoppers along the street. While this alternative was an acceptable compromise for the politicians and staff of the three levels of governments, the merchants thought it was insufficient, and the adjacent residents likened the result to "putting a glass mini-skirt on an old lady. It might as well be a glass tomb for the economy of the street."[977]

Unfortunately, the merchants and residents were right about the new design. The new pedestrian shelters attracted vandalism and homeless citizens. Many middle-class shoppers abandoned the street for the enclosed mall and bridges above. The stores on Rideau Street went bankrupt or moved out, and the Ogilvy and Caplan's department stores both failed. While these stores may already have been in decline, there is no doubt that the transit mall design hastened their demise. The Rideau Street pedestrian enclosures were removed in 1990, only a few years after their installations,[978] but it was too late. The once-vibrant Rideau Street retail strip was destroyed.

The new shopping mall developer reacted by turning its project inwards and developing a second level walkway from the new hotel/convention centre, through the mall and across Rideau Street to The Bay department store. The Rideau Centre shopping mall was a commercial success for the developers from its opening in early 1983, with 150,000 shopping in the complex on its first day. It reversed the decline in downtown Ottawa's share of regional retail sales, which increased for the first time in 30 years.[979]

Although the Rideau Street portion of the project was an unmitigated disaster from commercial and urban design perspectives, its participatory planning demonstrated a process that might be used in the future, even when the parties deeply distrusted each other. The key elements were joint retention of a neutral facilitator, extensive stakeholder participation, mutual respect for each other's objectives and shared management and funding.[980] The only missing element from the best modern participation practice was joint retention of technical consultants. The original urban designers and market researchers had excellent professional experience, but their recommendations were not acceptable to the mayor because they had previously been retained by the NCC. Unfortunately, it would take almost two decades of further battles before the three levels of government learned to work together.

Changing Local Political Dynamics

The Ottawa-Hull region included almost 50 local governments in 1970[981] and almost all of them were engaged in some form of community planning (Figure 11-20). This dramatic increase from the 1950s was the result of years of advocacy from groups like the Community Planning Association, combined with a much firmer line by Ontario and Québec. The provincial legislation in the immediate post-war period *permitted* local governments to plan, but by the 1970s, municipalities were *required* to plan their communities. The provincial governments also gave grants for smaller municipalities to develop comprehensive land-use plans and zoning bylaws, usually prepared by consultants.[982] Ottawa, Hull and Eastview (later Vanier) were focused on inner-city neighbourhood planning, but the rest of the municipalities prepared conventional land-use plans that attempted to control 'greenfield' new development in suburban and rural contexts.

A review of 54 local and regional plans from the 1970s and 1980s found that they focussed on residential development, with only generic consideration of employment issues. For example, only one plan mentioned the region's growing high-technology industries, and only one mentioned the federal government, which was the largest employer in the region.[983] While the earlier federally-sponsored plans of Bennett, Gréber and Hancock had always incorporated detailed consideration of local problems to complement their designs for capital city issues, the new municipal plans were entirely locally-focused, without any consideration of federal government concerns, and rarely acknowledged their setting in the nation's capital or even in a region with urban development on the other side of the river. The local, regional and federal governments were rapidly growing apart.

Local Opposition to Urban Renewal

Canadian urban renewal and expressway planning proposals from the 1950s and 1960s were often large-scale and destructive. By 1970, many planning proposals were questioned, often vociferously, by ordinary citizens and neighbourhood groups. Across Canada, big renewal projects were subject to intense debate: Pacific Centre in Vancouver, Sunnyside in Calgary, Trefann Court and the Spadina Expressway in Toronto, Lower Town in Ottawa, Cité Concordia in Montréal, and Quinpool Road in Halifax.[984]

The NCC probably did not realize it at the time, but downtown Hull was probably the last major example of unilateral federal action in the National Capital Region. The breathtaking scale and speed of the transformation was only possible because the citizens whose neighbourhood was destroyed had little access to the local or provincial governments, which were also involved in the redevelopment. If the Trudeau government thought that the investment would hold back the independence movement in Québec, they got a surprise in 1976 when a *Parti Québécois* MNA was elected in Hull, which had been a safe Liberal seat for the past 20 years. Although the federal investment in Hull was attractive from a symbolic and national perspective, the local residents bitterly opposed the expropriation, relocation and massive disruption associated with urban renewal and redevelopment.

Elsewhere in Hull, the residents of the Jardins Taché area also resisted the 1970 proposals by Dasken Enterprises for luxury high-rise development on a site on Taché Boulevard. The residents sued when Hull Council, acting on a legal opinion, allowed the project to proceed, even though the zoning for the site did not appear to permit high-rise development. After a series of legal battles, the Québec Supreme Court ruled in favour of the citizens in December 1971 and, after last-ditch attempts to retroactively re-zone the site failed, demolition of the buildings began in August 1972.[985] The Dasken case was nationally important because it demonstrated that developers and municipalities must follow their planning regulations or face severe consequences. Locally, it demonstrated to Outaouais citizen groups that you could fight city hall, and win.

In other Canadian cities, the late 1960s and early 1970s saw a great awakening of citizens' groups that opposed urban renewal, expressways and other centrally-planned projects that had major impacts upon neighbourhoods.[986] Many neighbourhood groups were inspired by Jane Jacobs' 1961 classic *Death and Life of Great American Cities*. Her attacks on urban renewal, expressways and Modern planning seemed more relevant after she relocated to Toronto in 1968 and became involved in the movement to stop the proposed Spadina Expressway from destroying downtown neighbourhoods.[987] These citizens' groups sometimes evolved from project opposition to city-wide political reform. Some neighbourhood advocates won seats on municipal councils and even the mayor's chair, such as Vancouver's Art Phillips and Toronto's David Crombie and John Sewell.[988] By the mid-1970s, the urban reformers in many North American cities had halted expressway network expansion, stopped urban renewal's demolition of existing residential areas and turned redevelopment funds to neighbourhood improvement and protection.

In a burst of creativity, the reform councils sponsored new forms of inner-city development such as Vancouver's False Creek South and Granville Island and Toronto's St. Lawrence Neighbourhood.[989] These programs effectively replaced urban renewal and were influenced by Jane Jacobs' ideas.[990] Her advocacy for mixed uses, higher density, greater diversity, and retention of older buildings supported the urban infill and rehabilitation programs that were proposed by many citizen groups. After the bitterly contested battles, the reformers also insisted that future urban planning should incorporate extensive public participation that included direct consultation with the citizens of affected neighbourhoods.[991] The traditional participants – politicians, planners, other bureaucrats, and business groups – began to accommodate citizens at the plan-making table. The provinces and municipalities made their planning processes more open with public meetings, newsletters, open houses, and design *charrettes* (Figure 12-7). Citizens became directly involved in articulating objectives, proposing alternatives and preparing detailed plans. New methods of participation emerged, such as consensus-building, and more attention was paid to the inclusiveness of planning processes to involve diverse groups such as women, the physically disabled, low-income households, ethnic populations, and the elderly. [992]

In Ottawa, the proposed Downtown Distributor (Figure 11-16) and other expressway corridors from the city's 1968 DeLeuw Cather expressway plan galvanized the inner city neighbourhoods like Ottawa Centre, Sandy Hill, Ottawa East and the Glebe. Local activists such as Lorry Greenberg and Michael Cassidy were elected to city council. Other neighbourhoods,

FIGURE 12-7: Citizen Participation at a charrette, Ottawa.
Local residents were rarely consulted about redevelopment proposals for plans in a meaningful manner by the municipal or federal governments during the 1950s or 1960s, which eventually fuelled opposition to most changes in their neighbourhoods.
(Source: Urban Strategies; reproduced with permission)

like Pinecrest-Queensway, stopped large-scale urban renewal/public housing projects. The urban renewal planners were replaced, and the City of Ottawa engaged new staff to help prepare neighbourhood plans coordinated by working committees of local residents. By 1970, a loose coalition of community organizations had formed across the Ottawa region. These neighbourhood groups would transform local planning.[993]

The City of Ottawa's urban renewal plans for Lowertown East were examples of the changed approach to redevelopment. The 1966 *Lowertown East Neighbourhood Study* estimated that 61 percent of the housing in the area was in poor condition, and was illustrated with stark photographs of dilapidated wooden structures. It called for wide-scale expropriation of the blocks on both sides of St. Patrick Street and their replacement with the King Edward Expressway and many apartment buildings of public housing.[994] By 1970, the city's planners had prepared a formal proposal for CMHC funding for a huge urban renewal district, and expropriation began for the expressway corridor and relocation of St. Patrick Street[995] (Figure 12-8). However, neighbourhood protests about the demolitions and new roads caused the new city council to cancel the King Edward expressway in 1973. Unfortunately, two large swaths of houses had already been demolished for the expressway and new arterial and many other expropriated buildings fell into poor condition. By 1976, the Urban Renewal Plan had become a "Redevelopment Plan," examining options for building rehabilitation, redevelopment of the demolished expressway blocks for non-profit and co-operative housing, and selective infill elsewhere. The new study was prepared after extensive public consultation and was the first city redevelopment plan printed in both official languages – an overdue reflection of Lower Town's identity.[996]

Figure 12-8: Lowertown East Urban Renewal Model, 1970
Note the King Edward Expressway (left), St. Patrick Street arterial (top) and new apartments and townhouses, requiring demolition of 16 blocks of older houses. The expressway was cancelled after the expropriation was started, but some of the redevelopment proceeded in a different form.
(Source: Murray and Murray, 1970, p. 2)

Regional Governments and Regional Planning

The NCC's primacy in regional planning disappeared during the 1970s. Although Ontario established the Regional Municipality of Ottawa Carleton (RMOC) in 1968, and the *Communauté Régionale de l'Outaouais* (CRO) was set up by Québec in 1970, it was a few years before their planning capacity was fully established. They both completed regional land use plans in the mid-1970s that co-ordinated with suburban township plans prepared by the new local professional staff. The plans called for extensive low-density, automobile-serviced suburban development on land held by private developers at the periphery of the metropolitan area.

The first official statement from Ottawa-Carleton's founding chairman, Denis Coolican, was that he expected planning to be the initial project of the new regional government.[997] Coolican, the former reeve of Rockcliffe Park, had an initial appointment of four and one-half years, and he drove the regional plan through to approval during that period.

The RMOC started from scratch, hiring planning staff and renting offices. There were two key initial decisions: the plan would be prepared with extensive public consultation, and it would be a new concept based upon extensive background research, rather than simply stitching together the official plans of the many local governments.[998] Extensive citizen participation in the preparation of a community plan was a new concept in the Ottawa-Hull metropolitan area region, but it was a good fit with the changing politics of planning.[999]

The RMOC planners put several alternative growth concepts out for public reaction but there was no public appetite for extensive redevelopment and infill within the Greenbelt (Figure 12-9, concepts I and II). Since it was clear that vacant

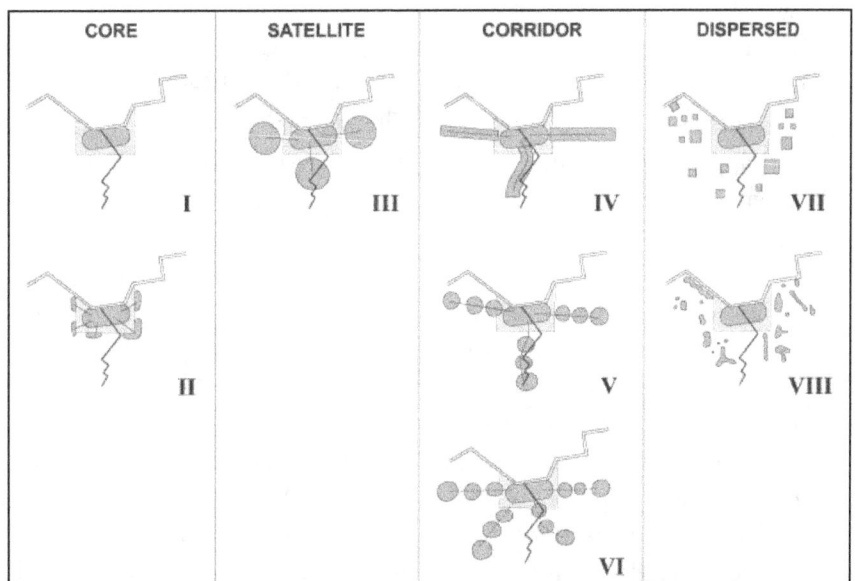

FIGURE 12-9: First RMOC Plan Concepts
Most stakeholders rejected intensification options I and II, while private developers who had large land assemblies outside the Greenbelt preferred the satellite concept III. Note that the large federal-provincial land assembly for a new town in the southeast is not shown in this concept. The north side of the Ottawa River is shown as a blank; there was little coordination with the regional planners in Québec.
(Source: RMOC 1973, adapted by Fullerton, 2005, Figure 3)

land within the Greenbelt was quickly running out, the essential debate was about the location of future development outside the Greenbelt.

There was not much debate about the form of future growth, since most stakeholders seemed content with conventional suburban development in the early 1970s. However, the location of the suburban growth areas was intensely controversial, since several organizations had assembled large areas of farmland just outside the Greenbelt. The provincial and federal governments had the largest assembly, with 3,800 ha. (9,400 ac.) located in the southwest quadrant, astride the new Highway 417 to Montréal. They proposed a satellite city with a substantial proportion of affordable housing. Four private developers controlled most of the lands to the west, south and east of the Greenbelt. Robert Campeau had taken over Bill Teron's Kanata lands, and Cadillac-Fairview also owned a major assembly to the west.[1000] Costain had large holdings in Kanata and Orleans, and the Greenberg family's Minto Corporation owned large sections of Orleans and the southwest land assembly, Barrhaven.[1001]

New development in the Kanata area was already underway in 1972, and a satellite community in Orleans appeared to be inevitable, given the eastern extension of the Queensway corridor. The developers and the reeves of Gloucester and Nepean townships lobbied hard for the southern extension to take place on the privately-owned Barrhaven lands, rather than the federal-provincial land assembly, even though these private lands had weak transportation connections and were located in the noise control zone of the Ottawa airport.[1002] The private developers and their political allies won this round. The Barrhaven land assembly was designated as the Southern Urban Community in the final 1974 plan (Figure 12-10) and RMOC was committed to servicing this large private land assembly by public transit, a promise that would come back to haunt Ottawa in the 21st century.[1003]

While many stakeholders supported the suburban land use proposals and the proposed regional bus transit network, other transportation components in the original RMOC plan proposals were rejected during the approval process. The regional planners had already discarded the inner city expressway network in Ottawa's 1964 plan, but they recommended two new bridges across the Ottawa River, four over the Rideau River and canal, and several new arterial roads to connect them. These bridges proved universally unpopular with adjacent Ontario residents and almost all were removed from the RMOC plan. Britannia residents stopped the western interprovincial bridge, New Edinburgh residents once again prevented the Vanier Parkway from connecting to the Macdonald-Cartier Bridge, and Centretown and Sandy Hill residents stopped new bridges across the canal and Rideau River.[1004] The CRO and Gatineau were not pleased, having designed their transportation plans around the bridge proposals and built some approach roads to implement them.

Regional Planning in the Outaouais

The regional government in the Outaouais started a year after the RMOC and moved more slowly, due to fierce inter-municipal rivalry. A further municipal reorganization in 1974 reduced the number of CRO municipalities from 32 to 8, but this set of amalgamations was deeply unpopular and may have weakened the political base of its sponsor, Hull MNA and Minister of State for Intergovernmental Affairs Oswald Parent. Constant friction remained between the City of Hull, which demanded that it be the main regional centre, and the suburban Town of Gatineau, which had exceeded its rival in population and continued to grow quickly. These local frictions may have diluted the effectiveness of Québec's *Société d'aménagement de l'Outaouais* (SAO), which had been established to encourage economic development in the region.[1005]

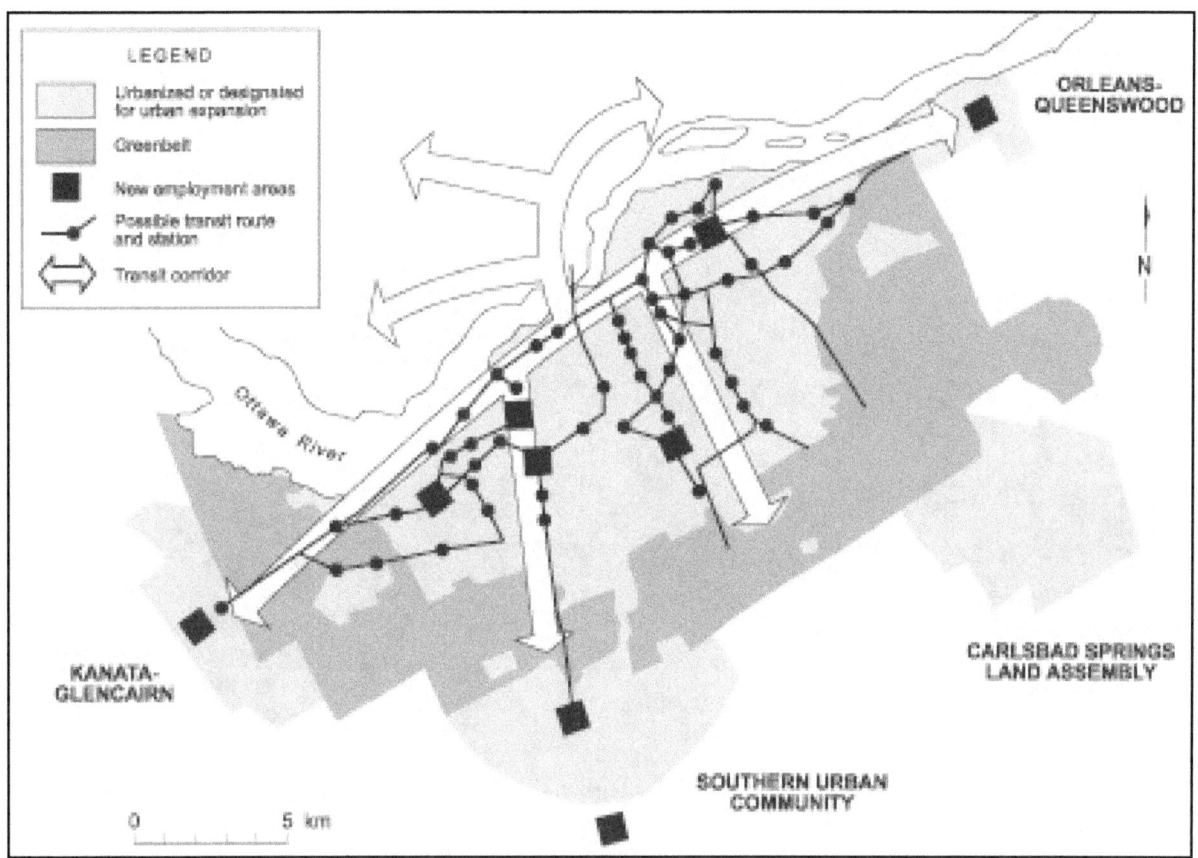

FIGURE 12-10: Urban Structure Plan for Ottawa-Carleton, 1974
The Carlsbad Springs Land Assembly by the provincial and federal governments was assigned the lowest priority for development, and eventually dropped from the regional plan. Three other land assemblies owned by large, politically-connected private developers were approved instead.
(Source: Fullerton, 2005)

Regional planning got off to a quick start at the CRO, and a 1973 interim plan called for Hull to be the regional centre and other city centres to be developed first in the east in Gatineau, and later in Aylmer, to the west. It also called for two new interprovincial bridges at Kettle Island and Deschênes, roughly in the locations proposed in Gréber's 1950 plan.[1006]

The 1970s were also a period when Outaouais local governments began to develop and use more modern planning instruments, such as master plans and comprehensive zoning bylaws, to replace the less effective post-war controls.[1007] The CRO's regional plan was delayed because although the provincial government had created the regional governments, its new municipal planning legislation was delayed. The CRO's plan was well ahead of similar efforts in Montréal and Québec, so it became the test case, officially adopted by the region in 1977[1008] (Figure 12-11).

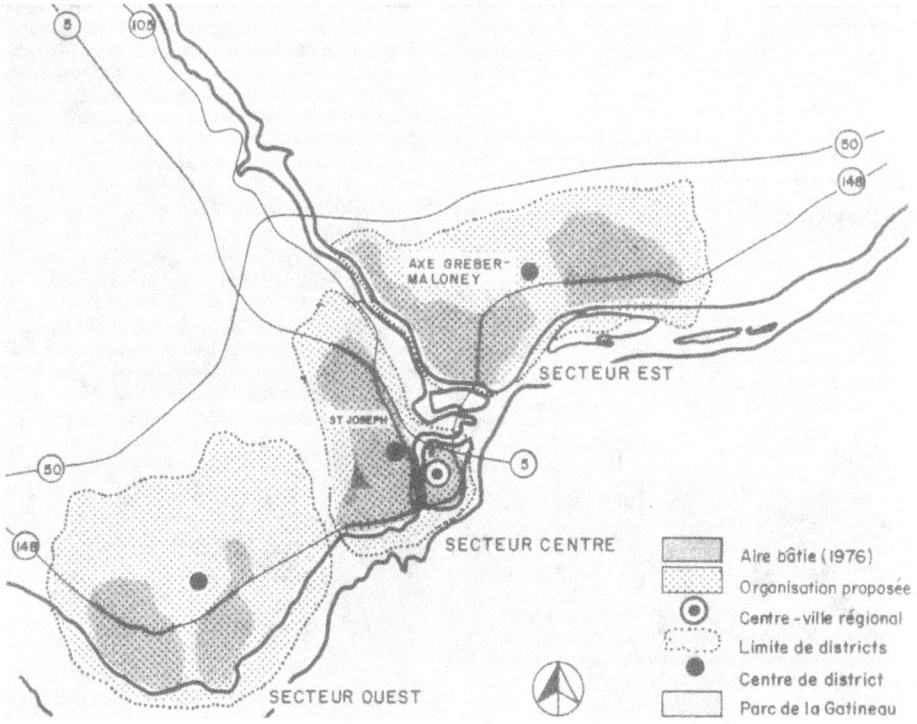

FIGURE 12-11: **CRO Regional Plan, 1973-77**
Note the regional downtown in downtown Hull and suburban district centres in Aylmer, north Hull and Gatineau. Once again, the area on the other side of the Ottawa River is a blank.
(Source: Tochon, 1978, Figure 2, p. 132)

Federal Responses to the New Regions

The emergence of the new regional governments and the flurry of regional planning activity in the early 1970s deeply concerned the popular NCC Chairman Douglas Fullerton. He believed that the local, regional, provincial and federal governments were working at cross-purposes, and that the National Capital Region was becoming ungovernable. He requested that Prime Minister Trudeau release him from his duties at the NCC to conduct a study of the topic, starting in early 1973.[1009]

Fullerton was the latest in a long line of critics of the governance arrangements for the national capital area[1010] but he now had first-hand experience with the complexity added by recent provincial activism, two new regional governments and the expanded planning capacity of rapidly growing suburban townships. Fullerton's two-volume report, released in November 1974, was a thorough description of the barriers to achieving federal objectives in planning and development of the National Capital Region (a "jurisdictional swamp"), perhaps only underestimating the emerging power of neighbourhood groups.[1011]

Fullerton stressed that the region needed a governing body that spanned both sides of the Ottawa River. He recommended a "supra-regional council," half elected and half composed of federal and provincial appointees.[1012] This suggestion met with the expected negative response from the local and regional politicians.[1013] However, Fullerton also pointed to the need for a stronger symbolic role for the national capital that could "inspire pride in all Canadians."[1014] Fullerton's promotion of bilingualism and the symbolic role of the capital would ultimately have more long-term effects than any governance proposal or perhaps even his aggressive leadership of the redevelopment of Hull.

While Fullerton was writing his report, the NCC planners were quietly preparing their response to the two new regional plans nearing completion. The federal agency had not provided any significant public feedback during the extensive consultations for the RMOC and CRO plans[1015] and prepared its proposals in secret.

In December 1974, the NCC released *Tomorrow's Capital: An Invitation to Dialogue*, a slim, handsomely produced monograph that contained the outline of a regional plan for both sides of the Ottawa River. The 90-page report was technically sophisticated and politically naïve, because the NCC proposed the exact opposite of the regional structure included in the draft RMOC and CRO plans.

The two regional governments proposed stronger east-west connections binding together the municipalities on their respective sides of the Ottawa River, while the NCC proposed strong connections across the river, to bind the two halves of the capital together (Figure 12-12). Secondly, the RMOC proposed to grow to the west, east and south, while the CRO draft plan initially pushed development to the east and north. *Tomorrow's Capital* proposed a northwest-to-southeast development corridor, with the federal-provincial satellite city as the southeast anchor. Finally, the two regional plans proposed low-density development served by automobiles and buses. In contrast, the federal plan proposed higher-density development along a rapid transit line in the southeast/northwest corridor, with an eight kilometre (five mile) tunnel through the central area. A second transit line with intensive development around the light rail stations was proposed for the abandoned CP Rail corridor from the southwest to the northeast across the region. Bus rapid transit was proposed from the Highway 550 corridor in the Outaouais and the Queensway corridor in the RMOC (Figure 12-12).

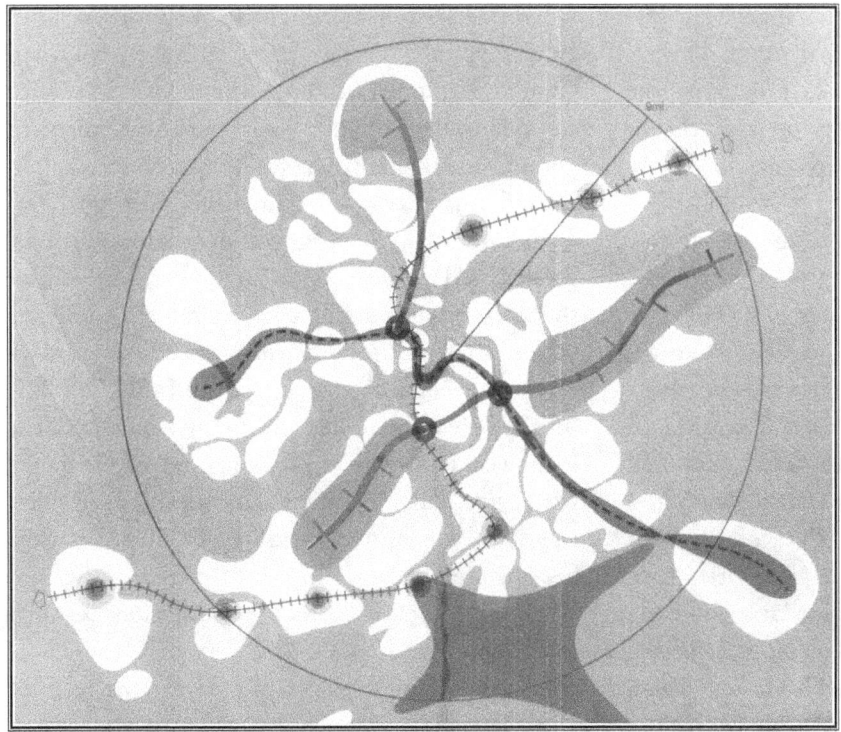

Figure 12-12: Tomorrow's Capital Regional Transit Structure Proposal, 1974
The NCC proposed a rapid transit line running from the southeast to the northeast with an 8 km tunnel through the central area. A light rail line was proposed to run from the southwest to the northeast.
(Source: NCC, 1974, p. 66)

The NCC also had social objectives for its northwest/southeast orientation, because the western Outaouais and eastern Ottawa were the most bilingual portions of the region, and strengthening that axis would strengthen the bilingual nature of the national capital.[1016] These national objectives meant nothing, of course, to the private developers and suburban politicians associated with the proposed regional plans. With hundreds of millions of dollars at stake, they objected strongly.[1017] The resistance of land speculators and their political allies should be expected, but *Tomorrow's Capital* also managed to offend regional and local politicians and professional staff because the NCC's "invitation to dialogue" arrived at the 11th hour, after years of participation by the general public in developing the RMOC and CRO plans.[1018]

After expressing their outrage, the regional governments simply ignored the Fullerton report and *Tomorrow's Capital* and approved their own plans.[1019] The NCC did not understand how to function effectively in the new political environment and had missed its chance to influence regional development. Since the new regional governments now had access to the municipal bond markets to fund their own capital works programs, the offer of massive federal spending for rapid transit infrastructure was less attractive than it was to Ottawa and Hull in the 1950s.

Tomorrow's Capital became simply a footnote marking the point at which the NCC's regional planning power evaporated. Later observers give it only a cursory glance.[1020] But before moving on, it might be useful to review what was lost by this complete failure of federal-regional cooperation. In effect, the NCC and federal government proposed to build an underground rapid transit line and a light rail line linking the two sides of the river and to develop model satellite communities with substantial components of affordable housing in each province. It was 1974, and the federal government was actively involved in urban development across the nation, through CMHC and the Ministry of State for Urban Affairs.

Vancouver's federal gifts included Granville Island and False Creek South, the first steps in that city's urban regeneration.[1021] Toronto received the St. Lawrence Neighbourhood and Harbourfront[1022] while Montréal had obtained federal subsidies for Expo '67 and the upcoming 1976 Olympics.[1023] There were other precedents for massive national investments in federal capitals in the 1970s. For example, the United States was building a subway system throughout the Washington region, and Australia was investing in Canberra.[1024] But in Canada, the 1975-1990 period was a time of such intense 'Town-Crown' conflict that federal spending on Ottawa actually declined.

'Town-Crown' Conflict Escalates

The combined effects of the Fullerton report, *Tomorrow's Capital*, massive redevelopment in Hull and the Rideau Centre placed the regional governments and biggest cities in constant conflict with the NCC in the mid-1970s. Almost all intergovernmental cooperation ground to a halt as the tensions escalated. In response, the federal government established another Joint Parliamentary Committee on the National Capital Region. Although the NCC was once again looking for federal support to implement an ambitious regional plan for the national capital, the circumstances were quite different from 1956. As before, many local governments and citizens' groups used the hearings as an opportunity to vent their frustration about the federal government's actions, but the nature of the opposition was more intense. Several groups suggested that the NCC be abolished altogether and many suggested that its powers be curtailed. The regional governments were particularly angry, recommending that the NCC's planning and development powers be withdrawn and any future interprovincial issues be settled by direct coordination between the RMOC and CRO. The City of Ottawa was concerned about the loss of federal jobs to Hull and Mayor Lorry Greenberg was a harsh critic of the NCC's methods.[1025]

The federal government also found itself with little support in the Outaouais and received much criticism of the construction and social impacts of the redevelopment of downtown Hull. There was also opposition to direct federal intervention in Québec territory from more sovereigntist organizations.[1026] Faced with severe local and regional resistance, NCC chairman Edgar Gallant was unable to get the Joint Committee to endorse the *Tomorrow's Capital* plan. The committee slowly dissolved and never issued a final report, while Gallant was eased out of the NCC chairmanship.[1027]

Interprovincial cooperation became even more difficult after the victory of the sovereigntist *Parti Québécois* (PQ) in late 1976, and the upset victory of Jocelyne Ouellette over Liberal powerbroker Oswald Parent in Hull. Since Parent had insisted that he be the main contact for the NCC in the Outaouais,[1028] the federal government had to rebuild its political network in the region. Of course, the PQ provincial governments wanted no further co-operation with the federal government on improving the Canadian capital, so any project that required federal/provincial or Ontario/Québec cooperation stalled. That was the end of the interprovincial bridge studies and the proposed federal parkways on the north shore of the Ottawa River. However, the NCC was eventually able to establish a better working relationship with the *Communauté urbaine de l'Outaouais* (CUO)[1029] to fund infrastructure, including a 50 percent subsidy for regional roads. This had the unusual effect of Outaouais road improvements stopping at the boundary of the National Capital Region for many years.

Provincial neglect and inter-jurisdictional conflicts and provincial neglect also left the Ottawa-Hull region as one of the few large metropolitan areas not connected to the continental interurban highway system in 1975. Ottawa was by far the largest urban area not connected to Ontario's 400 series of highways, and the Outaouais was the largest urban region not connected to Québec's interurban Autoroute system. The original Macdonald-Cartier Freeway (Highway 401/Route 20) had bypassed the region in the 1950s, passing 100 km. to the south. As the North American industrial system switched to truck transport for goods, the Ottawa-Hull region was being left behind, just as had happened in the railway era a century before.

Although Québec had no plans for an Autoroute, Ontario had plans for a Highway 417 from Ottawa southeast to Montréal and 416 southwest towards Toronto. These highways were stalled in the 1970s by disputes about how they were to connect to the Queensway, the spine of the Ottawa road network. The 1950 Gréber plan anticipated these interurban highways,[1030] and the FDC purchased the necessary road corridors through Alta Vista and Nepean when these lands were still farmer's fields in the early 1950s. However, the NCC made a tactical error by allowing grass to grow in the corridors. As the new suburbs grew up around them in the 1950s and 1960s, the residents used the road corridors as linear parks. When it came time to connect the much-delayed highways in the 1970s, the residents organized to prevent the projects for being built in their neighbourhoods, as part of the general rejection of the urban expressway network.

Since neighbourhood opposition prevented connecting the interurban highways to regional or local roads, the provincial government needed routes that did not touch *any* residential areas. The solution was to deflect both interurban highways into the Greenbelt, and construct new interchanges in the east for the 417 to Montréal and in the west for the 416 to Toronto. Since these projects only required the agreement of the federal and Ontario governments, the politics were manageable. Ottawa got a multi-lane highway connection to Montréal in the late 1970s, thirty years after the rest of southern Ontario. The 416 connection towards Toronto was built in stages, and completed in 1997, almost half a century after most other southern Ontario cities were connected by freeways. Gatineau is still waiting for a Québec Autoroute to Montréal, with no plans in sight.

The first phase of the long-delayed LeBreton Flats project managed to get started in the late 1970s, because it only required approval of the City of Ottawa. The NCC had removed the rail yards, built riverside parks and connected the Ottawa River Parkway to Wellington Street in the late 1960s. Although the federal offices proposed for the north portion of the site were cancelled in favour of development in downtown Ottawa and Hull, the southern part of the LeBreton site was proposed for high-rise housing (Figure 11-4). However, the reform council led by Mayor Marion Dewar pushed the NCC into considering a medium-density, low-rise neighbourhood, with a high proportion of social housing. CMHC adopted LeBreton as an urban demonstration project, pioneering some innovative environmental planning measures. The first phase was completed in 1982, with 424 units in the blocks south of Scott Street. These replaced, too late, the 225 units that were demolished in 1965 for the urban renewal project.[1031] The rest of the LeBreton site was criss-crossed by road right-of-ways owned by local and regional governments, and so required approval of all three parties to proceed, making implementation almost impossible in an era of constant inter-jurisdictional conflict.[1032]

Regional Growth and Expansion

The inter-jurisdictional quarrelling certainly did not affect the population growth in the suburbs of the National Capital Region. The Ottawa-Hull area grew from 516,985 to 920,780 people from 1971-1991, and was one of the fastest growing metropolitan areas in Canada.[1033] The two new regional governments did their jobs well, providing infrastructure for the rapid expansion of the suburban areas, although the central cities declined slightly. The CUO actually grew faster than the RMOC during this period, and the Québec side of the river grew from 21.8 percent to 29.7 percent of the metropolitan area.[1034] In the Outaouais, the CUO almost doubled in population from 102,739 to 201,536, even as Hull declined slightly from 63,588 to 60,707. The rapid growth of Gatineau (22,000 to 92,000) and Aylmer (7,000 to 32,000) more than made up for the slight decline in Hull.[1035] The rapid growth of the former Town of Gatineau created political problems within the CUO, since it was now 50 percent larger than Hull and demanded an equal place in the leadership of the region (Figure 12-13).

The RMOC also grew quickly during 1971-91, from 471,931 to 678,147, even though the City of Ottawa declined from 302,000 to 295,000 in the 1970s.[1036] Suburban development outside the Greenbelt accounted for most of the growth, with farm fields turning into subdivisions in Kanata, Barrhaven and Orleans (Figure 12-14). The local political dynamics were somewhat different than in the CUO, since Ottawa was clearly the largest city with a majority of the population in the region until 1986, and over triple the size of Nepean, the largest suburban municipality.

The planning and development issues were quite different in Ottawa and in the suburbs. The central city was essentially concerned with neighbourhood conservation, renewal and redevelopment issues, while the outer townships were managing rapid 'greenfield' suburban growth.[1037] The RMOC provided much of the infrastructure for suburban growth, and local political conflicts tended to be between Ottawa and the regional government, rather than between the central city and Nepean or Gloucester, as in the 1950s and 1960s. The RMOC's initial governance arrangements gave Ottawa wards a majority of the seats on the regional council but since the city politicians did not vote as a block, they did not control the council. When Nepean Reeve Andrew Haydon was elected as Regional Chairman in 1978, the RMOC's identification with suburban interests increased.

The new communities built in the 1970s and 1980s were conventional suburban development, planned using the neighbourhood unit principle (Figure 8-2). They were essentially bedroom communities at first, but some shopping malls and community recreation centres soon followed.

FIGURE 12-13: Urban Growth in the National Capital Region, 1890-1991
The independent satellite cities proposed by the regional governments in the 1970s became ordinary suburban bedroom communities.
(Source: NCC, 1950, Atlas Plate 6)

FIGURE 12-14: Greenbelt separation
Separation of suburban subdivisions by the Greenbelt in eastern Ottawa, looking toward downtown.
(Source: NCC)

Employment remained in the central area and federal nodes at first, but the townships soon developed industrial parks in an attempt to balance their tax assessment.[1038]

Although the Ottawa-Gatineau suburbs were rather ordinary, the RMOC developed several innovative transit systems to serve them, after it took over the Ottawa Transportation Commission in 1972. The first was the express bus, which picked up passengers along the standard collector loop road in a suburban neighbourhood unit, and then went directly downtown via the Queensway.[1039] Despite its fierce conflict with the RMOC over the *Tomorrow's Capital* plan, the federal government cooperated with the region to improve transit service. In 1974, the NCC began to close half of the Ottawa River parkway during rush hour, to provide a corridor for OC Transpo buses. This broke a seven-decade prohibition of commercial vehicles on the parkways, but it cut travel times to downtown and federal employment nodes like Tunney's Pasture by half on several bus routes. The federal government also improved transit's competitiveness by eliminating free employee parking and staggering work hours to spread out the peak demand periods.[1040]

These experiments were a prelude to the RMOC's greatest achievement, the Transitway system. The 1974 Official Plan considered several rapid transit alternatives, but concluded that the region could not afford a subway or light rail at the time. The plan opted for a bus rapid transit (BRT) system, largely on exclusive rights-of-way.[1041] BRT can be a cost-effective system for medium-sized cities, provided that the necessary transportation corridors are available at a nominal price. The RMOC was fortunate that the NCC had acquired many transportation corridors at rural prices in the 1950s and had held onto them, even as regional road network plans changed. The 1980s Transitway system used two former NCC road corridors, the Queensway landscape strips, part of the former downtown rail corridor and the Mackenzie King Bridge, all assembled decades earlier by the FDC and NCC. The RMOC built the Transitway in stages and then reorganized the regional bus service into a network that is acknowledged as the finest BRT system in North America, and one of the best in the world.[1042] Its only flaw was that the transit-oriented development anticipated around the new stations was slow to appear, if it emerged at all. The Transitway was a successful transportation innovation, but it had little effect upon the sprawling suburban form of growth in Ottawa-Carleton.[1043]

New National Institutions in the Core

Although the federal government largely abandoned the regional planning field in the 1970s, it continued to reinforce its presence in the core of the capital city area. Most capital cities have a collection of institutions that reinforce national cultural objectives near the symbolic core of the seat of government.[1044] Prior to the completion of the National Arts Centre in 1969, the core of Canada's capital was embarrassingly lacking in cultural facilities, with the National Gallery squeezed into an ill-adapted office building on Elgin Street, the natural history museum in a small Victorian structure in a residential area seventeen blocks south of Parliament, and the science and technology museum in a warehouse building in a suburban industrial park.

The National Museums Corporation (NMC) was responsible for improving these institutions, but had little to show for its efforts. The National Gallery had its sights on Cartier Square since the 1950 plan, but the Department of National Defence was reluctant to move from its 'temporary' buildings, and Ottawa wanted the site for a new city hall. In the mid-1970s, the Gallery was offered the site of another collection of war-time temporary buildings on Wellington Street, beside the Supreme Court. This was the era of mega-structures, and the gallery was to connect to a system of buildings and walkways binding the two sides of the river together[1045] (Figure 11-16).

The NMC ran a national architectural competition for the new gallery, which was won by Toronto's John Parkin and Associates in 1977. Alas, the funds to construct the gallery were not available during a period of fiscal restraint, and the gallery Director, Jean Boggs, departed to teach at Harvard.[1046] Perhaps it was just as well that the 1977 design was not built, since its series of interconnected concrete boxes arrayed along the cliff-top was not particularly inspiring. And while many building interconnections were established above downtown Hull at the time, it was doubtful that the proposed gallery could have been plugged into the system, given the conflicts between the federal, Ottawa and RMOC governments in the 1970s.

By the early 1980s, the condition of the museums and gallery were a "national disgrace"[1047] and Pierre Trudeau was considering his legacy in the national capital. The prime minister had always been interested in culture, and this was a period when great new museums were being commissioned internationally, most prominently the *grand projects* of Trudeau's colleague François Mitterrand in Paris.[1048] In February 1982, when Trudeau announced funding for new homes for the National Gallery and a National Museum of Man, he specifically referred to the value of these institutions in "the creating of a nation and preservation of values that make our identity possible."[1049]

To avoid the disappointments of previous projects, the buildings were to be constructed by a special-purpose implementation agency, headed by a repatriated Jean Boggs.[1050] She had to move quickly, since there were perhaps two years remaining in Trudeau's electoral mandate. Boggs dispensed with architectural competitions, which had produced mediocre results in past two attempts. She personally visited the offices of fifty architectural firms, short-listing ten for interviews. She also commissioned Roger du Toit Architects to compare and make recommendations on five museum sites in the core of the national capital. The study resurrected the NCC's 1971 idea of a "Boulevard Canada" – a ceremonial route connecting downtown Ottawa and Hull via the Alexandra and Portage bridges. Du Toit and Robert Allsopp argued that the best sites for national institutions could be connected by this route.[1051]

One year after her appointment, Jean Boggs announced the sites and architects. The National Museum of Man was to be designed by Métis architect Douglas Cardinal for a riverfront site in Hull, opposite the Parliament Buildings. The National Gallery was to be designed by Moshe Safdie and built on the northeast corner of Sussex Drive and St. Patrick Street, opposite Ottawa's Notre Dame Basilica. Both sites were federally-owned land, and the museums were to be built using a fast-track construction process.

Hull was pleased to finally receive a federal cultural institution that was expected to become a major tourist attraction. The NCC quickly produced planning guidelines for the site which required the architect to keep a view corridor open from Laurier Street to Parliament Hill.[1052] Cardinal's low rise, undulating Tyndall limestone structures are set into the riverbank and brilliantly frame the Parliament Hill view (Figure 12-15). The project was re-named the Museum of Civilization in 1986 and the Canadian Museum of History in 2013, after government changes. It became a "must-see" attraction for any visit to the national capital. The museum's Great Hall has become an iconic space with its collection of West Coast aboriginal totem poles overlooking the Ottawa River.

Prime Minister Trudeau was directly involved in the design of the new National Gallery. He cast the deciding vote for Safdie's 'extroverted' design, which carried the visitors up a long ramp from Sussex Drive to the Great Hall, a glass pavilion that faintly echoes the Library of Parliament on the skyline.[1053] The Great Hall offers another remarkable

FIGURE 12-15: Museum of Civilization
Douglas Cardinal's museum seems to grow out of the landscape. It frames another iconic view of Parliament Hill.
(Source: Museum of Civilization, Detail of photo CD95-731-099)

view of the Parliament Buildings, the Supreme Court, the National Library, the Ottawa River and Douglas Cardinal's new museum.[1054] Surprisingly, one of the halls of the new gallery contains the salvaged neo-Gothic interior of the Chapel of our Lady of the Sacred Heart, a significant remnant of Ottawa's built heritage. The Rideau Street convent had been purchased by private developers in 1972, and despite desperate appeals by citizens' groups, the historic buildings were demolished. The National Gallery stepped in to aid the rescue effort, salvaged the chapel's interior, and put it into storage until it could be reconstructed sixteen years later.[1055]

In contrast to Hull's support, the City of Ottawa opposed the construction of the new National Gallery on Sussex Drive, due to concerns about its visual impact on the Notre Dame Basilica across the boulevard. But Ottawa wasn't asked to approve the site or building, because the land was owned by the federal Crown and construction was by a federal agency. The CMCC used a constitutional legal provision that the federal government does not need permission to build a public work on federal property. They were also in a hurry to get a shovel in the ground before the government changed. As the buildings swirled in political controversy over their cost and design, the City of Ottawa announced that the NMCC had refused to purchase municipal building permits worth $800,000 and denied city building inspectors access to the site.[1056] Mayor Marion Dewar announced that she would pursue the new government for the building permit fees. When they didn't pay, Ottawa cut off electricity to the site.

Somehow, Boggs got the two new museum buildings out of the ground before Brian Mulroney's Conservative government took office in September 1984. The design process and fast-track construction had pushed the budgets 41 percent above the original estimates. In the end, the buildings were too prominent for the new Tory government to cancel and demolish, and they simply sacked Boggs, dismantled the CMCC and changed the name of Cardinal's building to the Canadian Museum of Civilization.[1057] Prime Minister Brian Mulroney got in front of the parade and presided over the opening of the Gallery and of the Museum in 1988 and 1989 respectively. Both institutions were smash hits with the public from their first days, although some Ottawa institutions complained that they drained the energy and volunteers out of civic arts activity.[1058]

Pierre Trudeau was long gone from Ottawa by the time the new institutions opened, but he seemed pleased with his legacy: "… one of the few capitals in the world where the arts are such a major symbol."[1059] They were certainly an improvement over the banal office buildings looming over the Parliament Buildings from the south, and they helped focus attention on a new strategy for the core of Canada's capital city.

Confederation Boulevard and a New Focus for the Core of the Capital

The search for the new museum sites helped the NCC re-focus their planning efforts on improving the symbolic core of Canada's capital city. The 1971 *Core Area Plan* suggested a loop road to support an enormous megastructure connecting Parliament Hill to the new buildings in downtown Hull via the Portage Bridge. However, the early results in Hull were not promising, and the expense and jurisdictional complexities of building megastructures made further implementation unlikely. However, during the evaluation of the museum sites, urban designers Roger du Toit and Robert Allsopp began to wonder if the same linking might be done with a boulevard and landscape, instead of interconnected buildings. Their 1983 report, *Ceremonial Routes,* marked a major change in the NCC's approach to urban design for the core of the capital city.[1060]

The plan for the ceremonial routes seems simple enough – a loop boulevard connecting Parliament Hill with Hull, and two extensions along Sussex Drive and Rideau Street (Figure 12-16). A closer look identifies nodes like Confederation Square, where the boulevard changes direction. These nodes are appropriate locations for important symbolic markers like the National War Memorial and the Peacekeeping Monument. However, it is only in cross-section that the strength of the concept becomes clear, with the boulevard serving as the border between a continuous street-wall of 'Town' buildings and 'Crown' institutions set as pavilions in a river's edge park (Figure 12-17).

While considering the views that needed to be protected along the Boulevard, the planners re-discovered the long-forgotten Ottawa River. The river had always been there, of course, but it had been terribly exploited for industrial purposes, and most buildings in Ottawa and Hull turned their backs upon it. When the lumber and pulp industries loosened their grip on the river's edge, it was once again possible to imagine the landscape that had captivated the Fathers of Confederation in 1864. A walk around the proposed loop revealed views of Parliament Hill that may be superior to the ones destroyed by Ottawa's new office towers. And the loop also reveals the Ottawa River at a point of important cultural significance to aboriginal, French and English Canadians.

The Ottawa River has other symbolic appeals, as a natural feature on the edge of the wilderness. As noted by Canadian philosopher John Ralston Saul:

"Rivers are sort of hinges.
They are interlocking and they swing;
They swing both ways.
That's the way Ottawa works, whatever the politics;
That's the classic Canadian evocation of the river:
Not as a border
But as a hinge,
A highway,
A joining."[1061]

The name "Core Area Ceremonial Routes" was a bureaucratic mouthful, so the project was re-branded as the Confederation Boulevard. The new design was first demonstrated on Wellington Street in the 1980s and gradually rolled out along the other roads in the next 20 years. Ottawa, Hull and the regions did not much object to the re-paving and embellishment of their roads, as long as the federal government was picking up most of the cost, and they also saw the boulevard's benefit as a visitor-orientation device.[1062]

Confederation Boulevard's other urban design features helped shape the federal government's strategy towards increasing symbolic content in the core of the capital in the decades ahead. Its design strategies were the foundation for the renovations to the Parliamentary Precinct, north of Wellington Street, to create a second triad of buildings focusing on the Supreme Court[1063] (Figure 12-18).

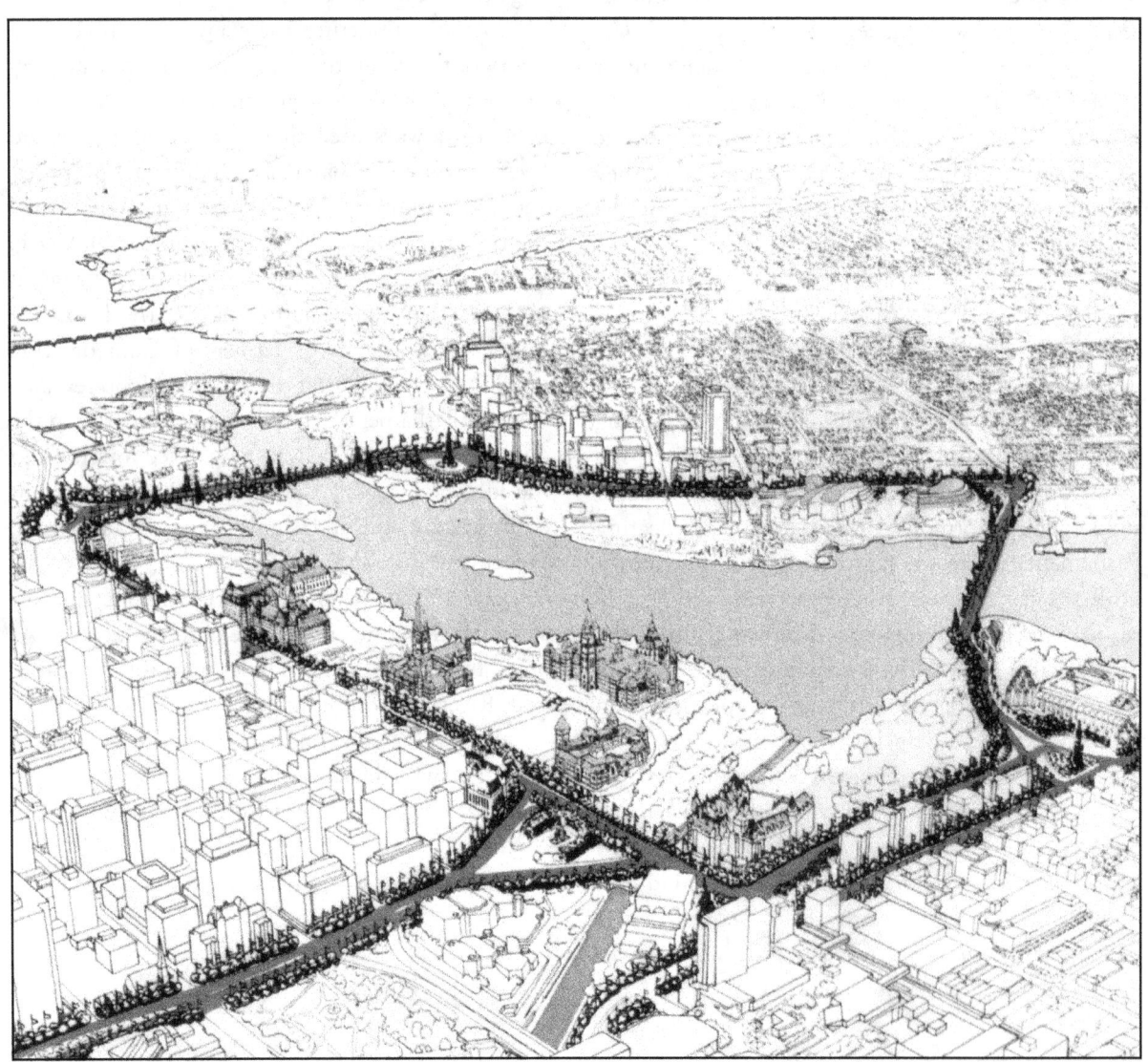

FIGURE 12-16: Confederation Boulevard Plan
du Toit and Allsopp's boulevard has become the key armature for the symbolic content in Canada's capital. The branch at the bottom right is Elgin Street, reconstructed by Gréber for Mackenzie King in the 1930s.
(Source: NCC, 1985)

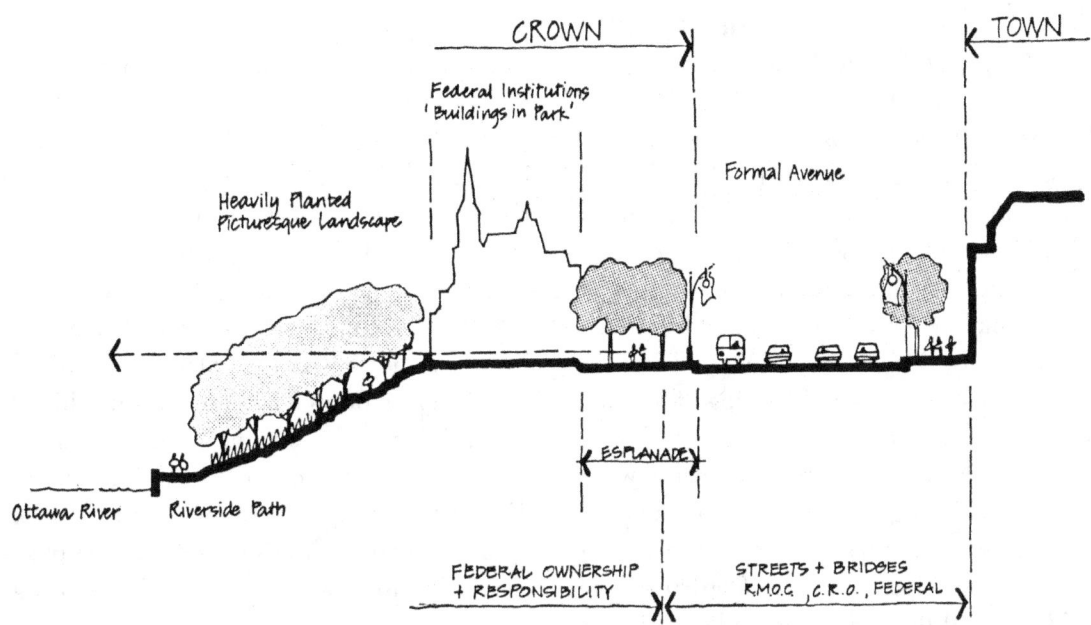

FIGURE 12-17: Ceremonial route cross-section on Wellington Street
The Confederation Boulevard provides a clear border between the 'Crown' and the 'Town.' Note the picturesque landscape along the river, federal institutions on the plateau as 'buildings in park;' the pedestrian esplanade on the inside edge of the loop; the formal avenue, with coordinated streetscape elements and the firm, continuous street edge of buildings (a street wall) along the 'Town' border.
(Source: du Toit Associates, 1983, Figure 50, p. 30)

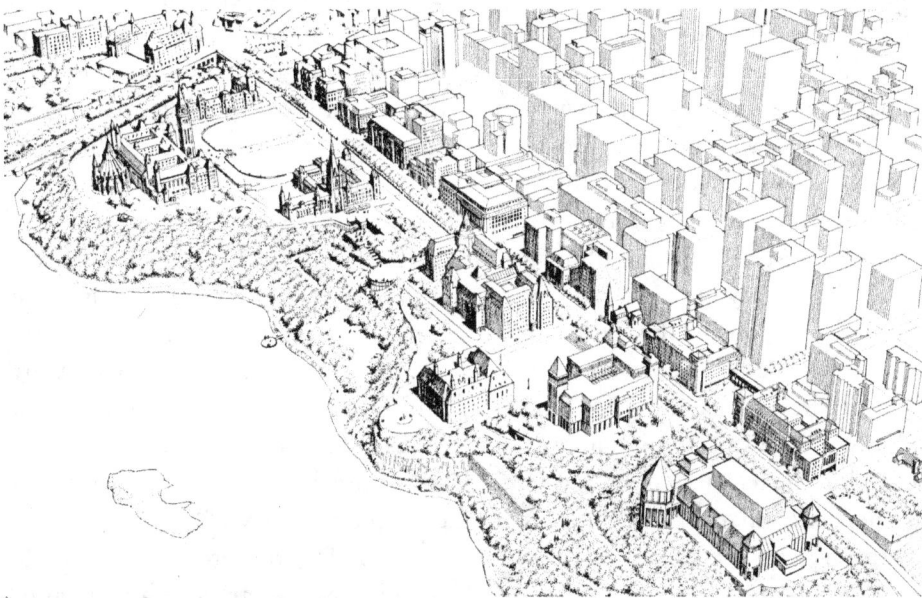

FIGURE 12-18: Parliamentary Precinct Plan, 1987
A brilliant simplification of the mess on Parliament Hill, removing the surface parking lots, regenerating the natural landscape along the cliffs and completing the Supreme Court area with a proposed federal court building.
(Source: du Toit Allsopp Hillier 1987, Figure viii)

Federal Retrenchment:
From City-Building to Nation-Building

The National Capital Region knew it was in for a shock when the new Progressive Conservative government swept into power in the fall of 1984. Prime Minister Brian Mulroney had promised "pink slips and running shoes"[1064] for federal civil servants, so the region suddenly realized that its major employer would be retrenching and decentralizing. The Department of Veterans Affairs offices were relocated to the PEI riding of its Tory minister, other budgets were slashed and federal capital expenditures were reduced nationwide. The early federal program reviews under Deputy Prime Minister Eric Nielsen recommended that the NCC be combined with the Department of Public Works and that federal expenditures in the National Capital Region be minimal. Even though NCC Chairman 'Bud' Drury had done a good job calming the political relationships with Ottawa and RMOC, he was a former Liberal Cabinet minister, and his days were therefore numbered. In January 1985, he was replaced by Jean Pigott, an Ottawa native and former Conservative MP.

Jean Pigott repositioned the NCC's mandate from capital-building to nation-building and, in the process, probably saved the organization from dissolution. The late 1980s were not an appropriate period for grand plans for the national capital. The regional and local governments had firmly seized control of planning and development within their jurisdictions and the uneasy truce to the inter-jurisdictional warfare negotiated by Drury had been on condition that the NCC stay out of their way. The NCC withdrew to planning for federal property holdings, which made up almost 10 percent of the land in the region. Not by accident, this cautious portfolio management approach was a much better fit with the strategic planning orientation of the new Tory government than the dramatic and visionary schemes of the 1960s and 1970s. The 1988 *Federal Land Use Plan* (FLUP)[1065] made no bold proposals for satellite cities or futuristic rapid transit facilities. It merely identified the medium-term outlook for federally-owned lands in the region. This caused little political backlash, and the FLUP was largely ignored by the regional and local governments.

The FLUP had one section that illustrated Pigott's new approach towards the region. She was passionately convinced that the national capital had an important role to play in fostering pride and unity among Canadians, during this period of painful constitutional negotiations and concern about the Québec independence movement. The first substantial section of the FLUP dealt with "Capital Institutions and Attractions" and the NCC took a leadership role in using the capital to interpret Canada's national identity to Canadians.[1066] The NCC expanded its role in public programming, marketing the National Capital Region, and reinforcing Canadian identity within the capital. This was a successful strategy at almost every level. It supported the federal government's national unity program, the regional governments liked the economic development benefits of increased tourism, and the cultural attractions and festivals improved the quality of life for many local residents. Canada Day became a huge, nationally-televised celebration on Parliament Hill, and a multi-media show was developed to interpret Canadian history on the Hill for other nights of the year. The open spaces in the core of the capital became venues for a wide range of music and cultural festivals spanning the seasons. Jacques Cartier Park in Hull welcomed Winterlude. Parliament Hill became the focus of New Year's Eve celebrations, and Confederation Boulevard was illuminated for the winter holidays.[1067]

Jean Pigott's programming initiatives gave the NCC an enlarged mandate and a new lease on life, but the agency lost some of its financial independence and was required to rationalize its land holdings.[1068] The NCC prepared a detailed classification of its property holdings, to determine which lands were essential for federal requirements (the National Interest Land Mass, NILM). The other lands might be eligible for disposal, if they could not be shown to be needed for the future development of the national capital.

The NCC's transformation from an urban development authority to a public programming agency was followed in other federal capitals, such as Canberra and Washington.[1069] As these cities matured, their agencies had less need for expertise in bricks and mortar and placed more emphasis on developing their capitals as stages to interpret national identity and promote national unity.[1070]

FIGURE 12-19: Jean Pigott
This portrait of the former NCC Chair hangs in Jean Pigott Hall – the room just outside the council chambers of Ottawa City Hall. Pigott greatly improved relations with a City of Ottawa and RMOC, which had descended into ugly conflicts in the 1970s and 1980s.
(Source: City of Ottawa portrait hanging in Jean Pigott Hall; painting by Bernard Poulin, 1999)

Reflections

By the end of the 1980s, the federal government had withdrawn from routine participation in local and regional planning, for which it had no constitutional authority, and somewhat repaired its relationships with most local and regional governments. The NCC retreated to strategic planning for federally-owned lands, while the regional governments made little effort to coordinate development on their respective sides of the Ottawa River and almost no attempt to link across the provincial boundary. Many local governments tended their own patches of turf and interacted with the numerous neighbourhood organizations that created a new level of political activity. Peace, or at least a cease-fire, had broken out among the various levels of government engaged in 'Town-Crown' conflict.

Unfortunately, after the smoke of battle cleared, it slowly became evident that the metropolitan area was deeply flawed on several levels. The regional governments had facilitated a tremendous volume of suburban growth in both provinces but the transit and road infrastructure had not been connected. The regional transit systems each served their side of the river and barely interconnected. The road system was not much better, since only one new inter-provincial bridge had been built, and the vehicular access to the other bridges was awkward. The poor truck circulation was a major problem, because the North American goods distribution system had moved away from rail. The downtown retail districts of both Hull and Ottawa were both in decline, and by 1990, the NCC had yet to articulate a clear vision for the national capital to replace the out-moded concepts from the 1950s and 1960s.

CHAPTER 13

From Red Tape to Blue Chips? (1990-2011)

It was 1990 before many people noticed that the Ottawa Valley had grown a significant cluster of activity in high-technology research development and employment.[1071] Many small high-technology companies had spun off from Bell Northern Research (BNR, later Nortel), the National Research Council,[1072] and other federal research facilities located in the Greenbelt.[1073] The evolution from "white pine to red tape to blue chips"[1074] had been masked by the high-profile decline of the lumber and pulp industries in the core, and the federal government's expanding presence after 1950.

Many high-tech employees lived in the new suburbs adjacent to the Greenbelt, and the new firms located in the modern industrial parks developed by Ottawa, the NCC, Nepean and March townships (Figure 13-1). One western suburb, Kanata, was particularly popular for both employees and firms. It initially appealed to high-tech employees because of its high neighbourhood design standards and excellent recreational opportunities at the doorstep. William Teron named his first industrial area 'Technology Park' and recruited Atomic Energy of Canada and Digital Equipment Canada as lead tenants, while BNR alumni Terence Matthews and Michael Cowpland were Kanata residents and located their Mitel Corporation there.[1075] After Robert Campeau took over the project from Teron, the local government pushed him to maintain the design quality, and began their own aggressive recruiting of other high-tech firms.[1076]

The high-tech cluster that emerged in the 1990s had particular strengths in software, telecommunications, defence/security, microelectronics and photonics. It was led by companies like Nortel, Corel, Mitel and JDS Uniphase, which were significant players in the 1990s. High-tech employment more than doubled in the 1990s, from less than 40,000 in 1995 to over 80,000 in 2001.[1077] This was welcome news for the National Capital Region, since the federal government had been cutting jobs, reducing the civil service by over 25,000 positions by 1996.[1078] The region was re-christened 'Silicon Valley North,' and there were triumphant predictions that the high-tech sector would soon pass the federal government as the region's largest employer.[1079]

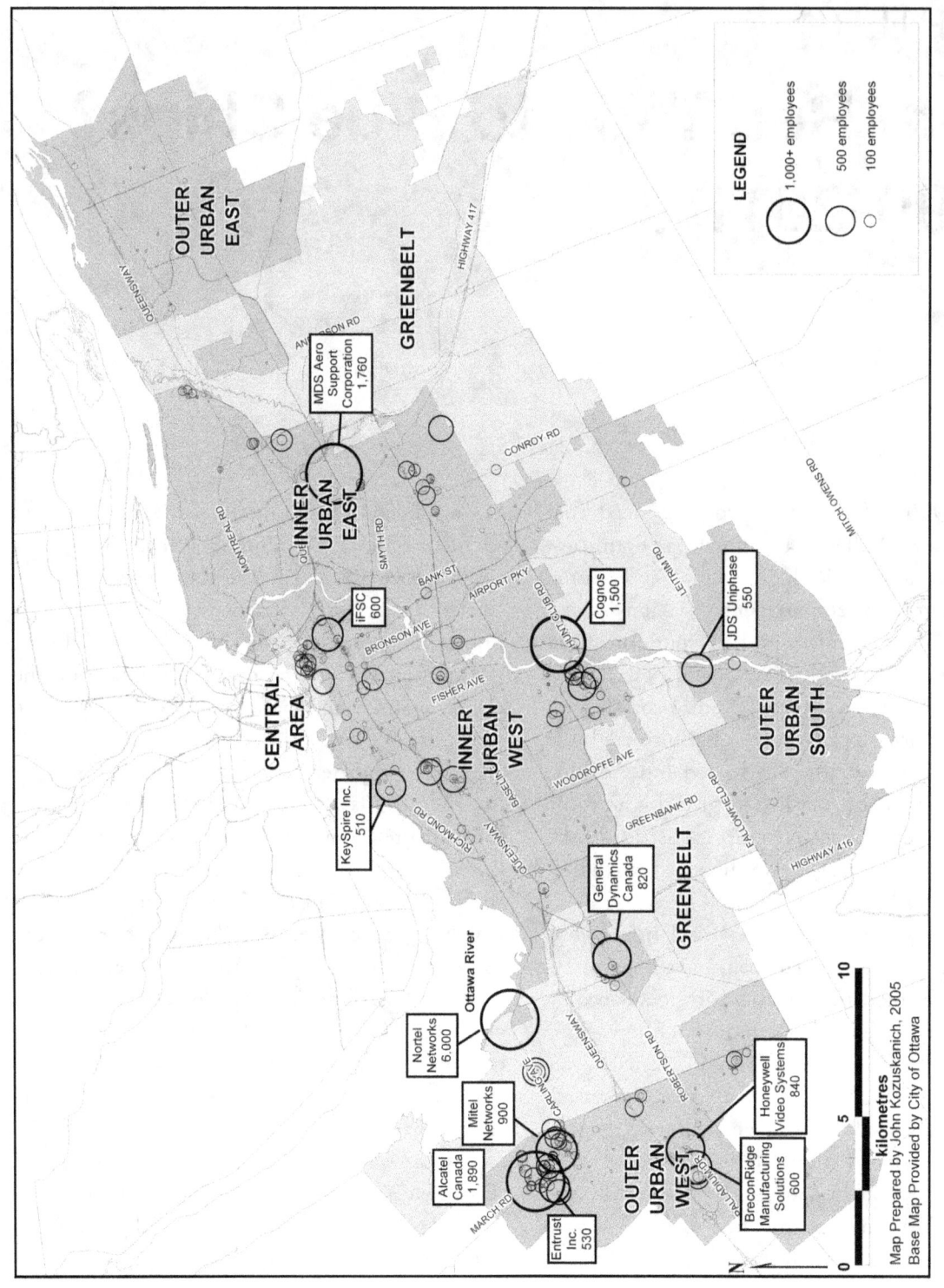

FIGURE 13-1: **Ottawa Region High-Tech Employment, 2004**
Note that most of the employment is south at the Ottawa and west of the Rideau River.
(Source: Gordon, Donald, Kozuskanich 2007; drawn by John Kozuskanich)

The high-tech boom of the 1990s was greeted with acclaim and relief by local and regional governments – at last, some quality jobs emerged in another sector to diversify the region's economy. RMOC identified high-tech as the most important of three sectors it targeted for growth, along with tourism and bioscience. The regional government supported the establishment of partnerships and networks led by the private sector, through the Ottawa Centre for Research and Innovation (OCRI) and the Ottawa Tourism and Convention Authority (OCTA). Leadership and strategic direction came from the private sector, and the RMOC supported OCRI with facilities, research and financial assistance.[1080] This approach to fostering the growth of a 'thick cluster' of specialized firms followed the best economic development advice of the day.[1081]

The background studies for the 1997 RMOC official plan included an economic development strategy based upon these principles, but rather remarkably, it almost completely ignored the region's largest employer, the federal government.[1082] The NCC and the federal government were essentially cut out of economic planning for the region, even though they played a key role in the tourism sector, developing many major attractions, and coordinating festivals and national outreach. And the federal government was expected to assemble, service and donate valuable land for many important facilities, such as the convention centres (Hull and Ottawa), research parks (Nortel), colleges and universities (*UQAH, Outaouais, Cité collégiale*), research hospitals (Ottawa General, Children's' Hospital of Eastern Ontario) or sports facilities (Nepean Sportsplex, Lynx baseball stadium).

The good news about high-tech employment was that its booms and busts seemed to run counter to the cycle of federal employment, so that it added some stability to the region's economy. The bad news was that Ottawa's high-tech firms liked suburban sites that contributed to the outward dispersion of the region. The locational preferences of the high-technology firms were for suburban industrial parks in the southwest quadrant of the region.[1083] The dispersed employment distribution for high-technology firms would prove difficult to serve by public transit and awkward to access from the Outaouais, since every attempt to build a new bridge was rebuffed by Ottawa neighbourhoods.

Regional Planning and Suburban Expansion

By 1990, the Québec government had concluded that the *Communauté régionale de l'Outaouais* (CRO) was too dysfunctional to continue. The large rural community in the Gatineau hills had little in common with the urban area, and the CRO was not effective in mediating the many disputes between Aylmer, Hull and Gatineau. The provincial government split the CRO into two regions – the urban *Communauté urbaine de l'Outaouais* (CUO) and the Rural *municipalité régionale de comté* (MRC) des *Collines-de l' Outaouais* on January 1, 1991.[1084] The provincial government was clearly concerned that the local disputes among the urban communities were preventing a strong Québec voice within the National Capital Region, but it hesitated to simply order an amalgamation, perhaps mindful of the political backlash from the 1974 restructuring. Instead, the province held a referendum in which Hull voted 65 percent in favour of amalgamation, and the four suburban municipalities voted overwhelmingly against it.[1085]

The referendum result caused concern among the political and financial elites of the Outaouais, who had lobbied the Bélanger-Campeau Commission for a stronger voice for the region during this period of constitutional uncertainty.[1086] Consequently, the Québec government appointed a committee to study changes to the economy of the Outaouais, chaired by Marcel Beaudry, a local lawyer and strong federalist who had been a member of the Bélanger-Campeau Commission. The committee recommended a strong program to diversify the regional economy, and Beaudry followed by successfully running for election as mayor of Hull in November 1991.[1087]

The CRO's new plan was used as a tool to slowly build regional consensus about development objectives. From the beginning, the regional government was concerned about the area's dependency on the federal government for employment, because 60 percent of its residents travelled to Ontario for work and 30 percent of its employees came from Ottawa-Carleton.[1088] The Outaouais had more success in the tourism sector, where it attracted the *Casino de Hull* (1996), a major visitor destination and employer.

However, the new region took almost a decade to formulate and adopt a new regional plan, since the Québec legislation required extensive coordination and consensus-building among member municipalities. Hull, Aylmer and Gatineau all had their own visions, and each wanted to develop as separate cities with separate downtowns, full arrays of institutions and links to Ottawa. All three wanted lots of suburban development, and for their downtown vision to happen quickly.[1089]

The former Town of Gatineau was particularly successful at attracting suburban retail development, as its urbanized area stretched eastwards towards the pulp and paper plants. The commercial strip along Boulevard Maloney attracted big-box retail outlets and the Outaouais' first regional shopping centre, three decades after the first big mall on the Ontario side. But as Gatineau's population overtook Hull's, it also wanted a city centre. The cash-strapped NCC agreed to give Gatineau a large parcel of vacant land adjacent to the new National Archives warehouse in exchange for the local government's agreement to build a long-planned parkway along the north shore of the Ottawa River. Gatineau designated the new land as its city centre, and added a new cultural centre, community college, athletic centre, and site for a new city hall.[1090] The federal government chipped in with another office building in 2002, but private-sector construction of apartments and offices in Gatineau's city centre was slow, an experience that mirrored similar proposals in Orleans, Nepean and Kanata (Figure 13-2).

One thing that the Outaouais municipalities all agreed upon was the need for more bridges to Ontario. The 1999 CUO plan showed two corridors for links that dated from the 1950 Gréber plan: a western corridor at Deschênes, where Highway 550 would connect to the western parkway and Queensway, and the Kettle Island corridor, connecting to the Aviation Parkway and Highway 417 in the east. However, neighbourhood opposition had long ago knocked these bridges out of the RMOC plan, much to the frustration of the Outaouais planners.[1091] As late as 2001, the City of Gatineau's street map showed a dotted line for a bridge extending across Kettle Island and ending in the middle of the Ottawa River, at the provincial boundary (Figure 13-3). However, the map does not show the riverside parkway promised in exchange for the town centre lands, which slowly disappeared from Gatineau plans.

On the Ontario side of the river, the costs of unchecked suburban expansion slowly became an issue in Ottawa-Carleton. The developers working in the suburban municipalities (Kanata, Nepean, Gloucester and Cumberland) encouraged rapid population growth outside the Greenbelt from 1986-1996,[1092] and RMOC continued to provide the regional infrastructure to support this low-density outward expansion. Perhaps the most spectacular example of suburban land speculation changing government policy came from the Firestone family, which had bought farm land west of Kanata's urban growth boundary. They offered to bring an NHL hockey team to Ottawa if their lands were re-designated from agricultural to urban uses.[1093] A major league hockey team proved to be an attractive incentive, and the prospect plunged the region into excited debate. Many people recognized the folly of locating a professional sports arena 30 km. from downtown, when every other North American city was moving its sports and entertainment facilities as close as possible to the central business district to maximize economic spin-offs from events.[1094] Several other locations were suggested, most prominently a proposal by RMOC Chair Andrew Haydon to build the arena on LeBreton Flats.[1095] However, the suburban land developers were adamant that the arena had to be the centrepiece of their proposed office/hotel/entertainment centre. The offer of a big-league team in Canada's most cherished sport was too much for the local politicians to resist, and the Kanata and RMOC plans were amended to let the Firestones develop their land in 1990.

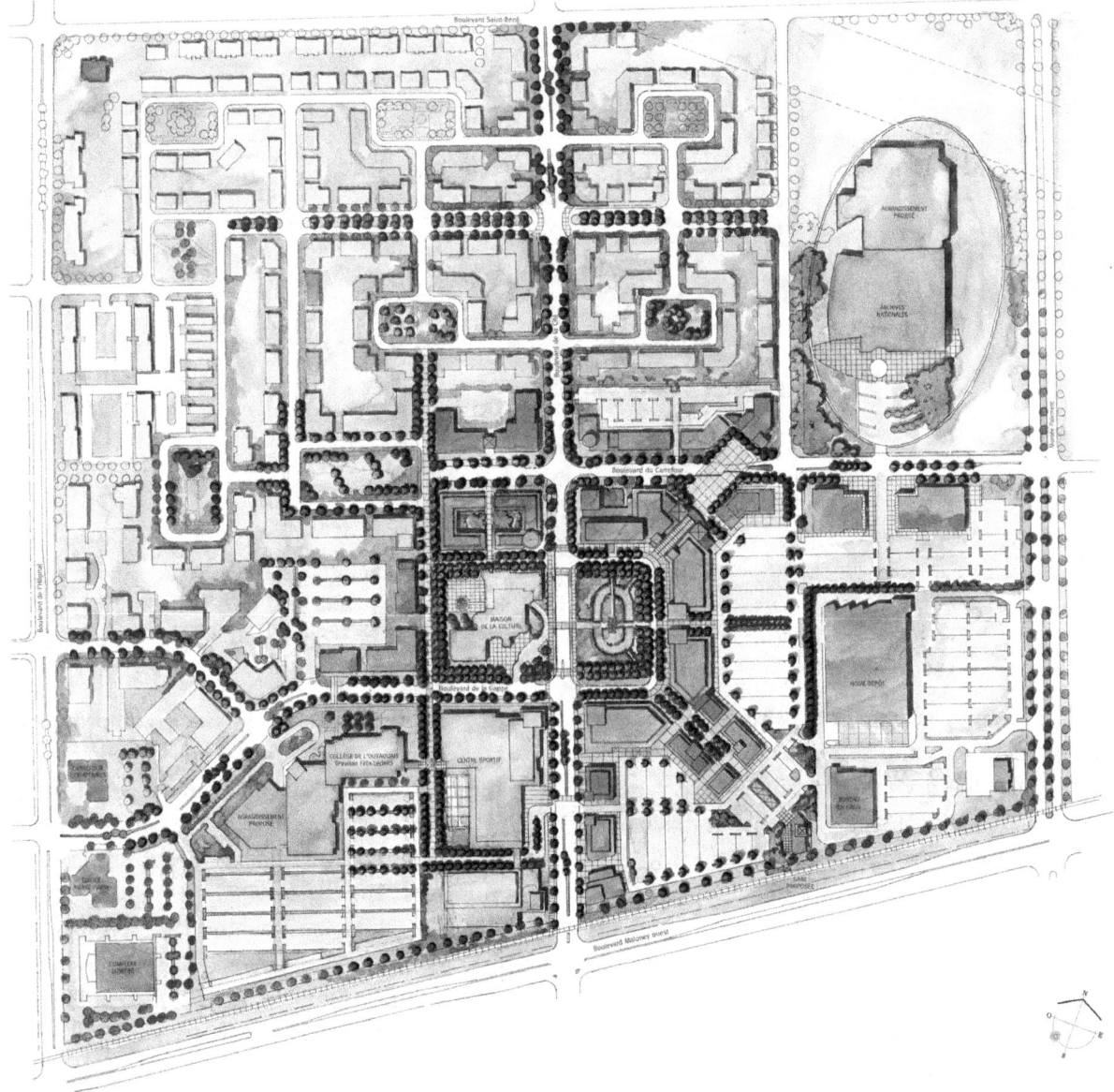

FIGURE 13-2: Gatineau City Centre Plan
Suburban town centres had slow development, but this one in Gatineau was perhaps the most successful.
(Source: Lemay +DAA; reproduced with permission)

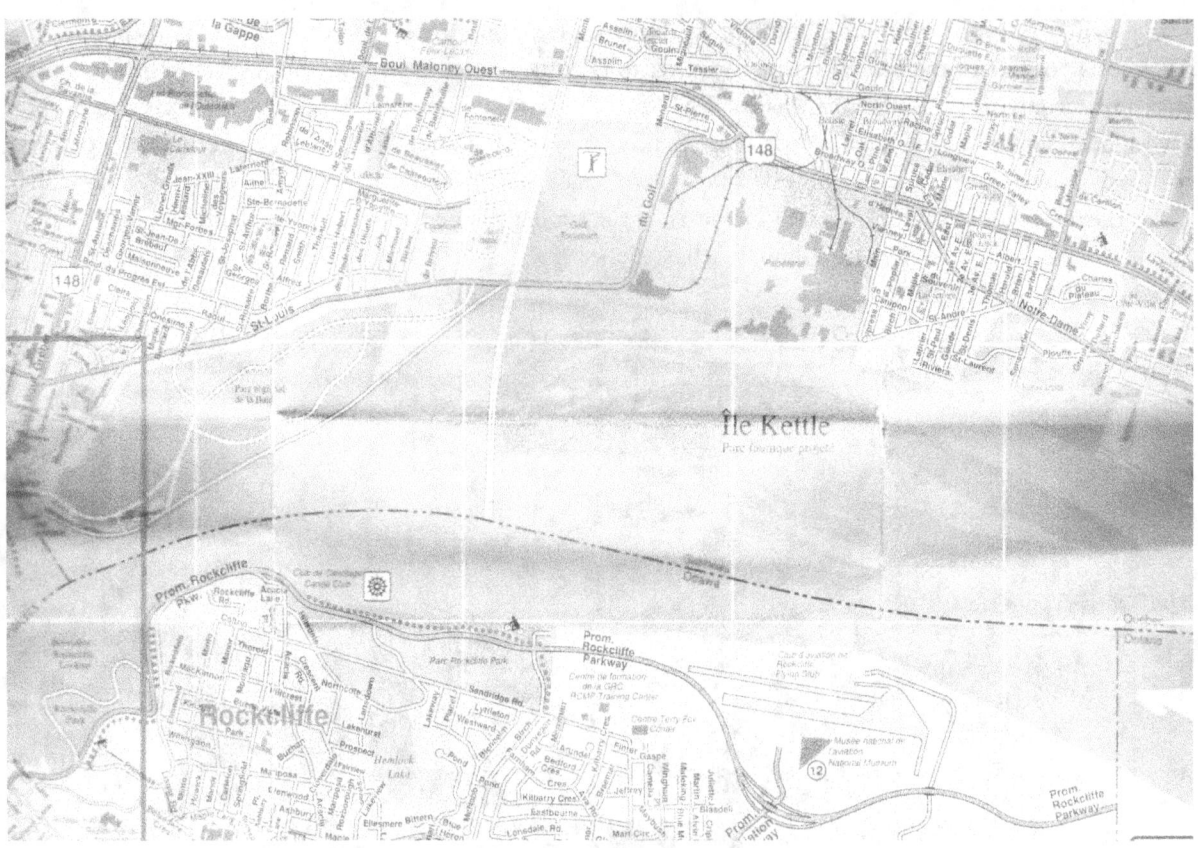

FIGURE 13-3: Bridge to Nowhere, 2001
Gatineau street map from 2001 shows continued hope for a connection to Ottawa. This one was twice vetoed by the residents of Manor Park and Rockcliffe Park, south of the river.
(Source: Author's collection)

The arena opened in 1996 as the Corel Centre (named after the local software firm), and traffic jams on the Queensway are a feature of every event. While new major league arenas in Vancouver, Toronto, Montréal and even Detroit have added to the vitality of their downtowns, an auto dealership was the only amenity added to the sea of parking lots surrounding Kanata's folly, more than a decade after it opened.

Ontario approached the need for better regional planning less directly than Québec. Ottawa-Carleton became a more active player on planning issues in the mid-1990s, after the provincial government mandated direct election to the regional council. RMOC politicians were also local councillors from 1969-1994, and their dual allegiance may have compromised their effectiveness on some regional issues. The Conservative provincial government elected in 1995 downloaded responsibility for transit funding, social housing and social services to the regional governments. The late 1990s, therefore, saw a directly elected regional council responsible for both the costs and benefits of urban development for the first time.

The RMOC's growing independence from its local governments was symbolized by the new regional headquarters building, built on the Cartier Square site previously coveted by both the City of Ottawa and the National Gallery. The regional government had lived in rented quarters in non-descript downtown office buildings for over two decades. It had a very low public profile, even though it was responsible for more than half of all local expenditures. Relations between RMOC and the NCC had improved dramatically during the late 1980s, under Jean Pigott and Andrew Haydon. The RMOC acquired the prime location first envisioned as a site for Ottawa's city hall in 1948, adjacent to historic buildings of the 1875 Ottawa Normal School teacher's college.

Despite objections and appeals by the City of Ottawa, the new regional headquarters opened in 1990, based on a relatively modest design by noted Toronto architect Raymond Moriyama (Figure 13-4). The City of Ottawa replied by commissioning

FIGURE 13-4: The constant competition between RMOC and Ottawa is symbolized by their new civic buildings
Top: RMOC Regional Headquarters, 1990
Bottom: Ottawa City Hall, 1994
RMOC got the central site on Cartier Square thanks to improved relations with the NCC. The city replied with a loud addition to its rather anonymous Modern style City Hall.
(Source: City of Ottawa; Photographer: William P. McElligott; reproduced with permission)

a large expansion of its city hall by Moshe Safdie, fresh from his triumph at the National Gallery. John Bland's simple modern slab was swamped by the geometric volumes that Safdie used to fill Green Island, including a cube, a pyramid, an undulating river edge and the enormous frame for an observation tower that was never completed. Its splashy symbols appeared to be an unsuccessful attempt to demonstrate that the city was still a more important local institution than RMOC.[1096]

The RMOC therefore entered the mid-1990s with some self-confidence in its ability to provide leadership and direction to the Ontario portion of the metropolitan region. It proposed a substantial diversification of the regional economy away from federal employment and used landscape ecology techniques to identify environmentally significant lands for protection at a regional scale.[1097] Much to the dismay of the suburban municipalities and developers, the 1997 Regional Plan had few extensions to the urban growth boundary and called for compact, transit-friendly development, a higher proportion of new housing inside the Greenbelt, and more jobs outside the Greenbelt. The plan also had "teeth" – measureable targets on its key development objectives and a regular monitoring program making it unpopular with the suburban land development industry, which appealed its provisions to the Ontario Municipal Board, with little success.[1098]

Although the suburban interests disliked the limits on low-density residential development, they did appreciate the RMOC's outward expansion of the Transitway and many wide new regional roads built in the 1990s. The suburban municipal councils also liked the idea of suburban town centres with substantial employment, because commercial assessment might improve their tax base. Unfortunately, none of the Ottawa suburbs were able to develop a walkable, mixed use, transit-oriented town centre like Burnaby's Metrotown, North York City Centre, or the Town of Mount Royal. For example, Gloucester's "city hall" was a few floors in a generic suburban office building, set in an un-walkable wasteland of parking lots and malls.[1099]

Central City Renewal?

Hull and Ottawa continued to stress neighborhood preservation during the 1990s, and both inner cities expanded their heritage activities to protect their older neighbourhoods.[1100] While both cities were concerned about maintaining their central roles within their regions, their other objectives were quite different. Hull's 1990 plan focused upon the economic impacts of the collapse of its older industries and cleaning up the damage done by federal and provincial urban renewal in its core. It had specific policies about economic and social development and a strategy to diversify into tourism.[1101] Many of Hull's remaining downtown buildings had been occupied by taverns and "adult entertainment." Visitors to the new Museum of Civilization faced bars and distasteful shops – not quite right for encouraging additional tourist expenditures in the Outaouais region. Hull quietly began buying up the offending properties and cancelled their tavern licences, but it was slow work reviving other forms of retail development along the remaining downtown streets.[1102]

Both Hull and the City of Ottawa continued to prepare sector plans in consultation with the citizens of neighbourhoods that were under development pressure throughout the region.[1103] Most of these plans were based upon standard land use and economic development policies. The City of Ottawa's 1991 Official Plan had many neighbourhood plans that were the culmination of the urban reform period that began in the 1970s.[1104] However, the plan had much more urban design content, with guidelines for "design control areas," and character diagrams for the downtown sectors (Figure 13-5). Although Rideau Street had been tarnished in the 1980s, the city recognized that the adjacent ByWard Market was a jewel and adopted policies that encouraged small-scale infill and historic preservation. The results were encouraging: a mix of shops, entertainment uses and housing that revived a lively downtown neighbourhood,[1105] although by 2010 there were concerns about over-development and gentrification.[1106]

Ottawa's 1991 Official Plan was a breakthrough for the city – the first truly comprehensive plan for the entire municipality, after 40 years of producing policies for specific problems (roads, parks, urban renewal) or individual neighbourhoods. The city followed up with a new comprehensive zoning bylaw, which had detailed designations for every property and, finally, height limits that protected the prominence of the Peace Tower.[1107] So, by 1996, the City of Ottawa finally had a strong vision of the future of its neighbourhoods and downtown, and fairly sophisticated policy instruments in place to protect it. Unfortunately, it was a purely local vision, affecting less than a third of the region's population, with little connection to the surrounding Ontario suburbs and even less with the Outaouais or the federal designs for a better national capital.

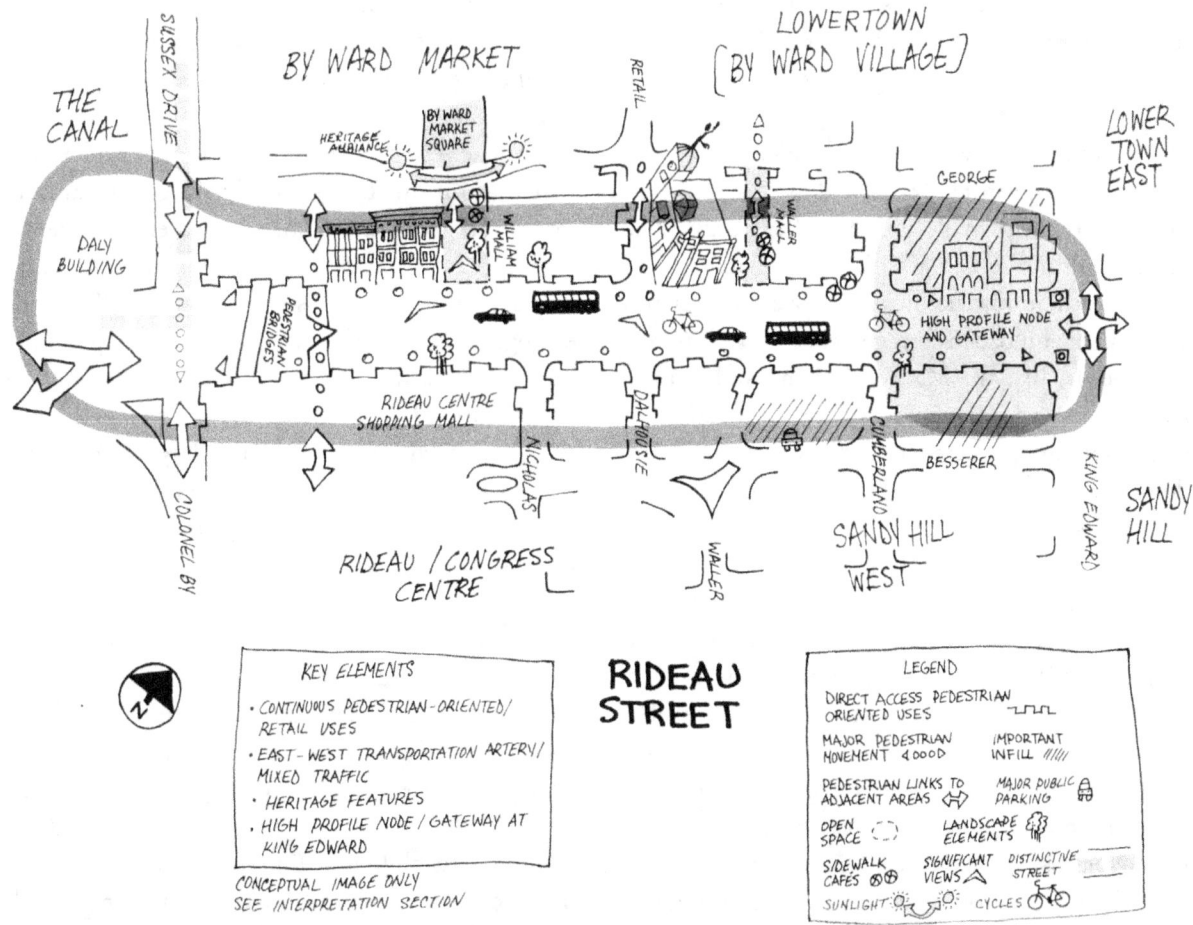

FIGURE 13-5: **Character sketch for Rideau Street, 1991**
This is an urban design policy sketch from the 1991 Official Plan, based upon public participation.
(Source: Ottawa 1991, Volume II)

Federal Reorganization

The portrait of Jean Pigott hanging outside the council chambers at the new RMOC headquarters (Figure 12-19) was a symbol of her success in repairing the broken relationships between the NCC and the regional and local governments. When she left the NCC in 1992, the agency had a new focus on promoting Canada, during a period when the country seemed on edge, after the rejection of the Meech Lake constitutional accord. Prime Minister Brian Mulroney's choice to succeed Pigott may have been influenced by these national concerns, since Hull Mayor Marcel Beaudry was a well-known federalist. He was also a well-known Liberal, so the prime minister's non-partisan appointment was a surprise to many, including Beaudry.[1108]

A new Liberal national government was elected within a year, and Beaudry was left in place. However, the NCC was burdened with an enormous budget cut, and specific instructions to sell surplus property to help make up the difference.[1109] The NCC could no longer afford to maintain the vast array of local infrastructure it built over the previous century. It unloaded bridges that served purely local needs, like the Mackenzie King and Laurier Avenue bridges downtown. The RMOC did not want to maintain them either, but was mollified by donations of valuable corridors for regional transit and road systems.[1110]

The federal land rationalization scheme was far more controversial. The NCC had begun to classify its property in the 1988 Federal Land Use Plan (FLUP) and National Interest Land Mass (NILM), but these rather colourless documents had attracted little attention. Similarly, the implications of the 1996 *Greenbelt Master Plan* were not well understood at first. The new plan repositioned the Greenbelt as an ecological feature, rather than an urban separator, using landscape ecological analysis similar to the Michael Hough's plans for Central Ontario (Figure 13-6).[1111] As a result, the NCC no longer considered the 1950 boundaries of the Greenbelt to be sacred. More land might be added to the outside of the Greenbelt for ecological purposes. However, if a parcel of land had little ecological value and was not critical element of the NILM, it might be sold. Needless to say, there was little protest when large and ecologically-valuable new areas of Mer Blue bog and Stony Swamp were added to the outside of the Greenbelt, but every small parcel sold inside the Greenbelt was a *cause célèbre* in the adjacent neighbourhoods. Similarly, purchase of 643 hectares of forest to expand Gatineau Park met little opposition, but setting aside 10 percent of these lands for a road corridor for Route 5 was intensely controversial.[1112] Ironically, suburban municipalities that had lobbied to allow the Greenbelt properties to be developed as low-density, un-serviced sprawl 40 years earlier, now fought any proposal to develop small parcels of the same lands.

The environment became a major planning focus again in the 1970s.[1113] The federal and provincial governments all adopted environmental impact assessment (EIA) or environmental assessment (EA) processes in the mid-1970s. The ecological basis for this environmental planning improved steadily in the final two decades of the century. Landscape ecology developed more advanced techniques to design large regions for improved biodiversity[1114] and these techniques were applied to large urban regions such as Toronto, Ottawa, Hamilton, and smaller suburban areas such as Markham.[1115]

Environmental planning was applied to entire metropolitan areas in the work of Michael Hough, who stressed the ecological values of urban open space systems and incorporating natural processes into urban development. He showed how degraded urban valleys such as Toronto's Don River could be rehabilitated and re-naturalized, while incorporating extensive citizen participation.[1116] Hough also had a major influence on the Crombie Royal Commission on the Toronto waterfront, pushing it to expand its frame of reference to the entire Toronto bioregion.[1117]

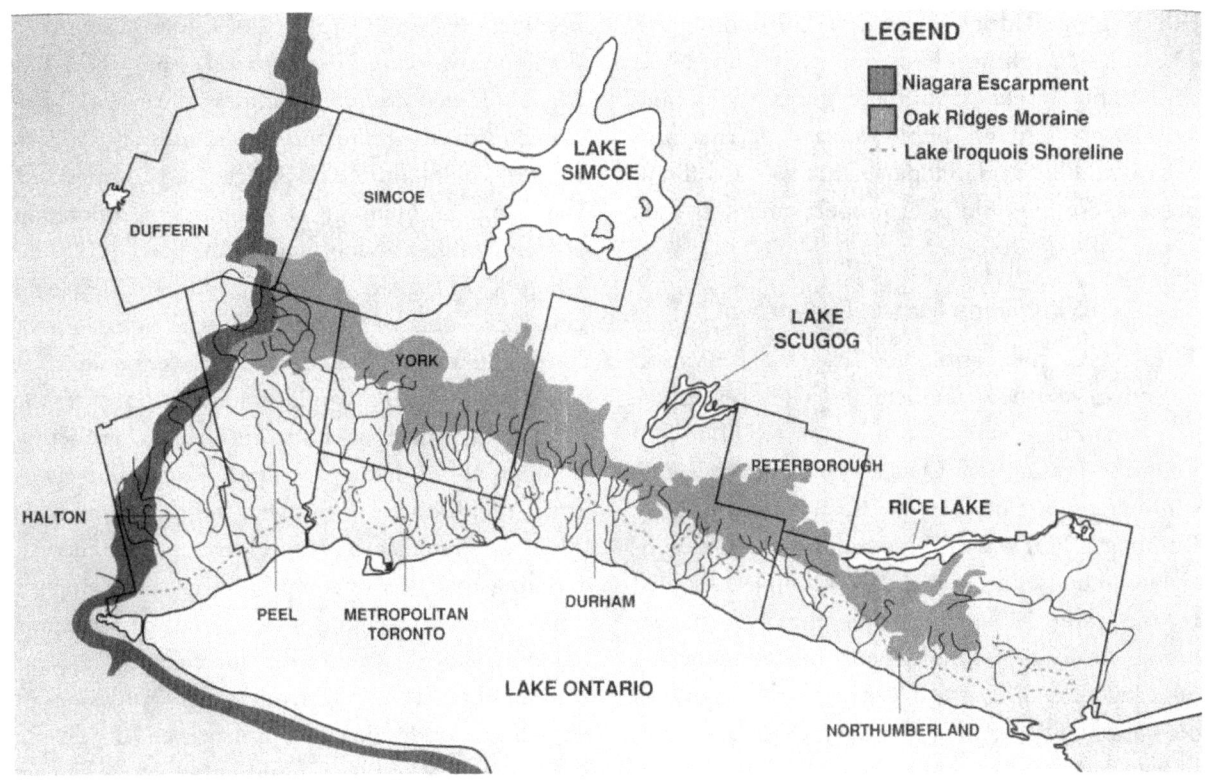

FIGURE 13-6: Ecological Planning and Sustainable Development: Crombie Commission Toronto Bioregion plan
The urbanized area is to be framed by natural features defined by landscape ecology – the Niagara Escarpment to the west and the Oak Ridges Moraine to the north.
(Source: David Crombie, *Regeneration*, 1992, Map 1.1)

The Greenbelt's change to an ecological feature and RMOC's 1997 regional plan marked the rise of the environment as a key component of metropolitan planning. Modern environmental planning practice also incorporates rehabilitation of former industrial sites that often contain contaminated lands.[1118] Extensive and expensive remediation of contaminated lands is a characteristic of projects such as Victoria's Dockside Green, Ottawa's LeBreton Flats and the Moncton Yards. Innovative financial tools are slowly emerging to make these brownfield projects more competitive with new greenfield development.[1119]

Finally, ecological planning, social planning, and economic development were combined in the concept of sustainable development, which became a primary goal in many Canadian community plans at the end of the 20th century.[1120] This broad concept was pushed along by public concerns about global warming, climate change, and other long-term legacies. Individuals and communities were invited to reduce their "ecological footprint" – the size of a natural area required to sustain the impact of their lifestyle on the environment.[1121]

Property development in the core area was also a major problem, but after the Place de Ville experience, the NCC wanted to control development of publicly-owned parcels close to Parliament, rather than simply sell them and trust local planning policies to meet federal objectives. The key properties in the core were the Chambers Buildings on Confederation Square, the Daly

Building on Rideau Street and LeBreton Flats. The budget cutbacks meant that the NCC could not simply rebuild these properties, and so had to rely on public-private partnerships with commercial developers. This was a difficult process, especially in poor property markets such as the 1990-94 recession.[1122]

Crown Plans for the Downtown

The NCC had strong heritage preservation objectives for the Chambers and Daly buildings. The Central Chambers Buildings (1890, 1883) were fine examples of Queen Anne and Italianate commercial architecture in Canada. The Daly Building (1905) was the best example of a Chicago-style warehouse in Ottawa.[1123] Both projects stalled in the early 1990s recession, since the private promoters could not find tenants for the renovated buildings. The NCC was able to rescue the Chambers project when the original developer, Perez-Bramalea, backed away.[1124] The completed project was perhaps Ottawa's best office development of the late 20th century, combining good rehabilitation of the two Chambers Buildings and a fourteen-story infill office tower designed by local architects Brisbin Brook Beynon.

The Daly Building proved to be a much more difficult proposition. The historic structure took up the entire block on Rideau Street beside the Château Laurier. The developer CoopDev won the original competition in 1987 with a proposal to rehabilitate the building in a manner similar to their successful re-use of the Ogilvy's department store in Montréal. They gutted the heritage building immediately, but could not obtain long-term financing to complete the project. By the time the NCC was able to repossess the project in 1991, the shell of the Daly Building was in ruinous condition and needed to be demolished, to everyone's dismay.[1125]

It took five years to redevelop consensus about appropriate new uses for the site. The *Ottawa Citizen* openly lobbied for the entire parcel to become a park and the City of Ottawa imposed a development freeze on the parcel, while the NCC negotiated new design guidelines for a plaza on the front third of the site and public uses at grade.[1126] In June 1998, the NCC selected the proposal of the Canadian Gateway Development Corporation (CGDC) for an indoor aquarium, hotel and retail complex on the site.[1127] Once again, the developer could not obtain financing for the aquarium or hotel, and an embarrassed NCC took the site back again when CGDC would not sign a lease.[1128] The NCC was luckier on its third attempt, attracting a proposal for luxury condominiums and shops from the Ottawa developer Claridge Homes.[1129] Montréal architect Dan Hanganu designed a building that was uncompromisingly modern, yet appropriate in scale and materials, using limestone cladding and copper trim that matched the adjacent Château Laurier. Despite containing Ottawa's most expensive condominium apartments, 700 Sussex is a quiet background building with reasonably good manners, deferring to the grand hotel next door (Figure 13-7). However, given how well the Chambers Buildings turned out, it is a pity that the Daly Building could not also have been re-used.

The LeBreton Flats saga was perhaps the worst example of interjurisdictional conflict in the region. Jean Pigott was able to get the City of Ottawa and RMOC to agree to restart the planning for the second phase of redevelopment in May 1985. Unlike the social housing in the first phase of the project, the agreement of all four levels of government was needed to redevelop the remaining lands, even though 78 percent of the land was owned by the NCC. The LeBreton Flats were cut up by small strips of property owned by the city and region along the alignment of the old streets. In addition, much of the land was heavily polluted from the former industries, requiring provincial and federal environmental approvals. The proposed development process was fairly simple: the site was to be jointly planned by the city, region and NCC, then the lands for the old streets and new roads were

FIGURE 13-7: 700 Sussex Drive
(Source: NCC)

to be swapped, and the NCC was to clean up the site to provincial and federal standards.

The planning went fairly well at first. The city, region and NCC sponsored a new round of urban design studies that had extensive civic consultation from 1986 to 1989. Five redevelopment concepts were produced by separate teams of design consultants and evaluated with public input at the three-day open house. The plan "An Agora for the Capital," designed by Calgary architect James McKellar, was selected as the preferred concept[1130] (Figure 13-8).

The tripartite planning process assumed that the new plans would go forward to city and regional council for approval in 1990, but it would take 13 additional years to complete this step. A large vacant site close to downtown attracts large ideas, and it seemed that every mayor, regional chairman and federal minister had a proposal for the LeBreton Flats, and a veto over the tripartite plan until his or her latest scheme collapsed. The LeBreton project was delayed while various parties advocated a district heating plant/incinerator (federal, 1970s/80s); a STOL airport (private, 1970s/80s); a hockey arena (RMOC, 1998); a domed stadium (city, 1990s); a high-speed railway station (city, 1990s); a World's Fair (city, 1990s); a transit terminal (RMOC, 1995+); and a War Museum (federal, 1999+).[1131] The regional Transitway and federal museum were worked into the plan, but all the other proposals eventually withered away.[1132] The Canadian War Museum was the final breakthrough, since by 1999 the NCC's capital budget had been cut to the point that it had no money for infrastructure. The cost of environmental remediation was added to the capital budget of the War Museum to prepare its site. It was just enough to clean up the Flats soils, but the infrastructure for other phases would have to be funded from private sources.[1133]

The NCC had agreed to follow the city's regular planning approvals process for LeBreton, and Ottawa finally approved the necessary amendments to the regulations in September 2003.[1134] Another controversy erupted as the NCC began to solicit private developers for the second phase. It had been so long since the extensive public participation for the 1990 plan that a new set of politicians, planners and citizens were involved, many of whom had new ideas, or didn't like the design guidelines or the winning proposal by Claridge Homes.[1135] But the federal government plowed ahead, and the Canadian War Museum opened to acclaim in 2005. The large central park and first residential building in Phase 2 opened two years later (Figure 13-9).

Figure 13-8: LeBreton Flats Plan, 1990
This concept, titled "An Agora for the Capital" was preferred because of its large, wedge-shaped park (centre) pointing towards Parliament Hill. National institutions were to be to the north (right) along the river, and a mixed-use neighbourhood to the south (left).
(Source: NCC, June 1990, IBI Group, Plate 1)

FIGURE 13-9: Canadian War Museum and New Park in LeBreton Flats
This dramatic museum kick-started the development of the second phase of LeBreton Flats, after more than 20 years of arguments between the federal, regional and local governments. The adjacent park is used for large outdoor concerts and festivals, with a fine view of Parliament Hill.
(Source: NCC)[1136]

LeBreton Flats, and the Chambers and Daly buildings are cautionary tales about the difficulty of redevelopment in the core of a capital city, during a period when the federal agency did not have the capital resources or political support to implement plans unilaterally. A modern urban redevelopment agency needs to be able to finance infrastructure, approve plans and react quickly to changes in market conditions,[1137] but the budget cuts and interjurisdictional warfare in Ottawa during the 1980s and 1990s frequently made this impossible. Under normal conditions, it often takes decades to implement major redevelopment projects, but the political volatility caused by frequent changes in the lead actors made progress more painfully slow. During the period that Jean Pigott and Marcel Beaudry stubbornly pushed these projects forward, the city mayor, RMOC chair and prime ministers changed frequently.[1138]

Planning For a Capital City

The NCC bought a measure of peace in the 'Town-Crown' wars during the 1980s and 1990s by leaving most planning and development to the many local and regional governments. After the 1974 *Tomorrow's Capital* debacle, the NCC withdrew to planning for federally-owned property for two decades.[1139] It rebuilt its planning credibility by focusing future efforts on elements that related to the region's role as the nation's capital. Other federal capitals, such as Washington, Canberra, Berlin and New Delhi, began to take a similar approach in the late 20th century, shifting from detailed hands-on metropolitan planning to more limited, higher-level concerns more unique to their role as the seat of government.[1140]

The 1999 *Plan for Canada's Capital* (PCC) was a significant change in the federal government's approach to planning the region. It identified the political, cultural and administrative functions of the federal capital, and specific roles for lands, buildings and infrastructure:

- *... convey through their location, design and built form, the political, cultural and administrative functions of the capital;*
- *provide support facilities for events and activities that express our culture;*
- *provide an appropriate setting for the Capital's historic and archaeological sites and monuments that help communicate the story of this country or significantly enhance the unique character of the Capital;*
- *provide highly visible sites for, and enhance access to, Capital destinations such as Parliament Hill, national museums, Gatineau Park and the Greenbelt;*
- *support the accommodation and space needs of federal or national political, administrative or cultural institutions, including official residences, national museums and galleries;*
- *meet the accommodation needs of foreign delegations whose requirements are not met by other means (e.g., the commercial real estate market);*
- *provide locations for the headquarters of Canadian or international non-governmental organizations;*
- *meet the special needs of the federal government (e.g., departmental headquarters, research and development facilities, and high-security activities for federal agencies);*
- *help tell the story of Canada through the Capital's cultural landscapes, shape the urban form, and preserve the character of the region through the ownership of large parcels of land such as Gatineau Park, the Greenbelt, the Central Experimental Farm, park lands or environmentally sensitive areas and river shore lands; and*
- *facilitate inter-provincial transportation between the Ontario (Ottawa-Carleton) and Québec (Outaouais) parts of the National Capital Region and beyond.*[1141]

Although the PCC represented a regional vision, it focused upon capital-city issues for which the federal government had a legitimate claim for action. Only the last two roles listed above seem to stray outside the capital-city issues: the first through accidents of land ownerships and the second left over from the difficulties of planning a region that spans two provinces.[1142]

The *Plan for Canada's Capital* proposed that the capital be developed as a visitor attraction, reviewing the role of the Parliamentary Precinct, Confederation Boulevard, public art, national institutions, the official residences and diplomatic missions. Unlike the dry strategic planning of the 1980s, the *PCC* document was filled with images and illustrations of the type of capital the plan envisioned (Figure 13-10).

Unfortunately, the federal government lost some of the momentum and credibility around capital planning issues during the 1996-2004 public consultation process over the detailed plans for the core area of the capital. The NCC put forward several good urban design concepts for consideration:

- completing Confederation Boulevard, which had stalled after 1989 (Figure 12-16),
- rehabilitating the Parliamentary Precinct (Figure 12-18),
- building new diplomatic missions on Sussex Drive,
- completing a new neighbourhood and park on LeBreton Flats (Figure 13-9),
- connecting northern Hull and Aylmer to Gatineau Park,
- extending Bank Street to the Ottawa River bluff (Figure 13-10),
- redeveloping the aging E.B. Eddy industrial lands on the Ottawa River (Figure 13-11), and
- adapting the Chaudière and Victoria islands for industrial heritage and an aboriginal centre (Figure 13-12).

But almost all of these proposals were ignored in the furor that emerged over a proposal to open up a broader view of Parliament Hill by widening Metcalfe Street.

The Confederation Boulevard, Parliamentary Precinct and LeBreton Flats proposals would complete plans that had started in the 1980s, but stalled. A plan for new diplomatic missions was another capital-city initiative that was long overdue. The relocation of the US Embassy was especially important, because as Jan Morris observed: "Directly opposite the front gate of Parliament, like an ever-watchful command post, stands the United States embassy, flag on the roof, iron posts in the sidewalk ... the symbolism of the site is brutal."[1144] The Americans needed room to expand, and were sold a good site on Sussex Drive, between the ByWard Market and Major's Hill Park. They produced a handsome urban building with two

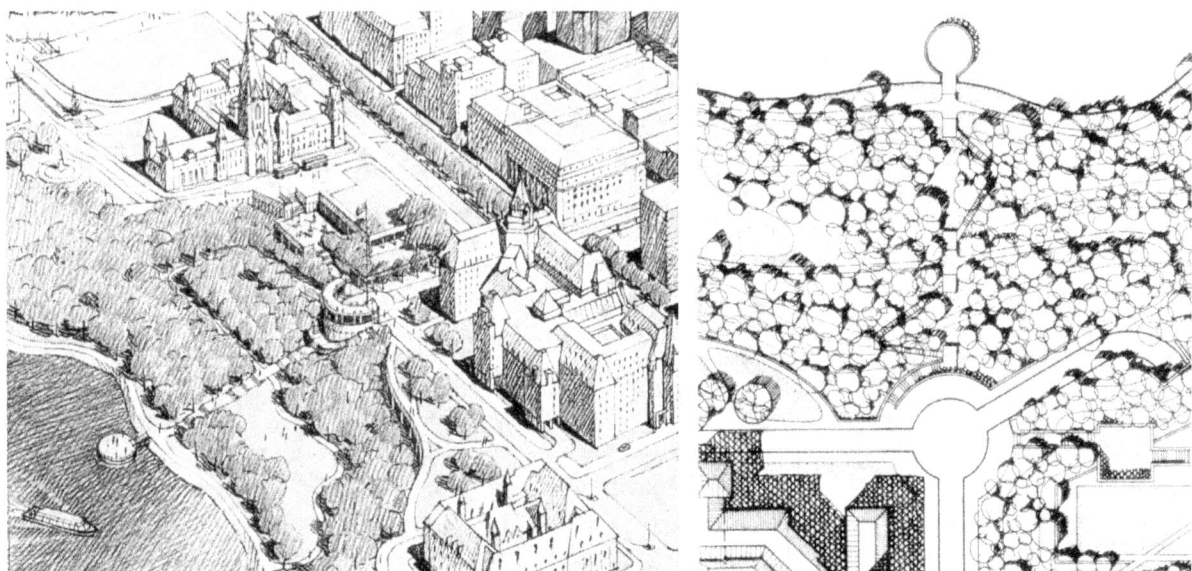

FIGURE 13-10: Bank Street Axis Development, *Plan for Canada's Capital,* **1999**
This image is one of many in the 1999 plan. Edward Bennett's 1915 plan had a similar proposal. It was elaborated in the 1987 *Parliamentary Precinct Plan*, illustrating an extension of Bank Street to the top of the escarpment, with a lookout and stairway to the river. The idea was put on hold for security reasons.
(Source: NCC, *Plan for Canada's Capital*, 1999, p. 57. Original image from du Toit Allsopp Hillier, *Parliamentary Precinct Plan*, 1987, Figure 163)

FIGURE 13-11: Victoria and Chaudière islands proposals
Planning for these islands in the Ottawa River will require a complex interplay between natural, aboriginal and industrial history. Proposed First Nations centre in the lower right, and industrial heritage complex in the middle. The Chaudière Falls would be visible, but still trapped behind the ring dam.
(Source: NCC)[1143]

faces – a stone façade of modest scale towards the Market and a glass wall with small towers facing the park and National Gallery.[1145]

Negotiations to close the toilet paper factory opposite Parliament Hill required more delicacy because the plant was still in production, even if it had lost its regional source of pulp logs decades earlier. The NCC negotiated a long-term agreement to purchase the property for future national uses, yet maintain the plant and jobs for up to 25 years[1146] (Figure 13-12).

The final decline of the 19th century lumber and pulp mills at the Chaudière was another opportunity worth seizing. Victoria Island was proposed to be restored as a natural area and aboriginal centre interpreting this key site for First Nations' history. Chaudière Island was a more difficult proposition, since it was packed with mill buildings. The NCC proposed new uses for industrial heritage buildings, in the manner of Vancouver's Granville Island, and opening up views of the Chaudière Falls, which had been closed off for a century[1147] (Figure 13-11).

The hydraulic power at the site no longer provides thousands of jobs sawing logs into lumber or crushing them into pulp, so there may be opportunities to reconfigure the dams to bring back the Chaudière Falls. Algonquin elder Ojigkwanong (William Commanda) proposed that the Asticou should be restored (Figure 13-13). The management of Niagara Falls for both tourism and hydraulic generation indicates that there are engineering precedents for dual use of the Chaudière.

However, all these worthy plans were ignored in the rush to condemn the proposal to recreate a view of Parliament Hill from the south. The proposed Metcalfe Street widening (Figure 13-14) was the headline in every media report. The response to its proposals to demolish heritage buildings to create the vista was almost uniformly negative.[1149] The NCC's monitoring of public consultation on the plan showed that the idea was intensely unpopular, but it did not go away quickly because, as in the days of Borden and Mackenzie King, it was favoured by the prime ministers who were impressed by Paris.[1150] The plan for a grand boulevard was a favourite of

FIGURE 13-12: Redevelopment proposal for the north shore of the Ottawa River, 2000
Left: Industrial site, 2000
Right: Proposed green space
When the toilet paper factory opposite Parliament Hill closes sometime in the next quarter century, its site will be used for a riverfront park and another national institution beside the Museum of Civilization.
(Source: NCC, *Core Area Concept for Canada's Capital*, 2000)

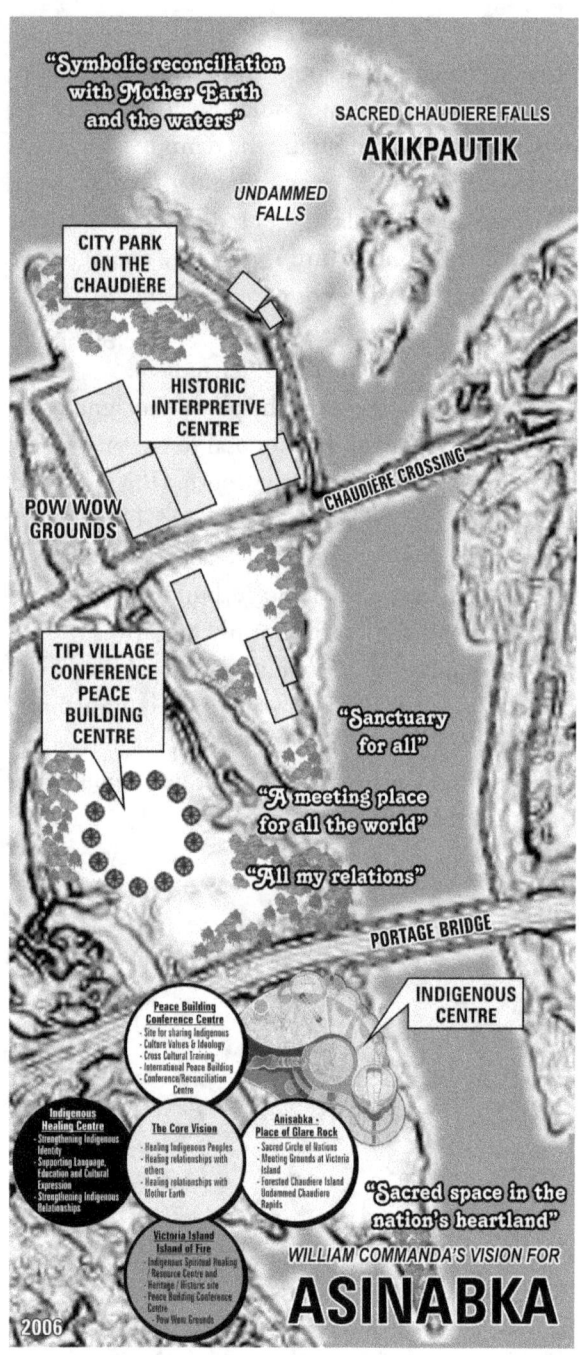

FIGURE 13-13: Asinabka Proposal
A vision by Indigenous elder William Commanda of a return to undammed Chaudière Falls and an indigenous peoples' centre on the islands
(Source: W. Commanda:[1148] Asinabka and Circle of All Nations; © Asinabka and Circle of All Nations, reproduced with permission)

Prime Minister Jean Chretien. The Metcalfe Street proposal ultimately disappeared from the 2005 final version of the plan[1151] but by then the delicate relationship between the NCC and Ottawa was severely damaged and inter-regional planning had once again fallen apart.[1152]

The Collapse of Regional Planning

Although the two regional governments barely acknowledged each other's existence in their 1990s land use plans, the interprovincial boundary along the Ottawa River could not deflect the area's transportation problems. Most Canadian metropolitan areas have major river bridges, but Ottawa-Gatineau is the only one where transit passengers must switch systems after crossing the river. The NCC attempted to encourage interconnection by assisting the Outaouais Transit System (STO) with a bus loop across the river along Wellington Street, but the vaunted Ottawa Transitway System does not extend into Gatineau, not even to serve the huge federal employment node just across Portage Bridge in downtown Hull.

The need for additional bridge capacity across the border increased steadily, and a multi-jurisdictional staff committee, the Joint Administrative Committee on Planning and Transportation (JACPAT), reviewed alternatives throughout the 1980s and early 1990s. The staff finally recommended a new bridge on the Kettle Island corridor, east of the downtowns. The proposal was strongly supported by the east Outaouais communities, but was greeted with howls of protest from Ottawa's Manor Park and Rockcliffe Park neighbourhoods. The City of Ottawa Council quickly moved to oppose it. The RMOC and provincial governments would not intervene, and both the bridge proposal and the JACPAT collapsed in the mid-1990s.[1153] It was clear that staff collaboration without advance political support would not work.

FIGURE 13-14: The Metcalfe Street Widening Proposal
Any proposal to create a grand boulevard centered on the Peace Tower would require demolition of a broad swath of downtown. Jacques Gréber argued against this City Beautiful proposal in 1950, but the idea seems to rise from the dead every quarter-century.
(Source: NCC)

The NCC would have to act alone to add any connections between the two provinces, and an opportunity arose with the deterioration of the Champlain Bridge west of downtown. The 50 year-old, two-lane structure needed major reconstruction and it was relatively easy to add an additional lane. The NCC optimistically believed that the proposition would be simple to adopt, since the agency owned both the bridge and the Ottawa River Parkway at its southern terminus. After considerable public discussion, the NCC proposed adding widened sidewalks, bicycle lanes, and a reversible transit and high-occupancy vehicle (HOV) lane to the rehabilitated bridge. Not so fast: the western Ottawa neighbourhoods, fearing an onslaught of rush-hour traffic from Québec, vigorously opposed the bridge widening and mobilized their allies at the City of Ottawa. The mayor became an outspoken critic of the Champlain Bridge proposal and the city opposed the project through every step of the local, regional, provincial and federal approval process and then into the courts. The approval process took seven years, but the NCC finally opened the rebuilt bridge in 2002.[1154] However, the collapse of the JACPAT and the bitter fight over the Champlain Bridge crushed any further thoughts of collaboration between the NCC, Ottawa and Gatineau.[1155]

Local Government Reform

The 'Town-Crown' conflicts seemed to peak in the late 1990s, at least in the media and in the City of Ottawa. The regional governments were quietly working with the NCC to achieve mutual objectives for transit and road connections, but the many local governments were in constant conflict among themselves and with the RMOC and CUO. The relationship between the City of Ottawa and NCC deteriorated as the problems with high-profile incomplete projects (LeBreton Flats, the Daly Building, the Champlain Bridge) and dislike for the Metcalfe Street proposal fed local anger. At the same time, the rapid growth of the high-tech industry and the cuts in federal employment led some people to assume that Ottawa's status as the national capital was no longer a priority. The Ottawa mayor and downtown councillors were constant critics of any proposals that had neighbourhood impacts, and the *Ottawa Citizen* heaped invective on every federal initiative:

It apparently hasn't come to the attention of the National Capital Commission but Ottawa has become something more than a backdrop for the federal government. Most people here don't work for the government and many find it little more than a costly annoyance. Two-thirds of tourists don't even bother making a trip to Parliament Hill. Surely even the people who regularly breathe the rarified air on the Hill occasionally make it far enough out into the real world to realize that we're not just a government town anymore.[1156]

A new round of local government reform reduced interjurisdictional in-fighting at the end of the millennium. Surprisingly, this reform cycle was initiated by the two most ideologically distant provincial governments in Canada – Ontario's Conservative's "Common Sense Revolution" and the Parti Québécois. Ontario moved first, eliminating 229 municipalities around the province, with most of the attention going to the "megacity" consolidation in Metro-Toronto.[1157]

The Ottawa region was plunged into controversy about municipal governance for several years. At this point, the Outaouais and Ottawa-Carleton regional governments were both mature organizations with sophisticated urban development controls and a track record for delivering infrastructure. The smaller municipalities like Rockcliffe Park and Vanier could see their demise, but the larger suburban governments in Kanata, Nepean and Gloucester fought hard to survive. In the end, the provincial government created a new City of Ottawa, with jurisdiction over the area formerly governed by the RMOC, and dissolved the other municipalities.[1158] The newly united City of Ottawa, with a population of 800,000 on the south side of the river, combined the usual urban-suburban divisions with a large rural area. In effect, the regional government became a new city both legally and symbolically, as the RMOC headquarters in Cartier Square was designated as the new city hall.[1159] The first mayor of the new city was Bob Chiarelli, the former regional chairman, who had a wide electoral base after the direct elections to the Ottawa-Carleton council in 2000 and 2003.

In Québec, Lucien Bouchard's government eliminated 212 suburban governments and replaced them with 49 amalgamated municipalities, with much of the attention on the proposed amalgamations in Montréal and Ville de Québec. The Montréal and Outaouais reforms were overlaid with language politics, as the English-speaking minorities in the West Island and Outaouais clung to their suburban municipalities. Nevertheless, Québec amalgamated the five local governments in the CUO region into the new City of Gatineau on January 1, 2002.[1160] The provincial Liberal Party promised local referenda on the unpopular amalgamation issues and defeated the Parti Québécois in the provincial election. In June 20, 2004, parts of Montréal voted to de-amalgamate but, surprisingly, the Outaouais referenda did not result in a change.[1161] The new Ville de Gatineau established its City Hall in the Maison des Citoyens, former headquarters of the City of Hull and the CUO. Its first mayor was Yves Ducharme, formerly the mayor of Hull.

The two provincial amalgamations greatly simplified urban governance in Canada's capital region and set the stage for improved 'Town-Crown' collaboration.[1162] For most urban issues, there were now only three major players – the Ville de Gatineau (2011 population 265,349), the City of Ottawa (2011 population 883,391) and the NCC. Both new local governments used the creation of new municipal plans as an exercise to consolidate their visions for the future. Remarkably, both municipalities also decided it was time to put aside old grievances and cooperate with the federal government.

Small Steps towards Collaboration

It took about a decade for the poisonous interjurisdictional atmosphere to disperse in the National Capital Region. The NCC's irrepressible Jean Pigott laid the foundations at the federal level by promoting popular cultural programming and improving relations with the RMOC.[1163] Her successor, Marcel Beaudry, was previously mayor of Hull and maintained a good relationship with the local and regional governments in the Outaouais for over a decade. He also enjoyed a close relationship with Bob Chiarelli, who was the RMOC chair (1998-2001) and then mayor (2001-06).[1164]

At the provincial level, the 2003 defeat of the Parti Québécois removed a government that actively resisted all attempts to improve the federal capital or even connect the two sides of the river. The Ottawa valley's influence in Queen's Park also increased in 2003 when Ottawa's Dalton McGuinty was elected as Ontario's premier.

The provincially-mandated amalgamations ended the ceaseless competition between local and regional governments. The disappearance of the former City of Ottawa also removed the largest 'Town-Crown' conflict. Marcel Beaudry simply outlasted the NCC's numerous critics in the old city, and some of the irritating long-term issues (Daly, Chambers, LeBreton, Metcalfe Street) gradually faded in the new century.

By 2002, there were only three real players left in Canada's capital region: the mayor of Gatineau, the chair of the NCC and the mayor of Ottawa. The three chief executives formed a tri-partite planning committee to consider transportation, environmental and economic issues. However, the first item for both new local governments was to build consensus within their newly amalgamated cities by preparing new visions for their own futures.

New City Visions: Town and Crown Collaborate Downtown

Ottawa started its new plan first, because its amalgamation was completed a year ahead of Gatineau's. The first hint of a wider outlook was the new municipal website, where the home page proudly announced: "The City of Ottawa: Canada's Capital / La Ville d'Ottawa: La Capitale du Canada." The municipal government's new branding acknowledged that it was a capital city for the first time in decades, and it did so in both official languages.

The new city had a difficult task ahead, combining eleven urban and rural municipalities into one local government structure serving almost 800,000 people. It began a two-year strategic planning process, branded as "Ottawa 20/20", starting with widespread community consultation and many background studies to prepare the new city to manage growth and change.

Ottawa 20/20 was quite different from a conventional land-use plan in the Ontario context. It was a comprehensive growth management strategy, combining a land-use plan with human services, arts and heritage plans, and economic and environmental strategies (Figure 13-15). The Official Plan's land-use strategies were also supported by master plans for transportation, infrastructure and green space. The plans were extensively interconnected and designed to be monitored annually with a broad

FIGURE 13-15: Ottawa 20/20 Structure
(Source: *Ottawa 20/20 Official Plan*, Figure 8, p. 1.1)

range of progress indicators. This strategic planning structure was based upon best practices from other North American cities.[1165]

The substantive content of Ottawa's 20/20 plans sometimes broke new ground. The Human Services and Arts and Heritage plans gave new prominence to these municipal activities and tied them to the city's strategic planning framework.[1166] The environmental and economic strategies extended the excellent work done for the 1997 RMOC regional plan, based upon extensive ecological analysis and tactics to diversify Ottawa's economy.[1167]

The 20/20 Official Plan contains many elements of the 1997 RMOC regional plan, combined with the secondary plans from the former City of Ottawa and other local government. But the 20/20 Plan's prologue signaled an additional feature, since it directly placed the new city in its national and regional context:

Today, Ottawa functions as both a national capital city on the international stage, and as an exciting yet comfortable place to call home. Parliament Hill is both a powerful national symbol and a familiar landmark to residents, a landmark carefully preserved in urban design plans prepared by both the federal government and the City of Ottawa. The green parkway system owned by the National Capital Commission, charged with coordinating the planning of federal properties in the National Capital Region, hosts motorcades for visiting dignitaries as well as streams of resident joggers and cyclists. The people of Ottawa celebrate Canada Day on Parliament Hill on national television, but also get together in neighbourhood parks to share their fireworks on the Victoria Day weekend. As part of the National Capital Region, the City of Ottawa partners with federal government as well as with the City of Gatineau in Québec on a range of issues, from the health of the river that runs between them to plans for new bridges to cross it. Together with the City of Gatineau, Ottawa is part of the fourth largest metropolitan area in Canada, with an economy to match.[1168]

Ottawa's 20/20 Plan specifically acknowledged the city's dual role as part of a national capital and regional metropolis. It referenced the objectives and policies of the NCC's 1999 *Plan for Canada's Capital*, and plainly supported them when the proposals were in the city's interest. The biggest changes were the downtown policies, which stated that the area was "the economic and cultural heart of the city and symbolic heart of the nation …" The city's plan promotes a livable, mixed-use downtown, but it also acknowledges that the area is the main tourism destination of the National Capital Region.[1169] The 20/20 Plan also included a commitment to prepare an urban design policy for the downtown, working with local stakeholders, but also pledging to protect "the visual integrity and symbolic primacy of the Parliament Buildings and other national symbols."[1170]

The new plan also supported the NCC's policy approaches for Confederation Boulevard, LeBreton Flats and the Greenbelt. However, despite the encouraging Prologue, neither the 20/20 Plan, nor its supporting documents, included any proposals for new bridges across the Ottawa River or cross-river rapid transit. The *Transportation Master Plan* did propose a new network of Light Rail Transit (LRT) lines and bus Transitway extensions throughout the new city.[1171, 1172]

Ottawa quickly followed up the 20/20 Plan with its promised downtown urban design strategy and secondary plan. The city retained one of Canada's leading urban design firms to prepare 41 targeted strategies to improve the downtown area. Its first strategy was to put Ottawa's downtown into its regional and national context, using the NCC's *Core Area Concept* plan. The policies that followed showed design improvements to protect and improve the ByWard Market, downtown shopping, mixed-use neighbourhoods, cultural centres and the university.[1173] The city also committed to following the lead of Vancouver and the NCC in convening a design review committee.[1174]

Planning in the new Ville de Gatineau got off to a slightly slower start, due to the amalgamation battle extending into 2004. The Gatineau planners had a recent foundation to build upon, since the CUO had adopted a revised regional plan in 2000, after years of local debate. The new Gatineau *urbanistes* adapted and extended it into a new municipal *Plan d'urbanisme* by June 2005, calling for a regional structure with a mosaic of urban villages and a primary core on the Île de Hull. The Gatineau Plan discussed the importance of diversifying the regional economy, promoting high-technology industries and tourism. It also contained a plan showing how the proposed mosaic of urban villages fit with the larger regional structure on both sides of the Ottawa River.[1175]

Building suburban "downtowns" proved more difficult. Nepean's ambitious plans for Centrepointe were only partially complete when the municipality was amalgamated with Ottawa. Gloucester City Centre never really got started, while the plans for Orleans and Kanata also lost momentum after Ontario's reforms and the loss of mayors and professional staff exclusively dedicated to their development. Ville de Gatineau quietly built the best suburban centre at La Cité (Figure 13-2) with federal land and employment and Québec's contribution to the transit station.

The NCC supported the new local governments with its 2005 sector plan for the core area, connecting the downtowns on both sides of the Ottawa River. To ensure a close fit with the City of Ottawa, the federal agency retained Urban Strategies, the same urban design consultants who prepared the municipal policy (Figure 12-7). This tactic of hiring a common consultant ensured a level of trust in the skilled professional advisors preparing the plan that would not be possible in other arrangements seconding local staff. The plan started with a clear statement of the areas where the federal government would take the lead to protect national interests – the international presence, federal offices, national cultural facilities, Confederation Boulevard, the "capital experience," national monuments, security and views of Parliament Hill. The NCC agreed to support Ottawa and Gatineau in planning for downtown neighbourhoods, heritage districts and local shopping areas, and also agreed to joint responsibility with the local governments for the river, Sparks Street, LeBreton Flats, and the Portage and Brewery Creek districts.

The three new core area plans went beyond urban design for the built environment to include strategies for promoting tourism and new 'capital stages' for national and local festivals in LeBreton and Hull. This strategy took some of the stress off the Parliament Hill and Confederation Park landscapes, which were being trampled by the crowds in popular programs such as Winterlude and the Blues and Jazz festivals[1176] (Figure 13-16). These diverse cultural events are crucial components for both local economic development and planning a national capital to reflect a multicultural society.[1177]

Local governments on both sides of the river pursued new entertainment and tourism facilities with the assistance of their provincial governments. The *Casino de Lac Leamy* (initially the Casino de Hull) was developed by the *Société des casinos du Québec* on the site of an abandoned cement plant in central Gatineau. It opened in 1996, with a hotel added in 2004. The drab Ottawa Congress Centre built on federal land in 1982 was demolished and replaced by the larger Ottawa Convention Centre, including a dramatic glass front overlooking the Rideau Canal. The federal, provincial and city governments split the cost of the new centre, with a minimum interjurisdictional wrangling.[1178]

The controversy over the redevelopment of Lansdowne Park was a contrast to the smooth sailing for the casino and convention centre. In 1847, Bytown received the 10-ha site beside the

FIGURE 13-16: **Drawing from the NCC's Core Area Plan**
The large circles illustrate potential commemoration sites at gateways. The small circles indicate "capital stages" for programming.
(Source: Core Area Concept 2006, Figure 16)

Rideau Canal from Canada, and it has been used continuously for exhibitions and sporting events, including the Stanley Cup (hockey) and Grey Cup (Canadian football). By 1900, Lansdowne was surrounded by housing and a century later, the site was in obvious need of redevelopment. The stadium stands were condemned, the heritage buildings in poor condition and the "park" was entirely asphalt, with an enormous parking lot stretching from Bank Street to the canal. The City of Ottawa started public consultation and an international design competition for the site, but the lure of professional sports franchises derailed the planning process once again. A local consortium obtained a Canadian Football League franchise and made an unsolicited bid for redevelopment of the entire site. They proposed a new stadium, condominium apartments, shops and a proper park. The design competition and consultation were suspended, provoking both local outrage and a counter-proposal for a professional soccer franchise and stadium on the vast parking lots surrounding the hockey arena outside the Kanata. City council briefly flirted with the idea of compounding the Kanata mistake, but instead permitted the consortium to redevelop Lansdowne Park. More local outrage and two years of lawsuits ensued, until the new stadium opened in 2014.[1179]

In the 1960s, the federal government might have got burned by trying to seize control of this project to create a national stadium, similar to Paris' Stade de France. However, 50 years later, the NCC was wise enough to let local residents make their own decisions on a project with mainly local implications. The NCC and Parks Canada quietly assisted with a design competition for the new park and guarded the canal's World Heritage status. The overall Lansdowne Park redevelopment process was awkward, but the early results seem broadly right – a new park near the canal, mixed-use along Bank Street and a refurbished stadium and arena.[1180]

The final strategies to improve the functional and symbolic content in the core of Canada's capital city fell into place with new plans for the Parliamentary Precinct, a commemoration strategic plan and a detailed strategy to protect views of capital symbols. The Parliamentary and Judicial Precincts Area plan addressed difficult issues around new space for Parliament and the Supreme Court and visitor access and security in the post 9/11/2001 world (Figure 13-17). The

FIGURE 13-17: **Parliamentary Precinct Plan, 2006**
This plan cleans up the landscape of Parliament Hill and would improve security, with minimal visual or physical barriers. Note the proposed new federal court building to complete the Supreme Court square.
(Source: du Toit Allsopp Hillier, 2006)

commemoration plan relieves the congestion on Parliament Hill by identifying a range of sites around Confederation Boulevard for new monuments and memorials.[1181] These sites, and Parliament Hill, are protected by the view protection strategy, prepared using 3-D computer modeling of the complex topography and future built form options for the core area (Figure 13-18). The City of Ottawa's adoption of these height limits closed the loop on a 40-year struggle to protect views of the strongest national symbols in the Canadian capital.[1182]

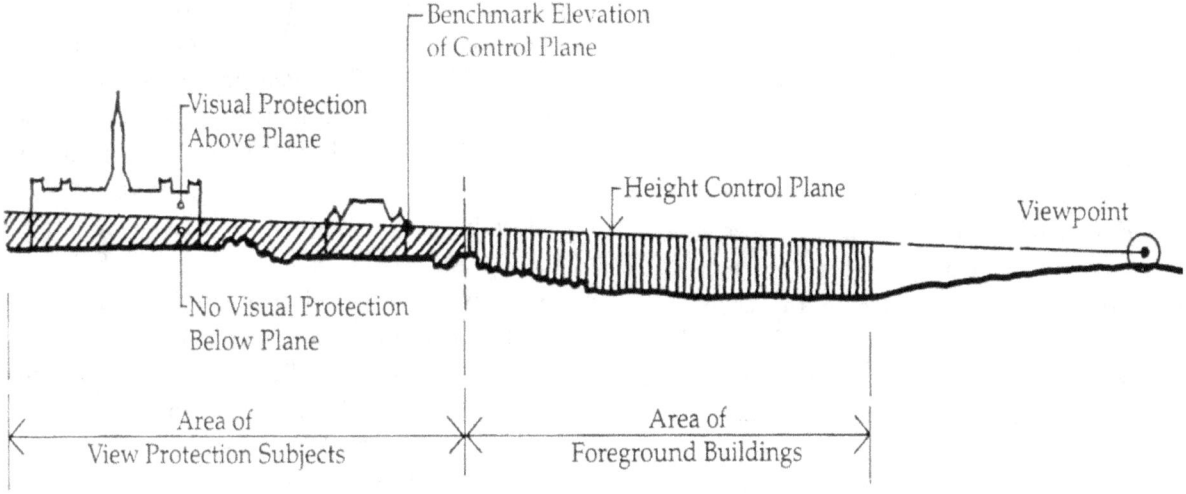

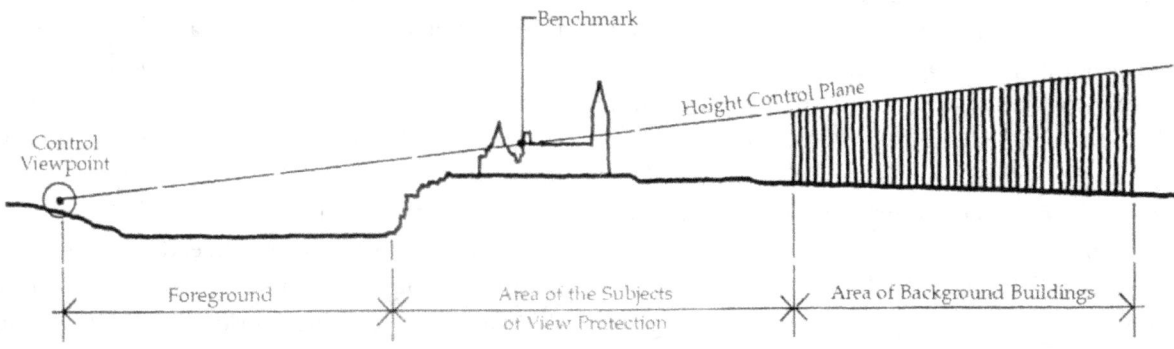

Figure 13-18: View Control Planes
The view of Parliament Hill can be ruined by a taller building in front, blocking the vista, or a taller building behind, preventing the silhouette of the towers on the skyline.
(Source: du Toit, Allsopp Hillier *et. al.*, 2007, Figure 118, p. 110 and Figure 87, p. 86)

Building Transportation Systems that Don't Connect

The new spirit of co-operation between the federal and municipal governments did not extend past downtown development to transportation systems. Gatineau and Ottawa both planned major expansions of their transit systems as part of their new regional plans in the first decade of new century. Unfortunately, the regional municipalities did not plan these systems together, and the NCC was unable to encourage them to collaborate after the failure of the JATPAC bridge process in the 1990's.

The early moves looked promising. Ottawa leased an abandoned CP Rail line for a light rail pilot project that ran eight kilometres south from the Prince of Wales Bridge to the edge of the Greenbelt. OC Transpo built its O-Train pilot for only $21 million, a pittance compared to the million dollar price-tags for new light rail, or even bus rapid transit (BRT) projects. Some critics suggested that the O-train went from "nowhere to nowhere" starting in green fields in the south and ending at an abandoned bridge and contaminated dump in the north. Surprisingly, the O-train attracted riders almost from the moment it opened, because it served two major employment nodes in the inner suburbs – Carleton University and the federal government's Confederation Heights office park. Carleton students used the new line to settle in the older Mechanicsville and Hintonburg neighbourhoods to the north, while some federal employees found that they had a simple transfer from their bus to the train. The O-Train pilot project won several transit awards, and the service was upgraded in 2015.[1183]

The O-Train's modest early ridership masked the long-term potential for the route. The green fields at the south end were the South Nepean Urban Area, the third major expansion area under the 1997 RMOC regional plan. Major developers had assembled these lands decades before but they were planned to be served by transit since, unlike Orleans and Kanata, they were not connected to expressways. The O-Train's north terminus was the Bayview Station at the existing east-west bus Transitway. The vacant City of Ottawa works yards were proposed as a major transit oriented development (TOD).[1184] From a regional perspective, the O-Train line also had a wonderful bonus as it came complete with an underpass below the Queensway and an unused bridge across the Ottawa River – piercing the two most serious east-west transportation barriers. It also offered the tantalizing opportunity to connect a new transit line across the river to Gatineau.

The Ottawa 20/20 Plan made the north-south O-Train route the centrepiece of its transportation strategy in 2003. The 29 km. system plan went through several more years of thorough public review in the environmental assessment process. The design, finance and construction of the new system was procured in an international process won by a consortium led by the German light rain contractor Siemens and PCL, the largest Canadian construction firm. With a $778 million contract signed in July 2006, Ottawa seemed well on the way to having the first leg of its LRT ready for 2009.[1185]

Unfortunately, all this transportation planning happened without consideration of the north side of the river. In the heady early days of collaboration between the new Ville de Gatineau, City of Ottawa and the NCC, all three agreed to collaborate in a "blue-ribbon" technical study of options for a new bridge across the Ottawa River to help deal with the truck, bus and automobile connection problems, as the regional population surged towards 1.5 million. The technical committee recommended Kettle Island for the crossing, connecting the existing Aviation Parkway to an existing corridor in the Gatineau plan.[1186] These connections were proposed in the 1950s, to serve a regional population of 500,000 and the necessary corridors were subsequently protected by the NCC and Québec municipalities. Since the Aviation Parkway had already been connected to the Queensway and Highway 417, the crossing offered the opportunity to rid downtown Ottawa of cross-river truck traffic. However, the vigorous opposition of stakeholders on the Ottawa side of the crossing once again prevented political approval of the bridge, and the proposal was scrapped in 2013, after both provincial governments refused to fund it.[1187]

Not surprisingly, Gatineau decided that it would not wait for federal/provincial/City of Ottawa collaboration to improve its regional transit system. The new city considered that it was too small (242,000 people in 2006) to support an LRT system and had the internationally acclaimed example of Ottawa's Transitway in easy view across the river, so the decisions to adopt bus rapid transit (BRT) was understandable. The *Société de Transport de l'Outaouais' Rapibus* system was approved in 2007 and opened in 2013 with $200 million funding from Québec and Gatineau.[1188] The first phase was a 17 km. east-west line, with most of the route using the same underutilized rail corridor that connects to the O-Train. The new system directly services the casino, several large suburban malls, *La Maison de la Culture, Cégep de l'Outaouais* and the new campus for the *Université du Québec en Outaouais*. Unfortunately, it does not serve the major federal employment nodes at Portage, Les Terraces or central Ottawa.

While the Outaouis was building the Rapibus systems, plans for Ottawa's long-awaited O-Train fell apart, even though the city had spent over $73 million in planning and a construction contract had been awarded. The 2006 mayoral campaign was a tight, three-way race between the incumbent Bob Chiarelli, former councillor Alex Munter and Larry O'Brien, a retired businessman with no political experience. The LRT's route and the contract's commercial confidentiality clauses became election issues.[1189] Munter proposed an alternate plan and O'Brien proposed to re-open the contract (at no cost to the taxpayers) if elected. In an extraordinary move, the federal minister responsible for Ottawa supported O'Brien's campaign by withholding the promised $200 million federal contribution until after the mayoral election and leaking the confidential contracts to the press.[1190]

O'Brien was narrowly elected and proceeded to dismantle the city's transportation plans during his first months in office. Council voted to break the Siemens' contract, and the consortium sued,[1191] eventually settling for $37 million. A thoughtful Ottawa councillor, Clive Doucet, wrote:

It took Colonel John By six years to build the Rideau Canal from Ottawa to Kingston. It has taken the City of Ottawa six years to plan its new north-south rail line. Those six years included 55 separate votes of City Council, a tripartite contribution agreement with the federal and provincial governments, a successful international competition, the contract signed, construction ready to begin – and then the whole thing fell apart... if you're looking for what's wrong with Canadian cities at the beginning of the 21st century, you need look no further than Ottawa's light rail project.[1192]

Doucet spoke too soon – although the 2007 collapse of the Ottawa LRT project is regarded as a serious public policy failure by many observers,[1193] Toronto repeated the mistakes on a larger scale after the 2009 election of Mayor Rob Ford. Planning and implementing transportation systems takes decades and is more difficult if a region's transportation plan is discarded whenever a new mayor or minister is elected.[1194]

The Ottawa transportation planning process was re-started in 2007, eventually settling on replacing some of the current Transitway with an east-west LRT from Blair Road to Tunney's Pasture, including an expensive tunnel through the rock underneath downtown Ottawa. Once again, the main downtown federal employment cluster is not directly serviced by the new transit stations planned by the local government, even after the feds increased their contribution from $200 to $600 million.[1195] Ironically, the new LRT, branded the Confederation Line, will serve neither Confederation Square nor Parliament Hill.

The 12.5 km. first phase of the new LRT is expected to open in 2018, at a cost of $2.6 billion, versus the 2009 opening and $780 million total cost of the cancelled 29 km. O-Train project.

Ottawa created an ambitious set of Transit-Oriented-Development (TOD) plans for the LRT stations in the eastern suburbs, which had seen little development interest as Transitway stops in the past.[1196] So it might be argued that the new Confederation Line could support more sustainable intensification, rather than suburban sprawl, except that rapid suburban growth continued in Nepean South, which was not cancelled, or even put on hold, after it lost the early, high-quality transit upon which it was planned.

Reflections

In the first decade of the new millennium, it appeared that the Ottawa-Gatineau region had emerged from 40 years of interjurisdictional conflict with a real chance to improve Canada's capital. The number of combatants had been drastically decreased; the political planets seemed aligned; the local economy was booming and excellent plans were in place. The provincial governments were less hostile after 2003, following the election of federalist Liberal Jean Charest as Québec premier and Ottawa native Dalton McGuinty in Ontario. The local agencies started to collaborate on cross-border environmental issues with the *Ottawa River Integrated Development Plan* and *Choosing our Future*, a 50-year plan dealing with community resilience and climate change. Quiet diplomacy by region-wide, non-governmental environmental organizations assisted in reshaping agreement on long-term policies, but the local governments resisted formal adoption of cross-border plans.[1197]

The 2006 election of a new Conservative federal government caused only a brief bump compared to the restructuring by the 1984 Mulroney regime. The new federal government was not openly hostile to the national capital.[1198] An expert panel reviewed and renewed the NCC's mandate and the government showed a flash of local insight by appointing the former publisher of the *Ottawa Citizen* as the NCC's new chair.[1199] Russell Mills promptly opened up the NCC's board meetings, removing the media's biggest complaint. The government moved the NCC into a planning and property-management mode, cut its capital budget, and transferred its popular programming to the direct ministerial control in the Heritage Department. The Canada Lands Company, a Crown corporation that has had considerable success across Canada, took over redevelopment of most surplus federal lands with the NCR, including CFB Rockcliffe. Keeping most federal land redevelopment activities separate from the NCC may assist with local relations. CLC acts as a regular land developer in the municipal planning process and can borrow funds for infrastructure and brownfields cleanup, which are desperately needed for projects such as CFB Rockcliffe and LeBreton.[1200]

'Town-Crown' relations in the capital simmered quietly in the new century, while the federal government occasionally put a foot wrong with the ill-fated proposals to move the proposed National Portrait Gallery to Calgary, or build a monument in the wrong place.[1201] But the NCC may have missed a golden opportunity to target federal spending power to insist on better connections across the river. The federal government invested mightily in infrastructure across Canada through Infrastructure Canada and the Economic Action Plan stimulus program following the 2008 recession. However, the NCC remained somewhat tentative during the post-amalgamation period and strong tripartite leadership on cross-border issues never emerged.[1202] With billions of dollars on the table in the National Capital Region, the NCC might have influenced the interconnection of the two transit systems, if only to better serve the federal government's own interests as the region's major employer.

The outbreak of peace in the mid-2000s may simply have been another temporary cease fire in the 'Town-Crown' conflicts, and a hostile minister, collapse of the economy or a clumsy mayor could easily upset the delicate balance again.[1203] As the new century unfolded, there was little doubt that Canada's capital still needed a lot of work to make it a place worthy of the nation's affection and pride,[1204] but the prospects for progress rarely seemed better.[1205]

CHAPTER 14

Town and Crown: Lessons for the Future of Canada's Capital

This final chapter will compare Ottawa-Gatineau to other metropolitan areas and Canada's capital region to other national capitals.[1206] It will also compare the objectives of local and national governments (the 'Town and Crown') and draw lessons for the future of Canada's capital from the history related in the earlier chapters.

Building a capital city is a complex and long-term undertaking that must work on at least two levels. Like all cities, a national capital needs to build functional and attractive places for its residents to live, work and play. A capital city must also meet the symbolic and functional needs of its sponsoring government. The tensions between these 'Town' and 'Crown' roles are a normal part of capital-city planning around the world, but have proved especially complicated for Canada's seat of government.[1207] The evolving Canadian cultural context adds another groundbreaking dimension, because the capital must move beyond separating the original aboriginal/French/Anglo stakeholders to reflect a more multicultural society.

Ottawa-Gatineau as a Canadian Metropolitan Region

The results of the past half-century have been quite positive in many functional issues, despite the interjurisdictional conflicts. The regional population and economy have grown; the metropolitan area has expanded, infrastructure has improved and the quality of life in the community compares favourably with other Canadian and world cities.[1208] These are not achievements to be taken lightly.

Most Canadian metropolitan areas have grown substantially since the end of the Second World War, as part of the general trend of increased Canadian urbanization. The population within the Ottawa-Gatineau region has grown six-fold, from about 250,000 to almost 1.4 million in 2014, now comprising Canada's sixth-largest metropolitan area. In comparison, Montréal has grown slower than the national capital, and Toronto, Calgary and Edmonton have grown faster. Both Calgary and Edmonton's metropolitan populations overtook Canada's capital region since the 2011 census.[1209]

The Ottawa-Gatineau economy has stabilized over the past century, as the region made the transition from natural resources to the knowledge economy and tourism. The collapse of the wood-based industries was offset by the expansion in public administration, technology and tourism, leaving the region with the nation's most highly-educated work force and a more balanced economy.[1210] Although the high-tech boom did not displace government as the region's primary employer, it counter-balanced periods of public sector cutbacks. The high-tech sector lost momentum after the 1999 JDS sale; 2001 'tech' bust and 2009 Nortel bankruptcy.[1211] Although OCRI's activities were scaled back,[1212] the region's economy proved rather resilient, with smaller companies replacing the loss of many Nortel and JDS jobs, while the federal government purchased their buildings.[1213]

While federal employment is relatively concentrated in the core and inner suburbs, the high-tech industry is clustered in the Ottawa suburbs, particularly in the southwest quadrant of the region. Their general preference for low density suburban environments and auto access has accelerated Ottawa's sprawl to the west, and the federal government's purchase of the Nortel and JDS sites will increase the dispersion of federal employees. These are powerful centripetal forces, especially when combined with the good road infrastructure built in the post-war years. Ottawa, like Canberra, benefited from national infrastructure investment during the 1950s and 1960s, during the height of the road-building era – the 1950 Gréber plan embraced General Motors' "city of the future" a little too fervently.[1214] The regional transportation system was somewhat re-balanced by RMOC's Transitway, lauded as North America's best bus network.[1215] Newman and Kenworthy's global transportation review suggests that Ottawa's transit system was "under-performing" in 2005-6, with *per capita* transit standing 31st among the 44 cities studied, last among the fifteen capital cities and last among the five largest Canadian metropolitan regions, including Calgary.[1216]

Canada became a suburban nation in the post-war years[1217] and since a large proportion of Ottawa-Gatineau's population growth occurred in that era, the region has a relatively smaller core and larger proportion of suburbs than older Canadian cities such as Halifax and Ville de Québec. It also has a relative high proportion of exurban development, compared to similar-sized cities, as significant population growth occurred in formerly rural areas such as Manotick, Richmond, Buckingham and Mississippi Mills. Despite most planning policies encouraging intensification, low-density housing and automobile use remain popular, and 92 percent of the region's population growth occurred in automobile suburbs and exurban areas from 2006-2011.[1218]

Although many observers have concerns about the economic, environmental and actual sustainability of this development pattern,[1219] it certainly delivers a high quality of life for the current residents. The region's strong economy, excellent healthcare, good public education, ample greenspace, cultural institutions, public safety and good housing cause Ottawa-Gatineau to be highly-ranked in many quality of life surveys, both within Canada and internationally.[1220]

The region's strong economy and good quality of life make it an attractive location for new immigrants, ranking only behind Toronto and Vancouver. As a result, the Ottawa-Gatineau has become more ethnically diverse, and more reflective of the modern multicultural nation that is Canada.

The Town's Priority: Building a Functional City with a High Quality of Life

Ottawa-Gatineau is probably Canada's most difficult metropolitan region to plan, build and govern. Although many Canadian urban areas straddle a river, no other metropolis straddles a provincial boundary.[1221] The numerous local, regional, provincial and federal agencies constantly quarreled from the 1970s to 2000, until the provinces reorganized local governments at the end of the century.

The Fathers of Confederation must take some blame for this muddle because, with the exception of New Brunswick's J.H. Gray,[1222] they did not give the local government of the national capital much thought from 1864-67. Even with hindsight, it is hard to criticize them too much since Washington was their only precedent for a federal capital, and the City of Ottawa was still somewhat accommodating towards national objectives, only seven years after its victory in the seat of government competition.

Any chance of having a federal district or a regional government straddling the two provinces had evaporated by the time of the 1915 Federal Plan Commission, due to political and demographic change at the local level.[1223] Any further discussion of the federal district issue poisoned regional planning efforts in the 20th century.[1224] Although the concept is theoretically attractive, it has only succeeded elsewhere when it is imposed at the beginning of the development of a federal capital city. In other federal districts like Canberra and Washington, power has gradually devolved in the opposite direction, from the national governments to the local government. There are few successful precedents for powers to be obtained by a national authority from local and provincial governments.[1225] And when we add the language issues, a federal district becomes even more problematic for Canada's capital.

So perhaps it is time to retire the federal district concept as a high-level solution to Ottawa-Gatineau's intergovernmental problems. If skilled political operators such as Mackenzie King and Douglas Fullerton cannot make it work, then perhaps we should drop the idea. There are other methods to implement capital city plans in complex jurisdictions.[1226]

The provincial governments must also accept a fair share of the responsibility for the interjurisdictional conflict. Ottawa and Hull were at the centre of the united province of Canada in 1857, but snapped back into peripheral locations in the new provinces of Ontario and Québec after 1867. Both provinces largely ignored the settlements in the distant Ottawa Valley, or intervened to assert provincial rights in opposition to national and cross-river planning objectives, especially in transportation and environmental infrastructure. Although local government reforms in both provinces drastically reduced the number of players in the regional planning game and increased the potential for cooperation, Québec and Ontario did little to increase linkages across the Ottawa River.

Local infrastructure also lagged in the Outaouais and Ottawa. Basic municipal services such as paved streets, sanitary sewage, transit, potable water, fire and police protection arrived later than in many other metropolitan areas and were often ineffective in their early stages. The environmental services systems are completely separate, running counter to all modern ecosystem principles that recommend organizing environmental planning on a watershed basis.[1227] Metropolitan-scale regional infrastructure planning must be considered a failure for the past quarter century. The transit systems barely interconnect and the newest bridge across the Ottawa River was built in 1973. Since that time, the regional population has doubled to 1.5 million people. In comparison, the Saskatoon region (2011 population 260,600) has seven bridges compared to Ottawa-Gatineau's five[1228] while serving a population one-fifth the size. The difference must be mainly in the jurisdictional arrangements, since the South Saskatchewan River Valley is deeper or wider than the Ottawa at several points. Saskatoon has one city straddling both sides of the river, within one province.

Our collective inability to build bridges across the Ottawa River is unfortunate at both the functional and symbolic levels. The repeated failures to approve bridges at long-planned locations due to Ottawa neighbourhood opposition corroded good will with Outaouais and Québec governments. It may be necessary to abandon inner suburban sites such as Kettle Island and build where there are no adjacent neighbourhoods to object – where the Greenbelt meets the river, following the example of the 1970s relocation of provincial highways 417 and 416.

The Canadian federal government did not deliberately hobble local governments in the capital city, similar to Washington, Canberra, London or Paris.[1229] However, there were many examples of the national government seizing leadership in local development issues or trampling on civic toes, especially in the Mackenzie King era.[1230] The large expanses of tax-exempt Crown lands also reduced local governments' fiscal capacity in the first half of the 20th century. As a result, both Hull and Ottawa may have deferred too much to the federal technical leadership and funding, reducing their capacity to take action in areas of clear local responsibility.[1231] Local disasters like fires and typhoid epidemics only reinforced paternalistic tendencies at the federal level. Even after the local and regional governments developed their own capacity to shape urban development, a peculiar relationship continued, where the 'Town' complains mightily about federal interference, yet is hesitant in assuming full responsibility for major initiatives in hopes of securing strategic 'Crown' cash and land contributions.[1232]

In the late 20th century, 'Crown' and 'Town' may finally have learned how to collaborate more effectively on local development issues. The federal government backed away from attempting to influence most local development in the 1980s, and defined its interest in capital-city issues more clearly in the 1999 *Plan for Canada's Capital*. Gatineau and Ottawa reinforced the 'Crown' interest in cultural programming to support local economic development through tourism. The coordination of leadership in the core area plans of the three governments early in the new century appears to be a promising approach.

There is also good potential for collaboration outside the core of the region. A capital city has an advantage because the national government is a large employer that can act in a coordinated manner to ensure that its employees have efficient access to good workplaces. The FDC and NCC achieved this objective in the 1950s and 1960s by building peripheral office nodes like Tunney's Pasture and Confederation Heights that were well-served by the new road system and had convenient access to the new suburban neighbourhoods. These were a big improvement on the immediate post-war conditions, but we now recognize that the 1950 Gréber plan went too far in promoting automobile dependence. However, the employment clusters that were a legacy of the 1950 plan are now a remarkable opportunity for transit-oriented development in the early 21st century.[1233] The suburban office parks and other large federal parcels from the 1950s are now considered inner-suburban locations and have excellent transit access. Their low density, vast parking lots, and single land-ownership make them ideal candidates for intensification and redevelopment, compared to downtown, suburban, or brownfield sites. A large, centralized employer like the federal government can facilitate transportation demand management, such as staggered work hours, transit incentives, and elimination of free parking. In contrast, the region's other major employer, the high-tech industry, has shown less sustainable development preferences for outer suburban locations and extensive automobile access.

These simple suggestions on physical planning can be matched by a few observations on planning agencies and process. First, the effects of land speculation across the past two centuries have been such that early acquisition of land by public agencies has been a good strategy in almost every case starting with Dalhousie's purchase of Parliament Hill and the NCC's early purchase of transportation corridors. Secondly, collaborative planning efforts have proved more effective for implementation than unilateral action by any single level of government. As the numbers of government actors at the local, regional, provincial and federal levels multiplied in the 1970s, collaboration became almost impossible.

Recent local government re-organizations show some promise for improving co-operation, but the Ottawa River will continue to be a barrier, not because it is a river, but because it is a provincial boundary.

Building a functional capital city is a collaborative enterprise, and both 'Crown' and 'Town' initiatives are found in most lists of triumphs and disasters (see Tables 14-1 and 14-2). A closer examination often reveals shared responsibility even in projects where leadership is clearly identified with one level of government. For example, OC Transpo's excellent bus Transitways are often located on transportation corridors assembled decades in advance by federal planners, or the NCC's ill-fated LeBreton Flats scheme in the 1960s was implementing the No. 1 priority of the City of Ottawa's 1950s urban renewal plans.

Table 14-1: Good Planning Ideas

Great Planning Decisions
- Parliament Buildings competition, 1858
- Todd's parks system report, 1903
- Creating Gatineau Park, 1935
- Freight railway relocation, 1950-65
- Gréber's parkway system, 1950-70
- Preserving the Mile of History, 1960
- Doing nothing to the ByWard Market, 1969
- Express buses from the suburbs, 1972-
- Ottawa Transitway, 1974-
- National Gallery and Museum of Civilization, 1982-89
- Confederation Boulevard, 1983-2005
- RMOC / City Hall at Cartier Square, 1990 and 2001

It Worked Out Fine in the End – Good Decisions for the Wrong Reasons
- Lord Dalhousie's purchase, 1823 (Parliament Hill, not a citadel)
- OIC Driveways, 1900-14 (bicycles, not horses)
- Preserving the Rideau Canal, 1900-40 (touring and skating, not a military canal)
- Uplands Airport, 1942-1960 (convenient airport, not air force base)
- Gréber plan road corridors, 1950-70 (Transitways and bike paths)
- Greenbelt purchase, 1959 (ecological feature, not sprawl girdle)

Sins of Omission – Good Ideas That Were Never Built
- Wright's Town plan, 1826
- Bennett's capital skyline silhouette, 1915
- Bank Street river terminus, 1915
- Gréber's downtown plan, 1939
- Satellite towns instead of bedroom communities, 1950-74
- Vanier Parkway connection to Macdonald-Cartier Bridge, 1964
- Macklin Hancock's ecosystem plan, 1967
- *Tomorrow's Capital* rail transit plan, 1974

Missed Opportunities
- LeBreton Flats passed over for the Rideau Canal Terminus, 1820
- Poor Wright's Town / Bytown townsite plans, 1826
- Parliament Buildings not connected to the city, 1858
- No Capital City district at Confederation, 1864-7
- Frederick Todd not hired as OIC Landscape Architect, 1904
- Rideau River waterfront not acquired, 1911-14
- Not implementing Holt Commission, 1914-21
- Not connecting Gatineau Park to the Ottawa River, 1936
- Ottawa River bridges, 1974-
- Missing Ottawa River pathway/parkway extensions, 1980-

Table 14-2: Bad Planning Ideas

Bad Ideas That Were (Thankfully) Not Implemented
- Barrack Hill citadel, ca. 1830
- Noulan Cauchon's Hexagonopolis, 1928
- Underground Confederation Square, 1962
- King Edward Expressway, 1965
- It's The Downtown Distributor! 1965
- LeBreton Flats Redevelopment Plan, 1967
- Chaudière megastructure, 1969
- LowerTown East Urban Renewal Plan, 1970
- Metcalfe Street axis, 1915/1926/1948/1998

It Seemed Like a Good Idea at the Time...
- Stegmann's township surveys, 1794
- The Bytown and Prescott Railway, 1855
- Damming the Chaudière Falls, 1856
- Central Experimental Farm, 1886
- Replacing the streetcar lines with buses, 1945-59
- Population forecast for the *National Capital Plan*, 1948
- *National Capital Plan* road network, 1950
- Relocating the railway stations, 1950-1966
- Federal suburban office parks, 1955-85
- Low-density Kanata, 1959-68
- LeBreton Flats urban renewal, 1959

Bad Ideas That Were Implemented Anyway
- Colonel By's townsite plan, 1827
- Long-term leases in Wright's Town and Bytown, 1827-57
- Sparks and Besserer's subdivisions, 1842
- Lumber piles along the Ottawa River, 1874
- E.B. Eddy sulphite pulp plant, 1890
- Lemieux Island water treatment plant, 1912
- Green Island City Hall, 1956
- Place de Ville, 1965
- Hull megastructures – Portage/Centre/Montferrand, 1970-77
- Barrhaven too close to the airport, 1974-
- The Palladium/Corel Centre/Scotiabank Place/Canadian Tire Centre, 1990-96

Canada's Capital Compared to Other National Capitals

Although Ottawa's residents enjoy a high quality of life, Canada's national capital has received many critiques from outsiders over the past 150 years, as quoted in the epigrams that open the previous chapters. Andrew Cohen's *The Unfinished Canadian* contains an entire chapter bemoaning Ottawa's ugly architecture, dull streets, ordinary neighbourhoods and winter weather, especially compared to other capital cities.[1234] Cohen's critique set off a blizzard of local rebuttals[1235] and some thoughtful responses.[1236]

Cohen has a point – Ottawa is a long way from inspiring the level of national pride or exciting urban living found in London, Paris, Tokyo or New York. Canada's capital still lacks some of the facilities found in other world capitals (Table 14-3).

But the great metropolitan capitals such as Paris and London are unfair comparisons for Ottawa-Gatineau. These larger cities are the dominant commercial and cultural hubs of their nations and their role as the seat of government is almost incidental to their world city status. Indeed, Japan recently considered moving its capital out of Tokyo, when it was thought to be interfering with its position as a global financial centre.[1237] The capital cities for countries that are federations are better comparisons for Ottawa-Gatineau. Most other federal capitals are also compromises between the interests of the dominant cities of the constituted states (Canberra vs Sydney/Melbourne; Washington vs Philadelphia/New York; New Delhi vs Mumbai/Kolkata) and they are often sited inland to spur development of the interior (Brasilia; Nigeria's Abuja; Tanzania's Dodoma).[1238]

Table 14-3: Capital City Elements

(Source: D.L.A. Gordon, "Ottawa" in H. Mayer (ed.), *Im Herzen der Macht? Haupt-städte und ihre Funktion*, (Bern, CH: Universität Bern, Geographisches Institut, 2013), Table 1, p. 239)

Capital City Types	Multi–Function			Global Capitals		Political Capitals						Former Capitals		Pr.	Super Capitals		
	PARIS	MOSCOW	HELSINKI	LONDON	TOKYO	WASHINGTON	CANBERRA	OTTAWA	BRASILIA	NEW DELHI	BERLIN	BONN	ROME	CHANDIGARH	BRUSSELS	BRUSSELS EU	NEW YORK

Legend:
- Many/All ●
- Some/Shared ▼
- Few/None ○
- Not Applicable N

Elements located in most capitals

Seat of Government	●	●	●	●	●	●	●	●	●	●	●	●	●	●	●	▼	N
Key Government Dept. Headquarters	●	●	●	●	●	●	●	●	●	●	●	●	●	●	●	▼	N
Official Residence of the Head of State	●		●	●	●	●	●	●	●	●	●	●	●	●	●	N	N
Official Residence of the Chief Political Leader				●	●	N		●	N	N			○	○		●	N	N
Embassies, Legations, Consular offices	●	●	●	●	●	●	●	●	●	●	●	●	●	N	●	●	▼
Final Court of Appeal	●	●	●	●	●	●	●	●	●	●	●	●	○	●	▼	●	N	N
Places for National Celebrations	●	●	●	●	●	●	●	●	●	●	●	▼	○	●	▼	●	N	●

Repositories of National Culture

• National Library	●	●	●	●	●	●	●	●	●		●		○	●		●	N	N
• Archives	●	▼			●	●	●	●			●	●	○			●	N	N
• State Art Museum	●	▼	●	●	●	●	●	●	▼	●	●	●	●	●	●	●	N	▼
• National Cultural Museums	●	▼	●	●	●	●	●	▼	▼	●	●	●	▼	▼	▼	▼	N	▼
Political and Cultural Visitors Facilities	●	●	●	●	●	●	●	●	▼	▼	▼	▼	▼	○	●	●		●
Memorials and Monuments	●	●	●	●	●	●	●	●		●	●	●	●	▼	●	N	●

Elements Usually in National Capitals

Government Dept. Offices	●	●	●	●	●	●	●	●	●	●	●	▼	●	●	●	▼	○
National Bank	●	●	●	●	●	○	●	●	●	●		●	●	○	●	N	●

National Performance Venues

• State Theatre		●	●	●	▼	▼	▼	▼	▼	▼	▼	▼	▼	○	●	N	●
• National Opera House	●	●	●	●	▼	▼	▼	▼	▼	○	▼	▼		○	●	N	●
• State Concert Hall			▼	●	▼	▼	▼	▼	▼	○	▼	▼		○	●	N	●
• National Ballet Theatre	▼	▼	▼	▼	▼	▼	▼	▼	○	○	○		○	●	N	●
• National Sports Stadia	●	●	●	●	●	▼	▼	○	▼	▼	●	▼		○	●	N	▼
National Place of Worship	●	●	●	●		●	○	○	●	○	●	●	▼	○	●	N	○
NGO Headquarters	●	●	●	●	●	●	▼	▼	●	▼	○	●	●	○	●	●	●

Elements Sometimes Found in a Capital

Research Institutes	●	●	●	▼	▼	▼	●	▼	▼	▼	▼	▼	▼	▼	▼	○	▼
Major University	●	●	●	▼	●	▼	●	▼	▼	▼	▼	▼	▼	▼	▼	▼	▼
Major Religion Headquarters	○		○	○	○	○	○	○	○	○	○	○	●	○	○	○	N
City Hall and Mayors Residence	●	●	●	●	●	●	●	●	●	▼	●	●	○	●	N	●

Elements NOT Usually Found in a Capital

Private Corporation Headquarters	●	●	●	●	●	▼	○	○	○	▼	○	▼	▼	○	●	N	●
Stock Exchange	●	●	●	●	●	○	○	○	○	○	○	○	○	○	●	N	●
Large Industrial Complexes	●	●	●	●	●	○	○	○	○	○	○	▼	○	▼	▼	N	●

Urban Elements Found in Capitals

Parks (capital grander)	●	●	●	●	●	●	●	●	●	●	●	●	●	▼	●	N	●
Transportation gateways	●	●	●	●	●	●	●	▼	▼	▼	▼	●	●	●	●	N	●
Residential Areas	●	●	●	●	●	●	●	●	●	●	●	●	●	●	●	N	●
Retail and Shopping Facilities	●	●	●	●	●	●	●	●	●	●	●	●	●	▼	●	N	●

How does Canada's capital compare to other capital cities? Well, it is certainly has the coldest winter, (save perhaps Mongolia's Ulaanbaatar). More seriously, residents of Canada's capital enjoy plenty of open space within the metropolitan area and easy access to vast wilderness areas for recreation and retreat compared to most other capitals. As mentioned above, most Ottawa and Gatineau citizens enjoy a good quality of life – only Vienna, Bern and Berlin are typically ranked higher among capital cities.[1239]

The financial and administrative arrangements for federal capitals are always controversial because, beyond the universal national-local tensions, there are an additional reluctance from state/provincial interests to invest in the federal capital in competition with the major cities in their jurisdiction.[1240] Tassonyi notes that, compared to other federal capitals, Ottawa and Gatineau have considerable autonomy as municipalities and benefit from the national government making payments in lieu of property tax.[1241] However, Ottawa and Gatineau are over-reliant on property taxes compared to other cities, as are all Canadian municipalities.[1242] In comparison, other federal capitals have often had federal districts that limit municipal government autonomy, and some national governments do not pay property taxes at all. Almost all federal capitals have national capital agencies similar to the NCC. In the early years they tend to be powerful development corporations and transition to regional planning agencies as the metropolitan region matures.[1243]

So the problems of building Canada's capital are not unique, as shown over a century of sustained effort to develop a mature capital city in a federal state. Washington had a great plan proposed by L'Enfant in 1793, yet the American capital was a laughing-stock throughout the 19th century. It only recently completed the last museum and memorial on its Mall, over 200 years after the monumental core was originally planned and over a century after the re-start from the 1902 Senate Parks Commission. Brasilia and Nigeria's Abuja had fast starts as capital cities and are slowly maturing as regional communities. Canberra's 1912 plan was only crowned by Australia's magnificent Parliament House in 1988, and that capital city still has a long way to go before it matches the sophistication of Melbourne or Sydney.[1244]

The physical setting of Canada's capital is remarkable, with one of the great natural sites, at the confluence of three rivers and two waterfalls. The Parliament Buildings, art gallery and history museum are magnificent, but much of the remaining architecture is mediocre and uninspiring in comparison to capitals in countries with a strong design culture, such as Finland, Germany or Brazil. Confederation Boulevard is a good symbolic framework, but somehow the density of national institutions and symbolic context is not quite there yet.[1245]

The Crown's Priority: Building a National Capital that is Worthy of Canada

What should be done to build a better Canadian capital?

Better governance would help, given the interjurisdictional difficulties noted above. There does not seem to be a magic bullet, such as a federal district, that would work in Canada's capital region, just better tri-partite co-operation between the federal, Ottawa and Gatineau governments. And given the interjurisdictional conflicts and language issues across the provincial boundary, Canada needs a national capital agency more than most federal countries. It also helps to recognise that issues can be local (utilities, housing), federal (embassies; monuments) or shared (tourism), and allow appropriate leadership in each area.[1246] The NCC's 1999 *Plan for Canada's Capital* was a breakthrough in this area, clearly articulating the federal interest in planning issues. Although angry local governments have called for the National Capital Commission's abolition in the past, it remains clear that a federal agency is needed to provide leadership on these national capital issues.[1247]

Most other nation-states have higher-order objectives for their seat of government, which go beyond the quality of life desired by local residents. This situation is especially common for federal 'political capitals' such as Ottawa-Gatineau, Canberra, New Delhi, Washington, or Brasilia.[1248] These relatively new political capitals are intended to be one tool used in nation-building in a federal state. Such 'invented traditions' can be retrogressive (imperial New Delhi) or even evil, depending upon the values of the sponsoring governments – most notoriously Hitler's plans for Berlin or Mussolini's evocation of Imperial Rome. In contrast, the best capital-city design can showcase the cultural and democratic values of the sponsoring government, such as Paris' *grand projects* or the Lincoln, Jefferson and Vietnam War memorials on the Mall in Washington. Similarly, L'Enfant's plan demonstrates the clear separation of the executive and legislative branches of the US government through the relative positions of the Capitol and White House.[1249]

However, Washington or Paris may not be good models for planning Ottawa-Gatineau, not only because their sites are different, but especially because their national characters are different. Political philosophers such as Charles Taylor and Will Kymlicka have demonstrated that Canada is an extraordinarily complex nation-state, and therefore simple expressions of national identity are rarely possible. Canada is a bilingual, multi-cultural, federal state with three founding peoples (aboriginal, French and British) and the world's largest and most diverse complement of new immigrants.[1250] Building a capital city that reflects this nation is not an easy task, especially in a federation where the central government has fairly weak powers compared to the provinces and there is a history of constitutional conflict.[1251]

Canada is not a monolithic state that was peopled by a single ethnic group, which makes defining a simple and clear national identity rather difficult. This complexity can be seen as a national strength in accommodating diverse new immigrant groups, one of the most difficult tasks in the modern world.[1252] However, Canada's character means that few of the traditional nation-building tools are appropriate. We cannot promote a single language (as in France), or limit immigration to a single ethnic group, or promote the experience of compulsory military service, or mythologize patriotic wars against colonial oppressors. A bilingual, multicultural Canadian federation must work with a more limited set of nation-building tools – adapting national symbols, renaming geographic features, supporting national sports, celebrating culture and promoting shared values.[1253]

Will Kymlicka argues that combining nation-building and multiculturalism is difficult work, but not a zero-sum game, provided that we do not encourage patriotism by promoting the interests and culture of a single ethnic group. Canada is something of a model for the modern multinational state, since it is one of the world's oldest democracies, the first state to peacefully negotiate its freedom from colonial rule, and a country with a relatively good record of tolerance while accommodating a large and diverse population of new immigrants. The best approach to nation-building under these circumstances seems to be to avoid the corrosive effects of 'ethnic nationalism' and focus instead on 'civic nationalism' – promoting the shared liberal democratic values and history of the country.[1254] Unfortunately, 'civic nationalism' provides relatively few strong symbols for building a national identity or a capital city. Baldwin and Lafontaine's coalition for responsible government or the Fathers of Confederation negotiating a federal union seems a bit dull compared to storming the Bastille or the Winter Palace.[1255]

So, if the traditional nation-building symbols are less appropriate in a multi-cultural state, what strategies can we adopt for symbolic content in building a capital city? Urban planners, like doctors, might start by a commitment to "do no harm," by avoiding introducing symbols that privilege one ethnic group. The next step might be to adjust other symbolic elements to become more inclusive. The

Peace Tower replaced the Victoria Tower, the maple leaf flag replaced the Red Ensign, and the maple leaf replaced the British crown as the dominant symbol of the federal government throughout the national capital. More recently, a statue of an aboriginal guide kneeling at the feet of Samuel de Champlain's monument was moved elsewhere on Nepean Point, reducing its patronizing appearance.[1256]

Similarly, Pierre Trudeau recognized the poor symbolism from federal government buildings concentrated in Ontario. The Canadian Museum of History and huge departmental buildings in Hull are highly visible symbols of a capital city that includes Québec. Replacing common English street names in Hull not only improved regional way-finding, but it reflected the vastly changed character of the Outaouais since the Wright family's founding settlement.[1257] Similarly, the NCC's unceasing effort to promote bilingualism on both sides of the Ottawa River allows the capital city to visibly reinforce Canada's official language policies.

The next step to programming a capital that inspires pride among Canadians is to make the best use of common national symbols. This is an imperfect strategy, because many of these elements are perceived differently within the country. The armed forces are a positive focus near Confederation Square[1258] and the new War Museum. However, the "Changing of the Guard" on Parliament Hill is an 'invented tradition' that may suggest membership in a long-vanished British Empire. The Royal Canadian Mounted Police seem to be a more authentic presence, for many Anglophone Canadians, at least. The Governor General can be a positive force in nation-building, by making Rideau Hall the centre of Canadian culture during ceremonies of the Order of Canada, the G-G's Literature Awards, and similar prizes.[1259] In a more limited fashion, the national currency and postal service are celebrated by displays at the Mint, the Bank of Canada and Museum of Civilization. International sport is another nation-building tool that is clearly underutilized in Ottawa-Gatineau. It is a pity that so few national championships and national teams are seen in the national capital, in comparison to Australia's Institute of Sport for high-performance athletes in Canberra.

Perhaps the most important contribution our capital city could make could be to act as teaching machine for Canadian history and values. Public education on common histories is one of the best nation-building tools available to a multicultural state.[1260] The programming of the national cultural institutions in Ottawa-Gatineau can play an important role in reinforcing a multicultural, bilingual image for the country. In effect, the national museums are a flexible stage, where exhibits can entertain and educate visitors about the various strains of the country's past, which is the context of its present and future. The great outdoor festivals supported by the NCC – Canada Day, Winterlude and music festivals – can also play a major role here by reflecting the complex and constantly changing content of Canadian culture. Plans for more outdoor programing venues in the core area will reinforce this activity.[1261]

Flexible programming content is a good strategy for reflecting multiculturalism, but the form of the national institutions and symbols, and their setting in the capital city can also reinforce Canadian values and inspire pride. Ottawa was the right choice for the seat of government in 1857 and 1864 for political, economic and military reasons. Its location on the border between Ontario and Québec and its history as a post on the main trade route to the West were powerful symbols that addressed the French-English tensions of the day and reflected the young country's determination to span a continent.[1262]

Confederation Boulevard and the recent core area plans re-focus the major institutions around the much-abused Ottawa River. These designs tap into Canadians' strong interest in the natural environment and beautiful landscapes, without denying their urban culture and northern location.[1263] By a stroke of good luck, the site of the portage around the Chaudière Falls and the Ottawa River's names are also significant for our First

Nations. This is why Confederation Boulevard is a masterful piece of symbolic urban design, because it retroactively links the nation's three founding groups – aboriginal, French and British. It was significant that the river-side Museum of History was designed by a Métis architect, Douglas Cardinal. However, the proposed First Nations centre on Victoria Island will be an important component of the overall ensemble, to reflect the role of the aboriginal peoples in the country's history.[1264]

However, the symbolic landscape of the National Capital Region does not need to be rebuilt to incorporate every new ethnic group in the nation. The complicated relationship between the First Nations, French and British peoples is an essential element of Canadian history, and the many past accommodations between those three founding groups within one nation-state are an essential context for the multicultural present.[1265]

Politicians and planners must take care when adjusting the symbolic content of a capital city. Monuments and memorials can privilege ruling elites, undermine minority rights or reduce patriotism in other groups.[1266] Once again, the best strategy appears to switch from ethnic nationalism to civic nationalism (i.e., from "Hail to our group's great leader" to "Hooray for our collective effort to reinforce this national value").[1267] Canada's National War Memorial in Confederation Square was an early and surprisingly diverse example of this approach. Vernon March's *The Response* (1926) shows members of all Canada's armed services, including women and aboriginal soldiers, struggling for peace.[1268] More recent good examples include the Peacekeeping Monument on Confederation Boulevard and the memorial on Parliament Hill to the 'Famous Five' who fought to have women recognized as legal persons (Figures 14-1 and 14-2). The NCC's 2006

FIGURE 14-1: *Reconciliation*, **Peacekeeping Monument, Jack Harmon, 1982**
Located on Confederation Boulevard, opposite the National Gallery of Canada.
(Source: NCC, *Canada's Capital Commemoration Strategic Plan*, June 2006, p. 15)

FIGURE 14-2: *Women Are Persons*, **Barbara Peterson, 2000**
One of the few depictions of women located on Parliament Hill.
(Source: NCC *Canada's Capital Commemoration Strategic Plan*, June 2006, p. 12)

commemoration plan appears to be a good guide for future action, calling for more emphasis on the nation's core values and its intellectual, cultural and community life.[1269]

Finally, Canada's National Capital Region should be beautiful. It should connect to Canadian values by celebrating the region's remarkable landscape and by promoting excellence in the design of the public buildings, streets and public spaces in the symbolic core of the capital city. The shoddy appearance of Ottawa and Hull in 1945 could be tolerated as a wartime hardship, but it was a national embarrassment for a country that wished to take its own place in the world. Laurier, Mackenzie King, Diefenbaker and Trudeau were right to make building a more worthy capital a national priority because good urban design and attractive architecture communicate Canada's quality to international visitors. They are also a benefit that local residents can appreciate every day.

It is slow work undoing a century of damage to the Ottawa River and redeveloping declining industrial areas near Parliament Hill. The 'Crown' also needs to work closely with the 'Town' to prevent further design atrocities such as Place de Ville and Place du Portage. A good first step might be a government policy not to rent space in ugly and tall buildings that undermine the national objectives for the capital city as contained in NCC plans.

Building a capital city that is worthy of Canada is a long-term endeavour, requiring a sustained effort for perhaps a century. The important work began in the early 1950s, so the job is about half complete. The density of national institutions and visitor attractions in the symbolic core has not yet reached critical mass, and there are still many mistakes to be undone. Increasing the natural institutions around Confederation Boulevard and building new links across the Ottawa River can benefit both 'Town' and 'Crown.' These projects would make the Ottawa-Gatineau region a place with a higher quality of life for both its residents and federal workers. More importantly, it would create a Canadian capital that would inspire more pride in its citizens, by physically expressing the history and interconnection of its three founding peoples and setting the stage for celebrating the country's values and cultures.[1270] However, our national habit of abandoning the previous regime's projects[1271] makes progress difficult within the brief political cycles available.

So perhaps Andrew Cohen was correct in *The Unfinished Canadian* – our collective reluctance to finish building our national capital is a disgrace.[1272] But that doesn't mean that we should abandon our incomplete capital half-way through the project. Great progress has been made, and the potential is dazzlingly clear to anyone who has gazed at Parliament Hill from the Museum of History (Figure 14-3). Our unfinished capital, like Cohen's unfinished Canadian, is a work in progress with magnificent prospects.

Let's take a long-term view, aim high and get on with the job.

FIGURE 14-3: View of Parliament Hill from the Museum of History
(Source: NCC)

Epilogue

It was another beautiful Ottawa summer day in late June, with the brilliant sunshine and humid warmth that sometimes surprises visitors who have only heard about the world's coldest winter capital city. Our research team decided to take a break from the library and eat lunch outdoors.

We slipped across Confederation Square, passing the War Memorial, and I was once again reminded of my grandfathers at Ypres and Normandy, and my father in Korea. They all came home, but many of their generations did not. The students paused briefly at the new Tomb of the Unknown Solider, who was probably younger than any of them when he fell at Vimy Ridge.

We were looking for shade, and heard the sound of a sitar wafting up from below. The new stairs down to the Rideau Canal had been cleverly designed to act as an informal amphitheatre, and an unlikely-looking ensemble was playing South Asian music below the bridge.

The acoustics were lovely and my mind drifted – thinking of the many layers of history on this spot where the Rideau Canal met Wellington Street:

- Colonel By and Lord Dalhousie hiking down this valley to check the canal's connection to the river that was the aboriginal peoples' trade route to the west;
- the Sappers who built a bridge so strong we sat on its foundation stones almost two centuries later;
- the Shiners terrifying Upper Town residents trapped on the bridge;
- the small knot of troops keeping the Tories and Reformers from killing each other after the Stony Monday riot;
- the Fathers of Confederation, ascending from the river landing in a torchlight procession on their first visit to the city they chose as the nation's capital;
- Mackenzie King's 20-year struggle to build a memorial to the fallen of the Great War on this spot; then 100,000 people gathered for its unveiling in 1939, only a few months before many of them would head overseas for a second world war;
- the revival of the Rideau Canal, first for summer pleasure boats, then for winter skating; and
- Canada's Charter of Rights and Freedoms negotiated in the abandoned railway station opposite.

And yet, despite the weight of history at this place, the music made me think of Canada's future. Who were these musicians? One man appeared to be of South Asian descent, but he was accompanied by a francophone man and a red-haired woman, whose Gaelic complexion might have been from Scotland or the upper Ottawa Valley. After they introduced the songs in French and English, one of our graduate students, recently landed from Bangladesh, quietly explained the sources of the music, which skipped across the Indian subcontinent.

After the recital wound down, we became aware of a group of people practicing Tai Chi a little further along, at the head of the locks. The leader was softly calling out the movements in a French accent that I couldn't quite place. Vietnamese, suggested another student, bilingual from her French immersion in Ontario schools. Of course.

As we headed back, we discussed our plans for the long weekend. I was joining my extended family at our lakeside cottage near Algonquin Park. In contrast, the students from our future generation decided to join the 100,000 others who would celebrate Canada Day throughout its national capital.

Their eyes were shining the next time we met.

Cast of Characters

Adams, Thomas

Thomas Adams (1871-1940) was born in Scotland, and was a farmer, town councillor and journalist as a young man. He went on to become secretary of the Garden City Association and the founding president of Britain's Town Planning Institute. In 1914, the Commission of Conservation scored a major coup to entice him to Ottawa, then a city of 90,000, as their Town Planning Advisor. A prolific journalist and gifted political organizer, Adams sowed model planning acts across Canada.[1273] He quickly proved his worth, producing scores of articles and speeches that addressed the value of town planning and the first Canadian planning textbook.[1274] Adams remained in Ottawa for a decade, and tirelessly promoted town planning. He founded both the Civic Improvement League and the Town Planning Institute of Canada.

Thomas Adams' arrival was a strong boost for housing and social planning in Ottawa. In addition to organizing town planning, Adams prepared garden suburb plans for affordable housing in Halifax's Richmond and Hydrostone districts (1917) and Ottawa's Lindenlea (1919). He also prepared plans for new industrial towns in Temiscaming, QC (1917) and Corner Brook, NF (1923).[1275] Following his Canadian decade, Adams led the preparation of the *Regional Plan of New York and Environs* (1929), ran a British consulting practice and taught planning at Harvard and MIT.[1276]

Ahearn, Thomas

Thomas Ahearn (1855-1938) was born in LeBreton Flats of Irish parents, and was already an expert telegrapher as a teenager. Fascinated by all things electrical, he pioneered the telephone in Eastern Ontario and was the first Ottawa manager for the Bell Company. In 1882, he partnered with Warren Soper to form an engineering and contracting firm that constructed and equipped some of Canada's largest electrical works. They built a hydraulic generating station at the Chaudière Falls to provide electric street lights in downtown Ottawa, and later expanded power service throughout the city. In 1897, Ahearn and Soper illuminated the Parliament Buildings with thousands of electric lights, to celebrate Queen Victoria's Diamond Jubilee.[1277]

Ahearn and Soper formed the Ottawa Electric Railway in 1891, and won the franchise for the city for $5,000 after an American consortium failed. They added a federal contract to haul mail with streetcars connecting the post office with the CP and Canada Atlantic stations, correcting one of the major flaws in Ottawa's railway network. Ahearn and Soper started with ten electric streetcars purchased from a St. Catharines firm, but quickly decided they could build their own. The Ottawa Car Manufacturing Company sold streetcars across Canada until the 1940s. Ahearn invented special vehicles to sweep the snow off the tracks with a large rotating brush, and organized the clearing of major city streets, which were almost impassable during many winter months. He also patented a system to electrically heat streetcars by circulating hot water under the floors.[1278] Ahearn was a trendsetter in other areas, developing the first electric stove and driving the first automobile on an Ottawa street in 1899. Not surprisingly, it was an electric car.[1279]

Thomas Ahearn was an astute businessman and made a fortune with his electrical companies. He also reorganized the Ottawa Gas Company and developed suburban property along his streetcar lines through the Ottawa Land Association.[1280] He was also a pioneer in developing Canada's long-distance telephone network. Prime Minister Mackenzie King asked Ahearn to organize the broadcasting for the 1927 Diamond Jubilee of Confederation. He arranged for the Prime Minister to make the first transatlantic telephone call to England, and built a 32,000 km. telephone network to carry a simultaneous, nation-wide radio broadcast of the celebrations on Parliament Hill (Figure 8-12).

A grateful prime minister appointed Ahearn, a lifelong Liberal, as chairman of the Federal District Commission (FDC) in 1927. Although Ahearn was 72 when he took responsibility for improving Canada's capital city, he had not slowed down. The FDC's pace of activity quickly accelerated; new parkways were built, the Champlain Bridge was completed (with donations from the chairman) and the site for Confederation Square was assembled.

Although Thomas Ahearn accomplished more as FDC chairman in three years than any of his predecessors, he was replaced by new Conservative Prime Minister R.B. Bennett in 1932.

By, John

Lieutenant-Colonel John By (1783-1836)[1281] was the principal designer of the Rideau Canal, and the founder of the settlement that became Bytown and later Ottawa. He was born into a middle-class family in London and educated at the Royal Military Academy in Woolwich. By was one of the new breed of army officers who earned their positions via specialized military training and education, rather than purchasing their commissions. He was trained in artillery, surveying, finance and in the design and construction of military and civil engineering works.[1282] By was commissioned into the Royal Artillery, but quickly transferred into the Royal Engineers, where he spent his entire career. In 1802, he was posted to Lower Canada, where he built a small canal on the St. Lawrence River and built a model of Québec's fortifications. By served with some distinction under the Duke of Wellington in the war against Napoleon's armies in Spain and Portugal.

Colonel By[1283] was one of the Royal Engineers' most senior officers when he was selected in March 1826 for the challenging task of building a canal through the wilderness to connect Kingston to the Ottawa River. He returned to England in 1832 with the Rideau Canal complete and in operation, only to find he had been censured by Parliament for allegedly exceeding his budget allocations. John By died in 1836, aged 52, of a stroke and complications from the malaria he contracted while personally supervising the most difficult portions of the project.[1284] His legacy, the Rideau Canal, was declared a UNESCO World Heritage Site in 2007.[1285]

Cauchon, Noulan

Joseph-Eusèbe Noulan Cauchon (1872-1935) had an unusual background among the founders of the Canadian planning profession. He was born in Ville de Québec, the son of an Irish mother and a French-Canadian politician, journalist and entrepreneur. His father, Joseph-Édouard Cauchon, was the former mayor of Québec and was Speaker of the Canadian Senate when Noulan was born.[1286] Noulan's stepmother, Emma LeMoine, was part of a prominent Québec family with French, English and Scots background. Thus, Noulan grew up in a family where bilingualism and biculturalism were the norm, and politics and the press were ever-present.[1287]

Cauchon received a classical French-Canadian education in Manitoba and Québec, but pursued a non-traditional career as a railroad surveyor and engineer. He apprenticed with the Canadian Pacific Railroad, first as a surveyor, then draftsman and finally as an assistant engineer. Noulan left the CPR after 20 years, to become an assistant engineer with the Board of Railway Commissioners of Ottawa in 1908. Two years later, Cauchon left the civil service to establish a consulting engineering practice with J.E. Haycock that would be his principal employment base for the next quarter century. He prepared railway and infrastructure plans for Chicoutimi, Hamilton, London, Montréal and St. Catherines and might have enjoyed a quiet professional career as a consulting engineer, except that he developed an interest in town planning during the early years of his new firm.[1288]

Cauchon was a member of the organizing committee and a founding member of both the Civic Improvement League of Canada (CIL) and the Town Planning Institute of Canada (TPIC). He was the chairman of the Ottawa Town Planning Commission (OTPC) from its inception in 1921 to 1935, and was twice elected president of the TPIC (1924-6). It was a rare month in the 1920s when Cauchon's opinion on planning issues could not be found in the local or national press. While his role on the OTPC was focused on small-scale local issues, his national work included unusual proposals for more esoteric issues such as new canals, hexagonal planning and resettlement of veterans. Although he passed away at the nadir of Canadian planning, Cauchon's City Scientific ideas influenced the early evolution of the profession in Canada and the redevelopment of the national capital after 1945.[1289]

Gray, Col. John H.

John Hamilton Gray (1814-1889) was born in Bermuda, educated in Nova Scotia and settled in Saint John, New Brunswick, where he was a successful lawyer and militia commander. In 1849, he was one of the first proponents of a federal union of the BNA colonies, and Gray entered politics the next year. He was briefly elected NB premier in 1856-7, and represented the province at the 1864 Charlottetown and Québec confederation conferences.[1290]

Gray was not a prominent negotiator at the Confederation conferences, but he may have been the only member who carefully considered the governance arrangements for the new country's capital city. His 1872 book contains little original material, but his discussion of the Confederation delegates' rationale for Ottawa's designation as the seat of the new federal government is unique in the contemporary literature.[1291]

Gray may not have been a great statesman, but he was a good lawyer, and he highlighted the potential and administrative problems that the federation's capital city might encounter:

> ... it is apparent that at the time of the Convention one mistake occurred: no provision was made for creating a federal district for the capital, and withdrawing it from the exclusive control of the local legislature of one of the Provinces. ... The expenses incident to its civic control must necessarily be far greater than would devolve upon it if merely an ordinary municipality. It is no answer to say that the increased value in property is sufficient consideration for the increased burden put upon the inhabitants. That does not meet the question. They may not choose to accept the responsibility; and the Dominion Parliament, under confederation, has no power to legislate upon the matter.[1292]

Gray then examined the American legislation and operation of Washington, D.C. He recommended a federal district for Ottawa, including territory from both Ontario and Québec. His proposal might have been possible in 1864 or even 1872, before provincial jealousies arose. The federal district proposal continued to be an idea that intrigued public administration scholars for the next century, including William Lyon Mackenzie King. However, it appears to be a concept that can only be implemented early in the history of a federal capital city.[1293]

John Gray was one of New Brunswick's strongest advocates for Confederation, crossing party lines to support Liberal Premier Leonard Tilley's difficult campaign for its ratification. Gray was elected MP to the first federal Parliament, but he was not brought into the Cabinet. Instead, Sir John A. Macdonald appointed him to the British Columbia Supreme Court in 1873, where he distinguished himself with his defence of the rights of Chinese immigrants and his scholarship on the Canada/Alaska boundary dispute.

Gréber, Jacques Henri-Auguste

Jacques Henri-Auguste Gréber (1882-1962) was born into an artistic family in Paris and admitted into architecture at the *École des Beaux Arts* in 1901.[1294] He was a fine student, winning several prizes during the arduous training at the *École*. On his graduation in 1909, he missed the Rome Prize for architecture, which changed the direction of his career. Instead of spending years in Rome studying classical architecture, he left for the United States, where American architects who had trained at the École immediately engaged his talents to design *jardins á la française* for the large houses they built in New England.

Gréber quickly developed a reputation as a landscape architect and collaborated with Horace Trumbauer of Philadelphia on mansions in Newport, Rhode Island and Elkinspark, Pennsylvania. Gréber's work with Trumbauer helped him win his first major commissions in urban design, the 1917 Fairmount Parkway in Philadelphia. It is a diagonal avenue cut through William Penn's 1682 grid plan from the art museum to city hall.[1295] While completing the parkway, Gréber was commissioned by the French government to make a systematic study of American construction practices. Characteristically, he expanded the study to include architecture, housing, landscape architecture and urban design. It became his influential book, *L'Architecture aux États-Unis*.[1296]

Gréber returned to France in 1919. The book and his winning plans for the land released by the removal of the Paris fortifications secured his reputation as one of France's leading urban designers. He was appointed to the faculty of the Institut d'urbanisme in Paris, and took a leading role in the reconstruction and expansion of French cities between the wars. Gréber prepared plans for Lille (1923), Belfort (1925), Marseilles (1930-37), Abbeville (1932) and Rouen (1940) among many others. He designed two Parisian garden suburbs, numerous gardens and parks, and the 1937 World's Fair grounds.[1297] Gréber also maintained his North American connections as consultant to Philadelphia, the 1939 New York World's Fair and lecturer at the Université de Montréal.[1298]

As a landscape architect, Gréber designed formal gardens across Europe, won competitions for public parks and designed six American war cemeteries in France, including Belleau Woods and the Argonne.

During the 1920s, his architecture changed from his Beaux-Arts training, seen in the Rodin Museum (1926-9, with Paul Cret),[1299] to a classically-proportioned Modern style, most notably in the *École de plein air* at Roubaix, and the Esso Building at *La Défense* (1962, with his son, Pierre Gréber).[1300] Gréber's multidisciplinary expertise was recognized by election to the Legion of Honour and presidency of the French societies for planning and landscape architecture during his career.

In the post-World War II period, Gréber's most prominent commission was the plan for Canada's capital. However, he also completed plans for the reconstruction of Rouen, Ville de Québec (with Édouard Fiset) and the Montréal region.[1301]

When Jacques Gréber died in 1962, *La Vie Urbaine* mourned him as "*le plus grand des urbanistes français.*"[1302] Yet within two decades he was practically forgotten in France, despite his prodigious output as an architect, planner, landscape architect and educator over a career spanning a half-century.[1303]

Gordon, Ishbel Maria
(Marchioness of Aberdeen and Temair)

Ishbel Maria Gordon, Marchioness of Aberdeen and Temair (1857-1939), was a reformer and political activist. She married the Earl of Aberdeen in 1877, and they melded their Presbyterian faith with Liberal politics and a social conscience. British Prime Minister W.E. Gladstone appointed the Earl as Lord Lieutenant of Ireland in 1886, and Lady Aberdeen immersed herself into Irish politics and social issues. She arranged immediate and effective action on the famine, promoted Irish crafts and supported Home Rule.

Lady Aberdeen toured Canada in 1890, to examine conditions for immigrants and recharge after her Irish endeavours. Her trip journal was serialized and then published as the book, *Through Canada with a Kodak*.[1304] While the earl was Governor-General of Canada (1893-1898), Lady Aberdeen was a force for social reform, founding the National Council of Women and the Victorian Order of Nurses.[1305]

The Aberdeens were intensely involved in Canadian politics in the late 19th century, using their prestige to attack religious and ethnic bigotry and support the reforms of new Liberal Prime Minister Wilfrid Laurier. Lady Aberdeen disliked Ottawa, and had her own brush with the capital's atrocious roads when she almost drowned after her ponies slipped and threw her carriage into the swollen Gatineau River.[1306] However, her interest in town planning for Ottawa appears to have evolved from a broader interest in social reform and a desire for improving the capital so that it would be a source of pride for Canadians.[1307]

Head, Sir Edmund

Sir Edmund Walker Head (1805-1868) was one of the most successful colonial administrators to serve in British North America. He was educated at Oriel College, Oxford, receiving a first-class degree in classics and toured Europe before returning to lecture at Merton College after 1830. He continued to travel widely, to write on public issues and served on Britain's Poor Law Commission from 1836-47.[1308]

Edmund Head was appointed Lieutenant Governor of New Brunswick in 1848, where he managed the successful transition to responsible government. While in Fredericton, he continued his scholarly activities, publishing books on European painting, and promoted public education, particularly in the reorganization of King's College (UNB). His interest in railways and a larger federation in British North America (BNA) made him an obvious choice to succeed Lord Elgin as BNA Governor-General in 1854. Elgin had carefully nurtured the responsible government initiated by Robert Baldwin and Louis-Hippolyte Lafontaine, but there were still many tensions within the United Province of Canada. Head arrived in Canada in 1854, to find that the divided legislature could not agree on a location for his seat of government, so the capital alternated between Québec and Toronto.[1309]

After the government of Sir Allan McNabb collapsed, Head worked closely with emerging leader John A. Macdonald to facilitate coalitions with first E.P. Taché and then Georges-Étienne Cartier. The seat of government deadlock was a symptom of the difficult partisan politics of the era, with Lower Canada concerned about losing its control of the combined legislature (and French culture) because the population of Upper Canada grew rapidly in the 1850s. The Reformers in Upper Canada, led by George Brown, demanded "representation by population" and opposed Macdonald and Cartier's coalition at every turn. Head carefully navigated this political swamp for some years, but the seat-of-government issue continued to paralyze the legislature, with a toxic mixture of civic, regional and cultural differences. Head's proposal that the rival cities submit their case to Queen Victoria for arbitration defused the issue temporarily. Careful archival research by David Knight demonstrated that Head's confidential memorandum recommending Ottawa was the crucial element of the decision. The Governor General sailed to London to ensure that his recommendation was accepted.[1310]

The capital city issue continued to plague the Macdonald-Cartier administration, since the Legislature refused to accept the choice which Head had orchestrated. After Macdonald's government was defeated, George Brown formed a ministry which also collapsed. Controversy erupted when Head refused dissolution of the Legislature to Brown. Instead, Cartier and Macdonald regained the government with the infamous "double shuffle." Head endured the enmity of the Reformers, and Brown's *Globe*, until his administration ended in 1861.[1311]

Head's connections with Canada continued after his return to Britain, and he was elected the governor of the Hudson's Bay Company in 1863. He was active in London's literary circles, receiving honourary degrees from Oxford and Cambridge, before his sudden death in 1868.

King, William Lyon Mackenzie

William Lyon Mackenzie King, (1874-1950) was Canada's longest-serving prime minister, holding that office for most of the period from 1921 to 1948. He was the grandson of William Lyon Mackenzie, leader of the 1837 rebellion in Upper Canada.[1312]

Mackenzie King was Canada's best-educated prime minister, and certainly its most widely travelled when he came to power in 1921. He held arts and law degrees from the University of Toronto, studied political economy at the University of Chicago and took his doctorate in economics at Harvard.[1313] King spent 1899-1900 in Europe, as part of his doctoral studies, and returned frequently to the continent.[1314] Prior to entering the federal Cabinet as Minister of Labour in 1909, Prime Minister Sir Wilfrid Laurier sent King on a round-the-world tour. King filled his diary with detailed observations on the architecture, landscape and cities of the countries he visited, and often called upon leading reformers during his travels.[1315]

Unlike previous prime ministers, King had a strong personal interest in town planning as a result of education and travel. While a graduate student at the University of Chicago, he was an intern at Jane Addams' pioneering university settlement house, where he was exposed to early social planning advocates.[1316] King spent 1899 in London, when Ebenezer Howard's Garden City was promoted in social reform circles. There was some overlap between British town planning advocates and settlement house leaders at that time, with Henrietta Barnett and Earl Grey's involvement in settlement houses, Hampstead Garden Suburb and Letchworth.[1317] Although King's main professional interest was labour relations, he regarded town planning as a component of an overall program for social reform, devoting several sections to planning in his 1918 book, *Industry and Humanity*.[1318]

King's interest in planning was complemented by a strong personal commitment to Ottawa's development as a capital worthy of the growing nation. As prime minister, he followed in Laurier's footsteps,[1319] personally managing almost every planning and design proposal of the federal government prior to 1950. Landscape planning was also an element in King's peculiar personal life, as he devoted his limited financial resources to enlarging his country estate in the Gatineau Hills, siting relics from demolished Ottawa buildings within its grounds.[1320]

King retired to his cottage in 1948, but kept a close watch on national planning. He contributed the foreword to the 1950 *Plan for the National Capital*, which was tabled in Parliament in 1950, just before he died. King left his country estate to the nation, and its farmhouse is now the official residence of the Speaker of the House of Commons. King's contribution to the planning of the Canada's capital is acknowledged as the first infrastructure element of the 1950 plan, the Mackenzie King Bridge across the Rideau Canal.

McKay, Thomas

Thomas McKay's (1792-1855) reputation as a master mason and honest businessman contributed to his rise from humble roots to become one of Bytown's leading citizens. He arrived in Montréal from his native Scotland in 1817 and found employment as a mason and then contractor on the Lachine Canal (1821-25) and Fort Lennox at Île aux Noix (1821-26). Colonel By brought him to Wrightstown on his first trip in 1826, and McKay promptly won contracts to build two spans of the Gatineau Bridge, the Commissariat Building (1827) and the tier of eight locks for the entrance to the

Rideau Canal. He replaced other contractors who failed at Hartwell's locks and the difficult Hog's Back falls.[1323]

McKay brought his family to Bytown in 1827 and shrewdly invested his canal profits in the local area. He bought property near the Rideau Falls, building a flour mill, distillery, cloth mill and sawmills that used the most modern technology. McKay also laid out the village of New Edinburgh on adjacent lands for his managers and workers. He invested in the region's first railroad, the Bytown and Prescott, to ensure that it would serve his village and industrial complex.

Thomas McKay also held important public offices, appointed to the earliest Bytown Council in 1828 and as a magistrate in 1833. He was elected as a Conservative to the provincial assembly from 1834 until 1841, and then appointed to the Legislative Council until his death. In 1842, McKay was also elected as the first Warden of the Dalhousie District (late Carleton County).

Thomas McKay designed and built Rideau Hall in 1838 as his estate north of New Edinburgh. It was leased by the Government of Canada as the Governor-General's residence in 1865 and purchased in 1868. McKay also designed and built a fine stone house on the cliff above the Ottawa River for his daughter Annie Mackinnon. Sir John A. Macdonald purchased Earnscliffe in 1882, and it later became the residence of the British Ambassador. The remainder of McKay's estate was developed as the suburb of Rockcliffe Park by his son-in-law, Thomas Keefer.[1324]

Meredith, Colborne Powell

Colborne Powell Meredith (1874-1967) had impeccable credentials as a member of English Canada's elite. His mother was Fanny Jarvis, a member of a prominent Toronto family, and his father was Edmund Allen Meredith, first Under-Secretary of State for the Dominion of Canada.[1321] Coly Meredith grew up in Ottawa and unlike his parents, he appreciated the city. He apprenticed as an architect in Frank Darling's Toronto office and returned to Ottawa to open his own practice. Meredith designed the former Murphy Gamble department store on Sparks Street and acted as the local architect for large commissions like Union Station.

In 1910, Meredith was young, aggressive and well-connected. Sir Wilfrid Laurier appointed Meredith to the Ottawa Improvement Commission despite his Conservative background, perhaps because he was active in the executive of the Ontario Architectural Association and the Royal Architectural Institute of Canada.[1322] After his attempt to obtain the consulting contract for the Federal Plan Commission failed, Meredith withdrew from architectural practice and immersed himself in the war effort. His last known planning and design project was Camp Petawawa, the large military base in the Upper Ottawa Valley.

Ramsay, George (9th Earl of Dalhousie)

George Ramsay, 9th Earl of Dalhousie (1770-1838) was a Scottish nobleman, educated at the University of Edinburgh. His family was not wealthy, and he embarked upon a military career at the age of 18. Young Ramsay served in the West Indies, Ireland, the Netherlands, Egypt and Gibraltar before joining the Duke of Wellington's army in Spain in 1812. Dalhousie was one of the few hereditary peers to have a respectable career as a general officer at the time, commanding the 7th Division at major battles in Vitoria, Spain and Toulouse, France from 1812-14, with solid, but not stellar results.[1325]

Dalhousie began a career as a colonial administrator after the Napoleonic wars, with a first appointment as Lieutenant Governor of Nova Scotia from 1816-1820. Halifax was a good fit with Dalhousie's aristocratic background and temperament. He was energetic, fit and accustomed to being obeyed after 28 years in the army. Nova Scotia's Scottish population and the large military presence in Halifax must have also been comfortable. Dalhousie attempted reforms in settlement policy, agriculture and education, founding a non-denominational college that would later bear his name.[1326]

Dalhousie was appointed Governor-in-Chief of British North America in 1820, following the untimely death of the Duke of Richmond. This position combined the roles of civil governor of Lower and Upper Canada, and military commander for a set of colonies that were nearly captured by the United States in a war that ended only five years before. Dalhousie was effective in his military role, touring the frontiers and arranging for new fortifications. He had less success as a civilian administrator. Lord Dalhousie's authoritarian manner aggravated the Canadian politicians in Lower Canada led by Louis Joseph Pappineau. He was also hostile to absentee land speculators in Upper Canada.[1327]

Lord Dalhousie left Québec in 1828, facing a cloud of civil opposition to his rule. He was appointed military commander in chief of India at age 58, but his health failed in the heat of the subcontinent. He returned to Scotland in 1832, spending his final years at his beloved Dalhousie Castle.

Todd, Frederick Gage

Frederick Gage Todd (1876-1948) became Canada's first resident landscape architect when he established an office in Montréal in 1900. A native of Concord, NH, Todd studied at the University of Massachusetts.[1328] From 1896-1900, he worked in the famous Olmsted office in Brookline, MA. Although Frederick Law Olmsted, Sr. retired due to health problems in 1895, Todd was exposed to outstanding landscape architects during his apprenticeship, including John C. Olmsted, Charles Eliot and Frederick Law Olmsted, Jr.[1329] The office was then implementing the remarkable "Emerald Necklace" regional parks system for Boston and had ongoing working with Mount Royal Park in Montréal, first planned by Olmsted Sr. in 1871.[1330]

When Todd opened the Montréal office, he started with a variety of local clients from the Olmsted firm, Mount Royal Park and Trinity College, Toronto.[1331] He designed parks across Canada in St. Johns (Bowring Park); Québec (Plains of Abraham); Montréal (St. Helen's Island); Winnipeg (Assiniboine Park) and Regina (Wascana).[1332] Todd was a founding member of the Town Planning Institute of Canada and designed attractive garden suburbs, such as Montréal's Town of Mount Royal and Shaughnessy Heights, Vancouver.[1333] One can only wonder how much better the OIC's parks system might have been had Todd been the consulting landscape architect and planner from 1903 until its successor, the Federal District Commission, hired its first designer in the mid-1930s.[1334]

Todd's only built legacy in Ottawa, Macdonald Gardens, is neglected and almost unknown today. Fortunately, Todd's landscape and belvedere have survived and the hospital buildings that bordered the park have been renovated into apartments and townhouses.

Wright, Philemon

Philemon Wright (1760-1839) was born in Woburn, near Boston, Massachusetts. He was the fifth child in a family that had been one of the region's earliest settlers 140 years before. His family had been farmers in the area for over a century, but good land was in short supply in New England in the late 18th century. Although Philemon had served for two years with the rebel forces in the Revolutionary War, he decided to seek a new homestead in Canada when the lands were opened to American settlers in the late 1790s. He was the founder of the Township of Hull, which is now the core of Gatineau.

Wright would have been considered a good candidate to receive land grants compared to other speculators, because he was an experienced farmer, had some capital, and a strong desire to build a community. He was a popular leader with a vision for an agricultural utopia for his settlers, but somewhat inept as an entrepreneur. His company, Philemon Wright and Sons, tried to control all commerce near the Chaudière, but flirted with bankruptcy several times. The family's extensive land holdings and restrictive policies showed in the development of the lands on the north shore of the river.

Wright wielded most of the offices in Hull Township over the years. He was the original justice of the peace, (followed by his sons) and was elected to the House of Assembly for Lower Canada from 1830-34. Wright was a captain of the Argenteuil militia, but tried to keep his family out of the War of 1812. As his settlement prospered, he became a favourite host for visiting governors and other important tourists in the 1820s and 1830s.

Philemon Wright passed the business to his sons Tiberius (1787-1841) and Ruggles (1791-1863), but neither shared his passion for agriculture. Tiberius' early death split the family, after his heirs launched lawsuits against Ruggles for control of the assets. Tiberius' son Alonzo (1821-1894) became a gentleman farmer and popular politician, representing the riding of Ottawa (most of Hull Township) in the Canadian Parliament from 1863-1891 for John A. Macdonald's Liberal-Conservative Party. After Alonzo's death, the riding was re-named Wright in his family's honour from 1896-1949, before being re-christened Gatineau. The Wright family's name disappeared from the local business scene in the late 19th century, after their lumber interests were bought by E. Eddy and the Gilmour family.[1335]

Bibliographic Essay

Research sources for investigating the planning and development of Canada's capital region have become much richer since 1980, so this essay provides a brief overview of the scholarly landscape. A bibliography of works consulted for this study runs to over 100 pages and is available for online searching at www.TownAndCrown.ca.

Gilbert Stelter's *The Urban Past* was the best Canadian urban history bibliography, while the National Capital Commission's *Bibliography of the History and Heritage of the National Capital Region* is the best guide to the archival sources and literature prior to 1978. David Hulchanski's *Canadian Town Planning and Housing* (Toronto Centre for Urban and Community Studies, 1978-79) is the best bibliography for the early literature on Canadian planning movement.

Primary Sources

The collections of Library and Archives Canada (LAC) contain the widest coverage of material relating to the region's role as the national capital. The most important collections are the papers of William Lyon Mackenzie King (MG 26 J1, J2), Canada's longest serving prime minister and an active participant in the shaping of the national capital for the entire first half of the 20th century. King's papers are so extensive that George Henderson's *W.L. Mackenzie King: A bibliography and research guide* (Toronto 1998) is a valuable introduction to the collections. The official biography volumes by Dawson, Neatby and Pickersgill (Toronto 1958, 1970, 1973, 1976) deliberately omit King's interests in the capital to accommodate his career as a politician and statesman, but his involvement is amply documented in thousands of letters, memoranda and reports in the official papers. King's personal opinions on capital city issues are most clearly revealed in his remarkable diary (MG 26 J6). We spent many fruitful months reading this diary, which is now available online. King's personal library is integrated with the National Library collection, but individual items may be retrieved from the catalogue to view his pencilled marginal notes. A smaller selection of volumes remain intact in King's study in Laurier House, including a presentation volume of model photographs of from 1950 *Plan for the National Capital*, which remains on the coffee table beside his reading chair.

The federal agencies directly responsible for capital city issues reported to the prime minister's office during most of the 19th and 20th centuries, so the papers of other activist prime ministers were also important sources, especially Macdonald (MG 26 A); Laurier (MG 26 G); Borden (MG 26 H); St. Laurent (MG 26 L) and Diefenbaker (MG 26 M). Parliamentary debates relating to capital city issues may be retrieved from the indexed editions of *Hansard* in the LAC main reading room.

Useful collections of private papers included those of Edward Bennett (Art Institute of Chicago, 1973.1), the Bronson family (LAC MG 28 III 26), Daniel Burnham (Art Institute of Chicago, 1943.1), Noulan Cauchon (LAC MG 30 C105), Fred Cook (LAC MG 20 C12), Wilfrid Eggleston (LAC MG 30 D282), the Freiman family (LAC MG 30 A82), H.P. Hill (LAC MG 24 I9), C.P. Meredith (LAC MG 29 E62), Olmsted Associates (US Library of Congress, Manuscript Division), Oswald Parent (ANQ-O), Horace Seymour (LAC MG 30 B93), Gordon Stephenson (U Liverpool D307), Eric Thrift (Queen's U. Archives), Charlotte Whitton (LAC MG 30 E256), and Ruggles Wright (LAC MG24 D8). The biographies of many key actors can be consulted in the *Dictionary of Canadian Biography*, now available over the Internet.

The diaries and published memoirs of people who were engaged in the capital region were also useful, especially Samuel de Champlain's *Des Sauvages* (1603), *Les Voyages du Sieur de Champlain* (1613) and *Voyages et Descouvertures faites en la Nouvelle France* (1619) (Champlain Society reprints 1922-36). David Fischer's *Champlain's Dream* (Knopf 2008) has the most authoritative discussion of Champlain's papers. Other valuable accounts included Philemon Wright's "Account of the First Settlement of the Township of Hull" (LAC MG24 D8: 136), Lord Dalhousie's *Journals* 1816-1828 (Oberon 1978,1981, 1982), John MacTaggart's *Three Years in Canada*, (Coulbourn 1829), Richard Scott's *Recollections of Bytown* (Mortimer 1911), J.H. Gray's *Confederation* (Copp Clark 1872); Frances Moncks' *My Canadian Leaves* (Bentley 1891) and Lord and Lady Aberdeen's *We Twa'* (Collins 1925) and *The Canadian Journal of Lady Aberdeen* (Champlain Society 1960).

Government Documents

The maps and drawings prepared by various government agencies are important primary sources for study of the development of the region. The LAC's National Map Collection (NMC) is a comprehensive collection that is strong for both sides of the Ottawa River. Some of the more popular plan drawings are available on the Internet, but the complete collection is readily accessible on microfiche at the LAC's building in Ottawa. The three volumes of the *Historical Atlas of Canada* (Toronto 1987, 1991, 1993) summarize much historical research in cartographic form, with especially valuable information on aboriginal peoples in Vol. 1. Many important maps are reproduced in Hayes' *Historical Atlas of Canada* (Douglas & McIntyre 2002) and Gentilcore & Head's *Ontario's History in Maps* (Toronto 1984).

The papers of the key federal agencies are also at the LAC. The Ottawa Improvement Commission (OIC, 1899-1927), the Federal District Commission (FDC, 1927-1959), and the National Capital Commission (NCC, 1959-) are in LAC RG 34. Some key OIC papers are with the Department of Finance records (LAC RG 19: 551). The Department of Public Works and its successors are in LAC RG 11, summarized in Douglas Owram's *Building for Canadians* (DPW 1979). Many other pre-Confederation government documents are available over the Internet through Early Canadiana Online (ECO) and the collections of the Champlain Society. The texts of Lord Dorchester's 1789 model town planning regulations are available in ECO as J. Williams "Rules and Regulations for the conduct of the Land Office Department" (Québec 1789), and their drawings are reproduced in *Ontario's History in Maps*.

The reports, minutes and briefs of several national commissions are valuable resources, especially the Advisory Committee on Reconstruction (1944), the joint parliamentary committees on the national capital (1944, 1956, 1976) and the Royal Commission on Bilingualism and Biculturalism (1969).

The largest collections of local primary sources are at the City of Ottawa Archives and Centre Régional d'archives de l'Outaouais (CRAO). The municipal council minutes and reports are collected at these locations, along with the papers of key local planning and development agencies. Michael Newton's *Lower Town Ottawa* (NCC 1979, 1980) reproduces many primary sources for Bytown.

Noulan Cauchon's papers (LAC MG 30 C105) contain the best overview of the work of the Ottawa Town Planning Commission, since its plans were lost in a 1931 fire at Ottawa City Hall. Research on the development of Hull is hampered by the loss of municipal documents after its city hall was destroyed by fire in 1900 and 1970. Municipal and regional planning departments maintained collections of background studies and consultant reports in the past, but these small libraries appear to have been casualties of the many government restructurings since 1970. The last to go was the National Capital Commission's library, which had the most comprehensive collection of planning studies and reports.

Comprehensive urban and regional plans began to appear in the 20th century. The key federal reports were Frederick Todd's *Report to the Ottawa Improvement Commissioners* (1903), Edward Bennett's *Report of the Federal Plan Commission on a General Plan for the Cities of Ottawa and Hull* (1916) and Jacques Gréber's *Plan for the National Capital* (1950). These plans are available online at www.TownAndCrown.ca. More recently, the *Greenbelt Master Plan* (1996) and *Plan for Canada's Capital* (1999) marked major shifts in policy. The most influential regional and local plans may be the 1974 Regional Municipality of Ottawa-Carleton *Official Plan*, the Communité Regional de l' Outaouais' 1977 *Schema D'amenagement du Territoire* and the 2003 City of Ottawa *Official Plan*.

Professional historians from Parks Canada prepare detailed local histories for National Historic Sites. These reports are available for review at the Parks Canada headquarters in Gatineau. At a smaller scale, Parks Canada's Federal Heritage Buildings Review Office (FHBRO) has a library of detailed research reports for historic buildings owned by the Canadian government. At the local level, heritage district studies provide neighbourhood-scale histories prepared by professional researchers. They are available for several older districts in Gatineau and Ottawa, from the municipal government heritage offices. The local governments also maintain some historical background on designated heritage buildings, although the quality of the information is variable.

Books and Journals

The political history of the selection of Ottawa as capital of the United Canadas is thoroughly analyzed in David Knight's *Choosing Canada's Capital* (Carleton 1991). Surprisingly, the only history of Canada's capital is Wilfrid Eggleston's *The Queen's Choice* (Queen's Printer 1961). Although superbly written, it lacks even a single reference to its sources, so researchers must consult his papers at the LAC. The NCC published an in-house history to mark its centenary (Gyton, *A Capital for Canadians*, 1999).

Although capital city planning history is neglected in Canada, it is a significant international topic, addressed in Slack and Chattopadhyay's *Finance and Governance of Capital Cities in Federal Systems* (McGill-Queen's 2010), Lawrence Vale's *Architecture Power and National Identity* (Routledge 2008), David Gordon's *Planning Twentieth Century Capital Cities* (Routledge 2006), Carola Hein's *The Capital of Europe* (Pergamon 2005), Taylor et al.'s *Capital Cities: International Perspectives* (Carleton 1993), and Donald Rowat's *Government of Federal Capitals* (Toronto 1973). Significant regional comparisons can be found in Thomas Hall's *Planning Europe's Capital Cities* (Spon 1997) and Arturo Almandoz's *Planning Latin America's Capital Cities* (Routledge 2002).

The capital cities of other federal nations typically have multiple histories in print. For Washington examples, see Gutheim and Lee's *Worthy of the Nation* (Johns Hopkins 2006) and John Rep's *Monumental Washington* (Princeton 1967). The Australian capital's planning history is the topic of several books, including Paul Reid's *Canberra Following Griffin* (Australia Archives 2002) and John Reps' *Canberra 1912* (Melbourne 1997). For New Delhi, see Andreas Volwahsen's *Imperial Delhi* (Prestel 2004) or Robert Irving's *Indian Summer: Lutyens, Baker and Imperial Delhi* (Yale UP 1981).

The best urban history of Ottawa is John Taylor's *Ottawa: An Illustrated History* (Lorimer 1986), which focuses on local governments and social history on the Ontario side of the river. Chad Gaffield's *History of the Outaouais* (Laval 1997) is probably the most comprehensive volume on the Québec region, again focusing on social history and local politics. Chattopadhyay and Paquet's *The Unimagined Canadian Capital* (Invenire 2011) is a useful collection of essays on governing the federal capital region. Caroline Andrew's chapters in Gaffield and Chattopadhyay and Paquet are the best overviews of local government in the region. The social history of the capital in the late 19th century is superbly documented in Sandra Gwyn's *The Private Capital* (McClelland and Stewart 1984), while Margaret Macmillan et al. address the social and landscape history of Rideau Hall in *Canada's House* (Knopf 2004).

Several specialist volumes illustrate important topics in the National Capital Region, most notably Carolyn Young's *The Glory of Ottawa: Canada's First Parliament Buildings* (McGill-Queen's 1995) and Janet Wright's *Crown Assets* (Toronto 1997) which both place the architectural histories of federal buildings in a larger context, using approaches grounded in art history. Similarly, Robert Leggett's *Rideau Waterway* (Toronto 1986) and *Ottawa Waterway* (Toronto 1975) are based on engineering history.

Municipal infrastructure and some early urban development issues are systematically addressed in Lucien Brault's *Ottawa, Old and New* (Ottawa 1946); *Hull 1800-1950* (Ottawa 1950) and *Links Between Two Cities* (Hull and Ottawa 1989). A special issue of *Urban History Review* (8:1 1979) focuses on difficult fire, disease and water problems in the late 19th and early 20th centuries. Bob McKeown's *Ottawa's streetcars* (Railfare 2006) addresses the early history of Ottawa transit, while the best analysis of the demise of the streetcars is D. Davis, "A Capital Crime?" in Keshen and St-Onge's *Construire une capitale* (Acte 2001).

The timber trade, lumber and other woods-based industries have a key role in the economic history of the Ottawa Valley. Arthur Lower's research on these subjects is still relevant, especially *The North American Assault on the Canadian Forest* (Ryerson 1938) and *Great Britain's Woodyard* (McGill-Queen's 1973). Social history in this era is illustrated by three articles by Michael Cross: "The Age of Gentility" (*CHA Historical Papers*, 1967); "The Shiner's War" (*Canadian Historical Review* 54 1973) and "Stony Monday, 1849" (*Ontario History* 63:4 1971).

National institutions are now attracting their own histories, including D. Ord, *The National Gallery of Canada* (McGill-Queen's 2003); R. Hubbard, *Rideau Hall* (McGill-Queen's 1977) and Sarah Jennings, *Art and Politics: The History of the National Arts Centre* (Dundurn 2009). The history of other theatres in Ottawa-Gatineau is illustrated in Alain Miguelez' *A Theatre Near You* (Penumbra 2004).

The Ottawa Room at the central branch of the Ottawa Library and the Centre Régional d'Archives de l'Outaouais (CRAO) maintain collections of local histories for towns, villages and neighbourhoods. Other local publication series are sponsored by Société d'Histoire de l'Outaouais, the Gatineau Valley Historical Society and the Ottawa Historical Society. Bruce Elliot's *The City Beyond* (Nepean 1991) is the best of these local studies, combining thorough scholarship with excellent illustrations. Phil Jenkins' *An acre of time*: (Macfarlane Walter & Ross 1996) is perhaps the most innovative approach, looking at the histories of a single acre of LeBreton Flats over thousands of years.

Valuable resources for the rural areas include the *Illustrated Historical Atlas of the County of Carleton* (Belden 1879), A. de Barbezieux, *Histoire de la province Ecclésiastique d'Ottawa et de la Colonisation dans la vallée de l'Ottawa* (Impr. d'Ottawa 1897) and H. and O. Walker's *Carleton Saga* (Carleton County 1968).

John Grodzinski's *The War of 1812: An annotated bibliography* (Routledge 2008) is a good guide to the region's military history in the first half of the 19th century. The revised edition of Mackay Hitsman's *The Incredible War of 1812: A military history* (Robin Brass Studio 1999) is a fine Canadian perspective on the war that influenced the location of Canada's capital city. Jon Latimer's *1812: War with America* (Harvard 2007) is a good general history from the British perspective. C.P. Stacey's research is perhaps the most influential among the military histories that affected the development of the national capital, including "The Myth of the Unguarded Frontier, 1815-1871," *American Historical Review* 41:1 (1950); "An American Plan for a Canadian Campaign," *American Historical Review* 46:2 (1941), and "Fenianism and the Rise of National Feeling in Canada at the Time of Confederation," *Canadian Historical Review* 13:3 (1931). The key document that advocated the construction of the Rideau Canal was the 1825 Smyth report to the Duke of Wellington, available at the National Library on microfilm. George Raudzens' *The British Ordnance Office and Canada's Canals* (Wilfrid Laurier 1979) covers the construction of the canals and the influence of the Ordnance on Bytown.

Newspapers

The *Perth Courier* covered some Bytown issues before the 1836 establishment of the settlement's first newspaper, the *Independent and Farmer's Advocate*, which continued as the *Bytown Gazette* until 1845. The *Packet* began in 1845, and has been in continuous publication as the *Citizen* since 1851. There were many small French language newspapers in the 19th century, and *Le Droit* has continued since 1913. The *Ottawa Journal* (1885-1980) was a second major English daily, which was reliably Conservative in its politics through most of the 20th century. The *Citizen* was usually the Liberal paper until the 1990s, when its editorial politics took a sharp turn to the right.

The *Globe* (1844-) is a leading Toronto daily that established national editions in the 1970s as *The Globe and Mail*. Its complete run is searchable online, which makes it a valuable research tool. Many small Ontario newspapers were searchable online through the late, lamented *Cold North Wind* service, which was swallowed by Google in 2008 and disappeared.

Several newspaper collections were particularly useful for researching major political issues. David Knight's *Choosing Canada's Capital* (Carleton 1991) contains many excerpts from the local papers of the cities vying for the seat of government. Whelan's *The Union of the British Provinces* (Haszard 1865) and Waite's *The Life and Times of Confederation* (Robin Brass 2001) contain wide coverage of the Charlottetown and Québec conferences and their aftermath.

Images

Prior to the advent of photography, military engineers and surveyors were trained to produce accurate perspective sketches and watercolour drawings to document sites. The most extensive set to survive are the sketches of Thomas Burrowes at the Ontario Archives. The documentary art collection of the LAC contains drawings from military officers such as John By, Philip Bainbrigge and Henry du Vernet and landscape artists such as Edwin Whitefield and W.H. Bartlett. Well-researched bird's-eye views, such as Herman Brosius' 1876 drawing can be a valuable historical resource in the era before aerial photography.

The most extensive collections of photographs of the National Capital Region are found at the LAC, but only a small fraction of the millions of images are catalogued. Some of the most useful collections included the vast holdings of W.J. Topley's firm, Samuel McLaughlin's remarkable images of the construction of the Parliament Buildings, Noulan Cauchon's lantern slides, Mackenzie King's photographic archives and the National Film Board stills associated with their Ottawa features.

The lumber industry and the terrible destruction of the 1900 fire are documented in the E.B. Eddy, J.R Booth and Bronson family collections at the LAC. Another LAC collection of Department of Public Works' images taken as background for Jacques Gréber's planning studies is featured in Alain Miguelez' *Transforming Ottawa* (2015) The Notman photographic archive at Montréal's McCord Museum is another good source of images, particularly of personal portraits.

The City of Ottawa Archives contains thousands of images documenting its public works since the 1940s and the urban renewal studies of the 1950s and 1960s. It also has a good collection of general views of the city. The most extensive historic photograph collection for the Outaouais is at the Archives Nationale du Québec – Outaouais (ANQ-O). The Canadian Museum of Civilization also collects local images, some of which were exhibited in Harry Foster's 2005 exhibition *Remember When? My encounter with the architecture of Old Hull*, which is available online: www.historymuseum.ca.

The Canada Mortgage and Housing Corporation and the National Capital Commission also maintain large image collections of projects from the region. Some of these have been transferred to the LAC and others remain in their corporate collections.

The National Film Board produced a remarkable series of documentary films about the development of the national capital, including *Ottawa: Wartime Capital* (1942), *A Capital Plan* (1949), *Planning Canada's National Capital* (1949), *Ottawa: Today and Tomorrow* (1951), and *Capital on the Ottawa* (1967). The NFB's *A Bus-For Us* (1972) documents the birth of the region's express bus network.

Theses and Dissertations

There are many graduate theses relating to the Ottawa-Gatineau region at the history and geography departments of Carleton University, the Université d'Ottawa and at Queen's University's School of Urban and Regional Planning. Some particularly useful theses included Léo Rossignol, *Histoire documentaire de Hull* (Ottawa 1941), Hans Hosse, *Projected Development Trends and Conceptual Structure of the Ottawa Region* (Ottawa 1962), Walter Van Nus, *The Plan-Makers and the City* (Toronto 1975), Sally Coutts, *Science and Sentiment: The Planning Career of Noulan Cauchon* (Carleton 1982), Vincent Asselin, *Frederick G. Todd Architecte Paysagiste* (Montréal 1995), Andre Lortie, *Jacques Gréber (1882-1962) et L' Urbanisme le temps et l'espace de la ville* (Paris XII 1997), Aidan Carter, *Planning a "Capital Worthy of the Nation," the Federal District Controversy and the Planning of the Canadian Capital* (Queen's 2001).

Recent History

Two collections of scholarly articles cover the planning and development of the Ottawa-Gatineau region – R. Wasche and M. Kugler-Gagnon *Ottawa-Hull: Spatial Perspectives and Planning* (Ottawa 1978) and J. Keshen and D. St-Onge *Construire une capitale* (Acte 2001). C. Fullerton's "Regional Planning in Ottawa, 1945-1974" *Urban History Review*, 24:1 (2005) is perhaps the best overview of regional planning south of the Ottawa River. For the evolution of "Silicon Valley North" see Nick Novakowski and Rémy Tremblay's *Perspectives on Ottawa's High-tech Sector* (Lang 2007).

Many pre-2000 documents may be found at the local university libraries, but recent collections are weakened by the practice of posting new planning studies in digital files on the World Wide Web. This provides broad access to current documents, but older studies are often lost when websites are re-organized. Sadly, it appears that no library is storing these digital files for future research.

The Internet became a useful scholarly tool during the last decade of research for this book. Some heavily-used collections of primary sources have moved online, which provides wonderful access to collections like *Early Canadiana Online*, the *Champlain Society* and the *Dictionary of Canadian Biography*. Retrieving recent refereed articles has become almost effortless, and triangulation with contemporary newspaper resources is much easier.

One of the lessons from a decade of Internet research is that careful judgement is needed about the quality of many online sources. We learned that if material has not been refereed or edited by scholars, then it should be treated with great caution. For example, the online *Dictionary of Canadian Biography* is magnificent and *Canadian Encyclopedia* articles were generally accurate, but some Wikipedia entries contained errors or omitted important themes. Most blogs were undocumented and many appear to be quite biased – making the electronic landscape even more slippery than the politics of competing party newspapers in the 19th century.

Future students of Canada's capital will have a much easier time with primary research as more of the collections of the LAC and local archives are posted on the Internet. But only a small portion of the collections are online and these are usually the materials that have already been well-used by previous researchers. The exciting new gains in urban history scholarship will likely continue to emerge from extensive time consulting documents in archives and libraries. After almost 20 wonderful years among the collections relating to Canada's capital, our research team still had the feeling that we were barely stirring the surface of the pool. Our advice to future researchers is: find a quiet spot and dive in.

Acknowledgements

First, some essential thanks to the public agencies that funded the research foundation for this project. Four Canadian Social Sciences and Humanities Research Council grants supported this book and the associated capital city research. A Fulbright Senior Fellowship supported a sabbatical year at the University of Pennsylvania, where Gary Hack and Eugenie Birch were gracious hosts at Penn's Graduate School of Fine Arts. The Richardson Fund at Queen's purchased historic city plans, French language newspapers, archival photographs and maps that were essential to the research. The Institute of Advanced Studies at the University of Western Australia provided a collegial home for the final revisions. The first grant is often the smallest and the most important, so special thanks to the Advisory Research Committee of Queen's University, which took a chance on this untried idea in 1996.

The research for this book was prepared with the aid of a dedicated group of research assistants over the past 18 years including Angus Beaty, Mehdi Bouhadi, Annamarie Burgess, Aidan Carter, Mathieu Cordary, Cheryl Dow, Laura Evangelista, Emma Fletcher, Aurélie Fournier, Kathryn Gilmore, Tiffany Gravina, Wesley Hayward, Richard Hernden, Anthony Hommik, Mark Janzen, Benjamin Jean, Geraldine Johnston, John Kozuskanich, Pooja Kumar, Dayna Lafferty, Denise McCormick, Kelly McNicol, Michael Miller, Raktim Mitra, Andrew Morton, Greg Newman, Michelle Nicholson, Tyler Nightingale, Jeffrey O'Neill, Sarah Orovan, Krystal Perepeluk, Sarah Piasetzki, Will Plexman, Marie-Claude Rioux, Jennifer Sandham, Inara Silkalns, Bramhanand Singh, Amanda Slaunwhite, Daniel Tovey, Miguel Tremblay, Farah Ward and Xiao Zhiliang. They did much of the primary archival research, reviewed images, drew maps, prepared bibliographies, chronologies, web sites and the extensive endnote documentation. Jo-Anne Tinlin prepared large sections of the manuscript and Angie Balesdent provided administrative support for the project at the Queen's University School of Urban and Regional Planning.

Several graduate students also contributed research through their theses and Master's reports, including Aidan Carter, John Kozuskanich, Peter Linkletter, Denise McCormick, Michael Miller, Gerald Schock, Stéphanie Gmernicki and Christopher Vandyk.

Many librarians and archivists helped, but special thanks should go to Marc Bisaillon and Guy Tessier at the Library and Archives Canada, Serge Barbe at the City of Ottawa Archives, Thomas Rooney at Ottawa Public Library, Renée de Gannes-Marshall and Rota Bouse at the National Capital Commission, Mary Woolever and Nathaniel Parks at the Art Institute of Chicago, and Mary Fraser, Jeff Moon, Barbara Teatero and Peter Waldron at the Queen's libraries.

The staff of many planning agencies in the National Capital Region helped find information and interpret results, especially Éric Boutet (Gatineau); Sally Coutts, Alain Miguelez (Ottawa); Pierre Dubé, Richard Scott, François Lapointe, and Lynda Villeneuve (NCC). I would also like to thank the 28 politicians and planners who agreed to in-depth interviews to support the recent planning chapters.

Many Canadian professors shared their research, collaborated on earlier papers or provided strategic advice, including Caroline Andrew (Ottawa), Carl Bray (Queen's), Betsy Donald (Queen's), Gerald Hodge (Queen's), Peter Jacobs (Montréal), André Juneau (Queen's), Larry McCann (Victoria), Gilles Paquet (Ottawa), Léon

Ploegaerts (Ottawa), Ted Regehr (Calgary), Mark Seasons (Waterloo), Gilbert Stelter (Guelph), John Taylor (Carleton) and Rémy Tremblay (UQO). The Canadian Centre for the Study of Capitals provided a venue for the discussion of the other capital cities, with Caroline Andrew and John Taylor as hosts. Perhaps most importantly, Brian Osborne provided endless counsel on heritage, the late Donald Swainson instructed me on the finer points of historical research and George Henderson guided me through the national and local archives.

Internationally, I have benefited from collaboration and advice from many colleagues from the Society for American City and Regional Planning History and the International Planning History Society, especially: Genie Birch (Penn), Eran Ben-Joseph (MIT), the late Joan Draper (Colorado), Sylvia Ficher (Brasilia), Rob Freestone (UNSW), Isabelle Gournay (Maryland), Jenny Gregory (Western Australia), the late Sir Peter Hall (UCL), Dennis Hardy (Middlesex), Carola Hein (Delft), Sauro Joardar (Delhi), Laura Kolbe (Helsinki), Michael Hebbert (Manchester), Michael Lang (Rutgers), David Massey (Liverpool), Heike Mayer (Bern), Mervyn Miller (Hampstead Garden Suburb Trust), Nihal Perera (Ball State), Giorgio Piccinato (Rome), Chris Silver (Florida), Wolfgang Sonne (Dortmund), the late Tony Sutcliffe (Leicester), Stephen Ward (Oxford Brookes), Shun-Ichi Watanabe (Tokyo), Larry Vale (MIT) and Christopher Vernon (Western Australia).

Some of the research behind this book has previously been published in other books and academic journals. I am grateful for comments from the editors and peer-reviewers at *Canadian Journal of Urban Research* (13:2. 2002; 18:1, 2009);

Journal of Architecture and Planning Research (30:3, 2013); *Journal of Historical Geography* (30:4, 2004); *Journal of Planning History* (1:1, 2002); *Journal of Urban Design* (5:3 2000); *Journal of Urban History* (28:1, 2001); *Planning History Studies* (12:1, 1998); *Planning Perspectives*, (13:3, 1998; 17:2, 2002; 23:3, 2008; 25:2, 2010); *Town Planning Review* (83:3, 2012) and *Urban History Review* (29:2, 2001). The larger themes in this book are explored in a wider context in the books *Planning Canadian Communities* (Nelson 2014, with Gerald Hodge) and *Planning Twentieth Century Capital Cities* (Routledge 2006).

Several brave souls read draft chapters of this book and helped correct errors of fact and interpretation: Don Akenson, Keith Banting, John Grodzinski, Brian Osborne and Gilles Paquet. I am especially indebted to Len Husband and four anonymous reviewers who examined the entire manuscript and provided many useful suggestions for its improvement.

At Invenire Press, McE Galbreath, Ruth Hubbard, Sandy Lynch, Gilles Paquet and Anne Phillips guided a complex manuscript through the publishing process.

The book is far better for the involvement of these many people, but I must take full responsibility for any shortcomings or errors.

My greatest debts are to Katherine Rudder and Sarah Gordon, who cheerfully allowed me to abandon them for extended periods of research, travel and writing. They know how much I owe them and that it can never be properly repaid.

Kingston, Ontario
(Canada's first capital city…)
Summer 2015

Endnotes

Preface

1. John Taylor, *Ottawa: An Illustrated History*, (Toronto, ON: Lorimer, 1986); Chad Gaffield (ed.), *History of the Outaouais*, (Québec, QC: Les Presses de l'Université Laval, 1997).

2. For the symbolic content of capital cities, see Lawrence Vale, *Architecture, Power and National Identity*, (New York, NY: Routledge, 2008); for broader capital city issues, see J. Taylor, C. Andrew, et al (eds.), *Capital Cities*, (Ottawa, ON: Carleton University Press, 1993). The case studies in this book were largely drawn from the work of my colleagues in D.L.A. Gordon (ed.), *Planning Twentieth Century Capital Cities*, (London, UK: Routledge, 2006/2010).

3. For the seat of government issues, see D.B. Knight, *Choosing Canada's Capital: Conflict Resolution in a Parliamentary System*, (Ottawa, ON: Carleton University Press, 1991); the scholarly books on Confederation are too numerous to mention here, but the work of P.B. Waite was particularly useful for this study.

4. The work of Caroline Andrew, Gilles Paquet and other scholars at the Université d'Ottawa sometimes addresses both Gatineau and Ottawa; see C. Andrew and L. Quesnel (eds.), *L'Aménagement des centre-villes*, (Ottawa, ON: Sciences Sociales, Université d'Ottawa et M. Éditeur, 1990); Association canadienne-française pour l'avancement des sciences, *Le capitale du Canada: Réflexions sur le passé et perspectives d'avenir*, (Ottawa, ON: NCC, 1999); Rupak Chattopadhyay and Gilles Paquet (eds.), *The Unimagined Canadian Capital: Challenges for the Federal Capital Region*, (Ottawa, ON: Invenire Press, 2011). In the professional field, only the National Capital Commission routinely considers both Ontario and Québec portions of the region.

Prologue

5. "Visit of the Delegates to Ottawa," *Ottawa Citizen*, November 4, 1864; "The Delegates of Ottawa," *The Daily Globe*, (Toronto, November 2, 1864); Edward Whelan, *The Union of the British Provinces*, (Charlottetown, PEI: GT Hazard, 1865), p. 135-37.

6. *Globe*, November 2, 1864, *op. cit.*

7. *Ibid.*

8. Edward Whelan, *The Union of the British Provinces*, *op. cit.*, p. 137

9. *Globe*, November 2, 1864, *op. cit.*

10. *Ottawa Citizen*, November 4, 1864, *op. cit.*

11. *Globe*, November 2, 1864, *op. cit.*, Whelan, *op. cit.*, p. 155.

Chapter 1

12. J.H. Gray, *Confederation; or The Political and Parliamentary History of Canada*, (Toronto, ON: Copp, Clark, 1872), p. 105.

13. J.M. Soucy, "The Changing Natural Environment" in Chad Gaffield (ed.), *History of the Outaouais*, (Québec, QC: Les Presses de l' Université Laval, 1997), p. 23-28. See also, W.G. Dean, "The Ontario Landscape, circa A.D. 1600" in E.S. Rogers and D.B. Smith (eds.), *Aboriginal Ontario: Historic Perspectives on the First Nations*, (Toronto, ON: Dundurn Press, 1994), p. 3-20.

14. J.M. Masterton, "The Climatic Factor in the Outdoor Recreation of the National Capital Region" in R. Wesche and M. Kugler-Gagnon (eds.), *Ottawa-Hull: Spatial Perspectives and Planning/Perspectives Spatiales et Aménagement*, (Ottawa, ON: Éditions de l'Université d'Ottawa, 1978), p. 43-52.

15. At latitude 45° 25' N, Ottawa-Gatineau is several hundred km. further south than Paris, London, Vienna, Berlin, or Moscow.

16. Agriculture Canada, *Canada Land Inventory, Solid Capability for Agriculture*, (Ottawa, ON: Agriculture Canada, 1967), Map Sheet 31G; Agriculture Canada, *Canada Land Inventory: Land Capability for Forestry*, (Ottawa, ON: Agriculture Canada, 1973), Map Sheet 31G, Leda Clay.

17. Agriculture Canada, *Canada Land Inventory: Land Capability on Wildlife-Ungulates*, (Ottawa, ON: Agriculture Canada, 1971), Map Sheet 31G.

18. Perhaps the best summary of the archaeological evidence is Gérald Pelletier, "The First Inhabitants of the Outaouais: 6,000 years of history" in Chad

Gaffield (ed.), *History of the Outaouais*, (Québec, QC: Les Presses de l'Université Laval, 1997), p. 43-66. See also, J.V. Wright, "Before European Contact" in Rogers and Smith, *op. cit.*, p. 21-30; and R.C. Harris and G.J. Matthews, *Historical Atlas of Canada, Vol. 1, from the Beginning to 1800,* (Toronto, ON: University of Toronto Press, 1987), Introduction and Plates 7-9 and 18. The oral histories of the aboriginal peoples dispute the wider archaeological conclusions about the First Nations, which assert that human beings first migrated to North American 20,000 years ago. The histories of the First Nations assert that their peoples have evolved from their lands and have always been present. See J. de Lotbinère, "Of Wampum and Little People: Historical Narratives Regarding the Algonquin Wampum Record" in D. Clément (ed.), *The Algonquins*, (Ottawa, ON: Canadian Museum of Civilization, [now the Museum of Canadian History] Mercury Series No. 130, 1996), p. 93-122.

[19] Samuel de Champlain gave an eyewitness account of one deer hunt in October 1615, illustrated by a wood cut. Samuel de Champlain, *The Works of Samuel de Champlain*, Vol. III, H.P Biggar (ed.), (Toronto, ON: The Champlain Society), p. 81-86.

[20] Pelletier, *op. cit.*, p. 407-60; Peter Hessel, *The Algonkin Tribe: The Algonkins of the Ottawa Valley: An Historical Outline* (Arnprior ON: Kichesippi Books, 1987), chapter 3.

[21] M. Lescarbot, *The History of New France*, Vol. II, W.L. Grant (trans.), (Toronto, ON: Champlain Society, 1911), p. 121-22 from Cartier's journal for October 3, 1535.

[22] It appears that Champlain misunderstood the reference to the people dancing in the celebration (in the Malecite language "a'llegon kin" meaning "dancer") and recorded the sound in his diary as "Algonkins." See Champlain *op. cit.*, Volume II, p. 98-102, May 27, 1603 and Hessel *op. cit.*, p. 11-14. Although Hessel recommends the spelling Algonkin, the more usual "Algonquin" will be used in this volume, following his practice of contemporary historians like Gaffield, *op. cit.*, "Algonkian" will be used to identify the language group of the bands that occupies the lands from Ville de Québec to North Bay in 1603.

[23] Champlain, *op. cit.*, Vol. 1, p. 149-52.

[24] Lescarbot, *op. cit., Vol. 11*; Champlain *op. cit., Vol. 11.*

[25] E. DeVille, "Radial Hamlet Settlement Schemes," *Plan Canada*, Vol. 15 (March 1975), p. 44 (reprinted from *Conservation of Life,* April 1918); Charlesbourg is now part of the Québec metropolitan area, but its radial street and lot pattern can still be discerned.

[26] F. Divorne, B. Gendre, B. Lavergne and P. Panerai, *Les Bastides d'Aquitaine, du Bas-Languedoc du Béarn*, (Brussels, BE: Aux Archives d'Architecture Moderne, 1983).

[27] Samuel de Champlain, *The voyages of the Sieur de Champlain*, (1613), reprinted in H.P. Biggar (ed.), *The Works of Samuel de Champlain, Vol. 1*, (Toronto, ON: Champlain Society, 1922), p. 275-76; David H. Fischer, *Champlain's Dream*, (Toronto, ON: Knopf Canada, 2008), p. 74-104; for Spanish colonial towns, see D.P. Crouch, D. Garr and A. Mundigo, *Spanish city planning in North America*, (Cambridge MA: MIT Press, 1982) and J.W. Reps, *The Making of Urban America*, (Princeton, NJ: Princeton University Press, 1965), p. 26-55.

[28] Ste. Croix and Port Royal are illustrated in Champlain *op. cit.*, p. 279, plate LXXI and p. 372-73, plate LXXVI.

[29] Peter Moogk, *Building a House in New France*, (Toronto, ON: McClelland and Stewart, 1977).

[30] See C. Graham, *Mont Royal-Ville Marie: Early Plans and Views of Montréal*, (Montréal, QC: McCord Museum of Canadian History, 1992); Phyllis Lambert and Alan Stewart, *Opening the Gates of Eighteenth-Century Montréal*, (Montréal, QC: Canadian Centre for Architecture, 1992); Jean-Claude Marsan, *Montréal in Evolution: Historical Analysis of the Development of Montréal's Architecture and Urban Environment*, (Montréal, QC and Kingston, ON: McGill-Queen's University Press, 1990).

[31] See J.W. Reps, 1965, *op. cit.*, chapter 3. Note that the original French town-site was one of the few areas that did not flood in 2005's Hurricane Katrina.

[32] Étienné Brûlé (1592-1633) was born near Paris and migrated to New France with Champlain in 1608. He was first sent inland with the Huron nations at age 18, and spent most of the remainder of his life with them. His most famous expeditions were to Lake Ontario and Lake Huron (1611), Chesapeake Bay (1615-17) and Lake Superior (1621-23). Brûlé

32 aided the English after they captured Québec in 1629, and Champlain accused him of treason. He was killed and eaten by the Hurons in 1633. See J.H. Cranston, *Étienné Brûlé discoveries and explorations 1610-1626*, (Cleveland, OH: Helman-Taylor, 1898), and Olga Jurgens, "Étienné Brûlé" in *Dictionary of Canadian Biography, Vol. I*, (Toronto, ON: University of Toronto Press, 1966).

33 The Ottawa River, named by Champlain "La Grande Rivière des Algonumequins."

34 The historical record on de Vignau relies on Champlain's diary, *op. cit.*, *Vol. II*, p. 255-307 and *Vol. IV*, p. 151-204. See also M. Trudel, "Nicolas de Vignau" in *Dictionary of Canadian Biography, Vol. I*, (Toronto, ON: University of Toronto Press, 1966).

35 de Vignau's story had the ring of truth, since the English explorer Henry Hudson had been trapped in the ice in James Bay in 1610 and lost two of his ships. Hudson's crew had mutinied, chasing the captain, his young son and seven sailors adrift in a boat. See D. Hunter, *God's Mercies: Rivalry, Betrayal and the Dream of Discovery*, (Toronto, ON: Doubleday, 2007). This story was known to the French; see Champlain *op. cit.*, *Vol. II*, p. 257 and Plate x 'Hudson's map of 1612.'

36 Champlain, *op. cit.*, *Vol. II*, p. 267. Champlain overestimated the height of the Rideau falls, which are about ten metres. The island in the centre is Green Island, which was the site of Ottawa City Hall from 1995 to 2001. The 'mountain' is the escarpment along the Ottawa River between the Rideau River and Parliament Hill.

37 *Ibid.*, p. 268.

38 de Vignau recanted his story under threat, and it is unclear whether he actually reached Hudson's Bay the year before. The Kichesipirini may not have wanted Champlain to continue further inland to meet other bands (See Trudel, *op. cit.*; Hessel, *op. cit.*, p. 25-29).

39 Champlain, *op. cit.*, *Vol. II*, p. 301-02.

40 A. Cellard, "Kichesippi: The Great River of the Algonquins (1600-1650)" in Gaffield, *op. cit.*, p. 67-84.

41 Hessel, *op. cit.*, chapters 5 and 6; A. Cellard and G. Pelletier, "The Ottawa River: 1650-1692" in Gaffield (ed.), *op. cit.*, p. 85-104; M. Ratelle, "Location of the Algonquins from 1634-1650," in Clement (ed.), *op. cit.*, p. 41-68.

42 A name from the Algonkian word for 'trader.' The English translation was Ottawa.

43 B.G. Trigger and G.M. Day, "Southern Algonquin Middlemen: Algonquin, Nipissing and Ottawa, 1550-1780" in E.S. Rogers and D.B. Smith (eds.), *Aboriginal Ontario: Historical Perspectives on the First Nations*, (Toronto, ON: Dundurn Press, 1994), p. 64-77.

44 J. Frenette, "Kitigan zibi Anishinabeg: The Territory and Economic Activity of the River Desert (Maniwaki) Algonquins, 1850-1950" in Clement (ed.), *op. cit.*, p. 69-92. In the late 19th century, two reserves were established for the remaining Algonquin bands at Golden Lake and the River Desert. See Hessel, *op. cit.*, chapters 7 and 8.

45 Gaffield, *op. cit.*, p. 121.

46 Now Kingston.

47 See Shackelton, "Francis Anne (Hopkins) Beechey" in *Dictionary of Canadian Biography, Vol. XIV*, (Toronto, ON: University of Toronto Press, 1998).

48 R.J. Surtees, "Land Cessions, 1763-1862" in Rogers and Smith (eds.), *op. cit.*, p. 92-120; "A Proclamation, October 8, 1763," reprinted in *Canadian Archives Documents Relating to the Constitutional History of Canada, 1759-1791, Part I*, (Ottawa, ON: Kings Printer, 1918), p. 163-68.

49 J. Williams, "Rules and Regulations for the Conduct of the Land Office Department," (Québec, QC: Québec (Province) Land Office Department, February 17, 1789); J. Williams, "Additional Rules and Regulations for the conduct of the Land-Office Department," (Québec, QC: Québec (Province) Land Office Department, August 25, 1789).

50 Reps, *Making of Urban America*, *op. cit.*, chapter 6; A.E.J. Morris, *History of Urban Form*, (New York, NY: Wiley, 1994), chapters 8 and 9; Reps, *Making of Urban America*, *op. cit.*, chapter 6; S. Kostof, *The City Assembled: Elements of Urban Form Through History*, (Boston, MA: Bullfinch, 1992), chapter 3.

51 Reps, *Making of Urban America*, *op. cit.*, p. 185-95. In contrast, James Oglethorpe's 1733 Savannah plan did not attempt to lay out an entire future city. Instead, he designed a repeatable neighbourhood module based on small squares that was used for the expansion of the town until the late 1800s. The Savannah plan made more frequent use of the

Georgian square by providing one in each ward of 40 houses, while the major streets that formed the boundaries of the neighbourhoods were 23 m. (75 feet) wide.

52 M. Hugo-Brunt, "The history of city planning: a survey," *Plan Canada*, vol. 1, no. 2, 1972.

53 J.V. Watson, *Historic Charlottetown*, (Halifax, NS: Nimbus, 2007), p. 7.

54 J. Williams, "Rules and Regulations for the conduct of the Land Office Department," (Québec, QC: Québec (Province) Land Office Department, February 17, 1789).

55 To follow the procedures from the 1763 Royal Proclamation, land had to be purchased from the aboriginal owners before settlement could begin. The Mississauga land sold lands along Lake Ontario from present day Trenton to Kingston in 1783 and the Oswegatchie band sold lands north of Brockville in 1784. See Surtees, *op. cit.*, p. 101-06. But the remaining Algonquins were not consulted and dispute the purchase of the Ottawa valley lands. See Hessel, *op. cit.*, p. 68-72.

56 B.S. Osborne and D. Swainson, *Kingston: Building on the Past*, (Westport, ON: Butternut Press, 1988), p. 18-47.

57 See L. Gentilcore, *Ontario's History in Maps*, (Toronto, ON: University of Toronto Press, 1984), p. 58-64.

58 J. Williams, *Rules and Regulations for the conduct of the Land Office Department, op cit.* J. Williams, *Additional Rules and Regulations for the Conduct of the Land-Office Department, op cit.*

59 J. Williams, *Additional Rules and Regulations, op. cit.* p. 1.

60 J. Williams, *Rules and Regulations, op. cit.*, p. 1.

61 Bruce Elliott, *The City Beyond*, (Nepean, ON: City of Nepean, 1991), p. 6.

62 *Ibid.*, p. 6-7.

63 The survey had to be corrected by another provincial land surveyor in the 1820s, see H. Beldon and Co., *The Illustrative Historical Atlas of the County of Carleton*, (Toronto, ON: H. Beldon, 1879), p. xxxix; Stegmann was rumoured to have died by falling into the Rideau during the survey, but actually drowned in Lake Ontario in the 1804 shipwreck of the *Speedy*. See Phil Jenkins, *An Acre of Time*, (Toronto, ON: Macfarlane Walter & Ross, 1996), p. 94-100.

64 H. Beldon and Co., *op. cit.*, p. 7-9; to make matters worse, many of these lots were only given verbal descriptions with "metes and bounds," leading to more ownership disputes in the future; see H. Beldon and Co., *op. cit.*, p. xxxv-xxxvii.

65 Bruce Elliot, *op. cit.*, p. 7-10; Hamnett Pinhey Hill, *Robert Randall and the LeBreton Flats*, (Ottawa, ON: James Hope and Sons, 1919), p. 6-13; E.A. Cruikshank, "An Experiment in Colonization in Upper Canada," *Ontario Historical Society Papers and Records*, 25 (1929), p. 32-77.

66 Wright, "An Account of the First Settlement of the Township of Hull, on the Ottawa River, Lower Canada," manuscript of 1820 address to the Lower Canada House of Assembly, Ruggles Wright papers, LAC, MG24 D8 Vol. 136, p. 4.

67 Chad Gaffield (ed.), *History of the Outaouais*, (Québec, QC: Les Presses de l'Université Laval, 1997), p. 121-26.

68 Wright, *op. cit.*, p. 2.

69 Wright, *op. cit.*, p. 9-11; Lucien Brault, *Hull 1850-1950*, (Ottawa, ON: Les Éditions de l'Université d'Ottawa, 1950), p. 24-25; B.S. Elliott, "The Famous Township of Hull: Images and Aspirations of a Pioneer Québec Community," *Histoire sociale/social history* 12 (1979), no. 24: 343-47.

70 Elliott, *op. cit.*, p. 349, ff. 37.

71 F. Ouellet, and B. Thériault, "Philemon Wright," in *Dictionary of Canadian Biography, Vol. VII*, (Toronto, ON: University of Toronto Press, 2003).

72 Wright, *op. cit.*, p. 11.

73 J. Bouchette, *A Topographical Description of the Province of Lower Canada*, (London: W.U. Faden, 1815), p. 251-52; J. MacTaggart, *Three Years in Canada*, (London: Henry Coulburn, 1829), Vol. 1, p. 266; Vol. 2, p. 264; J. Bouchette, *General Report of an Official Tour Through the New Settlements of Lower Canada*, (Québec, QC: Thomas Cary, 1825), p. 27-45.

74 A.R.M. Lower, "The Trade in Square Timber," *Contributions to Canadian Economics*, 6 (1933), p. 40-61; A.R.M. Lower, *Great Britain's Woodyard: British America and the Timber Trade, 1763-1867*,

(Montréal, QC and Kingston, ON: McGill-Queen's University Press, 1973).

75 Wright, *op. cit.*

76 Gaffield, *op. cit.*, p. 129-34.

77 Gaffield, *op. cit.*, p. 204-09.

78 The huge rafts were made up of smaller 'cribs,' each about eight metres wide, that could pass down the timber slide unscathed. Shooting down a timber slide and a crib was the 19th century equivalent of an amusement park flume ride, and an entertainment highlight for dignitaries visiting Ottawa. See Lower, *Great Britain's Woodyard, op. cit.*, p. 209-13.

79 Lower, *Trade in Square Timber, op. cit.*, Diagrams 1 and 2.

80 J.M. Hitsman, *The Incredible War of 1812: A Military History* (Toronto, ON: Robin Brass Studio, 1999, D.M. Graves, ed.), p. 15-16; Jon Latimer, *1812: War with America*, (Cambridge, MA: Belknap Press of Harvard University Press, 2007).

81 In June 1812, there were 6,034 British regular troops in the Canadas and Northwest, of which only about 1,200 were scattered across Upper Canada; see Hitsman, *op. cit., The Incredible War of 1812*, p. 31-32 and App. 3.

82 T. Jefferson in Loney (ed.), *The Papers of Thomas Jefferson, Retirement Series,* (Princeton, NJ and Oxford, UK: Princeton University Press, 2008). August 4, 1812, Jefferson to William Duane, editor of the Philadelphia *Aurora*, "The acquisition of Canada this year, as far as the neighbourhood of Québec, will be a mere matter of marching, & will give us experience for the attack of Halifax the next, & the final expulsion of England from the American Continent," p. 293.

83 The American troops were enraged by 263 casualties from the explosion, including the death of their commander, Brigadier Zebulon Pike. See R. Malcomson, *Capital in Flame: The American Attack on York, 1813,* (Toronto, ON: Robin Brass Studio, 1998), p. 224-30 and App. 2.

84 Naval power on the Great Lakes was a crucial element of the war, and the British dockyard at Kingston was the critical facility for building a fleet to control Lake Ontario. See Hitsman, 1999; R. Malcomson, *Lords of the Lake: The Naval War on Lake Ontario 1812-14,* (Toronto, ON: Robin Brass Studio, 1998).

85 On October 26, 1813 over 4,000 Americans attacked the Châteaugay defences manned by a mere 430 Voltigeurs Canadiens commanded by Lt. Col. Charles-Michel de Salaberry. The Canadians drove the American invaders back, and the defeated troops retreated to New York State. See Hitsman, *The Incredible War of 1812, op. cit.,* p. 184-86. De Salaberry was a professional soldier from a distinguished *canadien* family. He was ably supported by Upper Canada's Lt. Col. "Red George" Macdonell, who cleared the left bank of the river with 1,000 Voltigeurs, militia and 150 aboriginal warriors. Thus, Châteaugay was one of the few victories in the War of 1812 which was entirely won by Canadian troops. A similar mixture of troops from Canada's three founding peoples – aboriginal, French and English – assisted the British regulars at Crysler's Farm. See D.E. Graves, *Field of Glory, The Battle of Crysler's Farm 1813,* (Toronto, ON: Robin Brass Studio, 1999), Apps. C and F.

86 D.E. Graves, *Field of Glory, op. cit.,* p. 99-110; R.L. Way, "The Day of Crysler's Farm: November 11, 1813," *Canadian Geographical Journal,* 62 (1961): 184-217.

87 Latimer, *Battle of Crysler's Farm, op. cit.,* p. 204-16.

88 Hitsman, *The Incredible War of 1812, op. cit.,* p. 240-46; after their surprise victory in Washington, the Royal Navy tried to capture Baltimore, bombarding the outer forts with rockets and mortar bombs. When Fort McHenry would not yield, the Navy returned to Halifax, and "the rockets' red glare, and bombs bursting in air" from the attack were celebrated in the US national anthem.

89 Plenty of inexpensive land was available near the village of Georgetown, and President George Washington knew the area well, since his estate was nearby.

90 Scott W. Berg, *Grand Avenues: The Story of the French Visionary Who Designed Washington, DC,* (New York, NY: Pantheon Books, 2007).

91 John Reps, *Monumental Washington,* (Princeton, NJ: Princeton University Press, 1967).

92 F. Gutheim, and A. Lee, *Worthy of the Nation*, 2nd ed. (Baltimore, MD: John Hopkins University Press, 2006), chapters 3 and 4.

93 The 1817 Rush-Bagot naval agreement is a good example of an early mutual arms-reduction treaty. The naval arms race on the Great Lakes was a particularly expensive part of the War of 1812. Both sides agreed to place their fleets in storage and restrict themselves to a few small gunboats in active service.

94 The Great Lakes naval arms race was a serious affair. By 1814, the Royal Navy's Kingston dockyard had launched the 102-gun *HMS St. Lawrence*, a three-deck warship with similar firepower to *HMS Victory*, Lord Nelson's flagship from the Battle of Trafalgar. See R.A. Preston, *Historic Kingston, vol. l*, no. 1, (1950).

95 C.P. Stacey, "The Myth of the Unguarded Frontier, 1815-1871," *The American Historical Review*, 41, no. 1, (Oct. 1950): 1-18.

96 Yeo to Viscount Melville, May 30, 1815, LAC Admiralty Papers M 389.6, Transcripts 307-12; cited in C.P. Stacey, "An American Plan for a Canadian Campaign," *American Historical Review*, 46, no. 2 (Jan 1941): 348.

97 C.P. Stacey, *An American Plan for A Canadian Campaign, op. cit.*, p. 349-55; J.M. Hitsman, *Safeguarding Canada: 1763-1871*, (Toronto, ON: University of Toronto Press, 1968), p. 121-22. Hitsman's chapter 6 is a fine overview of defensive planning from 1815 onwards.

98 George Raudzens, *The British Ordnance Department and Canada's Canals, 1815-1855*, (Waterloo, ON: Wilfrid Laurier University Press, 1979), p. 12-25.

99 Hitsman, *op. cit., Safeguarding Canada*, p. 117-18; Charles Lennox, the Duke of Richmond (1764-1819), had been an army officer, but was retired in 1815. He was present at the Battle of Waterloo as Wellington's guest. The Duchess of Richmond had been the hostess of the famous ball in Brussels on June 15, 1815, from which Wellington and his senior officers were called away into battle near Waterloo, after Napoleon's surprise attack. See A. Roberts, *Waterloo, June 18, 1815: The Battle for Modern Europe*, (London, UK: Harpers Collins, 2005).

100 Stacey, *An American Plan for a Canadian Campaign, op. cit.*, p. 354-56.

101 J.C. Smyth, *Copy of a Report to His Grace the Duke of Wellington, Master General of His Majesty's Ordnance, etc. Relative to His Majesty's North American Provinces* dated September 9, 1825, p. 45 (Microfilm copy held by LAC, National Library). One portion of the report was suppressed as secret and deleted from all copies of the report. Paragraph 52 considered the "Vulnerable Points of America" and recommended that should another war break out, New York should be blockaded by seizing Long Island and Staten Island. This proposed strategy demonstrates the level of tension, still high in 1825, and both sides were still preparing for war. See J.J. Talman, "A Secret Military Document, 1825," *The American Historical Review*, 38, no. 2, (January 1933): 295-300.

102 Smyth, *op. cit.*, p. 39-43. These works were constructed from 1832-1848 and are still in place as Fort Henry and four Martello Towers. See Robert Passfield, *Engineering the Defence of the Canadas: Lt. Col. By and the Rideau Canal*, (Ottawa, ON: Parks Canada, 1980), p. 174-76.

103 Passfield, *op. cit.*, p. 71.

104 *Ibid.*, p. 72.

105 *Ibid.*, p. 16-77.

106 Mark Andrews, *For King and Country: Lieutenant Colonel John By, R.E., Indefatigable Civil-Military Engineer*, (Merrickville, ON: Historic Merrickville Foundation, 1998), p. 105-13.

107 M.S. Cross, "The Age of Gentility: The Formation of an Aristocracy in the Ottawa Valley," *Canadian Historical Society, Historical Papers*, 1967, p. 105-17.

108 R. Reid, "The End of Imperial Town Planning in Upper Canada," *Urban History Review*, 19, no. 1 (June 1990): 30-41.

109 Hamnett Pinhey Hill, *Robert Randall and the LeBreton Flats*, (Ottawa, ON: James Hope and Sons, 1919), p. 7-13; Bruce Elliott, "Famous Township of Hull," *op. cit.*, Map 1, p. 346; Wright, *The City Beyond, op. cit.*, p. 7-9.

110 "Historical Sketch of the County of Carleton" in *Illustrated Historical Atlas of the County of Carleton*, (Toronto, ON: H. Belden & Co., 1879), p. xxxiv. The Richmond Road passed only five farms along its length in 1818.

111 Beldon, *Illustrated Historical Atlas of the County of Carleton, op. cit.*,; Phil Jenkins, *An Acre of Time*, (Toronto, ON: Macfarlane, Walter & Ross, 1996).

112 E.A. Cruikshank, "Charles Lennox, the fourth Duke of Richmond," *Ontario History*, 24, (1927), p.

323-51; For a contemporary account of Richmond's death, see M. Whitelaw, ed., *The Dalhousie Journals, Vol 2, 1816-20*, (Ottawa, ON: Oberon Press, 1978), p. 42-44.

113 Hill, *op. cit.*

114 Whitelaw, *op. cit.*, p. 42.

115 Bruce Elliott, *The City Beyond*, (Nepean, ON: City of Nepean, 1991), p. 44, Appendix 2. According to the 1822 assessment roll, LeBreton owned 9,080 acres, or over 67 percent of the assessed land in Nepean Township. The next largest owner had 370 acres, and nobody else owned more than the standard 200 acre farm lot.

116 Randall's solicitors were Boulton & Boulton; Henry Boulton became first a judge and then Attorney General of Ontario as part of Upper Canada's "Family Compact." Randall claimed never to have been informed about the sale and attempted to retrieve the lands for the rest of his life, both through lawsuits and political action after he was elected as a Reform member for Lincoln. His cause was taken up by William Lyon Mackenzie King, See Hill, *op. cit.*, chapters IV, VI and VIII.

117 LeBreton managed to acquire the lots without using his own cash, by convincing Brockville lawyer Livius Sherwood to advance the funds in exchange for half the land. LeBreton kept the half with Richmond Landing and the mill site on the islands. See Hill, *op. cit.*, p. 24-28.

118 Dalhousie to LeBreton, 9th May 1827, LAC, UC Sundries, RG5, A1, Vol. 63, reel C-4612, "Claims of Capt. John LeBreton 1829-39." The letter is reprinted in Hill, *op. cit.*, p. 37-39, and the original is reproduced in Nick Mika, *Bytown: The Early Days of Ottawa*, (Belleville, ON: Mika Publishing, 1982), p. 31.

119 Lord Dalhousie purchased the lands with his own funds, so the deed is made out in his name. LeBreton made the feud worse by publishing a letter claiming that he had been offered the Fraser's lot for £15; see LeBreton to Dalhousie, March, 30, 1827, LAC UC Sundries *op. cit.*; also reprinted in Hill, *op. cit.*, p. 31-36. LeBreton's 1827 letter seems to be an *ex-post facto* attempt to salvage his reputation after Dalhousie had been disparaging him and supporting the squatters on his lands for six years. But the weight of evidence seems to be against LeBreton, since his £3000 offer of the land is not contested and Dalhousie's August 1820 diary entries clearly indicate his dissatisfaction with the Richmond Land and Richmond Road, and LeBreton's presence at the events with the half-pay officers. See *Dalhousie Journals, Vol. 2, op. cit.*, p. 35-48.

120 Hill, *op. cit.*, p. 31-36.

121 Elliott, *The City Beyond, op. cit.*, p. 81-85.

122 *Ibid.*

123 John Taylor, *Ottawa: An Illustrated History*, (Toronto, ON: Lorimer, 1986), p. 35.

124 Fern Graham, *An Annotated History of Blocks 1, 2 & 3 Wellington and Sparks Streets Ottawa*, (Ottawa, ON: Federal Heritage Buildings Review Office, 1999), p. 2.

125 The small blocks south of Rue Frontenac and west of Rue Leduc appear to be remnants of this plan. Each block is about one acre in size, divided into four lots in Ruggles Wright's plan. Streets were quite narrow at 40-50 feet wide, with lots about 105 feet square (Library and Archives Canada, National Map Collection, NMC-1443).

126 Library Archive Canada, National Map Collection NMC-11041, "Plan of the survey of the upper and lower village of Hull, the property of Ruggles Wright Esquire (1840)." The new plan had regular 66 foot by 99-foot lots (one chain by 1.5 chain) set in blocks that were 198 x 396 feet (3 x 6 chains) with 66 foot road widths.

Chapter 2

127 Dalhousie to By, Sept. 26, 1826, LAC RG8 C Series, *Vol. 42*, 97-98.

128 Philemon Wright's settlement had various spellings in the maps and texts of the era: i.e. Wright's Town; Wrightstown; and Wrights Town. Wright's Town appears to be the most common.

129 Mrs. Firth's tavern and the government warehouse were essentially squatting on John LeBreton's parcel. LeBreton did not receive clear title to his lands until an August 20, 1828 court decision; see Nick Mika *Bytown the Early Days of Ottawa*, (Belleville, ON: Mika Publishing, 1982), p. 25-28.

130 Sparks did not have clear title to his property, either, since John Burrows Honey's 1819 purchase from

the Crown was not recorded in the county registry until 1824. So Sparks' September 25, 1821 purchase for £95 was not registered until June 20, 1824. When it appeared that the Rideau Canal might go through his property, Sparks repurchased the land in June 20, 1826 to remove doubts about his title, and repurchased it again in 1830 for a token sum to further strengthen his title. See Michael Cross, "Nicholas Sparks" in *Dictionary of Canadian Biography, Vol. IX*, (Toronto, ON: University of Toronto Press, 1976).

[131] Lucien Brault, *Ottawa Old and New*, (Ottawa, ON: Ottawa Historical Information Institute, 1946), p. 34.

[132] By's birth date has been variously reported as 1779, 1781 and 1783 due to infant deaths and ambiguities in the By family baptism records. His most thorough biographer, Mark Andrew, suggests 1783 to match the memorial plaque approved by his widow. Mark Andrew, *For King and Country: Lieutenant Colonel John By, R.E., Indefatigable Civil-Military Engineer*, (Merrickville, ON: Historic Merrickville Foundation, 1998), p. 185, ff. 3.

[133] By's early establishment included Lt. Henry Pooley of the Royal Engineers and John MacTaggart, a British civil engineer/surveyor as clerk of the works. Capt. Daniel Bolton of the Royal Engineers joined them later. MacTaggart was invalided by malaria and dismissed for drunkenness. He attempted to salvage his reputation with a memoir; see John MacTaggart, *Three Years in Canada: An Account of the Actual State of the Country in 1826-7-8*, 2 volumes, (London, UK: Henry Colburn, 1829). Civilian managers included engineer John Burnett from the Lachine Canal, Thomas Burrowes, a former member of the Royal Sappers and Miners and surveyor John Burrows [Honey], who had sold Nicholas Sparks the 200 acres lot that is now downtown Ottawa; see R.W. Passfield, *Building the Rideau Canal: A Pictorial History*, (Toronto, ON: Fitzhenry and Whiteside with Parks Canada, 1982). Thomas Burrowes left an invaluable group of watercolour sketches and paintings of the project (see the Burrowes Collection, Ontario Archives, Toronto).

[134] Dalhousie stopped on his journey from Québec to inspect the locks at the Lachine Canal, fortifications on the Richelieu River, and the Grenville Canal. See M. Whitelaw (ed.), *The Dalhousie Journals, Vol 3, 1816-20*, (Ottawa, ON: Oberon Press, 1978), 77-78. American armies had attempted to invade Lower Canada via the Richelieu in 1775 and 1813. The Grenville Canal bypassed the Long Sault rapids, which were a major impediment to travel and settlement in the Ottawa Valley. Construction of the first canal began in 1819 under the supervision of Major Henry DuVernet of the Royal Staff Corps, a specialized regiment that was a competitor to the Royal Engineers. The work proceeded slowly due to the need to blast the canal through solid rock, and the Grenville and its sister Carillon canals were not completed until 1834. Dalhousie's inspection was no doubt influenced by the Duke of Wellington's request that the work be speeded up to complete the Kingston-Ottawa-Montréal military supply route recommended by the 1825 Smyth report. See R.F. Legget, *Ottawa River Canals and the Defence of British North America*, (Toronto, ON: University of Toronto Press, 1988), chapter 6; R.F. Legget, *Ottawa Waterway: Gateway to a Continent*, (Toronto, ON: University of Toronto Press, 1975), chapter 6 and 7; Andrew, *op. cit.*, p. 34-35; R.F. Legget, "Henry DuVernet" in *Dictionary of Canadian Biography, Vol. VII*, (Toronto, ON: University of Toronto Press, 1988). DuVernet's fine 1823 painting of Wright's mill and tavern (Figure 2) is at the Library and Archives Canada (LAC 028531).

[135] M. Whitelaw (ed.), *The Dalhousie Journals, Vol. 2, 1816-20*, (Ottawa, ON: Oberon Press, 1978), *Vol. 3*, p. 79.

[136] Colonel By shared some professional background with Dalhousie. However, they were from completely different social classes, since Dalhousie was an aristocrat who had purchased his initial army commissions. Dalhousie respected By's technical expertise and supported his work during the remainder of his tenure in Canada; see Whitelaw, *op. cit., Vol. 3*, p. 78-167.

[137] Robert Legget, one of Canada's leading civil engineers, speculates about the potential for the Richmond Landing site in *Ottawa Waterway, op. cit.*, p. 214-24.

[138] Brian Osborne and D. Swainson, *Kingston: Building on the Past*, (Westport, ON: Butternut Press, 1988), p. 54-61.

139 Neither By nor Dalhousie would have any trouble envisioning the effect of such a citadel after their Peninsular War service. By saw action at the second unsuccessful siege of the Bajadoz fortress, which ended in the slaughter of the British assault brigade (see Andrew, *op. cit.*, p. 61-67); Dalhousie's division assaulted French fortresses at Vittoria, Spain and Toulouse, France in 1813-14. See P. Burroughs, "George Ramsey" in *Dictionary of Canadian Biography, Vol. VII* (Toronto, ON: University of Toronto Press, 1988), p. 722-33; both officers were intimately familiar with the Québec citadel since By made a detailed scale model of the fortifications while stationed there from 1802-10 and Dalhousie had walked the battle sites with his son in 1819 (Andrew, *op. cit.*, p. 52-57; Whitelaw, *op. cit.*, *Vol. 1*, p. 152-54).

140 Whitelaw, *op. cit.*, Vol. 3, p. 79-80.

141 Dalhousie to By, *op. cit.*

142 M.S. Cross, "The Age of Gentility: The Formation of an Aristocracy in the Ottawa Valley," *Canadian Historical Society, Historical Papers*, 1967, p. 105-17; R.F. Legget, *Rideau Waterway*, (Toronto: University of Toronto Press, 1972), p. 47 reports that common labourers earned 2s/6p per day on canal work.

143 Gilbert Stelter, "Guelph and the Early Canadian Town Planning Tradition," *Ontario History*, 77, June, 1985, p. 83-106.

144 J.W. Reps, *The Making of Urban America*, (Princeton, NJ: Princeton University Press, 1965), p. 26-55; *Town Planning in Frontier America*, (Princeton, N.J.: Princeton University Press, 1969), p. 350, makes a similar point regarding the origins of the radial pattern of Buffalo, New York, which was laid out for the Holland Company by Ellicott.

145 Whitelaw, *op. cit.*, Vol. 3, p. 80.

146 Andrew, *op. cit.*, p. 117.

147 The leases were initially set at 2s/6d annually, but most of the original tenants did not build within the year, so By took the lots back. He re-leased the Upper Town lots for one pound per year for 30 years. Upper Town is now the site of the Supreme Court and the National Library. Lower Town lots were 2s/6d annually, but were leased to the highest bidders after the canal was under construction. See By to Capt. Airey (ca. 1829), LAC Hill Collection, MG24 I9, p. 4,462-64.

148 By paid £700 to build his house from his own pocket, and purchased Lt. Pooley's house after his 1827 departure. But he was later refused title to the lot. Worse, the Treasury refused to compensate him for the expense after the canal went over budget. See M. Newton, *Lower Town Ottawa, Vol 1. 1826-1854*, (Ottawa, ON: National Capital Commission, Manuscript Report 104, 1979), p. 80-81. When Major Bolton succeeded Lt. Col. By in 1832, the site became known as Major's Hill, which remains its name today.

149 Major Elliott of Dalhousie's staff attempted a survey in 1824, but had not been able to traverse the ground because of the swampy conditions (see Legget, *Rideau Waterway, op. cit.*, p. 202); but MacTaggart was made of sterner stuff and managed to lay out Lower Town in October 1832. The proposed canal route south of Lower Town almost defeated his survey crew. A flying level took three harrowing days cutting through thick bush to reach Dow's Lake, a journey that is a pleasant fifteen-minute bicycle ride today. The next leg of the survey had to wait until the swamps froze in December 1826. See John MacTaggart, *Three Years in Canada, Vol. 1*, (London, UK: Henry Coulbourn, 1829), p. 48-52.

150 See *Petition from the Inhabitants of Bytown to Lord Aylmer,* June 18, 1830, LAC, Hill Collection MG 24 I9, p. 5,579-81.

151 *Agreement between Nicklas [sic] Sparks and John By, L. Col., November 17, 1826,* LAC, MG-24 I9, Hill Collection.

152 Upper Canada, Legislative Assembly, *Statutes of Upper Canada*, 8 Geo. IV, chapter 1, section I, 3.

153 *Ibid.*, Section II, p. 5.

154 Unfortunately, the earliest surviving contour map of the area is Noulan Cauchon's 1912 drawing, where the land in this area has already been re-graded for urban uses. But examination of a relief map like Figure 1-1a in chapter 1 indicates that almost all of Sparks' land was *uphill* from the canal, which makes it difficult to argue that the land would be needed for canal purposes.

155 Sparks was not the only one to sue, since the Ordnance viewed most of the unoccupied swamp and bush along the canal route as having little commercial value. Landowners from Kingston to Bytown launched suits against the Ordnance, and

155 Col. By spent considerable time being vilified in courts in Brockville, Prescott and Cornwall, near the homes of the absentee owners. See Legget, *Rideau Waterway, op. cit.*, p. 43.

156 The building stands today as the Bytown Museum of the Ottawa Historical Society.

157 *Kingston Chronicle*, March 9, 1827. The 'Bytown' name become official upon opening of the first post office in April 1829; Brault, *Ottawa Old and New, op. cit.*, p. 172.

158 The bridge was so solidly constructed that it resisted explosives when it was demolished in 1912, finally requiring smashing the stone blocks by repeatedly dropping a huge weight. See Legget, *Ottawa Waterway, op. cit.*, p. 204-05.

159 Whitelaw, *op. cit., Vol. 3*, p. 116-17; the seventh span, which the Governor General did not mention, was the extension of Wellington Street over the gully at Richmond Landing, designed and built by Lt. Pooley of the Royal Engineers. This unusual structure was constructed entirely from unpeeled cedar logs, and the crossing became known as Pooley's Bridge.

160 Colonel By later admitted that it was his first time over the rope bridge too. Whitelaw, *op. cit.*, p. 117.

161 John MacTaggart supervised the bridge; see MacTaggart, *op. cit., Vol. 1*, p. 331-47; Passfield, *op. cit.*, p. 46-48; Lucien Brault, *Links between Two Cities: Historic Bridges between Ottawa and Hull*, (Hull, QC: City of Hull and Ottawa, ON: City of Ottawa, 1989), p. 11-15.

162 Tavern owners Firth and Berrie placed a competing advertisement in the paper on September 1, 1828 explaining that they were still open for business. See Mika, *op. cit.*, p. 28.

163 By 1853, there were 51 houses in LeBreton Flats (Bruce Elliott, *The City Beyond*, (Nepean, ON: City of Nepean, 1991), p. 96-99). One of the homes belonged to Dr. Hamnett Hill, author of a book sympathetic to Randall and LeBreton's plight. See Hamnett Pinhey Hill, *Robert Randall and the LeBreton Flats*, (Ottawa, ON: James Hope and Sons, 1919). These middle-class homes were burned in the great fire of 1900 and replaced with industrial buildings and more modest residences.

164 Michael S. Cross, "The Shiner's War: Social Violence in the Ottawa Valley in the 1830s," *Canadian Historical Review*, 54 (March 1973): 126.

165 MacTaggart, *op. cit., Vol. 2*, "Cranberry Marsh and Sickness," p. 13-16; for Corktown, see *Vol. 2*, p. 245.

166 By's peremptory actions to force an increase in the size of the canal were intensely controversial at the time. The Ordnance offices in London initially believed that he was out of control and he lost the confidence of Wellington and Smyth. See George Raudzens, *The British Ordnance Office and Canada's Canals 1815-1855*, (Waterloo, ON: Wilfrid Laurier University Press, 1979), p. 71-79. Although the Kempt Committee later approved By's recommendations, the Ordnance office in London remained wary of the financial estimates of their chief engineer for the Rideau project, and watched in dismay as the costs ballooned to over a million pounds sterling. *Ibid.*, "Completion of the Canal and Financial Chaos," p. 81-99.

167 Andrew, *op. cit.*, p. 108-09; Passfield, *op. cit.*, p. 24-29. Kempt's commission submitted a revised estimate of £576,756. Kempt (1765-1854) later replaced Lord Dalhousie as Governor-General of Canada (1826-30), and later returned to England to become Master General of the Ordnance (1830-34). See P. Burroughs biography in Volume VII of the *Dictionary of Canadian Biographies (DCB)*.

168 Joseph Bouchette, *The British Dominions in North America*, (London, UK: H. Colburn and R. Bentley, 1831), p. 81. John Taylor, *Ottawa: an Illustrated History*, (Toronto, ON: Lorimer, 1986) estimates the Bytown population in Table I, p. 210, note 3.

169 The two town-sites had approximately 240 lots (see LAC MG 24, I9, *Vol. 28*, p. 6,730-35); "Lots in Bytown Granted by Colonel By, 1827-32," reprinted in M. Newton, *Lower Town Ottawa, Vol 1. 1826-1854*, (Ottawa, ON: National Capital Commission, Manuscript Report 104, p. 1,979), Appendix 'B', p. 469-78. Two hundred forty lots at a minimum rent of 2s/6d per year would generate annual revenue of only £30. Colonel By spent £120 of rental income in August 1829 for wells and a market shed – see Legget, *Ottawa Waterway, op. cit.*, p. 206.

170 See Bouchette, *op. cit.*, p. 196-201.

171 See R. Reid, "The End of Imperial Planning in Upper Canada," *Urban History Review,* 19 (1990), no. 1: 30-41.

172 United Nations Educational, Scientific And Cultural Organization (UNESCO), World Heritage Committee, *Minutes,* June 23, 2007, p. 164-65, Decision: 31 COM 8B.35.

173 In contrast, the Ottawa River canals were started in 1819 and were not completed until 1834. See Legget, *Ottawa River Canals, op. cit.,* chapter 3.

174 Passfield, *op. cit.,* p. 64-67. Colonel By, with the assistance of Philemon Wright's woodsmen, Legget, *Ottawa Waterway, op. cit.,* p. 177-82.

175 Legget, *Ottawa Waterway, op. cit.,* p. 186-87.

176 MacTaggart, *op. cit.,* Vol. 2, p. 16-18; Legget, *Ottawa Waterway, op. cit.,* p. 51-53; Colonel By's health never fully recovered from the malaria and he died in 1836, only four years after his return to England. See Andrew, *op. cit.,* chapter 7.

177 Andrew Wilson, May 18, 1827 letter, LAC, S-1 Sundries, cited in Brault, *Ottawa Old and New,* 81. Wilson was one of four magistrates (three from Upper Town) subsequently appointed to keep the peace.

178 Peter Craske (ed.), *Law and Order in the Early Days of Bytown/Ottawa,* (Ottawa, ON: Historical Society of Ottawa, Bytown Pamphlet Series no. 41, 1992); also Brault, *Ottawa Old and New, op. cit.,* p. 126-32.

179 Brault, *Ottawa Old and New, op. cit.,* p. 80.

180 The Barrack Hill fortress cost was estimated at £205,000, (see Andrew, *op. cit.,* p. 158); James De Jonge, *Military Establishment at Bytown, 1826-1856,* (Ottawa, ON: Parks Canada, Microfiche Report Series, 1983), p. 109.

181 Fort Henry's stone redoubt was completed in 1836 and extended in 1841. During the Oregon Boundary Crisis in 1846-48, an additional four Martello Towers were built to defend the canal entrance and Kingston harbour, and a sea battery was constructed in front of Kingston City Hall (see Passfield, *op. cit.,* p. 174-75).

182 Passfield, *op. cit.,* p. 112, 138-39, 158-59.

183 Legget, *Ottawa Waterway, op. cit.,* p. 55-57.

184 Passfield, *op. cit.,* p. 19-32.

185 By purchased the lands from absentee owner William McQueen, grandson of the original Loyalist grantee, Thomas Fraser (see Newton, *op. cit.,* Vol. 1, p. 70-72 and Elliott, *City Beyond, op. cit.,* p. 7-9). Ironically, By retained John Burrows, previous owner of the Sparks property, to manage these lands after his departure. Burrows attempted to develop the land with 21-year leases, but had little success collecting rents. He was replaced by lawyer and future mayor John Scott and then Seth Thomas, who were equally ineffective in collecting rent or evicting the many squatters. The heirs of the By estate continued to insist on leases after the Colonel's premature death in 1836 and the property was not extensively developed until after this policy was changed in 1873. See Elliott, *City Beyond, op. cit.,* p. 90-92.

186 Robert Moon, *Colonel By's Friends Stood Up,* (Ottawa, ON: Crocus House, 1979).

187 By was caught in a dispute between Treasury Board and the Ordnance about controlling costs of military works, and also in an attempt by the new Reform government to discredit a project personally initiated by the previous prime minister, a military hero. See Andrew, *op. cit.,* chapter 7; Legget, *Ottawa Waterway, op. cit.,* p. 58-67; Passfield, *op. cit.,* p. 33-35. Even the new Master General of the Ordnance, Sir James Kempt, who had earlier recommended the expanded canal design, could not protect Colonel By, since the Whigs had appointed him on condition that he not be involved in party politics. See P. Burroughs' *DCB* biography of Kempt.

188 Dalhousie tried not to interfere with the prickly Lt. Governor of Upper Canada, Sir Peregrine Maitland (see Whitelaw, *op. cit.,* Vols. 2 and 3), but as Governor General and Commander in Chief of the military forces, he should have exercised his authority to extract a better *Rideau Canal Act* from the Upper Canada Legislature.

189 The provincial surveyors, who had laid out many towns, might have been able to assist. See R.L. Gentilcore and C.G. Head, *Ontario's History in Maps,* (Toronto, ON: University of Toronto Press, 1984), chapter 7.

190 Sparks had purchased his lot for £95 and might have been bought out for LeBreton's price (£2000) or less

while it was still assumed that the canal entrance was to be east of the Rideau, as recommended in previous engineering reports. The four lots to the south of Sparks were purchased by Colonel By for £1200 in 1832 *after* construction of the canal was complete; presumably they would have been available at a much smaller price from their absentee owners in 1826.

[191] See Frederick Gutheim and Antoinette Lee, *Worthy of the Nation*, 2nd ed., (Baltimore, MD: John Hopkins University Press, 2006), p. 1-24.

[192] J. Williams, *Additional Rules and Regulations for the conduct of the Land-Office Department*, (Québec, QC: Québec (Province) Land Office Department, August 25, 1789), p. 1.

[193] The construction of a second barracks building on Sussex Street was a better example. It was built by a civilian contractor and initially used as a hotel, before being converted to a barracks. After the departure of the imperial garrison it was converted into the Clarendon Hotel. See M. Newton, *Lower Town Ottawa, Vol. 1, op. cit.*; Lucien Brault, *The Mile of History*, (Ottawa, ON: NCC, 1981), p. 62-67. The arrangements for the canal workers were less successful. Although a 'civilian barracks' was built at Rideau and Sussex streets, it was not large enough for more than a few of the skilled trades. Some contractors provided shanties for their single men, similar to arrangements in the backwoods lumber camps, but the labourers with families were in desperate condition. In the best case, they might share a tenement in Lower Town with several other families. A temporary construction camp is a standard practice when the workforce is expected to leave after the project is completed, but conditions in Corktown were abominable. See William N.T. Wylie, "Poverty, Distress and Disease: Labour and the Construction of the Rideau Canal 1826-32," *Labour/Le Travailleur*, 11 (Spring 1983): 7-29. A planned construction camp, even in the 19th century, might have included a well for a supply of fresh water and free lumber to improve the labourer's shacks and burrows.

Chapter 3

[194] H. Labouchere to Sir E. Head, December 31, 1857, reprinted in Canada Legislative Assembly, *Journals*, 21 Vict., 1858: 139.

[195] John Taylor, *Ottawa: An Illustrated History*, (Toronto, ON: Lorimer, 1986), Table I.

[196] A.R.M. Lower, *Great Britain's Woodyard: British America and the Timber Trade, 1763-1867*, (Montréal, QC and Kingston, ON: McGill-Queen's University Press, 1973), chapter 16; Chad Gaffield (ed.), *History of the Outaouais*, (Québec, QC: Les Presses de l'Université Laval, 1997), p. 157-60.

[197] Taylor, 1986, *op. cit.*, p. 23-45.

[198] Linda Tresham, *Bytown and the Cholera Epidemic of 1832*, (Ottawa, ON: Historical Society of Ottawa, Bytown Pamphlet Series no. 14, 1993). Fifteen people died at the hospital in 1832 and 52 in 1834, see Lucien Brault, *Ottawa Old and New*, (Ottawa, ON: Ottawa Historical Information Institute, 1946), p. 233-36; M. Newton, *Lower Town Ottawa, Vol 1., 1826-1854*, (Ottawa, ON: National Capital Commission, Manuscript Report 104, 1979), p. 114-17.

[199] The local primary sources for this episode are scanty, with just a few desperate letters from the magistrates, and no local newspapers until 1836. Perhaps the best coverage was by Perth's Bathurst *Courier*, (1835-37) which was a bit smug about the lawless activities at the edge of its district. Michael S. Cross, "The Shiner's War: Social Violence in the Ottawa Valley in the 1830s," *Canadian Historical Review*, 54 (March 1973) appears to be the most completely researched account, although there are interesting perspectives in Brault, *Ottawa Old and New, op cit.*, p. 65-67; Newton, *op. cit.*, Vol. 1, p. 109-17, and Gaffield (ed.), *op cit.*, p. 209-14.

[200] Most Protestant and Catholic Irish immigrants to Eastern Ontario became successful small farmers; as shown by D. Akenson, *The Irish in Ontario: A Study in Rural History*, (Montréal, QC and Kingston, ON: McGill-Queen's University Press, 1984). The smaller number of poor, unskilled Catholic Irish immigrants to Bytown had a more difficult experience.

[201] The source of the nickname is obscure. It may have referred to *chêneurs* (hewers of wood), to the shiny hats of the immigrants, the new coins with which the timber crews were paid, or that their members were to 'shine' among others. See A.R.M. Lower, *Great Britain's Woodyard, op. cit.*, p. 188; Brault, *Ottawa Old and New, op. cit.*, p. 65-66; Cross, "The Shiners' War," *op. cit.*, p. 2.

202 Newton, *op. cit., Vol. 1*, p. 109-10.

203 Aylen (1799-1868) was more than a gang leader. A small timber cutter who expanded his network by marriage into a Nepean timber family, he joined the Wrights and other Hull merchants as part of the 'Gatineau Privilege,' a monopoly for cutting pine on the Gatineau River from 1832-46. Although arrested several times in 1835, the magistrates could not hold him, as his Shiners rioted, destroying a canal steamer in the turning basin. The other timber merchants attempted to co-opt Aylen into the Ottawa Lumber Association, set up to control violence on the rivers in 1836. After his defeat in Bytown in 1837, Aylen leased his substantial holdings in the village and Nepean township, and moved his operations to Aylmer in Lower Canada, where he was out of reach of the Upper Town magistrates. There Aylen switched tactics, becoming the pillar of society, even being appointed a justice of the peace in 1848! See M. Cross, "Peter Aylen" in *Dictionary of Canadian Biography, Vol. IX*, (Toronto, ON: University of Toronto Press, 1976), p. 13-14; also M. Stewart, "King of the Shiners" in E. Stafford (ed.), *Flamboyant Canadians*, (Toronto, ON: Baxter Publishing, 1964,), p. 63-81; and M. Cross, "The Shiners' War," *op. cit.*

204 Cross, "Peter Aylen," *op. cit.*, p. 14-17.

205 G. Goyer and J. Hamelin, "Joseph Montferrand" in *Dictionary of Canadian Biography, Vol. IX* (Toronto, ON: University of Toronto Press, 1976).

206 Cross, "Shiners' War," *op. cit.*, p. 18-19.

207 Brault, *Ottawa Old and New, op. cit.*, p. 6-9, 201; see also R. Reid, "James Johnston" in *Dictionary of Canadian Biography, Vol. IX*, (Toronto, ON: University of Toronto Press, 1976). Johnston's *Bytown Independent and Farmer's Advocate* commenced in February 1836 and was short-lived. He sold his new press to Dr. Christie, who began to publish the *Bytown Gazette* in June 1836.

208 M. Cross, "Shiners' War," *op. cit.*, p. 21-22.

209 M. Cross, "Peter Aylen," *op. cit.*

210 David Knight, *Choosing Canada's Capital: Conflict Resolution in a Parliamentary System*, (Ottawa, ON: Carleton University Press, 1991), p. 47-96; also Brault, *Ottawa Old and New, op. cit.*, p. 144-46; for Christie's advocacy for Bytown on the seat of government, see "The Seat of Government," *Bytown Gazette*, Aug. 27, 1840; "Bytown ought to be the Capital," *Bytown Gazette*, Sept. 17, 1840; "Seat of Government," *Bytown Gazette*, Jan. 19, 1844. On March 7, 1844, the *Gazette* published a letter from 'Vesper' recalling an 1820 conversation with Lord Dalhousie on the banks of the Ottawa River, during his first visit. The Governor General was quoted as "…on that eminence" (pointing to Barrack Hill) "may one day be the Seat of Government."

211 The Governor General was deceiving the Bytown population by holding out the possibility of the seat of government, since he had already decided on Kingston; see C.P. Thomson, (Governor General, Lord Sydenham) to Lord John Russell (Colonial Secretary) Private and Confidential, May 22, 1840, reprinted in D.B. Knight, *Choosing Canada's Capital: Conflict Resolution in a Parliamentary System*, (Ottawa, ON: Carleton University Press, 1991), p. 53-55.

212 Gaffield (ed.), *op. cit.*, p. 214-17.

213 There were only 85 eligible voters in Bytown's general population of perhaps 3,500 in 1841, since the property ownership required for the franchise was rare in the Lower Town's Ordnance lands. Derbishire defeated Lower Town merchant William Stewart 52 to 29. Stewart protested the partisan actions of Returning Officer George Baker, an Upper Town magistrate, postmaster and prominent Tory. See Brault, *Ottawa Old and New, op. cit.*, p. 141-45. The franchise was similarly limited by the Wright's ownership of land in Hull township.

214 C.P. Thomson, (Governor General, Lord Sydenham) to Lord John Russell (Colonial Secretary) Private and Confidential, May 22, 1840, reprinted in Knight, *op. cit.*, p. 54.

215 Gaffield (ed.), *op. cit.*, p. 211-12.

216 Brault, *Ottawa Old and New, op. cit.*, p. 83.

217 The Tory *Gazette* owned by A.J. Christie was not happy that the courthouse was going to Lower Town, and that Christie's son did not win the construction contract. See Newton, *op. cit., Vol. 1*, p. 135-37.

218 After 1850, districts were reorganized into counties and the Dalhousie District became Carleton County. See "Historical Sketch of Carleton County," in *Illustrated Historical Atlas of the County of Carleton* (Toronto, ON: Lt. Belden & Co.,

1879) and H. Walker and O. Walker, *Carleton Saga*, (Ottawa, ON: Carleton County Council, 1968).

[219] Brault, *Ottawa Old and New*, *op. cit.*, p. 84. The other Nepean councillor was timber merchant John Thomson, brother-in-law of the notorious Peter Aylen. See M. Cross, "Peter Aylen," *op. cit.*

[220] The court began in 1844. See Lucien Brault, *Hull 1800-1950*, (Ottawa, ON: Les Éditions de l'Université d'Ottawa, 1950), p. 55-68.

[221] The Union Suspension Bridge was designed by the engineer Thomas Keefer, and was the longest in Canada until Keefer's later bridge across the Niagara Gorge. The suspension bridge was replaced by a more utilitarian steel truss in 1889. See Lucien Brault, *Links between Two Cities: Historic Bridges between Ottawa and Hull*, (Hull, QC: City of Hull and Ottawa, ON: City of Ottawa, 1989), p. 17.

[222] Gaffield (ed.), *op. cit.*, p. 200-07; Brault, *Ottawa Old and New*, *op. cit.*, p. 204-13; Brault, *Hull*, *op. cit.*, p. 210-28. The College achieved university status in 1866 and become the bilingual Université d'Ottawa, still located in Lower Town and the adjacent neighbourhood of Sandy Hill. See Brault, *Ottawa Old and New*, *op. cit.*, p. 270-77.

[223] Taylor, 1986, *op. cit.*, p. 40-42, Figure 4, 68.

[224] Canada, Legislative Council, *An Act to define the limits of the Town of Bytown, to establish a Town Council therein, and for other purposes*, 10 and 11 Vict. Cap.4, July 28, 1847, p. 1,459-71; Brault, *Ottawa Old and New*, *op. cit.*, p. 85-86.

[225] E. Welch, ed., *Bytown Council Minutes 1847-48*, (Ottawa, ON: City of Ottawa, 1978).

[226] Sparks had donated the land for the failed Upper Town market. Conversion of the market to a city hall would improve the value of his adjacent property, and bring another civic institution to Upper Town. The Tories could force the city hall relocation because they had a 4-3 majority on council in 1849, even though Lower Town had a much larger population. The Lower Town ward boundaries had been gerrymandered by the Tories in the provincial legislature so that the "South Ward" might elect a merchant, which they did in 1849 and 1850, giving the Tories control of the town council. The 1850 Reform regime in the provincial government produced another set of ward boundaries that elected Reform mayors from 1851-55. A further revision in 1855 produced Tory mayors until the population growth in the new wards finally overwhelmed the Upper Town residents. See Taylor, 1986, *op. cit.*, p. 41-42, 68-70.

[227] *Bytown Packet*, August 25, 1849; Brault, *Ottawa Old and New*, *op. cit.*, p. 92-93.

[228] The Orange Order had been active throughout the 1840s, provoking riots during Governor Metcalfe's visit on August 19, 1843; several days of rioting also took place after the 1846 Orange parades. See Brault, *Ottawa Old and New*, *op. cit.*, "The Arch Riot," p. 70-72. The Orangemen continued the Shiners' tactic of rescuing prisoners by mob assaults on the magistrates conveying them to jail. Unfortunately, the new Bytown jail was poorly designed, with windows adjacent to the street, so that prisoners' friends could pass tools useful for jailbreaks. See "Memorial of the Sheriff of the District of Dalhousie to the Governor General," 1986 LAC PSO Correspondence, RG5 C1, *Vol. 195*, December 23, 1845, cited in Taylor, 1986, *op. cit.*, p. 40. A more secure jail was built after the original building burned in 1860; see Brault, *Ottawa Old and New*, *op. cit.*, p. 132.

[229] Seventeen of the 19 nuns had contracted typhus and one died while treating the 3,100 Irish immigrants who arrived in July 1847. No accurate count of the victims could be maintained, but hundreds died and were buried in mass graves. Lett was a fervent Orangeman whose newspaper never lost an opportunity to attack Catholics, even nuns who put their lives at risk treating an epidemic. The Tory majority on City Council appointed him as the City Clerk in 1855. See Newton, *op. cit.*, *Vol. 1*, p. 260-63; Brault, *Ottawa Old and New*, *op. cit.*, p. 236-37.

[230] The newspaper accounts of this event are probably not reliable. Bytown's two major papers in 1849 had strong partisan connections – the Tory *Gazette* and the Reform *Packet*. Michael Cross reconstructs the events from official correspondence in "Stony Monday, 1849: The Rebellion Losses Riots in Bytown," *Ontario History*, 63 (1971), no. 4: 177-90; Michael Newton incorporates extensive excerpts from the subsequent trials in "Lower Town," *op. cit.*, chapter 15, "The Stony Monday Riot of 1849," p. 276-334.

[231] For more details on the riot, see Cross, *op. cit.*, p. 186-87 and Newton, *op. cit.*, p. 278-81.

[232] Brault, *Ottawa Old and New, op. cit.*, p. 76-77. The Wrights sided with the Reformers as 'Yankees'; M. Cross, "The Age of Gentility: Construction of an Aristocracy in the Ottawa Valley," *Canadian Historical Association Papers*, 2 (1967), no. 1: 105-17.

[233] Taylor, 1986, *op. cit.*, p. 45. The troops raided the Wright's armoury the next day in an attempt to secure the rest of the arms. Joshua Wright, Ruggles Wright Jr. and Shiner leader Andrew Leamy were arrested while allegedly trying to fire a cannon at the soldiers. But the officers discovered that they had no authority in Lower Canada and had to release their prisoners. See Cross, "Stony Monday," *op. cit.*, p. 188-89.

[234] Brault, *Ottawa Old and New, op. cit.*, describes the conflict mainly as a political dispute, while Newton, 1979, *op. cit.*, p. 279, regards the incident as a "religious riot thinly covered by partisan political affiliation;" Cross, "Stony Monday," *op. cit.*, p. 190, describes the conflict as economically-driven, caused by the recession.

[235] See the editorial in *The Globe and Mail* (Toronto, ON), Sept. 20, 1849, p. 2; the news of Bytown riots even reached the papers in Scotland, see "The Scottish Guardian on Canada," Toronto *Globe*, Nov. 20, 1849, p. 2. In 1851 Bytown had 70 licensed taverns for a population of about 7,760, or one legal tavern per 111 residents. Apparently the licenced establishments may have been out-numbered by the 'shebeen' shops, 'hotels' and other speakeasies. See Newton, *op. cit.*, p. 372-76.

[236] D. McCalla, "Forest Products and Upper Canadian Development, 1815-46," *Canadian Historical Review*, 68, no. 2, (1987): 176-77.

[237] The District of Hull, which also included several rural townships had a population of 2,811 in 1851 and 3,711 in 1861 (Brault, *Hull, op. cit.*, Appendix A, p. 229); while Bytown alone had a population of 7,760 in the 1851 census and 14,669 in 1861. See Taylor, 1986, *op. cit.*, Table II, p. 210.

[238] M. Newton, "The Decade of Efficiency, Expansion and Improvement in Lower Town" in *Lower Town Ottawa, Vol. 1, op. cit.*, p. 343-78.

[239] It would take large fires that burned out several blocks of Sussex and York streets in the early 1860s before Bytown would get serious about purchasing fire engines, establishing a professional fire brigade and providing a piped water supply. But given the power of the lumber industry, council would not pass regulations requiring fireproof masonry construction in place of the vital timber construction. See Brault, *Ottawa Old and New, op. cit.*, p. 117-24; M. Newton, "The Ottawa Fire Brigades" in *Lower Town Ottawa, Vol. 2*, (Ottawa, ON: NCC, 1981), p. 397-421.

[240] The new Reform legislature struck back by re-arranging the ward boundaries to further disadvantage the Tory political friends of the Ordnance. See Taylor, 1986, *op. cit.*, p. 39-40.

[241] See E.F. Bush, "Thomas McKay" in *Dictionary of Canadian Biography, Vol. VII*, (Toronto, ON: University of Toronto Press, 1985).

[242] R.W. Scott, "The Sawed Lumber Trade" in *Recollections of Bytown: Some Incidents in the History of Ottawa*, (Ottawa, ON: The Mortimer Press, 1911), p. 20.

[243] S. Coutts, *New Edinburgh Heritage Conservation District Study*, (Ottawa, ON: City of Ottawa Department of Urban Planning and Public Works, 2000), p. 2-6.

[244] Coutts, *op. cit.*

[245] Taylor, 1986, *op. cit.*, p. 52-56.

[246] R.W. Scott, "Coming of the American Colony," in *Recollections of Bytown, op. cit.*, p. 21-22.

[247] Newton, *Lowertown, Vol. 1, op. cit.*, p. 379-82.

[248] The other end of the railway was equally bad – it could not connect to the Grand Trunk's Montréal-Toronto line at Prescott because the tracks were constructed with a narrower gauge. And the B&P trains could not cross the St. Lawrence to connect to American railways for want of a bridge. See C.C.J. Bond, "Tracks into Ottawa: The Construction of Railways into Canada's Capital," *Ontario History*, 17, no. 1 (1965): 123-27.

[249] Taylor, 1986, *op. cit.*, p. 47-49.

[250] Taylor, 1986, *op. cit.*, Table 2.

[251] Brault, 1945, *op. cit.*, p. 87-89.

[252] Taylor, 1986, *op. cit.*, p. 68-70.

253 Taylor, 1986, *op. cit.*, p. 39. Although John By is now regarded as the founder of Bytown and his canal is now recognized as a masterpiece of 19th century engineering, Ottawa council refused to commemorate his name for almost a century. After pressure from the Ottawa Historical Society and the Engineering Institute of Canada, the parkway on the east side of the canal was named Colonel By Drive in the 1960s, and a memorial to By erected in Major's Hill park overlooking the entrance locks, see R. Legget, *Rideau Waterway,* (Toronto, ON: University of Toronto Press, 1972), p. 219-20.

254 Brault, *Ottawa Old and New, op. cit.*, p. 19-20. The Ottawa name is therefore tied both to the aboriginal voyageurs and the river itself. Ottawa also had a Québec connotation in 1854 – Ottawa County was a riding for the Legislative assemblies for Lower Canada, the United Canadas and the province of Québec from 1829 to 1919, and at the federal level from 1867 to 1896; Gaffield (ed.), *op. cit.* p. 825-31.

255 M. Newton, *op. cit.*, p. 98-99.

256 The Ordnance were disappointed that the Canadian government would not even contribute to the cost of the land for the canal, and were outraged when provincial politicians like attorney general William Draper and Stewart Derbishire advised their tenants not to pay rent. George Raudzens, *The British Ordnance Department and Canada's Canals, 1815-1855*, (Waterloo, ON: Wilfrid Laurier University Press, 1979), p. 109.

257 See Newton, *Lower Town Ottawa, Vol. 1, op. cit.*, p. 335-36.

258 "Petition of the Inhabitants of the Town of Bytown to Lord Sydenham requesting that their leases be terminated to Deeds," LAC; Hill collection MG24, I9, Vol. 25, p. 5,933; June 4, 1841; reprinted in Newton, *op. cit., Vol. 1*, p. 139-41.

259 "The Ordnance Question," *The Bytown Gazette*, August 31, 1843.

260 Canada, Legislative Assembly, "An Act for vesting in the Principal Officers of Her Majesty's Ordnance the Estates and Property therein described," Vict., chapter 21, December 9, 1843.

261 This set off another bout of land speculation, as people with a previous interest in a lot came forward to try to claim it. Most of the original grantees for lots in Upper and Lower Town had not built anything within a year, as the terms of Colonel By's leases required. Most of the lots reverted to the Ordnance after a year, upon lack of performance or non-payment of their nominal rents. Twenty years later, many of these lots were quite valuable downtown sites, and the original grantees re-appeared demanding the right to buy them. Even the newly elected Bytown MPP William Stewart got involved, claiming a valuable Lower Town lot on Sussex Street that Colonel By had allegedly rented to him in 1827, for which he could not produce a lease, and had never paid any rent. When a second person came forward with a similar allegation for the same lot, Stewart introduced a bill into the legislature supporting his own claim! The Ordnance had to be careful how it handled Stewart, because he was arranging the arbitration for Nicholas Sparks' land. See Newton, *Lower Town, op. cit., Vol. 1*, p. 154-61.

262 Newton, *op. cit.*, p. 152-54.

263 Canada, Legislative Assembly, "Report of Special Committee on the Petition of Nicholas Sparks and others" 8 Vict. 1st sess., 1845, March 4, 1845. Sparks was represented by former Bytown Tory M.P.P. Stewart Derbishire and the chair of the mediation panel was John A. Macdonald of Kingston, then a rookie Tory MPP, and future prime minister.

264 Newton, *op. cit., Vol. 1*, p. 156-59.

265 The canal made a profit of between £852 and £2731 from 1842 to 1845. It lost money in all other years. Raudzens, *op. cit.*, p. 112-14.

266 Robert Passfield, *Engineering the Defence of the Canadas: Lt. Col. By and the Rideau Canal,* (Ottawa, ON: Parks Canada, 1980), p. 181-82.

267 Mark Fram, *Central Area West Heritage Conservation District Study and Plan, City of Ottawa,* (Toronto, ON: Polymath Planning and Design, December 1999), p. 10-11.

268 Charles P. De Volpi, *Ottawa: A Pictorial Record,* (Montréal, QC: DEV SCO Publications, 1964), p. 66.

269 Brault, *Ottawa Old and New, op. cit.*, p. 218-22.

270 Donating sites for elite institutions improved Sparks' social position. He was the only Irish labourer to be accepted as a member of Upper Town's Tory gentility. See Cross "The Age of Gentility," *op. cit.*

271 Taylor, 1986, *op. cit.*, p. 14.

272 The Sparks family was reported to have made almost £500,000 in land sales by 1882. See F.A. Dixon, "Ottawa" in George M. Grant (ed.), *Picturesque Canada: The Country as it Was and Is, Vol. I*, (Toronto, ON: Art Publishing Company, 1875-1882), p. 165.

273 Reform governments in Britain had reduced imperial garrisons and attempted to consolidate the military departments, but the Duke of Wellington's support for the Ordnance delayed the re-organization until after his death in 1852. See Raudzens, *op. cit.*, p. 23-25.

274 Grant, *op. cit.*, p.163.

Chapter 4

275 S. Gwynn, *The Private Capital*, (Toronto, ON: Harper Collins, 1984).

276 See T. Hall, *Planning Europe's Capital Cities*, (London, UK: Spon, 1997).

277 E.G. Burrows and M. Wallace, *Gotham: A History of New York to 1896*, (New York, NY: Oxford University Press, 1999), chapters 16-21.

278 United States First Congress, Sess. II, Ch. 28, 179, *An Act for establishing the temporary and permanent seat of the Government of the United States*, approved July 16, 1790; Section 6 set a hard deadline of the first Monday of December 1800 to transfer the federal government from Philadelphia.

279 Frederick Gutheim and Antoinette Lee, *Worthy of the Nation, Washington, DC, From L'Enfant to the National Capital Planning Commission*, (Baltimore, MD: Johns Hopkins University Press, 2006), chapter 2.

280 See David L.A. Gordon (ed.), *Planning Twentieth Century Capital Cities*, (London, UK: Routledge, 2006), chapters 10, 12, 13, 14.

281 Charles Dickens, *American Notes for General Circulation*, (London UK: Chapman and Hall, 1842; rpt. ed. London UK: Penguin, 1972), p. 249.

282 Bagot to Lord Stanley (Colonial Secretary), January 19, 1842, reprinted in David Knight, *Choosing Canada's Capital: Conflict Resolution in a Parliamentary System*, (Ottawa, ON: Carleton University Press, 1991), p. 67-70, and "Joint Address of the Legislative Council and Legislative Assembly to Queen Victoria, November 8, 1843. Reprinted in Knight, *op. cit.*, p. 90-91.

283 Brian S. Osborne and Donald Swainson, *Kingston: Building on the Past*, (Westport ON: Butternut Press, 1988), chapter 6.

284 Peter B. Waite, "Between Three Oceans: Challenges of a Continental Destiny (1840-1900) in Craig Brown (ed.), *The Illustrated History of Canada*, (Toronto, ON: Lester & Orpen Dennys, 1987), p. 290-94.

285 See Wilfrid Eggleston, *The Queen's Choice: A Story of Canada's Capital*, (Ottawa, ON: National Capital Commission, 1961), p. 14-15, 226.

286 M.S. Cross, "Stony Monday, 1849: The Rebellion Losses Riots in Bytown," *Ontario History*, 63, no. 3 (1971): 177-190; Michael Newton, *Lower Town Ottawa (1826-1854)*, (Ottawa, ON: National Capital Commission, 1979), chapter 15.

287 For example, the government spent £71,726 to move the capital from Ville de Québec to Toronto in 1855. See Canada Legislative Assembly *Journals*, 19 Vict., 1856, Appendix 21.

288 Canada Legislative Assembly *Journals*, 19 Vict., 1856, Department of Public Works, April 10, 1856, p. 281-83.

289 Canada Legislative Assembly, *Journals*, 20 Vict., 1857, March 24, 1857, 131-34; Knight, *op. cit.*, p. 168, notes that the vote was 64 to 48, divided on a political party basis.

290 R.W. Scott, *The choice of the capital: reminiscences revived on the fiftieth anniversary of the selection of Ottawa as the capital of Canada by her late majesty*, (Ottawa, ON: Mortimer Press, 1907).

291 Memorial of the City of Ottawa, May 18, 1857; reprinted in Knight, *op. cit.*, p. 233.

292 Knight, *op. cit.*, chapter 7.

293 Memorial of the City of Ottawa, May 18, 1857; reprinted in Knight, *op. cit.*, p. 237.

294 Macdonald letter, see Knight, *op. cit.*, chapter 9

295 E. Head, "Confidential Memorandum" in *Papers Relative to the Seat of Government in Canada*, (London: Colonial Office, 1857) in LAC MG27, IA2, file B1067, p. 225-51. Also reprinted in Knight, *op. cit.*, p. 250-55.

296 H. Labouchere to Sir E. Head, December 31, 1857, reprinted in Canada Legislative Assembly, *Journals*, 21 Vict., 1858: 139.

297 Eggleston, *op. cit.*

298 Newspapers, see Knight, *op. cit.*, p. 278-80.

299 Knight, *op. cit.*

300 Canada Legislative Assembly, *Journals,* 21 Vict. 1858, July 28, 1858: 930.

301 Canada Legislative Assembly, *Journals,* 22 Vict. 1859, January 29, 1859: 9-10.

302 For the lobby, see Scott, *Choice of the Capital, op. cit.* Scott himself switched from the Reform Party to supporting Macdonald for over a decade. See Brian Clarke, "Sir Richard William Scott' in *Dictionary of Canadian Biography, Vol. XIV,* (Toronto, ON: University of Toronto Press, 1998). For the vote, see Canada Legislative Assembly, *Journals,* 21 Vict. 1858, February 10, defeated 59-64. See also David Knight's detailed description of the vote in Knight, *op. cit.*, p. 285-96 and Scott's memoir, "Seat of Government" in R.W. Scott, *Recollections of Bytown,* (Ottawa, ON: Mortimer Press, 1911), p. 25-27.

303 Canada, Department of Public Works, "Notice to Architects" Toronto, May 7, 1859; reprinted in Canada, Legislative Assembly, 25 Vict. *Sessional Papers* 1862, no. 3, April 9, 1862, "Appendices to the Report of the Commissioner of Public Works."

304 *Bytown Gazette,* March 7, 1844.

305 Carolyn A. Young, *The Glory of Ottawa: Canada's First Parliament Buildings,* (Montréal, QC and Kingston, ON: McGill-Queen's University Press, 1995), p. 90.

306 *Ibid.*, p. 29.

307 *Ibid.*, p. 90.

308 The driveways in Calvert Vaux's 1873 landscape plan were aligned with the gates to the Hill, rather than the proposed alignment of Metcalfe or O'Connor streets in Sparks' subdivision plan.

309 The Parliament Buildings began construction just after the Canadian government switched currency from sterling to dollars in 1858, with an exchange rate of just under $4.90 to the pound. The records of the day use pounds for the early appropriations and dollars for the expenditures, which only added to the confusion over the project.

310 Canada, Department of Public Works, "Notice to Architects," Toronto, May 7, 1859, *op. cit.*

311 "Reception of H.R.H. The Prince of Wales," *Ottawa Citizen,* September 1, 1860.

312 Ralph Greenhill, "The Camera as the Engineer's Witness," *National Gallery of Canada Journal,* 16 (1985): 4-5.

313 Canada, Legislative Assembly, 25 Vict. *Sessional Papers,* 1862, no. 3, April 9, 1862, report of Public Works commissioner Joseph Cauchon, "Ottawa Buildings," p. 55-57.

314 Canada, Legislative Assembly 25. Vict. *Debates,* 1862, p. 142, J.C. Chapais.

315 Canada, Legislative Assembly, 26 Vict. *Sessional Papers,* 1863, no. 3. "Report of the Commission Appointed to Inquire into matters connected with the Public Buildings at Ottawa," January 29, 1863, p. 1.

316 R.G. Trotter, "An Early Proposal for the Federation of British North America," *Canadian Historical Review,* 25 (1925): 142-54.

317 "Canadian Affairs," *New York Times*, February 11, 1859, 2; also, Knight, *op. cit.*, p. 333.

318 J.M.S. Careless, *Brown of the Globe, Vol. 2,* (Toronto, ON: Macmillan, 1963).

319 Brown to Macdonald, August 15, 1864; Brown papers LAC MG24-F122, reprinted in Eggleston, *op. cit.*, p. 131. On the same day, Brown also wrote to his wife, that the buildings were "…fit for the British, French and Russian Empires, were they all confederates … the whole stands on a high promontory, seen all around for a great distance, and amid scenery no where equaled…" Brown to A. Brown, August 15, 1864, LAC MG24-F122 Brown Paper – Letters, partial facsimile in Eggleston, *op. cit.* p. 132-33.

320 The delegates negotiated in private, and kept no minutes, or official records. So the best understanding of the proceedings was pieced together by P.B. Waite from dinner speeches and newspaper accounts. P.B. Waite, *The Life and Times of Confederation, 1864-1867: politics, newspapers and the union of British North America,* (Toronto, ON: Robin Brass Studio, 2001); Charles Tupper's minutes do not mention the seat-of-government issue, either, see Ramsay Cook and R. Craig Brown (eds.), "Charles Tupper's Minutes of the Charlottetown Conference," *The Canadian Historical Review,* 48 (June 1967): 101-12; no mention in the 1865 debates, either, see P.B. Waite, *The Confederation Debates in the Province of Canada, 1865,* (Montréal, QC and Kingston, ON: McGill-Queen's University Press, 2006).

321 But the room had a fine view of the St. Lawrence River, perhaps inspiring dreams of a wider nation. See "The Colonists in Council," *Montréal Gazette*, October 28, 1864, reprinted in Peter Waite, *Confederation, 1854-1867*, (Toronto, ON: Holt, Rinehart and Winston of Canada, 1972), p. 86. The river view was later used by Robert Harris for the background of his 1884 painting "The Fathers of Confederation" reconstructing the delegates in debate. The painting was hung in the Parliament Buildings and was destroyed in the 1916 fire. See Moncrieff Williamson, "Robert Harris and the Fathers of Confederation," *National Gallery of Canada Bulletin*, 6, no. 2 (1968).

322 A.G. Doughty (ed.), "Notes on the Québec Conference, 1864", *Canadian Historical Review*, 1 (1920): 26-47; Waite, *Life and Times of Confederation, op. cit.*

323 "Report of Resolution Adopted at a Conference of Delegates from the Provinces of Canada, Nova Scotia and New Brunswick and the Colonies of Newfoundland and Prince Edward Island, held at the City of Québec, October 10, 1864 as the basis of a proposed Confederation of those Provinces and Colonies." In *Resolutions Relative to the Proposed Union of the British North American Provinces*, (LAC, Sir John A. Macdonald papers, Vol. 49, Part 2, Roll C-1505, 19808-19814), p. 9; Macdonald appears to have kept the packet of original motions slips in the LAC Macdonald papers MG 26 A Political Papers, 1864.

324 Saint John lawyer, John H. Gray, who represented New Brunswick at the Charlottetown and Québec conferences later criticized the decision not to make Ottawa a federal district, but this appears to be hindsight; his memoirs make no mention of an objection during the conferences. See John Hamilton Gray, *Confederation; or, The Political and Parliamentary History of Canada from The Conference at Québec in October 1864*, (Toronto, ON: Copp Clark, 1872).

325 The $3.4 million spent on the Parliament Buildings by 1866 was about half the total public debt of New Brunswick ($7 million) at Confederation. See Québec Conference 1864 resolution 61 for the public debt of the provinces.

326 Edward Whelan (ed.), *The Union of the British Provinces*, (Charlottetown, PE: Haszard, 1865) contains reports of many of the pro-Confederation speeches from the two conferences.

327 Alexander Galt, Nov. 1, 1864, Ottawa speech, in Whelan, *op. cit.*, p. 139-44. See also the best-selling expedition diary by Canadian nationalist, George M. Grant, *Ocean to Ocean*, (Toronto, ON: James Campbell And Son, 1873).

328 Whelan (ed.), *op. cit.*, p. 126-28.

329 J.H. Gray, *Confederation: The Political and Parliamentary History of Canada*, (Toronto, ON: Copp Clark, 1872), p. 104-114. Gray's description of the delegates' November 1864 Ottawa tour appears to draw on Whelan (ed.), *op. cit.*

330 Knight, *op. cit.*, p. 333, and *Halifax Morning Chronicle*, June 9, 1866.

331 "Canada – The Seat of Government to be Removed," *New York Times*, January 18, 1867, p. 1.

332 United Kingdom, "An Act for the Union of Canada, Nova Scotia and New Brunswick and the Government thereof;" *30 & 31 Victoria, C.3* (U.K.), March 29, 1867, S.16.

333 F.A. Dixon, "Ottawa," in *Picturesque Canada: The Country as it Was and Is, Volume I*, George M. Grant (ed.) (Toronto, ON: Toronto Art Publishing Company, 1875-1882), p. 163.

334 C.C.J. Bond, "The Canadian Government Comes to Ottawa, 1865-66," *Ontario History*, 55, no. 1 (1963): 24-25.

335 John Page, "Report by John Page, Chief Engineer on the Condition of the Public Buildings at Ottawa" in Province of Canada, 29 Vict. *Sessional Papers, 1866*, Vol. 1, Report of the Public Works Department, p. 54.

336 Canada Legislative Assembly, *Journals*, 29 Vict. 1866, June 8, 1859, p. 13-24. Although the Governor General's first remarks were about the "magnificent buildings, erected in the city chosen by Her Majesty…" the legislators replies were more concerned about the Fenian raids.

337 C.P. Stacey, "Fenianism and the Rise of National Feeling in Canada at the Time of Confederation," *The Canadian Historical Review*, 13, no. 3 (Sept. 1931): 235-352.

338 L. J. Burpee, "Fenian and Other Raids" in *Military History of Canada, 1608-1914, Vol. 1*, (Toronto, ON: United Publishers, 1917); *Ottawa Times*, June 8, 1866, p. 2.

339 Knight, *op. cit.*, p. 333-43.

340 John Taylor points out that Ottawa City Council had mixed enthusiasm for the celebrations, and the $500 appropriation was approved by only one vote. Ottawa City Council minutes, January 17, 1867, cited in John Taylor, *Ottawa: an Illustrated History,* (Toronto, ON: J. Lorimer, 1986), p. 75.

341 Gordon, *op. cit.*, chapter 9, 10, 12, 13.

342 For Washington, D.C., the commissioners were authorized to buy land from the local farmers and re-sell lots to pay for infrastructure. George Washington was directly involved in the purchase of the District of Columbia sites and one reason why Pierre L'Enfant resigned in 1792 was because he would not produce the detailed plan needed for the sale of lots fast enough. See Gutheim and Lee, *op. cit.*, p. 28-31.

343 D.L.A. Gordon and M. Seasons, "Administrative and financial strategies for implementing plans in political capitals" *Canadian Journal of Urban Research*, vol. 18, no. 1 (2009) pp. 94-117.

Chapter 5

344 F. Monck, *My Canadian Leaves: An account of a visit to Canada 1864-1865,* (London, UK: R. Bentley & Son, 1891).

345 A.R.M. Lower, "The Trade in Square Timber," *Contributions to Canadian Economies,* 6 (1933): 40-61, see Diagram 5; A.R.M. Lower, *Great Britain's Woodyard: British America and the Timber Trade, 1763-1867,* (Montréal, QC and Kingston, ON: McGill-Queen's University Press, 1973).

346 R.W. Scott, *Recollections of Bytown,* (Ottawa, ON: Mortimer Press, 1911), p. 19-22.

347 A.R.M. Lower, *The North American Assault on the Canadian Forest,* (Toronto, ON: Ryerson Press, 1938), p. 110-14.

348 John Taylor, *Ottawa: An Illustrated History,* (Toronto, ON: Lorimer, 1986), p. 211, Table IV.

349 *Ibid.*, p. 212, Table VIII.

350 J.R. Trinnell, *J.R. Booth: Life and Times of an Ottawa Lumberking,* (Ottawa, ON: Treehouse, 1998), p. 11-12.

351 *Ibid.*, p. 24, 66-70.

352 But most of the original American investors' profits went elsewhere, and Ottawa accrued few secondary benefits in the early years. See Taylor, *Ottawa: An Illustrated History, op. cit.*, p. 52-56.

353 Taylor, *Ottawa: An Illustrated History, op. cit.*, p. 110-11; Chad Gaffield, *History of the Outaouais,* (Québec, QC: Institut québécois de recherche sur la culture, 1997), p. 393; W.E. Greening, "The Lumber Industry in the Ottawa Valley and the American Market in the 19th Century," *Ontario History,* 62 (1970): 134-36.

354 See J. Grove Smith, *Fire Waste in Canada,* (Ottawa, ON: Commission of Conservation, 1918); John Taylor, "Fire, Disease and Water in Ottawa," *Urban History Review,* 8 (June 1979): 7-37; Lucien Brault, *Hull 1800-1950,* (Ottawa, ON: Les Editions de l'Université d'Ottawa, 1950), p. 80-91; Gaffield, *op. cit.*, p. 391-92; Raymond Ouimet, *Une ville en flames,* (Hull, QC: Éditions Vents d'Ouest inc., 1996).

355 R. Peter Gillis and Thomas R. Roach, *Lost initiatives: Canada's forest industries, forest policy and forest conservation,* (New York, NY: Greenwood Press, 1986); R. Peter Gillis, "A Case Study in Resource Use: The Ottawa Lumber Industry, 1880-1914," *Alternatives,* 1, no. 2 (Fall 1971): 3-10, 14.

356 A.R.M. Lower, *North American Assault, op. cit.*, p. 162-64.

357 *Ibid.*

358 Gaffield, *op. cit.*, p. 390-92.

359 Taylor, *Ottawa: An Illustrated History, op. cit.*, chapter 2.

360 C.C.J. Bond, "The Canadian Government Comes to Ottawa," *Ontario History,* 40, no. 1 (1963): 28. The trip took from 9am to 5pm.

361 Lucien Brault, *Ottawa Old and New,* (Ottawa, ON: Ottawa Historical Information Institute, 1946), p. 191.

362 Gaffield, *op. cit.*, p. 112.

363 For Québec, see C.J. Bond, "The Canadian Government Comes to Ottawa," *op. cit.*, p. 25-28.

364 "Sickness on Sparks Street," *Ottawa Daily Citizen*, May 28, 1891, p. 4.

365 "The Spark Street Sewer," *Ottawa Daily Citizen*, July 9, 1891, see also July 23 and September 3 and 26, 1891.

366 N.R. Ball, Building Canada: a History of Public Works. (Toronto, ON: University of Toronto Press, 1988), p. 206; L. Brault, *Ottawa, Old and New.* (Ottawa, ON: Historical Information Institute, 1946), p. 102, 105, 117, 131, 136, 194; John

Taylor, *Ottawa: An Illustrated History*, (Toronto, ON: Lorimer & Co, 1986), p. 40, 102, 106; The Robert O. Pickard Environmental Centre, 2001, (City of Ottawa), http://ottawa.ca/city_services/waterwaste/27_2_1_en.shtml [Retrieved November 21, 2007].

367 N.R. Ball, *Building Canada: a History of Public Works*, (Toronto, ON: University of Toronto Press, 1988), p. 35, 60, 200; J. Benidickson, *Water Supply and Sewage Infrastructure in Ontario, 1880-1990s: Legal and Institutional Aspects of Public Health and Environmental History*, (Toronto, ON: Queen's Printer for Ontario, 2002), p. 153, 155; J. Careless, *Toronto to 1918: an Illustrated History*, (Toronto, ON: Lorimer & Co, 1984), p. 54, 101, 112, 138.

368 G. Dillon, *Kingston Portsmouth and Cataraqui Electric Railway: History of the Limestone City's Streetcar System*, (Kingston, ON: Kingston Division of the Canadian Railroad Historical Association, 1994), p. 7; B.S. Osborne, *Kingston: Building on the Past*, (Westport, ON: Butternut Press, 1988), p. 107, 116, 118, 124, 131, 136.

369 J. Careless, *Toronto to 1918: an Illustrated History*, op. cit., p. 64; J.P. Doyle, *Report on the Drainage and Sewerage of the City of Montréal: Shewing the Location and Estimated Cost of the System of Main Outlet and Intercepting Sewers Proposed to be Constructed for the Thorough and Effectual Drainage of the City*, (Montréal, QC: City of Montréal, 1857), p. 9; F. Kee, *Electric Utilities Across Canada*, (March 28, 2000, Institute of Electrical and Electronics Engineers (IEEE) Canada), http://www.ieee.ca/diglib/library/electricity/pdf/P_one_4.pdf (p. 6) [retrieved October 21, 2007]; O. Lavallee, *The Montréal City Passenger Railway Company*, (Québec, QC: Canadian Railroad Historical Association, 1961), p. 13, 36; J.-C. Marsan, *Montréal in Evolution: Historical Analysis of the Development of Montréal's Architecture and Urban Environment*, (Montréal, QC and Kingston, ON: McGill-Queen's University Press, 1981), p. 145, 182; Montréal Dept. of Public Works, *Montréal and its Public Works Department*, (Montréal, QC: Dept. of Public Works, Publicity and Public Relations Section, 1947), p. 18; *Petition for Incorporation – Democracy in Montréal*, (n.d.), (Montréal, QC: City of Montréal Official Portal), http://ville.Montréal.qc.ca/, [retrieved October 21, 2007].

370 C. Warfe, "The Search for Pure Water in Ottawa, 1910-15," *Urban History Review*, 8, no. 1 (1979): 66-90; also Brault, *Ottawa Old & New*, op. cit., p. 109-17; Brault, *Hull 1800-1950*, op. cit. p. 92-95; Taylor, *Ottawa: An Illustrated History*, op. cit., p. 104.

371 Canada Commission of Conservation, *Report on the Epidemic of Typhoid Fever Occurring in the City of Ottawa, Jan. 1st to March 19th, 1911*, (Ottawa, ON: City of Ottawa, 1911); S. Lloyd, "The Ottawa Typhoid Epidemics of 1911 and 1912," *Urban History Review*, 8, no. 1 (1979): 66-90; Taylor, *Ottawa: An Illustrated History*, op cit., p. 156-59.

372 Michael E. Mercier and Christopher G. Boone, "Infant mortality in Ottawa, Canada, 1901: assessing cultural, economic and environmental factors," *Journal of Historical Geography*, 28, no. 4 (2002): 486.

373 Brault, *Ottawa Old and New*, op. cit., p. 135-36.

374 Brault, *Hull: 1800-1950*, op. cit., p. 98-99.

375 Taylor, *Ottawa: An Illustrated History*, op. cit., p. 66; Brault, *Ottawa Old and New*, op. cit., p. 102.

376 "The New System of Street Lighting," *Ottawa Daily Citizen*, May 1, 1885, p. 2.

377 "The Electric Street Railway," *Ottawa Daily Citizen*, June 30, 1891.

378 Bill McKeown, *Ottawa's Streetcars: The Story of Electric Railway Transit in Canada's Capital City*, (Toronto, ON: Railfare DC Books, 2006), chapter 3; Taylor, *Ottawa: An Illustrated History*, op. cit., p. 97-104.

379 McKeown, op. cit., p. 65.

380 Quoted in Robert Haig, *Ottawa: City of the Big Ears*, (Ottawa, ON: Haig & Haig, 1969), p. 130.

381 S. Gwyn, *The Private Capital: Ambition and Love in the Age of Macdonald and Laurier*, (Toronto, ON: Harper and Collins, 1984), p. 39.

382 Roger Todhunter, "Preservation, Parks, and the Vice-Royalty: Lord Dufferin and Lord Grey" in *Canada, Landscape Planning*, 12 (1985): 141-160.

383 See the Edmond and Fanny Meredith diaries cited in "Drains, Drains, Nothing but Drains," in Gwyn op. cit., p. 45-58. Edmund Meredith was one of the federal government's first deputy ministers. His

wife Fanny Jarvis Meredith was from the Toronto Tory family.

384 M. Hebbert, *London: More by Fortune than Design*, (Chichester, UK: Wiley, 1998).

385 See T. Hall, *Planning Europe's Capital Cities: Aspects of Nineteenth Century Urban Development*, (London, UK: Spon, 1997), chapter 3; A. Sutcliffe, *Paris: An Architectural History*, (New Haven, CT: Yale University Press, 1993), chapters 6, 7.

386 P.G. Hall, *Cities in Civilization*, (New York, NY: Pantheon, 1998), p. 657-705.

387 D. Van Zanten, *Building Paris: Architectural Institutions and the Transformation of the French Capital, 1830-1870*, (Cambridge, UK: Cambridge University Press, 1994).

388 A. Almandoz (ed.), *Planning Latin American's Capital Cities, 1850-1950*, (London, UK: Routledge, 2002). Paris was the main stop on the grand tour of the McMillan Commission's design team; see F.L. Olmsted's pictures of Paris in the McMillan Commission report, C. Moore (ed.), *The improvement of the park system of the District of Columbia*, 57th Congress, 1st sess. S. Rept. 166,. (Washington, DC: U.S. Government Printing Office, 1902), and also Charles Moore's *Daniel H. Burnham: Architect, Planner of Cities*, (Boston, MA: Houghton Mifflin, 1921).

389 C.M. Robinson, *The Improvement of Towns and Cities: Or, The Practical Basis of Civic Aesthetics*, (New York, NY: G.P. Putnam's Sons, 1901); W.H. Wilson, *The City Beautiful Movement*, (Baltimore, MD: Johns Hopkins University Press, 1989); Robert Freestone, "The internationalization of the city beautiful," *International Planning Studies*, 12, no.1 (2007): 21-34.

390 Burnham, Daniel H., and Edward H. Bennett. *Plan of Chicago, Prepared Under the Direction of the Commercial Club during the Years MCMVI, MCMVII, and MCMVIII*, (Chicago, IL: The Commercial Club, 1909); see also C. Smith, *The Plan of Chicago: Daniel Burnham and the Remaking of the American City*, (Chicago, IL: University of Chicago Press, 2006).

391 Burnham and Bennett, *Plan of Chicago, op. cit.*, plate CX, "Comprehensive plan view of Chicago's Central Area"; Edward Bennett projected a lantern slide of this image in his 1914 speech "Some Aspects of City Planning, with General Reference to a Plan for Ottawa and Hull." Address to the Canadian Club at the Normal School, Ottawa, Ontario, April 21, 1914. EHB Papers, Box 40; see also the original hand-tinted lantern slide in the EHB collection, Art Institute of Chicago. This image source is from the copy of the 1909 plan held in the Jordan Special Collections Library, Queen's University.

392 The exception would be Maisonneuve, an industrial suburb of Montréal; see P.A. Linteau, *The Promoter's City: Building the Industrial Town of Maisonneuve, 1883-1913*, (Toronto, ON: Lorimer, 1985). For the failures in Kitchener and Calgary, see E. Bloomfield, "Town Planning Efforts in Kitchener-Waterloo, 1912-1925," in Alan Artibise and Gilbert Stelter (eds.), *Shaping the Urban Landscape*, (Ottawa, ON: Carleton University Press, 1982), p. 256-303; W.T. Perks, "Idealism Orchestration and Science in Early Canadian City Planning: Calgary and Vancouver Re-Visited, 1914-1928, *Environments*, 17, no. 2 (1985): 1-28.

393 Walter Van Nus, "The Fate of City Beautiful Thought in Canada, 1893-1930," in Gilbert Stelter and Alan Artibise (eds.), *The Canadian City: Essays in Urban History*, (Toronto, ON: McClelland and Stewart, 1977), p. 173-78.

394 J.W. Brennan, "Visions of a 'City Beautiful': The Origin and Impact of the Mawson Plans for Regina," *Saskatchewan History*, 46, no. 2 (1994): 19-33; Gilbert Stelter, "Rethinking the Significance of the City Beautiful Idea" in R. Freestone (ed.), *Urban Planning in a Changing World; The Twentieth Century Experience*, (London, UK: Spon, 2000), p. 98-117; Charles Hill (ed.), *Artists, Architects and Artisans: Canadian Art 1890–1918*, (Ottawa: National Gallery of Canada, 2013).

395 Monck, *op. cit.*, p. 113.

396 Lady Dufferin, *My Canadian Journal 1872-78*, Gladys C. Walker (ed.), (Toronto, ON: Longmans, 1969), p. 37.

397 R.H. Hubbard, *Rideau Hall: An illustrated history of Government House, Ottawa from Victorian times to the present day* (Montréal, QC and Kingston, ON: McGill-Queen's University Press, 1977), chapters 1-5; the building was purchased for $86,000 and the first additions were over $200,000, see p. 9-15.

398 M. Harris, "In a Canadian Garden" in *Canada's House: Rideau Hall and the invention of a Canadian*

399 *home*, M. MacMillan, M. Harris and A.L. Desjardins (eds.), (Toronto, ON: Knopf Canada, 2004).

399 Hubbard, *op. cit.*, p. 54-57.

400 A.H. Fréchette, "Life at Rideau Hall," *Harper's New Monthly Magazine,* vol. 63, 1881, p. 213-23.

401 Duke Argyll (Marquis of Lorne), *Passages from the Past, Vol. 2,* (London, ON: London Hutchinson, 1907), p. 444.

402 Margaret Angus, *John A. Lived Here,* (Kingston, ON: Frontenac Historic Foundation, Occasional Paper No. 1, 1984).

403 Haig, *op. cit.*, p. 117. Earnscliffe became the residence of the British High Commissioner in 1928; 24 Sussex Drive, although built in 1868, only became the prime minister's official residence in 1951.

404 See the Meredith diaries, "Drains, Drains, Nothing but Drains," referred to in Gwyn, *op. cit.*, p. 45-58.

405 Gwyn *op. cit.*, p. 40.

406 Gwyn, *op. cit.*, Hubbard, *op. cit.*, chapters 2-4.

407 For the role of the Department of Public Works, see Janet Wright, *Crown Assets: The Architecture of the Department of Public Works, 1867-1967,* (Toronto, ON: University of Toronto Press, 1997), especially chapters 4 and 8; also, Margaret Archibald, *By Federal Design: The Chief Architect's Branch of the Department of Public Works, 1881-1914,* (Ottawa, ON: National Historic Parks and Sites Branch, 1983); also, Doug Owram, *Building for Canadians: A History of the Department of Public Works, 1840-1960,* (Ottawa, ON: Public Relations and Information Services, 1979).

408 Canada, 26 Vict. Sessional Papers 1863, No. 3, *Report of the Commission Appointed to Inquire into Matters connected with the Parliament Buildings at Ottawa,* January 29, 1863.

409 For the scandal, see Wright, *op. cit.*, p. 41; Orwam, *op.cit.*, p. 160-56.

410 See the Meredith diaries, "Drains, Drains, Nothing but Drains," referred to in Gwyn, *op. cit.*, p. 45-58.

411 Gwyn, *op. cit.*

412 Thomas Coltrin Keefer (1821-1915) was one of Canada's most accomplished civil engineers of the 19th century. He was half-brother to Samuel Keefer, designer of the 1843 Union Suspension Bridge over the Ottawa River. T.C. Keefer married Elizabeth McKay in 1848, and became well-known for his work on the Erie and Welland canals. He consulted on the design of the water supply systems for several Canadian cities, including Montréal, Hamilton and Ottawa; see his biography by H.V. Nelles, "Thomas Coltrin Keefer" in *Dictionary of Canadian Biography, Vol. XIV,* (Toronto, ON: University of Toronto Press, 1998).

413 Keefer was assisted in the design by Robert Surtees (1835- ca. 1906), a local architect/engineer. Surtees consulted on the design of Beechwood Cemetery before becoming Ottawa's City Engineer, where he designed Major's Hill Park and the Minto bridges over the Rideau River. Surtees was later appointed chief engineer to the Ottawa Improvement Commission, where he designed the landscape improvements to Strathcona Park, the Rideau Canal parkways, and Rockcliffe Park. See "Robert Surtees" in *Prominent Men of Canada*, (Toronto, ON: G. Mercer Adams, 1892), p. 199 and J. Smith and V. Angel, *Village of Rockcliffe Park Heritage Conservation District,* (Ottawa, ON: Village of Rockcliffe Park, 1997), p. 11-12.

414 During the 1960s, Rockcliffe Park residents were angry that they could not stop a developer filling in the wetlands beside McKay Lake, and the resulting political fallout helped create Ontario's *Environmental Assessment Act.* The entire village was declared a Heritage Conservation District in 1997, and was absorbed into the newly amalgamated City of Ottawa in 2001. Smith and Angel, *op. cit.*; H.S.M. Carver, *The Cultural Landscape of Rockcliffe Park,* (Ottawa, ON: Village of Rockcliffe Park, 1985); E. Von Bayer and J. Mulligan, *Rockcliffe Park Landscape History,* (Ottawa, ON: National Capital Commission, 1996); M. Edmond, *Rockcliffe Park: A History of the Village,* (Ottawa, ON: Friends of the Village of Rockcliffe Park Foundation, 2005).

415 M. Newton, *LowerTown Ottawa 1854-1900, Vol. 2,* (Ottawa, ON: National Capital Commission, 1981), p. 275.

416 "Major's Hill as a Park: Conditions on which the Government will allow the Corporation to Use

416 It," *Ottawa Citizen*, August 22, 1874; reprinted in Newton, *op. cit.*, p. 276-78.
417 Newton, *op. cit.*, p. 284-85.
418 Lady Aberdeen, *The Canadian Journal of Lady Aberdeen*, (Toronto, ON: Champlain Society, 1960), p. 194.
419 *Ibid.*, p. 479.
420 Wilfrid Laurier, *Dearest Émilie: The Love Letters of Sir Wilfrid Laurier to Madame Émilie Lavergne*, (Toronto, ON: NC Press Limited, 1989), p. 84. Letter dated August 9, 1891.
421 "The Washington of the North," *Ottawa Evening Journal*, June 19, 1893, p. 3.
422 Among those on the platform were W.S. Fielding, (Premier of Nova Scotia), Henry Bate (Ottawa grocer) and Thomas O'Keefe, all of whom were later involved in the Ottawa Improvement Commission, *Ottawa Journal*, June 19, 1893, p. 3.
423 Frederick Gutheim and Antoinette Lee, *Worthy of the Nation Washington, DC: From L'Enfant to the National Capital Planning Commission*, (Baltimore, MD: Johns Hopkins University Press, 2006), chapter 2.
424 Gutheim, Frederick and A. Lee, *Worthy of the Nation 2nd ed.* (Baltimore, MD: Johns Hopkins University Press, 2006).
425 C. Moore (ed.), *The improvement of the park system of the District of Columbia*. 57th Congress, 1st. sess. S. Rept. 166, (Washington, DC: US Government Printing Office, 1902).
426 J.A. Peterson, *The Birth of City Planning in the United States, 1840–1917*, (Baltimore, MD and London, UK: Johns Hopkins University Press, 2003); also "The Nation's First Comprehensive City Plan: A Political Analysis of the McMillan Plan for Washington, DC, 1900-1902," *Journal of the American Planning Association*, vol. 55, no. 2, Spring 1985: 134-50.
427 F. Cook, *Struggle for the Capital of Canada*, (Ottawa, ON: Ottawa Historical Society, Canada Pamphlet 009, 1938); also D. Mullington, *Chain of Office: Biographical Sketches of the Early Mayors of Ottawa, 1847-1948*, (Renfrew, ON: General Store Publishing, 2005), p. 102-3. The municipal report was probably lost in the city hall fire in the 1930s.

428 W. Eggleston, *The Queen's Choice: A story of Canada's capital*, (Ottawa, ON: Queen's Printer, 1961), p. 155-56.
429 Aberdeen, *op. cit.*, p. 478-79; W.S. Fielding was Laurier's Minister of Finance and former Premier of Nova Scotia. He and his wife were invited to Lady Aberdeen's picnic with the prime minister.
430 Fielding speech to House of Commons, August 2, 1899, *Hansard*, p. 9,186, and *An Act Respecting the City of Ottawa*, 62-63 Vict. chapter 10. 7 (c), assented August 11, 1899.
431 *Ibid.*, s. 7 (c), p. 116.
432 *Ibid.*, s. 1, 7 (a); p. 9, 116-17.
433 *Ibid.*, s. 15-18.
434 *Ottawa Evening Journal*, June 19, 1893, p. 3.
435 The last three appointments broadened the OIC's reach and range of expertise. Forget was a financier and owner of the Montréal Street Railway, see Jack Jedwab, "Louis-Joseph Forget" in *Dictionary of Canadian Biography*, Vol. XIV, (Toronto, ON: University of Toronto Press, 2000); and Frost was the former mayor of Smith's Falls, see Roch Lauzier, "James Frost" in *Dictionary of Canadian Biography*, Vol. V, (Toronto, ON: University of Toronto Press, 2000).
436 See A. Gard, *The Hub and the Spokes; or The Capital and its environs*, (Ottawa, ON: Emerson Press, 1904), p. 49-57; see also the 1900-1904 annual reports of the OIC in the NCC Library.
437 Brault, *Ottawa Old & New, op. cit.*, p. 124.
438 Ouimet, *op. cit.*, p. 85-95.
439 *Hansard*; "The Chaudière is in flames," *Ottawa Free Press*, April 26, 1900, p. 1, 7.
440 J. Fear, "Ottawa's Lumber Interests and the Great Fire of 1900," *Urban History Review*, 8, no. 1 (June 1979): 38-65.
441 Gaffield, *op. cit.*, p. 260-69.
442 W.J. Topley, "The Ottawa Album," Collection of 57 photographs of Ottawa businesses, 1875, LAC, MIKAN no. 156542; see also LAC Photographs, C 2237 and C 2239.

Chapter 6

443 William Lyon Mackenzie King Diary, May 24, 1900.
444 William Lyon Mackenzie King Diary, July 14, 1915. The lake's name pre-dated King's visit and is not related to his family.

445 King was influenced by the Sir Galahad lithograph in Harper's study (Figure 6-2) in the apartment that they shared in Ottawa.

446 W.L.M. King, *The Secret of Heroism: A Memoir of Henry Albert Harper*. (New York: Revell, 1906).

447 As quoted in Elsie Marie McFarland, *The Development of Public Recreation in Canada*, (Toronto, ON: Canadian Parks/Recreation Association, 1974), p. 14.

448 Frederick Law Olmsted, *Mount Royal*, (New York, NY: G.P. Putnam's Sons, 1881), p. 64.

449 Nancy Pollock-Ellwand, "The Olmsted Firm in Canada: A Correction of the Record," *Planning Perspectives*, 21.3 (2006): 277-310; G. Hodge, and D.L.A. Gordon, *Planning Canadian Communities, 6th ed.* (Toronto, ON: Nelson, 2014), chapter 3.

450 $60,000 in 1900 was equivalent to $1.65 million in C$ 2014. All prices in this paper were adjusted using Statistics Canada, *CANSIM, 326-0021Consumer Price Index*; the pre-1914 CPI was adjusted using Gordon Bertram and Michael B. Percy, "Real Wage Trends in Canada 1900-26: Some Provisional Estimates," *Canadian Journal of Economics*, 12, no. 2, (1979): 299-312.

451 OIC minutes May 1, 1903; June 9, 1903, p. 103-06.

452 OIC minutes June 11, 1903, 110, $250,000 in 1903 was approximately $6.5 million C$ 2014.

453 Edward I. Wood, "Landscape Architecture in the National Capital," *Community Planning Review*, 6, no. 1, (March 1956): 13-25.

454 F.G. Todd, *Preliminary Report to the Ottawa Improvement Commission*, (Ottawa, ON: OIC), p. 39, (August 28, 1903). At least three copies of the report survived in their original condition because Todd sent them to his mentors: one donated to the library of the Massachusetts Agricultural College, (now the University of Massachusetts at Amherst) and two at the Loeb Library at Harvard University. The second copy at Loeb is stamped "Received Olmsted Bros. October 1 1903." The report was supported by five maps (now lost) and 39 photographs, of which 17 were included in the printed version.

455 F.G. Todd, *Preliminary Report*, (1903), *op. cit.*, p. 2.

456 *Ibid*, p. 1.

457 *Ibid*, p. 2-3.

458 *Ibid.*, p. 3: "With a natural location which cannot be compared with that of Ottawa, the original plan of Washington took advantage of every natural feature which the location possessed, and made the most of it, and from this plan have evolved a beautiful city."

459 For City Beautiful ideology, see W.H. Wilson, *The City Beautiful Movement*, (Baltimore, MD: Johns Hopkins University Press, 1989), p. 78-95.

460 F.G. Todd, *Preliminary Report*, (1903), *op. cit.*, p. 7.

461 *Ibid.*; also F. G. Todd, *Esthetic Forestry*, (Montréal, QC; Witness Printing Co. n.d. [1920s]). Book is in collection of LAC. The map included with Todd's report has not been found. Figure 2 was constructed by careful comparison of the 1912 contour map prepared by Noulan Cauchon, the 1912 and 1925 *Special Reports* of the OIC and the 1915 *Report of the Federal Plan Commission*.

462 F.G. Todd, *Preliminary Report*, (1903), *op. cit.*, p. 9-10.

463 *Ibid.*, p. 10; David Schuyler, *The New Urban Landscape: The Redefinition of City Form in Nineteenth-Century America*, (Baltimore, MD: Johns Hopkins University Press, 1986).

464 F.G. Todd, *Preliminary Report*, (1903), *op. cit.*, p. 23.

465 *Ibid.*, p. 26-27.

466 *Ibid.*, p. 35.

467 *Ibid.*, p. 39.

468 The OIC treated Todd in an appalling fashion, withholding fees and attempting to wiggle out of paying for park plans prepared at their request. See David Gordon, "Frederick G. Todd and the Origins of the Park System in Canada's Capital," *Journal of Planning History*, 1, no. 1, (2002): 38-40.

469 Ottawa Improvement Commission, *Special Report of the Ottawa Improvement Commission, from its inception in 1899 to March 13, 1912*, (Ottawa, ON: OIC, 1913), p. 10; $1.2 million in 1909 (average date) would be approximately $22 million in C$ 1999; L.M.M. Dicaire, "The Rideau Canal Driveway: Founding Element in Ottawa's Evolving Landscape," *Ontario History*, LXXXIX, no. 2, (June 1997): 141-59.

470 *OIC Annual Reports, 1903-1914*, NCC Library, Ottawa. King Edward Avenue connected to Rideau Street, the main commercial thoroughfare. Future governors general preferred a more dignified and scenic route along the Ottawa River to Sussex Drive.

471 Laurier to Sir Thomas Shaughnessy, (CPR President) October 22, 1910. WL correspondence reel #299, 176326.

472 OIC, *1906 Annual Report*, p. 4.

473 OIC, *Annual Reports, 1912-1915*, NCC Library, Ottawa.

474 Unwin's address was reported in the local newspapers: "Ottawa has opportunities, for obtaining ideal city." *Ottawa Evening Citizen*, May 22, 1911, p. 1; "Movement for Garden City," 1911. *Ottawa Evening Citizen*, May 23, 1911, p. 3. See also "Canada and Town Planning: Interview with Mr. Raymond Unwin," *The Record, Hampstead Garden Suburb*, 2, no. 2, (Feb. 1914), p. 87-89. Thanks to Mervyn Miller for providing this article.

475 T.H. Mawson "The Ideal Capital City and How to Plan and Build it," *Addresses Presented Before the Canadian Club of Ottawa, 1911-12*, (Ottawa, ON: Mortimer Press, Dec. 2, 1911), p. 167. Also, see "Improvement Commission Gets Criticism from Landscape Artist," *Ottawa Evening Citizen*, May 26, 1911, p. 10. "The Planless Capital (editorial)," *Ottawa Citizen*, May 26, 1911, p. 6; "Opinions of Commission," *Ottawa Evening Citizen*, May 26, 1911, p. 1, 10. "A Valuable Criticism," *Ottawa Citizen*, May 27, 1911, p. 6.

476 T.H. Mawson, *The Life and Work of an English Landscape Architect*, (London, UK: The Richards Press Ltd., 1927).

477 Meredith papers, May 1911 correspondence file.

478 *Ottawa Citizen*, "The Glebe Streets: Infusion of a new spirit into the Ottawa Improvement Commission," April 20, 1904; Letter from Charles Murphy to W.S. Fielding, Minister of Finance, August 9, 1910, Laurier papers, MF 214, 85188-85190; Letter from T.C. Boville, Deputy Min. of Finance, to OIC, August 24, 1910, calling attention to the Commission's over-expenditure of $108,416.42 relating to public works and maintenance. Boville also made "some suggestions as to the carrying on of the Commission's business." CPM files, vol.11.

479 Meredith visited the Olmsted office in an unofficial basis in 1910 to sound them out, but took no further action. Olmsted Bros. Papers, File 5070, "Ottawa City Plan, Ottawa Canada 1913-1914."

480 Meredith chaired the conference of the Ontario Association of Architects in Ottawa in 1911, and also headed the Ottawa chapter of the Royal Architectural Institute of Canada (RAIC) that year. He arranged for the RAIC and the associations of Ontario, Québec, Manitoba and Alberta to send briefs to the government attacking the policies of the Department of Public Works and the OIC. The RAIC report is included in a "blue paper" issued by the federal government: *Report and Correspondence of the Ottawa Improvement Commission*, 2, George V. Sessional Paper no. 51a, Ottawa, ON: C.H. Parmelee, 1912. For Meredith's behind-the-scene orchestration of events, see CPM 6, files 42-44.

481 For the McMillan Commission, see C. Moore (ed.), *The Improvement of the Park System of the District of Columbia*, 57th Congress, 1st sess. S. Rept. 166. Washington, DC: U.S. Government Printing Office, 1902 and also J. A. Peterson, "The Nation's First Comprehensive City Plan: A Political Analysis of the McMillan Plan for Washington, DC, 1900-1902, *Journal of the American Planning Association*, 55, no. 2, (Spring 1985): 134-50. On Daniel Burnham's role as principal consultant to the commission, see DHB papers, and T. S. Hines, *Burnham of Chicago: Architect and Planner*, (New York, NY: Oxford University Press, 1974), chapter 7. The District of Columbia's political model was also popular in Ottawa at the time.

482 Laurier speech in House of Commons, January 12, 1912, *Hansard*, p. 977-981.

483 CPM to RLB, January 13, 1912. Meredith also sent his memo to Laurier. CPM to WL, June 13, 1912, CPM papers, 1912 correspondence file.

484 *Report and Correspondance of the Ottawa Improvement Commission, op. cit.*

485 "Merciless Analysis of Commission's Work," *Ottawa Evening Journal*, February 23, 1912, p. 1, 10.

486 Ottawa Improvement Commission *Special Report, op. cit.*

487 Meredith repeatedly tried to pull Todd into the fray, encouraging him to put his disappointment with the OIC on the public record. CPM to Todd, January 18, 1912, CPM papers. Todd gave Meredith copies of his report, but refused to condemn the government, presumably hoping for future commissions. Todd to CPM, January 19, 1912, CPM papers.

488 Wilfrid Eggleston, *The Queen's Choice : A Story of Canada's Capital,* (Ottawa: National Capital

Commission, 1961), p. 154-66, and Appendix 6; William DeGrace, "Canada's Capital 1900-1950: Five Town Planning Visions," *Environments*, 17.2 (1985): 43-57; Kent Hillis, "A History of Commissions: Threads of an Ottawa Planning History." *Urban History Review*, 21.1 (1993): 46-60.

489 Edward I. Wood, "Landscape Architecture in the National Capital" *Community Planning Review*, 6, no. 1, (March 1956): 13-25.

Chapter 7

490 Rupert Brooke, *Letters from America*, (Toronto, ON: McClelland Goodchild & Stewart, 1916), p. 57.

491 Lucien Brault, *Hull 1800-1950*, (Ottawa, ON: Les Éditions de l' Université d' Ottawa, 1950), Appendix A. The population of French-speaking people had crept up to 90 percent by 1921.

492 Odette, Vincent-Domey, "Industry and the World of Work" in Chad Gaffield (ed.), *History of the Outaouais*, (Québec, QC: Les Presses de l'Université Laval, 1997), p. 257-81.

493 Chad Gaffield (ed.), *History of the Outaouais, op. cit.*, p. 390-91.

494 Bill McKeown, *Ottawa's Streetcars: An Illustrated History of Electric Railway Transit in Canada's Capital City*, (Pickering, ON: Railfare Books, 2007), p. 70-77.

495 Bruce Elliott, *The City Beyond, A History of Nepean, Birthplace of Canada's Capital*, (Nepean, ON: City of Nepean, 1991), p. 184-201.

496 Thomas Adams, *Rural Planning and Development*, (Ottawa, ON: Commission of Conservation, 1917), p. 109-10. Adams found over 65 sq. miles of subdivisions in the region.

497 Walter Van Nus, "The Fate of City Beautiful Thought in Canada, 1893-1930," in Gilbert Stelter and Alan Artibise (eds.), *The Canadian City: Essays in Urban History*, (Toronto, ON: McClelland and Stewart, 1977), p. 173-78.

498 Lucien Brault, *Ottawa Old and New*, (Ottawa, ON: Historical Information Institute, 1946), p. 28-30; Elliott, *The City Beyond, op. cit.*, p. 184-88.

499 S. Lloyd, "The Ottawa Typhoid Epidemics of 1911 and 1912: A Case Study of Disease as a Catalyst for Urban Reform," *Urban History Review*, 8, no. 1 (June 1979): 66-90.

500 Dr. C. Hodgetts, *Report on the Epidemic of Typhoid Fever Occurring in Ottawa in 1911*, (Ottawa, ON: Commission of Conservation, April 1911), p. 1.

501 *Ottawa Medical Officer of Health Report*, 1911, p. 138 reprinted in Lloyd, *op. cit.*, p. 75; the suggestion that typhoid was caused by the health habits and poor neighbourhoods was undercut by the 1907 death of Lady Victoria Grenfell, the adult daughter of Governor General Earl Grey, from typhoid contracted at Rideau Hall; see M. Edmond, *Rockcliffe Park: A History of the Village*, (Ottawa, ON: Friends of the Village of Rockville Park Foundation, 2005), p. 265, ff. 8.

502 *Ibid.*, p. 67-87.

503 R.D. Gunn, *Judicial Investigation Re: Ottawa Waterworks and Health Departments*, 1912. Copy at City of Ottawa Archives.

504 Lloyd, *op. cit.*, p. 82-87; Dave Mullington, *Chain of Office*, (Renfrew, ON: General Store Publishing, 2005), p. 111-17.

505 The results of the referendum are documented in a letter from John Henderson, Ottawa City Clerk, to Prime Minister Borden, LAC, MG26 H, R-4047, May 16, 1912. See also Ottawa City Council Minutes, No. 37, 1912, p. 773. A plebiscite on the same subject had previously been held in 1907 and again the establishment of a federal district had been supported (*Ottawa Evening Journal*, January 8, 1907, p. 9).

506 John Taylor, *Ottawa: An Illustrated History*, (Toronto, ON: Lorimer, 1986), p. 151-54. The French language daily newspaper *le Droit* was founded in 1913 to protect the rights of francophones in the region.

507 C. Wharfe, "The Search for Pure Water in Ottawa, 1910-1915," *Urban History Review*, 8, no. 1 (1979): 90-112; Taylor, *op. cit.*, p. 164-69; "Sanitary Conditions in Canadian Cities," *Conservation of Life*, 1, no. 4 (January 1915): 81-83.

508 Janet Wright, *Crown Assets: The Architecture of the Department of Public Works, 1867-1967* (Toronto, ON: University of Toronto Press, 1997), chapter 3.

509 Taylor, *Ottawa: An Illustrated History, op. cit.*, Table VIII, p. 212.

510 Wright, *op. cit.*, chapter 4.

511 Wright, *op. cit.*, p. 111-14.

512 Canada, Department of Public Works, *General Conditions for the Guidance of Architects in Preparing Competitive Designs for the Proposed New Department and Justice Buildings,* (Ottawa, ON: Government Printing Bureau, 1906).

513 Wright, *op. cit.*, p. 114-20; E. Maxwell, *The Architecture of Edward & W.S. Maxwell,* (Montréal, QC: Montréal Museum of Fine Arts, 1991); for the reactions of the architects see the Royal Architectural Institute of Canada brief in Canada, 2 George V, Sessional Paper no. 51a, *Correspondence of the Ottawa Improvement Commission,* (Ottawa, ON: C-H. Parmalee, 1912).

514 Canada Privy Council order No. PC 446, February 27, 1912; the Minister of Public Works noted that the federal government then had 365,221 square feet under rental, and this "site of unsurpassed magnificence" would allow for extension of the Parliament grounds and space for future expansion.

515 Todd's plan is found as NMC 121793; his general advice was in a letter to J.B. Hunter, deputy minister of Public Works, LAC, RG11, vol. 2950, file 5084-1, July 8, 1912.

516 See the White-Webb proposal in LAC drawing L-14903, and also in Wright, *op. cit.*, p. 120-22.

517 See Lawrence Vale, "The Urban Design of Twentieth Century Capitals" in David L.A. Gordon (ed.), *Planning Twentieth Century Capital Cities,* (London, ON: Routledge, 2006).

518 For Pretoria, see Christopher Vernon, "Projecting Power on Conquered Landscapes: Canberra and Pretoria" in N. Etherington (ed.), *Mapping Colonial Conquest: Australia and Southern Africa,* (Perth, AU: University of Western Australia Press, 2007); for New Delhi, see A. Irving, *Indian Summer: Lutyens, Baker and Imperial Delhi,* (New Haven, CT: Yale University Press, 1981); and S. Joardar, "New Delhi: Imperial Capital to Capital of the World's Largest Democracy" in David L.A. Gordon (ed.), *Planning Twentieth Century Capital Cities,* (London, UK: Routledge, 2006), p. 182-95; for Canberra, see Vernon, in *Planning Twentieth Century Cities, op. cit.*, p. 130-49, and John Reps, *Canberra 1912: Plans and Planners of the Australian Capital Competition,* (Melbourne, AU: Melbourne University Press, 1997).

519 Mervyn Miller, "New Delhi: Vision of Splendour." Paper presented at the 12th international conference of the International Planning History Society, held at New Delhi, December 11-14, 2006; since 1948, the building has been the Rashtrapati Bhavan, the residence of the President of India.

520 Christopher Vernon, "Projecting Power on Conquered Landscapes: Canberra and Pretoria" in N. Etherington (ed.), *Mapping Colonial Conquest: Australia and Southern Africa,* (Perth, AU: University of Western Australia Press, 2007).

521 R.G. Irving, *Indian Summer,* (New Haven, CT: Yale University Press, 1981).

522 Eran Ben-Joseph, and David L.A. Gordon, "Hexagonal Planning in Theory and Practice," *Journal of Urban Design,* 5, no. 3 (2000): 237-65.

523 Lawrence Vale, *Architecture, power, and national identity, 2nd Ed.*, (London, UK: Routledge, 2008), p. 104-13.

524 Irving, *op. cit.*

525 Delhi's planning in the second half of the 20th century has necessarily focused upon the problems caused by the explosive growth of its metropolitan region, and New Delhi has become a low-density inner suburb; Sunil Khilnani, *The Idea of India,* (London, UK: Penguin, 2003), especially chapter 3, "Cities"; Joardar, *op. cit.*

526 T.G. Birtles, "Scrivener's Ideas and Mapping Surveys for an Australia Capital City," *Cartography,* 17, December 1998: 15-25.

527 Australia Commonwealth Department of Home Affairs, *Information, Conditions and Particulars for Guidance in the Preparation of Competitive Designs for the Federal Capital City of the Commonwealth of Australia,* (Melbourne, AU: Australia Commonwealth Department of Home Affairs, April 30, 1911); Reps, *op. cit.*

528 Reps, *op. cit.*, chapter 3.

529 Christopher Vernon, "Walter Burley Griffin and Marion Mahony Griffin: from Canberra to Lucknow (via Perth)," *The Architect,* 01/07 (2007): 10-13.

530 P. Harrison, *Walter Burley Griffin: Landscape Architect,* (Canberra, AU: National Library of Australia, 1995); Robert Freestone, "Canberra as a Garden City, 1901-1930," *Journal of Australian Studies,* 19 (1986): 3-20.

531 Vernon, in *Planning Twentieth Century Capital Cities, op. cit.*; K.F. Fischer, *Canberra, Myths and*

Models: Forces at Work in the Formation of the Australian Capital, (Hamburg, DE: Institute of Asian Affairs, 1984).

532 David L.A. Gordon, "Ottawa-Hull and Canberra: Implementation of Capital City Plans," *Canadian Journal of Urban Research*, 11, no. 2 (2002): 1-16.

533 Canada, Department of Public Works, *General Conditions for the Guidance of Architects in Preparing Competitive Designs for the Proposed New Departmental and Courts Buildings for the Dominion of Canada in Ottawa, Ontario*, (Ottawa, ON: Government Printing Bureau, 1913), s.28; the assessors were British architects T.E. Collcutt and Canadian architects J.H.G. Russell and J.-O. Marchand. They wrote the DPW that "the problem of adequately dealing with the site comes entirely within the province of the Architect, rather than that of the landscape gardener," denigrating White's professional background. See letter from T.E. Collcutt and J.H.G. Russell to J.B. Hunter, deputy minister of Public Works, August 13, 1913, LAC, RG11, DPW file 5360-1A, "Proposed Departmental Buildings."

534 The best analysis of the 1906 and 1913 competitions is found in Janet Wright's, *Crown Assets*, *op. cit.*, p. 114-24. Unfortunately, there is no central file of the 1913 submission drawings because the competition was abandoned.

535 "Ottawa Has Great Possibilities from Viewpoint of Mr. Mawson, Town Planner," *Ottawa Citizen*, April 30, 1913, p. 4. Mawson was so committed to the classical style that his 1913 Calgary plan made the city look like Paris on the Bow, see Thomas H. Mawson, *Calgary: A Preliminary Planning Scheme for Controlling the Economic Growth of the City*, (London, ON: T.H. Mawson and Sons, 1914).

536 See Daniel H. Burnham and Edward H. Bennett, *Plan of Chicago*, (Chicago, IL: The Commercial Club, 1909). Copies of these plans can be found in the National Library in Ottawa.

537 Federal Plan Commission, *Report on of the Federal Plan Commission on a General Plan for the Cities of Ottawa and Hull*, (Ottawa, ON: Federal Planning Commission, 1915), p. 9.

538 Sir Herbert Holt (1856-1941) was president of the Royal Bank and one of Canada's richest men when appointed, see T. Regehr, *A Capitalist Plans the Capital*, (unpublished paper to the Canadian Historical Society 1984 meeting). He trained as a railway engineer, worked on the CPR, and controlled Montréal's streetcar network by 1914. By the end of his career he was perhaps Canada's most powerful businessman, and most hated; when his death was announced during a 1941 baseball game in Montréal, the crowd cheered; S. Brearton, "Hall of Fame/Hall of Shame," *Report on Business Magazine*, November 2003, p. 43-48.

539 Sir William Van Horne of the Canadian Pacific Railway was the Prime Minister's first choice to chair the FPC, but he declined the nomination. For the circumstances of the formation of the FPC, see the 1913 correspondence of the Deputy Minister of Finance in the OIC papers. For Holt's background, see Regehr, *op. cit.*; the background of the other members was obtained from the H.C. Charlesworth (ed.), *Cyclopaedia of Canadian Biography*, (Toronto, ON: Hunter-Rose, 1919); *The Oxford Encyclopedia of Canadian History*, (Toronto, ON: Oxford University Press, 1926) and *Who's Who and Why*, (Toronto, ON: International Press, 1914).

540 The government included $8,000 in its 1913-14 appropriations and $55,000 for the next fiscal year to cover the cost of the plan.

541 THC, *Toronto Waterfront Development, 1912-1920*, (Toronto, ON: Brigens, 1913). For Cousins' and Home-Smith's roles in implementation of the plan, see W. Reeves, *Visions for the Metro Toronto Waterfront I: Toward Comprehensive Planning, 1852-1935*, (Toronto, ON: University of Toronto Centre for Urban and Community Studies, Major Report no. 27, 1992).

542 R. Home-Smith to F. L. Olmsted, Jr. Oct. 13, 1913 and FLO to RHS 16, 22 and 24 Oct. 1913; Records of Olmsted Associates, Inc., Manuscript Division, U. S. Library of Congress, Washington DC, Job File 5070, "Ottawa City Plan, Ottawa Canada, 1913-1914" (OA). FLO was busy in Denver at the time and appears not to have visited Ottawa prior to his interview with Holt, if at all. He may have lost the job by his reluctance to quote a fixed fee to prepare the plan. FLO to Holt 19 and 25 Nov. 1913 and Holt to FLO 24 Nov. 1913 (OA). I am indebted to Dr. L.D. McCann for sharing copies of the Olmsted Bros. correspondence on the Ottawa plan.

543 For Mawson's lobby, see Thomas Mawson, *The Life and Work of An English Landscape Architect*, (London, UK: The Richards Press, 1927) and Meredith's 1911-1913 correspondence in Colborne P. Meredith papers, Library and Archives Canada, MG 29 E62 (CPM). Mawson peppered his Canadian speeches with tributes to the British Empire and courted his vice-regal contacts assiduously, even going so far as to dedicate the fourth edition of his book, *The Art and Craft of Garden Making*, (London, UK: Batsford, 1912) to the Duke of Connaught. See Gordon Cherry, "Thomas Hayton Mawson (1861-1933): a biographical note," *Planning History Bulletin*, 9, no. 2 (1987): 28-29. Like most consultants today, Mawson used his books as promotional material for potential clients. He gave another copy to Frank Darling of the Federal Plan Commission, which survives in the Fisher Rare Book Library at the University of Toronto.

544 Cauchon's articles for 1911 to 1913 are found in NC Vol. 2. Bennett's visit to Darling and Home-Smith in Toronto is noted in his Nov. 13th 1913 diary, in the Edward H Bennett papers, Art Institute of Chicago, Burnham Library of Architecture, Collection 1973.1 (EHB). Bennett agreed to serve jointly with Olmsted as landscape architect during the visit, EHB letter to F. Darling, Nov. 13, 1913 (OA), but the arrangement subsequently fell through. This visit was prior to his December 1, 1913 interview with Holt in Ottawa. Meredith's letters are found in CPM 1913 correspondence. Meredith had apprenticed in Darling's office in Toronto, so Darling was in a unique position to judge his ability and temperament. See Meredith's autobiographical manuscript, 'I' in CPM vol. 9.

545 The complete letter is in OIC papers of the Department of Finance, file 142-1.

546 Edward Bennett, "Some Aspects of City Planning, with General Reference to a Plan for Ottawa and Hull," (Address at the Normal School, Ottawa, Ontario, April 21, 1914. EHB Papers, Box 40, p. 7).

547 The published speech contains brief descriptions of Bennett's images. Several of Bennett's original lantern slides survive in the collection of the Art Institute of Chicago's Ryerson Library of Architecture. Many of the remainder were traced from the reports in the EHB and Daniel H. Burnham papers, Art Institute of Chicago, Burnham Library of Architecture, Collection 1943.1 (DHB) and Bennett's contribution to the 1909 Plan of Chicago, and W. Moody (ed.), *Wacker's Manual of Citizenship*, (Chicago, IL: Commercial Club of Chicago, 1914). See David L.A. Gordon, "Introducing a City Beautiful Plan for Canada's Capital: Edward Bennett's 1914 Speech to the Canadian Club," (Paper presented to the Society of American City and Regional Planning Historians Conference, October 24, 1997).

548 *Ottawa Citizen*, April 22, 1914.

549 W.T. Perks, "Idealism, Orchestration and Science in Early Canadian Planning: Calgary and Vancouver Re-Visited, 1914/1928," *Environments,* 17, no. 2 (1985): 1-28.

550 EHB diaries and correspondence in EHB papers, Boxes 50 and 51.

551 EHB 1914 diary, December 26-30, 1914.

552 See "Burnham, Guérin and the City as Image" in J. Zukowsky (ed.), *The Plan of Chicago: 1909-1979*, (Chicago, IL: Art Institute of Chicago, 1979). Once again, Bennett's role is hardly mentioned, even though he appears to have personally supervised the preparation of the critical drawings. For example, his original drawing of the 'Snow Scene' remains in the AIC lantern slide collection. It was used by Guérin as the base for plate CXXXVII.

553 The draft report is in EHB, Box 51. None of the text from first section of the FPC report is found in Bennett's draft, with the exception of a few paragraphs describing the site. The final draft was completed in 1915 and sent for printing by the commission staff.

554 See Jacques Gréber, *Plan for the National Capital-General Report*, (Ottawa, ON: National Capital Planning Service, 1950), chapter 3.

555 See Thomas Adams, *Outline of Town and City Planning: A Review of Past Efforts and Modern Aims,* (New York, NY: Russell Sage, 1935).

556 *Ibid.*, p. 11.

557 For the 'Château style', see H. Kalman, *History of Canadian Architecture. Vols. 1-2*, (Don Mills, ON: Oxford University Press, 1994), p. 718-22.

558 Federal Plan Commission of Ottawa and Hull, *Report of the Federal Plan Commission on a General*

Plan for the Cities of Ottawa and Hull, (Ottawa, ON: Federal Plan Commission, 1915), p. 117. List showing the results of the restrictions based on Drawing 19.

559 FPC, *op. cit.*, p. 117 and Drawing 19. All references to zoning in Germany were removed from the final draft due to the Great War.

560 Holt was subsequently involved in several charitable programs to improve the conditions of the working class in Montréal. See Regehr, *op. cit.*

561 See Gordon Cherry (ed.), *Shaping an Urban World*, (London, ON: Mansell, 1980), p. 23-58.

562 EHB papers, draft Ottawa plan in Box 51. For the fate of the housing provisions in the Burnham and Bennett's *Plan of Chicago*, *op. cit.*, see Kirsten Schaffer, "The Fabric of City Life: The Social Agenda in Burnham's Draft of the Plan of Chicago," in *Plan of Chicago*, (New York, NY: Princeton Architectural Press, 1993), introduction.

563 FPC, *op. cit.*, p. 13.

564 FPC, *op. cit.*, p. 21, 22.

565 See Wilfrid Eggleston, *The Queen's Choice: A Story of Canada's Capital*, (Ottawa, ON: National Capital Commission, 1961). Ottawa passed a referendum approving a federal district on its second try, prior to the Federal Plan Commission.

566 FPC, *op. cit.*, p. 97.

567 For Holt's background as a railway executive, see T. Regehr, *op. cit.* and *The Canadian Northern Railway: pioneer road of the northern prairies 1895-1918*, (Toronto, ON: Macmillan of Canada, 1976).

568 "Town Plan Report Provides for Creation of Federal District," *Ottawa Citizen*, March 11, 1916, p. 3, and "Keeping Alive Federal Town Planning report By Discussion, Metropolitan Area Suggested," *Ottawa Citizen*, March 30, 1916, p. 2. Bennett published the plan as "A Plan for Ottawa, the Capital of the Dominion of Canada," *American Institute of Architects Journal*, 4 (1916): 263-68.

569 See OIC papers for reference to the drawings. Adams requested all of the FPC's papers and drawings be shipped to his office. The Commission of Conservation papers have not been located to date, see Michel Girard, *L'écologisme retrouvé: essor et déclin de le Commission de la conservation du Canada*, (Ottawa, ON: Presses de l'Université d'Ottawa, 1994), preface.

570 City of Ottawa, 1914 bylaw.

571 Denise McCormick, *Building Heights in Downtown Ottawa: A Comparative Analysis with Washington D.C.*, (Unpublished Master's Report, School of Urban and Regional Planning, Queen's University, 2000).

572 Wilfrid Eggleston, *The Queen's Choice: A Story of Canada's Capital*, (Ottawa, ON: National Capital Commission, 1961), p. 170 and National Capital Commission, *A Capital in The Making*, (Ottawa, ON: National Capital Commission, 1987), p. 16-17.

573 Eggleston, *op. cit.*, p. 171 and National Capital Commission, *op. cit.*

574 Van Nus, *op. cit.*; John Taylor, "City form and capital culture: remaking Ottawa," *Planning Perspectives*, 4, no. 1 (1989): 79-105; Noulan Cauchon, "Town Planning, With Special Reference to Ottawa," *The Canadian Engineer*, 37 (1919): 455-78; and "A Federal District for Ottawa," *Journal of the Town Planning Institute of Canada*, April (1922): 3-6.

575 For example, Noulan Cauchon proposed several schemes to the Soldier's Settlement Board. See NC papers, vol. 8.

576 Regehr, *op. cit.*, p. 15.

577 The contrast with the powerful and long-term promotion of Burnham and Bennett's 1909 Chicago plan by the Commercial Club is particularly instructive here. It was not until 1927 that Prime Minister Mackenzie King re-organized the OIC and installed one of Ottawa's few business barons as its chairman. For Bennett's role in the Commercial Club and the later Chicago Plan Commission, see EHB papers Series VII and the DHB papers. See also Thomas Hines, *Burnham of Chicago, Architect and Planner*, (New York, NY: Oxford University Press, 1974), chapter XIV and Thomas J. Schlereth, "Burnham's Plan and Moody's Manual: City Planning as Progressive Reform," *Journal of the American Planning Association*, 47, no. 1 (1981): 70-82. For the 1927 reorganization of the OIC as the Federal District Commission under Thomas Ahearn, see Eggleston, *op. cit.*, p. 173-78.

578 OIC papers, File 142-1. The Hull share was $6,560.32.

579 Noulan Cauchon, "Federal district – town planning" *Ottawa Citizen*, March 23, 1912, p. 2;

Noulan Cauchon, "Reconnaissance Report on the Development of Hamilton, 1917," NC papers vol. 1 and "How Hamilton Might Become City Beautiful," *Hamilton Herald*, April 4, 1917, NC, *Vol. 3.*

580 Thomas Adams, "Ottawa-Federal Plan," *Town Planning and the Conservation of Life,* 1, no. 4 (1916): 88-89.

581 *Town Planning Review,* 7, no. 4 (1916): 268. Abercrombie later praised both the Plan of Chicago and the FPC report in 'Civic Study in Civic Design' a paper presented to the 43rd Annual General Meeting and Conference of the Institution of Municipal and County Engineers (UK), June 29, 1916, (NC papers Vol. 12).

582 Jacques Gréber, *L'Architecture aux États Unis: Preuve de la Force d'Expansion du Génie Français* (Paris, FR: Payot, 1920), p. 141-54.

583 Adams, *Rural Planning and Development, op. cit.,* p. 109-10.

584 Thomas Adams, "The Federal Housing Project," *Town Planning and the Conservation of Life,* 6, no. 2: 25-28; Michael Simpson, *Thomas Adams and the Modern Planning Movement: Britain, Canada, and the United States, 1900-1940,* (London, UK and New York, NY: Mansell, 1985).

585 T. Adams, *op. cit.,* p. 35.

Chapter 8

586 WLMK speech to House of Commons, April 24, 1928, *Hansard,* p. 2,315

587 Bruce Elliot, *The City Beyond,* (Nepean, ON: City of Nepean, 1991), p. 204-07.

588 Clarence Stein, *Toward New Towns for America,* (New York: Reinhold, 1957), p. 19.

589 Odette Vincent-Domey, "Industry and the World of Work" in Chad Gaffield (ed.), *History of the Outaouais,* (Québec, QC: Les Presses de l'Université Laval, 1997), p. 258-90.

590 Thomas Adams, *Report of the Planning and Development of the Lindenlea Estate, Ottawa,* (Ottawa, ON: July 25, 1919, City of Ottawa Archives, Ref no. RGI-3, File#1), Correspondence-Thomas Adams 1919-1920; see also "Proposed or Completed Developments: Site Planning at Lindenlea, Ottawa," *Journal of Town Planning Institute,* 1, no. 3 (1921): 4-5. The 1919 report is also available at www.PlanningCanadasCapital.ca

591 Bill McKeown, *Ottawa's Streetcars: The Story of Electric Railway Transit in Canada's Capital City,* (Pickering, ON: Railfare Books, 2006).

592 See L. Simpson, "Letter to the editor," *The Canadian Engineer,* 47, no. 10 (1924), and Adams' reply on September 30, 1924, also in LAC, MG 30 C-105, File: Ottawa Town Planning, September 30, 1924.

593 J. Delaney, "The Garden Suburb of Lindenlea, Ottawa: A Model Project for the First Federal Housing Policy, 1918-24," *Urban History Review,* 19, no. 3 (1991): 151-65.

594 Clarence Perry, "The Neighborhood Unit," in *Regional Survey of New York and Its Environs,* (New York, 1929), vol. 7.

595 Janet Wright, *Crown Assets: The Architecture of the Department of Public Works, 1867-1967,* (Toronto, ON: University of Toronto Press, 1997), p. 138-42.

596 Wright, *op. cit.,* p. 129-33.

597 Harland Bartholomew Assoc., *A Plan for the City of Vancouver, BC,* (Vancouver, BC: Vancouver Town Planning Commission, 1929); N. Johnston, "Harland Bartholomew: Precedent for the Profession" in Donald Krueckeberg (ed.), *The American Planner: Biographies & Reflections,* (New Brunswick, NJ: Center for Urban Policy Research, 1994), p. 217-41.

598 G.B. Ford, *Proceedings of the Fifth National Conference on City Planning,* (New York, 1913), p. 31-32; the article was reprinted as "Principles of Scientific City Planning," *Engineering Contract Record,* 27, no. 21 (1913): 42-5, and summarized as "Engineering and the Beautiful," *Canadian Engineer,* 24, no. 4 (1913): 219-20, which are in Cauchon's papers at the LAC.

599 C. McShane, *Down the Asphalt Path: The Automobile and the American City,* (New York, NY: Columbia University Press, 1994); C. Boyer, *Dreaming the Rational City,* (Cambridge MA: MIT Press, 1983).

600 J. Lemon, *The Toronto Harbour Plan of 1912: Manufacturing Goals and Economic Realities, Working Paper,* (Toronto, ON: Royal Commission on the Future of the Toronto Waterfront, 1990). THC chief engineer E.L. Cousins directed the project, but Boston's Olmsted Bros. landscape architecture firm designed the public parks and boulevards.

[601] Thomas Adams, "Editorial: Town Planning is a Science," *Journal of the Town Planning Institute of Canada,* 1, no. 3 (1921): 1-3.

[602] Ottawa City Council, City Council Minutes, April 18, 1921.

[603] For the typhoid epidemic and pure water, see Canada, Commission of Conservation, *Report of the Epidemic of Typhoid Fever Occurring in the City of Ottawa, January 1st to March 19, 1911,* (Ottawa, ON: Commission of Conservation, 1912), and C. Warfe, "The search for pure water in Ottawa, 1910-1915," *Urban History Review,* 8, no. 1 (1979): 90-112.

[604] D. Mullington, *Chain of Office: Biographical Sketches of the Early Mayors of Ottawa, 1847-1948,* (Renfrew, ON: General Store Publishing, 2006).

[605] J.D. Hulchanski, *The Origins of Urban Land Use Planning in Ontario, 1900-1946,* (unpublished PhD Thesis, University of Toronto, 1981), p. 106; *Proceedings of the Sixth National Conference on City Planning, Toronto, May 25-27, 1914* (Cambridge, UK: The University Press, 1914).

[606] Statutes of Ontario. 7 Geo V, chapter 44, *An Act respecting Surveys and Plans of Land in or near Urban Municipalities 1917.*

[607] Hulchanski, *op. cit.*, p. 123-26.

[608] Noulan Cauchon, "Ottawa Town Planning Commission," *Journal of the Town Planning Institute of Canada,* 1, no. 4-5 (June-August 1921): 22.

[609] Equivalent to about $105,000 in 2005 Canadian dollars; Statistics Canada, Consumer Price Index 1914-1999 SDDS 2301 and Statistics Canada 2005, Cansim Table 62-001-XPB, 1999.

[610] *Journal of the Town Planning Institute of Canada,* 1, no. 4-5, (June-August 1921): 16.

[611] The OTPC's records and drawings were destroyed in the 1931 city hall fire. Its activity was reconstructed from reports to Council held in the City of Ottawa Archives. Unfortunately, the surviving minutes only included the text; all the OTPC's original drawings and plans were destroyed. Copies of some larger plans are held in the National Map Collection, Library and Archives Canada; while many of the smaller plans were found in Cauchon's lantern slide collection.

[612] S. Coutts, *Science and Sentiment: The Planning Career of Noulan Cauchon,* (Ottawa, ON: Carleton University, Unpublished master's report, Dept. of History, 1982), p. 40.

[613] A content analysis of the 1921-34 OTPC reports demonstrates that the key issues were traffic regulation, rounding street corners, widening streets to ease traffic congestion, street extensions, railway reorganization and stations, traffic re-routing to improve traffic circulation, playground and local open space creation, proposals for zoning bylaws, removal of cross-town railway tracks; See OTPC minutes 1921-34, COA and David L.A Gordon, "Agitating people's brains': Noulan Cauchon and the City Scientific in Canada's Capital," *Planning Perspectives,* 23, no. 3 (2008): 349-379.

[614] *Journal of the Town Planning Institute of Canada,* 1, no. 10, (June 1922): 15.

[615] *Ibid.*

[616] Ottawa Town Planning Commission, *Report No. 7 of the OTPC,* (Ottawa, ON: Ottawa Town Planning Commission, September 5, 1922), p. 477; Ottawa Town Planning Commission, *Report No. 5 of the OTPC,* (Ottawa, ON: Ottawa Town Planning Commission, September 1923), p. 2.

[617] Ottawa Town Planning Commission, *Report No. 1 of the OTPC,* (Ottawa, ON: Ottawa Town Planning Commission, February 15, 1926), p. 106

[618] "Economics of Zoning," *Ottawa Citizen,* February 15, 1926 and, "Zoning – Its financial value," *Journal of the Town Planning Institute of Canada,* 2, no. 3 (May 1923): 11.

[619] N. Cauchon, "Memorandum on Zoning," *Journal of the Town Planning Institute of Canada,* 2, no. 5, (September 1923): 2-12.

[620] "Zoning bylaw ready for section of city," *Ottawa Citizen,* February 13, 1926, p. 1.

[621] Ottawa Town Planning Commission, *Report No. 1, op. cit.*

[622] "Zoning By-law Consideration," *Ottawa Citizen.* February 17, 1926.

[623] "Zoning bylaw is warmly attacked," *Ottawa Citizen,* February 19, 1926, p. 7; "Asserts 92 new offences under zoning measure," *Ottawa Citizen,* February 20, 1926, p. 26.

[624] "Realtors learn more about zoning measure," *Ottawa Citizen,* March 24, 1926, p. 9. J.M Kitchen

625 discussed the issue of zoning on March 24 and on April 20, 1926.

625 "Zoning measure makes progress among realtors," *Ottawa Citizen*, March 31, 1926, p. 4.

626 "Zoning bylaw of the City of Kitchener," *Journal of the Town Planning Institute of Canada*, 4, no. 1 (January 1925): 4-8.

627 E. Bloomfield, *City Building Processes in Berlin/Kitchener and Waterloo, 1870-1930*, (Unpublished PhD thesis, University of Guelph, 1981), p. 432.

628 "Where There is No Zoning Bylaw: Ottawa," *Journal of the Town Planning Institute of Canada*, 9, no. 1 (February 1930): 20.

629 "N. Cauchon, Retiring President's Address," *Journal of the Town Planning Institute of Canada*, 5, no. 1 (April 1926): 1.

630 Federal Plan Commission, *Report on of the Federal Plan Commission on a General Plan for the Cities of Ottawa and Hull*, (Ottawa, ON: Federal Planning Commission, 1915), p. 32, Diagram 10.

631 "Federal District and Town Planning: Traffic Diagonals and Outlets," *Ottawa Citizen*, February 26, 1912, p. 7, clipping in NC papers, Volume 2, file: Clippings, Town planning, 1911-1915.

632 "Town Planning Commission Favor Removal of Cross-Town Track Yards," *Ottawa Citizen*. November 25, 1925, p. 9; Ottawa Town Planning Commission, *Report No. 6 of the OTPC*, (Ottawa, ON: Ottawa Town Planning Commission, December 8, 1925), p. 625.

633 "Tunnel Scheme for Ottawa," *The Canadian Engineer*, August 26, 1924: 273; "New Scheme for Railway Tunnel Under the City," *Ottawa Citizen*, July 4, 1924, p. 8; Ottawa Town Planning Commission, *Report No. 4 of the OTPC*, (Ottawa, ON: Ottawa Town Planning Commission, July 7, 1924), p. 405.

634 "Majors Hill Park," *Ottawa Citizen*, June 29, 1925, p. 7.

635 "Colonel By Town Planner," *Ottawa Citizen*, March 22, 1924, p. 41.

636 WLMK diary, August 11, 1937, Gréber described the concept as "frightful," p. 572.

637 Although in the 1980s a traffic circle and Peacekeepers' Monument was created on the site Cauchon proposed for Courcelette Place

638 Thomas Adams, *Proposed Memorial Hall for the City of Ottawa*, pamphlet published March 27, 1919. NC papers, 1919, Proposed Memorial Hall.

639 John Pierce, "Constructing Memory: The Vimy Memorial," *Canadian Military History*, 1, no. 1-2, (1992): 1-3.

640 *General Conditions for the Guidance of Architects, Artists and Sculptors in Preparing Competitive Designs for the proposed National Commemorative War Monument for the Dominion of Canada in Ottawa, Canada*, (Ottawa, ON: Department of Public Works, Feb. 12, 1925). Copy in National Library.

641 WLMK in a letter to Charles Murphy, January 25, 1925, NAC, RG19, Vol. 549, File 139, no. 2. King was adamant that the memorial world be located on Connaught Square, in front of the Post Office.

642 Cauchon clipped 10 articles during the 1911 campaign for a federal district, NC fonds, Vol. 2. "Clippings 1911-15"; "Federal District is Proposed for Ottawa-Hull," *Ottawa Citizen*, October 12, 1911, p. 1.

643 Noulan Cauchon, "Town Planning in General: Ottawa in Particular," (LAC, MG 30 C105, 1918), Volume 1. Address with notes and slides, p. 10; Noulan Cauchon, "A Federal District Plan for Ottawa," *Journal of the Town Planning Institute of Canada*, 1, no. 9 (1922): 3-6.

644 Cauchon, "Town Planning in General" *op. cit.*; N. Cauchon, "A Federal District Plan for Ottawa," *op. cit.*

645 "Would Create a New Capital in Gatineau Hills," *Ottawa Citizen*, August 13, 1927, p. 37; and clipping in NC paper MG30, C-105, vol. 7.

646 The OIC was moribund after the war, with a mere five employees and no plans for future work. See G. Gyton, *A Place For Canadians: the Story of the National Capital Commission*, (Ottawa, ON: National Capital Commission, 1999), p. 22-23.

647 Gyton, *op. cit.*, p. 25-28; Lucien Brault, *Links Between Two Cities: historic bridges between Ottawa and Hull*, (Ottawa, ON/Hull, QC: City of Ottawa/City of Hull, 1989), p. 32-34.

648 *Hansard*, April 6, 1927, p. 1,975-80 and April 27, 1927, p. 2,039-41. See H. Guthrie speech, 1976; King personally recruited Thomas Ahern. Letter from Ahern to King, January 3, 1927; WLMK, Reel 3257, 119579-80.

649 *Ottawa Citizen*, July 2, 1927. For more on the Jubilee celebrations, see Robert Cupido, "Appropriating the Past: Pageants, Politics, and the Diamond Jubilee of Confederation," *Journal of the Canadian Historical Association,* 8, New Series (1998): 155-186.

650 For more on the day's events, see Bryan S. Osborne and G.B. Osborne, "The cast[e]ing of heroic landscapes: constructing Canada's pantheon on Parliament Hill," *Material History Review,* 60 (2004): 35-47.

651 King was a founding vice-president of the Canadian Club that invited Bennett to lecture on capital city planning in 1914.

652 WLM King speech, *Hansard,* April 24, 1928, p. 2,435. The United States Consulate was also interested in the Metcalfe Street proposal, to give a more imposing site for their new embassy on Wellington Street: US Ambassador Philips to King, February 14, and June 5, 1928. Harold Fisher to King, April 23, 1928; Baldwin (King's secretary) to W. Philips (US Ambassador), June 6, 1928, WLMK papers reel 3266, 129478-9; 132632.

653 WLMK speech to House of Commons, April 24, 1928, *Hansard,* p. 2,315.

654 King speech, April 24, 1928, *Hansard,* p. 2,313-19.

655 WLMK diary, April 24, 1928.

656 See "Federal Governments' Confederation Park Scheme," *Ottawa Citizen,* October 29, 1927, p. 1. Drawing by N. Cauchon, OTPC. Cauchon suggested similar schemes in an article in the *Ottawa Citizen,* January 15, 1912, p. 10.

657 After negotiation by Ahearn and a meeting with the prime minister, the city's agreement was sealed by an exchange of letters from King to Mayor J.P. Balharrie, October 22, 1927, WLMK papers V. 168, Reel C-2296, 119 828-833 and from the Ottawa Board of Control to T. Ahearn, dated October 25, 1927, MG26 V. 165, Reel C-2299 119 597.

658 John H. Taylor, "City form and capital culture: remaking Ottawa," *Planning Perspectives,* 4 (1989): 79-105; John H. Taylor, *Ottawa: An Illustrated History,* (Toronto, ON: Lorimer, 1986), chapters 4, 5.

659 Janet Wright, *Crown Assets: The Architecture of the Department of Public Works, 1867-1967,* (Toronto, ON: University of Toronto Press, 1997), especially chapters 4 and 8; Margaret Archibald, *By Federal Design: The Chief Architect's Branch of the Department of Public Works, 1881-1914,* (Ottawa, ON: National Historic Parks and Sites Branch, 1983); and Doug Owram, *Building for Canadians: A History of the Department of Public Works, 1840-1960,* (Ottawa, ON: Public Relations and Information Services, 1979).

660 Sproatt letter to WLMK, June 6, 1929; NAC, WLMK papers, Reel 3277, pp. 143941-2.

661 "Bird's Eye View of Plaza Traffic Plan on Trial," *Ottawa Citizen,* November 7, 1929, p. 12; MG 30 C105, Volume 5, Scrapbook 5, p. 28. "Noulan Cauchon Plan Works Well," *Ottawa Citizen,* November 11, 1929, p. 18.

662 WLMK diary, October 15, 1936.

663 G. Gyton, *A Place for Canadians,* (Ottawa, ON: National Capital Commission, 1999), p. 25-29.

Chapter 9

664 Cable from the Canadian Minister of Public Works to Gréber, August 22, 1945, cited in Gréber, *Plan for the National Capital,* (Ottawa, ON: King's Printer for the National Capital Planning Service, 1950), p. 1. The original telegram is on display in the lobby of the National Capital Commission planning offices, Ottawa.

665 Bruce S. Elliott, *The City Beyond: A History of Nepean Birthplace of Canada's Capital, 1792-1990,* (Nepean, ON: City of Nepean, 1991), p. 209-22.

666 Prime Minister Bennett and Governor General Lord Bessborough were also enlisted as patrons. Edwinna von Baeyer, *Garden of Dreams: Kingsmere and Mackenzie King,* (Toronto, ON: Dundurn Press, 1990), p. 210-14. King later became an honourary member of the Canadian Society of Landscape Architects and Town Planners.

667 WLMK debate in House of Commons, May 27, 1935, *Hansard,* p. 3,046-49. The speech was widely reported. See "Mr. King takes the lead," *Ottawa Journal,* Monday, May 27, 1935; "Ottawa's Wooded Background," *Ottawa Evening Citizen,* May 27, 1935.

668 Department of the Interior, "Lower Gatineau Woodlands Survey: Interim Report," (Ottawa, ON: King's Printer, 1935).

669 von Baeyer, 1990, *op. cit.*, p. 212.

670 WLMK diary, Library and Archives Canada (LAC), MG 26 J6, August 19, 1937; von Baeyer, 1990, *op. cit.*, p. 214-15; Leduc speech to Commons, *Hansard*, June 1938, p. 683.

671 Chad Gaffield (ed.), *History of the Outaouais*, (Québec, QC: Les Presses de l'Université Laval, 1997), p. 284-51.

672 J. Gréber, *Plan for the National Capital*, (Ottawa, ON: King's Printer for the National Capital Planning Service, 1950), vol. 2 and Atlas, see especially p. 129-33, 235-45.

673 J. Taylor, *Ottawa: An Illustrated History*, (Toronto, ON: James Lorimer, 1986), Table XIV. The 1933 value of building permits was one-sixth that of 1930.

674 We reconstructed the activity of the OTPC from the formal reports to city council and Cauchon's ample papers at the Library and Archives Canada, MG 30 C105. Although Cauchon's original OTPC drawings were destroyed, some copies survived in the National Map Collection and his lantern slide collection contains good images of scores of drawings that did not survive in paper form. See David Gordon, "Agitating People's Brains: Noulan Cauchon and the City Scientific in Canada's Capital," *Planning Perspectives*, 23, no. 3 (2008): p. 349-79; and the images at this book's website.

675 CIP fonds LAC; TPIC Secretary-Treasurer John Kitchen (Cauchon's loyal OTPC assistant) kept the Institute's corporate charter alive by paying the annual registration fees until the TPIC was revived in 1952.

676 King to Bennett, August 9, 1930, Richard Bedford Bennett papers, Section F, Prime Minister's Office Files, LAC, MG 26 K (RBB) correspondence, 312384-6. King speech to House of Commons, June 2, 1931, *Hansard*, p. 2,225-27.

677 Mayor Allen to Bennett, April 2, 1931; Bennett to Allen, April 2, 1931; Allen to Bennett, May 8, 1931; RBB, 312421-6. The municipal archives and the OTPC records were destroyed. The 'City Hall' moved to several floors of the Transportation Building at Rideau Street, near Sussex.

678 Wright, J., *Crown Assets – The Architecture of the Department of Public Works, 1867-1967*, (Toronto, ON: University of Toronto Press), chapter 6, "Building in the Depression," p. 161-93.

679 *Ibid.*, p. 130-33.

680 The authors are currently working on a paper, "Wars make nations, nations make war memorials: a political-iconographic analysis of the Canadian National War Memorial."

681 "War Memorial Is Impressive Sight: Canada's tribute to Heroic Dead Erected in Hyde Park, London," London *Evening Citizen,* quoted in *Ottawa Citizen*, October 29, 1932.

682 See *Hansard*, February 22, 1934, p. 864-67.

683 WLMK diary, October 15, 1936. Gréber was officially appointed by Canada Order-in-Council P.C. 63/185, January 28, 1937.

684 Gréber collection, NAC, 1937, plans for Confederation Square.

685 Jacques Gréber oral history, 1961, CBC kinescope 11854, 04:00.

686 WLMK diary, August 12, 1937. King later admitted the congestion was too severe.

687 WLMK diary, March 18, 1938. The Château style, named after railway hotels like Ottawa's Château Laurier, became something of a national architectural style in the first part of the 20th century. See H. Kalman, *History of Canadian Architecture. Vols. 1-2*, (Don Mills, ON: Oxford University Press, 1994), p. 718-22.

688 See "Order of Ceremony: Unveiling of the National War Memorial at Ottawa," Ottawa Public Library vertical files-Ottawa-War Memorial.

689 WLMK diary, February 27, 1939.

690 W.L.M. King, *The Secret of Heroism: a memoir of Henry Albert Harper*, (New York, NY: Fleming H. Revell Company, 1906).

691 WLMK Papers LAC MG 26 J1, J2, Reel 3659, C20177-180.

692 Gréber collection, 1937 plans for Confederation Square, May-November 1937; Jacques Gréber, "Report on City Improvements" (February 7, 1938); Jacques Gréber, *City of Ottawa, Consultation on Development of Government Grounds*, (June 24, 1937); Jacques Gréber, "Notes sur les Travaux

692 d'Embellissement de la Ville d'Ottawa," *La Vie Urbaine*, Paris, no. 52, (julliet-aout 1939): 199-210; Gréber also had input on the location of Ernest Cormier's Supreme Court building. See Isabelle Gournay and France Vanlaethem, *The Supreme Court of Canada and its Justices, A Commemorative Book*, (Ottawa, ON: Supreme Court of Canada, 2000), p. 200-01.

693 See Ottawa City Council minutes, (September 1939), p. 231; also Lucien Brault, *Ottawa Old and New*, (Ottawa, ON: Ottawa Historical Information Institute), p. 93.

694 J.H. Taylor, *op. cit.*, Table VIII, p. 212. 'Headquarters' civil service rose from 11,848 in 1939 to 19,593 in 1941 and 34,740 in 1945.

695 The Cartier Square "temporaries" lasted until the 1970s, while one of the other buildings still stands beside the Supreme Court.

696 Lucien Brault, *Hull 1800-1950*, (Ottawa, ON: Les Éditions de l'Université d'Ottawa, 1950), Appendix A; Taylor, *op. cit.*, Table II, p. 210.

697 W. Eggleston, *National Research in Canada, The NRC 1916-1966*, (Toronto, ON: Clarke, Irwin & Company Limited, 1978); Janet Wright, *Crown Assets – The Architecture of the Department of Public Works, 1867-1967*, (Toronto, ON: University of Toronto Press), p. 194-97.

698 *Ottawa: War-Time Capital*, National Film Board of Canada 0142-073, 1942, 10 min.

699 H. Clout, "The Reconstruction of Upper Normandy: a Tale of Two Cities," *Planning Perspectives*, 14, no. 2, (April 1999): 183-207; A. Lortie, *Jacques Gréber Architecte Urbaniste 1882–1962: Les Allers Retours France Amerique une Energie Cynetique au Service de l'art Urbaine?* (Paris, FR: Institut d'urbanisme de Paris, unpublished master's thesis, 1988), p. 48; ironically, the First Canadian Army damaged several of these towns during their liberation as it advanced along the coast of France in 1944-45.

700 P. Abercrombie and J.H. Forshaw, *County of London Plan 1943*, (London, UK: Macmillan, 1944); P. Abercrombie, *Greater London Plan, 1944*, (London, UK: HMSO, 1945); Gréber visited Abercrombie in London after several of his Ottawa trips; for the influence of the Greater London Plan, see P.G. Hall, *Cities of Tomorrow*, (London, UK: Blackwell, 1988), p. 165-73; S.V. Ward (ed.), *The Garden City*, (London, UK: Chapman and Hall, 1994); S.V. Ward, *Planning the Twentieth Century City: The Advanced Capitalist World*, (New York, NY: Wiley, 2002).

701 Abercrombie, 1945, *op. cit.*; E. Howard, *Tomorrow: A Peaceful Path to Real Reform*, 1898, (2003 reprint edited by P. Hall and C. Ward, London, UK: Routledge, 2003), Diagram 7; P. Hall and C. Ward, *Sociable Cities: The Legacy of Ebenezer Howard*, (Chichester, UK: Wiley, 1998).

702 Abercrombie, 1945, *op. cit.*, p. 8; 24-26; see also Marco Amati (ed.), *Urban Greenbelts in the 21st Century*, (London, UK: Ashgate, 2008); For Moscow, see M. H. Lang in David Gordon (ed.), *Planning Twentieth Century Capital Cities*, (London, UK: Routledge, 2006).

703 Gordon Stephenson, *On a Human Scale: A Life in City Design*, (South Fremantle, AU: Fremantle Arts Centre Press, 1992); K.C. Parsons, "British and American Community Design: Clarence Stein's Manhattan Transfer, 1924-1974, *Planning Perspectives*, 7, no. 2, (1992): 211-33.

704 S.V. Ward, *Planning the Twentieth Century City: The Advanced Capitalist World*, (New York, NY: Wiley, 2002); for Stockholm, see P. Hall, *Cities in Civilization*, (New York, NY: Random House, 1998), chapter 27; for Seoul, see J. Kim and T. Kim, "Issues with Green Belt Reform in the Seoul Metropolitan Area" in M. Amati (ed.), *Urban Green Belts in the Twentieth Century*, *op. cit.*, p. 37-57; for Washington, see 1961 plan; for Paris, see P. White from Gordon, 2006; Jacques Gréber was certainly aware of the *Greater London Plan* since he visited London during several of his Atlantic crossings for the commission to plan Canada's capital.

705 Eric Mumford, *The CIAM Discourse on Urbanism, 1928-1960*, (Cambridge, MA: MIT Press, 2000).

706 J.L. Sert, *Can Our Cities Survive?* (Cambridge, MA: Harvard University Press, 1943). The Athens Charter was named after the site of the 1933 CIAM conference.

707 Canada, Advisory Committee on Reconstruction, *IV. Housing and Community Planning*, (Ottawa, ON: King's Printer, 1944), Report of the Subcommittee, 161.

708 A.B. Copp, and J.A. Gregory, *Final Report of the Joint Committee of the Senate and House of Commons appointed to Review the Special Problems Arising out of the Location of the Seat of Government in Ottawa*, (Ottawa, ON: King's Printer, August 1, 1944).

709 WLMK diary, April 20, 1944.

710 WLMK diary, August 19, 1937; This diary entry shows King's wide knowledge of the settlement history of Hull and Bytown, before most scholarly histories were published; for the 1944 speech see WLMK speech to House of Commons, April 21, 1944, *Hansard*, p. 2,234-40; Bronson, F (FDC Chair) brief to the 1944 Committee, 70; Nationalist groups in Hull reacted with inflammatory language, Western Québec Chamber of Commerce brief to the 1944 committee; St Jean Baptiste Society brief, 1944 committee.

711 Canada, Central Mortgage and Housing Corporation, *Housing and Urban Growth in Canada*, (Ottawa, ON: CMHC, 1956), p. 9.

712 Albert Rose, *Regent Park; A Study in Slum Clearance*, (Toronto, ON: University of Toronto Press, 1958); Peter Oberlander and Eva Newbrun, *Houser: The Life and Work of Catherine Bauer, 1905-1964*, (Vancouver, BC: UBC Press, 1999); John Sewell, *The Shape of the City: Toronto Struggles with Modern Planning*, (Toronto, ON: University of Toronto Press, 1993).

713 King, quoted in J.W. Pickersgill, *The Mackenzie King Record*, (Toronto, ON: University of Toronto Press, 1970), p. 656.

714 Cable from the Canadian Minister of Public Works to Gréber, August 22, 1945, cited in Gréber *Plan for the National Capital, op. cit.*, p. 1. The original telegram is on display in the lobby of the National Capital Commission planning offices, Ottawa.

715 J.A. Hume, "Ottawa-Hull Area Planned As Great National Memorial," *Ottawa Citizen*, August 30, 1945, p. 13.

716 "Soul of Canada today" from King speech, April 24, 1928, *Hansard*, p. 2,313-319; Further, Canada's new role as a middle-power in the post-World War II political arena necessitated the accommodation of the embassies and consulates located in Ottawa.

Chapter 10

717 A. Gotlieb, *The Washington Diaries*, (Toronto, ON: McClelland and Stewart, 2006), p. 3. It added "Allan, if the day comes when you say to yourself, 'I like Ottawa,' that's the time to leave. It won't be because Ottawa has improved. It will be because your standards have deteriorated."

718 Canada Privy Council order #P.C. 5624, August 15, 1945.

719 J. Gréber oral history, 1961 CBC kinescope 11854, 62:00.

720 Montréal and Toronto both had staff who shared planning with other duties.

721 National Film Board short films include: "Ottawa: Today and Tomorrow" (1951, 10 min, NFB #113C0151 056); "Planning Canada's National Capital," (1949, 21 min, NFB #106B 0149 057); "A Capital Plan" (1949, 11 min, NFB #106C 0149 035). Examples of Gréber's speeches and radio talks include: "Conference by Mr. J. Gréber, Chateau Laurier, under the auspices of La Société d'Études et de Conférences d'Ottawa," (November 14, 1948); "Address given at a luncheon in honour of the national capital plan given by his excellency Francisque Gay, Ambassador of France," (November 25, 1948); "Address given to the Ontario Citizens' Planning Conference, Convocation Hall, Toronto University, under the auspices of the Community Planning Association of Canada," (October 15, 1948); "Address presented by Gréber to the standing committee on public buildings and grounds of the Senate," (April 21, 1948); "CBC Radio Interview of Gréber following convention of the Ontario branch of the Community Planning Association, Toronto," (October 20, 1948); "Address given to the corporation of land surveyors of the province of Québec," (April 19, 1950); All at the NCC Library, Ottawa in 2012; for analysis of the propaganda content of the films, see Roger M. Picton, "Selling national urban renewal: the National Film Board, the National Capital Commission and post-war planning in Ottawa, Canada." *Urban History*, 37, no. 2 (2010): 301-21.

722 Canada Privy Council Order no. 5635, (August 16, 1945).

723 Jacques Gréber, *The Planning of a National Capital*, address delivered by Mr. Jacques Gréber before the Honourable members of the Senate and the House of Commons, (Ottawa, ON: King's Printer, October

723 (cont.) 25, 1945). This speech was in many ways similar to Edward Bennett's 1914 speech to kick-off the Federal Plan Commission; see Bennett, 1914.

724 Patrick Geddes, *Cities in Evolution: An Introduction to the Town Planning Movement and to the Study of Civics*, (London, ON: Williams and Norgate, 1915).

725 Gréber, *Plan for the National Capital*, (Ottawa, ON: Kings Printer, 1950), p.81

726 E.L. Cousins, the engineer for the 1915 Plan, was a NCPC member and chaired the railway committee. Gréber, 1950, *op. cit.*, p. 13.

727 Jacques Gréber, *Plan for the National Capital – Preliminary Report*, (Ottawa, ON: King's Printer 1948).

728 NFB films, *op. cit.*

729 "Ottawa: A National Responsibility (editorial)," *The Calgary Herald*, April 17, 1954; and "A National Responsibility (editorial)," *The Ottawa Journal*, April 21, 1954.

730 Jacques Gréber, "War Memorial" memo to E.P. Murphy, Deputy Minister of Public Works, November 20, 1946. WLMK files 2110, Ref. 10112; see also Gréber, 1950, *op. cit.*, p. 261-64.

731 Transcript of a Radio Talk by Mr. Édouard Fiset, CKCH, November 28, 1947. NCC Library. See also J. Gréber, 1950, *op. cit.*, p. 261-64.

732 Gréber, 1946 memo to Murphy, Deputy Minister of Public Works, November 20, 1946; Teletype message from Washington, DC, March 30, 1948, signed by Mackenzie King, WLMK papers V. 463, File 0-25; King, "Foreword" in Gréber, 1950, *op. cit.*, p. iii.

733 King's diary noted his concern for the national capital plan, WLMK diary, May 25, 1948.

734 WLMK diary, April 29, 1949; A.R. Sykes, "Plan Crowns Years' Hopes of Mr. King," *Ottawa Journal*, April 30, 1949; "Idea Developed by MacKenzie King," *Ottawa Citizen*, April 30, 1949, p. 29; "MacKenzie King Gave Real Impetus to Movement For Greater Capital," *Ottawa Journal*, April 30, 1949, Special Capital Plan Section, p. 23. These newspaper clippings are bound into King's diary for the day, an indication that he was particularly pleased by the stories.

735 Gréber, 1950, *op. cit.*, p. iii.

736 Although printed towards the end of 1950, the plan was not tabled in the House of Commons until May 22, 1951. Federal District Commission, *Brief submitted to the Joint Committee of the Senate and House of Commons* Ottawa, March 1956, p. 18. English and French versions were tabled at the same time.

737 National Film Board of Canada press release 55411, December 5, 1950; Braquenié & Cie. (Paris), "Interview demandée à M. Jean Dautzenberg-Braquenié au sujet de la tapisserie d'Aubusson offerte au Canada par le Gouvernement Français," (Paris, October 31, 1950). NCC file 5-014, box 235; "French Tapestry Immortalizes the New Ottawa," *Ottawa Journal*, September 29, 1950. Unfortunately, the tapestry was destroyed in the October, 1979 fire in the adjacent Rideau Club. The watercolour remains in the NCC's collection.

738 Office decentralization was also promoted for civil defence against bombing, although this argument disappeared after the power of the hydrogen bomb was understood. See Federal District Commission (FDC), *Brief submitted to the Joint Committee*, 1956, *op. cit.*, p. 44.

739 Clarence Perry, "The Neighborhood Unit," *Regional Survey of New York and Its Environs*, 1929, p. 7; Clarence Stein, *Toward New Homes for America*, (New York, NY: Reinhold, 1949/56); see John Sewell, *The Shape of the City*, (Toronto, ON: University of Toronto Press, 1993), chapters 2-3, for discussion of how the neighbourhood unit was adopted in Canada.

740 Gréber, 1950, *op. cit.*, Plate XXVII.

741 Gréber did design one model neighbourhood at the request of the Village of Pointe-Gatineau. See Gréber, 1950, *op. cit.*, Figures 147 and 148, 202. The plan was partly implemented with a main street named Gréber Blvd.

742 See Phil Jenkins, *An Acre of Time: The Enduring Value of Place*, (Toronto, ON: Macfarlane Walter & Ross, 1996). Peter Linkletter, *Redevelopment in a jurisdictional swamp: a case study of the LeBreton Flats*, (Unpublished Master's Report, School of Urban and Regional Planning, Queen's University, Kingston, 1997).

743 Ebenezer Howard, *Tomorrow! A Peaceful Path to Real Reform*, (London, UK: Swan Sonnenschein 1898), Diagram 7; see also Peter Hall and Colin

Ward, *Sociable cities: the legacy of Ebenezer Howard* (Chichester, UK: Wiley, 1998) for a review of how this structure is returning in current British and American planning.

744 P. Abercrombie, *Greater London Plan*, (London, UK: HMSO, 1945); Gréber visited Abercrombie in London after several of his Ottawa trips.

745 See the Analysis in David L.A. Gordon, "Frederick Todd and the Origins of the Park System in Canada's National Capital," *Journal of Planning History*, 1, no.1 (2002), Table 1, 47.

746 WLMK diary March 29, 1946; "Investigation launched into Hull fire;" *Ottawa Evening Citizen*, March 30, 1946, p. 1, 14, 15.

747 José L. Sert, *Can Our Cities Survive?* (Cambridge, MA: Harvard University Press, 1942), p. 246-49. This "Town Planning Chart" was developed at the Fourth C.I.A.M. Congress, Athens, 1933; Eric Mumford, *The CIAM Discourse on Urbanism, 1928-1960*, (Cambridge, MA: MIT Press, 2000).

748 Although the avant-garde Modern architects had built few major projects between the wars, they produced an urban planning model (the Athens Charter) that was intended to be widely applicable. Le Corbusier had travelled widely and proposed visionary schemes for capital cities in Paris (1925), Buenos Aires (1929), Rio (1929) Algiers (1933) and Barcelona (1934). But all that came out of these efforts were some drawings admired in intellectual circles.

749 Nancy Pollock-Ellwand, "Gréber's Plan and the Washington of the North: Finding a Canadian Capital in the Face of Republican Dreams." *Landscape Journal*, 20. no. 1 (2001): 48-61; Kenza Benali and Caroline Ramirez, "Le plan de Jacques Gréber pour la capital nationale: un héritage urbanistique décrié," *Cahiers de géographie du Québec*, 56, no. 157 (2012): 51-80; Danilo Udovicki-Selb, "Le Corbusier and the Paris Exhibition of 1937," *Journal of the Society of Architectural Historians*, 56, no. 1 (1997): 42-63; T. Andresen, M. Fernandes dé Sa, J. Almeida (eds.). *Jacques Gréber, Urbanist and Garden Designer*, (Porto: Serralves Foundation, 2011).

750 Mackenzie King was adamant about his preferences for classical architecture, waxing eloquent over the National Research Council laboratories disliked by Gréber. See WLMK diaries; Gréber, 1950, *op. cit.*, Figure 67.

751 V. Newhouse, *Wallace K. Harrison, Architect*, (New York, NY: Rizzoli, 1989), p. 104-43. Le Corbusier dominated the ten members of the Board of Design, who also included Oscar Niemeyer (Brazil), Ernst Cormier (Canada) and Sven Markelius (Sweden).

752 G.A. Dudley, *Workshop for Peace: Designing the United Nations Headquarters*, (Princeton, NJ: Princeton Architectural Foundation Press, 1994); Eugenie Birch, "New York City: Super-Capital – Not by Government Alone" in David L. A. Gordon (ed.), *Planning Twentieth Century Capital Cities*, (New York, NY: Routledge, 2006) p. 253-69, esp. 259-61.

753 Le Corbusier's Modern approach influenced other capitals in the sub-continent including Bhubaneswar and Ghandinagar in India and Doxiadis' Islamabad and Kahn's Dhaka plans in Pakistan ihal Perera, "Contesting Visions: Hybridity, Liminality and Authorship of the Chandigarh Plan," *Planning Perspectives*, 19 (April 2004): 175-99; Vikramaditya Prakash, *Chandigarh's Le Corbusier: The struggle for Modernity in Postcolonial India*, (Ahemedahbad, IN: Mapin, 2002); Sarah Williams Goldhagen, *Louis Kahn's situated modernism*, (New Haven, CT: Yale University Press, 2001); Sharif Uddin Ahmed, *Dacca: a study in urban history and development*, (London, UK: Curzon Press, 1986).

754 The Library and Archives were designed by Mathers and Haldenby, while the Tupper building was designed by Hazelgrove, Lithwick and Lambert. See J. Wright, *Crown Assets, op. cit.*, p. 233-52.

755 Mark Fram, "Central Area West Heritage Conservation District Study and Plan," (Toronto, ON: Polymath Planning and Design, 1999), p. 56.

756 Jane Jacobs, *The Death and Life of Great American Cities*, (New York: Random House, 1961).

757 Gréber designed the vista as the ceremonial entrance to the city from Montréal; see Gréber, 1950, *op. cit.*, Figure 133. A portion of this view is present from the Nicholas Street exit of the Queensway, but the best view is from pleasure boat or ice-skating on the Rideau Canal.

758 *Ibid.*, p. 179-80.

759 This happened in the 1913 New Delhi plan with unfortunate results: the Viceroy's palace is only partly visible from the monumental Rajpath. This error is well-known among capital city urban designers

and would have influenced Gréber and his planning team. See Peter Hall, *Cities of Tomorrow*, 3rd Edition, (London, UK: Basil Blackwell, 2002), p. 198-206.

760 David L.A. Gordon and Mark Seasons, "Administrative and Political Strategies for Implementing Plans in Political Capitals," *Canadian Journal of Urban Research,* (2009): 82-105.

761 Federal District Commission bylaw no. 28, March 8, 1946.

762 NFB newsreels, *op. cit.*, Gréber interviews, *op. cit.*

763 *The Calgary Herald*, 1954, *op. cit.*; "Québecers see famed master plan of future Ottawa for first time," *Québec Chronicle Telegraph*, November 17, 1949; "Comment Ottawa deviendra la plus belle capitale," *La Tribune, Sherbrooke*, November 21, 1949; "City planning exhibit in Sherbrooke today," *Montréal Gazette*, November 25, 1950; St. Laurent speech; J. Diefenbaker, "Acquisition of land to establish a green belt around the nation's capital," *Community Planning Review*, 8, no. 3, (1957): 78-79.

764 WLMK diary, Nov. 15, 1948.

765 The Department of Public Works continued its role as the client and lessor of federal buildings, see Janet Wright, *Crown Assets – The Architecture of the Department of Public Works: 1867-1967*, (Toronto, ON: University of Toronto Press, 1997).

766 The provincial government built the expressway and paid for most of its capital cost.

767 Joint Committee of the Senate and the House of Commons, *Proceedings of the Joint Committee of the Senate and the House of Commons appointed to Review the Special Problems Arising out of the Location of the Seat of Government in the City of Ottawa, Final Report, August 1, 1944*. (Ottawa, ON: King's Printer. Ottawa 1944); Ottawa 1956 brief to 1956 Committee, *op. cit.*

768 Letter from Joseph Jolicoeur, Managing Director of *Le Progres de Hull*, to Mackenzie King, February 6, 1946; Letter from King to Jolicoeur dated February 9, 1946, King papers Vol. 464 File0-25-2(A).

769 Gréber *Conference* November 14, 1948 *op.cit.*; Fiset CKCH talk, November 28 1947, *op. cit.*, Donald C. Rowat, *The Government of Federal Capitals*, (Toronto: University of Toronto Press, 1973); D.H. Fullerton, *The Capital of Canada: How Should it Be Governed? Special Study on the National Capital*, (Ottawa, ON: Information Canada, 1974).

770 Ottawa, Brief submitted to the Journal Committee of the Senate and House of Commons, (Ottawa, ON: Federal District Commission, 1956). The Greenbelt boundary moved outward in the final versions of the plan leaving pockets of Gloucester and Nepean townships in the urban area.

771 Elliott, *The City Beyond*, *op. cit.*, p. 250-55.

772 *Ibid.*, p. 257-58. Ottawa and Nepean agreed to divide the Hall after a week's standoff, which Mayor Bourque compared to the Russian blockade of Berlin. The Ottawa staff eventually gave up and withdrew in 1951, not to return until 2001.

773 *Ibid.*, p. 258.

774 Nepean at least had some form of basic subdivision control after 1947; see Elliott, *op. cit.*, p. 252; Gloucester would not designate itself as an "urban development area" under the *Ontario Planning and Development Act*, so any property owner could subdivide land in any manner they wanted – exactly the system that had caused the subdivision problems in the early 1900s.

775 D.A. Moodie, 'Brief to the Joint Committee' in Joint Committee of the Senate and the House of Commons, (1956), p. 557.

776 It is not clear if Québec provincial laws were strong enough to protect a greenbelt, even if the Outaouais townships were so inclined. Québec had Canada's weakest planning legislation in the mid-century and did not get its first legislation until 1941, some 30 years after the other provinces. See J. Wolfe, "Our Common Past: An Interpretation of Canadian Planning History," *Plan Canada*, Special Edition (July 1994), p. 12-34; Gerald Hodge and David Gordon, *Planning Canadian Communities*, 5th ed., (Toronto, ON: Nelson, 2008), p. 93-97.

777 See M. Amati (ed.), *Urban Greenbelts in the 21st Century*, (London, UK: Ashgate, 2008).

778 Almos Tassonyi, "Ottawa, Canada," in Enid Slack and Rupak Chattopadhyay (eds.). *Finance and governance of capital cities in federal systems,* (Montréal: McGill-Queen's University Press, 2009), p. 55-78; "Ottawa as the National Capital: Fiscal Issues" in R. Chattopadhyay and G. Paquet, *The Unimagined Canadian Capital: Challenges for the Federal Capital Region*, (Ottawa: Invenire 2011), p. 53-65.

779 The demographers also had to work with limited information, since the 1941 and 1946 census were reduced by the war effort. Leroy Stone, *Urban Development in Canada*, (Ottawa, ON: Dominion Bureau of Statistics, 1969), p. 39.

780 R. Griffiths, *Who We ARE! – A Citizen's Manifesto*, (Vancouver, BC: Douglas & McIntyre, 2009), p. 112-47.

781 See J.H. Taylor, *Ottawa: An Illustrated History*, (Toronto, ON: J. Lorimor: Canadian Museum of Civilization, National Museums of Canada, 1986), Table VIII, p. 212. The "headquarters" civil service declined from 34,740 to 30,069 over 1945-51, but then climbed to 36,945 by 1961.

782 The 1951 census results, released in 1953, showed a regional population of 292,476, slightly above the Gréber forecasts. The 1956 census, showed the Ottawa-Hull Census Metropolitan Area at 345,460, far above the forecast range. But these results were first released in 1958, only four years before the plan's capacity was reached. A plan that had been expected to guide development from 25-50 years was obsolete in only 11 years.

783 Elliott, *The City Beyond*, op. cit., p. 270-75. Nepean did not outlaw 'metes and bounds' plots until 1957, or require subdivision agreements until 1958. Gloucester was even further behind. Subdivision planning controls had been available in Ontario since the 1917 *Planning and Development Act*, but township councils dominated by rural property owners often declined to adopt them. See G. Hodge and D. Gordon, *Planning Canadian Communities*, 5th edition, (Toronto, ON: Nelson 2008), p. 33-102.

784 Interviews with two of the new planners, Arnold Faintuck and Marion Seymour, June 20, 2000.

785 R. Hubbard, *Rideau Hall*, (Montréal, QC and Kingston, ON: McGill-Queen's University Press, 1977), p. 223.

786 City of Ottawa submission, *Papers and Proceedings of the Joint Committee of the Senate and the House of Commons Appointed to Review and Report upon the Progress and the Programs of the FDC in Developing and Implementing the Plan of the National Capital*, (Ottawa, ON: Queen's Printer, 1956). The federal government may also have been influenced by Australia, which established a similar committee to deal with the Canberra deadlock. See Australia, "Senate Select Committee Appointed to Inquire into the Report of the Development of Canberra." *Report from the Select Committee*, Parliamentary Paper No. S2, 1955, (Canberra, AU: Commonwealth Printer, September 1955), J.A. McCallum, Chairman; J. Overall, *Canberra: Yesterday, Today & Tomorrow, a Personal Memoir*, (Canberra, AU: Federal Capital Press, 1995); Dave Gordon, "Ottawa-Hull and Canberra: Implementation of Capital City Plans," *Canadian Journal of Urban Research*, 11, no. 2, (Winter 2002).

787 City of Ottawa submission, *Papers and Proceedings of the Joint Committee of the Senate and the House of Commons Appointed to Review and Report upon the Progress and the Programs of the FDC in Developing and Implementing the Plan of the National Capital*, (Ottawa, ON: Queen's Printer, 1956).

788 Canada, Joint Committee of the Senate and the House of Commons appointed to review and report upon the progress and programs of the FDC in developing and implementing the plan of the National Capital, *Papers and Proceedings*, (Ottawa, ON: Queen's Printer, 1956).

789 John Hamilton Gray, *Confederation, or, The political and parliamentary history of Canada, from the conference of Québec, in October, 1864, to the admission of British Colombia, in July, 1871*, (Toronto, ON: Copp, Clark & Co. Printers 1872).

790 The committee's proposed act – Bill 417, *An Act Respecting the Development and Improvement of the National Capital Region* was ultimately not passed.

791 Canada, *National Capital Act*, 7 Eliz II, chapter 37; it was passed on Sept. 8, 1958 and proclaimed as law on Feb. 6, 1959. The NCC's jurisdiction doubled from 2,330 sq. km. to 4,660 sq. km. on both sides of the Ottawa River.

792 The prime ministerial appointment meant that Thrift could not be fired by a future regime. Eric W. Thrift (1912-1995) was one of Canada's most distinguished urban planners. He was recruited to the NCC from Manitoba, where he was instrumental in establishing the metropolitan planning agency for Winnipeg. Thrift had been president of the Town Planning Institute of Canada (1953-1954; 1959-1962) and the only Canadian ever elected President of the American Society of Planning Officials (1964).

Thrift retired from the NCC in 1970 to become a founding faculty member of the School of Urban and Regional Planning at Queen's University, where he taught until 1986. See Eric Thrift Fonds, Queen's University Archives.

793 *Hansard* (June 18, 1958), p. 1,381-82; National Capital Commission. *A Capital in the Making*, (Ottawa, ON: NCC 1998), p. 28. Jacques Gréber and Mackenzie King, *The National Capital Plan*, January 28, 1983, Michael Newton, *Lower Town Ottawa 1854-1900*. Vol. 2. (Ottawa, ON: National Capital Commission, 1981), p. 5; CPAC, "Acquisition of land to establish a green belt around the nation's capital," *CPAC Review*, 8, no. 3, (September, 1958): 78; J. Gréber, (J.A. Hume-Staff Writer), "Regarding Greenbelt," *Ottawa Citizen*, Dec. 12, 1958.

794 D. McDonald & J. Cole, *The Conservation of Urban Greenbelts, with particular reference to the National Capital of Canada*, (Ottawa, ON: National Capital Commission, 1973); National Capital Commission (NCC), *Agriculture in the Greenbelt: Implementation Program*, (Ottawa, ON: NCC, 1974a); see also David Gordon and Richard Scott, "Ottawa's Greenbelt Evolves from Urban Separator to Key Ecological Planning Component" in M. Amati (ed.), *Urban Green Belts in the 21st Century*, (Aldershot, UK: Ashgate Forthcoming 2008), p. 187-217.

795 Supreme Court of Canada, *Munro vs. National Capital Commission* [1966] S.C.R. 663.

796 Gordon and Scott, 2008, *op. cit.*, p. 187-217.

797 J. Smart, *A City and a Technology: The Role of Government in the Growth of the Technology Industry in Ottawa, Canada to 1984*, (Unpublished PhD Dissertation, Department of History, Queen's University at Kingston, Canada, 2004), chapter 5: 175-206. Nortel later leased an adjacent 121 hectares from the NCC and its research campus has been the region's largest private employer and source of dozens of spin-off high-technology companies. See David Gordon, Betsy Donald and John Kozuskanich, "Unanticipated Benefits – the Role of Planning in the Development of the Ottawa Region Technology Industries" in Nick Novakowski and Rémy Tremblay (eds.), *Perspectives on Ottawa's High-tech Sector*, (Brussels, BE: Peter Lang, 2007), p. 104-08.

798 NCC, 1970; David L. A. Gordon, "Ottawa-Hull and Canberra: Implementation of Capital City Plans." *Canadian Journal of Urban Research*, 13, no. 2, (2002): 1-16; the NCC reported capital expenditures of $243.8 million from 1947-70; see "Expenditures for Development and Improvement within the National Capital Region" April 1, 1947 to March 31, 1970 in *NCC Annual Report 1960-70*, financial statement Appendix. These expenditures were adjusted for inflation to C$2014 using Statistics Canada, "Consumer Price Index, historical summary" CANSIM Table 326-0021; Gordon Bertram and Michael B. Percy, "Real Wage Trends in Canada 1900-26: Some Provisional Estimates," *Canadian Journal of Economics*, XII, no. 2, (1979): 299-312.

799 A. Jacobs, E. Macdonald, Y Rofé, *The Boulevard Book*, (Cambridge, MA: MIT Press 2001); A. Jacobs, *Great Streets*, (Cambridge, MA: MIT Press, 1991).

800 Gréber suggested that the Queensway be designed as a "wide boulevard" and only function as the limited access Trans-Canada Highway on a temporary basis, until "The Real Transcontinental Highway By-Passing the City on its Southern Limit, is Finally Completed." See "Report by Jacques Gréber to Alan K. Hay, Federal District Commission," (July 1957), p. 9. The 1950 plan showed a route for the southern bypass and the FDC acquired the corridor, but the ring road was never completed.

801 Mayor Whitton directly lobbied Ontario Premier Leslie Frost for early implementation of the DeLeuw Cather Report. See Whitton to L. Frost, June 12, 1956, CW papers MG 30 E 256, Vol.49, "Queensway, 1954-56."

802 Ontario Department of Highways, *General Plan: The Queensway-Limited Access Highway*, (Toronto, ON: Ontario Department of Highways, July 1955), prepared by DeLeuw Cather & Company Consulting Engineers. DeLeuw Cather was an American firm with substantial expertise in expressway design. The United States was starting a vast expansion of its interurban expressway network through Interstate Highway program. American designers adopted pre-war parkway and German rural autobahn designers to create an unprecedented new form of highway in the city. See Jane Holtz Kay, *Asphalt Nation: How the Automobile Took over America, and How we Can get it Back*, (Berkeley CA: University of California Press, 1998).

803 Robert Haig, *Ottawa: City of the Big Ears – The intimate, Living Story of a City and its Capital*, (Ottawa, ON: 1969); *Ottawa Citizen*, "City's turn to play host at ceremony," October 15, 1957.

804 Ottawa, *Official Plan*, (Ottawa, ON: National Capital Planning Service, 1948); adopted August 7, 1951 Ottawa City Council, *City Council Minutes*, August 7, 1951, copy in the Ottawa City Archives; The city followed by adopting the open space plan from Gréber's 1950 report as Official Plan amendment no. 19, 1962.

805 Ottawa made a 50 percent financial contribution to the Dunbar and Hurdman's Bridges over the Rideau River in the late 1950s, the first major city to invest in the post-war era. The original 1954 cost-sharing agreement for the Queensway had the FDC contributing the land and the City of Ottawa paying one half of the roadway costs, but the federal government was persuaded to designate the route as part of the Trans-Canada Highway, which substantially increased its share. See C. Whitton memo to file, December 19, 1956; CW papers Vol. 49, "Queensway 1954-56."

806 Whitton papers Vol. 46. Industrial Land Development (Russell Rd. area).

807 See capital budget summaries in FDC/NCC annual reports from 1955-1969. The NCC contributed over $42 million in $2007 to utilities projects in the region. The federal subsidy of local sewers in the National Capital Region in the 1950s and 1960s set the precedent for CMHC funding of sewage treatment across Canada during the 1960s and 1970s.

808 Gréber, *op. cit*. The Lyon Street site was rejected in a 1938 plebiscite – City Council minutes (Dec. 5, 1938), p. 703; alternative city hall sites shown in Gréber (1950), *op. cit*., p. 215-20; City Hall Building Committee suggests structures on *both* sides of the canal, (Nov. 17, 1952, City Council minutes), p. 1,374-85; new committee considers 22 sites (Dec. 21, 1953), p. 1,587-93.

809 H. Kennedy to Whitton, Nov. 14, 1955; Whitton agreed to consider the Green Island site, but refused to provide clear title to the former city hall site. She offered instead 41 small parcels of city roads required for the Queensway, since the small downtown site was assessed at a much higher value than the 9.8 acre Green Island. Whitton to Kennedy Nov. 15, 1955, CW papers, "Queensway 1955-56." This was an unusual argument, since the land was granted to ByTown by Nicholas Sparks on condition that it be used for public purposes only, and therefore had no commercial value.

810 For the competition, see Ottawa City Council minutes, (January 3, 1956), p. 40, 202, 660 and Bylaw 8A-56. For the final selection of Green Island, see City Council minutes (January 30, 1956), p. 172-87. Ottawa refused to sell the old city hall site to the Federal District Commission, finally agreeing only not to erect a building on it without FDC permission. CC minutes (August 7, 1956), p. 1,171-77.

811 L. Brault, *Hull 1800-1950*, (Ottawa, ON: Éditions de l'Université d' Ottawa, 1950), p. 121-24.

812 B. McKeown, *Ottawa's Streetcars: The Story of Elective Rail Transit in Canada's Capital City*, (Pickering, ON: Railfare DC Books, 2006), chapter 6. When the OTC took over the system, it had only four new streetcars; almost half of the fleet was from the 1913-15 era; see McKeown's Appendix; D.F. Davis, "A Capital Crime? The Long Death of Ottawa's Electric Railway" in J. Keshen and N. St-Onge (eds.), *Construire une capitale: Ottawa: Making a Capital*, (Ottawa, ON: Acte Press, 2001), p. 349-81.

813 The FDC did not support a similar proposal for Sussex Street. B. McKeown, *Ottawa's Streetcars: The Story of Elective Rail Transit in Canada's Capital City*, (Pickering, ON: Railfare DC Books, 2006), p. 170.

814 McKeown, *op. cit*., p. 178. Ridership took another big hit the next year after the Civil Service went from a six to a five day week.

815 The exception was Toronto, which had invested in its streetcar system in the 1930s, and began a subway in the 1950s. M. Filey, *The TTC Story: The first seventy-five years*, (Toronto, ON: Dundurn Press, 1996), p. 53.

816 McKeown, *op. cit*., p. 170, 175.

817 Urwick, Currie Limited, report to Ottawa City Council, Report on the Ottawa Transportation Commission, March 18, 1958, copy in City of Ottawa Archives (COA) The report also criticized the OTC management for not investing in the system and concealing the upcoming deficits from Council. The general manager resigned, see McKeown, *op. cit*., p. 180-81.

818 *Ottawa Citizen*, "All trolleys to vanish from city in next year," May 15, 1958, p. 1. *Ottawa Citizen*, "The FDC and street-car removal," May 15, 1958, p. 6; *Ottawa Citizen*, "Eliminating the street-cars," May 17, 1958, p. 6.; *Ottawa Citizen*, "Board of Control against OTC sale," August 5, 1958, p. 7; *Ottawa Citizen*, "Children take first and last tram ride," May 2, 1959, p. 3; Phyllis Wilson, "Thousands watch city street cars ride into history," May 4, 1959, p. 3. Few people were sad to see the trams go. Davis found only four letters in support of the streetcar system during a review of newspapers from the 1950s, and critical letters every week. See Davis, *op. cit.*, Whitton papers, vol. 48, (OTC 1951-1953), Secretary, Board of Control, to W.R. Creighton, December 14, 1951; *Ibid.*, Whitton to Members of Board of Control, December 3, 1951; *Ibid.*, Whitton to the Members of Council, May 16, 1952; *Ibid.*, Whitton to D. McMillan, November 15, 1955; *Ibid.*, C. K. Pearce, Secretary, Board of Control to H.R. Welch, December 16, 1953; *Ottawa Citizen*, May 19, 1952; *Ibid.*, December 12, 1953 and December 29, 1953; *Ibid.*, January 6, 1954; *Ibid.*, September 14, 1956; *Ibid.*, January 7, 1959; *Ottawa Journal*, January 8, 1959. When Macdonald resigned, six others also resigned to protest the interference from the consultants. Women all, they include the company's secretary-treasurer, Elizabeth Baron, an employee since 1912. The organization, already very "male" became more so. See *Ottawa Citizen*, October 21, 1958, p 6, 17.

819 Community Planning Association of Canada, "The City Nuclear: A Regional Pattern for Urban Growth," (presentation to the Canadian Federation of Mayors and Municipalities Conference, 1952). The first slide was a map of the national capital with the caption: "Targets Fatten Since Hiroshima – Will They Continue."

820 J. Wright, *Crown Assets, op. cit.*, p. 218-23.

821 *Ibid.*, "Into the Modern Era, 1953-67," chapter 8: 231-45. The Central Mortgage and Housing headquarters was the exception to the Modern rule, built in the Georgian style to suit its President's taste. It was excoriated by the architectural press as retrograde. See H.S.M. Carver, *Housing a Nation: Forty Years of Achievement*, (Ottawa, ON: CMHC, 1986); Gréber's plan for Tunney's Pasture was lampooned by *Canadian Architect* for its monumental vista, grid streets and stripped classical design – one photo annotation sneered "the only thing lacking is the chateau roof," which was a serious insult among the avant-garde in 1960; see J.A. Murray and Z.M. Stanksewicz, "A Comment by the Editors," *Canadian Architect*, 5, no. 5, (May 1960): 62-63.

822 R. Harris, *Creeping Conformity: How Canada became suburban 1900-1960*, (Toronto, ON: University of Toronto Press, 2004), chapter 6; "The Rise of Corporate Suburbs, 1945-1960," p. 129-54.

823 It was quickly followed in the western suburbs by the Carlingwood Shopping Centre (1956), Billings Bridge in the southern suburbs (ca. 1960), and the St. Laurent regional centre in the east (1967).

824 Community Planning Association of Canada, *What's New in Planning: Report for 1965.* no. 8, (1966), a bulletin for citizens in the National Capital Region issued by the National Capital Region Branch, (May 1966); Community Planning Association of Canada, *A Further Report on Long-Range Planning for CPAC*, (Prepared for the National Council, 1972).

825 L. Ploegaerts, *Étude Critique et Comparative des Plans D'Urbanisme et de Développement Municipaux Préparés Depuis 1967 sur le Territoire de la Communauté Régionale de L'Outaouais*, (Geography and Regional Planning, Research notes, Université d'Ottawa, 1973); L. Ploegaerts, *Étude Comparative des Règlements de Zonage sur le Territoire de la Communauté Régionale de L'Outaouais*, (Geography and Regional Planning, Research Notes, Université d'Ottawa, 1976).

826 Todd letter to WLMK, July 15, 1937; Letter from Edwin Kay to WLMK, re: The Appointment of a Member of the Canadian Society of Landscape Architects, January 9, 1937; Anonymous, "Behind the scaffolding-a critical preview of official architecture in Ottawa," *Canadian Art*, 8, no. 2, (1950): 72.

827 Jacques Gréber, 1948. Radio interview of Gréber following convention of the Ontario branch of the Community Planning Association, (Toronto, ON: October 20, 1948).

828 Anonymous, 1950, *op. cit.*, p. 72-74; R.C. Hale and H.A. Elarth, "Architectural Competitions – Can They Help Us Obtain Better Public Buildings?" *Canadian Art*, 8, no. 3, (Spring 1950): 120-21;

Alex Colville, "Deplores the Gap Existing between Architects and the Public," *Canadian Art*, 8, no.3, (Spring 1950): 121-22.

829 Harold Spence-Sales, "The Preliminary Report on the Plan for the National Capital of Canada: a Review," *Layout for Living*, (Ottawa, ON: Community Planning Association of Canada, 1949), p. 3.

830 *Ibid*.

831 *Ibid*., p. 7.

832 Harold Spence Sales, "The Preliminary Report of the Plan for the National Capital of Canada: A Review," *Layout for Living*, (Ottawa, ON: Community Planning Association of Canada, 1949), p. 3.

833 *Ibid*., p. 35. Ironically, the rights-of-way of some of the abandoned roads in the 1950 plan were recently converted for extensions of Ottawa's acclaimed busway system.

834 Blumenfeld immigrated to Canada in 1955, after a distinguished European career and a brush with McCarthyism in Philadelphia. See Hans Blumenfeld, *Life Begins at 65: The not Entirely Candid Autobiography of a Drifter*, (Toronto, ON: University of Toronto Press, 1987); Hans Blumenfeld, "Glories and Miseries of a Master Plan," *Architecture Canada*, (April 1967): 32-35.

835 *Ibid*., p. 35.

Chapter 11

836 John English, *Citizen of the World: The Life of Pierre Elliott Trudeau, Vol. I, 1919-1968*, (Toronto, ON: Knopf Canada, 2006), p. 220-37.

837 Kenneth McRoberts, *Québec: Social Change and Political Crisis*, (Toronto, ON: Oxford University Press, 1999), chapters 5 and 6.

838 L.B. Pearson, *Mike: The Memoirs of the Right Honourable Lester B. Pearson*, (Toronto, ON: University of Toronto Press, 1975), *Vol. 3*.

839 P.H. Aykroyd, *The Anniversary Compulsion: Canada's Centennial Celebration*, (Toronto, ON: Dundurn Press, 1992).

840 Sue Hendler, "A dammed-up reservoir of ability: Women on the National Council of the Community Planning Association of Canada," *Plan Canada*, 45, no. 3 (2005): 15-7; Barbara Lambert, interviewed by Sarah Orovan, August 1, 2006. The women in the CPAC NCR Branch in the 1950s were usually drawn from elite groups like the University Women's Club or the Imperial Order of the Daughters of the Empire.

841 CPAC, NCR Branch, *"What's New in Planning,"* (May 1960), p. 18.

842 Bruce S. Elliott, *The City Beyond: A History of Nepean, Birthplace of Canada's Capital, 1792-1990*, (Nepean, ON: City of Nepean, 1991); Andrew Haydon, interviewed by David Gordon and Sarah Orovan, July 25, 2006; Nepean appointed its first planner in 1965; CPAC "What's New in Planning," *op. cit.*, 1966.

843 CPAC NCR *What's New in Planning, op. cit.*, 1965, 1966; Bob MacQuarrie, interviewed by Sarah Orovan, August 22, 2006; the quality of these secondary plans was variable, since many were prepared by the subdivision developers. Blackburn Hamlet was a typical example of 1960s era neighbourhood unit planning, while the design of Beacon Hill North omitted local parks and pedestrian walkways. Instead, the developers made a cash contribution to a hockey arena named after the township reeve, located 3 km. to the west.

844 Ottawa's first comprehensive plan would be adopted in 1991; *City of Ottawa Official Plan: A vision for Ottawa*, (Ottawa, ON: City of Ottawa, 1991, adopted October 16, 1991).

845 Ottawa, City Bylaw AZ-62, adopted and approved by the Ontario Municipal Board in 1964.

846 R.M. McGuire writing for the Ontario Municipal Board. In the matter of Section 30 of the *Planning Act* and in the matter of an application by the City of Ottawa for the approval of its restricted are Bylaw 159-68, P-6446-68, (October 29, 1968); interview with Arnold Faintuck and Marion Seymour, June 20, 2000.

847 FDC/NCC annual reports 1956-69; Community Planning Association of Canada, *What's New in Planning: Report for 1961*, (Ottawa, ON: CPAC, no. 4, 1962). A bulletin for citizens in the National Capital Region issued by the National Capital Regional Branch, June. The CPAC's annual bulletin is the best review of the expansion of planning capacity during the 1955-66 period.

848 J.A. Hume, "Need of New Hull Span Emphasized by Planner," *Ottawa Citizen*, Dec. 8, 1958, p. 1;

"Brief on the urgent need of a new bridge linking Ottawa and Hull," (Hull, QC: Hull Junior Chamber of Commerce, 1959).

[849] Wilber Smith and Associates, *Traffic and Transportation Plan for Ottawa*, (1955); DeLeuw Cather and Company, *Ottawa River Crossing Study*, (1956); both at NCC Library.

[850] LAC, National Film Board Container No. 2000783685, Accession No. 1986-004 Box 5249, NCP 1229.

[851] Gréber collection, 1937 plans for Confederation Square, (May-November 1937); Jacques Gréber, "Report on City Improvements," (February 7, 1938); Idem, *City of Ottawa, Consultation on Development of Government Grounds*, (June 24, 1937); Idem, "Notes sure les Travaux d'Embellissement de la Ville d'Ottawa," *La Vie Urbaine* 52 (juillet-août 1939): 199-210; Gréber also had input on the location of Ernest Cormier's Supreme Court building. See Isabelle Gournay and France Vanlaethem, *The Supreme Court of Canada and its Justices, A Commemorative Book*, (Ottawa, ON: Supreme Court of Canada, 2000), p. 200-01.

[852] The CPR was appeased by new tracks and a new station built by the NCC. I am indebted to David and Andrew Jeanes, who shared their research from Donald Gordon's papers in CN's archives on this issue.

[853] J. Gréber, *Plan for the National Capital*, (Ottawa, ON: King's Printer, 1950), chapters I-9 and I-12. See also Federal District Commission, "Program for the relocation of the railways in Ottawa-Hull metropolitan area and for the establishment of joint terminal rail operations," (Ottawa, ON: FDC, NCC Library copy, 1958); see the depiction in the National Film Board's *Ottawa: Today and Tomorrow* (1951), Dir. Bernard Devlin, (Ottawa, ON: National Film Board, 113C0151056).

[854] See J. Palmer, "Recent Heritage" in *Ottawa: A Guide to Heritage Structures*, (Ottawa, ON: City of Ottawa Local Architectural Conservation Advisory Committee, 2000), p. 171-72.

[855] Also, the diesel electric engines adopted in the early 1960s would have mitigated the smoke and soot issues.

[856] Over 5,400 dwelling units were inspected, and most were photographed. See H.A. Hosse, "Ottawa's Greenbelt and its anticipated effects," *The Canadian Geographer*, 4, no. 17, (Nov. 1960): 35-40. Reviewing these photographs in the City of Ottawa archives is a sobering task due to the appalling conditions of many homes. Samples are reprinted in, *City of Ottawa Urban Renewal Study: Analysis of Urban Renewal Surveys 1959/1962*, (Ottawa, ON: Ottawa, City Planning Branch, 1962), p. 46-57.

[857] Bland was a professor of architecture and Issalys was a local architect. Gordon Stephenson (1931-1932) studied with Le Corbusier and was a co-author of the 1944 *Greater London Plan*. He was prevented by McCarthy-era policies from entering the United States to assume the chair of MIT's urban planning school, and settled as head of the University of Toronto's school instead. Stephenson led urban renewal studies for Halifax (1957), Kingston (1960) and London, ON (1960) as well as chairing the Ottawa panel. See P. Abercrombie, *Greater London Plan*, (London, UK: HMSO, 1945); G. Stephenson, *Planning in a Human Way*, Christina DeMarco (ed.), (Australia: Fremantle Arts Centre Press, 1992); D.L.A. Gordon and J. Gregory (eds.). "Gordon Stephenson Special Issue," *Town Planning Review*, 83:3 (March 2012).

[858] *City of Ottawa Urban Renewal Study: Analysis of Urban Renewal Surveys 1959/1962*, (Ottawa, ON: Ottawa, City Planning Branch, 1962); *Urban Renewal*, (Ottawa, ON: Ottawa, City Planning Branch, 1967), p. 153-54.

[859] LAC DPW Collection, Container 2000 729 112

[860] P. Jenkins, *An Acre of Time*, (Toronto, ON: Macfarlane Walter & Ross, 1996), chapter 18; *Ottawa Urban Renewal*, op. cit., p. 152; R. M. Picton, "Rubble and ruin: Walter Benjamin, post-war urban renewal and the residue of everyday life on LeBreton Flats, Ottawa, Canada (1944–1970),"*Urban History*, 42, no. 1 (2015): 130-56.

[861] N. Campbell, "3 giant towers: $100 million cost for new defense HQ," *Ottawa Citizen*, June 2, 1966, p. 1.

[862] LAC, NCP 1301, container 2000783685.

[863] Le Corbusier's Brazilian collaborators from Rio and the UN building outshone their mentor. Niemeyer and Costa's Brasilia is the most influential Modern capital, and the only 20th century plan

on UNESCO's list of World Heritage sites. The monumental axis of the Pilot plan draws upon Beaux Arts planning principles, but the buildings and public spaces are strikingly Modern. N. Evenson, *Two Brazilian Capitals*, (London, UK: Yale University Press, 1973); Edmund Bacon, *Design of Cities*, (New York, NY: Penguin, 1976); Lawrence Vale, *Architecture, Power, and National Identity*. 2nd ed. (London; Routledge, 2008), p. 132-45.

864 Later examples began to attract criticism for their bombastic style, especially Wallace Harrison's Nelson Rockefeller Plaza for the New York state capital in Albany. Vale, 2008, *op.cit*.

865 The Department of Transport had initially been scheduled to occupy the building, which was designed by John Parkin. But Transport was moved into Robert Campeau's Place de Ville complex instead, and Defence officials were rumoured to be happy to stay near their historic home in Cartier Square. See P.R. Linkletter, *Redevelopment in a Jurisdictional Swamp: A Case Study of LeBreton*, (Kingston, ON: Unpublished Master's Report, Queen's University School of Urban and Regional Planning, April 1997).

866 *Ibid*.

867 G.N. Batista, S. Ficher, F. Leitão and D.A. de França, "Brasília: A Capital in the Hinterland" in David L.A. Gordon (ed.), *Planning Twentieth Century Cities*, (London, UK: Routledge, 2006), p. 164-81; N. Evenson, *Two Brazilian Capitals*, (London, UK: Yale University Press, 1973).

868 For Le Corbusier in Latin America, see Arturo Almandoz, *Planning Latin American Capital Cities*, (London, UK: Routledge, 2002). For Le Corbusier in Rio, see Evenson, *op. cit*.

869 Subsequent estimates by scholars and financial analysts put the initial cost at between US $400 and $600 million, with another $1 billion spent in the next decade to complete the existing projects. See Evenson, 1973, *op. cit*. The economic cost was almost more than the country could bear in such a short period. It was estimated that Brazil's new political capital consumed between 2 and 3 percent of the GNP for the period, driving up inflation and devaluing the cruzeiro; Celso Lafer, *The Planning Process and the Political System in Brazil: A Study of Kubitschek Target Plan, 1956-1961*, (Ithaca, NY: PhD Dissertation, Cornell University, 1970).

870 *Ottawa Urban Renewal, op. cit*., p. 72-81, 180-83.

871 Hull Town Planning Commission, *Master Plan for Hull, Aylmer, Hull South, Deschênes, Hull West*, (Hull, QC: City of Hull, 1964); E. Fiset, chief consultant, CPAC, 1965, *What's New, op. cit*.; Marcel D'Amour, interviewed by David Gordon and Sarah Orovan, July 25, 2006.

872 National Capital Commission, *The Sparks Street Mall*, (Ottawa, ON: National Capital Commission, 1968), p. 1. The trip followed a 1958 suggestion by Jacques Gréber that Sparks Street might be appropriate for such a pedestrian mall; see Shirley E. Woods, *Ottawa: The Capital of Canada*, (Toronto, ON: Doubleday, 1980).

873 National Capital Commission, 1968, *op. cit*., p. 1, Figure 7.

874 *Ibid*., p. 2-7; Ottawa Bylaw 142-60.

875 See Lewis Mumford, *The City in History*, (New York, NY: Harcourt Brace & World, 1961), plates 60-64. Gréber certainly would have known these precedents as part of his trans-Atlantic planning practice. See I. Gournay, "Revisiting Jacques Gréber's *L'Architecture aux États-Unis*: from City Beautiful to Cité-Jardin," *Urban History Review*, 29, no. 2 (March 2001): 6-19 and André Lortie, *Jacques Gréber (1882-1962) et L'Urbanisme le temps et l'espace de la ville*, (Paris, FR: PhD thesis, Université Paris XII, vol. 1-4, 1997).

876 Rotterdam included a 1,200-metre-long pedestrian street as the retail centre of its post-war reconstruction plan. The Lijnbaan (1953), with its trees, sitting areas, and play-spaces, was a big success. Thirty-two German cities built malls in the 1960s, and there were many other examples in England (Norwich), France (Rouen), Sweden (Gotëborg), Austria (Vienna), and the Netherlands. American urban designer Alan Jacobs calls Copenhagen's Strøget (1963) one of the world's great streets; A. Jacobs, *Great Streets*, (Cambridge, MA: MIT Press, 1993). Copenhagen has expanded the network extensively; See Jan Gehl and L. Gemzoe, *Public Spaces, Public Life*, (Copenhagen, DK: Danish Arch Press, 1999).

877 Minneapolis' Nicolet Mall (1967), Louisville's Fourth Street (1973), Portland's Transit Mall (1977), and Denver's 16th Street Mall are other prominent

examples, some of which were designed to include buses or streetcars as well as pedestrians. Alexander Garvin, *The American City: What Works, What Doesn't*, (New York, NY: McGraw-Hill, 1996), p. 143. Gruen's 1956 plan for Fort Worth, Texas, proposed that vehicular traffic be placed underground and all downtown streets be converted into pedestrian malls, but no city could afford such a dream, Garvin, *op. cit.*, p. 142-43.

878   National Capital Commission, 1960, *op. cit.*, p. 3-4; Watson Balharrie was a prominent Ottawa architect and son of a former mayor.

879   After its first year, retail sales increased by almost 10 percent, restaurant sales by 30 percent, and, of most significance, over 90 percent of the people surveyed liked the mall. See Sparks Street Mall Research Committee, *Sparks Street Mall: An Experiment in Downtown Revitalization*, (Ottawa, ON: National Capital Commission, 1960), p. 32-41.

880   Many pedestrian malls failed and important lessons were learned. To be successful, malls needed a good location, a firm retail market, an imaginative design, solid financing, and dynamic entrepreneurship. Sparks Street had all of these in the 1960s, and the Mall became an attraction to both residents and tourists. Kenneth Orski (ed.), *Streets for People* (Paris, FR: Organization for Economic Cooperation and Development, 1974), p. 123-25.

881   D. Ord, *The National Gallery of Canada: Ideas, Art, Architecture*, (Montréal, QC and Kingston, ON: McGill-Queen's University Press, 2003), p. 123-27.

882   Janet Wright, *Crown Assets: The Architecture of the Department of Public Works, 1867-1967*, (Ottawa, ON: University of Toronto Press, 1997), p. 265-71.

883   For Campeau's ties to the Liberal Party, see S. Goldberg, *Men of Property*, (Toronto, ON: Personal Library 1981), p. 166-7; G. Connolley, "McIlraith the New Trouble Shooter," *Ottawa Citizen*, July 10, 1965, p. 17.

884   P. Wilson, "Campeau's 'audacity' blasted," *Ottawa Citizen*, December 12, 1964, p. 4.

885   *Ottawa Citizen*, October 14, 1964, p. 21

886   P.T. Rooke and R.L. Schnell, *No Bleeding Heart: Charlotte Whitton, a Feminist on the Right*, (Vancouver, BC: UBC Press, 1987), p. 166-78.

887   D. MacRae, "Merchants Angry Over City's Plan to Sell Parking Lot," *Ottawa Citizen*, April 10, 1965, p. 3; R. Appleton, "Council Rejects Sale of City Parking Lot," *Ottawa Citizen*, May 18, 1965, p. 13; "The Albert Street parking lot," *Ottawa Citizen*, June 9, 1965, p. 6; "Campeau Getting OTC lot," *Ottawa Citizen*, June 22, 1965, p. 1.

888   Norman Campbell, "Question Government on Plans for New Campeau Building," *Ottawa Citizen*, June 29, 1965, p. 14; *Ottawa Citizen*, "Twin-tower hotel for old OTC site," June 26, 1965.

889   "23-Story Hotel Planned," *Ottawa Citizen*, September 14, 1965, p. 1; R. Appleton, "High-rise hotel facing objection from NCC," *Ottawa Citizen*, October 21, 1965, p. 5; R. Appleton, "City Skyline Faces Drastic 'New Look,' *Ottawa Citizen*, November 4, 1965, p. 1; "Piercing the Ottawa Skyline," *Ottawa Citizen*, November 5, 1965, p. 6; R. Appleton, "Builder Wins, City Waives High Rise Rule," *Ottawa Citizen*, November 16, 1965; "Scrap the 150-foot Ceiling," *Ottawa Citizen*, November 17, 1965, p. 6; only four aldermen opposed the project, noting that council's action had just handed the developer a fortune, since he had bought land from the city at a low price and got them to change their policies to vastly increase the amount of development upon it. *Ottawa Citizen*, "Council Challenged: Planners Will Take Height Bylaw Battle to OMB," November 24, 1965, p. 3.

890   "Council Challenged: Planners Will Take Height Bylaw Battle to OMB," *Ottawa Citizen*, November 24, 1965, p. 3; Controller Fogarty blasted the city's planners for volunteering their views, "Planners Must not Volunteer Views - Fogarty," *Ottawa Citizen*, November 26, 1965, p. 28; R.M. McGuire, writing for the Ontario Municipal Board, 1968, *In the Matter of Section 30 of the Planning Act and In the Matter of an application by the City of Ottawa for the Approval of its Restricted Area By-Law 159-68*, P-64446-68, October 29th, council approved February 8, 1966, see City Council minutes, p. 458-59.

891   Editorial, *Ottawa Citizen*, July 9, 1965, p. 6.

892   See D. McCormick, *Building Heights in Downtown Ottawa: A Comparative Analysis with Washington, D.C.*, (Kingston, ON: Unpublished Master's Report, School of Urban and Regional Planning, Queen's University, September 2000), chapter 3. The Department of Public Works found that buildings commissioned for specific government departments

892. were expensive and was moving to a general purpose office building design, or leased space, see "Chevrolets-not-Cadillacs: The General Purpose Office Building" in J. Wright, *Crown Assets, op. cit.*, p. 265-71.

893. "New Campeau bid to lift limit," *Ottawa Citizen*, December 16, 1965, p. 1.

894. J. Sewell, *The Shape of the City: Toronto Struggles with Modern Planning*, (Toronto, ON: University of Toronto Press, 1993), p. 44, 119, 122.

895. Hammer Green Siler Associates, *Ottawa Central Area Study, 1969*, prepared for City of Ottawa, National Capital Commission and the Ontario Department of Highways. The lead consultants were economists and the urban design consultant was Willo Von Moltke, a member of the CIAM and professor of architecture at the Harvard Graduate School of Design.

896. www.omb.on.ca/hearing/practise12.shtml; letter from John P. Nelligan to the Ontario Municipal Board, "Re: City of Ottawa Restricted Area By-law 42-69," Application for section 42 review, June 9, 1969; Ontario Municipal Board, "In the matter of the Corporation of the City of Ottawa By-law number 42-69," affidavit provided by Robert M. Leary of the City of Ottawa, June 12, 1969; see also McCormick *op. cit.*, p. 3-7 to 3-10.

897. "Piercing the Ottawa Skyline," *Ottawa Citizen*, November 5, 1965, p. 6.

898. J. L. Sert, "The Athens Town Planning Chart," *Can our Cities Survive?* (Cambridge, MA: MIT Press, 1947); E. Mumford, *The CIAM discourse on urbanism 1928-1960*, (Cambridge, MA: MIT Press, 2000).

899. The building was preserved as the Bytown Museum thanks to the Society's efforts.

900. The NCC was guided by noted local historian Lucien Brault and R.H. Hubbard, curator of Canadian Art at the National Gallery. See G. Gyton, *A Place for Canadians: A Story of the National Capital Commission*, (Ottawa, ON: NCC, 1999), p. 53-55.

901. John Leaning, interviewed by Sarah Orovan, June 8, 2006.

902. Hammer Green Siler, *Ottawa Downtown Study*, (Ottawa, ON: National Capital Commission, 1969), p. 126-27; Leaning, 2006 interview, *op. cit.*, Faintuck interview.

903. J.B. Parkin Association, *Confederation Square Development, Volume 1*, (Ottawa, ON: NCC, December 1962).

904. DeLeuw Cather and Beuchemin-Beaton-Lapointe, *Ottawa-Hull Transportation Study*, (Ottawa, ON and Hull, QC: City of Ottawa and City of Hull, August 23, 1965); "Plan for new Ottawa," *Ottawa Citizen*, Sept. 9, 1965, p. 1

905. "It's the Downtown Distributor," *Ottawa Citizen*, Sept. 9, 1965, p. 17; "Expropriation gets reluctant approval," *Ottawa Citizen*, January 18, 1966, p. 11; the only argument being whether the expropriation should be north or south of Gladstone Avenue, and whether bus rapid transit was worthwhile. Some councillors preferred a full subway system, while the mayor suggested a monorail over the Queensway.

906. A. Garvin, *American Cities: What Works, What Doesn't*, (New York, NY: McGraw Hill Professional, 2002), p. 122-26.

907. Hammer Green Siler, *op. cit.*

908. See Larry Smith and Company, "Economic Prospects – National Capital Region," (Ottawa, ON: NCC, 1963); this was one of the first population projections for a North American city to use the cohort-component technique, which is now a standard method to avoid the problems of simply extrapolating past trends.

909. NCC, "Statistical Review, with Explanatory Notes," (December 1964).

910. William Teron, interviewed by David Gordon and Sarah Orovan, July 28, 2006; David Guy and Tony Lofaro, "'Father of Nepean' served to the end; Farmer dragged into public life became one of city's smartest politicians," *Ottawa Citizen*, May 18, 2008, p. 1. The Nepean reeve claimed that the purchase of the Barrhaven lands was not a conflict of interest, but he was defeated by Andrew Haydon in the next municipal election, see B. Elliott, *The City Beyond*, *op.cit.*; Andrew Haydon, interviewed by David Gordon and Sarah Orovan, July 25, 2006.

911. City of Kanata, *Kanata – An Economic Profile: Spreading the Good News to the Rest of the World*. (Kanata, ON: Economic Development Office, 1999).

912. C. Timusk, "Kanata: A New Community Approaches its Tenth Year" in N. Pressman (ed.), "Special Issue:

New Communities in Canada: Exploring Planned Environments," *Journal of Urban and Environmental Affairs,* 8, no. 3, (1976): 222-32.

[913] J. Smart, *A City and a Technology: The Role of Government in The Growth of the Technology Industry in Ottawa, Canada to 1984,* (Kingston, ON: Unpublished PhD Dissertation, Department of History, Queen's University, 2004).

[914] R. McKay interview, October 16, 2004.

[915] D. Thomas, *Knights of The New Technology: The Inside Story of Canada's Computer Elite,* (Toronto, ON: Key Porter Books, 1983), p. 60.

[916] Bruce S. Elliott, *The City Beyond: A History of Nepean, Birthplace of Canada's Capital 1792-1990,* (Nepean, ON: City of Nepean, 1991).

[917] Denis Jacobs 2004 interview.

[918] As M.E. Porter, "Clusters and New Economies of Competition," *Harvard Business Review,* (November-December, 1998): 77-90 noted, the scattering of high technology across several Standard Industrial Classification codes used in the census makes it difficult to discern the emergence of a new cluster.

[919] Sketch attributed to Jacques Gréber. Found in NCC corporate files with his December 1958 report of his visit to Ottawa.

[920] CMHC history; H.S.M. Carver, *Cities in the Suburbs,* (Toronto, ON: University of Toronto Press, 1962).

[921] John Sewell, *The Shape of the City: Toronto Struggles with Modern Planning,* (Toronto, ON: University of Toronto Press, 1993); Macklin Hancock, "Don Mills: A Paradigm of Community Design," *Plan Canada,* (July 1994): 87-90.

[922] Project Planning Associates, *National Capital Development Concept,* (Ottawa, ON: NCC and CMHC, March 1967), Figure 3 and Figure 10; M. Hancock, June 18, 2004; Ian McHarg would publish his environmental planning method in *Design with Nature,* (New York, NY: Doubleday, 1969), one of the most influential books on planning. His land suitability analysis would be the foundation of current day Geographic Information Systems (GIS), but was almost unknown in 1964. PPL's use of this technique is likely the first use of modern environmental planning techniques in Canadian suburban planning.

[923] C.F. Hull submission to the 1956 Joint Parliamentary Committee, "Mémoire sur la nécessité d'un regain industriel à Hull," (Hull, QC: Chambre de Commerce de Hull, 10 décembre 1964); Marcel D'Amour, interviewed by David Gordon and Sarah Orovan, July 25, 2006; A. Beaucage, "From Manufacturing to Service" in C. Gaffield (ed.), *History of the Outaouais,* (Québec, QC: Les Presses de l 'Université Laval, 1997), chapter 13.

[924] J. English, *Just Watch Me: The Life of Pierre Elliott Trudeau, 1968-2000,* (Toronto, ON: Knopf, 2009), chapter 1; *Citizen of the World, op. cit.,* chapters 9 and 10.

[925] Canada, Constitutional Conference, 21st meeting, February 1969, document no. 96.

[926] Norman Campbell, "NCC Plans for Hull Still Thorny Issue," *Ottawa Citizen,* May 13, 1969, p. 3; Greg Connolly, "Govt. will help Hull catch up," *Ottawa Citizen,* May 16 1969, p. 1.

[927] Hammer Green Siler, *op. cit.,* June, 1969.

[928] NCC, *Hull 1969-1995,* (Ottawa, ON: NCC, 1969).

[929] NCC, *Royal Commission on Bilingualism and Biculturalism,* (Ottawa, ON: Queen's Printer, February 14, 1979).

[930] Murray V. Jones, and Donald B. Paterson, *Ottawa, Eastview & Carleton County local government review: final report and recommendations,* (Toronto, ON: Ministry of Municipal Affairs, 1965); H.B. Mayo, *Report of the Ottawa-Carleton Review Commission,* (Ontario: Ottawa-Carleton Review Commission).

[931] Henry Dorian, *Rapport de la commission d'étude sur l'intégrité du territoire du Québec,* (March 23, 1973); A.C. Carter, *Planning a "Capital Worthy of the Nation", the Federal District Controversy and the Planning of the Canadian Capital,* (Kingston, ON: Master's Thesis, School of Urban and Regional Planning, Queen's University, 2001).

[932] C. Gaffield, *op. cit.,* p. 464-68.

[933] See R. Harris, *How Canada Became Suburban,* (Toronto, ON: University of Toronto Press, 2004).

[934] Hans Blumenfeld did suggest that the 1950 plan went a little too far in promoting auto-mobility; see Hans Blumenfeld, "Glories and Miseries of a Master Plan," *Architecture Canada,* (April 1967): 32-35.

935 Peter Newman and Jeff Kenworthy, *Sustainability and Cities: Overcoming Automobile Dependence*, (Washington DC: Island Press, 1999); *Cities and automobile dependence: An international sourcebook*, (Brookfield VT: Gower, 1989). Ottawa-Gatineau was included in their international dataset.

Chapter 12

936 John English, *Just Watch Me: The Life of Pierre Elliott Trudeau, 1968-2000*, (Toronto, ON: Knopf, 2009), chapter 3; Kenneth McRoberts, *Québec: Social Change and Political Crisis*, (Toronto, ON: Oxford University Press, 1999), chapter 7.

937 English, *op.cit.*; P.H. Russell, *Constitutional Odyssey*, 3rd edition, (Toronto, ON: University of Toronto Press, 2004).

938 The City of Hull followed the federal lead with its own master plan for the community, see *Hull, Service d'urbanisme, Cité de Hull: Plan directeur d' urbanisme: Rapport Sommaire*, (Hull, QC: City of Hull, October18, 1971).

939 The general program was outlined in NCC, *Hull 1969-1995*, (May 1969); see also National Capital Commission, *Hull 1970/80*, (Ottawa, ON: NCC, 1982), p. 14-15. The federal government expropriated 6.07 ha. and the provincial government 1.45 ha.

940 C. Andrew, A. Blais and R. DesRosiers, *Les Élites Politiques, les Bas Salariés et la Politique du Logement à Hull*, (Ottawa, ON: Éditions de l'Université d'Ottawa, 1976), Tables 4.2, 4.3 and 7.2.

941 Ironically, the AGIH was funded by federal government grants for community organizing that were available in the late 1960s and early 1970s.

942 C. Andrew, "Social Movements in the Outaouais" in C. Gaffield (ed.), *History of the Outaouais*, (Québec QC: Les Presses de l'Université Laval, 1997), p. 569-73.

943 J. Lang, *Urban Design: A Typology of Procedures and Products*, (Burlington, MA: Architectural Press, 2005); R. Trancik, *Finding Lost Space: Theories of Urban Design*, (New York, NY: Van Nostrand Reinhold, 1986); R. Banham, *Megastructure: Urban Futures of The Recent Past*, (New York, NY: Harper & Row, 1976).

944 Edmond N. Bacon, *Design of Cities*, (New York, NY: Penguin Books, 1974).

945 David Gordon, *Battery Park City: Politics and Planning on the New York Waterfront*, (New York, NY: Routledge, 1997).

946 Alexander Garvin, *The American City: What Works; What Doesn't*, 2nd edition, (New York, NY: McGraw-Hill, 2002).

947 Phases I and II of Place du Portage were designed by Montréal architect Daniel Lazosky, and Phase III by David, Boulva and Dimakopoulos. The Terrasses de la Chaudière was designed by ARCOP Associates, Montréal. Lazosky was also the architect for Place du Centre, the Montferrand building and Maison du Citoyen, the latter in conjunction with P. Cayer of Hull. See NCC Hull 1970/80, *op. cit.*, p. 39-71. Dimakopoulos and ARCOP were architects for the massive Place Bonaventure (1967-68) in Montréal. See C.M. Ede, *Canadian Architecture 1960/70*, (Toronto, ON: Burns and MacEachern, 1971), p. 104-13.

948 Parent was vilified by the displaced residents for his support for demolition. See R. Poirier, *Qui a volé la rue Principale?* (Montréal, QC: Éditions Départ, 1986); C. Andrew, A. Blais and R. des Rosiers, *op. cit.* He would lose his seat in the next provincial election.

949 C. Andrew, "Government" The Developing Presence" in Gaffield (ed.), *op. cit.*, p. 466-68; NCC, *Hull 1970/1980 op. cit.*, p. 55-56.

950 L. Brault, *Du premier Hôtel de Ville à la Maison du Citoyen*, (Hull, QC: Éditions Asticou, 1981).

951 R. Poirier, *Qui a Volé la Rue Principale?, op. cit.*

952 Hull had many clubs and bars from the Prohibition era. See O. Vincent-Domey and A. Cellard, "Prohibition, Illegal Activity and Political Morality" in Gaffield (ed.), *op. cit.*, p. 410-19. They continued to draw Ontario residents in the post-war period, since liquor was more tightly regulated in Ontario, and the drinking age was 21 vs. 18 in Québec. This competitive advantage declined after Ontario lowered its drinking age to 18 in 1971 and new entertainment districts gradually emerged in downtown Ottawa.

953 The Eddy lands cost $29.5 million, with $1.8 million in landscaping. Parc de l' Hôtel de Ville and connections to Place du Centre cost another $2.8 million, see NCC, *Hull 1970/80, op. cit.*, Appendix 5.

954 The Place de Portage complex and the Portage Bridge were named after the adjacent aboriginal trail

used to carry canoes around the Chaudière Falls. Unfortunately, the bridge crosses the portage trail, Wright timber slide and Richmond Landing along its route. See L. Brault, *Links between Two Cities: Historic Bridges between Ottawa and Hull*, (Hull, QC and Ottawa, ON: 1989), p. 42-45.

955 See the capital budgets in the NCC annual reports, (1970-1982); also NCC, *Hull 1970/80, op. cit.*, p. 33-37 and 81.

956 A. Beaucage, "From Manufacturing to Services" in Gaffield (ed.), *op. cit.*, chapter 13, esp. Table 4.10 and Figure 4.1.

957 *Ibid.*, Table 4.10; NCC, *Hull 1970/80, op. cit.*, Appendix 2.

958 G. Beaudry, "L'influence de L'implantation du Gouvernement Fédéral à Hull" in R. Wasche and M. Kugler-Gagnon (eds.), *Ottawa-Hull: Spatial Perspectives and Planning*, (Ottawa, ON: Université d'Ottawa Press, 1978).

959 The DND architect was John B. Parkin Associates, J. Wright, *Crown Assets: The Architecture of the Department of Public Works, 1867-1967*, (Ottawa, ON: University of Toronto Press, 1997), p. 268-70. This was the last purpose-built departmental office building. The Department of Public Works developed several "General Purpose Office Buildings" on a generic plan in the federal suburban office *nodes;* The R.H. Coats building at Tunney's Pasture was the prototype. The DPW later began to drive down office space costs even further by competitive bids to lease entire buildings from private developers. The results were cost-effective but bland.

960 NCC, *Core Area Plan*, (Ottawa, ON: NCC, 1971).

961 J. Leaning, *The Revitalization of Older Residential Districts*, (Ottawa ON: Central Mortgage and Housing Corporation, 1970); J. Leaning, *The Story of the Glebe from 1800 to 2000*, (Ottawa ON: MOM Printing, 1999); John Leaning, interviewed by Sarah Orovan, June 8, 2006.

962 NCC Annual Report 1972-3; by the end of the century, the network included more than 170 km.; see NCC, *Pathway Network for Canada's Capital Region: Strategic Plan*, (Ottawa, ON: NCC, with City of Ottawa and City of Gatineau, June 2006).

963 Among Canadian cities over 500,000, the Ottawa-Gatineau CMA has the highest proportion of people who commute to work by bicycle at 2.2 percent, despite its cold winters. See Statistics Canada 2006 census. Only Victoria (5.6 percent) and small college cities like Kingston (2.4 percent), Saskatoon, Peterborough and Guelph had a higher proportion of cycle commuters.

964 Ottawa held the title until the 2008 extension of Winnipeg's River Trail. B. Ward, "The Year in Review," *Ottawa Citizen*, December 31, 2008.

965 NCC Annual Report 1970-1, p. 33-31; G. Gyton, *A Place for Canadians: A Story of the National Capital Commission*, (Ottawa, ON: National Capital Commission, 1999), p. 70-1; D.H. Fullerton, *The Dangerous Delusion*, (Toronto, ON: McClelland and Stewart, 1978), p. 131.

966 Larry Smith & Associates, *Retail Study: Regional Municipality of Ottawa*, (Ottawa, ON: Regional Municipality of Ottawa Carleton, 1989), Table H-2, p. 168; Larry Smith & Company, Inc., *Market Study: The Sparks Street Site*, (Washington, DC: Larry Smith & Company, 1968).

967 Hammer Greene Siler, *Ottawa Central Area Study*, (Ottawa, ON: National Capital Commission, 1969).

968 P. Benoit to Douglas Fullerton (NCC), October 18, 1972, NCC files; cited by W. Baker and G. Baker, *Collaboration and Conflict in Public Decision Making: The Case of the Rideau Area Project: Part 1*, (Toronto, ON: Institute of Public Administration of Canada, 1987), Case 159 (C), p. 4.

969 *Ibid.*, p. 19.

970 W. Baker and G. Baker, *Project Management and the Policy Decision Process, the Case of Ottawa's Rideau Area Project, Part II*, (Toronto, ON: IPAC, 1987), p. 27-30.

971 Clack was previously the chief designer for Bastion Square in downtown Victoria, a sensitive infill project in an historic district that won several design awards.

972 B. Kuwabara and B. Sampson, "Diamond and Myers: the form of reform," *City Magazine*, (August/September, 1975).

973 Diamond and Myers, *Rideau Mall/Galleria*, (Ottawa, ON: NCC, February 1975).

974 A somewhat similar project, the Toronto Eaton Centre (1977-83) became North America's most

975 successful urban shopping centre; see Urban Land Institute, *Dollars and Cents of Shopping Centers*, (Washington DC: ULI, 1995). However, success was not guaranteed for the Rideau Galleria since department stores were generally in decline in the 1980s and many downtown mall projects failed, including Brantford and London in Ontario, and Cleveland and Boston in the US.

975 Baker and Baker, *op. cit.*, p. 32.

976 For Lash's approach, see H. Lash, *Planning in a Human Way*, (Ottawa, ON: Ministry of State for Urban Affairs, 1976); for Sankey's role, see Baker and Baker, *op. cit.*, p. 7-31.

977 Architect Barry Padolsky, quoted in A. Gilmore, "The Rideau Area Project: Changing the Face of the National Capital," *Habitat*, 27, (1984): 35-5.

978 F. Lapointe interview, May 18, 2006; Ron Eade, "Ottawa Council ready to tear down bus mall," *Ottawa Citizen*, August 6, 1992, p. B1; Rod Eade, "Cut glass: Ottawa set to rid Rideau St of enclosures," *Ottawa Citizen*, July 28, 1992, p. C1; François Lapointe, *Cities as Crucibles: Reflections on Canada's Urban Future*, (Ottawa, ON: Invenire Books, 2011), p. 204-05. The glass and street canopies were recycled to become the roof of the Perth Farmers' Market.

979 The CBD's share of department store type merchandise sales increased from 21 to 23 percent from 1980 to 1985, before declining again to 18 percent in 1989; see Larry Smith & Associates, *Retail Study: Regional Municipality of Ottawa*, (Ottawa, ON: Regional Municipality of Ottawa Carleton, 1989).

980 J. Cruikshank and L. Susskind, *Breaking The Impasse: Consensual Approaches to Resolving Public Disputes Edition 13*, (New York, NY: Basic Books, 2001).

981 The CUO had 32 municipalities and RMOC had 6; see D. Fullerton, *The Capital of Canada: How Shall It Be Governed? Volume 1*, (Ottawa, ON: Information Canada, 1974), p. 24-36.

982 Gerald Hodge, and David L.A. Gordon. *Planning Canadian Communities – an Introduction to the Principles, Practice, and Participants.* (Toronto, ON: Nelson, 2014), p. 130-34; J.B. Milner, "The Statutory Role of the Planning Board," *Community Planning Review*, 12, no.3, (1962): 16-18; J.B. Milner, *Development Control*, (Toronto, ON: Ontario Law Reform Commission, 1969), p. 12. The key legislation in Ontario is the *Planning Act* and in Québec it was the *Act Respecting Land Use Planning and Development*, later the *Land Use Planning and Development Act*; also Pamela Sweet interviewed by David Gordon and Sarah Orovan, May 18, 2006.

983 David Gordon, Betsy Donald and J. Kozuskanich, "Unanticipated Benefits: The Role of Planning in the Development of Ottawa Region Technology Industries" in R. Tremblay and N. Novakowski (eds.), *Ottawa in The New Economy*, (Brussels, BE: Peter Lang, 2007).

984 Donald Gutstein, *Vancouver Ltd.*, (Toronto, ON: James Lorimer, 1975); David Nowlan and Nadine Nowlan, *The Bad Trip: The Untold Story of the Spadina Expressway*, (Toronto, ON: New Press, 1970); Graham Fraser, *Fighting Back: Urban Renewal in Trefann Court*, (Toronto, ON: Hakkert, 1972); Claire Hellman, *The Milton Park Affair: Canada's Largest Citizen-Developer Confrontation*, (Montréal, QC: Véhicule Press, 1987).

985 J.C. Leclerc, "Dasken: Sous le Pic des Démolisseurs," *Le Devoir*, August 21, 1972; C. Andrew "Social Movements" in Gaffield, *History of the Outaouais*, *op. cit.*, p. 582-84.

986 *City Magazine* was the cross-Canada journal of the citizens' groups, with individual cities and cases celebrated in C. Hellman, *The Milton Park Affair: Canada's Largest Citizen-Developer Confrontation*, (Montréal, ON: Véhicule Press, 1987); D. Gutstein, *Vancouver Ltd.*, (Toronto, ON: James Lorimer, 1972); G. Fraser, *Fighting Back: Urban Renewal in Trefann Court*, (Toronto, ON: Hakkert, 1972); J. Granatstein, *Marlborough Marathon*, (Toronto, ON: James, Lewis and Samuel 1971); D. Keating, *The Power to Make It Happen*, (Toronto, ON: Green Tree Publishing, 1975); J. Sewell, *Up Against City Hall*, (Toronto, ON: James, Lewis and Samuel, 1972).

987 J. Jacobs, *The Death and Life of Great American Cities*, (New York, NY: Random House, 1961); N. Nowlan, *The Bad Trip*, *op. cit.*; J. Sewell, *op. cit.*

988 Jon Caulfield, *The Tiny Perfect Mayor: David Crombie and Toronto's Reform Alderman*, (Toronto, ON: James Lorimer, 1974); J. Sewell, *The Shape of*

988 (...continued) *the City: Toronto Struggles with Modern Planning*, (Toronto, ON: University of Toronto Press, 1993); D. Gutstein, "Vancouver" in Magnusson and Sancton, *City Politics in Canada,* (Toronto, ON: University of Toronto Press, 1983), p. 189-221.

989 John Sewell, *The Shape of the City: Toronto Struggles with Modern Planning*, (Toronto, ON: University of Toronto Press, 1993); David Hulchanski, *St. Lawrence & False Creek: A Review of the Planning and Development of Two New Inner City Neighbourhoods*, (Vancouver, BC: UBC Planning Papers, no. 10, 1984); and Stephen Ward, *Planning the Twentieth Century City*, (New York, NY: Wiley, 2002), p. 219-24 and 288-94.

990 Jacobs, 1961, *op. cit.*

991 For the American experience, see Paul Davidoff, "Advocacy and Pluralism in Planning," *Journal of the American Institute of Planners,* 31, no. 4, (1965): 331-37; Herbert Gans, "Planning for People, not Buildings," *Environment and Planning,* A 1, (1969): 33-46; Clay McShane, *Down the Asphalt Path: The Automobile and the American City,* (New York, NY: Columbia University Press, 1994); Raymond A. Mohl, "Stop the Road: Freeway Revolts in American Cities," *Journal of Urban History*, 30, no. 5, (2004): 676-706. For the Canadian experiences, see W. Magnusson and A. Sanction (eds.), *City Politics in Canada*, (Toronto, ON: University of Toronto Press, 1983); J. Lemon, "Toronto, 1975: The Alternative Future" in J. Lemon, *Liberal Dreams and Natures Limit: Great Cities of North America Since 1600*, (Toronto, ON: Oxford University Press, 1996); Hodge and Gordon, 2008, *op. cit.*, chapters 11 and 12; J. Grant, *Drama of Democracy: Contention and Dispute in Community Planning*, (Toronto, ON: University of Toronto Press, 1994); J. Punter, *The Vancouver Achievement: Urban Planning and Design*, (Vancouver, BC: UBC Press, 2003).

992 Judith Innes, "Planning Through Consensus Building: A New View of the Comprehensive Planning Ideal," *Journal of American Planning Association*, 62, no. 4, (1996): 460-72. Hodge and Gordon, *Planning Canadian Communities, op. cit.*, chapters 14 and 15.

993 John Taylor, *Ottawa: An Illustrated History*, (Toronto, ON: James Lorimer, 1986), p. 196-98; C. Andrew in W. Magnusson and A. Sanction (eds.), *City Politics in Canada*, (Toronto, ON: University of Toronto Press, 1983), p. 140-65; For Greenberg's role in the Centretown Redevelopment Plan, see J. Leaning, "The Grasshopper's Dream," memoir, (October 2004), p. 43-44; For the Federation of Citizens' Committees, see Taylor, *op. cit.*, p. 196; Ed Aquilina, interviewed by David Gordon and Sarah Orovan, June 29, 2006.

994 Ottawa, City Planning Branch, *Lower Town East Neighbourhood Study*, (March 1966), Figures 30-35, Table 43 and Map 27. The plan called for expropriation and demolition of most of 16 residential blocks in Lowertown, a larger residential area than LeBreton Flats, for example.

995 Murray and Murray Architects, *Lowertown East Urban Renewal Project: Urban Design Concept and Development Plan*, (Ottawa, ON: City of Ottawa, 1970).

996 Ottawa, Planning Branch, *Lowertown East Redevelopment Plan: Preliminary Report*, (January 1976); Caroline Ramirez et Kenza Benali. "Les luttes patrimoniales à l'heure de la densification urbaine: Le cas de la Basse-Ville Est d'Ottawa," *Canadian Journal of Urban Research,* 21, no. 1 (2012): 109-50.

997 Coolican was initially influenced by the Metro Toronto experience, see D. Sagi, "New regional chief stresses service," *The Globe and Mail* (Toronto), May 31, 1968, p. 1.

998 John Wright, "The Regional Municipality of Ottawa-Carleton: Planning Objectives, Concepts and Principal Policies" in R. Wasche and M. Kugler-Gagnon (eds.) *Ottawa-Hull: Spatial Perspectives and Planning*, (Ottawa, ON: University Ottawa Geography Dept., 1978), p. 117-26; C. Fullerton, "Regional Planning in Ottawa, 1945-1974," *Urban History Review*, 24, no. 1 (2005): 100-112; Nick Tunnicliffe, interviewed by David Gordon, September 12, 2006.

999 See C. Andrew, "Ottawa-Hull" in W. Magnusson and A. Sanction (eds.), *op. cit.*, p. 140-65; C. Fullerton, *op.cit.*; for Canada, see J. Grant, "Shaped by Planning: The Canadian City Through Time" in T. Bunting and P. Filion (eds.), *Canadian Cities in Transition: Local through Global Perspectives*, 3rd edition, (Toronto, ON: Oxford University Press, 2006), p. 320-337; G. Hodge and D. Gordon, 2014, *op. cit.*, chapters 5, 14 and 15.

[1000] Brian Bourns, an RMOC councillor, noted that Cadillac purchased control of its lands during supposedly secret regional planning committee meetings that recommended the designation. See B. Bourns, "Ottawa Regional Planning: Winners take $300,000,000," *City Magazine*, (Summer 1974): 24-7.

[1001] Bourns, *Ibid.*, p. 26-27; see also P. Spurr, *Land and Urban Development: A Preliminary Study*, (Toronto, ON: James Lorimer, 1978), for more on the oligopoly in the local land market.

[1002] See C. Fullerton, "Regional Planning in Ottawa," *op. cit.*, p. 106-9. The developers also argued that the federal provincial land assembly should be excluded because it was partially located on Leda clay soils, which were subject to landslides. However, Leda clay is present in many parts of Ottawa-Gatineau, including the developers' Orleans assembly, Rockcliffe Park and Confederation Heights. The "hill" in Campeau/Minto's Beacon Hill development is a ridge formed by a Leda clay landslide. See H.G.M. Parkes and J.C. Day, "The Hazard of Sensitive Clays, A Case Study of the Ottawa-Hull Area," *Geographical Review*, 65, no. 2 (April 1975): 198-213, esp. Figures 1 and 6.

[1003] Bruce Elliott, *The City Beyond: A History of Nepean, Birthplace of Canada's Capital, 1792-1990*. (Nepean, ON: City of Nepean, 1991), p. 319-21. Elliott also notes that the Barrhaven land that former Nepean reeve Aubrey Moodie and four partners had bought in 1969 for $32,500 was sold for $982,750 after the new regional plan was approved. See G. Westin, "Moodie land sale revealed," *Ottawa Citizen*, December 1, 1976, p. 1; A. Moodie, "An open letter to the residents of Nepean" [paid advertisement], *Ottawa Citizen*, December 4, 1946, p. 4. When this leaked to the press in the 1976 Nepean elections, Andrew Haydon narrowly defeated Moodie for re-election as reeve. Elliott, *op. cit.*, p. 336-37.

[1004] C. Fullerton, "Regional Planning in Ottawa," *op. cit.*, p. 107-08; A. Haydon interview, *op. cit*. The proposed Kettle Island Bridge survived the first approval of the RMOC plan, only to be deleted later after opposition from Rockcliffe and Manor Park.

[1005] C. Andrew, "Government: The Developing Presence" in Gaffield (ed.), *op. cit.*, p. 468-71.

[1006] CRO, *Schéma intérimaire d'aménagement du territoire*, (Hull, QC: CRO, 1973); N. Tochon, "Le concept d'aménagement de la Communauté régionale de l'Outaouais" in R. Wasche and M. Kugler-Gagnon (eds.), *Ottawa-Hull: Spatial Perspectives and Planning*, (Ottawa, ON: Université d'Ottawa Press, 1978), p. 127-34; Nelson Tochon interviewed by Sarah Orovan, August 18, 2006; D. Hargreaves, "La problémataique du transport dons le développement du l' Outaouais québécois" in Wasche and Kugler-Gagnon, *op. cit.*, p. 135-42.

[1007] Léon Ploegaerts, *Étude Critique et Comparative des Plans D'Urbanisme et de Développement Municipaux Prépares Depuis 1967 sur le Territoire de la Communauté Régionale de l'Outaouais*. (Ottawa ON: Geography and Regional Planning, Research Notes, Université d'Ottawa, 1973); *Étude Comparative des Règlements de Zonage sur le Territoire de la Communauté Régionale de l'Outaouais*. (Ottawa ON: Geography and Regional Planning, Research Notes, Université d'Ottawa, 1976). For zoning, see also Leon Ploegaerts, *Le Zonage dans l'amanagement de l'espace urbain au Québec*, (Montréal, QC: PhD dissertation, Faculté de l'aménagement, Université de Montréal, Sept. 1974), especially p. 182-206; G. Beaudry, "Le rôle de la municipalité dans la planification" Le cas de Hull" in Wasche and Kugler-Gagnon, *op. cit.*, p. 135-43.

[1008] CRO, *Schéma d'aménagement du territoire*, (Hull QC: August 1977, approved by the Québec minister of municipal affairs, August 9, 1978); Tochon in R. Wasche and M. Kugler-Gagnon (eds.), 1978, *op. cit.*

[1009] D.H. Fullerton, *The Dangerous Delusion: Québec's Independence Obsession*, (Toronto, ON: McClelland and Stewart, 1978), p. 117-42.

[1010] Noulan Cauchon, "Plan for Ottawa South," *The Journal of the Town Planning Institute of Canada*, March, II 2, no. 7, (1923); C. Ketchum, *Federal District Capital*, (Ottawa, ON: Ottawa, 1939); perhaps the best critique came from Carleton professor Donald Rowat, "The Proposal for a Federal Capital Territory for Canada's Capital", in H.I. Macdonald (ed.), *Ontario Advisory Committee on Confederation: Background Papers and Reports*, (Toronto, ON: Queen's Printer, 1967), p. 216-81.

[1011] D.H. Fullerton, *The Capital of Canada: How Should it be Governed?* (Ottawa, ON: Information Canada, 1974, 2001).

1012 *Ibid., vol. 1*, p. 212-23.

1013 Lynn Ball, "The Fullerton report: brickbats outnumber bouquets," *Ottawa Citizen*, November 5, 1974, p. 1; Alain Dexter, "La rapport Fullerton: Queen's Park veut plus d'explications avant de commenter," *Le Droit*, November 6, 1974, p. 3; Charles Lynch, "Fullerton Goes Too Far," *Ottawa Citizen*, November 6, 1974, p. 7.

1014 Fullerton, *The Capital of Canada, op. cit.*, vols. 1, 3.

1015 The NCC was pushed to comment publicly. See "Construction shows decline" *Ottawa Citizen*, February 4, 1972; "City wins new development powers," *Ottawa Citizen*, February 13, 1974, p. 4; "Ottawa-Carleton plan Orwellian double think," *Ottawa Citizen*, February 4, 1974, p. 2; see also C. Fullerton, "Regional Planning in Ottawa," *op. cit.*, p. 102.

1016 National Capital Commission, *Tomorrow's Capital – an Invitation to Dialogue*, (Ottawa, ON: National Capital Commission, 1975), p. 78-81.

1017 Paul Workman, "Tomorrow's Capital kicking up a storm," *Ottawa Citizen*, December 18, 1974, p. 2; Maurice Bigio, "Bilingualism: $105 million 'reasonable price to pay for being Canadian' says Spicer," *Ottawa Citizen*, December 16, 1974, p. 2.

1018 *Ottawa Citizen* and *Le Droit*, Dec-Jan 1974-5; J. Wright, *op. cit.*; A. Haydon, N. Tochon, N. Tunnicliffe interviews, *op. cit.*; Pierre Chabot, interviewed by Sarah Orovan, August 23, 2006.

1019 RMOC removed the Carlsbad Springs federal land assembly from the 1988 revision of their regional official plan.

1020 J. Taylor, *op. cit.*, p. 194; C. Andrew, "Regional Political Identity," in Gaffield, *History of the Outaouais, op. cit.*, p. 727

1021 J. Punter, *The Vancouver Achievement: Planning and Urban Design*, (Vancouver, BC: University of British Colombia Press, 2003); L. Berelowitz, *Dream City: Vancouver and the global imagination*, (Lunenburg, NS: Douglas & McIntyre, 2005); D. Hulchanski, *St. Lawrence and False Creek*, (Vancouver, BC: University of British Colombia School of Community and Regional Planning, 1984).

1022 Hulchanski, *Ibid.*; David Gordon, *Learning from St. Lawrence*, (Toronto, ON: Ryerson Polytechnical Institute, 1990); David Gordon, "What Went Wrong at Harbourfront" in G. Halseth and H. Nicol (eds.), *(Re)development at the Urban Edges*, (Waterloo, ON: University of Waterloo, Department of Geography, Faculty of Environmental Studies, 2000).

1023 M. Safdie, *Beyond Habitat*, (Cambridge, MA: MIT Press, 1970); J.R. Gold, *Olympic Cities: City Agendas, Planning the World's Games, 1986-2012*, (New York, NY: Routledge, 2007).

1024 Z. M. Schrag, *The Great Society Subway: a History of the Washington Metro*, (Baltimore, MD: JHU Press, 2006); F. Gutheim, *Worthy of the Nation: Washington, DC, from L'Enfant to the National Capital Planning Commission*, (Baltimore, MD: JHU Press, 2006); I. Gournay, "Washington: The DC's History of Unresolved Power of Planning," in David Gordon (ed.), *Planning Twentieth Century Capital Cities*, (London, UK: Routledge, 2006), p. 115; J. Overall, *Canberra – Yesterday, Today, and Tomorrow*, (Fyshwick, AU: Federal Capital Press of Australia Pty Limited, 1955); C. Vernon, "Canberra, Where Landscape is Pre-eminent," in David Gordon (ed.), *Planning Twentieth Century Capital Cities, op. cit.*

1025 Canada, Special Joint Committee of the Senate and House of Commons on the National Capital Region, 1976-76; D. Coolican, (RMOC brief 15): 4-31; L. Greenberg (Ottawa, brief 28): 4-40; J.M. Seguin (CRO brief 17): 4-33; 41: 4-23.

1026 *Canada, Special Joint Committee of the Senate and House of Commons on the National Capital Region*, (Ottawa, ON: Special Joint Committee of the Senate and House of Commons 1976); J.M. Seguin (CRO, brief 17): 34-90; Conseil Régional de Développement du l'Outaouais, (brief 29): 43-56; Société nationale des Québec de l'Outaouais, (brief 34): 53-71.

1027 G. Gyton, *A Place for Canadians*, (Ottawa ON: NCC, 1999), p. 77-81.

1028 See D. Fullerton, *Dangerous Delusion, op. cit.*, p. 134-36.

1029 La Communauté régionale de l'Outaouais (CRO) was created in 1970 and renamed as the Communauté urbaine de l'Outaouais (CUO) in 1986. The CUO ceased to exist in 2002 with the creation of the new Ville de Gatineau; incorporating the former cities of Buckingham, Gatineau, Hull and the towns of Aylmer and Masson-Angers.

[1030] The Montréal highway was to enter from the southeast and connect to the Queensway at Nicholas Street. Its southbound ramp connection is still there from the 1960s. The Toronto highway was originally to connect to Carling Avenue, but later this was switched to a corridor connecting to the western parkway along Woodroffe Avenue. See Jacques Gréber, *Plan for the National Capital*, (Ottawa, ON: King's Printer, 1950).

[1031] NCC, *LeBreton Flats Development*, (Ottawa, ON: NCC, 1983); M. Hough, *City Form and Natural Process*, (London, UK: Routledge, 1984), p. 100-10; Marion Dewar, interviewed by Sarah Orovan, August 16, 2006.

[1032] J. Pressman and A. Wildavsky, *Implementation: how great expectations in Washington are dashed in Oakland*, (Los Angeles, CA: University of California Press, 1984); P.R. Linkletter, *Redevelopment in a Jurisdictional Swamp: A Case Study of LeBreton*, (Kingston, ON: Unpublished Master's Report, Queen's University School of Urban and Regional Planning, April 1997).

[1033] Statistics Canada, Census of Canada 1971-91.

[1034] Statistics Canada, Census 1971-1991 for the Ottawa-Hull Census Metropolitan Area; Gaffield (ed.), *op. cit.*, p. 439-43 points out that this growth in the 1970s counter-acted a slow decline in the Outaouais' share of the metropolitan population since 1941.

[1035] Hull declined mainly for demographic reasons – like many North American inner cities, its average household size declined from 3.6 to 2.7 over this period. The effects of urban renewal on the total housing stock were modest, with the number of units increasing from 17,490 to 26,940 over 1971-1991.

[1036] Census of Canada 1971, 1981, 1991. Ottawa rebounded to 314,000 in 1991; the decline had been caused by a drop in the average household size from 3.2 to 2.6. The number of dwelling units in the city increased by 188 percent over the period.

[1037] Cité Vanier (Eastview before 1971) had similar problems to inner-city Ottawa, with the additional cultural concerns about maintaining a francophone community. Rockcliffe Park remained as an elite suburb governed as a village, with concerns about its landscape and heritage; see H.S.M. Carver, "The cultural landscape of Rockcliffe Park village," (Ottawa, ON: Village of Rockcliffe Park, 1985); Roger Todhunter, "Evolution and Redevelopment of a picturesque landscape: Rockcliffe Park," (Ottawa, ON: Todd Hunter and Associates, 1998); E. von Baeyer and J. Mulligan, "Rockcliffe Park Landscape History," in cooperation with the Landscape Architecture Section of the NCC, September, 1996.

[1038] B. Elliott, *The City Beyond, op. cit.*, p. 327-30, 354-60; A. Haydon interview July 25, 2006; R. MacQuarrie interview, August 22, 2006; P. Clark interview, July 25, 2006.

[1039] The first express bus was the 'Beacon Hill Bullet' organized by citizens of an eastern suburb. When OC Transpo service was extended to Gloucester, the transit commission was obligated to keep the service, which prospered and was replicated elsewhere. See Rex Tasker, *A Bus – for Us*, National Film Board of Canada, 14 min 35 sec, (1972).

[1040] C. Fullerton, *op. cit.*, p. 109-10; A. Haydon interview, *op. cit.*

[1041] RMOC, *Official Plan, Ottawa-Carleton Region*, (Ottawa, ON: Ottawa-Carleton Planning Department, June 1974).

[1042] R. Cervero, *The Transit Metropolis: A Global Enquiry*, (Washington, DC: Island Press, 1998); R. Cervero, "Urban Transit in Canada: Integration and Innovation at its Best," *Transportation Quarterly*, 40, no. 3, (1986): 293-316; S. Rothwell and S. Schijns, "Ottawa and Brisbane: comparing a mature busway system with its state of the art progeny," *Journal of Public Transportation*, 5, no. 2, (2002): 163-182.

[1043] The Transitway enabled intensification around shopping centres like St. Laurent and Bayshore, and it serves a cluster of rental apartment slabs at Lees Avenue. In the Transitway's first twenty years, only Holland Cross, a mixed-use, medium-rise redevelopment near the Tunney's Pasture station meets Peter Calthorpe's prescription for transit-oriented development (TOD), see P. Calthorpe, *The Next American Metropolis*, (New York, NY: Princeton Architectural Press, 3rd edition, 1993).

[1044] David Gordon, "Capital Cities and Culture: Evolution of Twentieth-Century Capital City Planning" in J. Monclus (ed.), *Culture, Urbanism, and Planning*, (Burlington, VT: Ashgate, 2006).

1045 Hammer Greene Siler Associates, *Ottawa Central Area Study: Final Zoning Report*, (Ottawa, ON: City of Ottawa and National Capital Commission, 1969), p. 126-7; NCC, *Core Area Concept*, (Ottawa, ON: NCC, 1971); Zeidler Partnership, *Mall Wellington West*, (Ottawa, ON: NCC, 1975).

1046 D. Ord, *The National Gallery of Canada: Ideas, Art, Architecture*, (Montréal, QC and Kingston, ON: McGill-Queen's University Press, 2003), chapter 12, p. 247-77.

1047 B. Lee, "Our National Disgrace: Unless Ottawa Moves Fast, Much of Canada's Heritage is in Danger of Being Lost," *The Globe and Mail*, March 28, 1981, p. 10; A. Fotheringham, "National Museums Suffer during Trudeau's Reign," *Ottawa Citizen*, January 7, 1982; Ord, *op. cit.*, p. 280-85.

1048 For the museum binge, see W. Rybczynski, *A Place for Art: The Architecture of the National Gallery of Canada*, (Ottawa, ON: NGC, 1993); for grand projects in Paris' planning, see P. White, "Paris: From the Legacy of Haussmann to the Pursuit of Cultural Supremacy" in David Gordon (ed.), *Planning Twentieth Century Capital Cities, op. cit.*, p. 38-57; also Ord, *op. cit.*, p. 280-83.

1049 John Gray, "National Gallery, Museum to Get New Home," *The Globe and Mail*, February 19, 1982, p. 8.

1050 The Board of the Canada Museums Construction Corporation included Boggs, the Chairman of the NCC, the deputy ministers of Public Works and Communications and the secretary-general of the National Museums Corporation. This influential group could move quickly through the federal bureaucracy.

1051 Roger du Toit Architects, *Five Museum Sites*, (Ottawa, ON: Canada Museums Construction Corporation, November 4, 1982). The study ranked Ottawa's Sussex Drive/St. Patrick Street and Hull's Parc Laurier as the top two sites.

1052 NCC, *National Museum of Man Planning Guidelines*, (Ottawa, ON: NCC, Spring 1983), p. 10.

1053 D. Turner, *Safdie's Gallery: An Interview with the Architect*, (Ottawa, ON: Ottawa Public Library copy, 1989).

1054 The panorama evokes the Canadian nation so strongly that critic Douglas Ord complains that it distracts from the importance of the art within the gallery. See Ord, *op. cit.*, chapters 1, 2 and epilogue.

1055 L. Noppen, *In the National Gallery of Canada: One of the Most Beautiful Chapels in the Land*, (Ottawa ON: NGC, 1988).

1056 K. Collins, "Gov't Won't buy Permits to Build Area Museums," *Ottawa Citizen*, April 5, 1984, p. 1 and 18. Federal construction is normally inspected by professional engineers of the Department of Public Works.

1057 S. Cameron, "Government Takes Over Museum Job," *Ottawa Citizen*, May 17, 1985, p. 1 and A10; S. Cameron, "Trouble Has Dogged New Museums," *Ottawa Citizen*, May 21, 1985, p. A4; Ord, *op. cit.*, p. 337-41; M. Dewar interview August 16, 2006.

1058 B. Evenson, "Gallery Bash Draws 10,000," *Ottawa Citizen*, May 21, 1988, p. A1 and the reviews were good. See A. Duncan, "Canada's Art Finds a Home," *Montréal Gazette*, May 21, 1988, p. D1; R. Fulford, "Is National Gallery Too Posh?" *Toronto Star*, May 16, 1987, p. M5; J.F. Burns, "For Canada's Art, a home of its Own," *New York Times*, May 21, 1988, p. 13; for the CMC, see Hume, Christopher, "Museum of Civilization put visitors right inside history," *Toronto Star*, June 21, 1989, p. C1; T. Boddy, *The Architecture of Douglas Cardinal*, (Edmonton, AB: NuWest, 1988), p. 105. See also, John Taylor, "The Crippling Influence of the National Authority" in R. Chattopadhyay and G. Paquet, *The Unimagined Canadian Capital: Challenges for the Federal Capital Region*, (Ottawa, ON: Invenire, 2011), p. 27-34.

1059 Trudeau quoted by M. Safdie in Turner, *op. cit.*, p. 31.

1060 du Toit Associates, *The National Capital Core Area: Ceremonial Routes*, (Ottawa, ON: NCC, November 1983).

1061 John Ralston Saul, quoted in the exhibit *Ottawa: On Display/Mise en Scène*, (Ottawa, ON: Ottawa Art Gallery, 2000), curated by M.K. Rombout. See also M.K. Rombout, "Ottawa: On Display" in N. St-Onge and J. Keshen (eds.) *Construire Une Capitale: Ottawa: Making a Capital*. (Ottawa ON: Université d'Ottawa and Acte Press, 2001), p. 479.

1062 See NCC *Annual Reports*, 1985-2005. The only significant controversy was a proposal to add iron oxide to the asphalt to colour it red, as at Pall Mall in London. Unfortunately, red is also the colour of the Liberal Party and the Canadian flag, so this proposal was unacceptable to both federal Conservatives and Québec provincial politicians.

[1063] du Toit Allsopp Hillier, *The Parliamentary Precinct Area*, (Ottawa, ON: NCC and Public Works Canada, May 1987); *Parliamentary and Judicial Precincts Area*, (Ottawa, ON: Public Works and Government Services Canada, 2006).

[1064] James Guthrie, Christopher Humphrey, L.R. Jones and Olov Olson, *International Public Financial Management and Reform: Progress, Contradictions, and Challenges*, (Charlotte, NC: Information Age Publishing, 2005), p. 64

[1065] NCC, *Plan for Canada's Capital: A Federal Land Use Plan*, (Ottawa, ON: NCC, January 1988).

[1066] NCC, *Federal Land Use Plan* (FLUP), *Annual Reports*, 1986-1991, Section 2.

[1067] NCC, FLUP, *op. cit.*, "Capital Attractions, Visitor Services and Urban Design Elements," Map 5; NCC, *Discussion Paper on Canada's Capital: The Capital Orientation Plan*, (Ottawa, ON: NCC, 1988); Gyton, *op. cit.*, p. 91-99.

[1068] The NCC was originally a Crown Corporation that reported directly to the prime minister for policy and directly to the Cabinet for finance. During the 1970s, the agency began to report to a variety of departmental ministries. A move to Treasury Board oversight and a budgetary scandal ended the NCC's financial independence; see Steve Cameron, "Dispute may halt museum work," *Ottawa Citizen*, May 16, 1985, p. A1; "NCC Manager suspended following RCMP visit," *Ottawa Citizen*, May 18, 1985, p. A1, "Internal Audit of NCC Brings About Changes in Contracting Procedures," *Ottawa Citizen*, May 22, 1985, p. A3; Jack Aubry and Jane Defalco, "Mounties Charge NCC General Manager with Fraud," *Ottawa Citizen*, June 28, 1985, p. A1; Jack Aubry, "Ex-NCC Official Had Work Done Free, Contractors say," *Ottawa Citizen*, September 1985, p. 21, A1; *Ottawa Citizen*, "Fourth NCC Employee Charged," March 11, 1986, p. A1; E. Aquilina interview, June 29, 2006.

[1069] D.L.A. Gordon (ed.), *Planning Twentieth Century Capitals*, (London, UK: Routledge, 2006), chapters 9 and 10.

[1070] *Ibid.*

Chapter 13

[1071] K. Sweetman, "Ottawa is Also Our High-Tech Capital," *Canadian Geographic*, 102, (1982): 20-31; G.P.F. Steed and D. DeGenova, "Ottawa's Technology-Oriented Complex," *Canadian Geographer*, 27, no. 3 (1983): 263-78; a review of 54 plans from 17 different local and regional agencies for the period 1957-1996 found only one reference to high-technology – in the 1990 Kanata plan. See David Gordon, B. Donald and J. Kozuskanich, "Unanticipated Benefits: the Role of Planning in the Development of the Ottawa Region Technology Industries" in R. Tremblay and N. Novakowski (eds.), *Ottawa in the New Economy*, (Brussels, BE: Peter Lang, 2008), p. 103. Michael Porter suggested that the scattering of high-technology firms across several Standard Industrial Classification codes used in the census made it difficult for analysts to notice the emergence of a new cluster. See M. E. Porter, "Clusters and the New Economies of Competition," *Harvard Business Review*, (November-December 1998): 77-90.

[1072] W. Eggleston, *National Research in Canada: the NRC 1916-1966*, (Toronto: Clarke, Irwin & Company Limited, 1978).

[1073] J.D. Smart, *A City and a Technology: The Role of Government in the Growth of the Technology Industry in Ottawa, Canada to 1984*, (Kingston, ON: Queen's University, Department of History), unpublished Ph.D. Dissertation, 2004; Doyletech Corporation, *The family tree of Ottawa-Gatineau high-technology companies*, 2002 poster.

[1074] D.J. Doyle, *From White Pine to Red Tape to Blue Chips; How Technology Based Industries can Provide Continued Prosperity for the Ottawa-Carleton Region*, (Ottawa, ON: Ottawa-Carleton Economic Development Task Force, 1991).

[1075] D. Thomas, *Knights of the New Technology: The Inside Story of Canada's Computer Elite*, (Toronto, ON: Key Porter Books, 1983), p. 29-46, 61; Bill Teron, interviewed by Sarah Orovan and David Gordon, July 26, 2006.

[1076] Kanata Mayor Marianne Wilkinson, quoted in Thomas, *op. cit.*, p. 60; R. Mackay, interviewed by David Gordon, October 16, 2004.

[1077] T. Chamberlin and J. de la Mothe, "Northern Light: Ottawa's Technology Cluster," in *Clusters Old and New*, D.A. Wolfe (ed.), (Kingston, ON: McGill-Queen's University Press, 2003), p. 213-34; N. Novakowski and R. Tremblay, "Ottawa-Canada's

Capital: The Emergent Knowledge City" in N. Novakowksi and R. Tremblay (eds.), *Perspectives on Ottawa's High-Tech Sector*, (Brussels, BE: Peter Lang, 2007), p. 23-42, Table 8.

[1078] Federal employment in the Ottawa-Hull CMA declined from 115,590 to 93,640 over the 1986-1996 period; see Statistics Canada 1986, 1996 Census of Ottawa-Hull CMA; it was the first decrease over a decade in the 20th century – see J. Taylor, *Ottawa: An Illustrated History*, (Toronto, ON: J. Lorimer, Canadian Museum of Civilization, National Museums of Canada, 1986), Appendix IX.

[1079] Doyletech Corporation and McSweeney Associates Management Consultants, Market Research Corporation, *Serving Ottawa, economic strategies to develop Ottawa's local economy*, (Ottawa, ON: City of Ottawa, 2002). Caroline Andrew and David Doloreux, "Economic Development, Social Inclusion and Urban Governance: The Case of the City-Region of Ottawa in Canada," *International Journal of Urban and Regional Research*, 36:6 (2012), p. 1,288-305.

[1080] Ottawa-Carleton, *Partners for the Future*. (Ottawa ON: Ottawa Economic Development Task Force, March 1992); Chris Wilson, "Civic Entrepreneurship at the Ottawa Centre for Research and Innovation," (Ottawa, ON: Centre on Governance, Université d'Ottawa, 1999).

[1081] M. Porter 1998, *op. cit.*; J. Leibovitz, *Barriers to Collaborative City-Region Governance: Institutions and Economic Governance in Silicon Valley North*, (Glasgow, UK:, University of Glasgow, Department of Urban Studies, 2000), unpublished Doctoral dissertation; J. de la Mothe and G. Mallory, *Industry-Government Relations in a Knowledge-based Economy: The Role of Constructed Advantage*, (Ottawa, ON: Université d'Ottawa, 2003); Chamberlin and de la Mothe, 2003, *op. cit.*; Gertler and Wolfe, "Local Social Knowledge Management: Community Actors, Institutions and Multilevel Governance in Regional Foresight Exercises," *Futures*, 36 (2004): 45-65; J. Leibovitz, "Reflexive Governance and City-Region Economic Change: Between Reflexivity and State Selectivity in the Governance of Ottawa's Economic Transition" in Novakowski and Tremblay (eds.), *op. cit.*, p. 199-222.

[1082] See Ottawa-Carleton Regional Municipality, *Partners for the Future: A Strategic Economic Vision for Ottawa-Carleton*, (Ottawa, ON: Economic Development Task Force, 1992); the study contains only two paragraphs and one recommendation regarding federal employment and the remaining 23 recommendations of the 28-page report were devoted to high-tech life sciences and tourism. The study originally had no mention of the federal government, until the NCC quietly complained.

[1083] D. Nixey, *Corel Centre Lands: Justification of Need*, (Ottawa, ON: Region of Ottawa-Carleton, Department of Planning and Development Awards, 2000); J. Kozuskanich, *High Tech Firm Locations and the Implications for employment area planning in Ottawa*, (Kingston, ON: Queen's University, School of Urban and Regional Planning, 2005), unpublished M.PL. research report; Donald Gordon and Kozuskanich, *op. cit.*, p. 104-08.

[1084] Québec, *Loi sur la Communauté Urbaine de l'Outaouais*, 1990; *Loi modifiant divers dispositions législatives concernant les organismes intermunicipaux de l'Outaouais*, 1990.

[1085] C. Andrew, "Regional Political Identity" in C. Gaffield (ed.), *History of the Outaouais*, (Québec, QC: Les Presses de l'Université Laval, 1997), p. 731-35.

[1086] *Report of the Commission on the Political and Constitutional Future of Québec*, (Société d'aménagement de l'Outaouais, November 1991), brief to the Bélanger-Campeau Commission.

[1087] Andrew, "Regional Political identity," *op. cit.*, p. 736-39; Marcel Beaudry, interviewed by David Gordon and Sarah Orovan, July 26, 2006.

[1088] Materazzi *et. al.*, *Étude d'organisation de l'espace économique de la CUO*; (Hull, QC: CUO, 1994), p. 22.

[1089] CUO, *Schéma d'aménagement révisé de la communauté urbaine de l'Outaouais*, (Hull, QC: CUO, October 14, 1999); Aylmer, *Plan d'Urbanisme* (Aylmer, QC: Ville d'Aylmer, August 21, 2001).

[1090] Gatineau, *Plan d'urbanisme et de Développement*, (Gatineau, QC: Ville de Gatineau, 1990); Gatineau, *Ville de Gatineau: Règlement de Plan d'urbanisme numéro 500*, (D. Arbour Associates Gatineau plan, final version, June 2005); NCC *Annual Report*,

(1995-6), p. 23-24; Gatineau later decided not to build the parkway.

[1091] N. Tochon interview August 18, 2006; Andrew Haydon, interviewed by David Gordon and Sarah Orovan, July 25, 2006.

[1092] The population of Kanata, Cumberland and Gloucester grew by 54,977 people over this 10 year period from 1986-1996 – a growth of 27.5 percent.

[1093] John MacKinnon, "Drawing a line: Senators Turn the Heat on OMB," *Ottawa Citizen*, June 12, 1992, p. A1; Cyril Leeder, "The Palladium: A Question of Land Use; No Palladium, No Senators," *Ottawa Citizen*, May 17, 1991, p. A11.

[1094] Patrick Dare, "Kehoe Maps out Downtown Palladium; Critics Question Scheme's Logic, Seller's Motives," *Ottawa Citizen*, August 23, 1993, p. B2; Patrick Dare, "The Push for Palladium; in Kanata, the Arena's Boosters Threaten to Drown Out Skeptics," *Ottawa Citizen*, May 20, 1993, p. B2; Susan Riley, "Plan to Erect Palladium Downtown has Merit," *Ottawa Citizen*, August 29, 1993, p. A7.

[1095] Mike Shahin, "LeBreton Flats Better Site for Palladium, Politicians say; Kehoe's Downtown Location Criticized as too Small," *Ottawa Citizen*, August 22, 1993, p. A7; Andrew Haydon, interviewed by David Gordon and Sarah Orovan, July 25, 2006; Nick Tunnicliffe, interviewed by David Gordon, September 12, 2006.

[1096] "Civic Lessons: The Striking Forms of the New City Hall Buildings in Ottawa and Edmonton Speak About the Nature of Civic Life in Our Times," *Canadian Architect*, 40, no. 2, (February 1995): 13-22; R. Philips, "City Hall Deserves Place in Architectural Heritage," *Ottawa Citizen*, November 23, 1985, p. F1.

[1097] D. Miller, C. Hostovsky, and C. Keddy "The Natural Environment Systems Strategy: Protecting Ottawa-Carleton's Ecological Areas," *Plan Canada*, 35, no. 6 (1995): 26-29.

[1098] RMOC, *Region of Ottawa-Carleton Official Plan*, approved by the Minister of Municipal Affairs and Housing, October 1997 and by the Ontario Municipal Board, (April 1999); N. Tunnicliffe interview, September 12, 2006, *op. cit.*; Pamela Sweet, interviewed by David Gordon and Sarah Orovan, May 18, 2006, FoTenn Consulting; Peter Clark, interviewed by David Gordon and Sarah Orovan, July 25, 2006.

[1099] Kanata had ambitious plans for a town centre led by the civic-minded CEO of the high-tech firm Tundra Semiconductor, but they evaporated in the technology bust of 2002. Kathryn May, "Kanata Eyed for Federal Offices: Glut of Cheap, Vacant Tech Space May be too Good to Pass Up," *Ottawa Citizen*, August 8, 2001 p. A1; Bert Hill, "Tundra hopes for break-even quarter," *Ottawa Citizen*, November 21, 2002, p. D3.

[1100] Hull had 3 heritage districts and Ottawa had 11 Heritage Conservation Districts by 2000. These heritage districts helped to stabilize older residential areas, and prevent development that was wildly out of context.

[1101] Hull, *Plan d'Urbanisme*, (Hull, QC: Ville de Hull, September 18, 1990), p. 93-98; Pierre Chabot, interviewed by Dave Gordon and Sarah Orovan, August 23, 2006.

[1102] Jack Aubry, "New Museum in Hull Jewel in Shoddy Setting," *Ottawa Citizen*, October 5, 1987, p. C1; Jack Aubry, "The Dark Side of Hull; At Midnight the Bar Strip Seethes with Drugs, Crime and Sleaze," *Ottawa Citizen*, December 11, 1988, p. C1.

[1103] Hull's most detailed policies were for the south part of the Île de Hull – the historic core that had been ravaged by urban renewal. Hull, *Plan d'Urbanisme* (1990), *op. cit.*, "Plan Particulaire d'urbanisme – Parte sud de l'Île de Hull," p. 140-59.

[1104] Ottawa, *City of Ottawa Official Plan: A vision for Ottawa*, (Ottawa, ON: City of Ottawa, Planning Department, July 3, 1991), *Vol. 3*; it included four detailed policy plans and nine neighbourhood plans in *Volume 2*.

[1105] Ottawa 1991 plan, *op. cit.*, *Vol. 2*: 22-31; *Ottawa 20/20 Plan, Volume 24*, Section 1.0 Central Area, Policy 1.5.3e, ByWard Market HCD; John Norris, "*An Assessment of the Effectiveness of the ByWard Heritage Conservation District Designations 1990 to 1999*," (Kingston, ON: Queen's University, School of Urban and Regional Planning, 2000), unpublished M.PL. research report; Erin Topping, "*Pedestrian Public Spaces in the Nation's Capital: The Sparks Street Mall and the ByWard Market*," (Kingston, ON: Queen's University, School of Urban and Regional Planning2005), unpublished M.PL. research report; Jon Tunbridge, "Heritage momentum or maelstrom?

The Case of Ottawa's ByWard Market," *International Journal of Heritage Studies*, 6, no.3 (2000): 269-291; J. Tunbridge and G. Ashworth, *Dissonant Heritage: The Management of the Past as a Resource in Conflict*, (New York, NY: J. Wiley, 1996); B.S. Osborne and J.F. Kovacs, "Cultural Tourism: Seeking Authenticity, Escaping into Fantasy, or Experiencing Reality," *Choice*, (February 2008), p. 927-37.

[1106] Caroline Ramirez and Kenza Benali, "Les luttes patrimoniales à l'heure de la densification urbaine: Le cas de la Basse-Ville Est d'Ottawa, " *Canadian Journal of Urban Research*, 21, no. 1 (2012): 109-150.

[1107] City of Ottawa Zoning Bylaw number 93-98, Section 21; J. Moser interview, July 19, 2006.

[1108] John Hay, "Huge stakes in land and buildings in West Québec have bound National Capital Commission boss Marcel Beaudry to a unique set of conflict rules; A man of connections," *Ottawa Citizen*, February 13, 1993, p. B3; M. Beaudry interview, July 26, 2006.

[1109] The initial cuts were announced as 15-25 percent; see NCC *Annual Report*, (1995-96): 14. The agency laid off over half its staff, and transferred maintenance of most properties to companies set up by former employees. See NCC *Annual Report* 1996-7.

[1110] NCC *Annual Report*, (1995-96): 5-23. Similar deals were made for the maintenance of NCC parkways and interprovincial bridge, although the assets were kept in federal hands.

[1111] NCC, *Greenbelt Master Plan*, (Ottawa, ON: NCC, 1996); the plan was much praised and won the Canadian Institute of Planners' national award; see R. Scott, "Canada's Capital Greenbelt: Reinventing a 1950s plan," *Plan Canada*, 36, no. 5:19-21; its approach was incorporated into the 1997 RMOC and 2002 Ottawa official plans.

[1112] NCC, *Meech Creek Valley Land Use Concept Joint Planning Report*, (Ottawa, ON: NCC, 1998).

[1113] Rachel Carson, *Silent Spring*, (Boston, MA: Houghton Mifflin, 1962); Ian McHarg, *Design with Nature*, (New York, NY: Doubleday/Natural History Press, 1969).

[1114] Richard Forman, *Land Mosaics*, (New York, NY: Cambridge University Press, 1995); W. Dramstad, J. Olson, and R. Forman, *Landscape Ecology Principles in Landscape Architecture and Land-Use Planning*, (Washington, D.C.: Island Press, 1996).

[1115] Charles Hostovsky, David Miller, and Cathy Keddy, "The Natural Environment Systems Strategy: Protecting Ottawa-Carleton's Ecological Areas," *Plan Canada*, 35, no. 6, (1995): 26-29; Ken Tamminga, "Restoring Biodiversity in the Urbanizing Region: Towards Pre-emptive Ecosystems Planning," *Plan Canada*, 36, no. 4, (July 1996): 10-15.

[1116] Michael Hough, *Cities and Natural Process*, (New York, NY: Routledge, 2004); and "Toronto, The Task Force to Bring Back the Don," *Bringing Back the Don*, (Toronto, ON: City of Toronto, 1992).

[1117] Royal Commission on the Future of the Toronto Waterfront, *Regeneration: Toronto's Waterfront and the Sustainable City, Final Report*, (Toronto, ON: Queen's Printer, 1992).

[1118] Chris De Sousa, "Brownfield Redevelopment in Toronto: An Examination of Past Trends and Future Prospects," *Land Use Policy*, vol. 19, (2002): 297-309.

[1119] Casey Brendon, David Bergman, Judy Dunstan, and Hon Lu, "Urban Innovations: Financial Tools in Brownfield Revitalization," *Plan Canada*, 44, no.4, (October-December 2004): 26-29.

[1120] World Commission on Environment and Development, *Our Common Future*, (Oxford, UK: Oxford University Press 1987): 43.

[1121] M. Wackernagel and W. Rees, *Our Ecological Footprint: Reducing Human Impact on the Earth*, (Gabriola Island, BC: New Society Publishers, 1995).

[1122] J. Stainback, *Public/Private Finance and Development: Methodology, Deal Structuring and Developer Solicitation*, (Toronto, ON: John Wiley and Sons, 2000); J. McKellar and David Gordon, *The RFP Process for the Disposition of Publicly-Owned Real Estate Assets* (Kingston, ON: National Executive Forum on Public Property, Queen's University, Working Paper, November, 2007).

[1123] NCC, *The Chambers Site: A Call for Pre-Qualification Submissions*, (Ottawa, ON: NCC, February 1987); NCC, *The Sussex-Mackenzie Site – Call for Pre-Qualifications*, (Ottawa, ON: NCC, 1984).

[1124] The NCC agreed to relocate its own offices into a portion of the building, and the Senate later leased more space, See NCC *Annual Report*, 1994-5, p. 3; S.F. Patterson, *Public-Private Partnerships: The Secret of Their Success? – Case Studies of the Chambers and the Sussex-Mackenzie Development Projects*, (Kingston, ON: Queen's University, School of Urban and Regional Planning, April 2001), unpublished M.PL. research report, chapter 3; G. Gyton, *A Place for Canadians, op. cit.*, p. 109-11.

[1125] R. Eade, "Daly Building Demolition Looms; Federal Heritage Body Can't Agree on Saving Controversial Building," *Ottawa Citizen*, October 5, 1991, p. A17; R. Eade, "Daly Building: Fired Developer Sues NCC; Coopdev Alleges Breach of Contract in Multi-Million Dollar Suit," *Ottawa Citizen*, October 8, 1991, p. C1; R. Eade, "Daly Building: Demolition This Month," *Ottawa Citizen*, October 12, 1991, p. A15; A. Trevor Hodge, "Heritage Falls off the Daly Tightrope," *Ottawa Citizen*, October 20, 1991, p. B3; *Ottawa Citizen*, "Let There be Light – Downtown," April 18, 1992, p. B6; Patterson, *op. cit.*, S. 2.4; Gyton, *op. cit.*, p. 103-05.

[1126] *Ottawa Citizen*, "Want a Park? Then Build One," May 2, 1992, p. A10; P. Dare, "Why NCC Doesn't Want a Park on the Daly Site," *Ottawa Citizen*, May 7, 1992, p. A1; *Ottawa Citizen*, "80 percent back park for Daly site, poll finds," May 23, 1992, p. A1; NCC, *Sussex-Mackenzie Site: Stage II – Call for Detailed Financial, Development and Design Proposals*, (November 1996); Gyton, *op. cit.*, p. 103; Patterson, *op. cit.*, S. 5.2.4; NCC, *Call for Expression of Interest: Sussex-Mackenzie Development Opportunity*, (September 1996).

[1127] *Canadian Gateway Development Corporation – A Proposal for the Development of the Sussex-Mackenzie Site*, April 1997, submission to the NCC. The commercial proposal failed, despite backing from Gordon Capital, C.P. Hotels, Indigo Books and Planet Hollywood

[1128] Patterson, *op. cit.*, p. 35-49.

[1129] NCC, *Sussex-Mackenzie Site: Call for Pre-Qualifications*, (November 2000).

[1130] NCC, RMOC, City of Ottawa, *Core Area West: LeBreton Bayview*, (1988); NCC, *LeBreton Bayview: The Five Concepts*, (May 1989); NCC, *LeBreton Bayview: Evaluation of the Concepts – Summary of Public Participation*, (December 5, 1989).

[1131] P.R. Linkletter, *Redevelopment in a Jurisdictional Swamp: A Case Study of LeBreton*, (Kingston, ON: Unpublished Master's Report, Queen's University School of Urban and Regional Planning, April 1997), Appendix A; M. Adam, "Why renewal has taken so long," *Ottawa Citizen*, May 24, 2004, p. B6; A. Haydon interview, July 25, 2006; J. Holzman interview, August 15, 2006; N. Tunnicliffe interview, September 12, 2006.

[1132] The City of Ottawa, RMOC and NCC finally signed a tripartite land agreement in 1996, but the lands were not transferred to the NCC until three years later; see NCC, RMOC, City of Ottawa, *LeBreton Flats Master Land Agreement*, (1996).

[1133] NCC, *Annual Reports*, 1999-2005.

[1134] City of Ottawa, Bylaw 2003-441, September 10, 2003, amending the city's zoning bylaw.

[1135] NCC, *LeBreton Flats; Private Development Design Guidelines*, (Ottawa, ON: NCC, February 2004); M. Cook, "NCC invites developers to draw up housing plans for LeBreton Flats," *Ottawa Citizen*, February 27, 2004, p. F1; D. Reeveley, "Keeping the Plan on Track: Concerned residents say the way the NCC consulted the public about plans for LeBreton Flats was 'right on'," *Ottawa Citizen*, May 24, 2004; M. Cook, "Urban design controls: Enhancement or encumbrance?" *Ottawa Citizen*, August 9, 2004, p. B1; "Let market set the look of the Flats" (editorial), *Ottawa Citizen*, May 28, 2004, p. E4; requests for additional public benefits continued as the selection process dragged on and two of the short-listed firms withdrew, causing further cries that the whole planning process should be scrapped and started over again; see C. Wood, "NCC Supports Affordable Housing in LeBreton Flats," *Ottawa Citizen*, May 20, 2004, p. B4; M. Adam, "LeBreton Prize by Default: Report," *Ottawa Citizen*, August 25, 2005, p. C1; K. Egan, "Let's Have Another go at LeBreton," *Ottawa Citizen*, August 24, 2005, p. C1.

[1136] Also printed in *Ottawa Citizen*, Friday, September 20, 1992, Section A1.

[1137] L. Sagalyn, "Public/Private Development," *Journal of the American Planning Association*, 73, no. 1, (Winter 2007): 7-22; David L.A. Gordon, "Implementing Urban Waterfront Redevelopment," *Remaking the Urban Waterfront*, (Washington, DC: Urban Land Institute, 2004): 80-99; David L.A Gordon and Mark Seasons, "Administrative and Political Strategies for Implementing Plans in Political Capitals," *Canadian Journal of Urban Research*, (2009): 82-105.

1138 During the 41 years LeBreton was being re-planned (1962-2003), the City of Ottawa had ten mayors and ten planning commissioners and the NCC had 17 ministers and ten general managers; the RMOC (1969-2000) had four chairs and two planning commissioners. Pigott and Beaudry's combined 22 years tenure as NCC chair was the only stable point in the political structure; see Linkletter, *op. cit.*, Table 4.1 updated.

1139 NCC, *Federal Land Use Plan*, (1988); NCC, *Gatineau Park Master Plan*, (1990); NCC, *Greenbelt Master Plan*, (1996).

1140 National Capital Planning Commission (US), *Extending the Legacy: Planning America's Capital for the 21st Century*, (1997); National Capital Authority (Australia), *National Capital Plan*, (2002); W. Sonne, "Berlin: Capital Under Changing Political Systems" in David Gordon (ed.), *Planning Twentieth Century Capital Cities*, (London, UK: Routledge, 2006), p. 196-212; S.D. Joardar, "New Delhi: Imperial Capital of the World's Largest Democracy" in Gordon (ed.), *Planning Twentieth Century Capital Cities, op. cit.*, p. 182-195; D. Headon, *The Symbolic Role of the National Capital*, (Canberra, AU: National Capital Authority, 2003).

1141 NCC, *Plan for Canada's Capital: A Second Century of Vision, Planning and Development*, (Ottawa, ON: NCC, 1999), p. 11-12; also François Lapointe, interviewed by David Gordon and Sarah Orovan, May 8, 2006.

1142 The *PCC* had no proposals for the location of future bridges, leaving this problem to the regional governments (p. 80-1). This made the plan easier for the RMOC to support. N. Tunnacliffe, "RMOC Response to NCC's Draft Plan for Canada's Capital," (Ottawa, ON: RMOC Report 02-98-0018, September 2, 1998); Nick Tunnacliffe, interviewed by David Gordon, September 12, 2006, Pamela Sweet, interviewed by David Gordon, May 18, 2006.

1143 NCC, Press Release, March 1, 2000, "NCC Unveils Planning Concept for the Core of Canada's Capital Region."

1144 J. Morris, "Ottawa: A Half-Imaginary Metropolis" in *City to City*, (Toronto, ON: Macfarlane, Walter & Ross, 1990), p. 65.

1145 The architect of the US Embassy was David Childs of Skidmore Owing and Merrill; see I. Gournay and J.C. Loeffler, "A Tale of Two Embassies: Ottawa and Washington," *Journal of the Society of Architectural Historians*, 61: 480-507. Confederation Boulevard lost one lane on either side of the embassy to new security barriers after the 2001 World Trade Center attacks.

1146 NCC, *Capital for Future Generations, op. cit.*, p, 33-34; D. LeBlanc, "A River Runs Through It," *Ottawa Citizen*, June 9, 1998, p. E4; Marcel Beaudry, interviewed by David Gordon and Sarah Orovan, July 26, 2006.

1147 NCC, "A Capital for Future Generations: Visions for the Core Area of Canada's Capital Region," (Ottawa, ON: NCC, 1998); K. Egan, "Stroke of Happenstance and Genius," *Ottawa Citizen*, June 9, 1998, p. E5.

1148 W. Commanda, http://www.asinabka.com/; http://www.circleofallnations.ca/

1149 L. Boback, "Ottawa 50 Years From Now: Foes Blast 'Bizarre' Plan," *Ottawa Sun*, June 9, 1998, p. 1; R. Denley, "The NCC's Metcalfe Madness," *Ottawa Citizen*, June 10, 1998, p. D4; T. Spears, "A 'Grand' Vision: What Stands in The Way," *Ottawa Citizen*, June 9, 1998, p. A1, E1-E3; perhaps the best criticism was from Witold Rybczynski, "Ottawa's Makeover," *Time*, 153, no. 14, (Nov. 9, 1998).

1150 M. Adam, "Metcalfe Grand Allée Dream is Dead," *Ottawa Citizen*, February 20, 1999; L. Rochon, "Ottawa's Second Class Citizens: Residents Ignored in Plans to Make the Capital a Symbol for the Country," *The Globe and Mail*, March 22, 2000, p. R4.

1151 NCC, *Canada's Capital Core Area Sector Plan*, (June 2005).

1152 Sussex Circle, *National Capital Commission: Enhancing Relations*, (October 2000), p. B7; NCC, *Core Area Concept: Public Consultation Report*, (2001).

1153 The senior staff were disappointed by the lack of support after 15 years of painful negotiations. Ed Aquilina, Pierre Chabot, Francois Lapointe, Pamela Sweet, Nelson Tochon, Nick Tunnacliffe, 2006 interviews, *op. cit.*

1154 *NCC Annual Reports* 2001-2002, 2002-2003; Marcel Beaudry, interviewed by David Gordon and Sarah Orovan, July 26, 2006; Graham Hughes, "Champlain

Bridge Ready to Open: Problem-Plagued Project 20 Months Late," *Ottawa Citizen*, July 31, 2002, p. B4.

[1155] The bridge opponents sued NCC Chairman Marcel Beaudry, claiming that he would personally benefit from the project, since he owned property in Hull, some distance from the bridge. Patrick Dare, "Community Groups Abandon Champlain Bridge Court Fight," *Ottawa Citizen*, September 11, 1997, p. B3.

[1156] R. Denley "The NCC's Metcalfe Madness," *Ottawa Citizen*, June 10, 1998, p. D4. The *Citizen* had been a moderate, Liberal newspaper for most of the 20th century, but the demise of the Conservative *Ottawa Journal* in 1980 and its replacement by the tabloid *Ottawa Sun*, gave the *Citizen* monopoly as the local English broadsheet. The national edition of *The Globe and Mail* scooped many of the readers interested in public policy issues in the capital region, but the *Citizen* developed strong links with the high-technology industry. After Conrad Black took over the *Citizen* in 1996, the paper improved in quality, but moved sharply to the right in its politics. See M. McDonald, "Black's New Look Ottawa Citizen," *Maclean's*, March 17, 1997; R. Fulford, "Conrad Black and Canadian Newspapers," *National Post*, August 10, 2000; the NCC lost the editorial support of the *Citizen* in the 1990s and, under publisher Russell Mills, ran articles harshly critical of NCC Chairman Marcel Beaudry, and the Commission's practice of in-camera board meetings. R. Denley, "Beaudry, NCC Top MPs' hit list," *Ottawa Citizen*, November 4, 2004, p. B1.

[1157] A. Sancton, *Merger Mania: The Assault on Local Government*, (Montréal, QC and Kingston, ON: McGill-Queen's University Press, 2000), p. 14; R. Fischler, J. Meligrana, and J.M. Wolfe, "Canadian experiences of local government boundary reform: a comparison of Québec and Ontario" in J. Meligrana (ed.), *Redrawing Local Government Boundaries: An International Study of Politics, Procedures, and Decisions*, (Vancouver, BC: UBC Press, 2004).

[1158] *City of Ottawa Act*, 1999, S.O. 1999, c. 14, Sch. E, September 27, 2000.

[1159] The former City of Ottawa's recently expanded city hall on Green Island was sold to the federal government as expansion space for the Public Works Department.

[1160] J. Meligrana (ed.), *Redrawing Local Government Boundaries, op. cit.* p. 100.

[1161] The provincial government cleverly required two conditions for de-amalgamation, 50 percent of the vote in the referenda and 35 percent of all registered voters. Hull voted in favour of the amalgamation by both conditions, and both Aylmer and Masson-Angers voted to de-amalgamate, but did not reach the 35 percent of eligible voters required by the legislation, so the new status quo prevailed. I. Teotonio, "We Didn't Lose – We Won," *Ottawa Citizen*, June 21, 2004, p. D1.

[1162] The MRC continued as a regional government in the rural areas north of the new Ville de Gatineau.

[1163] Pigott was a confidante of Prime Minister Brian Mulroney and 1995-97 RMOC Chair Peter Clark had been campaign manager for her earlier career as a Conservative MP; see Gyton, *op. cit.* p. 91-107; P. Clark 2006 interview.

[1164] Beaudry was appointed by Brian Mulroney, but was a life-long Liberal and close confidante of Jean Chrétien, prime minister from 1993-2003. Chiarelli, also a Liberal, appointed a retired deputy minister and former NCC general manager as an advisor to his office, responsible for improving relations with the federal government. See Gyton, *op. cit.* p. 109-26; Marcel Beaudry, interviewed by David Gordon and Sarah Orovan, July 26, 2006; Ed Aquilina, interviewed by David Gordon and Sarah Orovan, June 19, 2006.

[1165] City of Ottawa, *City of Ottawa Official Plan* adopted May 2003; *Ottawa 20/20: Human Services Plan*, May 2003; *Ottawa 20/20: Arts and Heritage Plan*, adopted April 2003; *Ottawa 20/20: Economic Strategy*, adopted April 2003; *Ottawa 20/20: Environmental Strategy*, adopted October 2003; *Ottawa Transportation Master Plan*, adopted September 2003; the method for the Ottawa 20/20 strategic planning process is an extension of the 1998 *Plan Edmonton*, which combined strategic, financial and land use planning. This plan received the Canadian Institute of Planner's Award for Planning Excellence in 1999 and its coordinator was hired as the new City of Ottawa's chief administrative officer; see G. Jackson & M. McConnell Boehm, "Plan Edmonton: A Plan and a Process," *Plan Canada*, 39, no. 5

(Nov. 1999): 17-19; M. Seasons, "Monitoring and evaluation in municipal planning: considering the realities, *Journal of the American Planning Association*, 69, no.4, (Autumn 2003): 430-41.

[1166] *The Arts & Heritage plan* was influenced by current ideas. It cited B. Graham, G.J. Ashworth and J.E. Tunbridge, *A Geography of Heritage: Power, Culture and Economy*, (London, UK: Oxford, 2000); and M. Gertler, R. Florida, G. Gates and T. Vinodrai, *Competing on Creativity: Placing Ontario's Cities in a North American Context*, (Toronto, ON: Ontario Ministry of Enterprise, November, 2002). The Arts plan is entirely focused on local work, with no mention of either Gatineau, federal institutions such as the National Gallery, or celebrations such as the Jazz Festival or Winterlude. However, the Heritage Plan suggests numerous opportunities for collaboration with the NCC.

[1167] The environmental strategy coordinated with the NCC's 1996 *Greenbelt Master Plan*, and the economic strategy acknowledged the role of federal employment in the regional economy, which was an improvement on previous plans based entirely upon high-technology, tourism and the biomedical industries. See D. Gordon and R. Scott, *op. cit.*; D. Gordon, B. Donald and J. Kozuskanich, *op. cit.*

[1168] *Ottawa 20/20 Official Plan*, p. i-ii.

[1169] Ibid., p. 85.

[1170] Ibid., p. 86-87; Moser, Jacobs, Lapointe, Dubé, 2006 interviews.

[1171] *Ottawa 20/20 Transportation Master Plan*, (September, 2003). The city steered the first LRT lines though extensive public consultation of the environmental assessment process, and awarded a design-build contract for the north-south route. However, mayoral candidate Larry O'Brien opposed the plan in the 2006 municipal elections, defeated incumbent Bob Chiarelli and cancelled the LRT contracts, causing over $200 million in lawsuits.

[1172] Laura, Drake, "City girds for massive fight over cancelled light-rail plan; No sign of settlement in $280-million lawsuits," *Ottawa Citizen*, January 28, 2008, p. A1; Jake Rupert, "City, O'Brien knew killing light rail was unlawful, firms' lawsuit claims," *Ottawa Citizen*, June 7, 2007, p. D1; Jake Rupert, "City slapped with another light-rail lawsuit; Third firm in consortium seeks $103.9 million in damages," *Ottawa Citizen*, September 20, 2007, p. C1.

[1173] Urban Strategies, *Ottawa Downtown Urban Design Strategy*, City of Ottawa, March 10, 2004; even the *Citizen* was complementary; see D. Reevely, "Blueprint for a better downtown," *Ottawa Citizen*, February 18, 2004, p. B1-B2. The *Ottawa Downtown Urban Design Strategy* won the Canadian Institute of Planners' 2006 Award of Excellence in the category of downtown planning

[1174] See J. Punter, "From design advice to peer review: the role of the urban design panel in Vancouver," *Journal of Urban Design*, 8, no. 2, (June 2003); D. Reevely, "City Staff to have greater voice in design of buildings," *Ottawa Citizen*, February 18, 2004, p. B1-B2; the NCC began a design review for federally constructed buildings on federal land in the 1950s, see A. Adamson, "Thirty Years of the Planning Business," *Plan Canada*, 13, no. 1, (1973): 10-11; Andrew McCreight, "Design Review: A Comparison Between the City of Ottawa and National Capital Commission," (Kingston, ON: Queen's University, School of Urban and Regional Planning, 2010), unpublished M.PL. research report. The new Ottawa panel reviewed the urban design of new private buildings in the downtown.

[1175] Ville de Gatineau, *Plan d'urbanisme*, (June 2005), www.ville.gatineau.qc.ca; the new Ville de Gatineau also launched a secondary plan: *plan particulaire d'urbanisme* for l'Île de Hull; Communauté urbaine de l'Outaouais, *Schéma d'aménagement révisé*, approved January 5, 2000; Chabot, Dubé, Lapointe, Tochon 2006 interviews.

[1176] Urban Strategies, *Canada's Capital: Core Area Sector Plan*, (Ottawa, ON: NCC, 2005); Dubé, Jacob, Moses, Lapointe, 2006 interviews; this plan also won the CIP national award of excellence for urban design in 2006.

[1177] Guy Chiasson and Caroline Andrew, "Modern Tourist Development and the Complexities of Cross-border Identities within a Planned Capital Region" in R. Maitland, and B. Ritchie (eds.) *City Tourism: National Capital Perspectives*, (Wallingford, UK: CAB International, 2009), p. 253-63; Robert Maitland, "Capitalness is contingent: tourism and national capitals in a globalised world," *Current Issues in Tourism*, 15, no. 1-2 (2012): 3-17.

1178 Lisa Rochon, "Ottawa's new Convention Centre: A glass spaceship on the Rideau Canal," *The Globe and Mail*, March 11, 2011; it was rebranded as the Shaw Centre for 10 years in 2014.

1179 Jeffrey Simpson, "Howling at the park: Ottawa's Lansdowne Sturm und Drang," *The Globe and Mail*, June 29, 2010; Patrick Dare, "Touchdown, Ottawa; Council OKs redevelopment of Lansdowne Park," *Ottawa Citizen*, November 17, 2009, p. A1; Andrew Duffy, "Glebe group vows to fight Lansdowne Live plan," *Ottawa Citizen*, October 21, 2009, p. C2.

1180 Kristen Gagnon, "The urban park at Lansdowne Park," *Spacing Ottawa*, August 18, 2014; Joanne Chianello, "'They did a fabulous job'; Design wins wide praise, but approval uncertain," *Ottawa Citizen*, May 28, 2010, p. A1; Kristen Gagnon, "Ottawa's 'Little Toronto': Lansdowne Park's lack of local," *Spacing Ottawa*, December 15, 2014.

1181 Quentin Stevens, "Masterplanning public memorials: an historical comparison of Washington, Ottawa and Canberra," *Planning Perspectives*, 30:1 (2015): 39-66; A. Dance, "Negotiating Public Space on Canada's Parliament Hill: Security, Protests, Parliamentary Privilege, and Public Access," *Journal of Canadian Studies/Revue d'études canadiennes*, 48:2 (2014): 169-97.

1182 du Toit, Allsopp Hillier *et al.*, *Parliamentary and Judicial Precincts Area: Site Capacity and Long Term Development Plan*, (Ottawa, ON: Public Works Government Services Canada, 2006); this plan won awards from both the Ontario and Canadian planning institutes; it takes a more passive approach to security than the unpopular retro-fitting of the American and British embassies, following experience in Washington and Canberra; see *Urban Design Guidelines for Perimeter Security in the National Capital*, (Canberra, AU: National Capital Authority, NCPC, 2003); *The National Capital Urban Design and Security Plan*, (Washington, DC: National Capital Planning Commission, 2002); *Canada's Capital Commemoration Strategic Plan*, (Ottawa, ON: NCC, June 2006); du Toit, Allsopp Hillier and University of Toronto Centre for Landscape Research, *Canada's Capital Views Protection: Protecting the Visual Integrity and Symbolic Primary of Our National Symbols*, (Ottawa, ON: NCC, 2007). The *Capital Views* plan won a 2007 National Citation from the Canadian Society of Landscape Architects; the views were protected by adoption into the new City of Ottawa, Zoning Bylaw 2008-250, June 25, 2008.

1183 Canadian Urban Transit Association Award, 2002; American Public Works Association's Project of the Year Award, 2003; FCM Sustainable Community Award, 2003; see Transport Canada, *O-Train Light Rail Project*, (Ottawa, ON: Transport Canada Case Study Library, August 26, 2010).

1184 City of Ottawa, *Bayview Station District Secondary Plan*, June 2013; Queen's University School of Urban and Regional Planning, *Bayview Area Redevelopment Strategy* (2005).

1185 "Light rail plan gets green light, but debate far from over," *Ottawa Business Journal*, July 12, 2006.

1186 Patrick Dare and Dave Rogers, "Kettle Island chosen as site for new bridge," *Ottawa Citizen*, September 4, 2008, p. A1; "Build bridge at Kettle Island" (editorial), *Ottawa Citizen*, September 26, 2008, p. F4.

1187 Maria Cook, "A bridge too close: Residents gird for Kettle Island fight," *Ottawa Citizen*, September 23, 2008, p. A1; Doug Hempstead, "Province says no to Kettle Island bridge plan," *Ottawa Sun*, June 17, 2013.

1188 Kenza Benali and Ella Bernier, "Le train léger sur rails d'Ottawa : les rebonds d'un projet de transport durable conflictuel," *Revue Gouvernance*, 10.2 (2014): 1-30.

1189 Dominique La Haye, "La Ville d'Ottawa va de l'avant avec son train nord-sud," *Le Droit*, April 10, 2006; Patrick Dare and Mohammed Adam, "Secret contract likely to remain so," *Ottawa Citizen*, January 13, 2007.

1190 Randall Denley, "Finally, someone's put a stop to light-rail madness," *Ottawa Citizen*, December 13, 2006; Ken Gray, "Mr. Baird's municipal preoccupation," *Ottawa Citizen*, January 26, 2007; Clive Doucet, "Here's what's wrong with City Hall," *The Globe and Mail*, December 27, 2007.

1191 Dominique La Haye, "Train léger: Siemens engage des poursuites de 175 millions $," *Le Droit*, June 6, 2007.

1192 Doucet, "Here's what's wrong with City Hall," *op. cit.*

1193 Eric Champagne, "Transportation Failure in the Capital Region," in R. Chattopadhyay and G.

Paquet (eds.), *The Unimagined Canadian Capital: Challenges for the Federal Capital Region*, (Ottawa, ON: Invenire Press, 2011), p. 62-74; Robert Hilton and C. Stoney, "Why Smart Growth isn't Working: An Examination of Ottawa's Failure to Deliver Sustainable Urban Transit," *Innovation, Science, Environment: Canadian Policies and Performance, 2008-2009*, (Montréal, QC and Kingston, ON: McGill Queen's University Press, 2008), p. 74-92; Olivier Roy-Baillargeon and Mario Gauthier, "Gouvernance et concertation métropolitaines à Ottawa-Gatineau: La planification et l'aménagement du territoire en contexte interprovincial," *Cahiers de géographie du Québec* 56, no. 157 (2012): 173-88; Benali et Bernier, "Le train léger," 2014, *op.cit.*

[1194] Pierre Filion, "Toronto's Tea Party: Right-Wing Populism and Planning Agendas," *Planning Theory & Practice*, 12, no. 3 (2011): 464-469; Alan Walks, "Stopping the 'War on the car': Neoliberalism, Fordism, and the politics of automobility in Toronto," *Mobilities*, 10, no. 3 (2015): 402-22.

[1195] Ottawa will also use $179 million of federal gas tax revenue, see Government of Canada and City of Ottawa, *Ottawa Light Rail Transit Project Contribution Agreement with the Federal Government*, February 12, 2013; "Ottawa MPs ask for LRT station at Confederation Square," CTV News, May 11, 2012.

[1196] City of Ottawa, *Transit Oriented Development (TOD) Plans: Train, St. Laurent, Cyrville*, November 14, 2012; many of these stations also had preliminary plans prepared by the Queen's University School of Urban and Regional Planning from 2006-15.

[1197] The *Ottawa Riverkeeper/Sentinelle Outaouais* are heroes of this process; see Ville de Gatineau, City of Ottawa and National Capital Commission, *Ottawa River Integrated Development Plan*, 2003; and *Choosing our Future*, 2012; D.L.A. Gordon and A. Juneau, "Bridging Mechanisms for the Ottawa-Gatineau Region" in R. Chattopadhyay and G. Paquet (eds.), *The Unimagined Canadian Capital: Challenges for the Federal Capital Region*, (Ottawa, ON: Invenire Press, 2011), p. 87-104.

[1198] Preston Manning, "A Capital for All Canadians," *Ottawa Citizen*, September 14, 2010, p. A13.

[1199] Gilles Paquet, "The National Capital Commission: Charting a New Course," *Report of the NCC Mandate Review Panel*, December 21, 2006; the new government kept Marcel Beaudry on through the mandate review, and then appointed Russell Mills as the new chair. "Door opens at the NCC," *Ottawa Citizen*, May 3, 2007, p. A14.

[1200] Steve Ladurantaye, "Turning Problem Properties into Profit," *The Globe and Mail*, August 23, 2010.

[1201] "What's wrong with this picture?" (editorial), *Edmonton Journal*, November 15, 2008, p. A18; Andrew Cohen, Chattopadhyay and G. Paquet "Demise of Portrait Gallery shows Canada in a bad light," *Kingston Whig-Standard*, November 15, 2008, p. 9; Roy Macgregor, "New Victims of Communism memorial in Ottawa a looming disaster," *The Globe and Mail*, January 30, 2015.

[1202] Champagne, *op. cit.*, p. 50; Gilles Paquet, "Governing the Re-imagination of the Federal Capital Region" in Chattopadhyay and Paquet (eds.), *op. cit.*, p. 131-32.

[1203] Jeffrey Simpson, "Another reason for despairing of Ottawa," *The Globe and Mail*, December 11, 2007, p. A23.

[1204] Andrew Cohen, *The Unfinished Canadian: The People We Are*, (Toronto, ON: McClelland & Stewart, 2007); Caroline Ramirez and Kenza Benali, "Ottawa, une identité urbaine en mal de définition: analyse des représentations médiatiques de la capitale canadienne," *The Canadian Geographer/Le Géographe canadien*, 58.4 (2014): 443-456.

[1205] For example, the NCC and the City of Ottawa, after the usual confrontations, actually managed to agree on a route for the western extension of the LRT that does not damage the Parkway: Matthew Pearson, "NCC, City agree in principle to bury Western LRT extension," *Ottawa Citizen*, March 7, 2015.

Chapter 14

[1206] These comparisons will draw heavily from the author's other research, reported in detail in Gerald Hodge and David L.A. Gordon, *Planning Canadian Communities*, 6th ed. (Toronto, ON: Nelson, 2014) and David L.A. Gordon, *Planning Twentieth Century Capital Cities*, (New York, NY: Routledge, 2006). The sources for ideas not referenced below are included in these books.

1207 Rupak Chattopadhyay and Gilles Paquet (eds.), *The Unimagined Canadian Capital: Challenges for the Federal Capital Region*, (Ottawa, ON: Invenire Press, 2011); Lawrence Vale, *Architecture, Power and National Identity*, (New York, NY: Routledge, 2008); Gordon, *Planning Twentieth Century Capital Cities*, op. cit.; Andrew, Taylor et al. (eds.) *Capital Cities*, (Ottawa, ON: Carleton University Press, 1993); John Taylor, "City Reform and Capital Culture: Remaking Ottawa," *Planning Perspectives*, 4, (1989): 79-104.

1208 Ottawa-Gatineau ranked at or near the top of comparisons of the best places to live in Canada in Richard Florida, *Who's Your City?* (Toronto, ON: Vintage Books, 2008), Appendix C; similarly, Ottawa-Gatineau was ranked as the top place to live in Canada by the Martin Prosperity Institute, Kimberly Silk, "Ottawa, Guelph and Victoria Are among Canada's Most Livable Cities," *Martin Prosperity Insights*, (Toronto, ON: University of Toronto Martin Prosperity Institute, April 21, 2009); see also *MoneySense*, (March 2011).

1209 Statistics Canada, "Canada's population estimates: Sub-provincial areas, 2014," *The Daily*, February 11, 2015; Pierre Filion, M. Moos, T. Vinodrai and R. Walker (eds.), *Canadian Cities in Transition: Perspectives for an Urban Age*, 5th ed., (Toronto, ON: Oxford University Press, 2015), chapter 2.

1210 Caroline Andrew and D. Doloreux, "Economic Development, Social Inclusion and Urban Governance: The Case of the City-Region of Ottawa in Canada," *International Journal of Urban and Regional Research*, 36:6 (2012): 1,288-1,305; James Bagnall, "Hot & Cold: JDS and Nortel are in a World of Hurt. Fortunately, They're Not the Only Game in Town. Welcome to the Bipolar Economy," *Ottawa Citizen*, June 18, 2001, p. B2.

1211 Geoff Bowlby and Stéphanie Langlois, "High-tech boom and bust," *Perspectives on Labour and Income*, 3:4, (Ottawa, ON: Statistics Canada, April 2002).

1212 Chris Wilson, "Civic Entrepreneurship at the Ottawa Centre for Research and Innovation," (Ottawa, ON: Centre on Governance, Université d'Ottawa, 1999); Nick Novakowski, "Ottawa: the knowledge city and a labyrinth of obstacles," *GeoJournal* 75, no. 6 (2010): 553-565.

1213 James Bagnall, "Tech's time," *Ottawa Citizen*, July 13, 2013, p. B1; Claire Brownell, "Nortel campus goes to DND – at last; Public Works confirms $208-million purchase, consolidation," *Ottawa Citizen*, December 18, 2010, p. A3; Katherine May, "RCMP move to JDS complex to cost $600M," *Ottawa Citizen*, May 10, 2006, p. A1.

1214 Andrew Scott, "Storied Infrastructure: Tracing Traffic, Place, and Power in Canada's Capital City," *English Studies in Canada*, 36:1, (March 2010): 149-174. Gréber was design consultant to the 1939 New York World's Fair, and would be familiar with General Motors' famous Futurama exhibit; see Dolores Hayden, "'I HAVE SEEN THE FUTURE': Selling the Unsustainable City," *Journal of Urban History*, 38.1 (2012): 3-15.

1215 Sami Al-Dubikhi and Paul Mees, "Bus Rapid Transit in Ottawa, 1978 to 2008: Assessing the Results," *The Town Planning Review*, 81.4 (2010): 407-24.

1216 Peter Newman and Jeff Kenworthy, *The End of Automobile Dependence*, (Washington, DC: Island Press, 2015), p. 51; Figure 2.6 showed Ottawa with public transit use of 849 passenger-km. travelled per capita in 2005-6, in comparison to 44 global cities; comparative data in the Appendix, p. 245-56.

1217 D.L.A. Gordon and Mark Janzen, "Suburban Nation? Estimating the size of Canada's suburban population," *Journal of Architectural and Planning Research*, 30, no. 3 (2013): 197-220; Maria Cook, "Suburban nation: An ambitious new study says it's time for Canadians to dispel our urban myth," *Ottawa Citizen*, September 6, 2013, p. B1-B3; Richard Harris, *Creeping conformity: How Canada became suburban, 1900-1960*, (Toronto, ON: University of Toronto Press, 2004).

1218 D.L.A. Gordon and Isaac Shirokoff, *Suburban Nation? Population Growth in Canadian Suburbs, 2006-2011*, (Toronto, ON: Council for Canadian Urbanism: Working Paper #1, 2014); available at www.canu.ca, Ottawa-Gatineau CMA 14 percent exurban in Appendix A; 2006-2011 population growth 81 percent Auto Suburb and 11 percent exurban in Appendix B; Maria Cook, "In search of the suburban ideal," *Ottawa Citizen*, September 6, 2013, p. B2-B3.

1219 Pamela Blais, *Perverse Cities: Hidden Subsidies, Wonky Policy, and Urban Sprawl*, (Vancouver, BC: UBC

Press, 2010); François Lapointe, *Cities as Crucibles: Reflections on Canada's Urban Future*, (Ottawa, ON: Invenire Books, 2011); Gordon and Isaac Shirokoff, *Suburban Nation? op. cit.*, p. 5-6.

1220 For example, Ottawa was ranked 16/382 of major world cities for quality of life in 2015 by Mercer (www.imercer.com, [accessed June 28, 2015]); and first in Canada by the Martin Prosperity Institute, *op. cit.*; and *MoneySense* magazine. The region is not included in the *Economist's* Intelligence Unit rankings.

1221 Lloydminster (population 30,798 in 2011) straddles the Alberta/Saskatchewan boundary. It has a history of reasonable cooperation and lacks the federal-provincial-regional dimensions that often erupt into conflict in the Ottawa valley.

1222 J.H. Gray, *Confederation: The Political and Parliamentary History of Canada*, (Toronto, ON: Copp Clark, 1872).

1223 The ethnic composition of Hull switched from 90 percent English to 90 percent French from 1851-1911, see Lucien Brault, *Hull: 1850-1950*, (Ottawa, ON: Les Éditions de l'Université d'Ottawa, 1950), Appendix A; Ontario's 1913 school language regulations also provoked conflict by prohibiting the use of French.

1224 Aidan C. Carter, *Planning a 'Capital Worthy of the Nation': The federal district controversy and the planning of the Canadian Capital*, (Kingston, ON: School of Urban and Regional Planning, Queen's University, 2001), unpublished Master's thesis.

1225 The US Congress increased oversight of Washington when the municipal government flirted with bankruptcy and Prime Minister Margaret Thatcher abolished the Greater London Council in 1986. Both actions caused an uproar and were soon reversed; see Gordon, *Planning Twentieth-Century Capital Cities, op. cit.*; chapters 7 and 9.

1226 D.L.A. Gordon and A. Juneau, "Bridging Mechanisms for the Ottawa-Gatineau Region" in Chattopadhyay and Paquet (eds.), *The Unimagined Canadian Capital, op. cit.*, p. 87-104; D.L.A. Gordon and Mark Seasons, "Administrative and Political Strategies for Implementing Plans in Political Capitals," *Canadian Journal of Urban Research*, (2009): 82-105.

1227 M. Hough, *Cities and National Process: A Basis for Sustainability*, 2nd Edition, (New York, NY: Routledge, 2004); I. McHarg, *Design with Nature*, (New York, NY: Doubleday, 1969).

1228 The only railway crossing over the Ottawa River, the Prince of Wales Bridge, closed in the 1990s, leaving the region with five road bridges.

1229 Gordon, *Planning Twentieth Century Capital Cities, op. cit.*, chapters 4 and 7; Jacques Chirac (1977 to 1995) and Ken Livingston (2000 to 2008) might be considered the first true mayors of Paris and London, for example.

1230 Charles Taylor, *Sources of the Self: The Making of the Modern Identity*, (Cambridge, UK: Cambridge University Press, 1992); David Gordon, "Weaving a Modern Plan for Canada's Capital: Jacques Gréber and the 1950 Plan for the National Capital Region," *Urban History Review*, 29, no. 2, (2001): 43-61.

1231 John Taylor, "The Crippling Influence of the National Authority" in Chattopadhyay and Paquet (eds.), *op. cit.*, p. 27-34.

1232 Clive Doucet, "Why Ottawa Always Gets It Wrong," *Ottawa Life Magazine,* 25, (2005); Doucet is a thoughtful Ottawa councillor who has written extensively on urban issues. See Clive Doucet, *Urban meltdown: Cities, climate change and politics as usual*, (Gabriola Island, BC: New Society Press, 2007).

1233 Public Works and Government Services Canada, *Tunney's Pasture Master Plan*, (Ottawa, ON: PWGSC, 2014); the plan won a Canadian Institute of Planners merit award for urban design in 2015.

1234 Andrew Cohen, "The Capital Canadian," in *The Unfinished Canadian: The People We Are*, (Toronto, ON: McClelland & Stewart, 2007), p. 174-94.

1235 "Andrew Cohen is wrong" (editorial), *Ottawa Citizen,* May 10, 2007, p. A12; T. Schrecker, "What we deserve," *Ottawa Citizen*, May 11, 2007, p. A11; M. Sutcliffe, "Ottawa-basher Cohen appears to be short on big ideas himself," *Ottawa Citizen*, May 12, 2007, p. E1; Jim Watson, "Our community of neighbourhoods makes city great," *Ottawa Citizen*, May 16, 2007, p. D1.

1236 Caroline Ramirez and Kenza Benali, "Ottawa, une identité urbaine en mal de définition: analyse des représentations médiatiques de la capitale canadienne," *The Canadian Geographer/Le Géographe canadien*, 58.4 (2014): 443-456; Chattopadhyay and Paquet (eds.), *op. cit.*

1237 Shun-ichi Watanabe, "Tokyo: Forged by market forces and not the power of planning" in Gordon, *Planning Twentieth Century Capital Cities, op. cit.*, p. 101-14; see also chapters 4 and 7.

1238 L. Vale, *Architecture, Power and National Identity, op. cit.* p. 142-94; Gordon, *Planning Twentieth Century Capital Cities, op. cit.*, chapters 9, 10, 12, and 13.

1239 For example, in the 2015 Mercer quality of life rankings, only Vienna (1), Copenhagen (9), Wellington (12) Bern (13) and Berlin (14) were ranked ahead of Ottawa (16) among world capital cities, see Mercer, *op. cit.*

1240 Enid Slack and Rupak Chattopadhyay, *Finance and governance of capital cities in federal systems*, (Montréal, QC and Kingston, ON: McGill-Queen's Press-MQUP, 2009), chapter 12.

1241 Almos Tassonyi, "Ottawa, Canada" in Slack and Rupak Chattopadhyay, *op. cit.*, p. 55-78; "Ottawa as the National Capital: Fiscal Issues" in Chattopadhyay and Paquet (eds.), *op. cit.*, p. 53-65.

1242 *Ibid.*

1243 Gordon and Seasons, *op. cit.*

1244 L. Vale, *Architecture, Power and National Identity, op. cit.* p. 84-101; D.L.A. Gordon, "Ottawa-Hull and Canberra: Implementation of Capital City Plans," *Canadian Journal of Urban Research*, 13: 2 (2002): 1-16.

1245 L. Vale, *Architecture, Power and National Identity, op. cit.*, p. 79-81.

1246 Gilles Paquet, "Governing the Re-imagination of the Federal Capital Region," in Chattopadhyay and Paquet (eds.), *op. cit.*, p. 131-45.

1247 Government of Canada, Panel on the NCC Mandate Review, and Gilles Paquet, *The National Capital Commission: Charting a New Course: Report of the Panel on the NCC Mandate Review*, (Ottawa, ON: NCC, 2006).

1248 Peter Hall, "Seven Types of Capital City" in Gordon, *Planning Twentieth Century Capital Cities, op. cit.*, p. 8-14.

1249 See E. Hobsbawm and T. Ranger (eds.), *The Invention of Tradition*, (Cambridge, UK: Cambridge University Press, 1983), p. 107-13, 126-27; Taylor Andrew et al., *Capital Cities, op. cit.*; L. Vale, "Mediated monuments and national identity," *Journal of Architecture*, 4, no. 4, (1999): 391-408; Vale, *Architecture, Power and National Identity, op. cit.*; M.C. Boyer, *The City of Collective Memory: Historical Imagery and Architectural Entertainments*, (Cambridge, MA: MIT Press, 1996), chapter 6; B.S. Osborne, "London Landscapes, Memories, Monuments and Commemoration: Putting Identity in its Place," *Canadian Ethnic Studies*, 33, no. 3 (2001): 39-77, esp. p. 55-57.

1250 C. Taylor, *Reconciling Solitudes: Essays on Canadian Nationalism and Federalism*, (Montréal, QC and Kingston, ON: McGill-Queen's University Press, 1993); W. Kymlicka, *Finding Our Way: Rethinking Ethnocultural Relations in Canada*, (New York, NY: Oxford University Press, 1998); W. Kymlicka, *Multicultural Odysseys: Navigating the New International Politics of Diversity*, (New York, NY: Oxford University Press, 2007); J.R. Saul, *Reflections of a Siamese Twin: Canada at the end of the twentieth century*, (Toronto, ON: Viking Penguin, 1997); J.R. Saul, *A Fair Country: Telling Truths about Canada*, (Toronto, ON: Viking, 2008); K. Banting, T.J. Courchene and F.L. Seidle (eds.), *Belonging: Diversity, Recognition and Shared Citizenship in Canada*, (Montréal, QC and Kingston, ON: McGill-Queen's University Press).

1251 R.L. Watts, *Comparing Federal Systems*, 3rd ed., (Montréal, QC and Kingston, ON: McGill-Queen's University Press, 2008).

1252 Kymlicka, *Multicultural Odysseys, op. cit.*

1253 Wayne Norman, *Negotiating Nationalism: Nation-Building, Federalism and Succession in the Multicultural State*, (New York, NY: Oxford University Press, 2006), p. 38-59; B.S. Osborne, "A Capital for a 21st Century Canada: Making Ottawa More Representative of Canada and Canadians," unpublished paper (ca. 2009) prepared for the NCC.

1254 Kymlicka, *Multicultural Odysseys, op. cit.*, p. 83; Kymlicka, "Ethno-Cultural Diversity in a Liberal State: Making Sense of the Canadian Model" in Banting, Courchene and Seidle, *op. cit.*, M. Ignatieff, *Blood and Belonging: Journeys into the New Nationalism*, (Toronto, ON: Viking, 1993); J.R. Saul, *Confessions of a Siamese Twin, op. cit.*, p. 435-63.

1255 Norman, *Negotiating Nationalism, op. cit.*, p. 60-2.

1256 G.H. Herb and D.H. Kaplan (eds.), "Constructions of national symbolic spaces and places: The state of place identity" in *Nations and Nationalism: a Global Historical Overview*, vol. 4, (Santa Barbara, CA: ABC/CLIO), p. 1,350-64.

1257 The adoption of Ville de Gatineau as the name for the amalgamated municipality and Ottawa-Gatineau for the Census Metropolitan Area are further reinforcements of the Outaouais' francophone heritage.

1258 The two world wars are divisive memories because of Québec's resistance to conscription. However, the war memorial in Confederation Square focuses upon the collective efforts of those who served and the NCC has added additional monuments to aboriginals, French and English military heroes. See Gordon and Osborne, *op. cit.*

1259 M. MacMillan, M. Harris and A. Desjardins, *Canada's House: Rideau Hall and the Invention of a Canadian Home*, (Toronto, ON: A.A. Knopf Canada, 2004).

1260 Kymlicka, *Multicultural Odysseys, op. cit.*, p. 8; "Ethno-Cultural Diversity" *op. cit.*, p. 79; Rudyard Griffiths, *Who we are: a citizen's manifesto*, (Vancouver, BC: Douglas & McIntyre, 2009); Norman, 2006, *op. cit.*, Cohen, *The Unfinished Canadian, op. cit.*, p. 244; Taylor, *Reconciling Solitudes, op. cit.*

1261 NCC, *Core Area Concept: Public Consultation Report*, 2001.

1262 Saul, *A Fair Country, op. cit.*, p. 244-50.

1263 B.S. Osborne, "From Native Pines to Diasporic Geese: Placing Culture, Setting our Sites, Locating Identity in a Transnational Canada," *Canadian Journal of Communication*, 31, (2006): 147-175; E. Manning, *Ephemeral Territories*, (Minneapolis, MN: University of Minnesota Press, 2003), p. 1-30; M. Adams, *Unlikely Utopia: The Surprising Triumph of Canadian Pluralism*, (Toronto, ON: Viking, 2007), p. 96-97.

1264 Saul, *A Fair Country, op. cit.*, chapters 1-10.

1265 Griffiths, *Who we are, op. cit.*; Saul, *A Fair Country, op. cit.*; Kymlicka, "Ethno-Cultural Diversity," *op. cit.*; Taylor, *Reconciling Solitudes, op. cit.*

1266 B. Osborne and G. Osborne, "The Cast[e]ing of Heroic Landscapes of Power: Constructing Canada's Pantheon on Parliament Hill," *Material History Review*, 60 (Fall 2004): 35-47; B. Osborne, "Constructing Landscapes of Power: The George-Étienne Cartier Monument, Montréal," *Journal of Historical Geography*, 24, no. 4 (1998): 431-458.

1267 David Headon, *Symbolic Role of the National Capital: From Colonial Argument to 21st Century Ideals*, (Canberra, AU: National Capital Authority Australia, 2003), p. 165-98; National Capital Planning Commission (US), *Memorials and Museums Master Plan*, (Washington, D.C.: NCPC, 2001); Osborne, "From Native Pines," 2006, *op. cit.*

1268 David Gordon and Brian Osborne, "Constructing National Identity in Canada's Capital, 1900-2000: Confederation Square and the National War Memorial," *Journal of Historical Geography*, 30, no. 4, (October 2004): 618-642.

1269 NCC, *Canada's Capital Commemoration Strategic Plan*, (Ottawa, ON: NCC, June 2006), p. 4. The report identifies fundamental Canadian values to include "peace, order, and good government"; equality; democracy; cultural diversity; linguistic duality; cultural excellence and environmentalism.

1270 Osborne, "From Native Pines to Diasporic Geese," *op. cit.*

1271 Most recently the Federal Court, cancelled by the Liberal Martin government and the National Portrait Gallery, abandoned by the Conservative Harper government; see Jeffrey Simpson, "Another reason for despairing of Ottawa," *The Globe and Mail*, December 11, 2007, p. A23.

1272 Cohen, *The Unfinished Canadian, op. cit.*, p. 174-94.

Cast of Characters

1273 M. Simpson, "Thomas Adams in Canada 1914-1930," *Urban History Review*, vol. 11, no. 2 (1982): 1-15.

1274 M. Simpson, *Thomas Adams and the Modern Planning Movement: Britain, Canada and the United States, 1900-1940*, (London, UK: Mansell, 1985), chapters 4 and 5; T. Adams, "Editorial: Town Planning is a Science," *Journal of the Town Planning Institute of Canada*, vol. 1, no. 3: 1-3, April 1921; T. Adams, *Rural Planning and Development*, (Ottawa, ON: Commission of Conservation, 1917); T. Adams, "Editorial: Town Planning is a Science," *Journal of the Town Planning Institute of Canada*, vol. 1, no. 3: 1-3, April 1921; Wayne J. Caldwell, *Rediscovering Thomas Adams: Rural Planning and Development in Canada*, (Vancouver BC: UBC Press, 2011).

[1275] For a guide to Adams' articles on Canadian planning, see J.D. Hulchanski, *Thomas Adams: A Biographical and Bibliographic Guide*, (Toronto, ON: University of Toronto, Papers on Planning and Design; no. 015, 1978); Jill Delaney, "The Garden Suburb of Lindenlea, Ottawa: A Model Project for the first federal housing policy 1918-1924," *Urban History Review*, vol. 19 (1991): 156-65.

[1276] See T. Adams, *Outline of Town and City Planning: A Review of Past Efforts and Modern Aims*, (New York, NY: Russell Sage Foundation, 1935) for the basis of his American teaching; his British practice is summarized in *Recent advances in town planning*, (London, UK: J. & A. Churchill, 1932).

[1277] "Hon. T. Ahearn, Canadian Electrical Engineer," *The Times (London)*, June 29, 1938; "Thomas Ahearn," *New York Times*, June 29, 1938.

[1278] Bill McKeown, *Ottawa's Streetcars: The Story of Elective Rail Transit in Canada's Capital City*. (Pickering ON: Railfare DC Books, 2006).

[1279] A gifted publicist, Ahearn presented the first meal cooked "by the agency of chained lightening" to a gala dinner at an Ottawa hotel, "An Electric Banquet," *Ottawa Evening Journal*, August 30, 1892, p. 2.

[1280] Although Ahearn was an innovative designer of electrical devices, his suburban subdivisions were quite ordinary. See Bruce Elliott, "Streetcar Suburbs 1891-1914," in *The City Beyond*, (Nepean, ON: City of Nepean, 1991), p. 175-202.

[1281] By's birth date has been variously reported as 1779, 1781 and 1783 due to infant deaths and ambiguities in the By family baptism records. His most thorough biographer, Mark Andrew, suggests 1783 to match the memorial plaque approved by his widow. See Mark Andrew, *For King and Country: Lieutenant Colonel John By, R.E., Indefatigable Civil-Military Engineer*, (Merrickville, ON: Historic Merrickville Foundation, 1998).

[1282] Military engineers and surveyors of this era were also trained in perspective drawing and watercolour techniques to produce accurate drawings of military sites before photography was available. Several of By's drawings are held by LAC and are reproduced in this volume. The Royal Engineers were also trained in building design, but there is no mention of town planning in the Royal Military Academy curriculum. See Andrew, *op. cit.*, p. 33-44.

[1283] By was promoted to Lieutenant-Colonel in 1824 and retired at that rank. He is often referred to as 'Colonel' By in the same way that all grades of lieutenant are familiarly addressed as 'Lieutenant' and all grades of general officers are 'General'.

[1284] The entire By family suffered from poor health after leaving Canada. Colonel By's widow Ester, passed away at age 40 in 1838. His daughter, Ester March By (1819-1848) and Harriet Martha By (1821-1842) followed at ages 27 and 21, and his only granddaughters died at ages 1 and 3. After 1851, John By had no direct heirs, and his estates, including the Ottawa lands, were sold in 1863. See Andrew, *op. cit.*, chapters 1 and 7.

[1285] For detailed portraits of Colonel By's life and engineering feats, see also R.F. Legget, "John By" in *Dictionary of Canadian Biography, Vol. VII*, (Toronto, ON: University of Toronto Press, 1988) and R.F. Legget, *John By Lieutenant Colonel, Royal Engineers, 1779-1836: Builder of the Rideau Canal, founder of Ottawa*, (Ottawa, ON: Ottawa Historical Society, 1982); for a more critical view of By's management of the canal project, see George Raudzens, *The British Ordnance Department and Canada's Canals, 1815-1855*, (Waterloo, ON: Wilfrid Laurier University Press, 1979), p. 54-99.

[1286] J.E. Cauchon, *The Union of the provinces of British North America*, (Québec, QC: Hunter, Rose & Co., 1865).

[1287] A. Desilets, "Joseph-Édouard Cauchon," in *Dictionary of Canadian Biography, Vol. XI*, (Toronto, ON: University of Toronto Press, 1982), p. 159-65.

[1288] Sally Coutts, *Science and Sentiment: The Planning Career of Noulan Cauchon*, (Ottawa, ON: unpublished MA thesis, Carleton 1982); LAC, Engineering Institute of Canada Collection, MG 28 1277, vol. 43, File: J.E. Noulan Cauchon; his membership application listed his credentials.

[1289] W. DeGrace, "Canada's Capital 1900-1950: Five Town Planning Visions," *Environments*, 17, no. 2 (1985): 43-57 and K. Hillis, "A History of Commissions: Threads of An Ottawa Planning History," *Urban History Review,* 21, no. 1 (1992): 46-60; David L.A. Gordon, "Noulan Cauchon and the City Scientific in Canada's Capital," *Planning Perspectives,* 23, no. 3 (2008): 349-379.

[1290] C.M. Wallace, "John Hamilton Gray" in *Dictionary of Canadian Biography, Vol. XI,* (Toronto, ON: University of Toronto Press, 1982), p. 372-76. We should not confuse New Brunswick's Gray with another Father of Confederation of exactly the same name, Prince Edward Island premier, J.H. Gray.

[1291] J.H. Gray, *Confederation: The Political and Parliamentary History of Canada,* (Toronto, ON: Copp Clark, 1872), p. 104-14. Gray's description of the delegates' November 1864 Ottawa tour appears to draw on Edward Whelan, *The Union of the British Provinces,* (Charlottetown, PE: G.T. Haszard, 1865).

[1292] Gray, *op. cit.*, p. 108.

[1293] C. Ketchum, *Federal District Capital Ottawa,* (n.p., 1939); WLMK speech to House of Commons, April 21, 1944, *Hansard,* p. 2,234-40; D. Rowat, *The Government of Federal Capitals,* (Toronto, ON: University of Toronto Press, 1973); A. Carter, *Planning a "Capital Worthy of the Nation": The Federal District Controversy and the Planning of the Canadian Capital,* (unpublished Masters' Report, Queen's University, 2001).

[1294] André Lortie, "Jacques Gréber Urbaniste," *Les Gréber: Une dynastie des artistes,* (Musée départemental de l'Oise, catalogue de l'exposition, 1993).

[1295] David Brownlee, *Building the City Beautiful,* (Philadelphia, PA: University of Pennsylvania Press, 1989); W. Hegemann and E. Peets, *The American Vitruvius: An Architects' Handbook of Civic Art,* (New York, NY: Architectural Book Publishing Co., 1922).

[1296] Jacques Gréber, *L'Architecture aux Etats-Unis: prevue de la force d'expansion du génie Français, heureuse association de qualités admirablement complémentaires,* (Paris, FR: Payot & cie., 1920); see also I. Gournay, "Revisiting Jacques Gréber's L'Architecture aux Etats-Unis: From City Beautiful to Cite-Jardin," *Urban History Review,* 29, no. 2, (2001): 6-19. For the book's European influence see Jean-Louis Cohen, *Scenes of the World to Come: European Architecture and the American Challenge 1893-1960,* (Paris, FR: Flammarion, 1995).

[1297] D. Udovicki-Selb, "The Elusive forces of modernity: Jacques Gréber and the Planning of the 1937 Paris World Fair," *Urban History Review,* 29, no. 2, (2001): 20-35.

[1298] There is no known archive of Gréber's papers. The most comprehensive review of his work is André Lortie, *Jacques Gréber (1882-1962) et L' Urbanisme le temps et l'espace de la ville,* (unpublished PhD thesis, Université Paris XII, Vol. 1-4, 1997); 1936 resumé in the files of Canadian Prime Minister Mackenzie King is also useful. See LAC, MG 26 J2, Vol 276, File O-303-1, "Mr. Jacques Gréber" dated October 27, 1936; and a promotional monograph for his consulting firm: *Jacques Gréber, Architecte SADG SC SFU Urbaniste et Architecte de Jardins,* (Strasbourg, FR: EDARI, n.d., est. 1935) held in the library of the National Capital Commission, Ottawa; while in Montréal, he prepared a plan for a garden suburb, see Léon Ploegaerts, "Un projet inconnu de Jacques Gréber: La cite jardin de Villeray du Domaine Sainte-Sulpice a Montréal," *Urban History Review,* 29, no. 2, (2001): 36-42.

[1299] See Brownlee, *op. cit.*, p. 77-81. Jacques Gréber commissioned his father, noted sculptor Henri Gréber (1854-1941), to execute the large marble copy of Rodin's *The Kiss,* for the main gallery.

[1300] Colette Felenbok, "1910-1920: L'avenement d'un architecte urbaniste franco-americain" in *Les Grébers: Une dynastie des artistes,* (Musée départemental de l'Oise, catalogue de l'exposition, 1993).

[1301] José M'Bala, "Prevenir l'exurbanisation: le Plan Gréber de 1950 pour Montréal," *Urban History Review,* 29, no. 2, (2001): 62-70.

[1302] Pierre Lavedan, "Jacques Gréber," *La vie urbaine,* (January-March, 1963): 1-14.

[1303] There has been a modest revival of interest in recent years. T. Andresen, M. Fernandes dé Sa, J. Almeida (eds.). *Jacques Gréber, Urbanist and Garden Designer,* (Porto: Serralves Foundation, 2011); André Lortie, *Jacques Gréber Architecte Urbaniste 1882-1962: les allers retours France Amerique une energie cynetique au service de l'art urban?* (unpublished thesis, Institut d'urbanisme de Paris); A. Lortie, "Jacques Gréber (1882-1962) et l'urbanisme, le temps et l'espace de la ville," (unpublished PhD dissertation, Université Paris, 1997); and Jean-Claude Delorme, "Jacques Gréber: Urbaniste Français," *Metropolis*, 3, no. 32, (July 15-August 15, 1978): 49-54.

[1304] Countess of Aberdeen, *Through Canada with a Kodak*, (Edinburgh, UK: W.H. White and Co., 1893), p. 71-89. Her first impressions of Ottawa were those of a tourist – the picturesque beauty of the Parliament Buildings, the awesome might of the sawmills, shooting the timber slide, tobogganing at Rideau Hall, etc.

[1305] Countess of Aberdeen, *The Canadian Journal of Lady Aberdeen*, J.T. Saywell (ed.), (Toronto, ON: Champlain Society, 1960), see introduction; also Sandra Gwyn, *The private capital: Ambition and love in the age of Macdonald and Laurier*, (Toronto, ON: McClelland & Stewart, 1984), chapter 20, p. 273-292. Both the NCW and VON survive to this day. Lady Aberdeen continued as president of the International Council of Women.

[1306] Lord and Lady Aberdeen, *We Twa': Reminiscences of Lord and Lady Aberdeen*, Vol. 2, (London, ON: W. Collins and Co., 1925), chapter 9.

[1307] The Aberdeens also promoted town planning in Ireland, especially for Dublin. See Lord and Lady Aberdeen, *op. cit.*

[1308] D.G.G. Kerr, *Sir Edmund Head, a scholarly governor*, (Toronto, ON: University of Toronto Press, 1954); James A. Gibson, "Sir Edmund Walker Head" in *Dictionary of Canadian Biography, Vol. IX*, (Toronto, ON: University of Toronto Press, 1976).

[1309] David Knight, *Choosing Canada's Capital: Conflict Resolution in a Parliamentary System*, (Ottawa, ON: Carleton University Press, 1991); Gibson, "Sir Edmund Walker Head," *op. cit.*

[1310] James A. Gibson, "Sir Edmund Head's Memorandum on the choice of Ottawa as the seat of government of Canada," *Canadian Historical Review*, 16, (Dec. 1935): 411-17; Knight, *op. cit.*, chapter 8.

[1311] Donald Creighton, *John A. Macdonald; The Young Politician*, (Toronto, ON: Macmillan, 1952), chapter X and XI; Richard Gwyn, *John A: The Man Who Made Us, Vol. 1*, (Toronto, ON: Random House, 2007), chapter 11; Knight, *op. cit.*, chapters 9 and 10.

[1312] Charlotte Grey, *Mrs. King: the life and times of Isabel Mackenzie King*, (Toronto, ON: Viking, 1997). Ironically, William Lyon Mackenzie, the prime minister's rebel grandfather, was impressed by his first visit to Bytown before the lumber industry despoiled the river. He wrote in the *Haldimand Independent* on October 11, 1851: "Bytown and its environs astonishes me... nature seems to have destined it for the site of a great city and I suppose that it would have been chosen for the capital of the United Canadas had it not been located above tidewater..." Reprinted in David Knight, *Choosing Canada's Capital: Conflict Resolution in a Parliamentary System* (Ottawa, ON: Carleton University Press, 1991), p. 139.

[1313] B.A. 1895; LL.B 1896 (Toronto); studied at Chicago with Thorstein Veblen 1896-97; M.A. (Toronto) 1897; Ph.D. 1909 (Harvard, Frank Taussig, supervisor). See George Henderson, *W.L. Mackenzie King: A Bibliography and Research Guide*, (Toronto, ON: University of Toronto Press, 1998), xvi-xix; Robert Dawson, *William Lyon Mackenzie King, A Political Biography*, (Toronto, ON: University of Toronto Press, 1958), chapters 2, 3. King abandoned his dissertation in 1900 on joining the Department of Labour. He later appealed to Harvard to accept some of his reports as deputy minister in lieu of a thesis. See Dawson, *op. cit.*, chapter 3; It is a measure of King's ability as a social climber that Harvard President Charles Eliot thought well enough of him to offer King the position of the founding dean of their Graduate School of Business Administration in 1908, against the advice of Taussig. King turned them down to enter politics. J. Cruikshank, *A Delicate Experiment: Harvard Business School 1908-1945*, (Boston, MA: Harvard Business School Press, 1992), p. 39-40.

[1314] King went on overseas trips in, among other dates, 1899-1900, 1906, 1908, 1909, 1910, 1928, 1934 and 1936.

[1315] Wilfrid Laurier hated to travel. He first crossed the Atlantic in 1897, at age 57. See J.L. Granatstein, and N. Hillmer, *Prime Ministers: Ranking Canada's Leaders*, (Toronto, ON: Harper Collins, 1999), p. 57.

[1316] William Lyon Mackenzie King, "The Story of Hull House," *The Westminster*, November 6, 1897, p. 350-53. Jane Addams, *Twenty Years at Hull House*,

[1316] (New York, NY: The Macmillan Company, 1910). Autographed copy given to WLMK, held in Laurier House, Ottawa.

[1317] King lived in the Passmore Edward Settlement house while he was in London and visited Henrietta Barnett, the Webbs and other reformers. King diary, Oct 11 and 18, 1899, Jan. 27, Feb. 6, Feb 24, 1900. Dame Barnett kept Earl Grey informed about the Hampstead Garden Suburb Trust while he was in Canada. See Barnett to Grey, Feb 21, 1910 in C.P. Meredith papers, (LAC, MG 29 E62) vol. 4, File 29.

[1318] William Lyon Mackenzie King, *Industry and Humanity: A study in the Principles Underlying Industrial Reconstruction,* (New York, NY: Houghton Mifflin Company, 1918), p. 359. Copy annotated by WLMK, held in his library at Laurier House, Ottawa; see also David L.A. Gordon, "William Lyon Mackenzie King, Town Planning Advocate," *Planning Perspectives,* 17, no. 2 (2002): 97-122.

[1319] King literally followed in Laurier's footsteps every day, since he lived in Laurier's house in Sandy Hill after he became prime minister. His diary records many observations on the development of Ottawa from his daily walk home.

[1320] Edwinna Von Baeyer, *Garden of dreams: Kingsmere and Mackenzie King,* (Toronto, ON: Dundurn Press, 1990). The majority of the relics are from a demolished Ottawa bank and the burned centre block of the Parliament Buildings. Several panels were presented to King by visiting British officials, other statues were bought by King during European visits. At least one fragment was extracted from the bombed Westminster Houses of Parliament by a future prime minister and shipped home by submarine at taxpayers' expense. See Lester B. Pearson, *Mike: The Memoirs of the Rt. Hon. Lester B. Pearson, Vol. 1,* (Toronto, ON: Signet, 1973), p. 187-88.

[1321] For an autobiographical essay see, C.P. Meredith papers, (LAC, MG 29 E62), *Vol. 9, Rambling Recollections,* "I" and Sandra Gwyn, *op. cit.,* p. 219-20.

[1322] Chas. Murphy (OIC Secretary) letter to Hal McGiverin, M.P. August 3, 1910, cc. WL correspondence, 9663-4.

[1323] E.F. Bush, *The Builders of the Rideau Canal, 1826-32,* (Ottawa, ON: Parks Canada, National Historic Parks and Sites Branch, Manuscript Report no. 185, 1976).

[1324] For more on McKay's life, see F. J. Audent, "The Honourable Thomas McKay, M.L.C., Founder of new Edinburgh 1792-1855," *Canadian Historical Society Report,* (1932): 65-79; and E.F. Bush "Thomas McKay" in *Dictionary of Canadian Biography, Vol. VIII,* (Toronto, ON: University of Toronto Press, 1985), p. 551-54.

[1325] P. Burroughs, "George Ramsey" in *Dictionary of Canadian Biography, Vol. VII,* (Toronto, ON: University of Toronto Press, 1988), p. 722-33.

[1326] M. Whitelaw (ed.), *The Dalhousie Journals, 1816-20,* (Ottawa, ON: Oberon Press, 1978), *Vol. 1;* Burroughs, *op. cit.*

[1327] Whitelaw, *op. cit.,* vols. 2 and 3; Burroughs, *op. cit.*

[1328] Peter Jacobs, "Frederick Gage Todd – Biographic Notes," undated, unpublished. Based on University of Massachusetts calendars and interviews. The author is indebted to Professor Jacobs, the authority on Todd's work, for making his research notes available.

[1329] Charles E. Beveridge and P. Rocheleau, *Frederick Law Olmsted: Designing the American Landscape,* (New York, NY: Universe, 1998). The firm was known as Olmsted, Olmsted and Eliot from 1895 to 1898 and as Olmsted Bros. from 1898 to 1950.

[1330] Cynthia Zaitzevsky, *Fredrick Law Olmsted and the Boston Park System,* (Boston, MA: Harvard/Belknap, 1982); Frederick L. Olmsted, "Mount Royal" reprinted in S.B. Sutton (ed.), *Civilizing American cities: writings on city landscapes/Frederick Law Olmsted,* (New York, NY: Da Capo Press, 1997).

[1331] Vincent Asselin, *Frederick G. Todd Architecte Paysagiste: Une Pratique de l'aménagement ancrée dans son époque 1900-1948,* (unpublished thesis presented at Université de Montréal, Faculté de l'aménagement, Annexe C, 1995).

[1332] P. Jacobs, "Frederick G. Todd and the Creation of Canada's Urban Landscape," *Association for Preservation Technology (APT) Bulletin,* XV, no. 4, (1983): 27-34.

[1333] L.D. McCann, "Planning and building the corporate suburb of Mount Royal, 1910-1923," *Planning Perspectives,* 11, (1996): 259-301.

[1334] Edward I. Wood, "Landscape Architecture in the National Capital," *Community Planning Review*, 6, no. 1, (March 1956): 13-25.

[1335] P.M.O. Evans, *The Wrights: A Genealogical Study of the First Settlers in Canada's National Capital Region*, (Ottawa, ON: National Capital Commission, 1978); B.S. Elliot, "The Famous Township of Hull" *op. cit.*; Chad Gaffield (ed.), *History of the Outaouais*, (Québec, QC: Les Presses de l' Université Laval, 1997), chapters 5, 6 and 7; Lucien Brault, *Hull 1850-1950*, (Ottawa, ON: Les Éditions de l'Université d'Ottawa, 1950), chapter 1; R. Ouellet and B. Therialt, "Philemon Wright," *Dictionary of Canadian Biography, Vol. VII*; P-L. Lapointe, "Alonzo Wright," *Dictionary of Canadian Biography, Vol. XII*.

INDEX

PERSONS

(**Bold** page numbers for images)

Abercrombie, Patrick ... 160, 190, 192, 200, 224

Aberdeen, Lady 108-**9**, 111-**2**, 117, 146, 242

Adams, Thomas 150, 159, 160-2, 164-7, 170, 172, 180, 335

Ahearn, Thomas **173**-4, 177, 335

Allsopp, Robert............ 165, 279, 281, 283, 303, 314-5

Aylen, Peter................. 56-7

Bate, Henry 101, 113-4, 124

Beaudry, Marcel 289, 296, 301, 309

Bennett, Edward.......... 104, **147**-57, 159, 164-7, 169, 170, 175-7, 180, 182, 184-5, 199, 206, 222, 224, 226, 265, 303, 323

Benoit, Pierre 262

Besserer, Louis 49, 65, 67, 324

Bland, John.................. 219, 229, 294

Blumenfeld, Hans........ 224

Boggs, Jean 279-80

Booth, John R. 93-4, 97, 114-6, 120, 137, 230

By, John 26, **35**, 37-9, 41-51, 53-5, 64, 71, 124, 133, 142, 171, 185, 317, 324, 328, 336

Campeau, Robert 237-8, 240, 249, 256, 260, 270, 287, 289

Cardinal, Douglas 279-80, 329

Carver, Humphrey....... 193

Cauchon, Noulan 82, 133, 146-9, 159, 166-7, **168**-73, 176, 178, 180, 182, 199-200, 224, 226, 324, 336

Champlain, Samuel 5, 7-14, 23, 31, 92, 173-4, 308, 32

Commanda, William ... 305-6

Coolican, Denis............ 259, 269

Cormier, Ernest............ 183-4, 203, 221-2

Dalhousie, Lord............ 25-6, **28**-31, 34-5, 37-41, 43, 45, 47, 49, 53, 54, 58-9, 65, 80, 117, 322-3

Dewar, Marion 276, 280

Diefenbaker, John........ 211-3, 227, 330

du Toit, Roger.............. 165, 279, 281, 283, 303, 314-5

Eddy, Ezra B. 93-4, 115-6, 137, 227, 258, 303, 324

Elgin, Lord 60, 74, 76, 97, 107, 150, 152

Fielding, W.S. 112

Fiset, Édouard 196

Fullerton, Douglas....... 252, **260**, 264, 269, 271-4, 321

Galt, John 40

Gray, John H. 5, **87**, 211, 321, 336-7

Gréber, Jacques 135, 160, 176, 180-**1** 182-6, 190, 193-**8**, 199-209, 213, 215-9, 222-6, 229, 237, 249-50, 253, 255, 265, 271, 275, 290, 307, 320-3, 337-8

Greenberg, Lorry 249, 264, 267, 270, 274

Grey, Lord & Lady 131-**2**, 242

Head, Edmund............. 55, 77-**8**, 79, 89, 117, 338-9

Holt, Herbert............... 146-8, 154, 157, 159-60, 209, 323

Hough, Michael........... 296

Howard, Ebenezer 190, 200, 224

Jacobs, Jane.................. 266

Keefer, Thomas 62-3, 107-8

Kitchen, John M.......... 168, 170, 196

L'Enfant, Pierre C. 24, 40, 54, 73-4, 110-1, 126, 326-7

Laurier, Wilfrid............ 108, **110**, **112**, 117, 133, 174

Le Corbusier 202-03, 219, 222, 232, 242, 256

LeBreton, John 29-31, 34, 38-9, 47, 53

Lésvesque, René........... **227**

Macdonald, Sir John A. 76-7, 79-80, 82-6, 89, 106-7

Mackenzie King, W.L. 119-**21**, 122, 151, 161, 167, 172-**4**, 175-82, 185-6, 193, 195, 197-8, 203, 206-7, 211-2, 221, 305, 321-2, 330, 339

Mawson, Thomas......... 131, 133, 146-9, 159

McHarg, Ian................ 250

McKay, Thomas........... 41, 43, 50-1, 58, 62-3, 92, 94, 105-7, 189, 219, 227-8, 242, 339-40

Meredith, C.P. 131, **133**-4, 146, 148, 159, 340

Monck, Lord & Lady ... 91, 102, **105**

Montferrand, Jos. **56**, 258, 324

Olmsted, Frederick Law 123, 125, 129, 135, 167, 224

Olmsted, Frederick Law Jr. 110, 127, 147, 150

Parent, Oswald **227**, 253, 256, 270, 275

Penn, William.............. 13-4

Perry, Clarence............. 163, 200, 224

Pigott, Jean 284-**5**, 293, 296, 298, 301, 309

Reid, Don 27, 237, 238

Safdie, Moshe 279, 294

Scott, John................... 59-60

431

Scott, Richard W. 62-3, 77-9, 80, 92
Smith, Goldwin 73
Soper, Warren 101, 107
Sparks, Nicholas 30, 35-6, 39, 43, 47, 49, 51-3, 58-9, 65-9, 80-1, 96, 185, 204-5, 220, 221
St. Laurent, Louis 210-1
Stein, Clarence.............161, 192
Stephenson, Gordon 192, 229

Teron, William 249, 270, 287
Thrift, Eric...................212, **227**
Todd, Frederick 111, **125**-31, 133-5, 137, 140, 142, 146, 150, 165, 180, 199, 201, 206, 224, 323, 341
Turpin, Armand **227**
Trudeau, Pierre E. 225, 251, 255, 266, 272, 279, 281, 328, 330

Victoria, Queen 74, 77, 89, 106
Vivian, Henry..............131

Whitton, Charlotte......210-1, 218-9, 221, **227**, 237, 260
Wright, Henry 161
Wright, Philemon 18, 19, 20, 21, 23, 28, 29, 30, 35, 43, 49, 50, 51, 55, 57, 60, 62, 341
Wright, Ruggles...........21, 30, 38, 57

PLACES

(**Bold** page numbers for images)

Abuja (Nigeria) 324-5
Asinabka, *also* Victoria Island **306**
Aylmer 57-8, 71, 96, 173, 253, 271-2, 276, 289-90, 303

Bank Street 124, 137, 165, 173, 235, **303**, 31-4, 323
Barrack Hill, *also* Parliament Hill 38, 43, 49-52, 54, 60, 65-6, 68, **70**-1, 80-1, 83, 90, 324
Brasilia........................89, 203, 230, **232**, 324, 326-7
Britannia.....................29, 47, 101, 137, 139, 270
Bytown 35-72, 74, 76, 105, 312, 323, 324, 336
ByWard Market 41, 59, 60, **61**, 242, 243, 264, 294, 303, 311, 323

Canberra......................89, 142, 144, **145**, 146, 173, 207, 274, 285, 302, 320-2, 324, 326-8
Charlesbourg (QC) 9
Charlottetown (PEI)....**14**, 49, 84, **85**, 86
Chaudière Falls 1-**2**, **7**, 10, 19, 26, **39**, 43, **46**, 47, 58, **59**, 63, 92-3, 304-6, 324, 328
Chicago 103, **104**, 110, 144, 146-7, 149, 150, 157, 159, 298
Confederation Square ...169, 171, 175, **176**-8, 180-2, **183**, 185, 206-7, 219, 235, 243-**4**, 281, 297, 317, 324, 328, 329
Corktown 47, 49, 55

Dalhousie District 58-9, 65, 340

Eastview, *see* Vanier 137, 220, 227, 229, 251, 265
Elgin Street..................59-60, 97, 107, 150, 152-4, 167, 171-2, 176, 183, 187, 206, 235, 243, 278, 282
Entrance Valley............41, 43, 50-1, 53

Gatineau Hills.............6, 100, 119, 150, 151, 173, 180, 196-**7**, 200, 214, 289
Gatineau Park.............180, 197, 201-2, 254, 296, 302, 303, 323

Gloucester....................16-7, 33, 35, 39, 137, 195, 207-12, 220, 222, 226, 246, 251, 270, 276, 290, 294, 308, 312
Goderich (ON)............**40**, 48
Government House 74, 112
Grand River................9-11
Green Island 51, 62, **189**, 219, 294, 324
Guelph (ON) 40

Halifax (NS)................3, 14, 22-3, 51, 53, 73, 84, 86-7, 123, 266, 320
Hampstead Garden Suburb 131, 143, 161, 339, 352
Hull (QC), *also* Wrightstown 3, 19-21, **32**, 58, 71, 90, 93-4, **95**-9, 114, **115**-6, 118, 128, **129**, **135**, 137, 139, 146-53, **154**-9, 161, 179-80, 192, 195-7, 200-1, 204, 207, 211-3, **216**, 219, 226-**8**, 229-**30**, 248, 286, 289-90, 309, 312, 321, 330
  federal presence 211, 221, 226, 251-3, 255, **258**, **259**, 266, 284, 303, 312, 322, 328
  planning and development 226, 230, 242-**245**, 256-60, 265, 270-1, **272**, 275-82, 294, 306, 312, 324
  streetcars.................101, 220
  water and sewage....98-9, 196, 218, 259, 321
Huron Tract (ON).......40

Kanata.........................249, 270, 276, 287, 290-2, 308, 312, 314, 316, 324
King Edward Avenue....130, 244
Kingsmere....................119, **121**, 180-1
Kingston (ON) 15, 22, 23, 25, 26, 28, 38-9, 41, 43, 51, 53, 57, 58, 64, 74, 76-8, 86-8, 98, 106, 123, 235, 317

Lake Champlain 12, 14
Lake Ontario................ 10, 12, 15, 22, 25, 78
Lansdowne Park 312-4
LeBreton Flats 29, 47, 93-4, 97-8, 115, 195, 200, 224, 229, **230**-1, 241, 251, 253, 260, 276, 291, 297-9, **300**, **301**, 303, 308, 311-2, 323-4

INDEX

Lemieux Island 139, 226, 324
Letchworth Garden City
   .... 131, 161, 339
Lindenlea 160-1, **162**
London (UK) 65, 77, 87, 103,
   110-1, 126-7, 142-3, 149, 161, 181,
   190, **191**, 192, 200, 207-8, 249-50,
   322, 324
Lower Town 9, 41, 47, 49-51,
   53, 55-8, 60-1, 63-5, 67-8, 71, 96,
   219, 228, 266, **268**

Macdonald Gardens **134**, 341
Mackenzie King Bridge
   .... **183**, **204**, 219,
   278, 339
Major's Hill, *also* Colonel's Hill
   .... 107-**9**, 111, 114,
   123, 141, **182**, 303
Metcalfe Street 80, 96, 153, 175,
   206, 303, 305-7, 308-9, 324
Montréal 8-15, 20, 22-6,
   28, 41, 56, 58, 60, 65, 74, **75**,
   76-80, 86-9, 96-8, 101, 103, 106,
   108, 114, 122-**3**, 125, 141-2, 146-7,
   179, 181, 196, 198, 215, 219, 221,
   225, 235, 240, 253, 255-6, 266,
   270-1, 274-5, 292, 298, 309, 319

National Capital Region
   .... **6**, 118, 196, 207,
   213, 224, 226, 229, 251, 253-4,
   266, 272, 274-7, 284, 287, 289,
   302, 309, 311, 318, 329-30
Nepean Bay 100, 138-**40**
Nepean Township 17, 28-9, 35, 50,
   57-8, 137, 161, 179, 208, 210, 270
New Delhi 89, 142, **143**-6,
   206, 302, 324, 327
New Edinburgh **63**, 107, 219,
   228, 270
New York 8, 13, 15, 23-4,
   40, 50, 73, 87, 89, 138, 161, **203**,
   207, 240, 240, **257**, 324

Orleans 249, 270, 276,
   290, 312, 316
Ottawa **6**, 64, 207, 308-9
   airport 213, 270, 323-4
   as capital 1-3, 57, 73-90,
      102-14, 124-58, 161-76, 179-93,
      195-204, 211-15, 255-7, 278-86,
      302-7, 314-5, 324-31

commercial growth .. 50, 96, **101**,
   234-5, 242-3, 262-5, 286, 294-5 298
demography and social relations
   .... 49, 59-60, 71,
   208, **209**-11
elite class 49, 56, 58-9, 68,
   94, 101-3, 107, 148-9, 168, 329, 339
ethnic composition .. 50, 60, 71, 320,
   327-9
federal presence 90, 106, **116**,
   140, 255, 278-**83**, 312-3, **314**,
   315, **331**
hydraulic power 62, **92**, **94**, 101,
   126, 305
industrial growth 21-2, 62-3, 91-**4**,
   101, 115, 126, 137, 161, 199-201,
   204, 208, 213, 218-9, 231, 249-54,
   278, 287-9, **305**, 308, 330
neighbourhood organization ... 63,
   161-3, 200-2, 221-6, 228, 266-8,
   275-8, 286, 298, 306-8, 321-2
planning and development
   .... 168-71, 176-8,
   207-8, 210, 229-49, 251, 262-70,
   290-**5**, **310**-8
police force 50, 56-9, 71, 98,
   176, 253, 321
public health 58, 65, 99, 137-8
religious composition and differences
   .... 60, 71, 338
site and settlement ... 5-34
streetcars **97**-8, 101-2, 107,
   137-9, 149-50, 162, 166, 177, 183,
   188, 195, **220**-2, 229, 234, 254,
   324, 335
suburban development
   .... 126, **139**, 160,
   162, **189**, 195, 200, 207, 210-3,
   221-4, 243, 249-50, 265-76, **277**-8,
   286-7, 294, 296, 316, 320, 323
traffic and transportation
   .... 146, 149-50,
   157-8, 166-**76**, 177, 198, 201-6,
   213-**6**, **220**, 222, 227, 229, 243-4,
   245, **246**, **247**, 260, 262, 292,
   308, 316
water and sewage 95, 98-**9**, **100**-3,
   111, 113, 138-9, **140**, 168, 196,
   218, 253, 259, 321
Ottawa River 6, **7**, 8, 11, 17-21,
   23-30, 33-**9**, 41, **46**-9, 53, 56, 58,
   62, 81, 90, 92-4, 97-8, 102, 105-**6**,
   115, 119, 121, 125, 129-32, 137-8,
   140, 149, 153, **156**, 180, 192-7, 200,
   213-4, 222, 226-7, 230, 251-4, 258,
   269-70, 272-81, 286, 290, 303-**5**,
   306-12, 316, 318, 321-4, 328, 330-1

Outaouais 6, 11, 18, 56, 58,
   97, 137, 139, 161, 179, 212, 229,
   244, 251, 253, 25-7, 259, 260, 266,
   269, 270-6, 289, 290, 294-5, 302,
   306, 308-9, 317, 321, 328

Paris 3, 9, 103, 110,
   119, 127, 142-3, 147, 149, 181, 192,
   196, 207, 213, 216, 242, 249, 279,
   305, 314, 322, 324, 327
Parliament Hill, *also* Barrack Hill
   .... 28-9, 38, 52,
   80-1, 82, 87-**8**, 90, **93**, 96-7, 106-7,
   109, 115-6, 117-9, 121-2, 131, 134,
   140, 146, 150, **151**, 153, 161, 164,
   165, 167, 171, 174-5, 180, 185-8,
   196, 200-1, 206-7, 214, 215, 221,
   225-6, 229, 238, 240, 242, 261,
   279-84, 300-3, 305, 308, 311-4,
   315, 317, 322-3, 328-**31**
Patterson's Creek 130-1
Perth 26, **27**, 28-30,
   34, 47, 49-50, 53, 56-8
Philadelphia **13**-4, 23-4, 49,
   73-4, 89, 181, 207, 226, 256, 324
Place de Ville 238, 240-**1**, 297,
   324, 330
Place du Portage 256-**8**, 330
Portage Bridge 151, 154, **259**,
   279, 281, 306

Québec City 20, 38
Queensway 206-7, 214-7,
   218, 227-9, 243, 253-4, 268, 270,
   273, 275, 278, 290, 292, 316

Rideau Canal 25-6, 29, 35-8,
   41-**2**, 47, 49, 50-**2**, 53-5, 60, 62,
   64-7, 71, 78, 97, 98, 107, 113, **124**,
   130-1, 150, 171, 173, 200, 206-7,
   213-6, 218, 230, 235, 242, 254-5,
   260-**1**, 312-3, 317, 323
Rideau Falls 7, 50, 62-3, **92**,
   219, 227
Rideau Hall 62, 102, **105**-7,
   130, 242, 328
Rideau River **11**-2, 17, 26-8,
   35, 41-9, 61, 126-32, 222, 228,
   270, 323
Rideau Street 29, 41, 43, 61,
   68, 98-9, 177, 228, 229, 262-5,
   280-1, 294-**5**, 298
Rockcliffe Park 62, 101, 107,
   108, 117, 126, **129**, 130, 132, 137,
   162, 251, 269, 292, 306, 308

433

Sandy Hill 107, 228, 267, 270
Sleigh Bay 36, 37, 38, 41
Sparks Street 68-**9**, 71, 96, 99, **100-1**, 107, 115, **117**, 137, 158, 167, 173, 205-6, 220-1, 234-7, 243, 262, 312
   Mall **234**-7, 243, 262
   streetcars 101-**2**, 107, 137, 220-2, 234
St. Lawrence River 8-9, 13, 15, 17, 22-3, 26, 33
Strathcona Park 131-**2**
Sussex Street/Drive 43, 51, 58, 112, 140-2, 166, 180, 190, 228, 242-3, 279-81, **299**, 303

Toronto, *also* York 1, 22, 25, 39, 57, 60, 74, 76, 79-80, 84, 86, 88-9, 96-9, 101, 103, 119, 122-3, 146-9, 166-7, 176, **193**, 220, 224-5, 229, 235, 240, 250-1, 256, 262-3, 266, 274-5, 279, 292-3, 296, **297**, 308, 317-20
   Don Mills 250
   Eaton Centre 263
   Regent Park **193**
   St Lawrence Neighbourhood
   .... 266, 274
   waterfront 147, **167**, 296
Tunney's Pasture 221, **223**, 278, 317, 322

University of Ottawa ... **215**
Upper Canada 14, 17, 22-8, 33-43, 49, 53, 57-60, 65, 73, 76-9, 84, 86
Upper Town 41, 43, 47-50, 53, 56-60, 64-**70**, 71, 91, 96, 107, 142, 158, 185, 187, 219, 333

Vancouver (BC) 123, 138, 235, 264, 266, 274, 292, 305, 312, 320
   False Creek 266, 274
   Granville Island 266, 274, 305
Vanier, *also* Eastview 137, 219, 228, 229, 251, 265, 270, 308, 323
Victoria Island, *also* Asinabka
.... 96, 303, 305, 329

Washington, D.C. 23-**4**, 40, 74, 87-90, 103, 107, 110, **111**-4, 125-7, 133-5, 142-3, 146, 149-50, 158, 173, 192, 207, 238, 274, 285, 302, 324-7
Wellington Street 36, 41, 49, 53, 65-7, 70, 80, 82-3, 96, 113, 122, 142, 150-51, 153, 165, 171, 175, 180, 206, 220, 230, 259, 276, 278, 282, **283**, 306
Westgate Shopping Centre
.... 222
Wrightstown, *also* Wright's Town
.... 19, **20**, 21, 28, 30, **32**, 35-7, 41, 47, 49, 53, 58, 62, 73

York, *also* Toronto 22-3, 25, 41, 57, 58, 99, 163, 294

SUBJECT

(**Bold** page numbers for images)

Aboriginal peoples 8, 11, 18-9, 31, 33, 329
Advisory Committee on Reconstruction
.... 190, 192, 210
Agencies 196, 212, 221, 250, 255, 285, 302, 318, 320, 322, 326
   local government 53, 57-8, 60, 64, 71, 81, 86, 90, 101, 118, 123, 137, 157, 171, 175-6, 179, 200, 208, 211-2, 222, 226, 249-51, 253-6, 264-5, 269, 271, 274, 284, 286, 287, 290, 292, 296, 301, 308-12, 317-8, 320-3, 326, 345-6
   planning 168-71, 180, 196-7, 226, 207-8, 211
   provincial 16-7, 21, 25-6, 33, 57, 64, 78, 90, 104, 173, 187, 208, 211, 225, 228, 253, 255-57, 265-6, 271, 275, 289, 292, 296, 306, 308, 312, 317-8, 321
Agriculture 6, 10, 19-22, 30, 33-5, 55, 138, 208, 213
Airports 213, 270, 299, 323, 324
Apartments 134, 163, 215, 268, 290, 298, 313
Athens Charter (CIAM)
.... 192, 202
Automobiles 166, 190, 273

Baby Boom 209-10, 224, 249, 254
Bank of Canada 221, 328
Beaux Arts style 81, 199, 202, 203-**4**
Bennett (1915) Plan, *also* Federal Plan Commission **155**, 175-6, 185, 303
Bilingualism 58, 251, 272, 328
British North America Act
.... 87, 211
Building
   codes 158
   height limits 155, 238, 241, 243, 295, 315
   preservation 226, 242-3, 295
   public 74, 89, 113, 146, 330

INDEX 435

Bytown and Prescott Railway 63-4, 96, 324

Canada Company 40
Canadian Mortgage and Housing Corporation (CMHC) 221, 250, 268, 274, 276
Canadian Commission of Conservation 157, 159, 180
Canadian Institute of Planners (CIP), *also* TPIC 162
Canadian Atlantic Railway 94, 97
Canadian Pacific Railway 131, 146, 229
Canals 20, 23, 25, 37, 51, 202
Capital city planning 125, 230, 237, 302, 321, 326-31
Capitol complexes 24, 74, 110, 144, 172
Carleton University 316
Census 63, 210, 249, 319
Central Business District (CBD) 150, 154, 155, 291, 262
Chicago World's Fair ... 110, 149
CIAM (*Congrès Internationaux d'Architecture Moderne*) 192, 202, 203, 224, 242
City Beautiful Movement 103-4, 224
City halls 59-60, **68**, 74, 96, 108, 153, 157, 167, 172, 176, 180, 185, 187, 204, **219**, 255-6, 266, 278, 285, 290, 293-4, 309, 323-4
City Scientific 159, 166-7, **169**, 176, 178
Civic Centre 104, 144, 150, 153, 154, 159
Civic reform 168
Civil service 79, 87, 93, 103, 105-7, 114, 119, 141, 143, 157, 188, 195, 204, 237, 264, 287
Communauté urbaine de l'Outaouais (CUO) 275-6, 289-90, 308-9, 312
Community planning .. 15-6, 160, 190, 192, 196, 198, 226, 249, 265
 as coordination 53

boards/commissions .. 168, **177**, 180, 196, 207, 211, 238
Community plans 40, 297, 269, 297
Community Planning Association of Canada (CPAC) 196, 226, 265
Comprehensive planning 104, 131, 133, 134, 146, 146, 147, 150, 157, 169, 170, 192, 196, 206, 226, 265, 271, 295
Confederation 3, 59, 73, 80, 83-**5**, 86-90, 92, 96, 102, 164-**6**, 169, 171, 174-**6**, 177, 178, 180-4, 185, 203, 206-07, 211, 219, 225, 235, 243-**4**, 281, **282-3**, 284, 297, 302-3, 311-2, 315, 317-8, 321-4, 326-9, 331

Density 157, 190, 207, 249, 266, 269, 273, 276, 290, 294, 296, 320, 322, 324, 326, 331
Design competitions 80, 90, 144, 164, 172, 177, 181, 219, 232, 313, 314
Department of Public Works 82, 103, 107-8, 140-1, 144, 164, 180, 221, 237, 256, 284, 344, 348
Depression 177, 179-93, 195, 209
Dominion Bureau of Statistics **189**, 223

E.B. Eddy Company 258
École des Beaux Arts, Paris 147, 149, 181
Embassies 103, 175, 192, 195, 303, 326
Environment
 built 312
 natural 5-8, 135, 296-9, 328
 protecting 250, 276, 294-7, 302, 310-2, 316, 318, 321
Expropriation 69, 81, 107, 206, 211, 212, 213, 231, 243, 256, 266, 268

Federal districts 24, 74, 87, 125, 137, 139, 157, 159, 173, 177, 180, 192, 206, 207, 210, 211, 212, 213, 226, 321, 326
 Canberra 89, 142, 144-**5**, 146, 173, 207, 274, 285, 302, 320-2, 324, 326-8

Washington, D.C. ...23-**4**, 40, 74, 87, 89, 90, 103, 107, 110, 111, 112-4, 125-7, 133, 135, 142-6, 149-50, 158, 173, 192, 207, 238, 274, 285, 302, 321-7
Federal District Commission (FDC) 125, 157, 173-7, 180, 195, 197, 206-12, 218-20, 222-7, 275, 278, 322
Federal government 73-4, 87, 89, 106, 111, 113, 118-9, 137, 141-6, 153, 157, 158-62, 164, 169, 171, 174-80, 192-3, 200, 203, 208-13, 218-9, 225-7, 230, 235, 238, 240, 250-6, 259, 262, 265, 267, 270-5, 278, 280-90, 300, 302, 308-22, 328
Federal Plan Commission (FPC), *also* Holt Commission 146-50, 157-60, 164, 167, 169, 172-5, 226, 321
Fires 21, 74, 94-**5**, 107, 114-**5**, **120**, 137, 157, **158-9**, 161, 175, 180, 195, 219, 227, 229, 256, 322
Fire protection 58, 61, **93**, 95, 99-100, 111, 115-6, 138, 201, 321
First Nations, *see* Aboriginal peoples 8, 13, **304-5**, 329

Garden cities 131, 162, 192, 200, 224
Garden suburbs 131, 143, 160-2
Globe (Toronto), *also The Globe and Mail* 1, 79, 339
Gréber (1950) Plan **199**, 200, **201-4**
Greenbelt 190-2, 200-1, 207-8, 211-3, 218, 223-4, 226, 245, 249, 250-1, 254, 269-70, 275-7, 287, 290, 294, 296-7, 302, 311, 316, 321, 323
Grey Cup 313
Growth management ... 310

Heritage districts 312, 345
Heritage preservation ... 243, 298
Highways 150, 155, 210, 213-4, 270, 273, 275, 281, 290, 316, 322
High-tech industry 249, 287, **288-9**, 308, 312, 320, 322
Holt Commission, *see* FPC 159, 160, 323

Housing..................88, 104, 116, 149, 155, 157, 160, 161-2, 188, **189**, 192-6, 200, 222, 226, 229-30, 233, 247, 250, 256-7, 268, 270, 274, 276, 292-5, 298, 313, 320, 326
    affordable.........104, 149, 155, 160, 161, 162, 254, 270, 274
    shortages...188-9, 192, 256,
Hudson's Bay Company
   86

Industrialization **92**
Industrial districts 155
Infrastructure 19, 23, 33-4, 49, **51**, 54, 61-5, 74, 89, 98, **100**-4, 118, 137-**40**, 166-9, 177, 179, 196, 207-13, **218**, 224, 249, 251, 253, **259**, 274-6, 286, 290, 296, 299, 300-02, 308, 310, 318-21
Irish 47, 49, 50, 55, 56, 58, 59, 60, 77, 88

Landscape architecture
    ....123, 125, 181
Land subdivision 168
Land use 149, 196, 200, 202, 207, 220, 224, 226, 243, 249, 269-70, 284, 294, 296, 306
    land-use planning 200, 207, 224
    mixed 230, 266, 294, 300, 311, 314
    regional..................161, 192, 199, 207-8, 225, 250-5, 265, 269, 270-1, **272**, 273-4, 278, 286, 289-94, 297, 306, 311-2, 316, 321, 326
    rural.......................208, 210
    plans......................196, 265, 269, 284, 296, 306, 310
Le Droit (newspaper)....169
Legislature buildings ...74, 90
Libraries......................74, 80, 91, 203, 258, 279, 280
Local government 53, 57-8, 60, 64, 71, 81, 86, 90, 101, 118, 123, 137, 157, 171, 175-6, 179, 200, 208, 211-2, 222, 226, 249-51, **252**-6, 264-5, 269, 271, 274, 284, 286, 287, 290, 292, 296, 301, 308-12, 317-8, 320-3, 326, 345-6
    restructuring 138, 207-11, 251, 270, 289, 309-12, 318
Lumber industry..........21, 55-6, **91-4**, 95-6, 101, 106, 115-16, 126, **131**, 161, 195

Memorials and monuments
    ....76, 77, 110, 120, 121, 140, **141**, 171, **172**, 176, 177, 178, 181, **182**, **183**, 185, **186**, 192, 193, 195, 196, 197, 205, 206, 212, 225, 244, 281, 302, 312, 315, 326, 327, 329
Metropolitan planning, *also* Regional planning 297, 302
Mile of History, *see* Sussex Street
    ....**242**, 243, 323
Minto Corporation.......270
Mixed-use planning.....230, 266, 294, 300, 311, 314
Modernism, *also* CIAM
    ....184, 190, 192, 202-**4**, 219, 221-24, 229-**32**, 234-5, 242-43, 266, 293, 298, 301
Multiculturalism 327, 328
Municipalities, *see* Local government
    ....**6**, 57, 58, 74, 64, 65, 90, 168, 169, 180, 196, 226-7, 242, 244, 249, 251, 253, 256, 265-67, 269-70, 273, 276, 289-90, 294-6, 308-10, 312, 316
Museums 111, 140-**1**, 278-**80**, 281, 294, 299-**301** 302, 305, 323, 326, 328-9, **331**, 337

National Arts Centre ...235, 278
National Capital Commission (NCC)
    ....201, 207, 212-21, 225-7, 230, 235, 238, 242, 249, 250-1, 253-5, 258-60, 262, 264-6, 269, 272-81, 284-90, 293, 296-300, 302-**13**, 314, 316, 318, 322-3, 326-30
National Capital Planning Service (NCPS)
    ....143, 195-6, 226
National Film Board (NFB)
    ....190, 196, 210
National Gallery..........106, 210, 235, 278, 279-80, 292, 294, 305, 323, 329
National Research Council (NRC)
    ....180, 190, 287
Neighbourhood units...161, **163**, 192, 200, 202, 222, 224, 276, 278

Ontario (province)........6, 17, 22, 40, 51, 73, 77, 80, 84, 89, 94, 99, 125, 137, 139, 157, 168, 170, 207, 208, 212-3, 222, 227, 250-1, 258, 265, 269, 270, 275, 289, 290, 292, 294-6, 302, 308-10, 312, 318, 321, 328
Orange Order 60
Ordnance, British 25-6, 38, 47-57, 61, 64-**6**, 67-9, 71, 107
Ottawa Citizen (newspaper)
    ....90, 147-9, 169, 298, 308, 318
Ottawa Electric Railway Company
    ....101, 102, 107, 137, 220
Ottawa Improvement Commission (OIC)
    ....**109**, **110**, 111, 112, **113**, 114, 117, 118, 119, 121, 124, 125, 126, 128, 130, 131, 132, 133, 134, 135, 140, 141, 146, 147, 212, 214, 218, 260, 289, 296, 323
Outaouais regional government, *see* CUO

Parks............................14, 15, 26, **27**, 28, 62, 101, 103, 104, 107, **108**, **109**, 110, 111, 113, 114, 115, 117, 119, 324, 326
Parks movement...........111, 119, 122, 124, 126
Parliament Buildings ...1, 3, 17, 76-7, 80-1, **82**-3, 84-**91**, 93-4, 102, 107, 117, 119, 135, 140-2, 146, 149, 153, 155, 157-**8**, **164**, 166, 171, 174, 183, 206, 238, **240**, 279-81, 311, 323, 326
Planning commissions
    ....168, **177**, 180, 196
Preservation, *see* Heritage preservation
    ....226, 242-3, 295, 298
Property developers 40, 62, 67, 156, 205, 213, 237, 240, 249-50, 257, 262, 264-6, 269-71, 274, 280, 290-1, 294, 298, 300, 316, 318
Provincial Assembly.....94
Provincial government ..16-7, 21, 25-6, 33, 57, 64, 78, 90, 104, 173, 187, 208, 221, 225, 228, 253, 255-7, 265-6, 271, 275, 289, 292, 296, 306, 308, 312, 317-8, 321
Public participation 266, 295, 300
Public space 31, 118-9, 171, 202, 204, 258, 330
    gardens 123
    squares....................9, 13, 185
Public-private partnership
   298

Québec (province) 6-10, 13-4, 20-1, 28-9, 57, 73, 76-9, 82-9, 94, 98, 102-3, 106, 137-9, 154, 157, 159, 173, 180-1, 196, 207-8, 212-3, 222, 225, 227, 244, 250-9, 265-6, 269, 270-1, 275-6, 284, 289-92, 302, 308-12, 316-21, 328

"Queen's Choice"..........73-90

Queensway 206-07, 214-**7**, 218, 227-9, 243, 253-4, 268, 270, 273, 275, 278, 290, 292, 316

Railways 63, 84, 86, 94, 96-7, 100-2, 104, 107, 110, 115, 131, 137, 146, 149-50, **152**, 154-5, 157, 166, 170-1, 177, 185, 195-6, 199-200, 207, 213, 215-20, 224, 226-30, 253, 262, 275, 299, 323-4

Redevelopment 192, 205, 226, 244, 251, 255, 256, 259, 266, 267, 268, 269, 273, 274, 275, 276, 298, 299, 301, **305**, 312, 313, 314, 318, 322, 324

Rebellion, 1837............57

Rebellion Losses Bill....74

Reform movement 262

Regional Municipality of Ottawa-Carleton (RMOC)
.... 251, 264, **269**-70, 273-4, 276, 278-9, 284-5, 289-**93**, 294, 296-9, 301, 306, 308-9, 311, 316, 320, 323

Regional planning 192, 225, 250-1, 253, 255, 269-72, 274, 278, 286, 289, 292, 306, 321, 326

Richmond Settlement...26, 29, 34

Rideau Canal...............25-6, 29, 35-8, 41-**2**, 47, 49-**52**, 53, 55, 60, 62, 64-5, 67, 71, 78, 97-8, 107, 113, **124**, 130-1, 150, 171, 173, 200, 206-7, 213-6, 218, 230, 235, 242, 254, 255, **260-1**, 312-3, 317, 323

Rural planning 207-12, 222-6, 249-50, 289, 310, 320

Satellite towns..............200, 224, 249, 250, 323

Sappers Bridge 43, 49, 57, 60, 62, **97**, 177

Seat of government 3, 23, 25, 28, 49, 57, 60-1, 63, 69, 73-4, **76**-80, 84-7, 89, 90, 97-8, 107, 111, 118, 144, 173, 232, 278, 302, 319, 321, 324, 327, 328

Setbacks........................10

Sewage systems 98

Shiners War 57-8

"Silicon Valley North", *see* High-tech industry 287

Slums............................193, 200

Smallpox epidemic........11

Sprawl..........................**139**, 211, 278, 296, 318, 320, 323

Squares 9, 13-4, 60, 113, 122, 126, 130-31, 169, 171, 175-**6**, 177-8, 180-**3**, 185, 187, 206-7, 219, 230, 235, 243-**4**, 260, 278, 281, 292-3, 297, 309, 314, 317, 323-4, 328-9

Stony Monday Riot 60-**1**, 76

Streets:
avenues 24, 41, 74, 113, 130, 131, 144, 150, 152, 153, 158, 162, 169, 173, 182, 215, 218, 228, 235, 243, 244, 260, 283, 296, 337
boulevards 24, 103, 125-6, 130, 144, 146, 159, 166, 173, 176, 183, 200, 207, 213, **215-6**, 217, 224, 228, 266, 279-**82**, 283-4, 290, 302-3, 305, 307, 311-2, 315, 323, 326, 328, 329, 331
highways..................150, 155, 210, 213-4, 270, 273, 275, 281, 290, 316, 322
parkways..................110, 124, 126, 128, 130, 132, 150, 171, 173, 180, 200-2, 213-4, 216-9, 228-31, 241, 254, 260, 270, 275-6, 278, 290, 308, 311, 316, 323

Streetcars, *see* Transit systems
.... 97-8, 101-**2**, 107, 137, 139, 149-50, 162, 166, 177, 183, 188, 195, **220**-2, 227, 229, 234, 254, 324

Subdivision **32**, 47, 65, 67-9, 80-1, 107, 137-**9**, 160-1, 168-9, 179, 195, 207-8, 210-2, 220, 226, 249, 250, 276-7, 324

Suburbs........................107, 131, 143, 153-4, 157, 160, 161-2, 173, **189**, 199-200, 207-8, 221, 229, 249, 250-1, 275-6, 278, 287, 294-5, 316, 318, 320, 323

Supreme Court 91, 106, 141, 144, 159, 165, **184**-5, 187, 195, 212, 221, 260, 266, 278, 280, 282, 283, 314

Sustainability **297**, 320-2

The Globe and Mail 1, 79, 339

Timber trade.................21-2, 35, 55-6, 60, 62, 91, 93

Tories 59, 60, 65, 86, 89

Town Planning Institute of Canada (TPIC), *also* CIP
.............................160, 168, 173, 180, 226

Traffic 12, 38, 78, 146, 149-50, 157, 163, 166-7, 169-71, 176-7, 182, 198, 201, 206, 213-4, 216, 220, 222, 227, 229, 235, 243, 244, 258, 260, 262, 292, 308, 316

Transit-Oriented Development (TOD)
............................278, 316, 318, 322

Transit systems 220, 278, 286, 306, 316, 317, 318, 320, 321
bus rapid transit (BRT) 273, 278, 316-7
light rail..................273-4, 278, 311, 316-7
streetcars.................97-8, 101-**2**, 107, 137, 139, 149-50, 162, 166, 177, 183, 188, 195, **220**-2, 227, 229, 234, 254, 324

Transitway...............243, 278, 294, 299, 306, 311, 316-18, 320, 323

Transportation.............146, 185, 192, 198, **201**, 220, 222, 228, 243, **245**, 249, 270, 278, 302, 306, 309-11, 316-7, 320-3

Typhoid epidemic 99, 138, **140**, 168, 322

Union of the Canadas...57, 73, 77, 79, 84

Union Station 98, 101, 150, 167, 200, 229, 340

Urban design 103-4, 142-4, 146, 149, 150, 160, 164, 176-7, 181, 196, 202, 223-4, 256-7, 262, 265, 281-2, 294-5, 299, 303, 311-2, 329, 330

Urban development 34, 96, 180, 192, 250-1, 253, 265, 274, 285, 292, 296, 308, 320, 322

Urban growth 225, **277**, 290, 294, 318

Urban landscape 93

Urban renewal **192**-3, 200, 202, 224, 226, 229-31, **233**, 242-3, **247**, 253, 255-6, 266, **268**, 276, 294-5, 323, 324

Urban sprawl 139, 211, 296, 318, 320

Victoria Memorial Museum 140-**1**

Views and vistas **7**, **39**, **59**, **81**, **106**, 124, 144, 150-1, 175, **187**, 196-7, 206, **215**, **261**, 279-**80**, 301, 303, 305, **315**, **331**

War of 1812 .... 22, 23, 26, 29, 34

War Memorial 121, 171-**2**, 173, 176-8, 181, **182**-**3**, 185-**6**, 192, 195-7, 212, 244, 281, 327, 329

"Washington of the North" 107-10, 114, 125, 135

Waterfronts 15, 29, 93, 104, 110, 147, 166, **167**, 296, 323

Watersheds 8, 321

Water supply 95, 99-100, 103, 111, 113, 138, 139, 168

World War I 138, 144, 161, 171

World War II 3, 107, 177, 187, 192, 197, 206, 219, 225

Zoning 149-50, 154-**5**, 157, 159, 160, 169-70, 208, 224, 226, 238, 240, 265-6, 271, 295

Indexes prepared by Ashley Taylor.

Titles in the Collaborative Decentred Metagovernance Series

9.	Linda Cardinal et Pascale Devette (sld) *Autour de Chantal Mouffe: Le politique en conflit*	2015
8.	Ruth Hubbard and Gilles Paquet *Irregular Governance: A Plea for Bold Organizational Experimentation*	2015
7.	Gilles Paquet *Unusual Suspects: Essays on Social Learning Disabilities*	2014
6.	Ruth Hubbard and Gilles Paquet *Probing the Bureaucratic Mind: About Canadian Federal Executives*	2014
5.	Gilles Paquet *Gouvernance corporative : Une entrée en matières*	2013
4.	Gilles Paquet *Tackling Wicked Policy Problems: Equality, Diversity and Sustainability*	2013
3.	Gilles Paquet and Tim Ragan *Through the Detox Prism: Exploring organizational failures and design responses*	2012
2.	Gilles Paquet *Moderato cantabile: Toward Principled Governance for Canada's Immigration Policy*	2012
1.	Ruth Hubbard, Gilles Paquet and Christopher Wilson *Stewardship: Collaborative Decentred Metagovernance and Inquiring Systems*	2012

Other titles published by INVENIRE

21.	David L.A. Gordon *Town and Crown: An Illustrated History of Canada's Capital*	2015
20.	Robin Higham *What Would You Say? ... as guest speaker at the next Canadian citizenship ceremony*	2015
19.	Richard Clément et Pierre Foucher *50 ans de bilinguisme officiel : Défis, analyses et témoignages*	2014
18.	Richard Clément and Pierre Foucher *50 Years of Official Bilingualism: Challenges, Analyses and Testimonies*	2014
17.	Gilles Paquet *Tableau d'avancement III : Pour une diaspora canadienne-française antifragile*	2014
16.	Marc Gervais *Challenges of Minority Governments in Canada*	2012
15.	Caroline Andrew, Ruth Hubbard et Gilles Paquet (sld) *Gouvernance communautaire : innovations dans le Canada français hors Québec*	2012
14.	Tom Brzustowski *Why We Need More Innovation in Canada and What We Must Do to Get It*	2012
13.	Claude M. Rocan *Challenges in Public Health Governance: The Canadian Experience*	2012
12.	Richard Clément et Caroline Andrew (sld) *Villes et langues : gouvernance et politiques Symposium international*	2012
11.	Richard Clément and Caroline Andrew (eds) *Cities and Languages: Governance and Policy International Symposium*	2012
10.	Michael Behiels and François Rocher (eds) *The State in Transition: Challenges for Canadian Federalism*	2011
9.	Pierre Camu *La Flotte Blanche : Histoire de la Compagnie de Navigation du Richelieu et d'Ontario, 1845-1913*	2011
8.	Rupak Chattopadhyay and Gilles Paquet (eds) *The Unimagined Canadian Capital: Challenges for the Federal Capital Region*	2011
7.	Gilles Paquet *Tableau d'avancement II : Essais exploratoires sur la gouvernance d'un certain Canada français*	2011
6.	James Bowen (ed) *The Entrepreneurial Effect: Waterloo*	2011
5.	François Lapointe *Cities as Crucibles: Reflections on Canada's Urban Future*	2011
4.	James Bowen (ed) *The Entrepreneurial Effect*	2009
3.	Gilles Paquet *Scheming virtuously:* *The road to collaborative governance*	2009
2.	Ruth Hubbard *Profession: Public Servant*	2009
1.	Robin Higham *Who do we think we are: Canada's reasonable (and less reasonable) accommodation debates*	2009